Pandemics, Politics, & Public Health

The U.S. Public Health Service Commissioned Corps, 1798—2023

A Strategic Health Security Asset for the 21st Century

PANDEMICS, POLITICS, & PUBLIC HEALTH

☐ ☐ ☐ ☐ ☐

THE U.S. PUBLIC HEALTH SERVICE COMMISSIONED CORPS, 1798 – 2023

JAMES E. KNOBEN, PharmD, MPH
CAPTAIN, U.S. PUBLIC HEALTH SERVICE (RET.)

BORIS D. LUSHNIAK, MD, MPH
Contributing Editor
REAR ADMIRAL, U.S. PUBLIC HEALTH SERVICE (RET.)
DEAN AND PROFESSOR
SCHOOL OF PUBLIC HEALTH
UNIVERSITY OF MARYLAND

Copyright © 2024 by the
PHS Commissioned Officers Foundation
for the Advancement of Public Health

All rights reserved. No part of this book may be reproduced,
transmitted, or utilized in any form or by any means,
including any information storage and retrieval system,
without written permission from the copyright holder.

The author and contributing editor have written this book in their
private capacity. The views expressed are those of the author and
contributing editor and do not necessarily represent official positions
of the Office of the Surgeon General, U.S. Public Health Service,
Department of Health and Human Services, or
the PHS Commissioned Officers Foundation.

ISBN 979-8-218-39167-6

Second Printing

PHS Commissioned Officers Foundation
for the Advancement of Public Health
P.O. Box 189
Cheltenham, Maryland 20623

Printed in the United States of America

To the officers of the
U.S. Public Health Service
Commissioned Corps
who, for over two centuries,
have given honorable service
to this nation and the world.

CONTENTS

	Foreword	ix
	Preface & Acknowledgments	xi
	Organizational Abbreviations	xiii
	Prologue	1
CHAPTER ONE	Introduction, Notable Events	5
CHAPTER TWO	Foundations of the Public Health Service *1798 to 1891*	15
CHAPTER THREE	Convergence of Immigration, Quarantine, Research *1891 to 1911*	29
CHAPTER FOUR	Public Health Expansion, War, Pandemic *1912 to 1920*	45
CHAPTER FIVE	Health & Research Transition, Veterans' Bureau, Bureau of Prisons *1920 to 1936*	63
CHAPTER SIX	Health Reset, World War II, Food and Drug Administration *1936 to 1948*	83
CHAPTER SEVEN	Research & Service Growth, Fluoridation, Indian Health Service *1948 to 1961*	107
CHAPTER EIGHT	Tobacco, Paradigm Shift, Immunization, Oral Rehydration *1961 to 1969*	127
CHAPTER NINE	Surgeons General & PHS in Transition *1969 to 1977*	141
CHAPTER TEN	Dual Role, Smallpox, National Institutes of Health, Healthy People *1977 to 1981*	153

Contents

Chapter Eleven	OBRA, Tobacco, AIDS, Corps Revitalization *1981 to 1989*	163
Chapter Twelve	New Challenges, Commotion & Quiescence *1989 to 1998*	175
Chapter Thirteen	Calm & Competent, 9/11 *1998 to 2002*	187
Chapter Fourteen	Transformation, Emergency Response, ICE Health Service Corps *2002 to 2009*	201
Chapter Fifteen	Affordable Care, Ebola, CDC *2009 to 2014*	223
Chapter Sixteen	Opioids, Coast Guard, NOAA *2014 to 2017*	241
Chapter Seventeen	Opioids, Modernization, Reserve Corps, Covid-19 vs. Politics *2017 to 2021*	253
Chapter Eighteen	Covid-19, Unaccompanied Children, Climate Change, COA & Foundation *2021 to 2023*	273
Chapter Nineteen	CCHQ, PHS Deployments, PHS Challenges	289
Chapter Twenty	USPHS Professional Categories & Their Histories	303
	Appendices	333
	A – USPHS Force Strength	334
	B – Officer Duty Stations	335
	C – Surgeons General, 1871–2023	336
	References	339
	Index	373
	About the Author	386
	About the Contributing Editor	387

FOREWORD

IN 1798, THE SECOND PRESIDENT OF THE UNITED STATES, John Adams, signed into law an *Act for the Relief of Sick and Disabled Seamen*. Twenty cents per month was deducted from the wages of seamen for the purpose of funding medical care for sick and disabled seamen and to build hospitals for their treatment. It can be argued that this was the first federal health care system and health maintenance organization. We must recall that at that time our national security, as well as local and global commerce, were dependent on our domestic and international waterways. Thus, seamen and their ships were essential to the health, safety and security of the new United States.

This Act of 1798 laid the foundation for creation of the Marine Hospital Service (MHS), which 73 years later in 1871 welcomed the first Supervising Surgeon of the Service. John Woodworth was a retired U.S. Army surgeon who was recruited to rebuild the Marine Hospital system by ending corruption, nepotism and patronage, and ensuring that competent personnel were hired and held accountable. The states had failed in managing these federal assets, so Congress resumed direct oversight. It was indeed coincidental that Dr. Woodworth had a clear vision of the nation's needs and the professional competencies and deliverables required to administer the MHS, much to the satisfaction of Congress and the President. Today, what Dr. Woodworth stated is still a guiding principle of the United States Public Health Service Commissioned Corps (PHSCC) – to build a cadre of uniformed officers who are fit and deployable to meet any and all health needs of the nation. He further stated that, like the Army and Navy, these uniformed officers would be part of a uniformed service that would be assigned to various locations based on the needs of the nation. Therefore, allegiance would be to the nation and the uniformed service, and not to the entity to which officers were assigned.

This well-articulated and much needed vision has been an ongoing challenge to the PHSCC since its inception. Initially, career PHS officers occupied most senior leadership positions in Public Health Service agencies. As the PHS grew in size and complexity, however, more leadership positions were assumed by Civil Servants and civilian political appointees, and operating divisions began to think of PHS officers as their employees rather than deployable uniformed officers. In no other uniformed service has there been such ongoing disruption, which diminishes the credibility of the PHSCC as a bona-fide uniformed service. The USPHS Surgeon General serves as the "nation's doctor". As with the Surgeons General of the Army, Navy and Air Force, the Surgeon General of the U.S. Public Health Service was, during an earlier time, a career officer who earned the right to become Surgeon General. In fact, the Public Health Service Act of 1944 specifies that the Surgeon General shall be promoted from the ranks of the Regular Corps. To circumvent this, political leaders began to nominate civilians to the position of USPHS Surgeon General and first commission them as a Captain, then immediately "promote" to Vice Admiral. Without the experience and credibility of a real flag officer, such individuals are not well received as peer flag officers and leaders in other uniformed services. Regrettably, this political process has extended to the civilian Assistant Secretary for Health, who now has the option to be an "instant" 4-star Admiral, thus further undermining the integrity of the PHSCC.

Our colleague, the late Fitzhugh Mullan, had done an admirable job of memorializing the first century plus of our Public Health Service history in his seminal offering of *Plagues and Politics*, which was very aptly titled! Despite the plague *of* politics, the PHS Commissioned Corps has much to be proud of in the service to our nation and the globe – from serving in all federal agencies, providing exceptional clinical care, public health services and research, exemplifying unparalleled leadership in many HHS and non-HHS agencies, deploying repeatedly to all-hazards challenges in the U.S. and globally, and serving in all wars for over a century. Even during peace time, our PHS officers are frequently in harm's way as they deal with emerging infections, epidemics, manmade and natural disasters and even terrorism. We are a selfless, often anonymous, yet unique uniformed service. The PHS Commissioned Corps is the only all-officer corps comprised of health professionals in the world. My hope is that we can return to that pure vision of service articulated by our first Surgeon General Woodworth where we once again are a true uniformed service, and where our positions, ranks and titles are earned, and any career officer can aspire to and become Surgeon General.

This current history of the U.S. Public Health Service Commissioned Corps – *Pandemics, Politics, & Public Health* – is a remarkable newcomer to the few books that deal with the proud record of accomplishment as well as the challenges that have confronted the Corps. This account, beginning in 1798 through 2023, provides detailed information that previously might not have been readily available. It is well researched and provides some thoughtful insight to round out the rich history of the Commissioned Corps. Dr. Boris Lushniak currently serves as Dean of the University of Maryland School of Public Health, and Captain Jim Knoben and Rear Admiral Lushniak, holding Master of Public Health degrees from Yale and Harvard Universities, are well versed in the field. I offer my sincere congratulations on the successful completion of this multi-year effort, which is a tribute to all USPHS officers.

Richard Carmona

VADM Richard H. Carmona, MD, MPH, FACS
17th United States Surgeon General
Distinguished Laureate Professor, University of Arizona

PREFACE & ACKNOWLEDGMENTS

Pandemics, Politics, & Public Health provides a comprehensive review of the United States Public Health Service Commissioned Corps in fulfilling its domestic and global mission. Several years were required to research a vast amount of documentation for this historical account. It revealed a fascinating story of personal and institutional resilience that allowed the Commissioned Corps to not only endure, but to advance through ongoing improvement and renewal. While the Corps is thematically central to the narrative, this history is presented within the context of public health more generally, as well it should. The narrative progresses chronologically, with each chapter beginning with the appointment of a Surgeon General. Surgeons General perform a key role as the operational head of the Corps and as the nation's doctor. PHS officers, however, are the people who give life and substance to the Commissioned Corps in their exceptional professional endeavors. In so doing, they have shown real officership by supporting one another as a team in fulfilling the PHS mission. While a historical account is unable to cover every person and event, the work of *every* PHS officer is contributory. We introduced a concept called *In Their Words* that are personal accounts of officers about their experiences while on active duty, thereby lending considerable interest to the narrative.

While researching the literature, we often pondered the achievements of and challenges to the Commissioned Corps. Despite some institutional shortcomings, it is clear that PHS officers have very ably served this nation for over 200 years. PHS officers have consistently performed their duties with dedication, compassion and integrity, which is revealed in the Corps' heritage and legacy of extraordinary accomplishments that date from 1798. Further, PHS officers have put themselves on the front lines in deploying to public health crises domestically and internationally. This all-officer uniformed service of medical, public health, and scientific personnel with significant roles in clinical care, environmental health, regulatory affairs, and research is truly unique in the world. The Public Health Service provides a very meaningful life experience for those who are part of this ever evolving institution. Yet, for all their service to the nation, the USPHS Commissioned Corps receives relatively little public recognition as the critically important national asset that it is. Interestingly, there are also few published histories about the Commissioned Corps. Notable among them are *The U.S. Public Health Service, 1798-1950* by Ralph C. Williams, *A Profile of the U.S. Public Health Service, 1798-1948* by Bess Furman, and *Plagues and Politics* by Fitzhugh Mullan. We have striven to present a comprehensive, balanced and objective review of the USPHS Commissioned Corps, including its institutional challenges and setbacks, that expands upon those previous Commissioned Corps histories.

The year 2023 marks the 225th anniversary of the Public Health Service and 2024 is the 135th anniversary of the formalization of its Commissioned Corps. We believe this new history of the activities, events and challenges of the Public Health Service Commissioned Corps presents an authoritative resource for comprehensive information about current actions as well as historical knowledge. Creation of the book was a collegial effort involving numerous active duty and retired PHS officers who provided written contributions to content as well as reviews of the manuscript. We are especially grateful to them and to all the officers, including former Directors of Commissioned Corps Headquarters and the Chief Professional Officers, who were partners in documenting the activities and heritage of the Corps, and to Kun Shen who handled photo issues. We offer our sincere appreciation to Jerry Farrell, former COA/COF Executive Director, who provided a thoughtful review of the final manuscript, and to Gene Migliaccio and Randy Gardner, current and past president of the Commissioned Officers Foundation and to Jacque Rychnovsky, COA/COF Executive Director, who were supportive of this project. Our special thanks to former Surgeon General Richard Carmona, who was steadfast in supporting this project from inception, and to former HHS Assistant Secretaries for Health Howard Koh and Brett Giroir for their participation. On a personal note, as the author, I want to convey my great appreciation to Boris, who knew the significance this history represents for the PHS Commissioned Corps and who committed to working together to further advance the book to its completion. And my heartfelt appreciation and esteem to my wife, Alice *(Captain, Ret.)*, for enduring seemingly endless years devoted to this project, yet who provided encouragement to see it through to fruition.

James E. Knoben   Boris D. Lushniak

ORGANIZATIONAL ABBREVIATIONS

ACF	Administration for Children and Families
ASPR	Administration for Strategic Preparedness and Response
	Formerly Office of the Assistant Secretary for Preparedness and Response
BARDA	Biomedical Advanced Research and Development Authority
BOP	Bureau of Prisons
CBP	Customs and Border Protection
CCHQ	Commissioned Corps Headquarters
CDC	Centers for Disease Control and Prevention
CG	U.S. Coast Guard
CMS	Centers for Medicare and Medicaid Services
DHS	Department of Homeland Security
DOD	Department of Defense
EIS	Epidemic Intelligence Service
EPA	Environmental Protection Agency
FDA	Food and Drug Administration
FEMA	Federal Emergency Management Administration
FSA	Federal Security Agency
GAO	Government Accountability Office
	Formerly General Accounting Office
HEW	Department of Health, Education, and Welfare
HHS	Department of Health and Human Services
	Formerly Department of Health, Education, and Welfare
IHS	Indian Health Service
IHSC	Immigration and Customs Enforcement Health Service Corps
MHS	Marine Hospital Service
MRC	Medical Reserve Corps
NCI	National Cancer Institute
NIAID	National Institute of Allergy and Infectious Diseases
NIH	National Institute(s) of Health
NLM	National Library of Medicine
NOAA	National Oceanic and Atmospheric Administration
OASH	Office of the Assistant Secretary for Health
	Formerly Assistant Secretary for Health and Scientific Affairs
OMB	Office of Management and Budget
	Formerly Bureau of the Budget
OSG	Office of the Surgeon General
USAID	U.S. Agency for International Development
USPHS	U.S. Public Health Service
USPHSCC	U.S. Public Health Service Commissioned Corps
WHO	World Health Organization

Pandemics, Politics, & Public Health

■ PANDEMICS, POLITICS, & PUBLIC HEALTH ■

PROLOGUE

THROUGHOUT HISTORY, PUBLIC HEALTH HAS REPRESENTED an essential component of societal well-being as well as a growing force for global stability. For hundreds of years, public health professionals have exemplified a profound call to service. Yet everyone who has ever heeded that call struggles to understand how their day-to-day work fits into a broader context. After all, none of the work is easy: the challenges are enormous in scale, stem from numerous and highly complex causes, regularly play out "on stage" before a public audience, and impact a vast array of stakeholders who usually require intense negotiation and compromise. Moreover, the yawning gap between infinite needs and finite resources regularly fuels the politics of "who got what, when, why, and how."

Pandemics, Politics, & Public Health, an exhaustive description of the U.S. public health journey over two centuries, admirably provides that context by highlighting lessons learned from leaders who have gone before. This comprehensive chronicle of public health achievement, in the face of always daunting odds, puts things into perspective. Reflecting years of dedicated work by James Knoben, PharmD, MPH, and Boris Lushniak, MD, MPH, this volume tells the complex and dynamic story of public health from 1798 to 2023 through the lens of the United States Public Health Service (USPHS) Commissioned Corps. Today, as an all-officer cadre of medical, public health, and scientific professionals located in the Department of Health and Human Services (HHS), the Corps is overseen by the Assistant Secretary for Health (ASH) and directed by the Surgeon General. Public health in general, and the PHS Commissioned Corps in particular, has saved lives by adapting to a constantly evolving array of threats featuring astonishing twists, turns, ebbs, and flows. Their collective stories over two centuries of progress and setbacks, opportunities and ordeals, and fulfillment and frustration reflect the commitment and flexibility that public health service always entails.

Early Years. The public health history begins in 1798 when national attention focused on infectious disease threats that risked becoming epidemics. Because certain diseases were being introduced by afflicted seamen returning from abroad, marine hospitals, established at the time to care for them, served as the forerunner for today's Commissioned Corps. From the start, teams of public health professionals focused on a mission of maximizing evolving strategies for disease treatment and prevention to protect people in time of need. As ensuing decades turned into centuries, public health professionals were regularly compelled to broaden skills and competencies to address new threats. Numerous examples can be cited. For example, in the 19th century, which witnessed a major focus on sanitation to prevent infectious disease transmission, the field saw rapid development of environmental, industrial and occupational standards. In 1889, after years of less formal structure, the PHS Commissioned Corps was officially established. The very end of the century witnessed the introduction of the bubonic plague to the U.S.

The early part of the 20th century featured the 1918 Great Influenza pandemic in which 675,000 Americans died; after that, public health had to rebuild. Moreover, the century witnessed national growth of a more dedicated infrastructure for regulation, research and public health. Key agencies established then included the Food and Drug Administration (FDA) in 1906 and the Centers for Disease Control and Prevention (CDC) in 1946, not to mention the historic public health insurance programs of Medicare and Medicaid in 1965. Meanwhile, national attention grew regarding the power of prevention. Efforts to prevent drug dependence, obesity, and the epidemic of cigarette smoking included the 1964 Surgeon General's *Report on Smoking and Health*, one of the most recognized public health milestones ever. These developments occurred on behalf of a nation rapidly diversifying by race and ethnicity, among many other dimensions, presenting mounting social justice themes. Over time, public health grew to encompass these challenges by increasingly addressing health equity and social determinants of health.

As they necessarily work in a state of continuous change, all public health professionals must exhibit adaptability and flexibility. In this regard, the PHS Commissioned Corps is notable not only for dedicated service in hardship locations, but also serving as a unique uniformed deployable force for public health emergency response. In fact, Corps officers today focus their day-to-day responsibilities throughout multiple HHS agencies (such as the Indian Health Service, CDC, FDA and NIH) as well as other federal agencies (such as the Department of Defense and Department of Homeland Security). At the same time, however, they must be ready to depart at a moment's notice to serve those in need in the aftermath of numerous natural or manmade events domestically and worldwide, including earthquakes, hurricanes, epidemics, and acts of terrorism. In this way they contribute also to national health security and health diplomacy. In recent history Corps officers have been deployed to New York City for 9/11 (2001), to Liberia to address Ebola (2014), and to Puerto Rico after Hurricane Maria (2017). Throughout the course of the COVID-19 pandemic, two-thirds of Corps officers have been sent emergently to areas of the country most in need. Through it all the Commissioned Corps has survived peaks and valleys with respect to support and recognition, as well as ongoing debates about its optimal integration with other public health stakeholders. It regularly faces impactful funding shortfalls and even an occasional threat of elimination; all Corps leaders work in administrations where political pressures can be enormous. *Pandemics, Politics, & Public Health* does not shy away from any of this. So many times, public health professionals, and the Corps in particular, have had to meet the moment, rise to the challenge and rebuild.

Legacy of Leadership. Every reader can glean key life lessons from historic Corps leaders. Before entering public service I had the privilege of meeting a number of them. Three in particular advised me and provided tremendous lifelong inspiration. As a researcher, I was awed by the vision of Dr. Julius Richmond who, by establishing *Healthy People* in 1979, created an enduring legacy for unifying the nation. Each decade since, through a community-based, federally-coordinated process, *Healthy People* serves as a compass and roadmap for the nation and sets health goals, tracks progress, and drives action. As an advocate, I was energized by Dr. C. Everett Koop's relentless courage taking on the tobacco industry to advance public health, and his deep compassion standing up for stigmatized people infected in the earliest days of the HIV/AIDS epidemic. Finally, as a son of immigrant parents who searched for – and discovered – the American dream, I treasured the pioneering voice of Dr. David Satcher who sounded the urgent call to tackle health disparities and achieve true health equity.

So when I became the HHS Assistant Secretary for Health in 2009 (after nomination by President Obama, U.S. Senate confirmation, and preceding service as Massachusetts Commissioner of Public Health), I felt a duty to first show my respect for the legacy of the PHS Commissioned Corps. I did so by, among other things, individually consulting with each of my living Assistant Secretary for Health and Surgeon General predecessors. To my delight, in an act of great solidarity, many of them attended the glorious HHS ceremony hosted by Corps officers where I was sworn in before new colleagues, old friends, family, and my loving wife and children. I felt everyone's passionate support as I took the oath to protect and defend the U.S. This legacy also served me well as ASH as the nation grappled with a host of historic public health challenges. They ranged from confronting the H1N1 influenza pandemic to implementing the 2010 Affordable Care Act; the latter has since provided health insurance coverage to over 30 million underserved people despite political opposition and multiple lawsuits. I felt the palpable tug of my predecessors' legacy when I unveiled *Healthy People* 2020, the first HHS Action Plan to Reduce Racial and Ethnic Health Disparities (2011), and the first Tobacco Control Strategic Action Plan for HHS (2010); joining Acting Surgeon General Dr. Lushniak at the White House 50th Anniversary of the 1964 Surgeon General's

Report on Smoking and Health was a special thrill. And after close collaboration with top HHS administrative leaders, I was pleased to unveil a new organizational structure for the Corps with the goal of improving management, logistics, operations, and personnel oversight for this sprawling and always complex organization. I will always treasure meeting so many Corps officers as I traveled around the country. Every one of them expressed pride in their work, their uniform, and their contributions to service and history.

Present and Future. *Pandemics, Politics, & Public Health* ends in 2023, as it began in 1798 – with the theme of protecting the country against infectious disease threats. Currently, the aftermath of COVID-19 has left our nation and the status of its public health capacity in an uncertain state. Despite the heroic efforts of so many, over one million Americans and over six million worldwide have died, and socioeconomically disadvantaged communities and communities of color have suffered disproportionately. Moreover, this fast pandemic has been fueled by a longstanding slow pandemic of preventable conditions, including heart disease, lung disease, tobacco dependence, obesity and diabetes. Further, the detrimental effects of climate change on health are now fully evident. Most troubling has been the steady, sometimes overt, hostility to science and evidence-based thinking that has compromised public health.

So, as of this writing, it is time to rebuild public health once more. We must again meet the moment and rise to the challenge. We must do so with a sense of dedicated purpose while striving to apply lessons from the past to strengthen the future. After all, throughout history, the profound mission of public health has remained constant and fundamental – to help each person reach their "highest attainable standard of health." And it will all be worth it. Because when public health works, absolutely nothing happens except the miracle of a perfectly normal day. When public health works, more people can enjoy healthier lives, spend more precious time with friends and family, and have a chance to build a lifetime of cherished memories. Then historians will have a chance to write the next chapter of public health achievement.

May every reader of this volume find their place in this long sweep of public health history. And may every reader come away humbled, motivated, and ready to answer the call to service when their moment comes.

Howard K. Koh

Howard K. Koh, MD, MPH
14th Assistant Secretary for Health, HHS
Fineberg Professor of the Practice of Public Health Leadership
Harvard T. H. Chan School of Public Health

CHAPTER ONE

INTRODUCTION, NOTABLE EVENTS

THE HISTORY OF THE UNITED STATES PUBLIC HEALTH SERVICE COMMISSIONED CORPS is a chronicle of extraordinary achievement amid recurrent challenge and transition, and that legacy provides a foundation for understanding the institution as it exists today. For many years, the Surgeon General served as the administrator of nearly all federal public health agencies and programs that comprised the Public Health Service (PHS), with authority over the broad expanse of agency activities that were usually headed by PHS commissioned officers. The PHS was the acknowledged leader when it came to managing public health and it functioned with relative autonomy. In 1953, the Public Health Service became a subsidiary agency within the newly formed Department of Health, Education, and Welfare (HEW). Then in 1968, the Surgeon General's overarching authority was transferred to a new Assistant Secretary for Health and Scientific Affairs, HEW. That administrative realignment resulted in a redistribution of public health leadership authority and responsibility away from the Surgeon General, a situation that has had profound implications for the nation due to the increasing influence of political advocacy in decision-making. Yet, the Surgeon General has remained "the nation's doctor" and spokesperson on matters of health and the operational head of the Commissioned Corps. The Commissioned Corps has continued, as well, to provide clinical innovations and public health advancements in regulatory, research, and service roles. The record of accomplishment of the men and women who comprise this institution has been, foremost, a story of resolute commitment to the well-being of the citizens of this nation.

TRADITION AND TRANSITION

The Public Health Service began in 1798 in response to the need to protect American citizens from infectious diseases that could rapidly become epidemic in the absence of effective preventive measures and treatments. Although certain diseases were endemic, other diseases were introduced by afflicted seamen who were returning from abroad. This led to the establishment of "marine hospitals" around the nation, principally in major ports, to care for sick and disabled seamen. In 1870, the marine hospitals were formalized as the U.S. Marine Hospital Service (MHS), which developed into today's Public Health Service. In 1871, Dr. John M. Woodworth became the first Supervising Surgeon of the Marine Hospital Service and he transformed the disorganized marine hospitals into an effective system for delivering medical care. Woodworth adopted a military model for his medical staff, which was formalized in 1889 as the MHS Corps under then Supervising Surgeon General John B. Hamilton. Within a few years the MHS was tasked with the medical screening of passengers and quarantine of ships arriving from foreign countries to stem the entry of communicable diseases into the United States.

The etiology and management of diseases became a principal focus of the Public Health Service for decades, led largely by the PHS Hygienic Laboratory and a dedicated contingent of medical and scientifically trained officers working at the Laboratory and in the field, sometimes at the risk of great personal peril. Advances in germ theory and the application of epidemiological methods bolstered biomedical discoveries and an understanding about many illnesses. This ultimately led to the control of high burden diseases with the development of preventive measures and treatment interventions that would alter the susceptibility of populations to such maladies worldwide.

Sanitation was an area of public health that had a major impact on the transmission and severity of infectious disease. Described by Charles-Edward Amory Winslow as the "great sanitary awakening" of the late 19th century, it pertained to the recognition of environmental cleanliness and personal hygiene as significant determinants of disease.[1] The industrial revolution in the late 1800s brought a tremendous influx of immigrants to the United States to sustain factory production, a situation that produced overcrowding in cities and fostered disease susceptibility. The PHS therefore undertook research related to environmental, sanitation, and industrial health issues, and PHS officers worked directly with state entities to improve environmental, occupational, and personal living standards. Occasionally, active duty officers were assigned to serve as a state's health officer. PHS officers were posted to other countries to screen passengers for communicable diseases prior to their boarding ships bound for the United States. Officers also worked overseas in various capacities during war years and participated in international health organizations. And many officers have worked to the present in foreign countries as medical and public health consultants to health ministries.

A Congressional Act approved on August 14, 1912 (Public Law 62-265) changed the name of the Service to simply the Public Health Service and authorized the PHS to "study and investigate the diseases of man and conditions influencing the propagation and spread thereof," thereby providing the PHS with a wide ranging mission to study whatever disease-related issues it deemed necessary. Over time, as substantive progress was being made in controlling communicable diseases, the Public Health Service pivoted toward the study of chronic illnesses as a cause of significant morbidity and mortality. This initiated a period of research expansion at the National Institutes of Health, carrying forward its heritage as the nation's preeminent research organization. Throughout its history, the USPHS Commissioned Corps has accepted responsibility for providing essential medical care and public health services to several special and underserved populations within the nation, and it also became an accomplished public health emergency response force.

By the late twentieth century, federal, state and local agencies assumed much greater roles in health education, planning, financing, and the provision of medical care and public health services. Health promotion along with disease prevention became the predominant public health framework. An understanding emerged about the significant impact of social determinants on overall health status and health outcomes, and the need to take this into account in addressing the issue of health equity. Health equity is a recurrent thematic issue of Surgeons General since first being highlighted by Dr. David Satcher, who recognized that racial, ethnic, and socioeconomic disparities pervaded health care throughout the nation. Other ongoing issues that have engaged the attention of Surgeons General are the detrimental effects of cigarette smoking, obesity, and alcohol and substance abuse, all of which inflict preventable harm to personal health and to public health more generally.

The impact of communicable disease epidemics and pandemics and how best to control their spread has become a top priority for the Executive Branch of government, due to the relative ease by which infectious agents can spread within the nation and worldwide. In those situations, the Surgeon General is called upon to serve as a national health educator, and PHS officers often deploy in various roles to carry out public health measures deemed necessary to mitigate the disease. From inception, the Public Health Service has served as the nation's public health department and has continued to grow in complexity and responsibility. Aside from its ongoing medical, public health and scientific responsibilities, health-related legislative initiatives may task the PHS with responsibility for implementing the provisions of a new law. When implementation of a law encompasses multifaceted components, Commissioned Corps officers at different agencies, with a full range of skill sets, can be involved at the forefront of that endeavor. Throughout its history, the Corps has been in a state of continuous change – new authorities intermingle with new challenges that are relentlessly forging a more resilient future. It has been essential that the Commissioned Corps swiftly adapt to such new imperatives and incorporate the changes necessary to maintain its reputation as a reliable and trustworthy organization that can respond to multiple challenges.

CORPS RESPONSIBILITIES

The institution of the Public Health Service is organizationally located in the Department of Health and Human Services, with a staff comprised of commissioned officers, civilian employees and contractors. It has evolved into the foremost science-based regulatory, research, and service enterprise in the  world. The PHS Commissioned Corps is unique. One of the eight United States uniformed services, it is an all officer Corps of medical, public health and scientific professionals who serve in multiple federal agencies such as the Indian Health Service, Centers for Disease Control and Prevention, Food and Drug Administration, Bureau of Prisons, Marshals Service, the Department of Defense, Department of Homeland Security, U.S. Coast Guard, National Oceanic and Atmospheric Administration, and National Institutes of Health. The Corps is also a trained cadre of first responders to medical and public health emergencies, deploying to numerous natural and manmade events domestically and internationally, including earthquakes, hurricanes, epidemics, terrorism, unaccompanied immigrant children health needs, and mental health issues. This vast network of specialized professional and scientific personnel in the PHS Commissioned Corps serves as a vital component of public health delivery for the nation and of national health security.

ISSUES

Challenges

Implementation of the PHS mission has occasionally been met with various challenges. One challenge takes the form of periodic assertions by an incumbent administration that the Commissioned Corps is declining. Those claims have been reviewed by senior Corps/HHS leadership and, when the critique was deemed to have merit, corrective steps were taken to improve and proactively move forward. Another challenge has been periodic assertions by the Office of Management and Budget that using Commissioned Corps officers in place of Civil Service personnel is substantially more costly. Those claims have been countered by HHS in every instance, mainly due to being based upon unreliable cost analyses that generally lacked incontestable validity. The essentiality of the PHS Commissioned Corps is readily apparent – no other enterprise and certainly no uniformed service in the world can replicate the breadth of professional and scientific knowledge and expertise to render medical, public health, environmental health, and research services, and respond to emergency health crises domestically and internationally. The Commissioned

Corps has long been hindered by a fractured command structure, unlike the Armed Forces that have one chain of command. PHS officers are accountable to the Office of the Surgeon General and also to the agency in which they are assigned. Further, financing of the Corps is cobbled together from various funding streams, and essential field training has been underfunded for many years. *(See Chapter Nineteen for a review of these issues.)*

Surgeon General, Assistant Secretary Appointment
Consistent with other uniformed services, the Public Health Service Act of 1944 specified that the Surgeon General shall be appointed from the active duty Regular Corps for a four-year term. However, civilian nominees are increasingly being chosen by presidential administrations based upon personal and political considerations, and such nominees receive the rank of a Vice Admiral upon confirmation. Similarly, a civilian political appointee to the position of Assistant Secretary for Health may now be commissioned at the rank of an Admiral. Such appointments are a cause for some concern. *(See Chapter Nineteen.)*

Stewardship Responsibility
The story of the Public Health Service Commissioned Corps is intertwined with an ever-evolving public health system in the United States. If the Corps is to retain its prominence in public health, the Office of the Surgeon General must continue to lead. In more recent years, the relatively low profile of Surgeons General has led to some media commentary regarding the whereabouts of the nation's doctor. During an earlier time, Surgeons General were routinely looked to for guidance and if required, the national leadership to propel change. It is not uncommon for other federal agency officials to now lead public discourse on health issues of national importance. This shared responsibility is a reasonable accommodation given the greater complexity of health-related issues and the relationship of certain issues to agency missions. Even so, Surgeons General need to remain conversant on a range of health issues to ensure their participation in high level deliberations and official pronouncements.

    C. Everett Koop was an exemplary role model – against political odds, he became an AIDS authority and was able to effectively reclaim the considerable national persuasive power of a knowledgeable and proactive Surgeon General. Surgeons General and Assistant Secretaries for Health must commit to preserving the institutional integrity and viability of the Commissioned Corps in protecting the nation's health, and remain steadfast against uninformed, shortsighted and/or possibly harmful political intrusions. The effect of politics in public health is dangerous when policy is dictated by ideology.[2] This was particularly evident during the 2020 response to the coronavirus pandemic, where politics overrode science and compromised national public health.

TIDE OF TIME – THE FUTURE

PHS officers are among those who strengthen national and global health by their work in clinical, public health, and research positions. There are inherent advantages that derive from this network of highly trained professionals and scientists with wide ranging expertise. In carrying out their comprehensive mission, the PHS has stationed its officers in over twenty federal agencies and at hundreds of locations worldwide. They provide compassionate health care and environmental health services to special and underserved populations, are a vital component in regulatory, biomedical and research agencies, and are an experienced force of emergency responders.

As noted in the *National Security Strategy* released in October 2022, communicable diseases, climate change, and food insecurity are among the shared challenges at the very core of national and international security.[3] These thematic areas will be of increasing concern as climate change alters the present-day natural order of the planet. Notably, as climate continues to evolve, its impact will require a whole-of-government approach, including the capabilities of the Public Health Service. PHS officers will be integral to that endeavor, involved in efforts to respond to the disruptive occurrences brought about by climate-induced extremes. Critically important will be an expansion of Corps recruitment to address current and future challenges for the nation.

The PHS Corps has forged alliances with the military and other partner organizations to shore-up a strong public health presence in the federal sector. Many PHS officers are detailed to the Department of Defense and, increasingly, military commands turn to the PHS Commissioned Corps for expertise as a public health leader. PHS officers also serve as a force multiplier by supplanting military healthcare provider positions. PHS officers train with their military counterparts in areas such as clinical care, leadership, and readiness. Thousands of PHS officers have deployed to medical/public health emergency events throughout the nation and globally, often in coordination with and alongside the military, and they have deployed on joint international health diplomacy and humanitarian missions with the military.

An unprecedented, multidimensional societal transformation has been underway over the last several decades, and it will continue to evolve and in the process impact the activities of the Commissioned Corps. The Corps will adapt and advance as it has so often done, validating its role as a vital strategic health security asset of the nation in the 21st Century. The passage of time will only reinforce the imperative for a robust U.S. Public Health Service Commissioned Corps as it continues to build upon an extraordinary heritage in fulfilling its mission to protect, promote, and advance the health and safety of the nation and help secure global health and stability.

USPHS Notable Events, 1798 – 2023

July 16, 1798 – President John Adams signs *An Act for the Relief of Sick and Disabled Seamen*, forming the U.S. Marine Hospital Service (MHS).

June 29, 1870 – President Ulysses Grant signs *An Act to Reorganize the Marine Hospital Service* to centralize administration of the MHS. John M. Woodworth is named the first Supervising Surgeon General in 1871.

1887 – MHS medical officer Joseph J. Kinyoun creates a small, single room laboratory at the Marine Hospital at Staten Island, New York, which the Service will expand and become known as the Laboratory of Hygiene; it was renamed as the National Institute of Health in 1930.

January 4, 1889 – President Grover Cleveland signs *An Act to Regulate Appointments in the Marine Hospital Service of the United States*, formalizing the Corps as the uniformed service component of the MHS.

Immigration Act of 1891 – Centralizes enforcement authority in the federal government and assigns responsibility for the medical inspection of immigrants to the Marine Hospital Service.

National Quarantine Act of 1893 – Places authority and responsibility with the Marine Hospital Service to oversee quarantine activities, including those administered by states, and promulgate regulations. The quarantine system was fully nationalized by 1921.

Medical Research in the Early 1900s – Within the Laboratory of Hygiene, relocated to Washington, DC, and in the field, MHS medical researchers pursue investigations of diseases such as cholera, yellow fever, hookworm, Rocky Mountain spotted fever, trachoma, typhus fever, pellagra, bubonic plague, and typhoid fever.

August 14, 1912 – *An Act to Change the Name of the Public Health and MHS ...and Other Purposes*, changes name to Public Health Service and provides it with a comprehensive investigative national mission.

USPHS Notable Events, 1798 – 2023
[Continued]

1917-1918 – The onset of World War I places new demands on the PHS, requiring a significant increase of professional personnel. Coincident with the war, the Spanish influenza pandemic impacts the nation, and a PHS Reserve Corps is authorized to assist with response efforts.

May 26, 1930 – The Ransdell Act renames the Laboratory of Hygiene as the National Institute(s) of Health, moving it from Washington, DC, to Bethesda, Maryland, the cornerstone being laid in 1938. The National Cancer Institute is the first institute, authorized in 1937.

August 14, 1935 – President Franklin Roosevelt signs the Social Security Act. The 1965 amendments, signed July 30, 1965, by President Lyndon Johnson, establishes the Medicare and Medicaid programs that have profoundly impacted the provision of health care and public health.

1939 – PHS is transferred from the Treasury Department to the Federal Security Agency (FSA).
1953 – FSA is terminated and its responsibilities, including the Public Health Service, are transferred to the newly created Department of Health, Education, and Welfare (HEW).
1980 – HEW is renamed the Department of Health and Human Services (HHS).

1941 – The U.S. entry into World War II brings many new responsibilities to the PHS, redirecting its efforts to wartime needs and build-up of healthcare personnel. The Nurse Training Act of 1943 creates a uniformed Cadet Nurse Corps within the PHS to bolster health providers.

Public Health Service Act of 1944 – Consolidates laws, stipulates authorities of the PHS, specifies leadership positions to which senior officers are appointed, and provides for inclusion of more professional disciplines in the Regular Corps, expanding upon the Parker Act of 1930.

June 21, 1945 – President Harry Truman issues an Executive Order that formally militarizes the PHS Commissioned Corps; numerous PHS officers had already been detailed to military services during WWII.

USPHS NOTABLE EVENTS, 1798 – 2023
[Continued]

1946 – The Communicable Disease Center is founded by PHS medical officer Joseph W. Mountin in Atlanta, Georgia, with a mission to control the spread of malaria within the nation. It is renamed in 1970 to Center for Disease Control, and in 1992 to the Centers for Disease Control and Prevention, with a significantly broader portfolio.

1951 – Creation of CDC's Epidemic Intelligence Service led by Alexander Langmuir, to provide fellowship training in scientific investigation methodology and public health response.

Transfer Act of 1955 – The responsibility for Indian health care is transferred from the Bureau of Indian Affairs to the Public Health Service and creates the Indian Health Service (IHS). In 1988, the IHS, which had been a Bureau within HHS, is elevated to Agency status.

January 11, 1964 – The report on *Smoking and Health* is issued by Surgeon General Terry; it receives widespread media coverage and initiates release of regular Surgeon General reports on the topic.

1968 – The Surgeon General's authority for all Public Health Service programs is transferred to a civilian political appointee in the new position of Assistant Secretary for Health and Scientific Affairs, HEW. The Surgeon General remains operational head of the Commissioned Corps.

1970 – The National Health Service Corps (NHSC) is created to provide health care services in underserved areas throughout the nation. The program offers tuition and a stipend to health professions students in return for one year of NHSC service for each year of support.

1979 – Surgeon General Richmond releases the report *Healthy People: The Surgeon General's Report on Health Promotion and Disease Prevention*, which includes health goals and quantifiable objectives. The report is updated every decade with specific ten year objectives.

1980 – The last recorded case of smallpox occurred in Somalia in 1977. On May 8, 1980, the World Health Assembly certifies the global eradication of smallpox.

Omnibus Budget Reconciliation Act of 1981 – Leads to closure of the eight remaining PHS (Marine) Hospitals and 27 PHS Clinics. Consolidates 77 categorical programs relating to health, social and other services under nine block grants to the states.

USPHS NOTABLE EVENTS, 1798 – 2023
[Continued]

1980s – Surgeon General Koop comes to prominence due to his forthright stance on AIDS. Koop institutes a revitalization effort, foretelling future initiatives to modernize the Commissioned Corps.

2001 – Over 1000 PHS officers, PHS and CDC specialized teams, deploy in response to the 9/11 terrorist attacks in New York City and anthrax attacks in Washington, DC and elsewhere.

2005 – The Public Health Service Commissioned Corps releases a new Mission Statement and, in 2006, the PHS releases its declaration of new Corps Values.

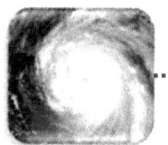

2005 – Hurricanes Katrina, Rita, and Wilma requires over one-third of PHS officers to deploy; new tiered response teams are formed.
2017 – Hurricanes Harvey, Irma, and Maria requires over 1800 PHS officers to deploy to Texas, Florida, Puerto Rico, and Virgin Islands.

2006 – The Pandemic and All-Hazards Preparedness Act creates the new HHS position of Assistant Secretary for Preparedness and Response, which in 2022 is elevated to an HHS Operating Division and renamed the Administration for Strategic Preparedness and Response.

2014 – World Health Organization declares the Ebola virus disease a public health emergency of international concern. PHS officers staff the Monrovia Medical Unit in Liberia for healthcare workers.

March 17, 2020 – The CARES Act provides authority to re-establish the USPHS Ready Reserve Corps to support the Regular Corps.

2020-2023 – The Coronavirus disease pandemic requires two-thirds of PHS officers to deploy for the response and accelerates Commissioned Corps modernization and readiness initiatives.

CHAPTER TWO

FOUNDATIONS OF THE PUBLIC HEALTH SERVICE
1798 to 1891

IN THE 1700s, there was an absence of state and federal health policy and little provision for an organized public health system in the United States. Infectious diseases spread and went largely uncontrolled due to a rudimentary understanding of medical science and a lack of effective treatments. A systematic approach to disease prevention and control, and the national public health infrastructure to administer corresponding policy were nonexistent. Individual states initially bore the responsibility for regulating quarantine of vessels, processing immigrants arriving from overseas and controlling epidemics, but by the late 1800s it was evident that ineffective and fractured capabilities among the states were inadequate to meet the public health needs of a growing nation – the federal government would, of necessity, assume public health obligations and powers. The origins of the organization known as the United States Public Health Service and its Commissioned Corps, in which provision of public health services is highly organized and complexly integrated, evolved from the implementation of a federal program in 1798 to render medical services to seamen.

The early American colonies needed a strong merchant shipping fleet in order to secure a flourishing commercial trade and provide for adequate resource support in times of military action. However, medical care services were generally unavailable to seamen who manned the ships that were often at sea for months. The work onboard ships was hazardous and the seamen endured poor and unsanitary living conditions. Further, contagious diseases could be acquired overseas, and the arrival in American port cities of merchant seamen with various maladies who were unable to provide for their own medical care made them dependent and a burden upon local resources. The potential hazards of injury and disease at sea, coupled with the lack of medical services aboard ship and in port, persisted for many years and were significant factors in discouraging men from a maritime occupation. Maintaining the health of merchant seamen was therefore recognized by legislators as necessary to improve working conditions and essential for ensuring the viability of a reliable merchant fleet.

The Act of 1798

The first Secretary of the Treasury, Alexander Hamilton, sent a report dated April 17, 1792, to Congress proposing the establishment of one or more marine hospitals in the "interests of humanity" as well as the "interests of navigation and trade."[1] That concept ultimately led to the legislative bill passed by the Fifth Congress and signed on July 16, 1798, by President John Adams, entitled *An Act for the Relief of Sick and Disabled Seamen*.[2] The Act provided for

> ...the temporary relief and maintenance of sick or disabled seamen, in the hospitals or other proper institutions now established in the several ports of the United States, or, in ports where no such institutions exist, then in such other manner as he [the Secretary of the Treasury] shall direct.

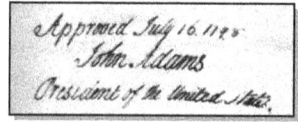

President John Adams signing *An Act for the Relief of Sick and Disabled Seamen*, July 16, 1798, which led to formation of the Marine Hospital Service.
[Painting by Garnet W. Jex, National Library of Medicine]

The 1798 legislation was built on earlier precedents, including an English hospital system established for seamen following the 1588 victory of the British Navy over the Spanish Armada, a program funded by royal grant, donations and supplemented with a tax of sixpence per month on seamen's wages. This was extended to the British merchant marine in 1696. During the 18th century, similar measures were passed in the American colonies to provide medical care to seamen in a few Atlantic ports including the Carolinas and Virginia.[3]

MARINE HOSPITAL FUND

Under the Act of 1798, twenty cents per month was deducted from the wages of each seaman onboard a U.S. vessel as revenue for a Marine Hospital Fund to be used in support of a system of hospitals for treating sick and injured seamen. An Act of 1799 extended the marine hospital care to U.S. Navy personnel, authorizing a deduction of twenty cents per month from the wages of naval officers, seamen and marines, until 1811 when a separate Navy fund was created. Other Acts extended coverage to seamen employed in inland water transportation.[4] The fund, administered by the Treasury Department, is cited as representing the first publicly funded system of health care in the United States. While the Act of 1798 dealt with administration and beneficiaries of the fund, other Acts dealt with construction, purchase, leasing or sale of marine hospitals and the provision of contract services. Existing hospitals were used to the extent possible and any surplus funds were used to build new hospitals in major port cities. Section 5 of the Act of 1798 specified that the President was to appoint directors of the marine hospitals in their respective port cities to "direct expenditure of the fund ...to provide for the accommodation of sick and disabled seamen." An unforeseen result was that the locally collected and administered fund often proved inadequate due to local political interference, inefficiency, graft and inconsistent application of eligibility rules. Even when funds were expended for the intended purposes, some hospitals were poorly located rendering them inaccessible to seamen, and some hospitals were unable to meet the seamen's demand for health care services. The inadequacy of the fund, coupled with mismanagement and lack of accountability, necessitated the imposition of restrictive economic measures, which ensured that the provision of medical care was substandard, leading to special appropriations by Congress beginning in 1804. Funding shortfalls contributed to minimal or nonexistent levels of care in many communities during the fund's first three or four decades.[5] Furthermore, public support waned and operation of the fund increasingly became disorganized and ineffectual.

MARINE HOSPITALS

In 1799, Castle Island in Boston Harbor was chosen as the temporary site for the first marine hospital. A former military barrack was restored and another built to deliver medical care. Dr. Thomas Welsh, a Harvard College graduate with excellent military as well as medical credentials, was appointed the first physician in charge (PIC) and he promptly prepared "Rules and Orders" of the Hospital that were approved in 1800. The first marine hospital to be owned by the federal government was originally built for merchant seamen by the state of Virginia; located at Washington Point in Norfolk County, it was purchased and designated a Marine Hospital in 1801. A new hospital,

Drawing of the first marine hospital built with Act of 1798 hospital funding at Charlestown, Port of Boston in Massachusetts, and occupied 1804 to 1825.
[National Library of Medicine]

using Congressionally authorized funds of $15,000, was built in the Charlestown section of Boston and occupied in January 1804, at which time Dr. Charles Jarvis succeeded Dr. Welsh. Upon Dr. Jarvis's death, Dr. Benjamin Waterhouse, who had introduced the smallpox vaccination technique to the United States and a friend of President Thomas Jefferson, was appointed the

PIC from 1807 to 1809. The Charleston hospital was sold to the Navy in April 1825, and patients were moved to a rented building in Charlestown pending the completion of a new Marine Hospital in Chelsea in 1827.[6] Until 1838, there were never more than three marine hospitals in operation simultaneously, mainly due to organizational disarray and a lack of funds. Furthermore, federal regulations often limited the services provided to seamen, with little regard for the legal stipulations of Congress. It was noted in the *First Annual Report of the Supervising Surgeon of the Marine Hospital Service, 1872*, that the standard plans for marine hospitals were materially unchanged since 1837 and that hospitals were poorly designed and often defective in construction.[7] By the mid-19th century, most services supported by the Marine Hospital Fund were provided through contractual arrangements with local hospitals, private physicians and boarding houses. Medical care services were concentrated at ports along the Atlantic Seaboard such as Baltimore, New York, Philadelphia, Wilmington, and Savannah, and on Pelican Island in Galveston, Texas. Compared with the unsatisfactory state of affairs on the Eastern Seaboard, the situation was far worse along western lakes and rivers. By the 1840s, the increasing commercial seagoing traffic on the Mississippi and Ohio rivers and Great Lakes led to the need to provide care and construct marine hospitals along riverways at places such as Natchez, Louisville, St. Louis, Chicago, New Orleans on the Gulf Coast, and at San Francisco on the Pacific coast.

The inefficiency and abuses relating to tax collection and disbursement of marine hospital funds led to an Act in 1849 authorizing the Treasury Secretary to commission a study of the marine hospitals. Drs. George Loring of the Boston Marine Hospital and Thomas Edwards of Ohio (later a member of Congress) reported on the extensive administrative deficiencies of the Marine Hospital Fund, and disorganization and lack of uniformity among the marine hospitals. They proposed that the hospitals be placed under the control of a chief surgeon whose bureau would be attached to the Treasury Department. Subsequently, hospitals were taken over by Union and Confederate troops during the Civil War such that, by 1864, only eight of the hospitals were operational. After the war, continued widespread concern about the marine hospitals led Treasury Secretary George S. Boutwell in 1869 to commission a study on the condition of seventeen specified hospitals. The study was conducted by Dr. John Shaw Billings who headed the Army Surgeon General's Library and Dr. W.D. Stewart of the Treasury Department. It resulted in the issuance of a critical report that detailed pervasive deficiencies among the marine hospitals and in the provision of medical care. A brief summarization of the Billings-Stewart report was included in Secretary Boutwell's 1869 annual report, and it led to the passage of important reform legislation the following year that would have a profound impact on the future of the Marine Hospital Service.

Marine Hospital Service Reform & the Supervising Surgeon

In January 1870, a bill for the reorganization of the marine hospitals was sent to Congress and signed into law by President Ulysses S. Grant on June 29, 1870. *An Act to Reorganize the Marine Hospital Service, and to Provide for the Relief of Sick and Disabled Seamen* provided for the administrative centralization of marine hospitals within the Treasury Department under the control of a supervising surgeon, and provided directives with respect to collection and accountability of the Marine Hospital Fund.[8] The reorganization Act of 1870 also increased the amount deducted from the wages of merchant seamen to forty cents per month. However, the tax was repealed in the Shipping Act of 1884 and the cost of maintaining the marine hospitals was then paid out of a tonnage tax until 1906.[9] Since that date, medical care for merchant seamen and other Service beneficiaries has been supported with direct appropriations by the Congress.

SUPERVISING SURGEON WOODWORTH

Perhaps the more significant change embodied in the Act of 1870 was the provision for appointment of a supervising surgeon to preside over the Marine Hospital Service (MHS). The Act provided that:

> the Secretary of the Treasury is hereby authorized to appoint a surgeon to act as supervising surgeon of marine hospital service, whose duty it shall be, ...to supervise all matters connected with the marine-hospital service, and with the disbursement of the fund provided by this act, ...who shall be required to make monthly reports to the Secretary of the Treasury.

The first person appointed to the position of Supervising Surgeon needed to be an administrator with integrity, who was both proactive and visionary in order to transform the wayward and disorganized hospital service into an effective and efficient system for delivering medical care. Treasury Secretary Boutwell's intention was to appoint Dr. John Billings to the post, but he was impeded by the Senate Commerce Committee, which amended the bill to require that the Supervising Surgeon come from civilian life. With the selection of Dr. John Maynard Woodworth as the first Supervising Surgeon, the Marine Hospital Service had a leader with the requisite character and ability to not only alter the course of the Service, but who would have an enduring impact on organized public health in the United States.

John M. Woodworth

John Woodworth was born August 15, 1837, in Big Flats, New York, the family moving soon thereafter to Illinois. He studied pharmacy at the University of Chicago (UChicago) and practiced for a while. An organizer of the Chicago Academy of Science, he became its museum curator in 1858; in 1859 he was asked by UChicago to establish a museum of natural history. He spent time at the Smithsonian Institution and then embarked on medical studies, graduating in 1862 from Rush Medical College. Woodworth joined the Union Army, eventually becoming medical director of the Army of the Tennessee while serving under General William Sherman. On the "march to the sea," he was in charge of the ambulance train, bringing over 100 sick and wounded to Savannah without the loss of a man, which was perhaps contributory to his selection as Supervising Surgeon. Following the Civil War, Woodworth spent a year in Europe training at hospitals in Berlin and Vienna. On return, he became an anatomy instructor at Chicago Medical College, Surgeon of the Soldiers' Home of Chicago, and Sanitary Inspector of the Chicago Board of Health.

Dr. John Woodworth was appointed to the position of MHS Supervising Surgeon and began on March 29, 1871, moving expeditiously to reform the marine hospital system. In 1872, only nine of the 31 marine hospitals established between 1798 and 1870 were in use, and Woodworth initiated the publication of annual reports containing meticulous detail about marine hospital conditions and MHS activities. Under his disciplined and resolute administration, Woodworth remedied many serious abuses and deficiencies within the Hospital Service and by 1873 the Service became self-sustaining. He sold hospitals at small inland ports and began construction of new or replacement hospitals at the great port cities of New York, Philadelphia, Baltimore, New Orleans, and San Francisco. In 1873, Woodworth adopted a military model for his medical staff – he prepared regulations directing the wearing of uniforms, provided for the maintenance of discipline on a military basis, and appointed officers for general service in any part of the United States. Of particular importance, Woodworth instituted rigorous examinations of applicants, thereby significantly raising the standard of MHS medical care. Local physician appointees at the various stations were either assimilated into the general service or replaced by regular officers.[10]

Dr. Woodworth published *Nomenclature of Diseases* in 1874, on the cover of which was the Marine Hospital Service insignia he designed and began to use in all annual reports. The seal consisted of a fouled anchor representing seamen cared for by the Service, and the caduceus of Mercury as a symbol of commerce to represent the merchant marine. With minor changes in design, this has remained the PHS seal to the present day.

The National Board of Health

John Woodworth envisioned broader public health responsibilities for the Marine Hospital Service that went beyond the provision of care to merchant seamen, and he was among those national public health leaders who founded the American Public Health Association (APHA) in 1872.[11] In 1873, a cholera epidemic led to an 1874 resolution in Congress authorizing an investigation of the causes of epidemic cholera and more specifically the outbreak of 1873. Dr. Woodworth joined Dr. Ely McClellan, Assistant Surgeon in the U.S. Army, in preparing a document in 1875 that was considered a significant contribution to understanding the disease. In recognition of the growing importance of the MHS and Woodworth's outstanding leadership, his title was changed to Supervising Surgeon General in 1875. In 1874, the National Association of State Health Commissioners was formed, and the American Public Health Association position was that each state should establish an effective state board of health. Woodworth noted in his *Annual Report* of 1875 that the nation's quarantine laws had been "...practically a dead letter," referring to earlier quarantine statutes including in 1799 *An Act Respecting Quarantine and Health Laws* that provided for federal assistance to state authorities to enforce state quarantine laws.[12] Woodworth's reports on cholera and yellow fever helped lay the foundation for new national legislation.

In 1878, a yellow fever epidemic spread from New Orleans up through the Mississippi River Valley causing an estimated 20,000 deaths. Some states, which heretofore had managed epidemics, albeit poorly, felt that a national approach was needed. Dr. Woodworth succeeded in gaining Congressional passage of the National Quarantine Act[13] in April 1878, which gave authority to the Marine Hospital Service to promulgate regulations for the detention of vessels having cases of contagious disease; however, such rules were not to conflict with state quarantine regulations and no appropriations were included for the MHS to implement provisions of the Act. The Act also required the preparation of weekly abstracts of U.S. consular reports on the sanitary condition of vessels departing for the United States, resulting in publication of the *Bulletin of the Public Health*, with the first issue on July 13, 1878. However, the *Bulletin* ended after just 46 issues. In 1887, *The Weekly Abstract of Sanitary Reports* replaced the *Bulletin* and, in 1896, it became *Public Health Reports*, the official journal of the Public Health Service that is still published.[14]

At a meeting of the APHA executive committee in 1878 that included Dr. John S. Billings as the committee vice president – a distinguished Army physician who had become increasingly adversarial toward Woodworth – a national board of health with quarantine powers was proposed. Although both men recognized the need for a national health service to oversee public health, Billings proposed a cooperative approach among federal, state and local municipalities, whereas Woodworth wanted to broaden the authority of the Marine Hospital Service. On March 3, 1879, the Congress passed an APHA-backed bill that was favored by Billings, entitled *An Act to Prevent the Introduction of Infectious or Contagious Diseases into the United States, and to Establish a National Board of Health*, which created the National Board of Health (NBH).[15] The legislation repealed quarantine authority given to the Marine Hospital Service in 1878 and transferred quarantine responsibilities to the NBH. Subsequently on June 2, 1879, another Act[16] was passed that strengthened NBH's state authority and its quarantine powers, and appropriated $500,000 for the quarantine activities. However, this Act also contained a provision that the National Board of Health quarantine authorities were limited to a four-year term, after which a reenactment bill was necessary.

Within days of the NBH enabling legislation, however, Dr. John Woodworth, who ably led and transformed the Marine Hospital Service and helped lay the foundation for a national public health system, died at age 41 on March 14, 1879, in Washington, DC, reportedly from pneumonia. Woodworth was a person of great ability, resourcefulness and perseverance who left an enduring legacy for the PHS Commissioned Corps. An elaborate funeral service was held in his honor, attended by dignitaries that included President Rutherford Hayes and Treasury Secretary John Sherman.[17,18] Woodworth was laid to rest at Saint Paul's Episcopal Parish Church, Rock Creek Cemetery in Washington, DC. MHS officers erected a memorial headstone at John Woodworth's gravesite.

New Supervising Surgeon General

John B. Hamilton

DR. JOHN B. HAMILTON assumed the position of Marine Hospital Service Supervising Surgeon General on April 3, 1879. Born 1847 in Illinois, Hamilton was educated at the Hamilton School, the country academy founded by his family. He enlisted in the Illinois 61st Regiment during the Civil War and, when the war ended, attended Rush Medical College in Chicago, earning his MD degree in 1869. Hamilton initially entered private practice but rejoined the Army as an Assistant Surgeon in 1874, and then resigned to enter the MHS in 1876. After one year, Hamilton was assigned to the Boston Marine Hospital at Chelsea, where he successfully resolved a serious sewage problem that was leading to infectious disease outbreaks. Hamilton, at 31 years of age, brought little national level experience to his position as the new Supervising Surgeon General. However, he was an able administrator and politically astute, and he was soon confronted with maneuvering by the National Board of Health, led by Dr. John Billings who served as vice president of its Executive Committee. The NBH was effective in coordinating its public health responsibilities with state boards of health, and Billings and the NBH were diligent in furthering national public health objectives. Hamilton realized, however, that if Congress did not reenact authorizing legislation at the end of its four-year term, NBH quarantine responsibilities would expire and revert to the Marine Hospital Service. Hamilton understood the significance of the situation and wanting to advance the public health authorities of the MHS, he set about to discredit the National Board of Health by making accusations against Board members and NBH activities. Although there was support for the NBH among the American Public Health Association and other national and state organizations, complaints from Congressional representatives about NBH encroachment upon states' quarantine rights led to failure of the NBH reenactment bill on June 2, 1883. As a result, the Marine Hospital Service was able to regain its quarantine responsibilities and functions and received more strengthened authorities over time. Yet, in the judgment of some public health experts, the NBH termination might have been a missed opportunity to form a centralized, national board of public health professionals, incorporating within it the central administrative authority and full-time career service of MHS officers.[19,20] Dr. Hamilton went on to establish the Laboratory of Hygiene and secure passage of legislation formalizing the MHS career corps of commissioned officers.

Laboratory of Hygiene

In 1888, some advocates of the former National Board of Health lobbied the Congressional Committee on Commerce to favorably report a bill to form a Bureau of Health in the Department of the Interior, which would have removed all public health functions of the MHS other than quarantine, and it included a provision for continuous scientific research. Supervising Surgeon General Hamilton testified at a Committee hearing that the Marine Hospital Service was already performing activities similar to those of the proposed Bureau. He noted that the MHS had already formed a Laboratory of Hygiene in the Marine Hospital at Staten Island, New York. The laboratory was, in fact, a small single room founded in 1887 by MHS medical officer Joseph J. Kinyoun, who had trained with the renowned bacteriologist Dr. Robert Koch in Europe. During testimony, Hamilton noted that Kinyoun also had identified the cholera bacillus among the immigrant passengers on a steamship in New York.[17] These revelations halted action on the proposed bill.

Joseph J. Kinyoun

Formation of the Hygienic Laboratory – the first federal bacteriology laboratory – was supported by Dr. Walter Wyman, the Surgeon in Charge of the Staten Island Hospital (and next Surgeon General) who also had studied bacteriology in Europe. Dr. Hamilton recognized the Laboratory's importance in infectious disease investigations for the entire Service and, in his 1888 *Annual Report*, recommended that the Laboratory be relocated in Washington, DC, where it could be housed in a proper facility and have the greatest usefulness to the Service and general public. Thus, in 1891, the Marine Hospital Service and its Laboratory did move to Washington, DC, and occupied the Butler building across the street from the U.S. Capitol. In 1901, Congress authorized $35,000 to construct a new building for the Laboratory on the Old Naval Observatory grounds, which it occupied from 1904 to 1941, becoming the forerunner of the National Institutes of Health.[21]

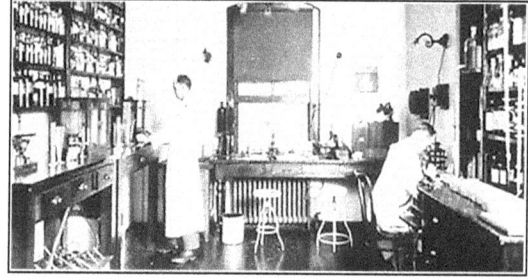

The Laboratory of Hygiene in the Marine Hospital at Stapleton, Staten Island, New York, founded by Joseph J. Kinyoun.
[National Institutes of Health]

The diagnostic work of the Hygienic Laboratory in support of quarantine activities initially focused on cholera, yellow fever, smallpox, and plague, with Dr. Kinyoun employing new techniques of Koch that allowed him to identify cholera. Kinyoun made several trips to Europe to study with Koch, Émile Roux of the Pasteur Institute, and other leading scientists. He modernized the Hygienic Laboratory, strongly orienting it toward research with applied clinical and public health applications, while supporting ongoing MHS infectious disease outbreak investigations. Research included studies of yellow fever etiology, pandemic influenza and plague, and it expanded to include production of antitoxins for infectious disease such as diphtheria and vaccines for diseases such as rabies. The Service also had a "traveling laboratory" that was used for bacteriological diagnoses in the field.

In 1902, an Act to rename the Marine Hospital Service[22] *(see Chapter Three)* included a provision to form three new divisions of chemistry, pharmacology, and zoology in the Laboratory. The importance of these new programs was underscored by allowing researchers, other than medical officers, to head them.

Concern about the dangers of impure biologics production led Congress to pass the Biologics Control Act of 1902, giving the Hygienic Laboratory authority to regulate the production of vaccines, antitoxins, antisera and serums before passage of the Pure Food and Drug Act in 1906. The renamed Public Health and Marine Hospital Service established standards and issued licenses to pharmaceutical firms to produce the biologicals. Passage of the two Acts contributed significantly toward the Hygienic Laboratory becoming a prominent center of research within the federal government.[21]

Formalization of the Corps

Doctors John Woodworth and John Hamilton both served in the U.S. Army prior to joining the Marine Hospital Service and they were strong proponents of a professional Corps based upon a military model. The regulations for MHS

MHS officers, Marine Hospital, Chicago. Truman Miller, seated in the center, Medical Officer in Charge, wearing the Service uniform that he designed, 1878. Joseph Kinyoun is to the right of Miller.
[National Library of Medicine]

officers that Woodworth had promulgated in 1873, however, did not have the force of law. Medical schools at the time were of variable quality and in his 1885 *Annual Report*, Hamilton noted that "Not only is it important, from a humanitarian point of view, that the (MHS) medical officers shall be of the first rank in their profession, but the interests of the Government now require them to be of such."[23] Further, the Service needed a mobile cadre of officers who could be assigned, as needed, to specific duty stations.

The Marine Hospital Service had become a national institution with ever-increasing public health authorities and responsibilities. It provided medical care to seamen, conducted surveillance and diagnosis of infectious diseases, and responded to disease outbreaks. Its quarantine activities, consisting of a foreign services component that inspected ships bound for the United States along with domestic inspection stations, were essential for monitoring and controlling infectious diseases. Hamilton's efforts ultimately succeeded in formalizing the MHS Corps of medical officers when, on January 4, 1889, *An Act to Regulate Appointments in the Marine Hospital Service of the United States* was signed by President Grover Cleveland.[24] The Act provided for the following:

(1) Appointment of medical officers to the Marine Hospital Service by the President with the advice and consent of the Senate;
(2) Appointment only after passing a satisfactory examination in the several branches of medicine, surgery and hygiene before a board of medical officers of the Service; and
(3) Specification of the uniformed service ranks to which appointment and promotions could be made, based upon time in service and examination.

As described by MHS medical officer Victor G. Heiser, who was among 42 young physician applicants arriving in Washington, DC, in July 1898, to take the entrance examination:[25]

> After a physical exam eliminated some, the remaining thirty candidates began a week's ordeal of daily written exams. Evenings were devoted to study and, in the mornings, some of their number would be quietly excused. Ten remained for the oral pre-medical exam where they were questioned on their knowledge of "history, philosophy, economics, literature, and kindred subjects." The final hurdle was clinical, where they were required to examine and diagnose six patients, and analyze specimens and identify bacteria under the microscope. At the end of a grueling two weeks, eight of the applicants had completed the ordeal. Two weeks later, three were offered commissions in the Service, including Dr. Heiser.

> **By this legislation, the Marine Hospital Service and its cadre of medical officers became a uniformed service of the United States.**

By this legislation, the Marine Hospital Service and its cadre of medical officers became a uniformed service of the United States. This small group of officers serving in hospitals, at quarantine stations and confronting disease epidemics throughout the nation acquired a broad range of professional experiences that contributed to a strong esprit de corps, which was so very important in holding together the career officer corps of the Service.[3] Dr. Hamilton had a further interest in wanting the name of the MHS changed to the Public Health Service. This had been proposed by others and in his 1889 *Annual Report*, Hamilton noted that Dr. J. Berrien Lindsley, in an address made at an American Medical Association meeting, suggested that the MHS had the components of a health department. Lindsley went on to state: "Thus it would seem that the United States Marine-Hospital Service has altogether outgrown its name. It should be styled the United States Public Health Service, while retaining essentially its present organization."[26] A partial success was achieved when in 1902 the MHS was renamed the Public Health and Marine Hospital Service.

Surgeon General Departure

Dr. John Hamilton was a capable administrator who made considerable progress in advancing the national agenda of the Marine Hospital Service. On June 1, 1891, he unexpectedly resigned as Surgeon General for personal reasons. At his request, he was reappointed an MHS Surgeon and assigned to the Chicago Marine Hospital as its director. Upon his departure, Hamilton recommended that Dr. Walter Wyman succeed him as the Supervising Surgeon General.

SHIP'S MEDICINE CHEST

An Act for the Government and Regulation of Seamen in the Merchants Service, enacted in 1790, required all United States ships of 150 tons or more with a crew of ten or more to maintain "...a chest of medicines, put up by some apothecary of known reputation, and accompanied by directions for administering the same."[27]

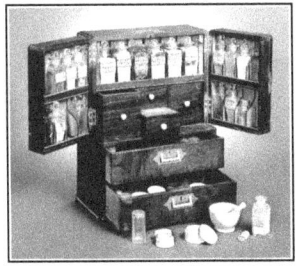

19th century ship's medicine chest. Most commonly, either the captain or first mate administered pharmaceutical products to any crew in need.

[National Museum of American History]

Aside from a few guides provided by private physicians, there was no federal government-issued manual for this purpose until 1881, when the Marine Hospital Service issued the manual entitled *Hand-Book for the Ship's Medicine Chest.* The book has since been issued in several revised editions by the U.S. Public Health Service. The title was modified for the 1929 edition to *The Ship's Medicine Chest and First Aid at Sea,* and with the 1978 edition to *The Ship's Medicine Chest and Medical Aid at Sea.* The most recent edition of *The Ship's Medicine Chest and Medical Aid at Sea* was issued in 2003.[28] As noted in the Introduction to this edition, earlier editions focused on specific medical treatments. Due to the availability of the internet and advanced communications technology, it departs from a how to book and provides, instead, sufficient information so that a person with the proper skills can examine a patient and communicate pertinent medical findings to a shore based practitioner. Further, the book provides public health information such as personal and communicable disease prevention and ship sanitation.

2003 Reprint Edition

> ## CHRONOLOGY • 1798–1891
> Supervising SG John Maynard Woodworth, March 1871–March 1879
> Supervising SG John B. Hamilton, April 1879–June 1891

1798	*An Act for the Relief of Sick and Disabled Seamen*. Creates the Marine Hospital Fund to support a system of hospitals to treat merchant seamen.
1798	English physician Edward Jenner publishes his work on vaccination as a preventive treatment for smallpox.
1861	American Civil War, 1861 to 1865.
1870	*An Act to Reorganize the Marine Hospital Service, and to Provide for the Relief of Sick and Disabled Seamen*. Provides for centralization of the Marine Hospital Service under the control of a Supervising Surgeon.
1871	John Woodworth is appointed as the first Supervising Surgeon; his title is changed to Supervising Surgeon General in 1875.
1872	American Public Health Association is founded.
1874	National Association of State Health Commissioners is formed.
1876	Robert Koch, studying the disease anthrax, validates the germ theory of disease that was introduced by Louis Pasteur, the idea that diseases are caused by infectious agents.
1878	*National Quarantine Act*. Provides the Marine Hospital Service authority to promulgate quarantine regulations that did not conflict with state rules; and authorizes publication of the *Bulletin of the Public Health* which became *Public Health Reports*, the official journal of the PHS.
1879	National Board of Health is established, transferring 1878 quarantine responsibilities from the Marine Hospital Service to the Board.
1881	Marine Hospital Service issues the first edition of *Handbook for [the] Ship's Medicine Chest*.
1882	Robert Koch identifies *Mycobacterium tuberculosis* as the causative agent of tuberculosis.
1883	Failure of the National Board of Health reenactment bill allows the Marine Hospital Service to reassume its quarantine responsibilities.
1884	Robert Koch identifies *Vibrio cholerae* as the causative agent of cholera.
1887	Formation of the Laboratory of Hygiene (Hygienic Laboratory) within the Marine Hospital at Staten Island, New York headed by Joseph Kinyoun; it was moved to Washington, DC, in 1901, becoming the predecessor of the National Institutes of Health.
1889	*An Act to Regulate Appointments in the Marine Hospital Service of the United States*. Formalizes the Officer Corps as the uniformed service component of the Marine Hospital Service.

CHAPTER THREE

CONVERGENCE OF IMMIGRATION, QUARANTINE, RESEARCH
1891 to 1911

D R. WALTER WYMAN was a graduate of the St. Louis Medical College and he served at the City Hospital at St. Louis and in private practice prior to joining the Marine Hospital Service (MHS) in 1876. He was assigned successively to the marine hospitals at St. Louis, Cincinnati, Baltimore, and then at Staten Island, New York as the Surgeon in Charge and where the Hygienic Laboratory was founded. In 1888, Wyman transferred from the Staten Island Hospital to Washington, DC, as Chief of the Quarantine Division. Wyman had taken on various tasks for Surgeon General Hamilton over the years and, following Dr. Hamilton's resignation as Supervising Surgeon General in 1891 and upon his recommendation, Dr. Walter Wyman was appointed to that position, which he held until his death in 1911. Upon his appointment, Wyman moved the Washington, DC, Marine Hospital Service headquarters to the Butler mansion (former residence of General Benjamin Butler, a Civil War Union officer and a member of Congress), which was located across the street from the U.S. Capitol. Wyman was known

Walter Wyman

as being industrious, meticulous and a strict disciplinarian, and he wrote comprehensive policies and procedures for all operational activities. Unlike his predecessors, Wyman did not have prior military service; nonetheless, as Surgeon General, he was a strong advocate for the MHS officers. He soon moved to broaden the powers of the MHS and, during his 20-year tenure, the authorities and responsibilities of the Service grew substantially.

The Immigration Act of 1891

The industrial revolution in the United States unfolded in several phases, with the latter stage being placed at around 1870 to 1920. During that period, the U.S. transformed from a predominately rural agrarian society to an industrial economy. Technological innovations of the earlier industrial age led to the creation of factories engaged in mass production. The consequent need to greatly expand the manufacturing labor force led to an influx of immigrants and the urbanization of society.[1] Beginning in the late 1800s, increasing numbers of immigrants were coming to the United States drawn in part to meet the demands of the growing industrial economy. This large migration necessitated that the federal government assume immigration jurisdiction from the states. Mounting immigration and the associated necessity for an expanded quarantine service to inspect foreign vessels arriving from overseas were issues immediately confronting the new Supervising Surgeon General. Just prior to Dr. Wyman becoming the Supervising Surgeon General, the Congress on March 3, 1891, passed *An Act in Amendment to the Various Acts Relative to Immigration and the Importation of Aliens Under Contract or Agreement to Perform Labor*.[2] The Immigration Act had several provisions relating to immigration rules, procedures and enforcement for the foreigners arriving from countries other than China, and extended regulatory authority to land borders with Canada and Mexico, as well as to coastal borders of the United States. Importantly, the legislation assigned responsibility for the medical inspection of all arriving immigrants entering U.S. ports to the Marine Hospital Service. While most immigrants entered the United States through New York Harbor, others sailed to ports such as Boston, Philadelphia, Baltimore, San Francisco, Savannah, Miami, and New Orleans.

The largest immigration inspection station was at Ellis Island in Upper New York Harbor, which opened January 1, 1892, replacing New York's Castle Garden Emigrant Landing Depot. The Ellis Island Immigration Station, built of Georgia pine, caught on fire in 1897; however, it was rebuilt in Beaux-Arts style with fireproof materials and reopened December 17, 1900. The enormous

The rebuilt Immigration Station on Ellis Island in New York. Originally opened in 1892, Ellis Island was the gateway for over 12 million immigrants from 1892 to 1924.

[c. 1905, Ellis Island Foundation]

station housed administrative offices, inspection facilities, a hospital, cafeterias, a railroad ticket office, and representatives of immigrant aid societies. The immigration law specified that "All idiots, insane persons, paupers or persons likely to become a public charge, persons suffering from a loathsome or a dangerous contagious disease" were to be denied admission into the

United States. A relatively small group of MHS surgeons (the term used in the legislation) were assigned to examine sometimes thousands of arriving immigrants on busier days. Service officers boarded arriving ships to conduct a perfunctory inspection of first- and second-class passengers. Steerage or third-class passengers, however, were transported by barge or ferry to Ellis Island to undergo a medical inspection.[3] Upon disembarking, the immigrants were guided to the main building. Then, arranged in passageways single file called "the line," the immigrants slowly filed by an MHS officer who rapidly surveyed

Marine Hospital Service physicians at Ellis Island Immigration Station inspecting immigrants on the line. Here they are everting eyelids to check for signs of trachoma.
[c. 1910, National Library of Medicine]

them for any apparent physical or mental deficiencies. Due to the large number of immigrants arriving daily, medical officers performed a diagnostic glance of each individual within a matter of several seconds, examining the face, scalp, throat, and hands of the immigrant, and turning back the person's eyelids to check for the presence of trachoma. If a suspected defect or disease was present, a letter (e.g., *B* for possible back problem, *C* for eye conjunctivitis, *CT* for trachoma, *H* for heart problem, *S* for senility) was written in chalk on the immigrant's clothing and those persons were directed off the line to semi-private rooms for additional evaluation.[4] About 20 percent of immigrants had a letter written on their clothes, most of which were due to eye disease. The further examination would generally determine whether the immigrant was sufficiently healthy to enter the United States. Some immigrants with acute medical conditions might be referred to the onsite hospital for treatment, prior to gaining admission into the country. Other immigrants might be "medically certified," meaning an individual had a specified condition or disease that could render him or her unfit for admittance. Persons diagnosed with infectious diseases such as favus, trachoma, tuberculosis or venereal disease were deemed to be inadmissible to the United States. In 1903, the Marine Hospital Service issued the *Book of Instructions for the Medical Inspection of Immigrants*, which described medical conditions that constituted grounds for exclusion or contributory evidence to justify exclusion from admission; lighting and other factors that were to be considered when conducting medical examinations; and the need for physicians to perform a thorough examination and use care when placing someone in an exclusionary category.[5]

Medically certified assessments were conveyed to an Immigration Service Board of Special Inquiry, where an individual received a hearing prior to the Board rendering a decision relative to exclusion. The final determination of whether an individual would be received in the U.S. or returned to their country of origin was made by the Immigration Service. Prior to 1898, only about 1 percent of arriving immigrants at Ellis Island were inadmissible based upon the medical certificates and deported back to their country of origin. Service physicians were discouraged by Special Inquiry Boards overruling medical decisions much of the time. Yet, deportations based on medical certifications steadily rose, accounting for 18 percent in 1898, 38 percent in 1908, and 69 percent of all deportations for medical reasons in 1916.[6,7]

Until 1914, Service physicians assigned to immigration duty in the Line Division considered it a hardship post that was often the first tour of duty for new medical officers. They worked long hours under continual physical and mental strain amid an ongoing shortage of staff to meet the demand. Until 1898, only a few medical officers were assigned to the medical inspection line, which was increased to eleven officers in 1914. By contrast, the Ellis Island Hospital was considered among the nation's best hospitals and an assignment to the Ellis Island Hospital Division was sought by Service physicians.[7]

Medical examinations at Ellis Island were brief and served as more a processing than exclusionary function. In comparison, Latin American and Asian immigrants arriving at stations along the Mexico border and Pacific Coast were subject to more stringent medical examinations. Asian immigrants arriving in San Francisco were usually detained at Angel Island in San Francisco Bay for up to fourteen days awaiting results of their interview with officials and routine laboratory tests. Further, in 1882 the Chinese Exclusion Act, enacted due to unemployment fears (and renewed in 1892 by the Geary Act), prohibited entry of Chinese laborers. Similarly, in the early 1920s following World War I, discomfort with Europeans led to legislation that stemmed the flow of immigrants from eastern and southern European countries.[4,6,7]

Federalization of Quarantine

Until the late 19th century, quarantine authority was largely within the purview of the individual states. However, the states were often unable to cope with the ongoing introduction of infectious disease and spreading epidemics, and the increasing number of immigrants to the United States. Spurred by a "grave" cholera situation, the New York Academy of Medicine formed a special quarantine committee in 1892 which found that the capabilities at the Port of New York were insufficient to deal with the situation.[8] The

Committee believed that a national approach was needed and prepared a bill to establish a bureau of public health within the U.S. Treasury Department. The bill did not pass, but it led Congress to enact the Rayner-Harris National Quarantine Act of 1893, *An Act Granting Additional Quarantine Powers and Imposing Additional Duties upon the Marine-Hospital Service.*[9] While allowing state-run quarantine to continue, Section 3 of the Act provided for federal review of the adequacy of state and municipal quarantine regulations, promulgation of additional and/or new regulations where necessary, and authority to supersede in the enforcement of those regulations when a state/local jurisdiction failed or refused to properly enforce quarantine rules. Section 4 of the Act placed full authority and responsibility with the MHS:

> That it shall be the duty of the supervising Surgeon-General of the Marine Hospital Service ...to perform all the duties in respect to quarantine and quarantine regulations which are provided for by this act, and to obtain information of the sanitary condition of foreign ports and places from which contagious and infectious diseases are or may be imported into the United States.

Many states voluntarily transferred quarantine stations to the federal government and new federal quarantine facilities were built to provide better coverage. By 1913, the Service operated 48 quarantine stations on the Atlantic, Gulf and Pacific Seaboards, and quarantine systems in Alaska, Puerto Rico, and the Hawaiian and Philippine Islands.[8] Ultimately, the federal government took over all municipally administered quarantine activities and facilities, culminating in 1921 with acquisition of the quarantine service at the Port of New York.

The Act of 1893 also required that vessels at any foreign port bound for the United States obtain from a consular office a "bill of health" attesting to the sanitary history and conditions of the vessel, and compliance with applicable regulations with respect to the vessel, its cargo, passengers and crew. Prior to issuing the certification, a U.S. consular or medical officer assigned to the consul's office must be satisfied that "the matters and things therein stated are true." MHS officers were stationed in the ports of China, Japan, India, Europe, Central and South America and the West Indies to sign the bills of health of vessels, examine immigrants and provide sanitary information.[8]

The Act of 1893 gave the MHS dominance over quarantine activities and, when combined with its other functions of providing medical care to seamen, medical inspection of immigrants, surveillance and prevention of infectious disease, and research, the Service had effectively become a health department. MHS officers were a cohesive group that generally knew one another and shared a special camaraderie and commitment to national service, despite oftentimes difficult and potentially dangerous work and frequent duty relocations. In May 1896, the American Medical Association adopted a report declaring that the Marine Hospital Service "...was, by the Act of 1893, converted into a national health department, with very large and far-reaching powers and abundant means. It is not called a department of public health, but is a department of public health in fact."[10]

NATIONAL LEPROSARIUM

Throughout history leprosy had been misunderstood, resulting in considerable stigma and isolation of those who were afflicted. It is believed to have first appeared within the United States in Louisiana during the mid-1700s, followed by other nodes in the upper Midwest, California and New York.[11] Fear of contagion convinced Congress in 1899 to authorize the MHS to survey the prevalence and issues related to leprosy and formulate a national policy to address the matter. The resulting November 1901 report recommended the establishment of a national leprosarium. Two existing communities for the quarantined treatment of persons with leprosy, the Louisiana Leper Home in Carville and the Kalaupapa Settlement on the Hawaiian island of Molokaʻi staffed by Catholic ministries, were the foundation upon which the federal government built its leprosy research and treatment program. In 1905, Congress appropriated $150,000 for the construction and maintenance of a hospital and laboratory in Hawaii and Surgeon General Wyman selected the site on Molokaʻi. However, from 1906 until its closure in 1913, the facility proved to be a failure, because few patients would accept the rigor of treatments and imposed confinement compared with a freer life in Kalaupapa.[12] It wasn't until some years later in 1917 that a special Act[13] authorized a national leprosarium which was to be administered by the U.S. Public Health Service. In 1920, the Leper Home in Carville, Louisiana, was sold to the federal government and in 1921 the Home became a Marine Hospital. *(See also Chapter Five.)*

PLAGUE IN SAN FRANCISCO

The spread of bubonic plague had an enormous impact on the development of modern civilization during a time in history when the cause of plague was unknown. There have been three major pandemics of plague: the Justinian Plague of 541 that began in Africa and during the next 200 years claimed over 25 million lives, mainly in the Mediterranean basin; the "Black Death" or Great Plague of 1334 that originated in China and spread along major trade routes to Constantinople and Europe, claiming up to 60 percent of the European population; and the Modern Plague which began in China in the 1860s, appeared in Hong Kong by 1894 and spread to port cities around the world by infected rats on steamships, causing 10 to 15 million deaths. During the last pandemic in 1894, French physician Alexandre Yersin identified the bacterium *Yersinia pestis* as the causative agent that infects small rodents and is transmitted to humans through the bite of an infected flea.

PHS–Political Controversy

In April 1899, Dr. Joseph J. Kinyoun was transferred by Surgeon General Wyman to direct the San Francisco Quarantine Station based on Angel Island. Medical experts as well as Kinyoun and Wyman believed that plague cases would eventually arrive in the United States from China, where an outbreak began around 1860. Plague etiology was poorly understood in 1899, although an association with rats was known. Of particular concern was the San Francisco port, which received many ships from Asian cities with ongoing plague epidemics. And, in fact, a plague epidemic did evolve in San Francisco, occurring from 1900 to 1904, followed by another outbreak in 1907 to 1908. In March 1900, Dr. Kinyoun confirmed a preliminary diagnosis by city health officials of the first case of bubonic plague in a Chinese American resident of Chinatown. The San Francisco Board of Health immediately imposed a quarantine of Chinatown, which was lifted after only a few days due to a clamorous response by state officials, Chinatown leaders and the local press. Nonetheless, the city Board of Health declared plague to be present and continued efforts to clean up Chinatown. The California governor, allied with business interests, publicly refuted the claim of plague in San Francisco, fearing that word about its presence would be detrimental to the city and state economy.[14] When the State Board of Health also concluded that plague existed in the city, the governor purged the Board members and replaced them with new members who would deny the existence of plague.[15] The city Board of Health nonetheless identified areas of infection and continued its house-to-house inspections to clean and disinfect Chinatown. Surgeon General Wyman recommended inoculating its residents with the Haffkine vaccine and, in May 1900, he was given authority to implement the interstate quarantine provisions of 1893 that limited residents'

Plague was endemic in San Francisco and a Public Health and Marine Hospital Service plague office was maintained for several years.
[c. 1907, National Library of Medicine]

travel. The Surgeon General regularly communicated with and provided direction to Dr. Kinyoun. However, resistance to PHS activities and Kinyoun's perceived "officious manner" led Chinese officials to file for a restraining order, resulting in a federal court ruling against the federal government. This coincided with an intensified state campaign to malign Joseph Kinyoun.

To further assess the situation, Dr. Wyman detailed Surgeon Joseph H. White of the division of domestic quarantine to the Pacific Coast in December 1900, who in January corroborated the reports of plague. In response to the ongoing recalcitrance of the state, Wyman recommended, and the federal Treasury Secretary appointed on January 19, 1901, a commission of three bacteriologist/medical scientist experts to travel to San Francisco to ascertain the "existence or nonexistence of bubonic plague." By February the commissioners had substantiated the presence of plague in San Francisco.[15,16] The governor continued to deny the plague's existence, so the standoff with the California politicians was resolved at a meeting held with President William McKinley in Washington, DC, whereby the state allowed the MHS to proceed with quarantine and plague control, if Kinyoun was removed from his post. Although supported by the special commission, fellow officers and organized medicine, Dr. Kinyoun was reassigned by Surgeon General Wyman and left for Detroit in May 1901; one year later, he resigned from the Service. The dishonorable political interference in San Francisco from 1899 to 1901 and scapegoating of Dr. Kinyoun would be a low point in Service history.

The San Francisco plague eradication program was taken over by Joseph White until June 1901. Wyman recalled White and, with the governor's consent, MHS medical officer Rupert Blue took charge of the Chinatown disinfection activities and maintenance of a plague laboratory. Dr. Blue was succeeded by medical officers Mark J. White, and then Arthur H. Glennan in October 1902. In November, city health officials began a comprehensive effort to eliminate rats and the following month Dr. Wyman visited San Francisco. In January 1903, the new governor of California, George C. Pardee, MD, was installed and he provided steadfast support for the Marine Hospital Service. The State and Territorial Health Officers also met with the Surgeon General and expressed their concern about the situation. Faced with a growing threat of a national quarantine, California State and local officials acceded to the MHS and cooperated with plague control efforts. In February 1903, Dr. Blue returned to take charge of a one-year campaign to eradicate bubonic plague in San Francisco through a massive clean-up effort that included the removal of unsanitary wooden additions erected by Chinese residents. By March 1, 1904, the last case of plague was reported, marking 120 people who died of the disease.[17] However, some believe that the obstructionist response to the 1900 infection may have contributed to rural spread of the pathogen in California and possibly other states through the squirrel population.

That was not to be the end of plague in San Francisco. In April 1906, much of the city was destroyed by a great earthquake and fire. The lack of sanitation during reconstruction allowed the emergence of a second plague epidemic throughout the city in 1907. This time, though, state and local officials and the public were very supportive of a comprehensive program to rapidly assess and eradicate the disease. Wyman again dispatched Rupert Blue to San Francisco to lead the control effort and work with health authorities to exterminate the rat infestation, identify human cases and clean-up the environment. Blue is credited with exceptional public relations efforts and an indefatigable campaign to eliminate the disease in San Francisco, which occurred in June 1908. By the end of the second plague outbreak, there were 78 deaths, a lower mortality than during 1900 to 1904.[18]

Angel Island Quarantine and Immigration Stations

Angel Island, among the largest islands in San Francisco Bay, provided an isolated location on a cove named Hospital Cove to build a quarantine station operated by the Marine Hospital Service. Opened on April 29, 1891, the station was comprised of forty buildings including a boathouse, warehouse for personal effects of steerage passengers, three detention barracks with dining room and kitchen, a disinfection plant with three large iron cylinders,

Marine Hospital Service Quarantine Station at Hospital Cove on Angel Island in San Francisco Bay, 1891–1946. Renamed Ayala Cove in 1969.
[c. 1920, Angel Island Conservancy]

a hospital for noncontagious diseases, a lazaretto (isolation hospital), pump house, laundry, laboratory, and staff quarters. Arriving ships were inspected at the entrance to the Bay and, when a contagious disease such as smallpox was discovered, a yellow flag was raised and the vessel anchored at the Quarantine Station. Upon reaching the station, ships could be fumigated, and clothing and luggage disinfected with pressurized steam. Steerage passengers, who were almost exclusively Chinese or Japanese, were held in detention for up to 14 days for observation and examination by MHS medical officers. As improved medical examinations at ports of embarkation made quarantines unnecessary, use of the Angel Island Quarantine Station diminished over the years and it was decommissioned in 1946.[19-21] On January 21, 1910, the Department of Commerce and Labor opened the Angel Island Immigration Station (AIIS) at North Garrison, also known as China Cove or Winslow Cove, about a mile and a half from the MHS Quarantine Station. Previously housed in buildings along San Francisco's waterfront, the AIIS became the major U.S. port of entry for immigrants coming from the West. The station included an administration building, a small hospital, a confined detention barracks, kitchen and dining facility, powerhouse, and wharf. PHS medical officers were detailed to the Immigration Station for the purpose of conducting examinations of arriving immigrants to detect conditions that were exclusionary for entering the United States and to provide care for common diseases. In operation from 1910 to 1940, the Immigration Station processed up to one million immigrants from over 80 countries, including 250,000 Chinese and 150,000 Japanese immigrants. Unless those arriving from China were in an exempt category, Chinese were targeted for exclusion from immigration by the Chinese Exclusion Act of 1882, which mainly barred skilled and unskilled laborers. Most arriving Chinese were detained on Angel Island from two weeks to six months to complete their immigration hearing and if necessary to file an appeal, until their applications were approved.[22,23]

The Act of 1902

By the late nineteenth century, the responsibilities of the Marine Hospital Service had expanded well beyond the provision of health care to merchant seamen. The medical inspection of immigrants to the United States, broad quarantine authority, and activities relating to the control of infectious diseases placed the Service in the forefront of national public health. Accordingly, the name of the Service was changed in 1902 to the "Public Health and Marine Hospital Service" (PHMHS). The *Act to Increase the Efficiency and Change the Name of the United States Marine-Hospital Service*,[24] signed by President Theodore Roosevelt on July 1, increased the statutory powers of the Service and included provisions of note:

> Section 1 renamed the Marine Hospital Service the Public Health and Marine Hospital Service and changed the title of the Supervising Surgeon General to Surgeon General.†
>
> Section 2 provided an annual salary of $5,000 for the Surgeon General.
>
> Section 4 authorized the President to use the PHMHS in time of war.
>
> Section 5 & 6 authorized an advisory board and the formation of three new divisions in the Hygienic Laboratory – chemistry, pharmacology and zoology.
>
> Section 7 authorized the Surgeon General to hold an annual conference of the health authorities of all States, Territories and the District of Columbia, and to call a special conference in the interests of the public health and/or upon the application of not less than five specified State or Territorial entities.

---

† An initial use of the title *Surgeon General* appears to be in the U.S. Army. A reorganization Act of March 3, 1813, cited *physician and surgeon-general* for medical superintendence, and the Act of April 14, 1818, reaffirms use of the title *surgeon-general*.[25]

Section 8 required the PHMHS, after the annual conference, to provide forms for the collection, compilation and publication of mortality, morbidity and vital statistics.

Section 9 required the Surgeon General to annually provide the Treasury Secretary, for transmission to the Congress, a full and complete report of the transactions of the Service.

Surgeon General Wyman was a very able administrator who constantly strove to improve the Service and its provision of hospital care, medical inspection and quarantine services, research endeavors, and response to communicable disease outbreaks. He slowly introduced female nurses into the Service, who were first employed in the early 1890s in the care of immigrants at Ellis Island Hospital.[26] The Service employed pharmacists to prepare medications and handle administrative duties at hospitals and quarantine stations. Under Wyman, the Service led the effort to study and recommend actions to accommodate those who were afflicted with leprosy; three Service officers served on the Leprosy Commission that reported on the disease. As has been noted, several proposals for a national health department or changes to the Service had been introduced in Congress by 1910. The Surgeon General, although generally supportive, was determined that the Service not be preempted by a health department and he deftly navigated the Service through a number of critical challenges to strengthen and advance the Service and its contribution to national public health.[27]

Medical Research (Part 1)

Dr. Walter Wyman served as Surgeon General until 1911. He was a formidable administrator who was relentless in his efforts to establish a medical laboratory that would rival the best scientific laboratories in Europe. The Marine Hospital Service's Laboratory of Hygiene, which began in 1887 in a room of the Marine Hospital at Staten Island, New York, and headed by Dr. Joseph Kinyoun, was the foundation upon which an extensive MHS research program and eventually the National Institutes of Health was built. In 1901, Wyman formed the Division of Scientific Research in the Service, which included the Hygienic Laboratory. During the tenures of directors Joseph Kinyoun (1887-1899), Milton J. Rosenau (1899-1909) and John F. Anderson (1909-1915), the Hygienic Laboratory became an epicenter of research – along with academic research centers such as the University of Michigan – on the etiology of infectious and other diseases. Many diseases were introduced into the United States by infected merchant seamen and immigrants on the ships arriving from foreign ports, and it was imperative that the Hygienic Laboratory form a robust research program to address the wide array of these diseases, some of which were becoming endemic in the Nation. It became Dr. Rosenau's mission to expand the important research program of his predecessor. Rosenau was an exceptional scientist who was previously involved in anti-cholera efforts and worked on pneumococcal immunizations, anaphylaxis, and milk safety, and in 1896 headed the San Francisco Quarantine Station on Angel Island. The newly authorized divisions of chemistry, pharmacology, and zoology were added to the bacteriology and pathology division in the Hygienic Laboratory. Scientific researchers as well as PHS medical officers staffed the divisions. In 1904, the Laboratory moved into the new building authorized by Congress and significantly increased its research activities on infectious diseases at the Laboratory and in the field, including typhoid fever, bubonic plague, yellow fever and Rocky Mountain spotted fever. Moreover, the 1902 Biologics Control Act[28] authorized the Laboratory to regulate the production of biologicals, set standards, issue biologics licenses to firms, and regulate the importation and transport of products.

Milton J. Rosenau

YELLOW FEVER

Yellow fever is transmitted to people through the bite of an infected female mosquito that acquired the yellow fever virus by feeding on and ingesting blood from a viremic human or other primate. Prior to 1900, little was known about the cause or treatment of yellow fever, and it was a feared pestilence and significant threat in many countries worldwide. In the United States, outbreaks occurred with some regularity in coastal cities, including severe epidemics in Philadelphia in 1793 and New Orleans in the 1800s. In 1898, MHS medical officer Henry Rose Carter, who was assigned to the quarantine station at Ship Island, Mississippi, performed epidemiological studies to determine the interval between onset of yellow fever and the occurrence of secondary cases, results suggesting that an intermediate host was the vector for yellow fever. At about the same time, yellow fever was having a devastating impact on U.S. troops who were deployed to Cuba during and after the Spanish American War of 1898. In 1899, Carter was assigned to Cuba as the chief quarantine officer, where he met members of the Army Yellow Fever Commission headed by Major Walter Reed. The Commission was in Cuba to conduct observational experiments to learn about the etiology of the disease. By 1900, taking into account Cuban physician

Henry R. Carter

Carlos Finlay's 1881 theory that a mosquito which bites a diseased victim could subsequently bite and infect a healthy person, and Dr. Carter's discovery of the "extrinsic incubation period" of yellow fever, the Commission confirmed that the mosquito *Aedes aegypti* was the carrier of yellow fever and that immunity was achieved following prior infection. Walter Reed subsequently wrote to Carter stating, "I know of no one more competent to pass judgment on all that pertains to the subject of yellow fever. You must not forget that your own work in Mississippi did more to impress me with the importance of an intermediate host in yellow fever than everything else put together." Dr. Carter was next assigned as the Director of Hospitals and, with other MHS officers, joined forces with Army Colonel William C. Gorgas, Chief Sanitary Officer, to stem the spread of yellow fever and malaria in the Canal Zone during construction of the Panama Canal. The early discoveries were a foundation for subsequent investigations of yellow fever. Dr. James Carroll, member of the Yellow Fever Commission, would later prove that an agent in the blood, compatible with a virus, caused the disease; and the work of Dr. Max Theiler on virus attenuation led to development of the initial 17D vaccine in 1937. Despite the availability of a vaccine, however, many regions in the world remained at risk.[29-31]

HOOKWORM

Charles Wardell Stiles was a zoologist and expert on intestinal parasites in the Department of Agriculture from 1891 to 1902. His work on the problem of parasites in farm animals introduced him to the parasitic hookworm and his identification of an American hookworm – *Uncinaria americana* (later called *Necator americanus*) – that differed from its European counterpart.

Charles W. Stiles

In the early 1900s, hookworm disease was endemic in the rural South due to lack of or open privies and the absence of shoes, causing widespread chronic illness. Transmission is via larvae in feces that enter the soil and penetrate the skin, particularly of the feet and hands. Hookworm larvae then inhabit the small intestine, attaching to capillaries to feed and causing progressive anemia. Left untreated and in susceptible individuals, the disease can cause severe physical and cognitive impairment in infected children. In 1902, Dr. Stiles transferred to the Public Health and Marine Hospital Service to become chief of the new Division of Zoology within the Hygienic Laboratory. That position allowed him to continue his hookworm research and beginning in late 1902, he embarked on regular field trips through the South, publishing a comprehensive report in February 1903 about the disease and its prevalence, entitled *Report Upon the Prevalence and Geographic Distribution of Hookworm Disease in the United States*. Stiles pressed a campaign for improved sanitation facilities and encouraged the practice of wearing shoes outdoors, but resources were unavailable and his efforts were not embraced by the public or the medical profession. In 1908, a chance meeting with Walter Page, a distinguished person of note, gave Dr. Stiles an opportunity to discuss the considerable disease burden on Southerners. Page connected with associates of John D. Rockefeller, which led in 1909 to the founding of The Rockefeller Sanitary Commission (RSC) for the Eradication of Hookworm Disease, with a grant of $1 million to be used over a five-year period. Stiles was appointed the RSC scientific secretary; the goals were to map and survey hookworm prevalence in the South, treat infections, and eradicate the disease. The RSC belief was that education was the most important factor in both curing hookworm and promoting public health in the South. The RSC adopted the model of local dispensaries to attract, screen, provide medication (thymol and Epsom salt), and educate the public about the need for sanitary privy construction. Cooperative work with the medical profession, medical schools and media raised awareness about the disease and importance of hygiene and sanitation.[32,33]

ROCKY MOUNTAIN SPOTTED FEVER

Rocky Mountain spotted fever (RMSF) can be a life-threatening disease that is spread to humans by a tick infected with the pathogen *Rickettsia rickettsii*. By the early 1900s, RMSF was reported in several Western states, but was most prevalent in heavily wooded areas of Montana and Idaho. In 1902, there was 80 to 90 percent mortality among adults including sheep herders and stockmen in the Bitterroot Valley of Montana, while in Idaho there was a much lower fatality rate. The inhabitants' fear of the disease, known locally as "black measles" due to its dark rash, led to declining land values and depopulation. The Montana State Board of Health invited pathologists Louis B. Wilson and Willliam M. Chowning of the University of Minnesota to study the situation; the Public Health and Marine Hospital Service sent Dr. Julius O. Cobb, whose arrival in 1902 began a multi-year association of the Hygienic Laboratory with spotted fever, with numerous Laboratory scientists making contributions toward understanding the disease.[34,35] Drs. Charles Stiles and John Anderson of the PHMHS were among those researching the disease. In 1906, Dr. Howard T. Ricketts of the University of Chicago discovered that the disease was transmitted through the bite of the Rocky Mountain wood tick, *Dermacentor andersoni* (named in 1908 to honor Dr. Anderson). Ricketts returned each summer and by 1909 he had isolated the bacterial pathogen that was later named in his honor. Uncertainty about continued funding led Ricketts to work on typhus in Mexico City.

The Montana legislature appropriated funds to continue the RMSF work and, upon request of the Board of Health, the effort was taken up by the Public Health and Marine Hospital Service. Assistant Surgeon Thomas B. McClintic was assigned in May 1911 to the state to continue work on eradication of the tick that was the causative agent. Accompanied by Dr. Thomas Tuttle of the Board of Health and medical officer William C. Rucker, the work was conducted in a manner similar to Rickett's method of testing and the destruction of wild animals in the vicinity of Victor, Montana. Most animals, both wild and domestic, harbored the tick, so ranchers were encouraged to drive their herds through dipping vats of arsenical solution to control the tick. McClintic continued his investigations in the Bitterroot Valley during the summer of 1912. However, early in August, Dr. McClintic became infected with spotted fever. Returning immediately to Washington, DC, he soon died on August 13, 1912. Surgeon Lunsford D. Fricks became the lead investigative officer in Montana in 1913.[34] Work on spotted fever continued for many years. In 1924, Dr. Roscoe R. Spencer of the PHS and Dr. Ralph R. Parker, Montana entomologist who was a special expert to the PHS working at the Hygienic Laboratory and at a makeshift laboratory in Hamilton, Montana, created a vaccine against spotted fever. In 1928, a new laboratory was built in Hamilton, which was leased by the PHS until 1932 when it was purchased by the federal government, becoming part of the National Institute of Health in 1937. Several additional buildings were constructed by 1940. During World War II, the laboratory produced vaccines to protect soldiers against spotted fever, typhus and yellow fever. It subsequently returned to its primary mission of scientific research on infectious diseases. Rocky Mountain Laboratories (RML) has become a state-of-the-art biomedical research component of the National Institute of Allergy and Infectious Diseases, NIH. It is comprised of

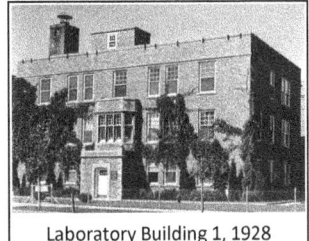
Laboratory Building 1, 1928

about 30 buildings on an expansive campus where research is conducted on infectious agents such as prions, intracellular and maximum containment pathogens. The RML Integrated Research Facility,

RML Integrated High Containment Research Facility, 2008

which opened in 2008, is the first NIH facility of its kind to house biosafety level-2 (BSL-2), BSL-3, and BSL-4 (highest level of biosafety precautions) laboratory space in one building.

SURGEON GENERAL PASSING

Walter Wyman, a bachelor who dedicated his life to advancing the Public Health and Marine Hospital Service, continued to serve as Surgeon General until the onset of a diabetic coma that led to his death in Washington, DC, on November 21, 1911. Within a month, a new Surgeon General would be named.

CHRONOLOGY • 1891–1911
(Supervising) SG Walter Wyman, June 1891–November 1911

1891	The *Immigration Act of 1891*. Assigns responsibility for the medical inspection of all arriving immigrants entering U.S. ports to the Marine Hospital Service.
1891	MHS Quarantine Station opens on Angel Island in San Francisco Bay.
1892	Immigration Station opens on Ellis Island in New York Harbor.
1893	The *National Quarantine Act of 1893*. Provides authorization for the Marine Hospital Service to administer a federal system of quarantine.
1899	Joseph Kinyoun assigned to San Francisco, Angel Island Quarantine Station.
1900	Onset of the first plague epidemic in the nation, in San Francisco.
1901	The U.S. Army Yellow Fever Commission, with epidemiological evidence from MHS officer Henry Carter, publishes its report on disease etiology.
1901	MHS releases report on the origin and prevalence of leprosy in the U.S.
1902	The *Act to Increase the Efficiency and Change the Name of the United States Marine-Hospital Service*. Renames the Service the Public Health and Marine Hospital Service; charges the SG with convening an annual conference of State health authorities and publish vital statistics; and expands the capabilities of the Hygienic Laboratory.
1902	The *Biologics Control Act*. Provides the Hygienic Laboratory with authority to regulate the production of biologicals.
1902	PHMHS begins work on Rocky Mountain spotted fever, culminating in the development of a vaccine in 1924.
1906	Leprosy research program is established at Moloka'i, Hawaii; closed 1913.
1907	Second outbreak of plague in San Francisco following a major earthquake.
1909	Founding of the Rockefeller Sanitary Commission for the Eradication of Hookworm Disease, with PHMHS officer Charles Stiles as scientific secretary.
1910	MHS Immigration Station opens on Angel Island in San Francisco Bay.
1910	[Abraham] *Flexner Report* is released about needed reforms in medical school education, which transformed medical training in the Unites States.

CHAPTER FOUR

PUBLIC HEALTH EXPANSION, WAR, PANDEMIC
1912 to 1920

THE PROGRESSIVE ERA in the United States covered the period from the 1890s through the end of World War I until 1920 when national sentiment rose to address economic and social reform in the United States. During this period there was a general belief that science and medical research could improve public health. Leading industrialists began making philanthropic investments in support of biomedical research, and Congress stood ready to provide greater funding for the important work of the Public Health and Marine Hospital Service (PHMHS).

Following the unexpected death of Walter Wyman in November 1911, Dr. Rupert Blue was appointed Surgeon General of the Public Health and Marine Hospital Service on January 13, 1912. President William H. Taft's appointment of Dr. Blue over other more senior officers was hailed in *The Medical Times* in April 1912 as a tribute to "one of medicine's truly great disciples." Surgeon General Blue was the beneficiary of a now robust Service with national responsibilities, a cadre of well educated and committed medical officers, and a strong research program. Born and raised in North and South Carolina, Blue earned his MD from the University of Maryland in 1892. Following an internship, he was commissioned in the PHMHS Regular Corps as an Assistant Surgeon on March 3, 1893. Blue spent earlier years in various duty assignments throughout the country including Cincinnati, Galveston, Charleston, Portland, OR, and Norfolk, VA; he served abroad in Genoa, Italy, performing medical screening of persons bound for the U.S. He led mosquito eradication efforts during the 1905 yellow fever outbreak in New Orleans, and he was nationally recognized for exemplary leadership in directing successful campaigns from 1903–1904 and 1907–1908 to eradicate bubonic plague in San Francisco. Blue conducted health surveys in South America, and in 1911 he was sanitary adviser in Hawaii to lessen disease impact on ships traveling through the new Panama Canal.

Rupert Blue

The Act of 1912

The mission of the Service continued to extend beyond the provision of care to merchant seamen, enforcement of maritime and interstate quarantine, medical inspection of immigrants, and investigation and containment of disease. Soon after the passing of Walter Wyman, Treasury Secretary Franklin MacVeagh used the opportunity in his report to Congress to "promote and expand" the role of the Public Health and Marine Hospital Service and to rename the organization.[1] Finally on August 14, 1912, the anticipated law was signed by President Taft that changed the name of the PHMHS to the Public Health Service (PHS). In the Surgeon General's *Annual Report* of 1912 Rupert Blue notes: "The passage of this law marks a new epoch in the history of the health activities of the Federal Government, and it is believed clearly recognizes the Public Health Service as the central health agency of the Nation."[2] The *Act to Change the Name of the Public Health and Marine-Hospital Service to the Public Health Service, to Increase the Pay of Officers of Said Service, and for Other Purposes*,[3] included the following provision:

> This law marks a new epoch in the history of health activities ...and clearly recognizes PHS as the central health agency of the Nation.

> Section 1 renamed the Public Health and Marine Hospital Service the Public Health Service; it authorized the Public Health Service to study and investigate the diseases of man and conditions influencing the propagation and spread thereof, including sanitation and sewage and the pollution either directly or indirectly of the navigable streams and lakes of the United States; and authorized the Public Health Service to issue information in the form of publications for the use of the public.

The importance of the Act's provision authorizing the Public Health Service to "study and investigate the diseases of man and conditions influencing the propagation and spread thereof, including sanitation and sewage and the pollution either directly or indirectly of the navigable streams and lakes of the United States" was profound. By this Act, the PHS was acknowledged as the lead federal public health agency with a comprehensive mission that would enable it to address whatever disease-related and environmental issues it deemed appropriate. On June 13, 1913, President Woodrow Wilson signed the Sundry Civil Appropriations Act which provided funding in support of the Public Health Service law of 1912. The PHS Division of Scientific Research was provided $200,000 for field investigations of diseases and the pollution of navigable waters. An additional $47,000 and $25,000 were earmarked for the study of pellagra and trachoma, respectively; and $20,000 in supplemental funds were provided for the Hygienic Laboratory.

Medical Research (Part 2)

Dr. John F. Anderson, who went abroad to study bacteriology, joined the Marine Hospital Service in 1898. He was assistant director of the Hygienic Laboratory under Milton Rosenau and was appointed its director in 1909, serving in the position until 1915. Dr. Anderson did early research on Rocky Mountain spotted fever and had worked closely with Rosenau on anaphylaxis and tuberculosis. His research interests were many and varied, and included cholera, poliomyelitis and typhus, as well as immunology and sanitation. Throughout his tenure, medical and scientific personnel of the Laboratory continued to make scientific advances through focused investigations of high burden diseases, bringing recognition of the Public Health Service as the preeminent federal research center in the United States. The Laboratory's prominence coincided with a growing societal awareness that disease etiology could be uncovered scientifically and controlled with sanitation and public education playing a pivotal role as preventive public health measures. PHS officers were at the front lines of research, such as Dr. George W. McCoy who in 1912 first isolated the tularemia bacterium; McCoy served as the fourth director of the Hygienic Laboratory from 1915 to 1937. Also, Dr. Leslie Lumsden, who investigated and then led a successful sanitation campaign in Yakima, Washington to control a typhoid fever epidemic; his efforts served as a civic action model for rural health reform.[4] The following are brief accounts of a few PHS officers and the diseases that they investigated during the early 1900s. *(See also Chapter Three, Medical Research [Part 1].)*

TYPHUS FEVER

Throughout history, millions of deaths have been ascribed to epidemic typhus caused by *Rickettsia* bacteria, often accompanying overcrowding in poor living conditions and during times of war. There are two major types of the disease: endemic or murine (flea-borne) typhus caused by *R. typhi* and involving an infected animal harboring flea vectors that, via flea fecal contamination of the flea bite wound, can infect humans; and epidemic (louse-borne) typhus, a more severe form caused by *R. prowazekii* that involves infected body lice vectors that, via lice fecal contamination, infect humans. Illness from epidemic typhus can vary from mild to severe, with high fever, headache, delirium, exanthema, vasculitis and absent treatment, up to a 60 percent fatality rate. Brill-Zinsser disease is a milder form of epidemic typhus when *R. prowazekii* bacteria reactivate in a previously infected person. MHS/PHS officers were involved in investigations of typhus from 1909 until the production of a vaccine in the 1940s. Charles Nicolle was a French bacteriologist who in 1909 showed that infected body lice were able to transmit typhus. Drs. John Anderson and Joseph Goldberger, in independent studies of typhus in Mexico and the United States, reported the first evidence implicating the head louse as a possible agent in transmission of epidemic typhus. In 1912, Anderson and Goldberger further determined that Brill's disease, first noticed in New York City in 1898, and typhus fever were identical. Subsequent work in Alabama and Georgia in the early 1920s by Dr. Kenneth F. Maxcy, who transferred to the Hygienic Laboratory for four years beginning in 1925, produced experimental and epidemiological evidence that there was likely a domestic rat reservoir of the typhus organism that was transmitted to humans by fleas and mites, as the causative agent of endemic typhus.[5] Dr. R. Eugene Dyer and other PHS officers took over typhus work in 1929, eventually confirming that endemic typhus is carried among rodents by fleas, which is transmitted to humans. The first basic typhus vaccine was created by Polish biologist Rudolf Weigl. In 1938, Dr. Herald R. Cox of the Rocky Mountain Laboratory showed that active immunity could be induced using a chick embryo yolk sac-grown typhus vaccine, from which Drs. Norman H. Topping and Ida A. Bengtson of the National Institute of Health produced a more efficacious product that was used to protect American troops during World War II.

TRACHOMA

Trachoma was especially prevalent in Europe during the 19th century as the leading cause of blindness. It was common in parts of the United States in the early 1900s, including a high rate of endemic trachoma among Native Americans. Presence of the disease was attributed to prior importation. Trachoma is an infectious disease caused by the bacterium *Chlamydia trachomatis*. It produces inflammatory granulation of the inner surface of the eyelids, which can lead to eye pain, corneal breakdown and blindness. Trachoma is spread by contact with an affected person's eye secretions and indirectly by contact with fomites such as towels that have the secretions.

The Immigration Act of 1891 assigned responsibility to the Marine Hospital Service for the medical inspection of immigrants entering U.S. ports. Trachoma is not only contagious, but those afflicted could also become a public charge, so trachoma was among the most prominent of diseases screened for by Service officers. In 1912, Dr. John McMullen, a medical officer who worked for many years at the Ellis Island Immigration Station, was assigned to Kentucky to conduct a trachoma survey that indicated a relatively high prevalence of the disease. The state health officer requested intervention by the Public Health Service to control the disease, leading in 1913 to a federal appropriation of $200,000 for further investigations and $25,000 to treat the disease in the field. MHS medical officers were detailed to several states during the next few years to further study trachoma prevalence. The surveys disclosed the presence of a "trachoma belt" extending from Virginia through the southern states to Kentucky.[6] Described as a large and kindly man who was known as "Big Doc," McMullen often rode by mule into Kentucky mountain country where he found that families had an average of eight to ten children. In the Surgeon General's *Annual Report* for 1912,[2] the observation was made:

> The whole family often sleep, live, and cook in the one room of the home, and in addition use the same towel for days without changing, and wash in the same basin, which is often a stone partially buried beside the well and having a depression on the top, the thorough cleansing or even emptying of this rudimentary basin being practically impossible. If a disease as contagious as trachoma is introduced, all the facilities for its rapid transmission will be found present.

Such factors were affirmed by medical officer Charles Bailey who completed a survey of the prevalence of trachoma in Tennessee and Georgia in 1914, where unsanitary cabins and use of common basins and towels were implicated in the dissemination of trachoma.[7] Dr. John McMullen's approach to prevention and control of trachoma included a health education campaign about the importance of hygiene, as well as clinical treatment of identified cases. In 1913, based in an office in Louisville, McMullen proceeded over the

John McMullen (pictured in white coat) on a mobile railway car that transported personnel, a clinic and surgical operating room throughout Missouri.[8]
[c. 1922, National Library of Medicine]

next decade to create a system of field clinics and trachoma hospitals in Kentucky, Tennessee, Arkansas, Georgia, Missouri, Virginia and elsewhere. The hospitals had a physician and at least two nurses who cared for convalescing patients and traveled to surrounding areas to identify trachoma patients and conduct health education.[1] McMullen traveled between these clinics and hospitals to oversee the program and perform corrective surgery. He also authored and had distributed thousands of copies of the pamphlet, *Trachoma: Its Nature and Prevention*. Working relentlessly until 1924, Dr. McMullen is credited with saving the sight of thousands of people in this country. Due to improved sanitation, living conditions, and the availability of effective treatments, trachoma has been mostly eliminated in the United States and the industrialized world, but it is still prevalent in the developing world.

Pellagra

Pellagra is a disease caused by a dietary deficiency of niacin (vitamin B3) or deficiency of the essential amino acid tryptophan which is found in eggs, fish, meat, poultry, and peanuts. The classic symptoms of pellagra include dermatitis, diarrhea, and dementia, and death within five years if not treated. Pellagra was first described in Spain in 1735 and was prevalent in Europe by the late 1800s, becoming endemic in rural areas and northern Italy. Disease outbreaks were often clustered within poorer areas where corn was a staple food crop; for that reason, a prevailing hypothesis was that spoilage of corn or maize produced a toxin as the causative agent. Another prominent theory espoused by Dr. Louis Sambon of the London School of Tropical Medicine was that pellagra was an infectious disease transmitted by an insect vector.

In the early 1900s, pellagra had become epidemic in the southern United States. By 1912, South Carolina reported 30,000 pellagra cases, with a mortality rate of 40 percent. Ultimately, there were over 3 million cases and 100,000 deaths from pellagra in the country by 1940. Initial cases were diagnosed in mental hospitals located in Alabama and South Carolina, but the disease rapidly spread to orphanages, prisons, and to poorer populations such as tenant farmers and sharecroppers throughout the South. The growing epidemic spurred a situation where those afflicted with pellagra became socially isolated. In 1912, the Thompson-McFadden Pellagra Commission, named for two philanthropists who funded the commission, investigated the disease in cotton mill districts of South Carolina, erroneously concluding that unsanitary waste disposal and not diet was a factor in disease causation. The Commission report also provided support for the theory of an infectious agent being the etiology of pellagra. Publicity about the association of pellagra with an impoverished citizenry was considered an affront to Southern pride, provoking political figures to condemn such reports about the disease.[9] In response to widening pleas for federal involvement, Surgeon General Walter Wyman appointed a study commission and in 1909 assigned medical officer and epidemiologist Claude H. Lavinder to try and identify the causative agent. Dr. Lavinder established a small laboratory at the South Carolina Hospital for the Insane, the superintendent of which was Dr. James Babcock who led the early American response to pellagra. Lavinder performed animal experiments that would prove to be helpful, but he was not successful in identifying the causative factor. A conceptual breakthrough occurred in 1912 when Casimir Funk, a chemist working in London, proposed that pellagra, like beriberi and scurvy, was a deficiency disease that could be prevented or cured by substances called "vitamines." Surgeon General Rupert Blue later noted Funk's hypothesis as one of the two most promising theories, the other being of infectious origin.[10]

In early 1914, Lavinder requested reassignment and in February, Surgeon General Rupert Blue sent an experienced infectious disease officer named Dr. Joseph Goldberger, who had distinguished himself in typhus and yellow fever research. Blue conveyed to Goldberger that there was considerable congressional pressure to deal more forcefully with pellagra.[11] Upon arrival at the Hygienic Laboratory, Goldberger began to tour Southern mental institutions and orphanages, confirming earlier observations that patients and younger children had pellagra, whereas nurses and attendants did not. He reviewed the available literature and within four months, Goldberger had determined that an inadequate diet was likely causing the disease. In June 1914, Goldberger suggested that a dietary change – the introduction of eggs, meats and milk – could be both curative and preventive, and the lack of such foods could induce pellagra. These conclusions were shown by subsequent studies in orphanages, a state sanitarium and in volunteer prison inmates. To prove that pellagra was not a communicable illness, Goldberger exposed himself, his wife and other volunteers to pellagrin body fluids and pellagrous lesions; none of the volunteers contracted the disease. Goldberger and PHS epidemiologist Edgar Sydenstricker conducted meticulous epidemiological studies in the cotton mill villages of South Carolina which showed that pellagra was associated with socioeconomic conditions. The usual "monotonous diet" of poor Southerners and institutional populations often included fat pork meat, cornmeal and molasses. The method of milling corn changed with the introduction of the degerminator in 1905, which reduced the niacin content in processed cornmeal and plausibly led to the widespread outbreak of pellagra, beginning in the South. Native populations in the Americas, in contrast, traditionally soaked corn in lime water (alkali) before grinding into meal and cooking, which released bound niacin for dietary consumption. By 1926, Dr. Goldberger found that dried yeast contained a high amount of what was termed the "pellagra-preventive factor," which would prevent pellagra, but he was unable to identify the specific nutritional deficiency before his death in 1929. It was not until 1937 that Conrad Elvehjem of the University of Wisconsin showed that nicotinic acid (niacin) deficiency caused the canine analogue of pellagra. At the same time, Dr. Tom Spies and other researchers determined that niacin could cure pellagra. By the 1940s, the enrichment of commercial foods with niacin helped eliminate pellagra in the United States. Goldberger committed his professional life to discovering the etiology of pellagra and provided the world with the knowledge to mitigate the dreadful effects and suffering brought about by the disease.

Joseph Goldberger

ENVIRONMENTAL HEALTH

Environmental health was increasingly being drawn into the arena of public health. It was known in the early twentieth century that the pollution of rivers and streams with sewage was a source of waterborne diseases. Typhoid fever was a particular problem in the Midwest and in 1910 the Public Health Service initiated a survey of interstate waterways with a focus on cities in the Great Lakes region. PHS medical officer Allan J. McLaughlin led the effort, with results showing a high prevalence of typhoid in Missouri River cities and especially Niagara Falls. Within a few years, Canada joined the effort, with McLaughlin directing field investigations of boundary waters for the U.S.–Canadian International Joint Commission. Then in 1914, at the request of the State of Massachusetts, he transferred to develop the state's health system as Commissioner of Health, setting a precedent for other PHS officers who would follow to act as commissioner or director of health in other states.

The responsibility of the states to monitor water supplies was assumed by the Public Health Service when the Congress passed the Act of 1912,[3] which authorized the PHS to investigate the conditions influencing the propagation and spread of diseases, "...including sanitation and sewage and the pollution either directly or indirectly of the navigable streams and lakes." The following year, the Sundry Civil Appropriations Act provided funds in support of that law, allowing for the establishment of the Stream Pollution Investigation Station at a former marine hospital in Cincinnati, Ohio, to be directed by PHS medical officer and epidemiologist Dr. Wade H. Frost.[12] Additionally, five branch laboratories were established along the Ohio River.

Two notable initiatives were a study of the pollution and natural purification of the Potomac River representing a tidal stream, and a study of the pollution and natural purification of the Ohio River representing a large inland stream, under the direction of officers Hugh S. Cumming (later Surgeon General) and Wade H. Frost, respectively. Numerous multidisciplinary PHS officers participated in these meticulous investigations, including sanitary engineers, bacteriologists and chemists. These studies provided invaluable information about local conditions and populations and the impact on stream pollution and consequent waterborne disease, including bacterial content and biochemical oxygen demand, and the conditions needed to optimize self-purification of natural streams. Surveys along the Ohio River also provided the basis for a rating system that served as a model for appraising health conditions and sanitation in other cities.[13] The work of Dr. Frost and other scientific personnel laid the foundation for conducting subsequent river surveys that led to a comprehensive understanding of water pollution and self-purification, helping improve the processes related to sewage and water treatment.

The Public Health Service extended its environmental efforts to include occupational health. In 1913, serious health hazards existed in the mining industry and the PHS assisted the Bureau of Mines in surveying the health of coal miners. The PHS established an Air Hygiene Unit in Pittsburgh where coal was used in the production of steel. During 1914 and subsequent years, the PHS and Bureau conducted field investigations of the dust and ventilation in mines, to include the first review of silicosis in the mining industry. Study results confirmed the harmful effects of breathing airborne siliceous dust, leading to the eventual passage of legislation and enforcement of health and safety standards for the protection of mine workers. In the 1950s, the PHS began to study uranium miners and the effects of long-term exposure to radon, results of which showed an increased incidence of lung cancer.[14]

National Health Insurance. Of note were the efforts of PHS officers Edgar Sydenstricker and Benjamin S. Warren who studied the sickness insurance programs in Europe in the early 1900s. These officers were early proponents of a national system of compulsory health insurance and in 1916 published *Health Insurance: Its Relation to the Public Health.*[15] Their investigations beginning in 1914 showed the detrimental impact of industrial conditions on health and, underlying this, the widespread economic impoverishment and substandard diet of low income workers in the country. Although this progressive era initiative had the support of organized medicine and public health officials such as Surgeon General Blue, momentum was slowed by growing opposition among conservative physicians and labor groups who believed that efforts to attain higher wages were more important. Within a few years, opposition of physicians, business leaders and conservative legislators stifled further progress as attention turned toward World War I, also called the Great War.

The War Years

Rupert Blue, appointed Surgeon General in 1912, remained for a second 4-year term under President Woodrow Wilson, from 1916 to 1920. In addition to the Service's other public health responsibilities, it would soon be tasked with responding to the significant new challenges of a world war and pandemic.

In 1916, Surgeon General Blue focused his efforts on educating the public about healthy practices. Various Federal agencies joined in an initiative to showcase their health and welfare-related activities using "Safety-First" as the national slogan. The Safety-First exhibit in Washington, DC, was sent throughout the nation via railroad, with a Public Health Service officer and two attendants presenting information about proper personal and environmental sanitation using motion pictures, lantern slides, and PHS literature.[1]

On July 28, 1914, the First World War began in Europe with the nations of Austria-Hungary and Germany pitted against Russia, Serbia, and the Western Allies Belgium, France and Great Britain. It was a grueling war that claimed the lives of over 9 million combatants and 7 million civilians, and subsequently led to major political change in several nations. The United States maintained a policy of neutrality until April 6, 1917, when, amid increasing pressure by Britain and France and the sinking of U.S. merchant ships by German submarines, Congress declared war on Germany. Because the United States was in many respects ill-prepared to enter the war, Executive Office and Congressional actions quickly followed, along with an immediate and massive build-up of the military and production of materiel and supplies.

PHS WAR-RELATED ACTIVITIES

While Rupert Blue's attention was directed toward domestic issues, he also recognized the looming threat of the ongoing European conflict. Just prior to America's entry into World War I, he convened a board of officers to prepare a framework of war-related activities that would correspond with the Service's capabilities. Nonetheless, the immediacy of the war emergency placed a tremendous burden of responsibility upon the Public Health Service.

PHS Militarization, Reserve Corps

On April 3, 1917, one day after President Woodrow Wilson asked Congress to declare war, under authority of the Act of 1902 the President issued Executive Order 2571 to militarize the Public Health Service Commissioned Corps.† The Order was published to the Army for guidance to all concerned:[16]

> Under the authority of the act of Congress, approved July 1, 1902, and subject to the limitations therein expressed, it is ordered that hereafter in times of threatened or actual war the Public Health Service shall constitute a part of the military forces of the United States, and in times of threatened or actual war, the Secretary of the Treasury may, upon request of the Secretary of War or the Secretary of the Navy, detail officers or employees of said Service for duty either with the Army or the Navy. All the stations of the Public Health Service are hereby made available for the reception of sick and wounded officers and men, or for such other purposes as shall promote the public interest in connection with military operations.

---

† The Executive Order of April 3, 1917, was overturned by an opinion issued by the Attorney General on October 29, 1921, ruling that the power to create a military force out of a civilian entity was a duty of Congress alone, and that the Act of 1902 authorized the President to utilize, but not convert the Service to a military force within the definition of "military or naval forces of the United States." During World War II, the President was provided the legislative authority to militarize the USPHS Commissioned Corps.[17]

Soon thereafter, on May 18, 1917, Congress passed the Selective Service Act,[18] which resulted in the relocation of hundreds of thousands of individuals to cantonments, with an eventual 4.8 million men (2.8 million drafted and 2 million volunteers) serving in the military services through the end of 1918. While regulations exempted PHS officers from the selective service draft, many draft age PHS officers felt they should be allowed to enter military duty. In November 1917, a representative committee of five PHS officers submitted a memorandum, signed by four of the officers with one dissenting officer, to Surgeon General Blue stating that the "U.S. Public Health Service in its entirety be ordered for duty either under the Army or the Navy for the duration of the war... constituting the U.S. Public Health Service a part of the Military Forces of the United States." The contrary view held by other PHS officers was that, once absorbed by the military, the Corps could lose its organizational identity. The Executive Committee of the General Medical Board of the Council of National Defense favored transfer of the PHS to the Army Medical Department and by memorandum so informed the Secretary of War. In January 1918, the proposal was taken to a Cabinet meeting; however, the Treasury Secretary was not present, and action was deferred pending receipt of his comments. Treasury Secretary William McAdoo determined that it was in the best interests of the PHS to maintain its organizational integrity and so declined to approve transfer of the Service to the Army.[13]

It was evident that there were insufficient medical officers and other personnel of the Public Health Service to carry out the responsibilities that had been thrust upon the Corps. A bill passed the Senate on June 18, 1917, authorizing the creation of a PHS Reserve Corps, but the House of Representatives delayed action and it did not become law until October 27, 1918:[19]

> That for the purpose of securing a reserve for duty in the Public Health Service in time of national emergency there shall be organized, under the direction of the Secretary of the Treasury, ...a reserve of the Public Health Service.

The PHS nonetheless had to greatly increase its professional staff reserve prior to enactment of the legislation to meet the critical needs of the war effort and an impending flu pandemic. By June 30, 1918, there were 1,472 professional and 3,515 other personnel working in the Service, and an Executive Order signed July 1, 1918, directed all federal civil health functions to be under PHS control.[20] The Congress appropriated considerably more to support activities of the PHS – about $3 million in 1917 and $50 million in 1918, with a concomitant increase in personnel to an eventual 23,000 employees.[13]

PHS medical officers were already detailed as sanitary advisors at military and shore stations of the Navy, to include each of the Naval districts in the nation and service aboard Coast Guard vessels in the Navy. Recognizing that these and other PHS officers would be serving in war zones, a joint resolution of Congress was approved July 9, 1917, as follows:

> ...That when officers of the United States Public Health Service are serving on Coast Guard vessels in time of war, or are detailed in time of war for duty with the Army or Navy in accordance with law, they shall be entitled to pensions for themselves and widows and children, if any, as are now provided for officers of corresponding grade and length of service of the Coast Guard, Army or Navy, ... and shall be subject to the laws prescribed for the government of the service to which they are respectively detailed.

As originally passed by the Senate, the resolution provided that PHS officers serving under the prescribed details should be entitled to "all the rights, privileges, benefits, and allowances, including rights to pensions ...as are now provided for officers of corresponding grade and length of service in the Coast Guard." However, that provision was stricken in the House of Representatives. In an August 6, 1917, determination by the Comptroller of the Treasury, PHS officers were entitled only to the specified pensions, and the regular pay and allowances that they received from the Department of the Treasury.[21]

Extra-Cantonment Sanitation; Industrial Oversight

The rapid construction of military encampments around the nation required that hygiene and other public health issues be addressed in and around the military camps. While the Army Medical Corps was responsible for sanitary matters within cantonments, the PHS was tasked with and redirected its resources toward instituting sanitation measures in the zones around military establishments. A lack of coordination of public health activities related to the national war effort compelled President Wilson to issue an Executive Order on July 1, 1918, that brought all Federal agency health functions under the supervision and control of the Public Health Service.[22] The PHS thereby became responsible for introducing public health initiatives attendant to munitions industries and workers engaged in war-related work. Beginning the summer of 1917, in cooperation with the Army and state and local health officials, the PHS initiated intensive sanitation activities within what came to be 47 zones, mainly around military cantonments and industrial areas. The PHS was significantly aided in its sanitation work in extra-cantonment areas by the American Red Cross, which provided units comprised of sanitary inspectors, bacteriologists, public health nurses, laboratory and other assistive personnel. By the end of 1918, 49 PHS medical officers, 72 acting assistant surgeons and nearly 400

professional and scientific personnel (exclusive of laborers) were engaged in the wide-ranging work that varied according to local needs. Extra-cantonment zone activities to prevent spread of disease and protect military and civilian personnel outside of camps and industrial plants included ensuring an adequate system of disease control and prevention, with a PHS officer directing each unit; control of communicable diseases, including anti-malaria work within a one mile wide area surrounding the camps, industrial plants, and city or town adjacent; supervision of water supplies; inspection and supervision of environmental sanitation, including proper human excreta and sewage disposal; food supervision and restaurant certification; industrial hygiene; provision of health education by public health nurses; smallpox and typhoid vaccinations; medical care; and daily morbidity reporting.[20,22]

Venereal Disease Control
The Public Health Service also was given responsibility for overseeing the nationwide control of venereal diseases. On July 9, 1918, the Chamberlain-Kahn Act[23] was approved, providing for the establishment of a Division of Venereal Diseases within the PHS, and an Interdepartmental Social Hygiene Board consisting of the Surgeons General of War, Navy and Public Health Service. The Division's comprehensive plan for venereal disease control included three phases – medical, educational, and enforcement. The law appropriated $1.2 million for the investigation and control of these diseases in cooperation with state boards of health. States received an allotment on a per capita basis, and a PHS officer was assigned to each state to work with the state health officer in supervising their programs for venereal disease control, prevention and treatment. The PHS initiated educational and treatment programs for civilians as well as personnel at military encampments. With the end of World War I in November 1918, however, the public health campaigns to control these diseases declined, and not until 1926 when Dr. Thomas Parran, Jr. was appointed head of the Division of Venereal Diseases was there renewed interest to deal with the diseases.

Biologics Production
The Biologics Control Act of 1902[24] authorized the Public Health Service to regulate the production and sale of vaccines and antitoxins, issue licenses to firms and regulate the transport of such products. This Hygienic Laboratory responsibility took on critical importance during World War I, as it was essential that large quantities of reliable biologic products be readily available for military forces. The Laboratory prepared biologic standards, conducted inspections of production facilities and, along with manufacturers, produced vaccines and antitoxins against diseases such as typhoid, tetanus, diphtheria, and smallpox.

HEALTH CARE FOR VETERANS

The cessation of the war brought with it an urgent need to provide care for wounded veterans. The Executive Order of April 3, 1917, directed that all Public Health Service marine hospitals be made available to treat personnel of the Army and Navy whenever needed, and particularly in geographic locations where there was no military hospital. Further, an Act of Congress[25] approved March 3, 1919, specified the following:

> ...That the Secretary of the Treasury be, and he is hereby, authorized to provide immediate additional hospital and sanatorium facilities for the care and treatment of discharged sick and disabled soldiers, sailors, and marines, Army and Navy nurses (male and female), patients of the War Risk Insurance Bureau, and the following persons only: Merchant marine seamen, seamen on boats of the Mississippi River Commission, officers and enlisted men of the United States Coast Guard, officers and employees of the Public Health Service, certain keepers and assistant keepers of the U.S. Lighthouse Service, seamen of the Engineer Corps of the U.S. Army, officers and enlisted men of the U.S. Coast and Geodetic Survey, civilian employees entitled to treatment under the U.S. Employees' Compensation Act, and employees on Army transports not officers or enlisted men of the Army, now entitled by law to treatment by the Public Health Service.

By an Act of Congress of September 2, 1914, the Bureau of War Risk Insurance (BWRI) was formed to insure American vessels and their cargoes against damage or loss from the hazards of war. The Act was subsequently amended on June 12, 1917, to extend insurance coverage to personnel of merchant ships against injury or death, and it was again amended on October 6, 1917, to provide disabled soldiers and sailors with similar coverage, including "reasonable governmental medical, surgical, and hospital services" and medical supplies for discharged personnel. The Bureau was responsible, therefore, for performing disability ratings, providing compensation for service-related disability based upon those ratings, rendering medical care and providing vocational training, when necessary. The Bureau, however, lacked the resources to provide medical care and vocational education. The BWRI and Public Health Service were both located in the Treasury Department and the March 3, 1919, law in effect made PHS the entity through which the BWRI would secure medical services. For vocational education, the Vocational Rehabilitation Act of June 27, 1918, amended the Smith-Hughes Act of 1917, directing the independent Federal Board for Vocational Education to provide rehabilitation services and vocational training to disabled military personnel.[26,27]

The PHS Division of Marine Hospitals and Relief (later called the Hospital Division), headed by Assistant Surgeon General William G. Stimpson and then Assistant Surgeon General Claude H. Lavinder, was the largest Division in 1920 and it had responsibility for the substantial expansion of hospital facilities to meet the immediate and rapidly growing demand for general medical, surgical, tuberculosis, and neuro-psychiatric treatment services of war veterans. Dr. Lavinder was ably assisted during this period by medical officers Robert W. Hart in surgery, Frederick C. Smith in tuberculosis, and Walter L. Treadway in psychiatry.[13] Further, the PHS supplied medical personnel to the Federal Board for Vocational Education for intrinsic medical functions and the care of disabled personnel. The American Red Cross, in cooperation with other agencies such as the American Legion, Catholic Knights of Columbus and Jewish Welfare Society, provided an extensive medical social service that ministered to the discharged sailors and soldiers.[27]

The law provided for the transfer of available federal/military hospitals and facilities to the Treasury Department for use by the PHS, for contracts with civilian hospitals, and for the lease, purchase or limited construction of hospitals to provide medical care to beneficiaries of the law, which was bolstered by significant, though constrained funding allocations totaling about $10 million. To better serve beneficiaries, the PHS established 14 districts within the nation to provide medical examinations (mainly for disability ratings), hospitalizations, treatments and specialty services. The Service greatly increased its total medical staff to approximately 3,000, including reserve and attending specialists, along with about 200 dental officers and 1,100 nurses. Lucy Minnigerode, who was detailed from the American Red Cross to assess PHS hospital nursing capabilities to handle the influx of returning veterans, was appointed the first PHS Superintendent of Nurses in 1919 and it led to the creation of a Department of Nurses within the Service. The enormity of the Public Health Service effort can be gleaned from the fact that in March 1919, the PHS was treating about 1,500 patients; by March 1921 there were reported nearly 26,000 patients.[27] Other reported data are the following:[28] there were fifty hospitals in operation with a total bed capacity of 12,500 by the end of fiscal year 1920; nearly 400,000 patients were treated during fiscal year 1920, of which about 270,000 (about 650,000 times) received outpatient treatments, and 119,000 (over 4 million hospital days) were inpatients, of which 87,000 were patients of the Bureau of War Risk Insurance. About 500,000 medical examinations were made during the year, of which 450,000 were BWRI-related, and 22,000 patients received dental treatments. Fiscal year expenditures for medical and hospital relief and expenses incident thereto totaled $10.5 million. The PHS effort, with all the complexities and difficulties involved in this post-war endeavor was fraught with extraordinary challenges, yet it was considered successful.

Lucy Minnigerode

The Spanish Flu

In the midst of the war raging in Europe, an unprecedented extremely virulent influenza pandemic emerged in Europe, the United States and Asia that would eventually infect an estimated 500 million civilians and troops, resulting in the death of an estimated 50 million and perhaps as many as 100 million people worldwide – more people than any other disease outbreak in history. It was called the "Spanish flu" because Spain's uncensored press was the first to report on the widespread nature of the disease. The unusually high case fatality, often due to bacterial pneumonia, was accompanied by a high prevalence of death among previously healthy younger adults, when ordinarily influenza mainly affects the very young and elderly.[29]

The influenza epidemic was caused by an H1N1 virus. First identified in the United States in March 1918, at Fort Riley, Kansas, it rapidly spread to the civilian population as well as to other military camps. It was also carried by

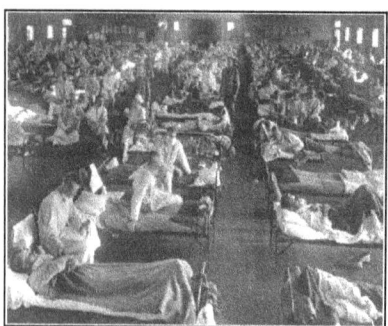

Emergency military hospital during the Spanish influenza epidemic, Camp Funston, a training camp at Fort Riley, Kansas, 1918.
[National Museum of Health and Medicine]

American troops bound for and returning from Europe. The U.S. epidemic came in three waves, the first being a relatively mild illness in the spring of 1918. The second influenza wave was highly lethal and appeared in the fall of 1918 among the military at Navy and Army facilities in Massachusetts, and also affected civilians, particularly along the Eastern Seaboard including New York and Philadelphia. Nationwide, October 1918 was very severe, with nearly 200,000 American deaths. Between late 1918 and March 1919, an equally intense third wave of the pandemic occurred in the U.S. and Europe, but with a somewhat uneven occurrence. Complicating the situation was a shortage of physicians and nurses due to their involvement in the war effort, and many healthcare personnel contracted the flu themselves. Then suddenly, following the third wave of influenza, the disease began to fade away. In total, about 675,000 persons died from the epidemic in the United States.[30,31]

While the U.S. Army and Navy Medical Departments were responsible for the care of military personnel, the Public Health Service was entrusted to lead the response to influenza outbreaks throughout the nation. PHS quarantine stations were notified to be alert for cases of highly communicable influenza on vessels arriving from European ports. The PHS promptly began to compile disease prevalence data from the states and publish the information in the weekly *Public Health Reports*. Six million copies of the pamphlet entitled *Spanish Influenza* with information on influenza spread and prevention were distributed to the public with assistance of the postal service, Red Cross and the Federal Railroad Administration. An informative article was also sent to 10,000 newspapers with a request to publish. On October 5, 1918, the Surgeon General issued an order to state and local health officials to close places of public assembly, resulting in churches, theaters and other public places being closed throughout the nation.[32] Then on October 1, 1918, the Congress passed a joint resolution to "enable the Public Health Service to combat and suppress 'Spanish influenza' and

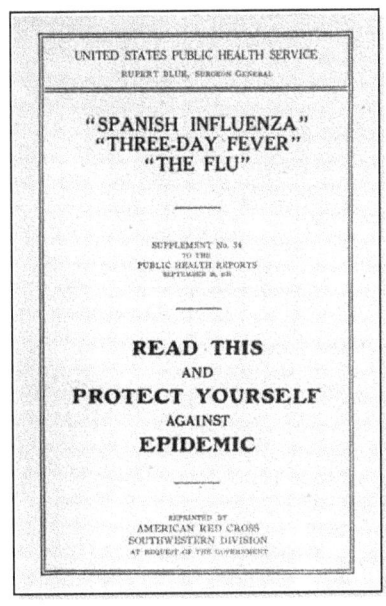

other communicable diseases", appropriating $1 million to aid state and local boards of health, including pay and allowances for personnel, materiel and other expenses. Sixty-four PHS officers, about one-third of the Corps, were assigned to influenza duty, including to assist with directing the states' relief activities. The Congressional resolution directed that personnel and facilities of the Medical Departments of the Army, Navy, and the PHS were to be utilized, so far as possible. The shortage of physicians and nurses prompted Surgeon General Blue to call upon the American Medical Association and the Volunteer Medical Service Corps to solicit physicians to respond to the influenza crisis, leading to the eventual appointment of 1,085 physicians as Acting Assistant Surgeons in the PHS; 703 nurses and nurses' aides, and 328 clerks were also hired to assist in the medical response to the influenza epidemic.[33] By the summer of 1919, the pandemic finally subsided.

Impact of Reserve Corps

As a result of the influenza pandemic, Congress belatedly passed legislation on October 27, 1918, that created a PHS inactive reserve – although too late to be of assistance in responding to the influenza outbreak. While Regular Corps commissions were restricted to medical professionals, Reserve Corps commissions were authorized and allowed for (in addition to physicians) dentists, nurses, pharmacists, sanitary engineers, scientists and other health professionals who could be called to active duty in the event of public health emergencies. The reserve legislation was opportune, because the War Risk Hospital Act of March 3, 1919, designated World War I veterans and other categories of individuals as new beneficiaries of the Bureau of War Risk Insurance. The Public Health Service was the entity through which the BWRI would secure medical services and, as a result, the responsibility of the Service was substantively increased with respect to providing examinations of beneficiaries and operating hospitals for the proper care of these patients.[33,34]

NEW SURGEON GENERAL

Upon his completion of eight years of exceptional service, Rupert Blue was succeeded by medical officer Hugh S. Cumming as Surgeon General. Dr. Blue was assigned to Paris, France, to administer Public Health Service operations in Europe. Then in 1924, he headed a bubonic plague suppression campaign in Los Angeles. He retired from active duty in the Service in 1932 and passed away in 1948 in Charleston, South Carolina.

CHRONOLOGY • 1912–1920
SG Rupert Blue, January 1912–March 1920

1912	*An Act to Change the Name of the Public Health and Marine-Hospital Service to the Public Health Service, to Increase the Pay of Officers of Said Service, and for Other Purposes.* Renames the Service; authorizes PHS to broaden its research to include diseases of man and contributing factors such as sanitation and pollution of navigable waters.
1912	Dr. John McMullen begins a twelve year campaign to control and treat trachoma in the South and Midwest.
1914	Dr. Joseph Goldberger theorizes that pellagra is caused by a dietary deficiency.
1914	World War I begins in Europe, with the U.S. declaring war in 1917.
1917	Executive Order issued that militarizes the PHS Commissioned Corps.
1917	Congress passes the Selective Service Act.
1918	Onset of the Spanish influenza pandemic.
1918	Executive Order issued that authorizes the PHS to administer all federal public health activities related to prosecution of the war.
1918	*Chamberlain-Kahn Act.* Directs the PHS to lead efforts to investigate and control venereal diseases.
1918	A U.S. Public Health Service Reserve Corps is authorized.
1919	The War Risk Hospital Act authorizes the PHS to provide medical care for discharged sick and disabled soldiers, sailors, and marines, patients of the War Risk Insurance Bureau, personnel of the Coast Guard, and others.

CHAPTER FIVE

HEALTH & RESEARCH TRANSITION, VETERANS' BUREAU, BUREAU OF PRISONS
1920 to 1936

THE NEW SURGEON GENERAL, Hugh Smith Cumming, was a medical graduate of the University of Virginia and the University College of Medicine (Richmond, VA) in 1893 and 1894, respectively. Commissioned an Assistant Surgeon in the Marine Hospital Service in 1894, Cumming served in an array of assignments prior to becoming Surgeon General on March 3, 1920. He served at quarantine stations on both the East and West Coasts, including Ellis Island in New York and Angel Island in San Francisco Bay. In 1906, Cumming was detailed for four years to the U.S. General Consul's office in Yokohama, Japan, where he dealt with issues relating to immigration and quarantine diseases. Cumming was assigned to the Hygienic Laboratory in 1913 where he and Dr. Wade Frost led an important investigation of tidal water pollution and the impact on shellfish, particularly oysters, within Maryland and Virginia. During World War I, he served as a sanitary advisor with the U.S. Navy, later surveying European ports from which troops would return to the U.S. to prevent the introduction of diseases. The appointment of Treasury Secretary and Virginian Carter Glass in December 1918 and the friendship of Dr. Cumming with White House physician Dr. Cary Grayson perhaps influenced the Secretary's decision to appoint Cumming as Surgeon General.

Hugh S. Cumming

Surgeon General Cumming, described as courtly in manner, consolidated and selectively expanded activities of the Public Health Service, while taking a conservative approach to advancing the scope of its responsibilities. The model of laboratory research coupled with field investigations by a relatively small group of individuals making remarkable discoveries would begin to give way to a new era of research consortiums. Nonetheless, external events would continue to impact the PHS agenda. The research of the Hygienic Laboratory increasingly disclosed a correlation of disease with poverty, and the Great Depression that began in 1929 would probe the PHS role of providing greater assistance to state and local health departments, something that Dr. Cumming did not favor. And, at the time of Dr. Cumming's appointment as Surgeon General, the PHS was continuing to fulfill its mandate of providing care to military veterans, pursuant to the Act of Congress on March 3, 1919, but that would change in 1922. A year after the appointment of Dr. Cumming, President Warren G. Harding, a Republican, came into office on March 4, 1921, and he chose to retain Dr. Cumming as the Surgeon General. It was that year that Cumming became an advisory member to the Health Section of the League of Nations, whose leaders would travel to Washington, DC, to visit the Public Health Service and the renowned Laboratory of Hygiene to learn about its research programs and laboratory methodology.

MATERNAL AND CHILD HEALTH

Women's organizations were the driving force behind establishment of the Children's Bureau in 1912 within the Department of Labor, having developed from the progressive era White House Conference on Child Welfare Standards in 1909.[1] Among the Bureau's initiatives were studies that showed a strong correlation between poverty and infant mortality, and a general inadequacy of medical care for women and children. This foray into maternal and child health led to enactment on November 23, 1921, of the Maternity and Infancy Protection Act (Sheppard-Towner Act),[2] which provided grants-in-aid to the states for teaching prenatal and newborn infant care to mothers. A Board of Maternity and Infant Hygiene was formed that was comprised of the Surgeon General, Chief of the Children's Bureau, and Commissioner of Education to review state implementation plans.

It is noteworthy that former Surgeon General Walter Wyman expressed no interest in the PHS taking on responsibility for the welfare of mothers and infants,[3] and Surgeon General Cumming was not favorably inclined toward the new law, considering it federal involvement in state welfare programs. Dr. Cumming nonetheless believed that the PHS should oversee the program, which was administered by the Children's Bureau.

Under the Children's Bureau, the program achieved a significant reduction in the infant death rate from 75 to 64 per thousand live births during its years of operation. The program's funding was authorized for only five years, which was extended in 1927 for two years, but increasing opposition by the American Medical Association and other conservative groups led to a lapse in support for the health program in 1929. Restoration of maternal and child protection came about with its incorporation in broader social legislation, specifically Title V of the Social Security Act of 1935. Title V provided a full range of maternity and infant health care and welfare services as a federal-state partnership and, although periodically amended, it remains among the most enduring of public health legislation.

Veterans' Bureau

There was growing recognition in Congress of the need for one agency to deal solely with all veterans' issues. Accordingly, legislation was signed on August 9, 1921, by President Harding that established the Veterans' Bureau,[4] incorporating the Bureau of War Risk Insurance (BWRI) and the Rehabilitation Division of the Federal Board for Vocational Education (FBVE). This newly independent agency's responsibilities included veteran compensation and the provision of medical services and vocational training. All equipment, facilities, records and personnel of the Public Health Service relating to beneficiaries of the BWRI and FBVE, as described in a Treasury Department order issued April 19, 1921, were transferred to the Veterans' Bureau. Section 9 of the Veterans' Bureau Act further allowed the agency to use existing or future medical care facilities of the PHS, War Department and Navy Department. Regarding PHS commissioned officers, the Act specified that:

> Section 4. ...all commissioned personnel detailed or hereafter detailed from the United States Public Health Service to the Veterans' Bureau, shall hold the same rank and grade, shall receive the same pay and allowances, and shall be subject to the same rules for relative rank and promotion as now or hereafter may be provided by law for commissioned personnel of the same rank or grade or performing the same or similar duties in the United States Public Health Service.

On April 29, 1922, pursuant to the Veterans' Bureau Act of 1921, an Executive Order was issued transferring all veterans hospitals then operated by the Public Health Service to the Veterans' Bureau,[5] leaving the PHS with responsibility for only marine hospitals. At the time of transfer, the PHS turned over to the Veterans' Bureau 57 hospitals (44 of which were operational) with a total bed capacity of 17,500 and 13,000 patients; and personnel numbering over 900 physicians, dentists and attending specialists, about 1,400 nurses and other employees for a total of 11,500 staff. Commissioned personnel were transferred by detail, with Regular Corps officers on temporary duty and Reserve Corps officers remaining with the Veterans' Bureau for as long as needed; all other personnel were transferred permanently. The PHS maintained control of its 24 operating marine hospitals with a total bed capacity of 3,000, and for a few years the PHS continued providing care to veterans in its marine hospitals during the transition period.[6]

The Veterans' Bureau was consolidated with the Bureau of Pensions and the National Home for Disabled Volunteer Soldiers on July 21, 1930, creating the Veterans Administration (VA). The VA was renamed the Department of Veterans Affairs and elevated to a cabinet-level executive department by President Ronald Reagan on October 25, 1988, which took effect in 1989.[7]

Organizational & Health Care Expansion

ORGANIZATIONAL CHANGES
Statistical Office
PHS epidemiologist Edgar Sydenstricker was nationally recognized for conducting meticulous epidemiological investigations that provided a foundation for understanding disease etiology. By 1920, a statistical office was considered a necessity to support the epidemiological studies that were such an important part of the public health mission of the Service. A sufficient number of staff were assembled to compile and analyze the extensive morbidity and mortality data from throughout the nation, and mechanical tabulating machines were procured. Accordingly, a Statistical Office was established in 1920 under the direction of Sydenstricker, supported by statisticians from other offices and expert consultants to the program.[8] Activities were far reaching and included research work in areas such as studies of pulmonary tuberculosis, epidemic influenza, venereal diseases, industrial morbidity, child hygiene, pellagra and stream pollution. Data and information on these topics were disseminated through various reports, including articles in *Public Health Reports*. In 1923, Sydenstricker was detailed for one year to direct the epidemiological intelligence service of the League of Nations' Health Section in Geneva, Switzerland,[3] remaining in charge of the PHS Statistical Office until 1928 when he became Research Director at the Milbank Memorial Fund. He continued as a consultant to the Public Health Service, overseeing the National Health Survey of 1935 to 1936, which was the first national survey to focus on chronic disease and disability.[9]

Edgar Sydenstricker

Public Health Districts
In 1923, the Surgeon General divided the nation into seven geographic areas, each encompassing several states. Dr. Cumming designated them Public Health Districts to bring about closer coordination of the various activities of the Service, to standardize methods and facilities and increase the efficiency of Service operations, and to provide savings in program expenditures. These modifications were also shown to promote cordial relations with state and local governments and other organizations. Interstate sanitary districts were simultaneously changed to coincide with the Public Health Districts, and an experienced Service officer was assigned as director to each Public Health District (reduced to six Districts in fiscal year 1925).

REGULAR CORPS EXPANSION – PARKER ACT

Initially, physicians and pharmacists were the only professionally trained personnel in the Public Health Service. Although not commissioned officers, pharmacists served in a variety of administrative, professional and technical capacities with a range of position designations. In addition to pharmaceutical responsibilities, senior pharmacists often served as the hospital superintendent, with general direction from the medical officer in charge.[10] In 1918, Congress authorized a Reserve Corps for the Public Health Service that allowed recruitment of healthcare professionals to supplant Regular Corps physicians for emergency duty. Surgeon General Cumming proposed the commissioning of nonmedical officers, which found its way into a bill introduced by New York Congressman James S. Parker. Though vetoed by President Coolidge, the bill was revived and on April 9, 1930, President Herbert Hoover signed the "Parker Act" (Public Law 71-106), which authorized expansion of the PHS Regular Corps to include the commissioning of dentists, sanitary engineers, and pharmacists, not to exceed at total of 55 officers.[11] The legislation also authorized commissioning of three research scientists annually at the level of a medical director to serve with the Hygienic Laboratory. (*Note:* The Public Health Service Act of July 1, 1944, extended commissioning to hygiene, nursing, "and related scientific specialties in the field of public health," which led to the inclusion of other professionals.) With certain restrictions, the 1930 legislation included a provision for pay equity with the military, specifying that PHS Regular Corps officers "shall be promoted according to the same length of service and shall receive the same pay and allowances as are ...authorized for officers of corresponding grades of the Medical Corps of the Army." Another provision renamed the Hygienic Laboratory's advisory board as the National Advisory Health Council, to advise the Surgeon General.

Health Care Expansion

NATIONAL INSTITUTE OF HEALTH *(See also Chapter Ten.)*

The Hygienic Laboratory in 1920 was under the direction of medical officer George W. McCoy, who had an illustrious PHS career as Hygienic Laboratory chief from 1915 to 1930. Dr. McCoy maintained an extraordinary research program with a comprehensive portfolio of infectious and other diseases, using field as well as laboratory investigations. The Laboratory had become preeminent in federal research since its origins in 1887.

On May 26, 1930, President Herbert Hoover signed the Ransdell Act[12] (for Senator Joseph E. Ransdell of Louisiana), renaming the Hygienic Laboratory as the National Institute of Health, and directing it to ascertain "...the cause, prevention, and cure of disease." The law provided for research fellowships and an appropriation of $750,000 for the construction and equipping of research facilities. Dr. McCoy became the Director of NIH, serving in that position until 1937. In 1938, the National Institute of Health moved from Washington, DC, to Bethesda, Maryland, where NIH Building 1 was built upon gifted land. By October 1940, construction of the original NIH campus comprising six buildings was nearly complete, and on October 31, 1940, President Franklin Roosevelt dedicated the National Institute of Health. The Ransdell Act also made it possible for the PHS in 1932 to purchase the Rocky Mountain Laboratory in Hamilton, Montana, which was being leased from the state. The Rocky Mountain Laboratory became part of the National Institute of Health in February 1937, within the Division of Infectious Diseases, eventually becoming part of the National Institute of Allergy and Infectious Diseases.

Soon after the Ransdell Act became law and prior to passage of the Social Security Act (SSA) in 1935, the groundwork was laid for securing sufficient financing to expand the research portfolio of the NIH. Assistant Surgeon General Lewis R. Thompson, chief of the Division of Scientific Research from 1931 to 1937, took the lead in working with Congress to promote the potential of a great medical research institution. He and others advocated for the President's Science Advisory Board, created by Executive Order in July 1933 for a two-year period, to study the scope of medical research in the Public Health Service with the prospect that a recommendation for expansion would result. A subcommittee consisting of Thomas Parran, Milton Rosenau and Simon Flexner performed the study, the report of which recommended intensified research in cancer, heart disease, tuberculosis, malaria, venereal disease, and dental problems, and that funding for the PHS's scientific work be increased by $2.5 million. Dr. Thompson and his colleagues organized a correspondence campaign to generate Congressional support, resulting in a SSA Title VI authorization of $2 million annually for research endeavors. However, Congress did not appropriate the maximum amount. Title VI appropriations began with $375,000 in 1936, increasing to $1.64 million by 1940.[13] Dr. Thompson was largely responsible for securing the Bethesda site as the permanent location of the National Institute of Health and its associated Institutes that would be authorized over the years. When the Scientific Research Division merged with NIH in 1937, Lewis R. Thompson was appointed NIH Director, serving in that position until 1942. And in 1948, the National Heart Act was enacted, in which the NIH was redesignated the National Institutes [plural] of Health.

George W. McCoy

Lewis R. Thompson

NATIONAL LEPROSARIUM

Leprosy has afflicted humankind for thousands of years. Leprosy is believed to have first appeared in the United States in Louisiana during the mid-1700s, followed by other nodes in the Midwest, California and New York. Fear of contagion led Congress in 1899 to direct the Marine Hospital Service to survey the prevalence of leprosy and formulate a national policy for its control. The resulting 1901 report recommended the establishment of a national leprosarium for treatment and research purposes. It wasn't until 1917 that a special Act[14] authorized the national leprosarium to be administered by the U.S. Public Health Service, making those persons afflicted with leprosy beneficiaries of the Service. World War I delayed site selection for the national leprosarium until 1920, when the Louisiana Leper Home in Carville was purchased by the federal government and in 1921 designated a marine hospital. Hospital improvements were made over the years, including provision for individual patient dormitory rooms and separate staff living quarters. PHS Captains Guy Henry Faget, and in the 1970s

Guy H. Faget

PHS Hospital for Hansen's Disease at Carville, Louisiana.
[c. 1950, National Library of Medicine]

Robert C. Hastings and Robert R. Jacobson, were instrumental in advancing the treatment options for leprosy patients. In 1941, Faget, National Leprosarium director and his staff showed the efficacy of sulfones in treatment of leprosy. In the 1950s, Englishman Dr. Robert G. Cochrane studied the use of dapsone, which became the treatment of choice; however, the *Mycobacterium leprae* bacterium developed resistance. Then in the early 1970s, Dr. Jacobson pioneered work on drug resistance and introduced rifampin, which became part of an effective multi-drug treatment (MDT) regimen of dapsone, rifampin, and clofazimine that was endorsed in 1981 by the World Health Organization.

Leprosy is properly known as Hansen's Disease, for Norwegian Gerhard-Henrik Hansen who identified *Mycobacterium leprae* in 1873. In 1981, Hansen's Disease became an outpatient diagnosis and outpatient clinics were opened around the nation. The PHS continued its medical ministry to patients at the Gillis W. Long Hansen's Disease Center, renamed for the U.S. Congressman who lobbied for Carville, but in 1999 the Center was closed and the facility returned to the state of Louisiana. In 2011, PHS officer Richard W. Truman published study results showing that armadillos and many leprous patients in the South were infected with the same strain of *M. leprae*.

TYPHOID AND RURAL SANITATION

Beginning in 1911, medical officer and epidemiologist Leslie L. Lumsden was sent from the Hygienic Laboratory to investigate a typhoid fever epidemic in Yakima, Washington. Typhoid fever is a bacterial infection due to *Salmonella typhi*, and Dr. Lumsden determined that it was likely being spread by food and water contaminated with fecal material from an infected individual or sewage. He led a successful campaign to control typhoid directed primarily at remedying contaminated water supplies and unsanitary outdoor privies, and he recommended to civic leaders that a Yakima County health department be established. Lumsden also collaborated with Dr. Charles Stiles, who was investigating hookworm disease and its association with soil contamination *(see Chapter Three)*. He continued to work on rural sanitation for many years with a nationwide campaign that served as a civic action model for rural health reform in the United States.[15] Dr. Lumsden and other PHS officers traveled to rural counties that had no health department and educated citizens about diseases related to unsanitary conditions and provided written materials and guidance on how to construct a fly-proof, ventilated sanitary privy. From 1917 to 1920, funding was allocated for surveys and demonstration work in rural sanitation, with one study showing that only 2 percent of rural homes consistently practiced basic principles of sanitation. By the fiscal year ending June 30, 1930, cooperative projects in rural sanitation were carried out in 202 counties and 24 states. Further, the counties with full-time health officers directing public health offices rose from 109 health departments in 1920 to 505 in 1930.[16] The federal-state demonstration project for rural sanitation was a resounding success and the 1930 *Surgeon General's Annual Report* included a suggestion of making the program an ongoing, cooperative partnership. A program of federal grants to the states for that purpose was received favorably by members of Congress, but the plan was opposed by organized medicine and perhaps Dr. Cumming due to divergent views regarding the federal role in health and a possible "quiet rivalry" between Cumming and Lumsden. On November 20, 1930, the Surgeon General inexplicably promoted and transferred Dr. Lumsden to New Orleans, Louisiana, to serve as District Director of Southern states, effectively ending further programmatic discussions.[3]

Leslie L. Lumsden

MILK PASTEURIZATION

Louis Pasteur was a French chemist and microbiologist who discovered the process of attenuating disease microbes to produce vaccines, but he is probably best known for his discovery of pasteurization. Although the preservation of wine by a process of heating had been known for centuries, in 1864 Pasteur offered a more efficacious process that would not diminish product quality and the process was subsequently used for beer and vinegar. Later, milk pasteurization began initially as an effort to extend shelf life; heating milk for the purpose of destroying spoilage microorganisms was not appreciated until the recognition of Pasteur's work.[17] Cow's milk is considered a good source of dietary nutrients that can benefit health. In the 1800s, raw cow's milk was typically consumed in the United States, although it would often be heated in the home before infant feeding. Commercial heat treatment of milk to kill pathogenic microbes was more common by the early 1900s, but strategies adopted by different jurisdictions were inconsistent and pasteurization methods of milk dealers were highly variable and controversial, particularly the "flash" method, resulting in an unreliable certification system. The Public Health Service became actively involved in the matter of milk pasteurization. In 1909, Dr. Milton Rosenau of the Hygienic Laboratory published investigatory findings that confirmed the effectiveness of a low temperature holding method, leading to general acceptance of that process for milk pasteurization. His book, *The Milk Question*, provided an overview of the value of milk in nutrition and the importance of pasteurization to ensure its safety.[18] The PHS worked with the New York Commission on Milk Standards and other research initiatives, reporting in 1925 on the findings of a study by four dairy plants that experimentally tested various heating and equipment methods for pasteurization.[19] In 1923, PHS sanitary engineer Leslie C. Frank was assigned to work with the Alabama State Board of Health to standardize inconsistent milk ordinances throughout the state, and a legislative effort in 1924 led to the first *Standard Milk Ordinance*, attracting the attention of other states and cities. The *Standard Milk Ordinance* of the Public Health Service (renamed in 1965 the *Grade "A" Pasteurized Milk Ordinance*), which provides pasteurization standards and technical guidance, was adopted as the national standard by the Conference of State and Territorial Health Officers in 1926, followed by a second document, the *PHS Milk Code*, to provide interpretive guidance. New equipment designs such as plate heat exchangers led to the introduction of high-temperature short-time (HTST) pasteurization methods that are mainly in current use, standards for which were first included in the 1933 PHS *Milk Ordinance and Code*.

Louis Pasteur

MARITIME TRANSPORTATION

Following passage of the National Quarantine Act of 1893, many states began to voluntarily transfer their quarantine stations to the federal government, and federal quarantine facilities were built to provide better coverage. In 1921, with the acquisition of the quarantine service at the Port of New York, the Public Health Service had taken over all municipal and state maritime quarantine activities and facilities in the nation. The Service was responsible for administration of the entire interstate and international quarantine system – inspection, fumigation, and quarantine – of cargo and passenger ships. The PHS had a small fleet of quarantine boarding launches, a type of tugboat, to carry medical quarantine officers and inspectors to incoming ships. PHS personnel would assess and clear the health of passengers and crew, and examine cargo to ensure diseases were not brought into the U.S.

USPHS W.H. Welch, Built in 1934

AIR TRANSPORTATION

Increasing international airplane transportation amplified the transmission of communicable diseases, and disease-carrying insects and animals had become a matter of serious concern. On May 20, 1926, the Air Commerce Act[20] was enacted, which charged the Department of Commerce to issue and enforce flight safety rules. Section 7 of the Act authorized the Treasury Secretary "to provide for the application to civil air navigation of the laws and regulations relating to the administration of the customs and public health laws to such extent and upon such conditions as he deems necessary." This provision allowed the PHS to begin quarantine and immigration inspection for air travel, which it began in December 1927 at the airport of entry at Meachem Field, Key West Florida, soon followed by the airports at New York City and Tampa, Florida. By 1930, there were 23 designated airports of entry, most of which had commenced inspection and quarantine procedures.[21] In the 1930s, after discovering the variety of mosquito carrying yellow fever, the PHS began spraying insecticide inside aircraft. International coordination of quarantine practice led to ratification in 1934 of the International Sanitary Convention for Aerial Navigation, under the auspices of the International Office of Public Hygiene in Paris.

NATIONAL PARK SERVICE

The National Park Service (NPS), an agency of the Department of Interior (DOI), was created on August 25, 1916, by the Organic Act (Public Law 64-235). The NPS is a vast system that includes national parks, historic sites, monuments, memorials, and recreational areas. In 1921, an agreement between the NPS and Public Health Service provided for consultative work in all national parks to be performed by PHS engineers, who provided for sanitary inspection of food, water and sewage disposal and vector control. PHS officers were detailed to NPS via CDC; in March 2000, the National Park Service formalized an Interagency Agreement directly with the PHS, which in 2009 was expanded to allow for the assignment of officers to DOI and all its Bureaus. Nearly 70 PHS officers are assigned to DOI, the vast majority with the NPS Office of Public Health directed by CAPT Sara B. Newman, an exemplary officer who served most of her career in the NPS. The Office is comprised of a Washington, DC, Support Office and PHS field officers who serve in every region of the park system, providing public health expertise in engineering, epidemiology, environmental health, occupational, human and veterinary medicine, and health services administration.[22]

Sara B. Newman

NARCOTICS DIVISION/MENTAL HYGIENE DIVISION

From 1913 to 1919, medical officer Lawrence Kolb served at the Ellis Island, New York Immigration Station specializing in the mental illness of incoming immigrants, and later studied patients suffering from neuroses brought about during World War I. Dr. Kolb transferred in 1923 to the Hygienic Laboratory for five years investigating drug addiction. He was among the first to advance the view of treating drug addicts as patients, not criminals. In 1929, on the premise that addiction is primarily a medical-social problem, the Narcotic Farms Act was enacted.[23] It provided for a new Narcotics Division, renamed the PHS Division of Mental Hygiene in 1930, and the establishment of two institutions to treat prisoners addicted to habit forming drugs. Kolb was an internationally recognized expert in psychiatry and narcotics, and in 1935 he was appointed superintendent and physician in charge of the institution (Narcotics Farm, renamed PHS Hospital in 1936) in Lexington, Kentucky. The other institution at Fort Worth, Texas, opened in 1938, with medical officer William F. Ossenfort in charge. Kolb and Dr. Walter L. Treadway, director of the Division of Mental Hygiene, used a treatment program of withdrawal, rehabilitation, and after-discharge assistance with assimilation into society that was later refined.[10]

Lawrence Kolb

FEDERAL BUREAU OF PRISONS HEALTH CARE

On May 14, 1930, President Herbert Hoover signed Public Law 71-218 creating the federal Bureau of Prisons (FBOP) within the Department of Justice, charged with the "management and regulation of all Federal penal and correctional institutions." This responsibility covered administration of the eleven federal prisons in operation in 1930, assigning about 50 PHS professional staff. The first Director's goals were to "promote a unified professional approach to management by centralizing administration and creating a consistent BOP-wide system policy." An Act authorizing the Public Health Service to provide health care services in the federal prisons, and an Act to provide a medical center for inmates with a mental affliction and degenerative disease were both approved May 13, 1930.[24,25] The latter Act established the Medical Center for Federal Prisoners at Springfield, Missouri, that is still in operation.

Prior to the 1970s, health care in prison systems, in general, was often substandard due to a lack of sufficient funding. A standard of care that must be provided to inmates was settled by a 1976 Supreme Court decision in the case of *Estelle v. Gamble* that, under the Constitution's Eighth Amendment, there is a right to health care for all persons in custody and that "deliberate indifference" – purposely ignoring the plight of prisoners in need of care – is forbidden. This is particularly important in that many incarcerated individuals come with a range of acute and chronic illnesses in need of medical attention, including dental disease, mental illness, and substance use disorders.

A memorandum of understanding was signed on September 30, 1991, between the Public Health Service and FBOP, setting forth the conditions and responsibilities governing the assignment of PHS officers to the Bureau of Prisons.[26] A BOP Assistant Director of the Health Services Division (HSD) is responsible for directing and administering Health Services in addition to the Food Service and Safety Programs, and in January 2023 RADM Christopher A. Bina was appointed to that position. A BOP Medical Director, who has been a PHS medical officer consistently from 1936 to 2015, is delegated final authority for clinical matters and is responsible for all health care provided by healthcare practitioners. The Bureau appoints Chief Professional Officers (CPOs) for the largest health disciplines, some of whom attain the rank of Rear Admiral befitting their overarching responsibilities. BOP health care, food service, and occupational safety and health are provided by approximately 6,500 authorized staff. These staff are comprised of civilian professionals and a variable range of about 700 to 900 PHS officers detailed to the Bureau of Prisons. Recruitment and retention of healthcare personnel is an ongoing challenge.[27]

Chris A. Bina

As of 2023, there were 121 federal prisons, each with an ambulatory care clinic known as a health services unit (HSU), with a Clinical Director and Health Services Administrator. The Clinical Director oversees all medical care provided at the facility. Most HSUs are composed of a staff of physicians, dentists, nurses, pharmacists, physician assistants (PAs), and nurse practitioners (NPs). Select institutions include social workers, therapists, and psychiatrists. PHS officers serve commendably in offering high quality, personalized medical care to inmates, as health care continues to be enhanced. The pharmacist's role, for instance, now encompasses clinical functions like medication use review, chronic disease management, patient counseling and education. Systemwide pharmacist delivered patient care is rendered pursuant to pharmacist-physician collaborative practice agreements.[28] Navy Corpsmen and Army medics initially supplanted the care provided by physicians before a formal physician assistant program was introduced at BOP in 1974. PHS and Civil Service PAs and NPs are critically important, accounting for much of the care provided. PAs and NPs perform an array of medical services to include physical examinations, minor surgical procedures, seeing inmates at sick call, and ordering laboratory and diagnostic tests and medications.[29] The provision of health care is guided by a four-tiered system to denote the level of care provided. Care Level 1 is for prisoners who are generally healthy and under 70 years of age; Level 2 for those who are stable outpatients; Level 3 for outpatients requiring frequent clinical visits; and Level 4 for those with specialized needs, or serious medical or mental health conditions requiring care at one of the seven accredited Federal Medical Centers or a contract provider. The first Medical Center for Federal Prisoners was opened in 1933 in Springfield, Missouri, under PHS superintendent Marion R. King. From 1936 to 1998 and 2006 to 2015, all PHS medical officers who were BOP Medical Directors served concurrently as the BOP Assistant Director, Health Services. In earlier years, some PHS officers served as the chief medical officer and as superintendent/warden of the prison to which they were assigned. BOP's first Medical Director, Justin K. Fuller, was also Chief Medical Officer of the War Shipping Administration, which included the Maritime Service, from 1942 to 1949.[30-32]

Federal Medical Center, Springfield, MO

PHS MEDICAL DIRECTORS OF THE BUREAU OF PRISONS, 1936-2015

RADM Justin K. Fuller, *1936-1942, 1947*	CAPT Harold M. Janney, *1953-1961*
CAPT Marion R. King, *1943-1946*	CAPT Charles E. Smith, *1962-1965*
CAPT Stanley E. Krumbiegel, *1948-1952*	RADM Ernest C. Siegfried, *1966-1968*

PHS MEDICAL DIRECTORS OF THE BUREAU OF PRISONS, 1936-2015

First Director
RADM
Justin K. Fuller
1936-1942, 1947

RADM
Robert L. Brutsché
1969-1987

RADM
Kenneth P. Moritsugu
1987-1998

RADM
Newton E. Kendig
1999-2015

In Their Words

by RADM (Ret.) Newton E. Kendig

The Commissioned Corps has been vital to implementing the Federal Bureau of Prison's (FBOP) health care mission since the agency's inception in 1930. In the FBOP's more recent history, major advances in correctional health care were implemented by my predecessor, Dr. Kenneth P. Moritsugu, who established a licensed FBOP health care workforce, a continuous quality improvement program, and secured Joint Commission accreditation for FBOP facilities. When I became Medical Director in 1999, the FBOP was experiencing unprecedented growth in its inmate population. Health care was complicated by the rural location of many new FBOP facilities and escalating medical expenditures. To meet these challenges a medical classification system was established that designated inmates to FBOP facilities that could best meet their health care needs. Evidenced-based clinical practice guidelines were promulgated to better define a standard of care for correctional medicine. Preventive health was enhanced by a national menu that met nutritional dietary standards and a prohibition of tobacco use by inmates. Corps officers were instrumental in leading these advancements and providing a stable workforce for the FBOP during a period of critical health care staffing shortages. FBOP Corps officers, with their strong clinical skills, were also valuable members of Corps deployments to natural disasters, the island of Saipan to support hospital accreditation, and the Ebola response in West Africa. Today, as we look to the future, the historic and unprecedented engagement of Corps officers within the FBOP is as important as ever. Bipartisan criminal justice reform efforts are resulting in more incarcerated persons returning to our communities. At the same time, we now have more effective interventions for treating incarcerated patients with serious health conditions such as opioid use disorder, hepatitis C, and serious mental illness. These represent strategic opportunities for FBOP Corps officers to make important gains in the health of incarcerated patients and substantively advance the public health of our nation.

VENEREAL DISEASES PROGRAM

After World War I ended in November 1918, congressional support for the control of venereal diseases waned and by 1926, federal appropriations were severely reduced to $58,000. That year, medical officer Thomas J. Parran, Jr. was appointed head of the PHS Division of Venereal Diseases. He began working with state health departments to try to expand research and treatment of venereal diseases and promote acceptance of syphilis as a medical condition and a public health issue. However, with inadequate federal appropriations and state health budgets and the onset of the Great Depression in 1929, funding became extremely scarce, making any real progress unattainable. Appropriations under the Social Security Act of 1935 and the National Venereal Disease Control Act of 1938, coupled with the leadership of Dr. Parran, would reinvigorate the latent venereal diseases program. *(See Chapter Six.)*

TUSKEGEE SYPHILIS STUDY

One of the most reprehensible human experiments in American history was conducted under the auspices of the U.S. Public Health Service. In 1932, the PHS in conjunction with the Tuskegee Institute initiated a study in Macon County, Alabama, to determine the natural course of untreated, latent syphilis in Black males. The study involved 399 men with syphilis, mostly impoverished sharecroppers, and 201 healthy men as a control group. Researchers told the men with syphilis that they would receive free medical care and treatments for "bad blood," a local term used to describe several ailments including syphilis. In fact, the men had been misled and were never given adequate treatment for their disease – they were deprived of the antisyphilitic drug arsphenamine available in 1910 and penicillin which became the drug of choice in 1947. Initially planned as a 6-month observational study, the study continued for 40 years. Then in July 1972, media reports about the Tuskegee Study led to public scrutiny and in November 1972 the study was ended. The Department of Health, Education, and Welfare convened an ad hoc advisory panel to review the study, which concluded that it was ethically unjustified. A class action lawsuit led to a $10 million settlement in 1974 that ultimately included lifetime medical and health benefits and burial services for all living participants and their wives, widows and offspring. In 1974, Congress passed the National Research Act, creating a national commission to write regulations governing human subject research and to oversee the use of human experimentation in medicine. President Clinton apologized to the African American study participants on behalf of the nation in 1997, and in June 2000 the Office for Human Research Protections was established in the Department of Health and Human Services to protect human subjects in future biomedical and behavioral research.[33,34]

Social Security Act of 1935

Against the backdrop of the Great Depression, the effects of which were still being felt, the President's Committee on Economic Security (CES) was formed in June 1934. Within six months, the CES proposed the first federal social insurance program for the nation. A health insurance plan prepared by Edgar Sydenstricker and Isidore Falk of the CES Technical Committee on Medical Care was not retained due to controversy surrounding the issue, including conservative opposition and the balance of individual medical care with the need to provide for public health preventive services.[35] In January 1935, the full CES report was sent to Congress as draft legislation, entitled the Economic Security Bill. The Social Security Act[36] which emerged from that bill was of historic importance and a major component of the New Deal programs being introduced by the Roosevelt administration. The Preamble of the Social Security Act set forth the legislative purpose:

> An Act to provide for the general welfare by establishing a system of Federal old-age benefits, and by enabling the several States to make more adequate provision for aged persons, blind persons, dependent and crippled children, maternal and child welfare, public health, and the administration of their unemployment compensation laws; to establish a Social Security Board; to raise revenue; and for other purposes.

President Franklin D. Roosevelt signing the Social Security Act in the Cabinet Room of the White House, August 14, 1935.

The principal elements of the Social Security Act of 1935 were means-tested public assistance programs, unemployment compensation, and old age benefit insurance. Title II, Federal Old-Age Benefits, was the new social insurance program known as Social Security. The four basic types of benefits are retirement, disability, survivors, and supplemental benefits. Along with subsequent amendments that created new programs such as the Medicare and Medicaid programs in 1965, the Social Security Act has had a profound and enduring impact on the provision of health care, public health and welfare services in the nation. The Act included two key provisions for maternal and child health and public health in Titles V and VI, respectively.

Title V – Maternal and Child Welfare

Title V of the Social Security Act of 1935 reinstated federal grants to the states for maternal and child protection after funding for the Sheppard-Towner Maternity and Infancy Protection Act was allowed to lapse in 1929. Title V provided appropriations as a federal-state partnership for a full range of maternal and infant health care services, especially in rural areas and in areas suffering from severe economic distress; medical care and services for special needs children (then known as "crippled children"); and child welfare services for homeless, dependent, and neglected children. The Children's Bureau of the Department of Labor administers the provisions of Title V. The authorizing legislation has been amended frequently over the years to include new areas of maternal and child health and prevention services, and it was converted to a block grant program as part of the Omnibus Budget Reconciliation Act of 1981.

Title VI – Public Health Work

The purpose of Title VI of the Social Security Act of 1935 was twofold: to support the expansion of state and local public health services, and to expand the scientific investigatory work of the Public Health Service.

State and Local Public Health Services

The law provided appropriations "for the purpose of assisting States, counties, health districts, and other political subdivisions of the States in establishing and maintaining adequate public health services, including the training of personnel for State and local health work." An $8 million annual appropriation was allotted for distribution to the states, with the amount determined on the basis of population, special health problems, and financial needs of the respective states. The Surgeon General was tasked with administration of the grants program, subject to approval of the Secretary of the Treasury. Once funds were received, the states were to make expenditures for health services in accordance with state plans that were approved by the Surgeon General. In anticipation of enactment, the Surgeon General met with officials at the Annual Conference of State and Territorial Health Officers in June 1935 to review proposed regulations governing the conditions under which state allotments would be made which, with some modification, was approved by the Conference and recommended to the Surgeon General for adoption.[37]

Investigations. The law also provided funding support to the Public Health Service "for investigation of disease and problems of sanitation." An annual appropriation of $2 million was provided for this purpose, to include pay and allowances and traveling expenses of PHS personnel engaged in such research or detailed to a state, upon request, to assist with state efforts.

DISCOVERY OF INSULIN AND PENICILLIN

During the 1920s, two events occurred that were among the great public health advancements of the 20th century – the discovery of insulin and penicillin.

Insulin

The year 2021 marked the 100th anniversary of the discovery of insulin in 1921, a hormone produced by the pancreas that is required for the body to utilize glucose. The lack of insulin is a hallmark of type 1 diabetes. Before 1921, people with type 1 diabetes were unlikely to live beyond a year or two. Building upon the work of scientists around the world, University of Toronto Dr. Frederick Banting and Charles Best, a medical student, successfully isolated insulin for the first time on July 27, 1921. Although difficult to purify and produce, insulin was successfully used in the treatment of a diabetic boy in January 1922, and by 1923 insulin had become widely available. Many purity and production advances were made in the ensuing decades, and in 1978 a major milestone was reached when the company Genentech produced biosynthetic human insulin in *Escherichia coli* bacteria using recombinant DNA techniques. Approved in 1982 by the FDA, the product (Humulin®) was manufactured by Eli Lilly and Company and was the first-ever approved genetically engineered human therapeutic.

Penicillin and Antimicrobials

The discovery of antimicrobial agents was another great public health milestone. Arsphenamine and sulfonamides were among early synthesized antibacterials, yet it was the discovery of penicillin in 1928 by Dr. Alexander Fleming, a scientist working at St. Mary's Hospital in London, that ushered in the modern era of antibiotics. Penicillin is produced by certain molds that have antibacterial properties. While Fleming believed that penicillin's antibacterial traits could be developed for chemotherapy, it was not until the early 1940s that scientists successfully purified the first penicillin. The FDA began testing penicillin in 1943 as part of the wartime development program and it was initially used by the Allied military during World War II. By the mid- to late 1940s, penicillin became widely available for the general public, and the application of medicinal chemistry yielded a vast array of new antibiotic substances during the 20th century.

Antimicrobial Resistance. For nearly a century, antimicrobial agents were thought of as essential lifesaving drugs that would overcome infectious diseases. However, their misuse and overuse in humans and animals has contributed to a global crisis of drug resistant infections. The emergence and re-emergence of infectious diseases, sometimes in drug resistant forms that may render a disease untreatable, has become a clear threat to public health.

The CDC's Emerging Infections Program (EIP) was established in 1995 in response to the Centers for Disease Control and Prevention's 1994 strategy, *Addressing Emerging Infectious Disease Threats: A Prevention Strategy for the United States*. An updated plan was released in 1998, *Preventing Emerging Infectious Diseases: A Strategy for the 21st Century*,[38] describing the CDC plan to combat infectious diseases as the second phase of the effort launched in 1994. The CDC affirmed that about 30 percent of all antibiotics prescribed in U.S. acute care hospitals were either unnecessary or suboptimal, and in 2014 called upon hospitals to implement antibiotic stewardship programs.[39] Such programs have arisen throughout the nation and have had some success in reducing inappropriate prescribing. Nonetheless, the seriousness of the situation is borne out by the World Health Organization's 2019 determination that antimicrobial resistance is one of the top ten threats to global health, as antibiotic resistant bacterial strains continue to emerge.[40]

CHRONOLOGY • 1920–1936
SG Hugh S. Cumming, March 1920–January 1936

1921	Canadians Dr. Frederick Banting and Charles Best discover insulin.
1921	Veterans' Bureau is established with improved facilities; War Risk Insurance Act is modified, including transfer of PHS activities related to WRIB beneficiaries to the new Bureau.
1921	Marine Hospital Service-administered national leprosarium is established at Carville, Louisiana.
1921	*Maternity and Infancy Protection Act (Sheppard-Towner Act)*. Provides state grants for teaching prenatal and newborn infant care to mothers.
1921	Agreement with the National Park Service for the Public Health Service to provide consultative work in all national parks.
1922	Executive Order transfers all PHS-operated veterans' hospitals to the Veterans' Bureau.
1926	The *Standard Milk Ordinance* of the Public Health Service adopted as the national standard for milk pasteurization.
1926	The *Air Commerce Act*, which led to expansion of PHS quarantine and immigration inspection authority for air travel.
1928	Scottish physician-scientist Alexander Fleming discovered penicillin.
1929	The *Narcotic Farm Act*. Creates the PHS Narcotics Division/Division of Mental Hygiene, forerunner of the National Institute of Mental Health, NIH.
1929	Stock market crash, beginning a 12-year Great Depression that affects Western industrialized countries.

1930	The *Parker Act*. Expands the PHS Regular Corps by new professional categories including healthcare providers, sanitary engineers and research scientists.
1930	The *Ransdell Act*. Creates the National Institute of Health, which replaces the Hygienic Laboratory.
1930	Creation of the Bureau of Prisons, and authorization of the Public Health Service to provide health care services in federal prisons.
1930	Executive Order 5398 consolidates the Veterans' Bureau with two other agencies to form the Veterans Administration.
1932	Initiation of the Tuskegee syphilis study, which continued for 40 years and was deemed ethically unjustified.
1935	*Social Security Act of 1935*. Authorizes health grants to states as an effective way to improve state and local public health programs and prevent the interstate spread of disease. Title VI expanded state public health services and scientific research of PHS.

CHAPTER SIX

HEALTH RESET, WORLD WAR II, FOOD AND DRUG ADMINISTRATION
1936 to 1948

A NEW ERA of expanding federal involvement in public health was about to begin with passage of the Social Security Act in 1935, while Americans were still contending with the ongoing, impactful effects of the Great Depression. Surgeon General Hugh S. Cumming retired from active duty in the Public Health Service on January 31, 1936, serving afterward until 1947 as director of the Pan American Sanitary Bureau. His successor as Surgeon General was Thomas J. Parran, Jr. Born and raised near St. Leonard, Maryland, Parran was named after an ancestor who was a physician in the Revolutionary War, and other relatives were physicians, thus preparing Thomas to enter the medical profession. While attending medical school, Parran worked two summers at the Washington, DC, Health Service laboratories under Dr. Joseph Kinyoun, the first director of the PHS Hygienic Laboratory, and in 1915 he graduated from Georgetown University Medical School. Dr. Parran was commissioned in the PHS in 1917. His initial assignments included rural sanitation work along with other officers in Oklahoma and Southern states, under the direction of Dr. Leslie Lumsden. He was chief medical officer at Muscle Shoals, Alabama, during the Spanish flu epidemic, worked in the Veterans' Bureau, and was assigned to a tristate health district in Missouri. Parran's experience in communicable diseases led him to a leadership position as head of the PHS Division of Venereal Diseases in 1926. He worked with state health officials to expand research and treatment of venereal diseases,

Thomas J. Parran, Jr.

but inadequate federal and state health funding made progress unattainable.

Edgar Sydenstricker, PHS statistician who had taken a position at the Milbank Memorial Fund, praised Dr. Parran's talents to the Milbank Fund director, a friend of Franklin D. Roosevelt, newly elected Governor of New York. In 1930, Thomas Parran accepted an appointment by Roosevelt to the position of state health commissioner, taking a leave of absence from the PHS.

Franklin Roosevelt was elected President in 1933, and in 1934 he appointed Dr. Parran to the Committee on Economic Security to draft proposals that would "promote greater economic security." The Committee report formed the basis of the Social Security Act (SSA) of 1935. In a speech titled *Health Services of Tomorrow* made in 1934, Parran advanced the concept that "the care of public health is a primary responsibility of government." Such a pronouncement was consistent with public health provisions of the soon-to-be enacted Social Security Act. Upon the retirement of Hugh S. Cumming in 1936, Roosevelt selected Thomas Parran to serve as Surgeon General. Reportedly, it was known in 1933 that Roosevelt would appoint Parran Surgeon General after the completion of Dr. Cumming's 4-year term.

SOCIAL SECURITY ACT OF 1935 *(See also Chapter Five.)*

A consequence of the Great Depression was a transformative expansion of the federal government's role in the economy. Passage of the Social Security Act[1] was an indicator of that change and a component of the New Deal programs being ushered in by the Roosevelt administration. The Preamble of the Social Security Act set forth the purpose of providing for the general welfare "...by establishing a system of Federal old-age benefits, and by enabling the several States to make more adequate provision for aged persons, blind persons, dependent and crippled children, maternal and child welfare, public health, and the administration of their unemployment compensation laws." The Social Security Act, along with subsequent legislation that created the Medicare and Medicaid programs in 1965, has had a profound impact on the provision of health care, public health and welfare services in the United States. The Social Security Act contained three key provisions for maternal and child health, public health, and research support for the National Institute of Health.

Maternal and Child Welfare. Title V of the Social Security Act reinstated federal grants to states for maternal and child welfare after funding for the Sheppard-Towner Maternity and Infancy Protection Act was allowed to lapse.

Public Health Work. Title VI provided support for the expansion of state and local public health services and expanded the scientific investigatory work of the Public Health Service.

Title VI Research Provision. Title VI authorizations were provided for scientific research endeavors of the PHS Division of Scientific Research and thereafter when the Division was merged with the National Institute of Health (NIH). This funding was the foundation from which the vast intramural and extramural research enterprise of the NIH began and indicated a shift toward public funding of biomedical research.

NIH CAMPUS

In 1935, philanthropists Luke and Helen Wilson donated their estate known as Tree Tops in Bethesda, Maryland, eventually totaling 70 acres, on which was built the National Institute(s) of Health.[2] On June 30, 1938, the Surgeon General along with Mrs. Wilson and Treasury Secretary Henry Morgenthau laid the cornerstone of NIH Building 1. With several laboratory buildings completed, President Franklin Roosevelt stood between the white columns of Building 1 to dedicate the NIH campus on October 31, 1940.

President Roosevelt at NIH

INFECTIOUS/CHRONIC DISEASE RESET

Whereas infectious diseases had been at the center of Public Health Service investigations since the founding of the Hygienic Laboratory in 1887, research discoveries had led to preventive measures such as improved hygiene and environmental sanitation, vaccines and antitoxin serums that were bringing these conditions under control. With an increasing lifespan among the general population, the National Institute of Health began to shift its research attention toward chronic diseases. In 1937 Surgeon General Parran declared:[3]

> The acute infectious diseases have declined rapidly during past years under the impact of public health effort. There has been an increase, however, in many of the diseases of adult life, particularly the chronic diseases. The emphasis of public health services needs to be shifted, therefore, to the prevention and treatment of the chronic diseases, particularly among the under privileged part of the population.

Even as infectious disease studies continued within the PHS, the National Cancer Institute Act of 1937 was an indication of congressional concurrence with the new PHS research approach.[4] The Act created the National Cancer Institute (NCI) as an independent research institute of the Public Health Service, merging an NIH pharmacology division with the Office of Cancer Investigations at Harvard University. The law authorized the Surgeon General, in cooperation with the National Cancer Advisory Council, to conduct, foster and coordinate research relating to "the cause, prevention, and methods of diagnosis and treatment of cancer." The NCI was directed to award fellowships and grants-in-aid for research projects outside the PHS, and promote coordination of research conducted by NCI and other agencies, organizations and individuals. The Act represents the first time Congress had

> The emphasis of public health services needs to be shifted to prevention and treatment of the chronic diseases.

provided funding to deal with a noncommunicable disease, serving as the prototype for other NIH Institutes that were to follow.

VENEREAL DISEASE CONTROL

From 1926 to 1930, Dr. Thomas Parran, Jr. was in charge of the PHS Division of Venereal Diseases. As New York State Health Commissioner, he continued at the forefront of efforts to educate the public about venereal diseases and to eradicate the disease that was becoming ever more prevalent in society. An anecdote is recounted about his direct approach to confront the public's reluctance in discussing the disease. For years, the word "syphilis" was not spoken in public venues. In November 1934, Dr. Parran was to speak on the Columbia Broadcasting System radio network. Upon arrival at the New York studio, he was informed that he could not mention the words "syphilis" and "gonorrhea" on the air, so he refused to go on the broadcast. Parran was not dissuaded and was unequivocal in using such words in public, including in magazine articles and at his first press conference as Surgeon General in 1936. An Associated Press reporter told Parran that the AP never used the word "syphilis," to which the Parran replied: "The Associated Press will use it from now on or it probably will have to omit all the pronouncements of the Surgeon General." By the fall of 1936, the popular press began to publicize the issue of venereal disease, with about 125 newspapers carrying articles concerning sexually transmitted diseases. In 1937, Dr. Parran published a book entitled *Shadow on the Land* that detailed the campaign against syphilis, which soon became a bestseller. Through these and other efforts, discussions about venereal disease gained wide public acceptance.[5,6]

The Social Security Act of 1935 authorized $8 million in grants to the states, which increased state health department budgets an average of 10 percent. Dr. Parran had determined that venereal disease was the most pressing of all public health problems and organized a National Conference on Venereal Disease Control that was held in December 1936. In a message sent to the Conference, President Roosevelt indicated the federal government was deeply interested in conserving resources and reducing the health care costs of "...the disastrous end-results of the venereal diseases." It was evident that federal support was needed for venereal disease control work and, ultimately, over 10 percent of SSA Title VI funds were allocated to states to help develop venereal disease programs, an amount more than any other communicable disease.[6] Congressional and public awareness about the pervasiveness of venereal diseases in the nation led to the enactment of the National Venereal Disease Control Act[7] on May 24, 1938. The purpose of the *Act to Impose Additional Duties upon the United States Public Health Service in Connection with the Investigation and Control of the Venereal Diseases* was to assist states, counties and health districts in providing "adequate measures for the prevention, treatment, and control of the venereal diseases;" conducting investigations to develop more effective control measures; and for training personnel and other expenses. Authorized appropriations to implement the law for the fiscal year ending June 30, 1939 was $3 million increasing in 1941 to $7 million, and for each year thereafter, such sum as deemed necessary to carry out the law's provisions. At the time, arsenicals were the primary treatment for syphilis until 1943 when penicillin was introduced, and in 1938 sulfanilamide was used to treat gonorrhea. The funding resulted in a significant expansion of clinic facilities and laboratories used for serologic tests for syphilis. Along with public subsidies, there was a substantive increase in the number of patients receiving therapy, jumping from 15 to 58 percent, and double the number of arsenical drug doses from 1933 to 1940.[6,8] An average of 20,053 syphilis-related deaths occurred each year from 1933 to 1939, which declined to about 10,000 deaths by 1950, indicating that the revived federal-state partnership made possible by the Venereal Disease Control Act was having a real impact on controlling the disease.[9]

GUATEMALA STD EXPERIMENT

Similar to the Tuskegee Syphilis Study *(Chapter Five)*, the Public Health Service engaged in unethical experimentation on human subjects in Guatemala from 1946 to 1948. While the Tuskegee Study followed the natural progression of syphilis, in Guatemala researchers intentionally infected healthy people with diseases. In 1946, the Surgeon General approved an NIH grant to the Pan American Sanitary Bureau (later, the Pan American Health Organization) to investigate venereal disease in Guatemala. The study purpose was to learn about effective prophylaxis of sexually transmitted diseases (STDs) for use among U.S. military personnel. Surgeon General Parran was knowledgeable about the nature of the research and PHS medical officer John C. Cutler was the lead researcher. About 1,500 study subjects were intentionally inoculated with syphilis, gonorrhea and chancroid, only about half of whom were provided some form of treatment. The subjects were members of vulnerable populations, and the research was conducted with deception and without valid informed consent. In 2010, President Barack Obama apologized to the Guatemalan President on behalf of the nation, and in September 2011 the U.S. Presidential Commission for the Study of Bioethical Issues produced the first of two reports, which provided a detailed account of how the research unfolded and was conducted. The report condemned the experiments and researchers as unethical and morally wrong.[10,11] Dr. Parran's awareness of the Tuskegee and Guatemala experiments prompted later considerations about whether an award and a building that bore his name should be retained.

FOOD AND DRUG ADMINISTRATION

Before the twentieth century, there was no federal oversight of domestically produced food and drugs. Adulteration and misbranding of food and drugs were problematic. Most drugs were prepared in local pharmacies. To provide uniform standards of composition, eleven physicians took action that in 1820 led to the creation the *U.S. Pharmacopeia* (USP) and later a *National Formulary* of medicinal substances and tests for purity, which ultimately became the official compendia for drugs. After the death of several children from contaminated diphtheria antitoxin, the Biologics Control Act of 1902[12] was enacted authorizing the PHS Hygienic Laboratory to regulate biological products such as vaccines. That was followed by the Pure Food and Drugs Act of 1906,[13] which prohibited the sale of adulterated or misbranded food and drugs in interstate commerce. Of note was Upton Sinclair's 1906 novel *The Jungle*, which revealed appalling working conditions and unsanitary practices in the meat packing industry, prompting public concern for reform that was reflective of the progressive movement of the time. Harvey W. Wiley, MD, known as the "Father of the Pure Food and Drugs Act," was chief chemist in the Department of Agriculture where, in 1902, a volunteer group of healthy men deemed the "poison squad" tested the effects of chemicals and adulterated foods on themselves. President Theodore Roosevelt signed the Pure Food and Drugs Act, largely written by Wiley, who with the Bureau of Chemistry would oversee its administration. Though not a PHS officer, Dr. Wiley was a prominent figure in public health and is often recognized as the first head of Food and Drug Administration (FDA). His activism was crucial to enactment of the Act of 1906, which first provided for the federal regulation of food and drugs. The 1906 Act was superseded by the Federal Food, Drug, and Cosmetic Act of 1938,[14] which assigned federal authority to the FDA to regulate the safety of food, drugs, medical devices, and cosmetics. That law was prompted by the death of over 100 persons, many being children, due to a preparation called Elixir Sulfanilamide in which diethylene glycol was the solvent. The Act of 1938 has been amended numerous times and is a cornerstone for the activities of the Food and Drug Administration, which was so named in July 1930. The FDA remained under the Department of Agriculture until June 1940, when the agency was moved to the new Federal Security Agency. It was again transferred in April 1953 to the Department of Health, Education, and Welfare, which became the Department of Health and Human Services, effective on May 4, 1980. From its inception, FDA has undergone a number of transformative changes to its authorities and organizational structure.

Harvey W. Wiley

There have been many legislative milestones that updated and modernized FDA's authorities and operations; two are noted here. In 1960, the William S. Merrell Company submitted a new drug application (NDA) for thalidomide, which was marketed in Europe for morning sickness in pregnant women. The FDA physician leading the NDA review was Frances O. Kelsey, who believed that the safety data were inadequate to support drug approval in spite of continued pressure upon Kelsey. Soon thereafter, the drug was being linked with the birth of deformed infants in Europe, and Kelsey was hailed for her steadfast position in not approving thalidomide for use in the U.S. President John F. Kennedy recognized Dr. Kelsey with the President's Award for Distinguished Federal Civilian Service. That event led to renewed interest in a bill sponsored by Senator Estes Kefauver of Tennessee to enhance drug regulation. In 1962, a major legislative advance was made with passage of the *Kefauver-Harris Drug Amendments*, which for the first time required drug manufacturers to prove the effectiveness and greater safety of their products in order to receive approval from FDA. In 1984, the *Drug Price Competition and Patent Term Restoration Act* (known as the *Hatch-Waxman Act*) went into effect, which expedited the availability of generic drugs by an abbreviated approval process, and expanded market and patent exclusivity periods for both branded and generic drugs.

FDA Headquarters. In 1995, the Naval Surface Warfare Center in the White Oak area of Montgomery County, Maryland, was closed and transferred to the General Services Administration. The site was renamed the Federal Research Center at White Oak and a major $1.15 billion project was undertaken which included the construction of fourteen new buildings. It now serves as the headquarters of the Food and Drug Administration, consolidating previously dispersed components of the FDA into a secured campus headquarters with offices, laboratories, and support facilities.

FDA Operations

The Food and Drug Administration is a scientific regulatory agency that has jurisdiction over food products (other than meat and poultry), prescription and nonprescription drugs, biologics such as vaccines, medical devices, cosmetics, radiation-emitting products, tobacco products, and veterinary products. FDA's authority reportedly oversees products accounting for 20 cents of every dollar spent by consumers. In fiscal year 2023, the FDA budget was approximately $6.5 billion, consisting of annual appropriations and user fees. The core functions of the agency are conducted within six Centers for:

- Biologics Evaluation and Research
- Devices and Radiological Health
- Drug Evaluation and Research
- Food Safety and Applied Nutrition
- Tobacco Products
- Veterinary Medicine

FDA Commissioners. Few FDA Commissioners have served with the PHS Commissioned Corps. James L. Goddard, MD, achieved the rank of Rear Admiral upon becoming Director of CDC, prior to FDA Commissioner. Arthur H. Hayes, MD, and Frank E. Young, MD, PhD, received the rank of Rear Admiral upon appointment as FDA Commissioner. Stephen M. Hahn, MD, was a PHS Commander in the early 1990s while at the National Cancer Institute.

James L. Goddard
1966-1968

Arthur H. Hayes
1981-1983

Frank E. Young
1984-1989

Stephen M. Hahn
2019-2021

FDA Staffing. As of 2023, the FDA staff was comprised of nearly 18,000 Civil Service employees, and over 1,000 PHS commissioned officers in all professional categories. The Center for Drug Evaluation and Research is the largest Center with approximately 5,000 civilian employees, and 500 PHS officers of which most are pharmacists. The Office of Regulatory Affairs, which is the lead office for all agency field activities, employed about 4,500 civilians and 350 PHS officers. Within the Centers for Biologics, Devices, Food Safety, and Tobacco Products, there was a smaller proportion of PHS officers relative to civilian employees, ranging from approximately 40 to 75 officers. Officers are principally engaged in an array of activities related to the review of biologic, drug and device applications, and regulatory imperatives of the Centers.

Center for Biologics Evaluation and Research

With the 1930 creation of NIH from the Hygienic Laboratory, biologics regulatory authority remained there until 1972, when it was moved to FDA and renamed the Bureau of Biologics. In 1982, it was merged with the FDA Bureau of Drugs to form the National Center for Drugs and Biologics. In 1987, under Commissioner Frank E. Young, drugs and biologics were split into their present organizational form of the Center for Biologics Evaluation and Research (CBER) and the Center for Drug Evaluation and Research (CDER).

CBER's mission is to ensure the safety, purity and effectiveness of biological and related products including vaccines, allergenics, blood and blood products, tissues, and cellular and gene therapies. Predecessor organizations collaborated with researchers of the polio, rubella and pertussis vaccines, and in ensuring the safety of blood and plasma products. The innovation of recombinant DNA was a foundation for biotechnology and a new era of genomics and proteomics, and the creation of new therapies such as monoclonal antibodies. During the COVID-19 pandemic, CBER worked on emergency investigational new drug applications, expediting clinical trials for vaccines and therapeutic biologicals, and supporting product development and scaling up manufacturing capacity. Of the several CBER Directors, as of 2023 only one was a PHS officer – RADM Harry "Hank" M. Meyer, Jr., MD. Dr. Meyer was a highly regarded medical virologist who served as the first Director of the Bureau of Biologics from 1972 to 1982, and first Director of the National Center for Drugs and Biologics from 1983 to 1986. His Deputy, Dr. Paul D. Parkman, served as the first CBER Director from 1987 to 1990.

Harry M. Meyer

Center for Devices and Radiological Health

The Center for Devices and Radiological Health (CDRH) approves new medical technologies, ensuring the safety and effectiveness of medical devices and electronic radiation-emitting products. Originating as the Radiological Health Unit within the PHS Bureau of State Services in 1948, the Unit underwent various organizational iterations. It was the Bureau of Radiological Health (BRH) in 1968, with authority to implement the Radiation Control for Health and Safety Act of 1968. In 1982, BRH merged with the Bureau of Medical Devices to form the Center for Devices and Radiological Health. An exemplary PHS engineering officer, John C. Villforth, served as the Director of the Bureau of Radiological Health, attaining the rank of Rear Admiral in 1971, and and he went on to serve as the first Director of CDRH until his retirement in 1990. RADM Villforth was a renowned radiological health specialist. He was first commissioned in the U.S. Air Force where he commanded the Radiological Health Laboratory, and transferred to the PHS Commissioned Corps to join the radiological health program. He also served as the PHS Chief Engineer from 1985 to 1989.

John C. Villforth

CAPT Brian Lewis, cardiologist, reviewing medical device clinical trials.

Center for Drug Evaluation and Research

CDER provides regulatory oversight of prescription and nonprescription drugs, including some biological therapeutics, and generic drugs to ensure  they are safe and effective. In 1982, FDA's Bureau of Drugs was merged with the Bureau of Biologics to form the National Center for Drugs and Biologics. It consisted of five offices, among which was the Office of Drugs with PHS pharmacy officer Jerome A. Halperin as first Director. Halperin held Master's Degrees from Johns Hopkins University and M.I.T. and achieved the rank of Rear Admiral. With the increasing number of new drug applications and to properly address the issues that were specific to the evaluation of drugs and biologics, FDA Commissioner Frank Young split drugs and biologics into their present form of the Center for Biologics Evaluation and Research and the Center for Drug Evaluation and Research, effective October 6, 1987. Dr. Carl C. Peck, formerly a Colonel in the U.S. Army Medical Corps, was appointed the first CDER Director from October 1987 until retiring in 1993,  receiving the PHS rank of RADM in October 1990. Senior executive Dr. Janet Woodcock became the Director from 1994 to 2004 and 2007 to 2021. In April 2001, RADM Steven K. Galson joined FDA as the CDER Deputy Director, becoming Acting Center Director and then the permanent Director in August  2005 until October 2007, when he was appointed Acting Surgeon General (see Chapter Fourteen).

Office of Orphan Products Development

 The Orphan Drug Act of 1983 supports the development of drugs, vaccines and diagnostic agents to treat diseases that affect fewer than 200,000 persons.[15] With about 7,000 rare diseases, nearly 30 million people are affected in the U.S. The Act provides tax and other benefits to companies that sponsor research and development of these agents. Pursuant to the law, the FDA Office of Orphan Products Development (OOPD) was established in 1983. OOPD evaluates submissions from sponsors to designate products for rare diseases. RADM Marlene E. Haffner, MD, MPH, assumed directorship of the Office in 1986, serving there until her retirement in 2007. Dr. Haffner introduced and advanced the enduring policies, strategies and major components of the program, receiving international recognition for her expertise.

In Their Words

by RADM (Ret.) Steven K. Galson

The fact that FDA-regulated products account for about 20 cents of every dollar spent by U.S. consumers, including some 20,000 prescription drug products, 78 percent of the U.S. food supply and 90,000 tobacco products means that the agency receives a lot of attention – from the public, the health care ecosystem, Congress and the press. With the expanded globalization of food and medical product production, FDA's scope is worldwide. In the spring of 2001, I left EPA and stepped into this fishbowl as the Deputy Director and Senior Commissioned Corps officer (as a Captain) of the Center for Drug Evaluation and Research (CDER). The Center at that point had some 2,500 staff, strong leadership from Dr. Janet Woodcock, who had recently reorganized to create a sole Deputy Director position and robust funding thanks to the Prescription Drug User Fee program whereby drug companies pay a fee to support the agency review process. At that time, the Center was involved in a series of high profile drug safety issues that would only expand during the next few years. A mere four months after joining the agency the 9/11 terrorist attacks happened, and the FDA was suddenly front and center in the government's effort to rapidly build-up counterterrorism capabilities. The anthrax attacks and the nation's supply of ciprofloxacin for anthrax treatment, in particular, occupied much of my time that first year. This enabled me to work closely with the CDC and other agencies on how to ensure the availability of critical drug supplies in nationwide public health emergencies. The first year also tested my mettle as a leader, as Dr. Woodcock moved into the FDA Deputy Commissioner post and I became the Acting Center Director at CDER, way before I had completed my full acclimatization of my initial job. My tenure at FDA went by in a flash mostly, as I look back, because of the crisis management nature of running such a diverse medical regulatory organization during a period of national emergency, exciting scientific advances, and a rapidly growing global drug industry. Corps officers were at my side working in many parts of the agency in key roles and the camaraderie from the Commissioned Corps inside and outside the FDA were key parts of my support system. I returned from summer vacation in August 2007 to calls from the White House personnel office and the Office of the Secretary. I was sure they were actually from my friends engaged in an elaborate ruse, but in fact they were asking me to be the Acting Surgeon General in a period of political tumult in Congress toward the end of the George W. Bush administration. The decision to leave FDA to take on this new role was enormously challenging. FDA Commissioner von Eschenbach told me he was supportive, but I felt it was not a great time in my FDA tenure to be departing. Nonetheless, CDER has continuously striven to advance its regulatory and scientific competences to keep ahead of new innovations in drug design, and I am proud that Commissioned Corps officers remain a vital component of the agency's professional and scientific staff.

REORGANIZATION AND CONSOLIDATION

Reorganization and Impact on Corps

On April 3, 1939, the Reorganization Act of 1939 was enacted as a planned reorganization of the federal Executive Branch to consolidate agencies with similar purposes, increase the efficiency of operations and reduce expenditures.[16] Various reorganization plans were prepared pursuant to the law. Plan No. 1, submitted April 25, 1939, created the Federal Security Agency (FSA), under which the Public Health Service was transferred from the Treasury Department, plus the Office of Education, the Civilian Conservation Corps and the Social Security Board (superseded by the Social Security Administration in July 1946). Reorganization Plan No. 4, submitted on April 11, 1940, transferred the Food and Drug Administration to the FSA from the Department of Agriculture, and Saint Elizabeth's Hospital and Freemen's Hospital from the Department of the Interior. The FSA was terminated on April 11, 1953, when its duties and responsibilities were assumed by the newly created Department of Health, Education, and Welfare (HEW).

The Public Health Service was generally allowed to function in a near-autonomous manner while located within the Treasury Department and later the Federal Security Agency. The Surgeon General was looked to as a respected leader in a position of authority managing a large medical portfolio in support of national public health, and that individual was widely considered above reproach. Though not immune to outside influences, Surgeons General were protective of the Service's institutional independence and adept at navigating partisan forces, whether doctrinal or political in nature. The new parent organization, Health, Education, and Welfare, would prove to be an encumbrance to the Public Health Service, and more specifically to the PHS Commissioned Corps. This was a turning point because HEW priorities, which would become increasingly subject to political considerations, marked the prospect of a coming gradual diminishment of authority and self-sufficiency of the Office of the Surgeon General, and a related vulnerability of the Commissioned Corps that prompted sporadic political assaults upon the Corps, its mission relevance and viability.

Public Health Service Act, 1943, 1944

As the Service continued to expand, the Public Health Service Act of 1943 was enacted to consolidate the PHS into four components: Office of the Surgeon General, Bureau of State Services, Bureau of Medical Services, and the National Institute of Health. On July 1, 1944, the Public Health Service Act of 1944 codified the authorities of the Public Health Service.[17] Title II–Administration, of the Act included several key organizational and personnel provisions, as follows.

Section 201 declared that the PHS in the Federal Security Agency shall be administered by the Surgeon General under the supervision and direction of the FSA Administrator.

Section 203 stated that there shall be in the PHS a commissioned Regular Corps and, for the purpose of securing a reserve for duty in time of national emergency, a Reserve Corps.

Section 204 specified that the Surgeon General shall be appointed from the Regular Corps for a four-year term by the President, by and with the advice and consent of the Senate.

Section 205 provided for the Surgeon General (SG) to appoint a Regular Corps officer as Deputy Surgeon General (DSG); to designate an Assistant Surgeon General to serve as SG in the event of absence, disability or absence of both the SG and DSG; and to assign Regular Corps officers as the Director of NIH, Chief of State Services Bureau, Chief of Medical Services Bureau, Chief Medical Officer of the U.S. Coast Guard, PHS Chief Dental Officer, and PHS Chief Sanitary Engineering Officer.

Section 206 specified that the grades of PHS officers shall correspond with grades of officers of the Army.

Section 208 specified that the appointment of Regular Corps officers may be made in the fields of medicine, surgery, dentistry, hygiene, sanitary engineering, pharmacy, nursing, and scientific specialties in public health.

Section 208 authority included dietitians, physical therapists, and subsequently veterinarians. By 1945, the Commissioned Corps had expanded by a few thousand personnel. Other provisions relating to pay and allowances, promotions, separation, retirement, and military benefits for PHS officers are contained in the Act. Title III of the Act stipulated the range of duties and powers of the Public Health Service, provided broad authority to conduct and support research into an array of diseases and disabilities, and allowed for grants to the states to carry out its provisions. Further, it clearly established federal quarantine authority and gave the PHS responsibility for preventing the introduction, transmission and spread of communicable disease from abroad.

World War II

The Second World War began in Europe on September 1, 1939, when Germany invaded Poland. Due to an alliance they had with Poland, Britain and France declared war on Germany two days later. World War II (WWII) involved most of the world's major countries, which were divided into two opposing military alliances: the Allies, which included Britain, France, United States, Canada, Australia, New Zealand, India, China and the Soviet Union; and the Axis, which included Germany, Italy and Japan. The United States' entry into World War II came about on December 8, 1941, when the U.S. declared war on Japan, one day after the Japanese attack on Pearl Harbor, and on December 11, 1941, when war was declared on Germany and Italy. The war came to an end with the formal surrender of Japan on September 2, 1945. WWII claimed an estimated 50 to 80 million lives – civilians and combatants – making it the deadliest conflict in history. The war led to creation of the United Nations on October 24, 1945, with the purpose of preventing future wars and to provide a platform for international dialogue. It replaced the League of Nations that was formed after World War I to maintain world peace.

PHS WAR-RELATED ACTIVITIES

On September 5, 1939, President Roosevelt proclaimed the neutrality of the United States and a state of limited national emergency, as the nation prepared for possible involvement in the war. The Lend-Lease program, enacted March 11, 1941, allowed the U.S. to supply materiel, warships and warplanes to the Allies from 1941 to 1945. On the domestic front, the war ended the Great Depression as hundreds of thousands of people were being employed in defense industries. The Public Health Service had to contend with problems created by the national emergency, while continuing the steady development of state health services and implementing preventive health measures throughout the country. Research was redirected from peacetime requirements to the wartime medical needs of military and industrial defense – industrial hygiene, aviation physiology, tropical diseases, and chemotherapy. Among the challenges outlined by the Surgeon General were a shortage of health personnel and sanitary engineers, a scarcity of components to manufacture drugs, medical and health supplies, and an increased demand for vaccines, antitoxins and serums.[18] However, the number of active duty PHS officers rapidly increased from 627 in 1940 to over 2,500 by 1946.

Selective Service Act; Extra-Cantonments

The Selective Training and Service Act of 1940,[19] which was amended after the U.S. entered WWII, required men 18 to 64 years of age to register for the draft and those ages 18 to 37 subject to military service. From 1940 to 1947, about 11.5 million men were inducted into the Armed Forces and over 6 million were volunteers. The Selective Service System required a physical examination with routine blood testing of all registrants. State laboratories and health officers were challenged by the demand for syphilis testing and providing treatment to infected individuals. Once treated, such individuals were referred to their Selective Service Boards for reexamination. In 1942, with an increasing need for manpower, the Army began inducting men with venereal diseases and curing them before they reported for active duty.[20]

As with World War I, the military encampments around the nation required that environmental sanitation, hygiene and other public health issues be addressed in and around these military bases. In 1940, a working resolution known as the Eight-Point Agreement was signed by officials of the Army, Navy, Public Health Service, and state health departments to control the spread of venereal disease in extra-cantonment areas. The military was responsible for health matters within cantonments, and state health departments, in cooperation with the PHS, agreed to institute control measures for venereal disease in civilian populations contiguous to military camps.[18]

Industrial Hygiene

On September 19, 1940, a Presidential Executive Order created the Health and Medical Committee (HMC) under the Council of National Defense (moved November 1940 to the Office of Health and Welfare Services), comprised of a former president of the American Medical Association, a representative of the National Research Council, and the Surgeons General of the Army, Navy, and PHS. In February 1941, the HMC subcommittee on industrial hygiene and medicine designated the PHS Division of Industrial Hygiene to coordinate all activities for the health protection of defense workers. The program included recruitment and training of professional personnel, provision of industrial hygiene services, research into the cause and control of occupational diseases, and aid to state industrial hygiene units. Under PHS leadership, the states investigated defense industry hazards, supervised plant construction and renovation, developed medical services in the industries, and provided educational programs.[18]

Nurse Training Act of 1943

In 1940, the American Nurses Association formed the Nursing Council on National Defense (renamed National Nursing Council for War Service in 1942) to study nursing resources and to determine the role of nurses in national defense. In cooperation with the Council, the PHS undertook a nationwide inventory of registered nurses which revealed a severe nursing shortage. In response, and to meet the increasing civilian and military need for nursing staff, the Labor-Federal Security Appropriation Act of 1942 provided $1.2 million (and $600,000 supplemental) to support basic nursing education, postgraduate courses, and refresher courses for inactive nurses, to be administered by the Public Health Service. However, the program was inadequate to meet the demand for more nurses, and the Nurse Training Act of 1943[21] (also known as the Bolton Act, for Congresswoman

Lucile Petry Leone

Frances P. Bolton of Ohio) was enacted into law on July 1, 1943. The Act created the Cadet Nurse Corps and the Division of Nurse Education in the Public Health Service under the direction of Lucile Petry, RN, the first woman to head a major division of the PHS. The Act provided grants to accredited schools of nursing to pay for reasonable tuition, fees, maintenance, Corps uniforms and insignia (silver Maltese Cross), and stipends for student nurses; and maintenance, tuition and fees for postgraduate and refresher courses. To discuss administration of the Corps, nurse education consultants visited 46 states and 158 nursing schools during the year, and an extensive public relations promotional and recruitment campaign was instituted. The recruitment quota for the year ending June 30, 1944, was set at 65,000 new student nurses, with an initial appropriation of $65 million.

A feature of the training program was its accelerated curriculum, compressing the traditional 36-month program into 30 months, with a further 6 months of service in a hospital prior to graduation. Of the nation's 1,300 nursing schools, 1,125 accredited schools participated in the program, with 124,000 student nurses graduating from those schools. The Act of 1943 specified that the program would cease at the end of the war and in September 1945, the President directed the Surgeon General to discontinue admission of Cadet Nurses to schools after October 15, 1945. Formal termination of the program came when the last Cadets were graduated in June 1948. The Cadet Nurse Corps was a highly successful program that provided the nation with a strong foundation of professional nursing services for years to come.[22,23] Lucile Petry was appointed in 1949 as the first Chief Nurse Officer of the PHS with the rank of Rear Admiral, with the distinction of being the first woman to achieve that rank in any uniformed service.[24]

PHS MILITARIZATION

Legislative authority was given to the President to militarize the Public Health Service during World War II. The Public Health Service Act of 1943 (Public Law 78-184) authorized military benefits for PHS commissioned officers and gave the President authority to declare the USPHS Commissioned Corps a part of the military forces in time of war. The Public Health Service Act of 1944,[17] which repealed the 1943 Act, included a similar provision:

> Section 216. In time of war, or of emergency proclaimed by the President, he may utilize the Service to such extent and in such manner as shall in his judgment promote the public interest, and in time of war he may by Executive order declare the commissioned corps of the Service to be a military service.

During the war, PHS officers were detailed for duty with the Army, Navy, and Coast Guard as well as to federal, state and local governmental entities, and to educational, research and other institutions engaged in health activities relating to public health. The PHS was formally militarized on June 21, 1945, when President Harry Truman issued Executive Order 9575 stating: "I hereby declare the commissioned corps of the Public Health Service to be a military service and a branch of the land and naval forces of the United States during the period of the present war."[25] This status remained in effect until July 1952, because it was not until the Treaty of San Francisco was signed by 48 nations on September 8, 1951, which became effective on April 28, 1952, that peace became official between Japan and some of the Allied nations. Interim legislation on April 14, 1952 (Public Law 82-313), and Executive Order 10349 on April 26, 1952, continued certain wartime powers of the President and included maintenance of the PHS Commissioned Corps as a military service, respectively. Public Law 82-450, approved July 3, 1952, again extended certain Presidential wartime powers, but absent a PHS provision, effectively ended the USPHS Commissioned Corps' status as a military service.[26]

Military Service
On February 1, 1942, Medical Director Lewis R. Thompson was appointed the Chief Inspection Officer in the Surgeon General's Office to coordinate national public health activities through the PHS District Offices and eleven PHS liaison officers who were assigned to the ten Army Service Commands and the Military Department of Puerto Rico. The liaison officers were responsible for communicating the health and medical needs of the military to state and local health officials, and advising the military about state and local capabilities to fulfill such needs. Duties and responsibilities of the District Offices and states increased tremendously, and critical wartime problems related to housing, sanitation, and a shortage of medical and hospital facilities, along with other duties of military and civilian authorities coupled with a declining availability of health department personnel, were common to all districts.[27]

Effective November 1, 1941, Presidential Executive Order 8929 directed that the Coast Guard (CG) would operate as part of the Navy (CG returned to the Treasury Department in 1946). This was followed on December 23, 1941, by Executive Order 8988, stating that Public Health Service commissioned officers detailed for duty on Coast Guard vessels and with other Coast Guard units were also constituted as a part of the naval forces of the United States. A PHS medical officer served as Chief Medical Officer of the Coast Guard, PHS officers staffed Coast Guard ships, and the Public Health Service was responsible for providing medical care, surgical and dental treatment and hospitalization to Coast Guard, Coast and Geodetic Survey, seamen, and Maritime Service and Merchant Marine personnel. Over 700 Public Health Service medical, dental, engineer, and nurse officers served with the Coast Guard from 1941 to 1945. PHS medical officers were first assigned to the 14 Coast Guard Districts and to several CG and Maritime Service training stations.

PHS physician James W. Todd on boatswain's chair traversing from a destroyer escort to a merchant ship to treat an injured seaman, 1944.
[New York Sunday News, National Library of Medicine]

Almost all PHS medical officers and nearly half of the dental officers were assigned to duty aboard Coast Guard ships, assisted by CG hospital corpsmen and pharmacist mates. Duty afloat could be very hazardous, with the Coast Guard vessels escorting supply ships and manning Naval patrol frigates, destroyer escorts, transports and landing craft. PHS medical officers also served as flight surgeons for aviation duty with the Coast Guard. With passage of the Nurse Training Act of 1943, nearly 40 PHS nurse officers were assigned to the Coast Guard to work in medical facilities. PHS officers sustained injuries and eight officers lost their lives in the service during the war.[28,29] Public Health Service officers also served with the Army during the war. Deputy Surgeon General Warren F. Draper was detailed to the War Department. PHS officers served in India, North Africa, and the Philippine Islands, and were assigned in various capacities throughout the world. In 1941, six PHS medical officers were in the Philippines to conduct quarantine service and provide medical care to merchant seamen and Coast Guard personnel. After the Philippine Islands were attacked by the Japanese on December 8, 1941, these officers reported to Army commands in the region. Five officers were captured and transferred to Japanese prison camps; Dr. Floyd A. Hawk died of exposure and malnutrition, and Dr. Fred J. Black lost his life on a Japanese transport sunk by a U.S. submarine. Dr. Victor H. Haas led 15 PHS officers on duty with the Army in the China-Burma-India theater. This group advised Chinese medical staff and provided preventive medicine and public health services for 150,000 workers building a railway from China to Burma to expand the Burma Road as a supply route to China. As Japanese forces advanced and Burma fell, the officers escaped and thereafter worked with the Army, being sent to an array of locations. Dr. Haas subsequently became the first director of the National Microbiological Institute, renamed in 1955 as the National

Institute of Allergy and Infectious Diseases, NIH. PHS officers also served with the American Mission in North Africa to assist with procurement and distribution of medical supplies and to study epidemic diseases that might impact military forces. These officers worked with the Allied Force Headquarters. A number of PHS officers, including Leonard Scheele (next Surgeon General), were detailed to the European theater where they served in Mediterranean countries and with Allied Force Headquarters; Scheele went on to serve with the Supreme Headquarters Allied Expeditionary Force commanded by General Eisenhower. During the summer of 1944, PHS officers were also assigned to the United Nations Relief and Rehabilitation Administration to implement public health activities in areas where they were on duty.[28,30]

MALARIA CONTROL, CREATION OF CDC

Malaria was a serious problem during World War II, both in the southern U.S. where military encampments were located and in combat operations areas, primarily in the South- and Southwest Pacific theaters. In response, a comprehensive research program underwritten by the National Research Council was undertaken in the United States that included the PHS, university research scientists and pharmaceutical companies, and in Britain to discover effective antimalarial drugs to replace quinine. This research produced new compounds, including drugs such as atabrine and chloroquine which altered malaria control throughout the world. To assist the Army in dealing with malaria around training camps, the Public Health Service detailed its chief malariologist, Dr. Louis L. Williams, Jr., to the Army's Fourth Service Command in Atlanta, Georgia. Backed by War Department needs, the PHS obtained an appropriation to operate an independent malaria control program and, in February 1942, established the office of Malaria Control in War Areas (MCWA) in Atlanta, headed by Dr. Williams and assisted by PHS sanitary engineers and entomologists. The program was administratively within the PHS State Relations Division headed by Dr. Joseph W. Mountin. The control program involved resources of the PHS, state and local health departments and the Work Projects Administration to implement water drainage and filling, larviciding with oil or Paris green, and beginning in 1945 spraying with DDT in areas contiguous to military and war industry facilities throughout the South and in the Caribbean. The MCWA also provided intensive malaria control training to state and local personnel and a community education program for residents. A growing concern was that servicemen returning from combat might harbor and transmit malaria or other tropical disease, so mobile units were employed to handle inspection and control efforts. In 1944, the MCWA took on typhus control and expanded training courses to include tropical diseases.[28] After World War II ended, Dr. Mountin, as director of the Bureau of State Services, envisioned a national agency that could support state and local health departments in monitoring, investigating and controlling communicable diseases.

Joseph W. Mountin

Upon the foundation of the MCWA, Mountin proposed creation of the Communicable Disease Center (CDC) based in Atlanta. After obtaining the concurrence of Surgeon General Parran and NIH Director Rolla E. Dyer, on July 1, 1946, the MCWA became the CDC with Sanitary Engineer Mark D. Hollis serving during the transition as its first director. The CDC expanded its coverage in 1947 taking over the San Francisco Plague Laboratory as the Epidemiology Division. Mountin brought university professor Alexander Langmuir to lead the division in 1949, who in 1951 created the CDC's Epidemic Intelligence Service (EIS). The CDC expanded its reach into chronic diseases, environmental health, nutrition and other areas, with several name changes until 1992 when "and Prevention" was appended and it became the Centers for Disease Control and Prevention, retaining the acronym CDC.

TUBERCULOSIS

Tuberculosis (TB) is a highly contagious disease associated with a high mortality rate. In 1882, Dr. Robert Koch isolated the causative agent, *Mycobacterium tuberculosis*, at a time when one in seven persons succumbed to the disease. TB sanitariums were built in the early twentieth century and drugs became available in the 1940s and 1950s to treat the disease. Aside from the need to screen military recruits for tuberculosis, there was concern that wartime conditions might increase the prevalence of tuberculosis in this nation. Dr. Herman E. Hilleboe, working in Minnesota to develop a tuberculosis case-finding device for the Public Health Service, transferred in January 1942 to Washington, DC, to take charge of a PHS emergency tuberculosis control program and to pursue development of a commercial X-ray machine by the Westinghouse Corporation. The Public Health Service Act of 1944[17] contained in Section 314(b) provision for the PHS to oversee a national tuberculosis control program, including grants-in-aid to states and other political subdivisions to develop and maintain effective measures for the prevention, treatment, and control of tuberculosis. On July 6, 1944, Surgeon General Parran officially established the Tuberculosis Control Division within the Bureau of State Services.[31] Eight mobile x-ray units were also deployed in various parts of the country during fiscal year 1944, examining 832,000 individuals. Hilleboe is credited with using radiographic equipment with an automatic camera to mass screen for tuberculosis, resulting in millions of persons including war workers and military personnel being examined.[5,22]

JAPANESE AMERICAN RELOCATION

On February 19, 1942, President Franklin Roosevelt issued Executive Order 9066, authorizing the Secretary of War to designate certain areas as military zones with the intent to relocate to those areas Americans of German, Italian, and Japanese origin. This very controversial action was never based on objective evidence of a perceived threat, yet it resulted in the relocation of about 110,000 American men, women and children of Japanese ancestry, 11,000 of German and 3,000 people of Italian ancestry to designated detention areas in the U.S. The Public Health Service was given overall responsibility for the provision of health care. The PHS performed pre-evacuation examinations so persons with communicable diseases could be treated and, with the assistance of local nurses and physicians, provided medical care en route from assembly areas to one of ten relocation centers. At the four largest centers – three in California and one in Washington State – the PHS established hospitals and supervised infirmaries at the smaller centers. Under the supervision of a PHS officer, a Japanese American physician was placed in charge of the hospital or infirmary and the professional staff. State and county health officers made regular inspections at each center and provided medical support within their jurisdictions. The need for healthcare professionals due to the war and ongoing shortages of Japanese American physicians and nurses was challenging, although other professionals such as dentists and pharmacists were readily available. Medical equipment and supplies were limited, yet a viable health care system emerged. Finally in 1945 to 1946, detainees were released and the relocation centers closed.[28,32]

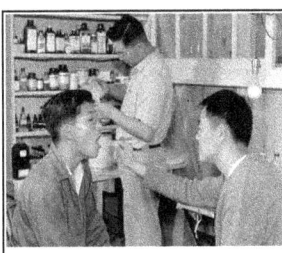

Japanese Americans Dr. K.H. Taria & pharmacist Tom Arase, Relocation Center, Jerome, Arkansas, 1942.
[U.S. National Archives]

On August 10, 1988, the Civil Liberties Act of 1988 signed into law by President Ronald Reagan provided financial redress of $20,000 for each former Japanese internee, and the Civil Liberties Act Amendments of 1992 appropriated an additional $400 million to ensure that all internees received the payment.

OFFICE OF CIVILIAN DEFENSE

On May 20, 1941, Executive Order 8757 established the Office of Civilian Defense to coordinate civilian defense activities for the protection of life and property in an emergency. The Public Health Service was tasked with overseeing the medical and public health activities. PHS personnel canvassed states to form a State Emergency Medical Service (EMS), and in most coastal states the State Chief or Deputy of the EMS was commissioned in the PHS Reserve Corps so that functions of a federal and state officer might be combined. A regional medical officer was assigned in nine regions of the country, most of whom were commissioned into the Reserve Corps. These officers were assisted by Reserve officer sanitary engineers and nursing staff.

POSTWAR PLANNING

The Public Health Service convened a Postwar Planning Committee to propose the reorganization and development of the nation's health resources, such that health and medical services necessary for the preservation and promotion of health, prevention of disease and treatment of illness would be available to the entire population. In 1944, the proposed plan envisioned a comprehensive program to include the following objectives:[22]

(1) assurance of a sanitary environment for the entire population
(2) a hospital system adequate for provision of complete medical services for all
(3) expanded public health services in every part of the country
(4) augmented research in the health and medical sciences
(5) training of health and medical personnel in adequate numbers
(6) a national medical care program.

LEGISLATIVE INITIATIVES

The National Institute of Health was tasked with conducting research necessitated by war and it discontinued most all other basic research except that pertaining to cancer. Dr. Rolla E. Dyer was appointed NIH director, as former director Dr. Lewis R. Thompson was transferred in 1942 to work with Dr. Parran in the Surgeon General's Office. During Dr. Parran's tenure as Surgeon General, several important pieces of legislation were passed. As noted earlier, the National Cancer Institute Act of 1937 created the National Cancer Institute as the first Institute of NIH. CAPT Robert H. Felix, a psychiatrist and chief of the PHS Division of Mental Hygiene, perceived a shortage of mental health professionals in the nation and he moved to incorporate mental health policy into federal biomedical policy. He proposed a national mental health program that led to legislation which, on July 3, 1946, became the *National Mental Health Act*,[33] signed by President Harry Truman. The Act was an acknowledgment of the mental health needs prevalent among the population, including active duty military personnel

Robert H. Felix

and veterans. The Act was comprehensive and included provisions for the conduct of research relating to the cause, diagnosis and treatment of psychiatric disorders; provided grants to conduct research, training of mental health professionals; and assistance to states in implementing mental health programs. The law called for a National Institute of Mental Health (NIMH), and on April 15, 1949, the NIMH was established from the Division of Mental

Hygiene, with a National Advisory Mental Health Council chaired by the Surgeon General. Dr. Felix became the first Director of NIMH and remained in that post until retiring from the PHS as Assistant Surgeon General in 1964.[34]

On August 13, 1946, the *Hospital Survey and Construction Act* (Hill-Burton Act, Public Law 79-725) was enacted to authorize state grants for the construction of nonprofit and local public hospitals and other health care facilities. The legislation responded to a perceived need for health care facilities to serve individuals in poorer rural areas of the U.S. The Public Health Service administered the law and was responsible for approving state plans. The Hill-Burton program had a major impact on the construction of hospitals, accounting for an increase of over 70,000 beds nationwide. From July 1947 through 1971, $28 billion (adjusted to 2012 dollars) were distributed for the construction and modernization of health care institutions.[35]

Throughout the 1940s, it was evident that the NIH needed a hospital to conduct clinical research. In 1944, Public Law 78-410, the Public Health Service Act authorized the establishment of the NIH Clinical Center. On July 8, 1947, the Labor-Federal Security Appropriation Act (Public Law 80-165) was enacted, providing funds for various PHS programs, and including construction of NIH research facilities and a clinical research hospital. The NIH Clinical Center hospital opened in July 1953.

PHS AND WORLD HEALTH ORGANIZATION

In January 1945, Surgeon General Parran informed the Department of State that the draft charter of the United Nations (UN) did not adequately provide for an international health agency. As a result, PHS officers were detailed to the State Department to organize an International Health Affairs Branch and work on proposals for an international health organization. Following intense review by health experts, Dr. Parran submitted their proposal at an International Health Conference held in New York City during the summer of 1946, where proposals were reviewed and at which he was elected president. The Conference, with representation from all UN member States, formed a World Health Organization (WHO) Interim Commission that laid the foundation for a permanent WHO. On July 22, 1946, the Constitution was formally approved, which led to its eventual ratification by member countries on April 7, 1948, making the World Health Organization official. Parran considered the formation of WHO as among his most important accomplishments as Surgeon General, second only to the expansion of medical research at the National Institute of Health.[5,28] WHO governance is carried out by the World Health Assembly which meets annually in Geneva, Switzerland, and an Executive Board which implements the decisions and policies of the Assembly. A Director-General heads the organization. Member States

are grouped into six regions; activities are directed through the regional offices: Regional Office for Africa, the Americas (Pan American Health Organization), Europe, Eastern Mediterranean, South-East Asia, and Western Pacific.

COMPLETION OF TENURE

Surgeon General Thomas Parran completed 12 years as Surgeon General on April 5, 1948. He retired on October 1, 1948, to become the first Dean of the Graduate School of Public Health, University of Pittsburgh, serving until 1958.

CHRONOLOGY • 1936–1948
SG Thomas J. Parran, Jr., April 1936–April 1948

1935   *Social Security Act of 1935.* Authorizes health grants to states to improve state and local public health programs and prevent interstate spread of disease. Title VI expanded state public health services and scientific research of PHS.

1937   *National Cancer Institute Act.* Creates the National Cancer Institute, providing support for cancer research and fellowships.

1938   *National Venereal Disease Control Act.* Provides state grants to support prevention, treatment, and control of venereal diseases.

1939   *Reorganization Act.* Transfers the PHS from the Treasury Department to the new Federal Security Agency.

1939   World War II begins in Europe, with the U.S. declaring war in 1941, the War lasting until 1945.

1943   *Nurse Training Act.* Establishes the Cadet Nurse Corps and Division of Nurse Education in the PHS.

1944   *Public Health Service Act.* Reorganizes the PHS; specifies that the SG shall be from the Regular Corps; specifies that PHS officer grades shall correspond with the Army; expands the professional fields from which to appoint Regular Corps officers; and authorizes militarization of the PHS.

1945   Executive Order declares the PHS a military service during the war, a status which remained in effect until July 1952.

1946   Communicable Disease Center is created, the predecessor of the current Centers for Disease Control and Prevention (CDC).

1946   *National Mental Health Act.* Provides for research relating to psychiatric disorders and establishes the National Institute of Mental Health in 1949.

1948   Formation of the World Health Organization, an agency of the United Nations.

CHAPTER SEVEN

RESEARCH & SERVICE GROWTH, FLUORIDATION, INDIAN HEALTH SERVICE
1948 to 1961

AN ERA OF OPTIMISM came about with the end of war and the realization of New Deal social reform programs. The Public Health Service was a beneficiary of many programmatic initiatives, which led to expansion of its public health authorities and substantially increased budgets. The National Institutes of Health (NIH) continued to gain prominence with the addition of new institutes and society's growing regard for biomedical research as a promising path toward curing chronic diseases. Dr. Leonard Scheele, then director of the National Cancer Institute (NCI), was named by President Harry S. Truman to serve as Surgeon General, effective April 6, 1948. Leonard Andrew Scheele received his medical degree from the Wayne State University School of Medicine in 1934. He entered the PHS on July 2, 1934, as an Assistant Surgeon, and served two years on quarantine duty at San Francisco and Honolulu. He then joined the PHS Division of Public Health Methods, serving briefly as a health officer in Maryland, and was sent to Memorial Hospital in New York City to receive special cancer training for three years. During World War II, Scheele served with the Office of Civilian Defense and then was detailed for three years with the U.S. Army, serving in Africa and Europe. He subsequently served in Britain with the Medical Division at the Allied Expeditionary Force Supreme Headquarters and, after Germany's surrender, was chief of preventive medicine of the Allied Control Council in Berlin. Following service with the Army, Dr. Scheele was appointed Assistant Director and in 1947 Director of the National Cancer Institute and Associate Director of the National Institute of Health (renamed *Institutes*, June 1948) for one year, prior to his appointment as Surgeon General. With the ardent support of philanthropists Albert and Mary Lasker and Congressional leaders who would promote expanded biomedical research, especially cancer research, and with support from the Lasker-backed American Cancer Society, the NIH became a clinical research beacon nationally and internationally.

Leonard A. Scheele

NIH RESEARCH INSTITUTES

Under Surgeon General Leonard Scheele, the National Institutes of Health experienced rapid growth, adding new institutes organized around specific medical conditions and chronic diseases, similar to the National Cancer Institute which was established by the National Cancer Institute Act of 1937 and made part of NIH with the Public Health Service Act of 1944.

National Heart Institute (1948)
PL 80-655, National Heart Act, June 16, 1948
National Institute of Dental Research (1948)
PL 80-755, National Dental Research Act, June 24, 1948
National Microbiological Institute (1948)
Pursuant to PL 78-410, Public Health Service Act, July 1, 1944
National Institute of Mental Health (1949)
PL 79-487, National Mental Health Act, July 3, 1946
National Institute of Arthritis and Metabolic Diseases (1950)
PL 81-692, Public Health Service Act, amendment, August 15, 1950
National Institute of Neurological Diseases and Blindness (1950)
PL 81-692, Public Health Service Act, amendment, August 15, 1950
National Institute of Allergy and Infectious Diseases (1955)
Under authority of PL 81-692, Public Health Service Act, amendment, replacing the National Microbiological Institute, August 15, 1950

In 1953, a 500-bed Clinical Center Hospital opened to accommodate patient care and clinical research on the NIH campus. The authorizing legislation for the construction of institutes and investigatory research typically included other complementary provisions such as national advisory boards, fellowship and training support, extramural research grants to public and private institutions and individuals, and grants-in-aid to states for support of their professional and scientific capabilities, community programs and activities.

DENTAL RESEARCH – FLUORIDATION

At the beginning of the 20th century, the presence of extensive dental caries was common, with no effective means for preventing the disease. In 1901, Dr. Frederick S. McKay opened a dental practice in Colorado Springs, Colorado, and observed scores of residents with brown stains on their teeth. Along with dental researcher Dr. Greene V. Black, they determined that children waiting for their secondary set of teeth to erupt were at high risk, yet teeth with the Colorado brown stain were inexplicably resistant to decay. Brown stains also appeared on children's teeth in Oakley, Idaho, after construction of a pipeline to a spring as a water source. McKay advised abandoning the pipeline and in a few years the younger children of Oakley grew healthy secondary teeth without staining or mottling. Dr. McKay and Dr. Grover Kempf of the PHS traveled to Bauxite, Arkansas, a town owned by the Aluminum Company of America

(ALCOA), to investigate reports of a prevalence of brown stain on teeth. They discovered that the mottled teeth enamel among children of Bauxite was not present in a town five miles away. ALCOA's chief chemist made a spectrographic analysis of the town's water, which showed high levels of fluoride. He advised McKay to collect water samples from other towns where staining occurred and within months Dr. McKay was able to conclude that high levels of water-borne fluoride caused the tooth enamel discoloration. Shortly thereafter, PHS epidemiology investigations began, led by Dr. H. Trendley Dean, head of the Dental Hygiene Unit at NIH. Dean and his staff traversed the country to compare fluoride levels in drinking water, and by the late 1930s they determined that fluoride levels up to 1.0 ppm did not cause enamel staining (fluorosis) in most people. Based on studies that mottled teeth were resistant to tooth decay, the PHS cooperated with Grand Rapids, Michigan, officials to introduce fluoridation in its water supply in 1945. The PHS program was taken over by the National Institute of Dental Research in 1948, with CAPT Dean as its first Director. By 1950, there was a significant reduction in the rate of dental caries among Grand Rapids children born after fluoridation of the water supply. On June 1, 1950, the Public Health Service announced its new policy: "Using scientific methods and procedures, communities desiring to fluoridate their communal water supplies should be strongly encouraged to do so." The scientific achievement that led to water fluoridation is considered one of the great preventive health measures of the time.[1,2]

H. Trendley Dean

WATER POLLUTION CONTROL

Investigations of water quality date from the Public Health Service Act of 1912, which authorized the PHS to "study and investigate the diseases of man and conditions influencing the propagation and spread thereof, including sanitation and sewage and the pollution either directly or indirectly of the navigable streams and lakes of the United States."[3] The PHS had the mission to address environmental issues that it deemed appropriate and led to stream pollution investigations centered at the Field Investigation Station (FIS) in Cincinnati, Ohio. On June 30, 1948, the Water Pollution Control Act[4] was enacted, which was very comprehensive in scope. While affirming the primary responsibility of the states to control pollution in their waterways, the law charged the Public Health Service with responsibility to ensure the sanitary condition of interstate waters and tributaries; to encourage cooperative activities for prevention and abatement of water pollution; investigate discharges of sewage, industrial waste and other substances that adversely affect such waters, provide notification to offenders and request the Attorney General to bring a law suit, if needed, to secure abatement; and to publish reports of surveys and research made under authority of the Act. In conjunction with the Federal Works Administration, the law also authorized technical assistance, loans and financial appropriations to states for investigations, surveys and research related to the prevention and control of water pollution. The PHS prepared principles of a "Suggested State Water Pollution Control Act" for guidance in developing uniformity among state laws.[5] The Water Pollution Control Act of 1956 added provisions for technical assistance, research and construction grants for waste treatment facilities. Since the Act of 1948, there have been major legislative revisions involving transfer of PHS and Departmental responsibilities to other agencies, culminating with the Federal Water Pollution Control Act Amendments of 1972, Clean Water Act of 1977, and Water Quality Act of 1987 that now vest environmental health authority in the Environmental Protection Agency, which was created in 1970. The Act of 1948 also provided funds to construct and equip a new PHS research facility in Cincinnati, Ohio, replacing the FIS. In 1954, the Robert A. Taft Sanitary Engineering Center was constructed for research, field investigations and training in the sanitary sciences relating to wastewater treatment, water and air pollution control, food protection and radiation. Another research laboratory was built in Cincinnati in 1975, the Andrew W. Breidenbach Environ-mental Research Center.

AIR POLLUTION CONTROL/DONORA INCIDENT

Soon after Dr. Scheele was appointed Surgeon General, one of the worst U.S. air pollution disasters occurred in the small steel mill town of Donora, Pennsylvania, about 20 miles south of Pittsburgh. During the last week of October 1948, an atmospheric temperature inversion led to the presence of toxic smog over Donora that was laden with industrial contaminants, likely due in large measure to airborne emissions of the Donora Zinc Works, a part of U.S. Steel. Visibility was extremely poor and about 6,000 of the town's 14,000 residents became ill (most affected were those 65 years of age and older), 400 of whom were hospitalized and 20 who died before rain dispersed the smog on October 31. In response, the Public Health Service fielded a 25-member team to conduct a comprehensive investigation of the incident to determine causative clinical and environmental factors in a systematic way – it was considered the most exhaustive study of air pollution ever made to date. In the *Foreword* to the PHS investigative report, Surgeon General Scheele noted that the study was "...the opening move in what may develop into a major field of operation in improving the Nation's health."[6] Recommendations included the reduction of noxious emissions and particulate matter from specified industrial processes, and institution of weather forecasting and community alerts about impending adverse weather conditions coupled with preventive measures. The Donora incident and other environmental disasters eventually led to Congressional passage of the Air Pollution Control Act of 1955,[7] which provided authority to the PHS relating to air pollution control that included the conduct of research into the causes of and methods to control air pollution, and provision of technical assistance and grants-in-aid to the states, institutions and individuals for research and training purposes. That Act was strengthened by the Clean Air Act of 1963, Air Quality Act of 1967, and Clean Air Act of 1970 which authorized federal and state regulations to limit emissions, and the Clean Air Act Amendments of 1977 and 1990, all of which provided for air emission control methods, standards and enforcement that have resulted in substantive improvements in the nation's air quality.[8]

EPIDEMIC INTELLIGENCE SERVICE

Surgeon General Scheele and PHS officer Dr. Joseph W. Mountin oversaw the 1951 creation of the Epidemic Intelligence Service (EIS) in the Communicable Disease Center (CDC). With the outbreak of the Korean War in June 1950, Army Major General Anthony C. McAuliffe conversed with Scheele about the threat of biological warfare and lack of information, and requested the Public Health Service to begin research on the topic. For physician-epidemiologist Alexander D. Langmuir, head of the EIS, this was the first major investigative undertaking of the EIS. Within a few years, the EIS would take on another important national issue, the Salk polio vaccine Cutter incident. Langmuir greatly broadened the epidemiologic scope of the EIS, and it has become internationally recognized as having an expansive portfolio and reputation for superior surveillance, epidemiologic and emergency response capabilities.

Alexander Langmuir

The Epidemic Intelligence Service accepts PHS officer, civilian and non-U.S. citizen applicants into its program. They must commit to a two-year fellowship that includes the conduct of field investigations, epidemiological methodology, public health surveillance systems, scientific writing, and public outreach activities. As of 2023, EIS had trained over 4,000 EIS officers since its inception, who are assigned to CDC offices, state and local health departments, federal agencies, and globally for investigative work in chronic diseases, infectious and noninfectious diseases, and environmental and occupational health. Responses have included its participation in the worldwide Smallpox Eradication Program, Legionnaires' disease, outbreaks and incidents related to anthrax, SARS, and flu subtypes H_1N_1 and H_5N_1, and providing on-the-ground support for Ebola, Zika, COVID-19, and mpox outbreaks.[9]

Polio Vaccine/Cutter Incident

Poliomyelitis has been present worldwide for thousands of years. It is a highly infectious disease that in a small percent of patients can lead to lifelong paralysis and death. Thus, it was very much feared during outbreaks, and in the early 1950s it caused over 15,000 cases of paralysis yearly in the United States. Poliovirus infections only occur in humans and are spread person to person by the fecal-oral and respiratory routes. The disease is more prevalent among infants and young children, and children living in poor hygienic conditions.

In 1952, Dr. Jonas E. Salk developed an inactivated poliovirus vaccine (IPV). Underwritten by the National Foundation for Infantile Paralysis (evolved from fund raising efforts by President Franklin Roosevelt, later renamed March of Dimes), a national trial of the Salk vaccine involving 1.8 million children was conducted, the largest drug or vaccine trial ever conducted at the time. The successful results of 1954 field trials were announced on April 12, 1955, by Surgeon General Scheele and Oveta Culp Hobby, Secretary of Health, Education, and Welfare (HEW). Five manufacturers were licensed to immediately begin vaccine production and mass polio vaccination was initiated. However, two weeks after vaccine release, there were reports about children in California who became paralyzed in the arm that was inoculated with polio vaccine made by Cutter Laboratories. On April 27, the Surgeon General requested Cutter Laboratories to recall its vaccine, although 380,000 doses had already been administered. An Epidemic Intelligence Service investigation determined that two production pools (120,000 doses) made by Cutter contained live poliovirus and among children who received the vaccine, 40,000 had developed abortive polio, 51 were permanently paralyzed and 5 had died. On April 28, Scheele created a new Poliomyelitis Surveillance Unit at the CDC and a national system of case reporting from the states. On May 7, 1955, the Surgeon General halted the national vaccination campaign for five days until all vaccines were cleared for safety. Although Scheele was relatively unscathed by the episode, it was apparent that the Public Health Service moved too hastily and did not ensure that proper manufacturing standards were in place and being followed, prior to launching the vaccination program. The matter also weakened public and Congressional confidence in the PHS and federal government.[10,11]

A live attenuated poliovirus vaccine was first developed in 1950 by virologist Hilary Koprowski, but it required more research before being ready for use, five years after the Salk vaccine. Another attenuated virus vaccine was being developed by Dr. Albert B. Sabin who had been investigating poliomyelitis for many years, and he showed that the virus entered via the mouth and was an infection of the alimentary tract, and then spread to nerve tissue. Sabin's attenuated poliovirus vaccine was administered orally on a sugar cube to confer long-term immunity. He conducted a study of millions of children in the Soviet Union that substantiated the vaccine's efficacy. In 1960, Surgeon General Burney approved the Sabin vaccine over Koprowski's vaccine as somewhat more attenuated and therefore safer, for licensure in the United States.[12] In 1961, the Sabin oral polio vaccine (OPV) became the nation's primary polio vaccine due to its relative lower cost and ease of administration. By 1979, the polio virus was eliminated in the U.S. In 1987, an enhanced potency inactivated polio vaccine became available as the preferred standard for childhood vaccination.

ORGANIZATIONAL TRANSITION

The Reorganization Act of 1939 was enacted to consolidate agencies that had similar purposes. Among the organizational changes was transfer of the Public Health Service from the Treasury Department to the Federal Security Agency (FSA). By 1953, FSA programs had grown in importance and budget to such an extent that President Eisenhower submitted a reorganization plan for dissolution of FSA, to be replaced by a new agency with Cabinet status – the Department of Health, Education, and Welfare (HEW). Upon approval, FSA organizational components and responsibilities were transferred to HEW, effective April 11, 1953, with the major operating components being the PHS, Office of Education, Food and Drug Administration, Social Security Administration, Office of Vocational Rehabilitation, and Saint Elizabeth's Hospital. The American Medical Association wanted provision for a new, high level position to advise the HEW Secretary on medically related issues, with the result that a special assistant for health and medical affairs was put in place. The first incumbents of that position had little impact on Surgeon General Scheele's ability to continue exercising his public health responsibilities and work directly with Secretary Hobby. However, the special assistant position foretold a future that ultimately would challenge the Surgeon General's line management authority to oversee federal public health policy and operations.

INDIAN HEALTH SERVICE

In the late 1700s, European immigrants coming to the United States brought infectious diseases that spread to the indigenous Indian population which lacked immunity. The War Department was given responsibility to provide health care to American Indians; however, the level of care was minimal and Army physicians primarily took measures to contain contagious diseases such as smallpox among Indian tribes, particularly those near military posts. In 1824, the Bureau of Indian Affairs (BIA) was formed within the War Department to oversee trade and treaty obligations, which in 1849 was transferred to the Department of the Interior, initiating the provision of more systematic medical care. The position of chief medical supervisor was established in 1908 and, in 1911, budgetary appropriations were designated for the provision of health care to the tribal population. Then in 1924, a health division was created in the BIA. PHS medical officers were detailed to the Indian health program beginning in 1926, with Marshall C. Guthrie serving as the first chief medical officer/adviser, followed by James G. Townsend in 1933 and Fred T. Foard, Jr. in 1948. Legislation that first authorized federal funding of health care, personnel, buildings and other services for American Indians and Alaska Natives (AI/ANs) included the Snyder Act of 1921,[13] which specified that such expenditures were for the "benefit, care, and assistance of the Indians." Nonetheless, the Lewis Meriam Report of 1928, commissioned by Interior Secretary Hubert Work, described a substandard level of health care for Indians that was prevalent throughout the nation. And the Thomas Parran Report released in 1954 described deplorable health conditions, including a 10 percent incidence of tuberculosis among Alaska Natives.

Although various proposals were widely supported for reassignment of the health care program to the Public Health Service, it was not achieved until passage of the Indian Health Transfer Act of 1954 (Public Law 83-568), which transferred responsibility for Indian health care from the Bureau of  Indian Affairs to the Public Health Service and created the Indian Health Service (then known as the PHS Division of Indian Health, Bureau of Medical Services), effective July 1, 1955.[14] About 2,500 BIA health program personnel, 48 hospitals, 18 health centers, 62 stations, 13 infirmaries and other facility locations were placed under the jurisdiction of the new Indian Health Service (IHS). PHS officer James R. Shaw, who was medical advisor to the BIA, had observed that BIA funding was often used for things other than health care and, importantly, he worked with Congress to obtain passage of the Transfer Act. Surgeon General Scheele appointed Dr. Shaw as the first director of the Division of Indian Health in 1955, where he served until 1962.[15] Appropriations for the Division increased substantially in 1956 to $35 million, with a request that PHS conduct a detailed evaluation of the health program status. Two reports were produced: a preliminary report of the most pressing needs and a more comprehensive report that was sent to Congress in February 1957. The latter report, *Health Services for American Indians*, was referred to as the *Gold Book* due to it being bound in a gold colored cover, and it became the basis for congressional appropriations for years.

In 1955 and 1957, public laws extended use of the Hill-Burton Act and appropriated funds for the construction of community hospitals. Enactment in 1959 of the Indian Sanitation Facilities Act was a major milestone, which authorized the construction of much needed safe water systems, sewer and solid waste facilities for AI/AN homes and communities. Numerous PHS engineer officers have participated in this effort, which is administered by the IHS Sanitation Facilities Construction Program.

President Richard Nixon advanced a concept of tribal self-rule, resulting in the Indian Self-Determination and Education Assistance Act of 1975 and subsequent amendments that codified federal policy to support tribal self-determination and self-governance. In 1976, Congress enacted the Indian Health Care Improvement Act (IHCIA)[16] "to meet the national goal of providing the highest possible health status to Indians and to provide existing Indian health services with all resources necessary to effect that policy." It contained a vast array of provisions to enhance health care services and was refined and reauthorized several times in ensuing years. The Patient Protection and Affordable Care Act of 2010 permanently reauthorized the IHCIA. On January 4, 1988, the Indian Health Service, which had been a Bureau in the Health Resources and Services Administration, was elevated to Agency status.

IHS Health Care System

Many IHS programs have been transferred to tribal authority over the years, with control of health care services increasingly coming under the direction of local tribal communities. Health care delivery is described as the I/T/U system – IHS/Tribal/Urban Indian health programs, emanating from Title V of IHCIA.[17] As of 2018, about 70 percent of American Indians and Alaska Natives lived in metropolitan areas, of which 25 percent were served by urban Indian Health programs. The Indian Health Service provides health care for about 2.2 million of the nation's 3.7 million AI/ANs (of a total 5.7 million AI/ANs alone or in combination with other races).[18]

Phoenix Indian Medical Center

As of 2020, the IHS consisted of 24 hospitals (and 22 tribal hospitals), 51 (and 279 tribal) health centers, and 24 (and 79 tribal) health stations. The facilities are located in the IHS administrative/health care delivery system comprised of twelve geographic areas of the nation, with each area having a unique group of tribes. As of 2020, the Indian Health Service employed about 15,000 personnel of whom 4,000 were healthcare providers. IHS practitioners represent an array of professions including dentistry, nurse, engineering, environmental health, medical technology, optometry, pharmacy, physical rehabilitation and physician.

Alaska Native Medical Center

Among those were over 1,600 PHS officers from every professional category who were assigned to IHS/tribal/urban Indian health programs throughout the country. Healthcare professionals often come from cultural backgrounds that differ from American Indian/Alaska Native heritage so understanding and respecting cultural practices and needs of their patients is important toward building trust and providing quality medical care. Healthcare professionals include advanced practice providers who serve as physician extenders and include physician assistants and nurse practitioners who are vital to ensuring the delivery of high quality care to all patients. Advanced practice nurses include nurse practitioners, behavioral health/psychiatric nurses, family practice nurses, nurse midwifes, and nurse anesthetists.

LCDR Jessica Van Den Berg
Family Nurse Practitioner

Pharmacy Practice Innovation

Over the years, noteworthy health care advances have been initiated within the Indian Health Service. One innovation was the transition of pharmacy practice from a product- to a patient-centered model. In 1953, CAPT Allen J. Brands became lead pharmacist in the Division of Health, BIA, who in 1967 was appointed pharmacy liaison officer to the Surgeon General. That title was changed to Chief Pharmacist Officer in 1979 with the rank of Assistant Surgeon General. With the support of Dr. Shaw, Brands justified hiring more pharmacists in the clinics and hospitals to relieve physicians and nurses of responsibility for pharmaceutical and administrative duties. Novel practices were introduced over the next few decades, including the use of patient medical records for prescription orders, providing education to improve medication compliance, and offering pharmacist counseling to patients on proper medication use. It was evident to Brands that many patient visits involved minor health issues that pharmacists could competently treat, which led in 1996 to the Indian Health Service designating pharmacists as primary care providers with direct patient care privileges, including medication and laboratory prescriptive authority. A National Clinical Pharmacy Specialist Program was formed by the Chief Pharmacy Officer in 1997 to credential federal pharmacists nationwide to ensure professional competency, and it was one of the catalysts for the entire profession to pursue healthcare provider status. These innovations are now standards of practice within IHS and other federal agencies where PHS pharmacists provide professional and more clinical services. Such advances were among

Allen J. Brands

the seminal projects that supported the national clinical pharmacy movement and the doctoral level degree programs that are now the professional practice model in all public and private clinics and hospitals nationally.[19,20]

Improper Sterilization

The General Accounting Office (GAO) conducted a study of medical research involving the American Indian population during fiscal years 1972 to 1975. Results of the study revealed that in four of the twelve Indian Health Service regions – Aberdeen, Albuquerque, Oklahoma, and Phoenix – sterilization procedures were performed on 3,406 women without their permission, of whom 3,001 were of childbearing age. The GAO investigation found that the IHS areas were noncompliant with IHS policies regulating consent to sterilization, using inadequate consent forms that were a persistent problem. There were also assertions that the number of sterilizations was at least 25 percent of Native American women during that period. Many such women were thereafter affected by various forms of long-term suffering in their lives. The 1976 Indian Health Care Improvement Act helped to strengthen tribal communities and the health care they received in the aftermath of the improper medical procedures.[21,22]

IHS Directors

As of 2023, eleven individuals had served as Director of the Indian Health Service, of whom eight were PHS officers. In 2022, Roselyn Tso became Director.

DIRECTORS OF THE INDIAN HEALTH SERVICE*

James R. Shaw
1955-1962

Carruth J. Wagner
1962-1965

Erwin S. Rabeau
1966-1969

Emery A. Johnson
1969-1981

Everett R. Rhoades
1982-1993

Michael H. Trujillo
1994-2002

Charles W. Grim
2002-2007

Robert G. McSwain
2008-2009

Yvette Roubideaux
2009-2015

Michael D. Weahkee
2020-2021

*2015-2020, Robert G. McSwain, Mary L. Smith, Chris Buchanan, and Michael D. Weahkee served as Acting IHS Directors. Civilian Directors: Robert G. McSwain, Yvette Roubideaux, Roselyn Tso [not pictured].

In Their Words
by RADM Michael D. Weahkee

The role and responsibilities of the Indian Health Service are rapidly evolving, as more of the 574 federally recognized tribes in the United States exercise their sovereign status and rights under the Indian Self Determination and Education Assistance Act to manage and govern their own health care programs. When first established in 1955, the primary focus of the IHS was on directly managing and operating the health care programs that serve American Indian and Alaska Native patients. Since passage of the ISDEAA in 1975, the agency's mission has been transitioning away from direct provision of health care toward a model that places the IHS in a fiduciary pass-through role, with loose oversight of the tribal contractors and compactors who now directly operate and govern their programs. In these first three-and-a-half years that I have served as the principal steward of the IHS, there has been an 8 percent increase in the number of tribes administering programs under the ISDEAA, now including 65 percent of tribes. This evolving role has required the agency to concurrently re-tool and adjust our staffing plans, our policies and procedures, and our agency's culture. Tribal governments continue to develop innovative solutions to the challenges facing their communities and the IHS is working hard to support them in meeting those challenges. The historical underfunding of the IHS unfortunately continues, yet the advocacy and education efforts persist. In recent years, tribal-federal workgroups have updated the formulas and benchmarks used to demonstrate the disparate funding levels of the agency, using the Centers for Medicare and Medicaid Services National Health Expenditures (NHE) as the yardstick. In fiscal year 2019, the U.S. NHE was $9,726 per person compared with an IHS expenditure of $4,078 per patient, or just 42 percent of the benchmark. Additional funding is needed to provide the 2.6 million American Indians and Alaska Natives served by the IHS with equitable health care services. Tribal leaders also continue to press Congress and the Executive Branch to fully implement all provisions authorized under the Indian Health Care Improvement Act, and they have also engaged the Judicial Branch in clarifying grey areas of the law through litigation. With each legal decision, the IHS makes the necessary adjustments and moves forward proactively with the mission of the agency in mind, "to raise the physical, mental, social and spiritual health of American Indians and Alaska Natives to the highest level." Every day there are other new challenges to confront, like the historic 35-day government shutdown in fiscal year 2019 and the current global COVID-19 pandemic. Despite ongoing challenges, the Indian Health Service and the American Indian and Alaska Native people that we serve will persevere and prove that we are a strong and resilient people, dedicated to the long-term improvement of the health status of our Native communities.

PHS AND ATOMIC ENERGY
Nuclear Testing

The Atomic Energy Act (AEA) of 1946, amended by the AEA enacted August 30, 1954, and other amendments thereafter, created the Atomic Energy Commission (AEC) to research the use of atomic energy for peaceful purposes consistent with defense and security, and the health and safety of the public. The AEC conducted atmospheric and underground nuclear tests in southeastern Nevada at the Nevada Test Site (NTS renamed Nevada National Security Site, NNSS, in 2010) from 1951 to 1992, and is now under the Environmental  Protection Agency (EPA). A 1954 Memorandum of Understanding with the AEC provided for the Public Health Service to assist with determining the health and safety risks of nuclear tests. The Offsite Radiological Safety Program was established within the Public Health Service, and hundreds of PHS commissioned officers staffed offsite radioactive fallout monitoring programs from 1954 until 1970, at which time the new EPA assumed that responsibility. Initially, monitoring involved collecting fallout on paper covered with sticky film, and later included measuring ambient radiation levels, radioactive gases, and collecting air, water, milk, soil, plant, and wildlife samples. Nuclear testing was held at the Pacific Proving Grounds in the Marshall Islands where offsite monitoring was mainly by aerial reconnaissance. For tests held at the Nevada Test Site, PHS officers staffed the Base Camp Mercury laboratory in the NTS and at all offsite monitoring stations located throughout Nevada, Arizona, Utah and California. The region was divided into zones, with each zone having a headquarters location and a USPHS officer as zone commander. The PHS and

Charles F. Costa

EPA also provided offsite surveillance for nuclear explosive tests at places other than the NTS/NNSS.[23-25] USPHS officer CAPT Charles (Chuck) F. Costa, a PHS engineer, served at the NTS in the 1960s and was one of the founders of an expanded surveillance system located in communities surrounding the NNSS – the Community Environmental Monitoring Program – which was formed in 1981. Upon retiring from the PHS, Costa served as the division director for the EPA's offsite environmental monitoring group. He subsequently joined with others to create the Smithsonian Affiliated National Atomic Testing Museum.[26]

Uranium Mining and Radon

From the late 1940s to 1970s, there was a uranium mining boom due to the AEC procuring uranium for nuclear power and weapons development. The largest source of uranium ore in the U.S. was at the Colorado Plateau in the Four Corners intersection of Colorado, Utah, Arizona and New Mexico. Most uranium mines are underground networks of shafts and caverns, where miners are exposed to radioactive dust and gases. It was well known that Czech and German uranium miners had excess lung cancer deaths, but for years miners in the U.S. were not informed of the potential hazards. In 1949, the Public Health Service initiated comprehensive environmental studies of the mines and epidemiologic studies of the miners. Because radiation-induced lung cancer has a 10- to 20-years latency, preliminary findings were that the conditions within mines might seriously affect miners' health. States began to enact standards in 1955, and finally in 1959 the PHS provided miners with a pamphlet about the hazards of radon exposure. However, it was not until 1960 that the PHS presented conclusive evidence that there was a correlation between uranium mining and lung cancer, and in 1967 the first federally enforceable standards for radon and isotopes in mines were promulgated.[27,28]

VETERINARY PUBLIC HEALTH

PHS officer James H. Steele, DVM, MPH, is often referred to as the father of veterinary public health. Commissioned a sanitarian in 1943, Dr. Steele was stationed in Puerto Rico and Virgin Islands during World War II working on food sanitation and zoonotic diseases. In response to a conversation with Dr. Joseph Mountin, Steele prepared a report for Mountin and Surgeon General Parran about the risks of zoonotic diseases and the benefit to PHS of employing veterinarians for research and response. Dr. Steele was assigned to NIH and then CDC to gather zoonotic information, and in 1953 Dr. Langmuir of CDC's EIS asked Steele to recruit veterinarians for the EIS program. Dr. Steele proposed forming a PHS veterinary medical officer category which became effective in 1947, and he was named the Chief Veterinary Officer in 1968.

James H. Steele

More than six of every ten known infectious diseases in people can emanate from animals,[29] and Steele was a proponent of the One Health concept – the association of human health with the health of animals and the environment, and veterinary public health as a framework for similar programs that he helped establish worldwide. Dr. Steele had an enduring impact on promoting veterinary medicine and setting up rabies and other vaccination programs in the nation. He was the first veterinarian to hold the rank of Assistant Surgeon General and he also served as Deputy Assistant Secretary for Health in 1970. Upon retiring in 1971, Steele became a professor at the University of Texas and he was editor of the first comprehensive compilation of zoonotic diseases, the *CRC Handbook Series in Zoonoses*.[30,31]

NATIONAL LIBRARY OF MEDICINE

The National Library of Medicine began in 1836 as a small collection of medical books and journals in the U.S. Army Surgeon General's office. Over the years, it was housed in Riggs Bank, Ford's Theatre, and the Army Medical Museum in  Washington, DC. In 1865, Army medical officer John S. Billings took charge and by 1895 he had transformed the collection into a world class medical library. In 1922, it was renamed the Army Medical Library and in 1952 re-designated the Armed Forces Medical Library (AFML). An amendment to Title III of the Public Health Service Act was enacted on August 3, 1956, transferring the AFML to the Public Health Service and renaming it the National Library of Medicine (NLM). A new building was erected for NLM on the National Institutes of Health campus which opened in 1962.[32] Congressionally authorized in 1968, the NLM Lister Hill National Center for Biomedical Communications building was dedicated in 1980. NLM is the world's largest medical library and provides global access to its biomedical information. NLM's National Center for Biotechnology Information also serves as the repository for GenBank®. In 2016, NIH tasked the Library to advance data science and informatics in order to accelerate the translation of biomedical findings to clinical solutions.

A New Surgeon General

SURGEON GENERAL SCHEELE carried forth the PHS's presence in international health, leading the U.S. delegation to the World Health Assembly for several years and serving twice as its President. In April 1956, President Dwight D. Eisenhower appointed Dr. Scheele to a third term as Surgeon General, but he soon resigned to take a position with a pharmaceutical company. Scheele's successor as Surgeon General was Leroy Edgar Burney, who was a conservative selection by the Eisenhower administration. Leroy Burney received his medical training at Indiana University, graduating in 1930, followed by a one year internship at the Chicago Marine Hospital and a fellowship at Johns Hopkins University. Burney entered the PHS Regular Corps in 1932, with his first postings being the Marine Hospital in Cleveland, a venereal disease clinic in Hot Springs, Arkansas, and at Marine Hospitals in New York and elsewhere.

Leroy E. Burney

In 1936, he was named assistant to Raymond A. Vonderlehr, Chief of the PHS Division of Venereal Diseases (who was CDC Director, 1947–1951). During World War II, Dr. Burney was detailed for five months to the Mediterranean on behalf of the War Shipping Administration and served as Assistant Chief of PHS's Division of State Relations from 1943 to 1944. In 1945, he accepted a nine-year detail as the Indiana State Health Commissioner and Secretary of the State Board of Health, returning to the PHS in 1954 as an Assistant Surgeon General and Deputy Chief of the Bureau of State Services, overseeing grants-in-aid to the states. Then in August 1956, President Eisenhower nominated Burney on a recess appointment and he was sworn in as Surgeon General on August 8, 1956, with Senate confirmation in January 1957.

INFLUENZA PANDEMIC

Among the immediate challenges was responding to an outbreak of pandemic influenza from 1957 to 1958. In February 1957, a new influenza virus (H2N2) called the Asian strain emerged in China and rapidly spread to Southeast Asia and then to other countries including the United States by summer. The initial U.S. cases were reported in military camps and aboard naval ships. Subsequently, localized outbreaks began in closed settings and spread to urban and community areas, with attack rates as high as 30 to 50 percent, but illnesses were mild. School openings in September, however, appeared to be a significant factor in instigating community epidemics and by the end of October more than half of the nation's counties were experiencing epidemics. New outbreaks declined and began to level in November, though a second more pronounced wave of influenza occurred from January into February 1958. The subtype of the Asian virus was identified in May 1957, but only 4 million vaccine doses were ready by August and the quantity of vaccine by October was sufficient to only cover 17 percent of the U.S. population. Surgeon General Burney announced on August 15 that the vaccine would be distributed to the states according to population size, recommending that it be prioritized for public services personnel, healthcare workers, and persons with a special medical risk. Because the disease mainly occurred within a few months and the limited availability of vaccine with an effectiveness of only 53 to 60 percent, it was concluded that the vaccine had a negligible impact on the epidemic.[33] Ultimately, the influenza caused an estimated 116,000 deaths in the United States.

CDC Surveillance Unit. In response to the need for information about the progress and severity of the influenza epidemic, the Surgeon General directed the Communicable Disease Center to form an Influenza Surveillance Unit in July 1957. The Unit systematically compiled national influenza data from state and county health department reports, including onset of influenza outbreaks, attack rate and number of deaths (influenza, pneumonia), and absenteeism data provided by large companies. Epidemic Intelligence Service staff then published the information in weekly *Influenza Surveillance Reports*. The influenza surveillance program was similar in approach to the successful poliomyelitis surveillance program of 1955 conducted by the EIS.[34]

NATIONAL HEALTH INTERVIEW SURVEY

The National Health Survey of 1935 to 1936 was the first national survey to acquire comprehensive data on the health status of the general population, with interviewers visiting nearly 750,000 households. Information from that survey provided the only estimates of disease prevalence until the 1950s, so the data were becoming increasingly outdated. HEW therefore proposed new legislation for a continuing survey, resulting in passage of the National Health Survey Act of 1956.[35] The Act specified that the Surgeon General was authorized to make continuing surveys and special studies of the U.S. population to determine the extent of illness and disability and related information, to develop improved methods to obtain such statistical information, and to periodically publish the survey and study results. The annual survey referred to in the Act, now called the National Health Interview Survey, was initiated by the Public Health Service in July 1957 under the direction of Forrest E. Linder, PhD.[36] In 1960, the National Health Survey was merged with the National Office of Vital Statistics to form the National Center for Health Statistics, which since 1987 has been part of the CDC.

RADIOLOGICAL HEALTH

Surgeon General Burney was cognizant of the increased scientific and public awareness about the impact of environmental contamination on matters of health and he took steps to position the Public Health Service in the lead on these issues. Although the PHS had been involved in studying radiation hazards for some time, the 1950s brought about a renewed interest in the effect on public health of atmospheric radiation from nuclear weapons testing and from other sources such as X-ray emissions. In 1958, Burney formed the National Advisory Committee on Radiation, which recommended consolidation of radiation control and protection authority in the PHS, leading to the formation of the PHS Division of Radiological Health. The Division assumed broad responsibility for studying environmental radiation levels, assessing all forms of radiation exposure, recommending acceptable exposure levels from air, water, milk, medical procedures, and the environment, and providing technical assistance to state radiological health programs. In 1967, the Division was renamed the National Center for Radiological Health and then again in 1968 the Bureau of Radiological Health, with regulatory authority to implement the Radiation Control for Health and Safety Act (Public Law 90-602). In 1971, personnel and budgets were reassigned to the newly created Environmental Protection Agency, and to the Food and Drug Administration where there was an eventual merger with the Bureau of Medical Devices to form the Center for Devices and Radiological Health.[37]

TOBACCO HAZARD

By the 1950s, statistical data compiled by the American Cancer Society (ACS) showed a significant increase in the prevalence of lung cancer during the previous two decades. Numerous investigative studies conducted during the 1950s produced similar results, namely, that there was a connection of cigarette smoking with lung cancer. For example, a study of 605 patients with bronchogenic carcinoma published in 1950 disclosed that excessive and prolonged use of tobacco, especially cigarettes, was an important factor in the induction of lung carcinoma.[38] Against the backdrop of a tobacco industry campaign that cast doubt about cigarette causation evidence and the manifest support of pro-tobacco members of Congress, the Public Health Service took a measured approach to making definitive pronouncements on the issue. In 1956, a Study Group on Smoking and Health was organized by the ACS, American Heart Association, National Cancer Institute, and the National Heart Institute, and in 1957 it issued its conclusion that scientific evidence "establishes beyond a reasonable doubt that cigarette smoking is a causative factor in the rapidly increasing incidence of human epidermoid carcinoma of the lung." On July 12, 1957, Dr. Burney took action, publicly declaring: "It is clear that there is an increasing and consistent body of evidence that excessive cigarette smoking is one of the causative factors in lung cancer."[39] The Surgeon General's statement, along with the Study Group report and research findings of the American Cancer Society, were sent to state health officers and the American Medical Association. Then in 1959, a Statement of the Public Health Service was published stating: "The weight of evidence at present implicates smoking as the principal etiological factor in the increased incidence of lung cancer."[40] Even after making such definitive statements, the Public Health Service elected not to pursue further public health control and preventive actions. Instead, the PHS leadership continued to gather substantiating data and left it to state health departments to take responsive measures.[41]

CHALLENGES AND ORGANIZATIONAL REVIEW

The Public Health Service began experiencing challenges to its mission in the form of two reports of the Hoover Commission on Organization of the Executive Branch – one in 1949 and another in 1955. The first report recommended that all federal government health care, including that provided by

PHS and the Veterans Administration, be consolidated under a United Medical Administration (which was never acted upon), and the second report recommended that all medical and hospital care provided by the PHS be taken over by community hospitals, where it was believed that care could be provided more economically. These proposals marked the start of long-term contention between the PHS and the Bureau of the Budget (now Office of Management and Budget) about the viability of PHS hospitals.[42] There were also looming issues related to the PHS handling of environmental matters. In Congressional testimony, Dr. Burney believed there was a distinction in the Public Health Service's role between eradicating infectious disease and its newer role in environmental health, stating that when dealing with the possible harmful effects of the byproducts of industry and of the wastes of nuclear technology, the goal cannot be complete conquest, but containment.[43] Although the PHS knew the importance that environmental protection had in public and political discourse, Congressional support for aligning environmental health authority within the Service was uncertain. The NIH and CDC were becoming somewhat independent power centers within PHS, with medical research the unquestioned domain of NIH. CDC continued to expand, acquiring the PHS Venereal Diseases Division in 1957 and Tuberculosis Control Division in 1960. And in 1960, *Morbidity and Mortality Weekly Report* was acquired by CDC from the National Office of Vital Statistics.

By 1959, Surgeon General Burney acknowledged the evolving change in the nation's health problems and the organizational and political issues attendant thereto by appointing a *Study Group on Mission and Organization of the Public Health Service*. The charge to the group was to study the present and probable future mission of the Public Health Service over the next decade and design the best possible organizational structure to accommodate its responsibilities. The *Final Report*[44] of the Study Group, or *Hundley Report* (for chairperson Dr. James M. Hundley), was released in June 1960, identifying functional areas where increased efforts were needed: biomedical research, application of research findings, development of health resources, environmental health, comprehensive health care, national systems for health statistics, collection and dissemination of scientific literature, and provision of health information and education. The Study Group concluded that "The next great nationwide health efforts may be expected in two broad areas: the physical environment and comprehensive health care." The Study Group proposed a new organizational structure comprised of six major operating divisions and the Office of the Surgeon General. While the new PHS organizational structure was a thoughtful roadmap for the future, the Surgeon General would not be present to see it come to fruition.

Precedent Change

The Public Health Service had been the beneficiary of many years of good working relationships with administrators of the Federal Security Agency and the Department of Health, Education, and Welfare. The agencies were deferential to and supportive of those who served in the position of Surgeon General. But the political imperatives of a changing national health policy and a new, more resolute presidential administration would result in the early departure of Dr. Burney. The office of the Surgeon General was considered to be a nonpartisan, apolitical position. For that reason, Surgeons General were traditionally reappointed, sometimes serving under both Democrat and Republican presidents. Yet, Leroy Burney's tenure ended in January 1961, which coincided with the beginning of the Kennedy administration. The new administration took that opportunity to replace Burney, whose last official day in office was January 29, 1961.

Chronology • 1948–1961

SG Leonard A. Scheele, April 1948–August 1956
SG Leroy E. Burney, August 1956–January 1961

1948 *Water Pollution Control Act.* Provides PHS with comprehensive authority including the control of interstate waterway pollution.

1950 *Public Health Service Act, Amendment.* Creates the National Institute of Arthritis and Metabolic Diseases, and the National Institute of Neurological Diseases and Blindness.

1950 PHS policy recommends water fluoridation to prevent dental caries.

1951 Creation of the Epidemic Intelligence Service, CDC.

1953 Federal Security Agency organizational components and responsibilities transferred to new Department of Health, Education, and Welfare.

1954 *Transfer Act of 1954.* Provides for the transfer of all health care authorities, responsibilities and facilities from the Department of Interior, Bureau of Indian Affairs to the Public Health Service, effective July 1, 1955.

1954 PHS–Atomic Energy Commission memorandum of understanding tasks PHS with responsibility for determining the health and safety risks of nuclear tests.

1955 Salk polio vaccine is licensed for use in the United States.

1955 *Air Pollution Control Act.* Provides PHS with authority for research relating to the control of air pollution.

1956 *National Health Survey Act.* Provides authorization for the PHS to conduct a continuing national survey and special studies of illness and disability.

1957 Surgeon General is the first federal official to state that cigarette smoking is a cause of lung cancer.

1960 Sabin polio vaccine is licensed for use in the United States.

CHAPTER EIGHT

TOBACCO, PARADIGM SHIFT, IMMUNIZATION, ORAL REHYDRATION
1961 to 1969

WITH THE NEW ADMINISTRATION of President John F. Kennedy came the promise of economic and social reform, including new programs to provide medical care for the elderly and poor. During a period of great political change through the end of the Lyndon Johnson administration in 1969, the Public Health Service continued to expand and flourish in many respects. In 1961, the PHS was well staffed and had a reorganization plan that would meet Service requirements for the next decade. Yet, the PHS was sidelined as certain health-related programs were ensconced in other agencies and PHS responsibilities, particularly as they related to the Surgeon General's authorities, were substantially diminished.

The incoming administration's choice for a Surgeon General was Luther L. Terry. Born and raised in Red Level, Alabama, Terry's father was the town doctor and he was named after his father's personal physician, Luther Leonidas Hill. Hill's son, Joseph Lister Hill, went on to become an influential U.S. Senator serving as chairman of the Labor and Public Welfare Committee, which dealt with health legislation. It was that connection which reportedly propelled Luther Terry to the position of Surgeon General, taking charge of the Public Health Service comprised of 4,000 commissioned officers and 24,000 civilian employees at the time.[1,2] Terry received his medical degree at Tulane University and, following internships, served on the faculty of the University of Texas. He joined the PHS in 1942, becoming the Chief of Medical Services at the Baltimore Marine Hospital. In 1950, Terry began as a cardiac specialist and then Chief of General Medicine and Experimental Therapeutics with the NIH's National Heart Institute. His program moved to the new NIH Clinical Center in 1953, where he developed a leading cardiovascular research unit. In 1958, Dr. Terry became Assistant Director of the National Heart Institute, serving until his appointment as Surgeon General, effective March 2, 1961.

Luther L. Terry

Smoking and Health

Surgeon General Burney and the Public Health Service had made official pronouncements in 1957 and 1959 that the scientific evidence indicated a causal relationship between excessive cigarette smoking and lung cancer. In 1959, a Statement of the Public Health Service specified "The weight of evidence at present implicates smoking as the principal etiological factor in the increased incidence of lung cancer."[3] In the following years, data continued to mount showing a clear correlation of smoking with lung cancer. The public's awareness about the possible link between cancer and cigarette smoking, along with the increased concern among professional organizations, called for a meaningful public health response to the matter. On June 1, 1961, the American Cancer Society, American Heart Association, American Public Health Association, and the National Tuberculosis Association sent President Kennedy a letter requesting formation of a national commission to study the "tobacco problem." Adding to the public pressure was a 1962 report published by the Royal College of Physicians of London on smoking and health which, based on a comprehensive review of the evidence, determined that cigarette smoking was a cause of lung cancer and bronchitis.[4] The British report came to the attention of the U.S. press; that report and the advocacy groups' request for a commission prompted Surgeon General Terry on June 7, 1962, to appoint the Surgeon General's Advisory Committee on Smoking and Health to conduct an evaluation of all relevant data to reach definitive conclusions. The Advisory Committee met from November 1962 to January 1964. Committee staff were housed at the National Library of Medicine where they had ready access to the 7,000 scientific articles, reports and other documents that were provided to Committee members. Special reports were prepared under contract with experts in the field. The Committee reviewed three main sources of evidence: animal experiments, clinical and autopsy studies, and epidemiologic studies. The final report, entitled *Smoking and Health: Report of the Advisory Committee to the Surgeon General of the Public Health Service*,[5] was released on January 11, 1964. The Advisory Committee concluded that cigarette smoking was:

- Causally associated with a 70 percent increase in age-specific all-cause mortality among men and to a lesser extent among women.
- A cause of lung cancer in men and probable cause of lung cancer in women, with average male smokers having a 9- to 10-fold risk and male heavy smokers a 20-fold risk of developing lung cancer.
- The most important among the causes of chronic bronchitis.
- A possible causative factor in other illnesses such as emphysema, cardiovascular disease, and various types of cancer.

Of note was the following conclusion of the Committee:

> On the basis of prolonged study and evaluation of many lines of converging evidence, the Committee makes the following judgment: Cigarette smoking is a health hazard of sufficient importance in the United States to warrant appropriate remedial action.

The release of the Advisory Committee Report was of immediate national and international interest that gained widespread media coverage. This Report and subsequent Reports pertaining to the use of tobacco cigarettes have had an enduring impact on the reduction of cigarette smoking. As the first *Surgeon General's Report*, it became a landmark event in the historical record of the Public Health Service.

Surgeon General Terry presents report on Smoking and Health at the State Department, January 11, 1964. *[National Library of Medicine]*

Soon after the 1964 Advisory Committee Report was released, legislative action was taken. The Federal Cigarette Labeling and Advertising Act of 1965 (Public Law 89-92) set national standards for cigarette packaging that required a health warning on the package, namely, *Caution: Cigarette Smoking May Be Hazardous To Your Health*. The law also required the Department of Health, Education, and Welfare and the Federal Trade Commission to transmit an annual report to the Congress on current information about the health consequences of smoking, and the status of cigarette labeling and advertising, respectively. The Act was amended by the Public Health Cigarette Smoking Act of 1969 (Public Law 91-222), which modified the health warning on the package to, *Warning: The Surgeon General Has Determined That Cigarette Smoking Is Dangerous to Your Health*. Further, this Act declared it unlawful to advertise cigarettes in the broadcast media.

Since the 1964 Report, over 30 Surgeon General's reports on cigarette smoking have been released on the adverse health effects of smoking and secondhand smoke exposure. On January 17, 2014, *The Health Consequences of Smoking–50 Years of Progress: A Report of the Surgeon General*,[6,7] was published, which updates the evidence about adverse effects of tobacco on health. The Report notes that cigarette smoking has now been causally linked to diseases of nearly all organs of the body. Although smoking prevalence declined from about 43 percent in 1965 to 18 percent in 2014, and to 12.5 percent in 2020, annual smoking-attributable deaths was estimated to be about 480,000 as of 2020 *[CDC data]*. Thus, considerable work remains to quell this leading preventable cause of premature disease and death in the U.S.

New Issues

ENVIRONMENTAL HEALTH

Environmental health programs such as water and air pollution control had long been a Public Health Service responsibility, beginning with the Public Health Service Act of 1912 which authorized the PHS to investigate disease-related water pollution. Recognizing the importance of a dedicated environmental health program within the PHS, the 1960 report of the *Study Group on Mission and Organization of the Public Health Service* recommended the formation of a PHS Bureau of Environmental Health. In 1961, a budget set-aside was made for site acquisition for a PHS Environmental Health Center, with the request that the PHS prepare a definitive proposal. On July 21, 1961, Surgeon General Terry formed the Committee on Environmental Health (Gross Committee) to prepare the proposal with resource and personnel requirements that was due by November 1. There was uncertainty within Congress, however, with a major concern being the cost of the proposed PHS environmental program.[8] That and other factors contributed to Congress ultimately deciding not providing funds for the Environmental Health Center.

Due to the escalating importance of environmental health issues, an abrupt transfer of water and air pollution control was made, moving it out of the PHS to a new Assistant Secretary of the Department of Health, Education, and Welfare (HEW) in late 1961. In 1962, Rachel Carson's book *Silent Spring* was published, documenting the adverse effects of indiscriminate pesticide use on the environment and inspiring an environmental movement in the nation. The movement led to a shared environmental concern within public discourse that was not limited to human health, and it required federal oversight. This belief contributed to the shift of the environmental health arena away from the PHS. In 1965, the Water Quality Act created the Water Pollution Control Administration in HEW. Executive action[9] soon led to the transfer of water pollution functions from HEW to the Department of the Interior in 1966, and in 1970 reassignment of those responsibilities to the new Environmental Protection Agency where environmental standards and regulations were promulgated.

LEGISLATIVE ACTIONS

Several health-related legislative actions were taken during Surgeon General Terry's tenure, including the following.

New NIH Institutes
Public Health Service Act, Amendment (Public Law 87-838)
- National Institute of Child Health and Human Development
- National Institute of General Medical Sciences

Education and Training [Administered by the PHS]
Health Professions Educational Assistance Act of 1963 (Public Law 88-129)
- Provides grants for construction of medical, dental, pharmaceutical, optometric, podiatric, nursing, osteopathic and public health teaching facilities.

Nurse Training Act of 1964 (Public Law 88-581)
- Provides grants for construction of nursing schools and nurse training.

Health Services [Administered by the PHS]
Community Health Services and Facilities Act of 1961 (Public Law 87-395)
- Provides grants to expand medical services facilities like nursing homes, medical programs and outpatient health services for the elderly.

Mental Retardation Facilities and Community Mental Health Centers Construction Act of 1963 (Public Law 88-164)
- Provides grants for community mental health centers and research facilities.

Community Health Centers

Certain agency actions bypassed the Public Health Service in administering health-related program activities. For example, Neighborhood Health Centers, renamed Community Health Centers, were initially funded under authority of the federal Office of Economic Opportunity, the lead agency in President Lyndon Johnson's "War on Poverty." Funding was first approved in 1965 for these clinics to provide health services for poor and medically underserved communities. The program was moved in the early 1970s to HEW (later Department of Health and Human Services), where the Health Resources and Services Administration, Bureau of Primary Health Care administers the program.

Medicare/Medicaid

On July 30, 1965, President Lyndon B. Johnson signed the Social Security Amendments of 1965 into law (Public Law 89-97), thereby creating Medicare (Title XVIII) and Medicaid (Title XIX).[10] The use of fiscal intermediaries to administer billing operations was a factor that helped persuade PHS and Congressional leaders not to involve the PHS in this insurance plan for the elderly and federal–state program for low income individuals. The landmark legislation produced a major new federal presence in health care finance, making the federal government the single largest health insurer in the nation.

Changing of the Guard – A New SG

SURGEON GENERAL TERRY HAD SECURED HIS LEGACY through release of the 1964 Surgeon General's *Report on Smoking and Health*. Although it seemed that President Lyndon Johnson would reappoint Terry for a second term, the need to expeditiously implement the Medicare and Medicaid programs with possible involvement of a more responsive Surgeon General may have factored into the decision to replace Dr. Terry, who served until October 1, 1965.[1] He continued for years afterwards as a leader in the campaign against smoking.

The administration's choice for a new Surgeon General was William H. Stewart. Born in Minneapolis, Minnesota, Stewart earned his medical degree in 1945 from the Louisiana State University School of Medicine, and was commissioned and served as an Army medical officer at Brooke General Hospital in San Antonio, Texas, from 1946 to 1947. Dr. Stewart joined the first class of Alexander Langmuir's Epidemic Intelligence Service at the Communicable Disease Center (CDC). In February 1951, he was commissioned in the PHS Inactive Reserve and dispatched to CDC's Thomasville, Georgia, Field Station. As an EIS Fellow, he worked under Dr. James Watt (future Director, National Heart Institute, NHI). He transferred to NHI, holding various positions until 1957 when Surgeon General Leroy Burney recruited Dr. Stewart to join his staff. Stewart managed projects related to planning, reorganization, and health professions education, and led the Public Health Methods Unit. He also became a resident expert on national health insurance and in 1961 headed the new Division of Community Health Services. It was propitious that from January 1963 through 1965 he worked as an Assistant to Dr. Boisfeuillet Jones, Special Assistant for Health and Medical Affairs along with Medicare proponent Wilbur Cohen, the Assistant Secretary for Legislation at HEW. On August 1, 1965, Stewart became NHI Director. However, he had the requisite background in the midst of burgeoning federal health programs and the need to rapidly implement the Medicare and Medicaid programs that led to his selection as Surgeon General, effective October 1, 1965. Perhaps not fully recognized by the new Surgeon General and PHS leadership was the tenuous position that the Public Health Service held within the federal health establishment and the pivotal change that would alter its future.

William H. Stewart

> Perhaps not fully recognized was the tenuous position the SG and PHS held within the federal health establishment.

A New PHS Administrator

In addition to overseeing all operational and research programs of the Public Health Service, Surgeon General Stewart would become involved in issues that had a profound impact on the Service. Foremost among these was the need to advance PHS capabilities in order to meet the expanding health legislation agenda. Commissioned officers comprised the leadership of the PHS, and it was plainly evident that the Public Health Service had ceded its authority and was passed over in areas such as environmental health, community health centers, health insurance, maternal and child health, and automobile safety. With enormous growth and a 1965 budget of nearly $1 billion (half the PHS budget), the National Institutes of Health was essentially operating independently of the PHS. The long-standing reputation of the Public Health Service as a vanguard organization with extensive competencies was being questioned. By the early 1960s, there was administration disenchantment toward the PHS, considered by many as "unwilling or unable" to effectively respond to the emerging health landscape.[11] This was acknowledged by Stewart, who recognized the perceived lack of PHS foresight: "The Commissioned Corps was more identified with the way things were," he said, "and not the way things were going to be."[1] In August 1965, John W. Gardner took over as Secretary of Health, Education, and Welfare. A former Carnegie Corporation president, education and leadership specialist, Gardner was a dynamic individual whose major task was to implement the Medicare program enacted on July 30, 1965. Gardner was a proponent of individual and organizational renewal and his strategy included a reorganization of the Department. He believed the PHS was made up of fiefdoms and was not sufficiently responsive.[12] As a result, pursuant to Reorganization Plan No. 3 of 1966[13] effective June 25, 1966, all statutory authorities of the Surgeon General and functions of the Public Health Service were transferred to the Secretary. By authority delegated from Gardner, Dr. Stewart remained in charge of the Service. However, by 1967, the decision was made to transfer line authority for all PHS programs to a new Assistant Secretary for Health and Scientific Affairs and political appointee Dr. Philip R. Lee. Surgeon General Stewart would become Lee's deputy and remain the operational head of the Commissioned Corps. This paradigm shift was made in March 1968 by Gardner's successor, HEW Acting Secretary Wilbur Cohen. The realignment ranks among the most significant milestones in PHS history.

Philip R. Lee

The Public Health Service was initially restructured into these agencies:
- National Institutes of Health
- Health Services and Mental Health Administration (new) Bureau of State Services, Bureau of Medical Services, National Institute of Mental Health, and other new programs
- Food and Drug Administration (FDA)

A later Executive Order created the Consumer Protection and Environmental Health Service which incorporated the FDA, CDC, National Air Pollution Control Center, and National Center for Radiological Health, among others.

The transfer of the Surgeon General's leadership authority over the Public Health Service was a momentous event, marking the first time that the nation's top public health official was not a career professional. The changeover was widely viewed as a significant misstep and major setback by PHS officers, but the opposing view had validity, as well – it was essential to maintain the relevancy of the PHS at a time when strategically important reforms were being made to the nation's health care enterprise. Even though the Surgeon General was no longer at the helm of the Public Health Service, the Service continued to grow programmatically to meet the nation's public health needs. Surgeon General Stewart remained at the forefront of public health issues as a senior spokesperson and public health representative for HEW. He continued to speak about the hazards associated with cigarette smoking and new issues would arise in which he would be involved. Dr. Stewart remained as the operational head of the Commissioned Corps, yet PHS officers, whose duty stations resided in multiple agencies, were no longer under the sole authority of the Surgeon General. Going forward, PHS officers had to respond to split authorities – the personnel and deployment authority of the Office of the Surgeon General and the administrative authority of the agency to which officers were assigned. This situation has continued to cause some disarray in the management of PHS officers' duties.

New Issues

MEDICARE – TITLE VI CERTIFICATION

With implementation of the new Medicare program came myriad issues. The Medicare program, which covered hospital medical services for people aged 65 and older, would involve virtually all the 7,000 hospitals in the U.S. In order to participate in Medicare and receive federal funds, hospitals were required to be in compliance with the anti-discrimination provisions of Title VI of the Civil Rights Act of 1964. In September 1965, HEW Assistant Secretary James Quigley told an audience at the American Hospital Association meeting that to be eligible for Medicare funds, hospitals would have to comply with the Civil Rights Act. With the knowledge that hospital discrimination was widespread, particularly in the South, HEW Secretary Gardner placed hospital desegregation as his top priority just months before Medicare was to go into effect on July 1, 1966. Secretary Gardner tasked Dr. Phil Lee with overseeing this effort, with Surgeon General Stewart, his deputy (and first medical director of the U.S. Peace Corps) Dr. Leo Gehrig, and PHS medical officer Richard A. Smith taking leading roles in the effort. Stewart and Gehrig were often on travel, meeting and speaking with involved parties. An Office of Equal Health Opportunity was established in February 1966, responsible for ensuring the Title VI compliance in Medicare. Hundreds of HEW temporary staff, along with PHS officers, traveled to hospitals and staffed information units for Medicare and Title VI at PHS headquarters and in regional offices. The PHS prepared a compliance packet that included a letter from the Surgeon General and a questionnaire that was sent to all 7,000 hospitals. On the basis of the questionnaire, noncompliant hospitals would be inspected by teams drawn from a group of over 300 personnel, including PHS officers, who were dispatched to the field. Preliminary data in April 1966 indicated that only 49 percent of hospitals met Title VI compliance standards; by June, 85 percent of hospitals were in compliance, a level that allowed a successful launch of the Medicare program. It resulted in a major transformation in hospitals throughout the nation, described by Secretary Wilbur Cohen as one of the most significant social reforms of the decade.[14,15]

LEGISLATIVE ACTIONS

Health-related legislative actions taken during Surgeon General Stewart's tenure include the following.

New NIH Institutes
Public Health Service Act, Amendment (Public Law 90-489)
 - National Eye Institute

Education and Training [Administered by the PHS]
Allied Health Professions Personnel Training Act of 1966 (Public Law 89-751)
 - Provides grants to construct teaching facilities for allied health professions personnel and support to strengthen training and student loan programs.
Health Manpower Act of 1968 (Public Law 90-490)
 - Extends and strengthens prior health professions education and training, student loan, and training and research facilities construction legislation.

Health Services [Administered by the PHS]
Social Security Amendments of 1965 (Public Law 89-97)
 - Creates the Medicare (Title XVIII) and Medicaid (Title XIX) programs.
Heart Disease, Cancer, and Stroke Amendments of 1965 (Public Law 89-239)
 - Provides grants for development of Regional Medical Programs.

REGIONAL MEDICAL PROGRAMS

In 1964, President Johnson established the Commission on Heart Disease, Cancer and Stroke (DeBakey Commission) to develop a plan to counter the three named diseases which accounted for over 70 percent of the deaths in the nation. The Commission published its report in December 1964, entitled *Report to the President: A National Program to Conquer Heart Disease, Cancer and Stroke*. Among the Report's recommendations was the institution of regional complexes for the care and clinical investigation of patients with heart disease, cancer and stroke. In October 1965, the Heart Disease, Cancer, and Stroke Amendments of 1965 became law,[16] providing grants to public and nonprofit organizations for the purpose of forming regional medical programs (RMPs) – cooperative arrangements among medical schools, research institutions and hospitals to make biomedical research advances in diagnosis and treatment more available to patients. The Public Health Service administered the program and Surgeon General Stewart served as chairperson of the National Advisory Council on RMPs. In 1968, the Regional Medical Program office transferred to the new PHS Health Services and Mental Health Administration. By 1970, new provisions emphasized primary care, added prevention and rehabilitation services, and used "physician extenders" such as nurse practitioners. Fifty-four RMPs were operational by year's end. The National Health Planning and Resources Development Act of 1974 (Public Law 93-641) consolidated RMPs with the Hill-Burton (Public Law 79-725) and Comprehensive Health Planning (Public Law 89-749) programs.

CDC – ACQUISITIONS

By the 1960s, the Communicable Disease Center, like the NIH, was expanding and becoming somewhat autonomous from the Public Health Service. Its more recent programmatic acquisitions had been the PHS Division of Venereal Diseases in 1957 (now Division of STD [Sexually Transmitted Diseases] Prevention), and Tuberculosis Control Division in 1960. Also in 1960, *Morbidity and Mortality Weekly Report* was acquired by CDC from the National Office of Vital Statistics. In 1967, the Foreign Quarantine Service, among the oldest and most prominent of PHS units, was transferred to the CDC. At the time, the program had 55 quarantine stations and over 500 personnel at every port, international airport and major border crossing. The CDC significantly reduced the inspection program due to recognition that the threat from communicable diseases was diminished. The focus was shifted from routine inspection to program management and problem intervention. By the 1970s, the number of quarantine stations was reduced to eight; however, due to periodic emerging diseases, there were 20 quarantine stations in 2020 located in the continental U.S., Anchorage, Alaska, Honolulu, Hawaii and San Juan, Puerto Rico.[17]

IMMUNIZATION PROGRAMS

Immunization programs are an important component of CDC operations and in March 1964 the Surgeon General appointed a new Advisory Committee on Immunization Practices (ACIP) to develop recommendations for use of vaccines licensed by the FDA. Two immunization schedules are updated annually – a childhood and adolescent immunization schedule, and an adult immunization schedule. In 1963, the Edmonston-B strain of measles virus vaccine was licensed for use in the U.S., replaced by the Edmonston-Enders attenuated strain vaccine licensed in 1968. A live, attenuated mumps vaccine for use in the U.S. was licensed in 1967. Rubella, also known as German measles, is an infection caused by the rubella virus that spreads via airborne droplets from coughs or sneezes of infected individuals. Rubella is usually mild with few if any symptoms. Those with rubella may be contagious from 7 days before to 7 days after symptoms appear. Symptomatic children generally develop a maculopapular rash as the first sign that may appear on the face and then appear on the rest of the body, lasting about three days. A pregnant woman infected with rubella can pass it to her developing fetus, causing serious birth defects or miscarriage. Led by PHS medical officer Harry M. Meyer, Jr. and Paul D. Parkman, an NIH team began research on developing

Doctors Meyer and Parkman holding a bottle of rubella HPV-77 virus strain.
[c. 1967, National Library of Medicine]

a rubella vaccine after a 1964 to 1965 epidemic in the U.S. that resulted in an estimated 12.5 million rubella cases, with 11,000 pregnant women having miscarriages, 2,100 neonatal deaths and 20,000 babies born with congenital rubella syndrome.[18] Prior to their collaboration, Drs. Meyer and Parkman had been researchers at the Walter Reed Army Institute of Research at different times. Dr. Parkman joined the Army Medical Corps in 1960. Meyer entered the PHS Commissioned Corps in 1959 and served as chief of the Laboratory of Viral Immunology in the NIH Division of Biologics Standards. In 1963, he was joined by Parkman (who led one of two groups that had isolated the rubella virus in 1962). By 1966, the Meyer-Parkman team successfully developed the first attenuated rubella virus strain, which was used to produce a live rubella virus vaccine that, in clinical trials, exhibited attenuation, immunogenicity and non-communicability.[19] Using the NIH virus strain, the first commercially available rubella vaccine was developed by Maurice Hilleman and licensed in 1969. And the combination measles-mumps-rubella (MMR) vaccine was licensed in 1971 (the rubella component was changed in 1979).

INFLUENZA PANDEMIC

In July 1968, an influenza outbreak emerged in Hong Kong that rapidly became a pandemic. The outbreak was caused by an influenza A (H3N2) virus, a variant of H2N2 (Asian flu pandemic in 1957–1958) through antigenic shift. It was first noted in the United States in September 1968 and rapidly became widespread by the end of the year. The availability of a vaccine was quite limited, but influenza activity began to decline in late January 1969. About 100,000 deaths occurred in the nation, with most excess deaths among persons 65 years and older. Worldwide, there were an estimated one million fatalities. The H3N2 virus remains in circulation as a strain of seasonal influenza.[20]

CHOLERA, ORAL REHYDRATION THERAPY

Cholera is a diarrheal illness that is caused by infection of the intestine with the bacterium *Vibrio cholerae*, which is acquired by ingesting food or water contaminated by feces of an infected person. Up to four million people worldwide are infected with cholera each year and, though symptoms may be mild or nonexistent, about ten percent of such persons will experience severe symptoms that include watery diarrhea, vomiting and leg cramps. The rapid and profound loss of body fluids can result in dehydration and hypovolemic shock, leading to death within hours. Prompt rehydration is of paramount importance, along with antibiotics that may diminish disease severity. There have been several cholera pandemics in the world over the past 200 years. Currently, cholera is endemic in a number of countries, primarily in Africa and Asia, with peaks typically associated with rainy seasons and with an incidence that is highest in children under five years of age. Cholera may also become epidemic in countries related to population-based immunity and climate. Treatment with oral replacement fluids is very efficacious, except when severe volume depletion or shock warrants the administration of intravenous fluids.[21]

While an effective rehydration treatment with expensive intravenous hypertonic saline solutions was available by the mid-1920s, it was essentially unobtainable to persons most afflicted by diarrhea in the developing world. The development of oral rehydration therapy (ORT) by 1968 is for that reason considered among the most important public health advances of the twentieth century. For context, the World Health Organization estimated in 1975 that there were about 500 million bouts of diarrhea in children under the age of five in Africa, Asia and Latin America, resulting in at least 5 million deaths yearly.[22]

Oral Rehydration Development

The endeavor to develop an effective oral rehydration solution spans a few decades. Among many prominent researchers involved in the effort were four USPHS Commissioned Corps medical officers, including David B. Sachar, Norbert Hirschhorn, David R. Nalin, and Richard A. Cash. Their contributions to oral rehydration research are the focus of this review. A complex path led to the development of a safe and effective oral therapy for cholera and other disease diarrheas. By the early 1960s, Captain Robert A. Phillips of the U.S. Navy fortuitously discovered that the presence of glucose in an oral solution enhanced the absorption of sodium.

> Oral rehydration therapy is among the foremost public health advances of the twentieth century.

However, the prevailing theory at the time was that a "poisoned sodium pump" altered the electric potential of a cholera patient's intestine, thus preventing oral rehydration. The sodium pump, a biological transport mechanism in the intestine, absorbs water and salts and is therefore critical to keeping a person hydrated. In 1965, PHS officer David Sachar arrived at the Cholera Research Laboratory in Dacca, East Pakistan. He was then sent to Copenhagen to work with a distinguished physiologist, Hans Ussing, tasked with designing an apparatus to measure electric potential in the intestines of cholera patients. Dr. Sachar returned to Dacca and successfully showed that active sodium absorption was intact and that it was stimulated by the infusion of glucose into the intestinal lumen of a cholera patient, thus disproving the paralyzed sodium pump hypothesis. Sachar and his senior colleague, Dr. Norbert Hirschhorn, recognized the therapeutic implications that the addition of glucose to a salt solution would stimulate the sodium pump to transport water and salt out of the intestine and into the circulation, where it was needed to sustain life.[23] Hirschhorn moved forward with clinical studies to confirm that a net positive fluid balance could be achieved with glucose and sodium solutions. Dr. Nathaniel F. Pierce of The Johns Hopkins Center for Medical Research and Training in Calcutta, India, was working on similar issues and was able to advance Dr. Hirschhorn's conceptual framework. Hirschhorn left Dacca but was unable to return, so in 1967 PHS medical officers David Nalin and Richard Cash, both 26 years old and lacking prior experience with cholera, were assigned to Dacca. Nalin and Cash went to the

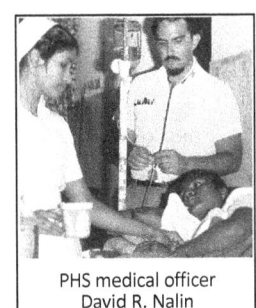

PHS medical officer David R. Nalin with a patient at Matlab, Pakistan.

Chittagong district to help establish a clinic and conduct studies of their own. Dr. Rafiqul Islam, a local investigator, prepared an oral therapy protocol that subsequently failed. Dr. Nalin soon determined that if the dosage of the therapy had corresponded with intake and output measurements, then it would be a success. Upon returning to Dacca, Nalin, Cash, Islam and others forged ahead using a new protocol that included an oral solution of glucose and electrolytes in volumes that were equal to diarrheal losses, with success. The support of Dr. Alexander Langmuir of the CDC Epidemic Intelligence Service allowed Drs. Nalin and Cash to conduct field trials in Matlab Bazaar in rural Pakistan. Their studies confirmed that cholera patients could be rehydrated with oral rehydration therapy alone and that field staff could administer the therapy with ease.[24]

SURGEON GENERAL'S LEGACY

William Stewart was a very capable administrator who made important contributions to the PHS, yet he will also be associated with the loss of authorities that had defined the Office of Surgeon General since its inception.

CHRONOLOGY • 1961–1969

SG Luther L. Terry, March 1961–October 1965
SG William H. Stewart, October 1965–August 1969

1962	Surgeon General Terry appoints the Surgeon General's Advisory Committee on Smoking and Health.
1964	Surgeon General's Advisory Committee on Smoking and Health releases its Report, which indicates that lung cancer and chronic bronchitis are causally related to cigarette smoking.
1964	Advisory Committee on Immunization Practices is founded at CDC.
1965	*Social Security Amendments of 1965*. Creates the Medicare (Title XVIII) and Medicaid (Title XIX) programs.
1965	Community Health Centers open; program is now administered by HHS.
1966	PHS/HEW water pollution functions transferred to Department of the Interior.
1966	First efficacious attenuated rubella virus strain is developed.
1967	PHS Foreign Quarantine Service transferred to Communicable Disease Center.
1968	Reorganization transfers line authority for all PHS programs from the Surgeon General to the Assistant Secretary for Health and Scientific Affairs, HEW.
1968	PHS officers prove that oral rehydration therapy effectively treats dehydration.
1969	*Public Health Cigarette Smoking Act of 1969*. Requires a health warning on cigarette packages.

CHAPTER NINE

SURGEONS GENERAL & PHS IN TRANSITION
1969 to 1977

THE NEW ADMINISTRATIONS of Richard M. Nixon and Gerald R. Ford, spanning 1969 to 1977, were beset with many issues, but the need to reduce inflation would permeate much of the decision-making. The landmark health initiatives of the Johnson era would go largely unaltered, and the health sector continued its expansion as much as the economy and politics would permit. A succession of four Secretaries of the Department of Health, Education, and Welfare (HEW) and four Assistant Secretaries for Health and Scientific Affairs (renamed Assistant Secretary for Health, 1972) confounded the situation for the Public Health Service as it settled into its new organizational structure, with leadership authority now residing with the Assistant Secretary for Health. It was also a period when the very existence of the Office of the Surgeon General and the Commissioned Corps were at risk.

In July 1969, HEW Secretary Robert Finch chose Roger O. Egeberg as the Assistant Secretary for Health and Scientific Affairs. Egeberg was Dean of the University of Southern California, School of Medicine at the time and he called upon former faculty member Dr. Jesse Steinfeld to assist him during the start-up of his tenure as Assistant Secretary. A new Surgeon General was sought to replace William Stewart who was still in office and it was felt that Steinfeld had the requisite capabilities. Dr. Stewart resigned August 1 and Steinfeld was confirmed as Surgeon General December 18, 1969. Jesse Leonard Steinfeld received his medical degree from Western Reserve University in 1949. He entered the PHS Commissioned Corps, taking a fellowship at the Atomic Energy Commission, and he later rejoined the Service serving at the National Cancer Institute (NCI) from 1954 to 1958. In 1959, Dr. Steinfeld

Jesse L. Steinfeld

joined the University of Southern California, School of Medicine, rising to professor in 1967. He returned to NCI in 1968, and in 1969 was appointed Deputy Director of the Institute. Unlike prior Surgeons General who were appointed in accordance with the Public Health Service Act of 1944, Steinfeld was not a

PHS career officer. His appointment as Surgeon General represented the first among successive Surgeons General who were civilian appointees. When Roger Egeberg assumed the position of Assistant Secretary, duties of his Office were unsettled and some larger agencies went around him; relations between Drs. Egeberg and Steinfeld also became contentious.[1] Surgeon General Steinfeld was a spokesperson for PHS and continued his involvement in a range of issues, whereas Egeberg was replaced on July 1, 1971, by Merlin K. DuVal and the position title was renamed in 1972 to Assistant Secretary for Health.

Organizational Issues

In June 1970, not long after Surgeon General Jesse Steinfeld took office, Robert Finch left the HEW Secretary position to serve as counselor to the President; he was replaced by Elliot L. Richardson. Due to growing administration pressure for dissolution of the PHS Commissioned Corps, Secretary Richardson appointed former HEW undersecretary John A. Perkins to chair a committee on the future of the Commissioned Corps. The resulting committee report, *Report of the Secretary's Committee to Study the Public Health Service Commissioned Corps*, was released in 1971. Its conclusion was that the Corps was obsolete and too reliant on military conscription, inasmuch as PHS officers could meet their military obligation by joining the PHS (the military draft ended in 1973). The committee recommended that the Corps be disbanded and the position of Surgeon General be abolished. In its place, it proposed that all personnel be hired within the Civil Service framework. Dr. Steinfeld strongly opposed the recommendations and was able to gain support for the Corps among key members of Congress, notably Congressman Paul Rogers of Florida, who served as chairman of the House Subcommittee on Health. Rogers was a strong proponent of the Commissioned Corps and reportedly threatened "trouble on the Hill" if the Department were to proceed with implementation of the Perkins Report. Secretary Richardson backed down and the report was shelved.[2,3] Although the PHS Commissioned Corps survived this episode, criticism of the Corps continued to be lodged by the Office of Management and Budget, which claimed that Civil Service employees could just as effectively do the work performed by many, if not most, PHS officers.[4]

The Public Health Service had been acquiring new programs as well as losing some of its more traditional responsibilities over a period of years. Beginning in 1965, there was a gradual transfer of the environmental health responsibilities out of the PHS. On December 2, 1970, a new Environmental Protection Agency (EPA) was created to consolidate federal environmental programs that had been spread among various agencies. Reorganization Plan No. 3 of 1970[5] provided the framework for the process, transferring to the new agency relevant authorities and functions from the Department of the Interior,

Department of Agriculture, Council on Environmental Quality, and Atomic Energy Commission; and from the Department of Health, Education, and Welfare, functions of the National Air Pollution Control Administration, Air Quality Advisory Board, the Bureau of Solid Waste Management, Bureau of Water Hygiene, portions of the Bureau of Radiological Health, and certain pesticide functions from the Food and Drug Administration. The Clean Air Amendments of 1970 (Public Law 91-604) enacted December 31, 1970, authorized the transfer of PHS officers to the EPA, most of whom moved with their programs on detail to the EPA, an arrangement that remains in place.

HEALTH ISSUES

Cyclamate

Surgeon General Steinfeld became involved in certain issues that entered the public discourse. On October 18, 1969, Secretary Finch announced that the artificial sweetener cyclamate was being removed from the list of substances designated Generally Recognized as Safe (GRAS) due to a 1969 study finding that large doses of cyclamate (for humans, about 400 bottles of cyclamate-containing soda per day) over prolonged periods caused an increased incidence of bladder tumors in rats. Seventy percent of cyclamate usage was in sodas, and a ban of all soft drinks containing cyclamate went into effect on January 1 and all food products with cyclamate on February 1, 1970. At the press briefing, Dr. Steinfeld noted that "there is absolutely no evidence ...that the use of cyclamates has caused cancer in man," thus calming public reception of the news.[6]

Lead-Based Paint

Most exposure to lead with resultant poisoning occurred in occupational settings during and after the Industrial Revolution. Toxic exposures also arose from leaded gasoline additives and lead-based house paint. Interior lead paint was used until the 1940s, with childhood poisoning occurring due to contaminated dust and ingestion of paint chips. The industry began replacing lead with titanium dioxide and zinc oxide white pigment. In 1967, Children's Bureau pediatrician Dr. Jane Lin-Fu prepared an authoritative informational pamphlet which drew attention to the problem of lead paint that remained in houses. In the fall of 1970, her pamphlet and draft guidelines for childhood lead poisoning programs were sent to HEW for review. Recognizing its significance, Dr. Steinfeld used the draft report as the basis for a policy statement and national guidelines for screening programs on the prevention and treatment of lead poisoning in children. He estimated that up to 400,000 children had blood lead levels above 40 micrograms per deciliter in 1970 and introduced the concept of undue lead absorption, a phase that preceded clinical symptoms. On January 13, 1971, the Lead-Based Paint Poisoning Prevention Act was enacted, providing grants to local government units for testing and treatment programs, paint elimination and research programs, and it prohibited the use of lead-based paint in residential structures. In 1978, the Consumer Product Safety Commission also banned residential use of lead-based paint.[7,8]

Leaded Fuel

Tetraethyl lead (TEL) is a gasoline additive that can increase octane rating and vehicle performance. General Motors discovered the additive in 1921, and it partnered with the DuPont Company to create the Ethyl Corporation to produce and market the product, which was soon in wide use as an engine anti-knock agent. Lead toxicity was a concern at the time, which was heightened in 1924 when five workers died and 35 others experienced severe neurological symptoms of lead poisoning at Standard Oil Company's laboratories. This and similar occurrences at the DuPont chemical plant served to undermine an earlier industry-sponsored study by the Bureau of Mines that found TEL to be safe. Ongoing controversy about the safety of TEL led Surgeon General Cumming to convene a conference on the topic in May 1925, and production of TEL was temporarily halted for about a year. Industry spokespersons were advancing the contribution of TEL to industrial progress and propagating disinformation, while some public health experts were warning of a potential health calamity. With inconclusive evidence, Cumming was urged to form a blue ribbon scientific committee to investigate leaded gasoline. The study was of limited scope and short duration, and could not predict the long-term health effects of TEL. Thus, the conclusion was that there were insufficient grounds to prohibit leaded gasoline provided its use was controlled by proper regulations, and further government study was recommended.

Scientific authorities continued to express concern about TEL, noting that it should not be introduced for general use until proven harmless. Most public health professionals, however, did not concur, arguing that there should be definitive proof of harm before banning the use of TEL, so for the next few decades leaded gasoline consumption increased steadily. In the late 1940s, geochemist Clair C. Patterson developed the uranium–lead dating method, and in measuring the lead content of rocks and ice core samples he determined that lead was contaminating the environment, dating it to the timeframe that TEL was being added to gasoline. The environmental movement of the 1960s, coupled with scientific reports identifying automobile tailpipe emissions as the main source of environmental lead pollutants, and studies indicating a relationship between gasoline lead and elevated lead levels in infants and children raised public awareness about the health hazards associated with leaded gasoline. By 1970, government officials including Surgeon General Steinfeld and legislators recognized that lead toxicity was a very serious health hazard in the country. This realization led the Environmental Protection Agency to issue regulations that took effect in 1976 and later in 1985 to phase-down the lead content in fuel over a period of years. Then in 1990, in amendments to the Clean Air Act, lead was finally banned from gasoline for use in automobiles, allowing companies to phase out leaded gasoline by 1995.[9-11]

Tobacco Use
Steinfeld was passionate about discussing the health hazards associated with cigarette smoking. He reportedly posted a sign in his office that read *"Thank You for Not Smoking."* The 1972 report on the health consequences of smoking, released by Surgeon General Steinfeld provided data indicating an association between smoking and coronary heart disease, peripheral vascular disease, and bronchopulmonary diseases and lung cancer. New evidence also revealed that maternal smoking during pregnancy exerted a retarding influence on fetal growth. At a January 11, 1971, meeting of the National Interagency Council on Smoking and Health, Steinfeld ended his presentation stating:

> Non-smokers have as much right to clean air and wholesome air as smokers have to their so-called right to smoke, which I would redefine as a so-called 'right to pollute.' It is high time to ban smoking from all confined public places such as restaurants, theaters, airplanes, trains, and busses [sic]. It is time that we interpret the Bill of Rights for the Non-Smoker as well as the Smoker.[12]

The 1972 Surgeon General's report *The Health Consequences of Smoking*[13] was the first to identify that secondhand exposure to tobacco smoke was a health hazard for nonsmokers, noting that carbon monoxide levels in a smoke-filled room could exceed EPA limits for ambient air quality. A public interest movement was spawned to promote the concerns of nonsmokers and new rules limiting smoking began to appear at the federal and local levels. The data showing the harmful effects of secondhand smoke was reported in subsequent Surgeon General reports, with secondhand smoke being the topic of the entire 1986 Surgeon General's Report, *The Health Consequences of Involuntary Smoking* issued by Surgeon General C. Everett Koop.

LEGISLATION

Soon after Surgeon General Jesse Steinfeld took office, there was an upsurge in health- and safety-related legislation that resulted in the enactment of several important laws covering a range of topics, among which were the following.

Mine Safety
The Federal Coal Mine Health and Safety Act of 1969 (Public Law 91-173), enacted December 30, 1969, provided for the establishment and enforcement of health and safety standards for coal mines, with HEW as the lead agency for standards development.

Occupational Health

Public Health Service involvement in industrial hygiene formally began with the establishment of the PHS Office of Industrial Hygiene and Sanitation in 1914. Over many years, the Office conducted workplace hazard investigations in a range of industries. During World War II, the PHS Division of Industrial Hygiene coordinated all activities for the health protection of defense workers. Reorganization in 1943 placed the Division of Industrial Hygiene (redesignated Division of Occupational Health, 1951) within the Bureau of State Services, after which the PHS assisted state programs in carrying out their occupational health and safety responsibilities. The need for uniform occupational standards led to the Occupational Safety and Health Act of 1970 and creation of the National Institute for Occupational Safety and Health (NIOSH) and the Occupational Safety and Health Administration (OSHA) within the Public Health Service and in the Department of Labor, respectively.[14] The law tasked NIOSH with research and training, while OSHA was tasked with the development and enforcement of health and safety standards. Initially located within the PHS Health Services and Mental Health Administration, NIOSH was transferred in 1973 to the CDC.

National Health Service Corps

On August 20, 1969, PHS medical officer Laurence J. Platt, on his own initiative, completed a proposal that the U.S. Public Health Service create a National Health Service Corps (NHSC) to provide scholarships for healthcare professionals in training, who in turn would commit to practicing for at least two years in areas that had a severe lack of healthcare providers.[15] Remarkably, the proposal rapidly gained wide support and resulted in the enactment of the Emergency Health Personnel Act of 1970[16] to enlist health care personnel to provide medical services in underserved communities. The Act created the National Health Service Corps, which became operational in 1972. By this legislation, the Public Health Service became responsible for rendering care to the general public for the first time. Although there was initial emphasis on utilizing Commissioned Corps officers in the program, it would ultimately be staffed primarily by civilian healthcare professionals. The difficulty of recruiting primary care personnel led to enactment of the Emergency Health Personnel Act Amendments of 1972 (Public Law 92-585) which established the Scholarship Training Program, whereby health professions students would receive tuition and a monthly stipend in return for one year of clinical service for each year of scholarship support, with a minimum service commitment of two years. To remedy a healthcare practitioner shortfall within Health Professional Shortage Areas at the time, the American Recovery and Reinvestment Act of 2009 included $300 million in expansion funds for the NHSC.[17]

In 2010, the Patient Protection and Affordable Care Act permanently reauthorized the NHSC and created a mandatory funding stream to sustain the program. As of 2020, over 16,000 NHSC civilian and PHS officer practitioners were providing health care to about 17 million people throughout the nation, with more than 60 percent serving at 8,400 community health centers. The National Health Service Corps is organizationally located in the Health Resources and Services Administration, HHS. There have been fifteen NHSC directors as of 2023, eight of whom were PHS medical officers:

PHS OFFICER DIRECTORS, NATIONAL HEALTH SERVICE CORPS, 1972–2010

H. McDonald Rimple	Fitzhugh Mullan	Donald L. Weaver
Martin P. Wasserman	Kenneth P. Moritsugu	Richard J. Smith III
Edward D. Martin	Audrey F. Manley	

Alcoholism Institute

The Comprehensive Alcohol Abuse and Alcoholism Prevention, Treatment, and Rehabilitation Act of 1970 (Public Law 91-616), enacted December 31, 1970, established the National Institute on Alcohol Abuse and Alcoholism within the National Institute of Mental Health. The Act authorized grants to the states and public and private nonprofit organizations for the development of more effective prevention, treatment and rehabilitation programs to deal with alcohol abuse and alcoholism. It provided that the Secretary of HEW would conduct comprehensive education, training, research and planning programs for the stated purposes.

Health Manpower/Nurse Training

In order to expand health professional resources and improve the educational quality and distribution of healthcare professionals in the nation, the Comprehensive Health Manpower Training Act of 1971 (Public Law 92-157) and Nurse Training Act of 1971 (Public Law 92-158) were enacted November 18, 1971. The chief intents of these Acts were the provision of construction grants, special project and financial distress grants, per capita assistance to the institutions, student assistance and education initiative awards.

Cancer Institute

The National Cancer Act of 1971 (Public Law 92-218) was enacted December 23, 1971, representing the national commitment to what President Richard Nixon described as the "war on cancer." The Act expanded the authority of the NCI Director, with input from a new National Cancer Advisory Board, to create cancer centers and manpower training programs, award research contracts, expand the NIH and other research facilities, conduct cancer control activities, establish an international cancer research data bank, and collaborate with other federal, state or local public agencies and private industry.

Heart, Lung, and Blood Institute

The National Heart, Blood Vessel, Lung, and Blood Act of 1972 (Public Law 92-423), enacted September 19, 1972, expanded the authority of the National Heart, Lung, and Blood Institute to advance the national effort against heart, blood vessel, lung, and blood diseases. The Act provided for intensified Institute activities in accordance with a comprehensive plan by the Director and Advisory Council. It also called for prevention and control programs; and development of 15 new centers for basic and clinical research, training and prevention programs for heart, blood vessel, blood and chronic lung diseases.

Health Maintenance Organizations

The Health Maintenance Organization Act of 1973 (Public Law 93-222) was enacted December 29, 1973. Health maintenance organizations (HMOs) are a form of managed care intended to reduce health care costs while improving the quality of that care. HMOs are prepaid plans that use a health care provider group or network to provide care to enrollees and include preventive care services. The Health Maintenance Organization Act provided grants and loans to plan, start or expand an HMO, removed state restrictions if the HMOs were federally certified, and required companies with 25 or more employees to offer federally certified HMO options.

Survival of the Corps

ALTHOUGH SURGEON GENERAL Jesse Steinfeld was expecting to serve another year to complete his four-year term of office, Richard Nixon asked for his resignation upon reelection as president. Steinfeld's last day in office was January 20, 1973. The Nixon administration, which had earlier attempted to dismantle the Public Health Service Commissioned Corps, declined to fill the position of Surgeon General. However, someone was needed to discharge the duties and ceremonial functions of the position, so the Department appointed S. Paul Ehrlich, Jr. to serve as Acting Surgeon General, effective January 31, 1973. Ehrlich received his medical degree at the University of Minnesota. He entered the Public Health Service in 1957, interned at the Staten Island PHS Hospital, and earned a master's degree in public health at the University of California, Berkeley, in 1961. He began at the National Heart Institute and was Director of the HEW Office of International Health at the time of his appointment as Acting Surgeon General. Ehrlich joined Dr. Steinfeld and others in fending off earlier efforts to diminish the Surgeon

S. Paul Ehrlich, Jr.

General's office and the Corps. Dr. Ehrlich did, in fact, accomplish his primary mission, which was to secure the future of the PHS Commissioned Corps at a perilous moment in time. C. Everett Koop, Surgeon General under President Reagan, told the Associated Press, "The role of a man like Paul Ehrlich is not to make big discoveries or to move mountains. It is to provide the steady, experienced leadership for the public health in this country."[18] Ehrlich had the unflinching support of Congressman Paul Rogers, chairman of the House Subcommittee on Health and protector of the Commissioned Corps, who would not allow any attempt to eliminate the Office of the Surgeon General.[1]

During his tenure, Paul Ehrlich very ably sustained the role of the Surgeon General with its delimited authority and responsibilities. Gerald R. Ford assumed the office of President August 9, 1974, and Dr. Theodore Cooper, a former PHS officer who served as Director of the National Heart Institute, in 1974 became Deputy Assistant Secretary and then on July 1, 1975, Assistant Secretary for Health. Surgeon General Ehrlich was personally respected and supported by Dr. Cooper. On the other hand, the Surgeon General was often sidelined in the administration of Departmental and PHS-related activities.

Reorganization
In 1972, the Public Health Service consisted of three principal agencies: NIH, the Health Services and Mental Health Administration, and the Consumer Protection and Environmental Health Service, which included the FDA. Assistant Secretary for Health Merlin DuVal and his successor in April 1973, Charles C. Edwards, were tasked with building-up the capabilities of the Assistant Secretary's Office to better manage and restructure the PHS. In July 1973, followed in October 1973 when the Alcohol, Drug Abuse, and Mental Health Administration was created, a major reorganization occurred, realigning the Public Health Service into six agencies:
- Alcohol, Drug Abuse, and Mental Health Administration (ADAMHA)
- Center for Disease Control (CDC)
- Food and Drug Administration (FDA)
- Health Resources Administration (HRA)
- Health Services Administration (HSA)
- National Institutes of Health (NIH)

National Health Planning
The National Health Planning and Resources Development Act of 1974, enacted January 4, 1975,[19] authorized the development of national health planning guidelines and the establishment of improved federal, areawide and state health planning and resources development in response to issues related to the delivery of health care services, distribution of health manpower and health care facilities. The overall intent of the Act was to provide more equal access

to high quality health care at reasonable cost. Three existing programs were consolidated under this Act: the Hill-Burton health facilities construction program, Regional Medical Programs, and Comprehensive Health Planning. The legislation provided for a National Council on Health Planning and Development to advise the HEW Secretary on the development of national health planning guidelines. State Health Planning and Development Agencies – a government agency like the state health department – were created to perform planning and resource allocation functions, and other entities called Statewide Health Coordinating Councils were formed to approve state plans and disburse grants. Finally, a network of Health Systems Agencies was designated in 205 health service areas for determining area needs and implementing the plans to meet those needs.[20]

Health Issues

Swine Flu

In February 1976, two Army recruits at Fort Dix, New Jersey, acquired an influenza-like illness, one of whom died. Virus isolate was identified as a new swine flu strain that appeared to be antigenically similar to the strain involved in the 1918 flu pandemic. A variant of H_1N_1 known as A/New Jersey/1976 (H_1N_1), it did not spread beyond Fort Dix. However, the increased surveillance uncovered another strain in circulation, A/Victoria/75 (H_3N_2), which spread simultaneously and infected over 200 soldiers. On March 10, the Advisory Committee on Immunization Practices concluded that the H_1N_1 New Jersey strain could foretell a possible pandemic. A meeting of military, NIH, FDA and state health officials decided action must be taken to prevent a pandemic, although there was some disagreement on the need for mass vaccination. CDC recommended that the federal government contract for vaccine production sufficient to immunize the entire population. The HEW Secretary and President Gerald Ford concurred, and Dr. Theodore Cooper and CDC Director David Sencer took the lead in advancing the initiative. The National Influenza Immunization Program (NIIP) began immunizations on October 1, 1976. However, cases of Guillain-Barré syndrome (GBS) were soon being reported, eventually totaling an estimated 500 GBS cases and 58 fatalities. Epidemiologists' consensus was that the number of GBS cases was in excess of normal prevalence. As a result, the immunization program was ended on December 16, 1976. Within the brief program period of 2½ months, about 45 million persons had been immunized, yet the prospect of a potential pandemic did not materialize beyond Fort Dix. Although decisions related to the NIIP had been based on scientific judgment, it was believed that the perception was the program was driven by politics rather than science and was a misstep by the federal government.[21,22]

Legionnaires' Disease

On July 21, 1976, more than 2,000 American Legion members gathered in Philadelphia for their annual state convention. In the following weeks, about 200 Legionnaires and other persons became ill with a severe atypical pneumonia, and 29 persons eventually died. Most of those affected had attended the convention at the Bellevue-Stratford Hotel in Philadelphia. Initially thought to be an outbreak of swine flu, the CDC sent a 30-member team of Epidemic Intelligence Service officers to conduct an intensive investigation.

Finally in January 1977, CDC microbiologist Joseph McDade identified the causative agent of "Legionnaires' disease" as the bacterium, *Legionella pneumophila*. *Legionella* can cause Legionnaires' disease and also Pontiac fever, a mild flu-like illness, collectively known as legionellosis. By the summer of 1977, it was determined that *Legionella* bacteria thrive in warm water such as in cooling towers of large buildings, which can be aerosolized and spread through the air conditioning systems. Legionnaires' disease continues to be a public health risk wherever maintenance problems exist in building complexes. According to CDC, health departments reported nearly 10,000 cases of Legionnaires' disease in the United States in 2018, noting that this number may underestimate the true incidence.[23,24]

Reye Syndrome

Reye syndrome (also known as Reye's syndrome) is a rare, acute and life-threatening condition characterized by lethargy and vomiting that may progress to delirium, coma and death. The syndrome is named for Australian pathologist Ralph D.K. Reye who first described a syndrome in young children where acute encephalopathy and fatty degeneration of the liver occurred after an acute febrile illness, usually influenza or chickenpox (varicella). In 1963, he published a report on the condition's clinical and pathological features in the medical journal *The Lancet*.[25] The Centers for Disease Control and Prevention initiated a National Reye Syndrome Surveillance System in December 1973 to monitor the incidence of the disease and, during the winter of 1973-1974, the first nationwide outbreak of Reye syndrome was described.[26] Although the anecdotal reports during the 1970s suggested a possible link between Reye syndrome and salicylates, it wasn't until the 1980s that researchers began to more definitively associate Reye syndrome with aspirin, which was then commonly given to children with viral infections. There is no specific treatment for Reye syndrome, other than providing supportive care.

In June 1982, the Surgeon General issued an *Advisory on the Use of Salicylates and Reye Syndrome*.[27] Citing recommendations of the CDC, American Academy of Pediatrics and the FDA, the Surgeon General advised against the use of salicylates and salicylate containing medicines in children with influ-

> **Warnings**
> **Reye's syndrome**: Children and teenagers who have or are recovering from chicken pox or flu-like symptoms should not use this product. When using this product, if changes in behavior with nausea and vomiting occur, consult a doctor because these symptoms could be an early sign of Reye's syndrome, a rare but serious illness.

enza or chickenpox. Reports of Reye syndrome began a precipitous decline thereafter, and there are now few cases. In 1986, the FDA issued rules that all nonprescription aspirin products must be labeled with a warning that children and teenagers with or recovering from chickenpox or flu-like symptoms should not use the product. Reye syndrome is now a rare diagnosis.

CHRONOLOGY • 1969–1977
SG Jesse L. Steinfeld, December 1969–January 1973
Acting SG S. Paul Ehrlich, Jr., January 1973–July 1977

1970	*Occupational Safety and Health Act*. Creates the National Institute for Occupational Safety and Health (NIOSH) and Occupational Safety and Health Administration (OSHA).
1970	*Emergency Health Personnel Act*. Creates the National Health Service Corps.
1970	*Comprehensive Alcohol Abuse and Alcoholism Prevention, Treatment, and Rehabilitation Act of 1970*.
1971	Release of the *Report of the Secretary's Committee to Study the Public Health Service Commissioned Corps*.
1971	*Lead-Based Paint Poisoning Prevention Act*. Prohibits the use of lead-based paints in residential structures.
1972	The Office of the Assistant Secretary for Health and Scientific Affairs is renamed Assistant Secretary for Health.
1972	Surgeon General Steinfeld releases report on smoking and health, the first to identify secondhand cigarette smoke as a health hazard.
1973	Environmental Protection Agency issues regulations to phase-down the lead content in fuel, and in 1990 unleaded gasoline was banned.
1973	*Health Maintenance Organization Act*. Provides grants and loans to start or expand a health maintenance organization.
1973	Initiation of CDC National Reye Syndrome Surveillance System to monitor incidence of the disease.
1975	*National Health Planning and Resources Development Act of 1974*.
1976	Swine flu and Legionnaires' disease outbreaks occur.
1982	Surgeon General issues an advisory on use of salicylates and Reye Syndrome.

CHAPTER TEN

DUAL ROLE, SMALLPOX, NATIONAL INSTITUTES OF HEALTH, HEALTHY PEOPLE
1977 to 1981

PRESIDENT JAMES EARL "JIMMY" CARTER JR. took office on January 20, 1977, and soon thereafter appointed Joseph A. Califano Jr. as Secretary of the Department of Health, Education, and Welfare. Califano was an activist and forward looking administrator who previously served in high level positions at the Department of Defense and as Special Assistant to President Lyndon Johnson. Califano chose Julius B. Richmond to serve as the next Surgeon General, a person with a distinguished professional career who had served as first director of the child development program Head Start in 1965. Advantages to combining the prominence of the position of Surgeon General with the administrative authority vested in the position of Assistant Secretary for Health (ASH) led to Richmond being granted the rare distinction of serving both as Surgeon General and Assistant Secretary for Health. Julius Richmond was the son of Russian immigrant parents, something that shaped a strong social conscience throughout his adult life. He received his medical degree in 1939 from the University of Illinois and interned at Cook County Hospital, followed by a pediatric residency. In 1942, Richmond was inducted into the Army Air Corps, serving until 1946 as chief flight surgeon at the Flight Training Command at Randolph Field, Texas. He returned to the University of Illinois from 1946 to 1953, rising to professor of pediatrics. From 1953 to 1970, he was professor and chairman in the department of pediatrics at the State University of New York at Syracuse College of Medicine. In 1965, he took a leave of absence for two years to direct the new Project Head Start program, which supported educational day care for preschoolers from poor families. In 1971, he moved to Harvard as professor and chair of the department of preventive and social medicine and psychiatrist-in-chief of Children's Hospital Medical Center, when he was selected and then confirmed as Surgeon General on July 13, 1977. Although he

Julius B. Richmond

was a federal official at Head Start, Dr. Richmond was the first Surgeon General who had never served in the PHS Commissioned Corps. In March 1978, RADM John C. Greene was appointed Deputy Surgeon General, the first nonphysician in that position, serving until January 1981, and from then until May 1981 he was the Acting Surgeon General. Dr. Greene was Chief Dental Officer from 1973 to 1981, and he was considered legendary in dental public health. He was known for developing the Greene–[Jack] Vermillion Simplified Oral Hygiene Index, a simplified method to quantify plaque, debris and calculus on teeth.

A principal focus of the Carter administration was the need to control inflation and it strove to contain expenditures in the health care sector with various, though oftentimes unsuccessful proposals. A limited health insurance plan to provide catastrophic health insurance and a proposed cap on hospital charges were unable to sustain Congressional support. Assistant Secretary for Health Richmond was aware that 20 to 30 million people – about 10 percent of the population – still did not have good access to health care. Among his goals were to improve health outcomes within the framework of extending health services to those persons who were underserved or unserved; taking actions for the prevention of noninfectious disease, while minimizing the development of disabilities associated with illness of all kinds; and to provide support for research.[1]

Community Health Centers

The Community Health Center (CHC, formerly Neighborhood Health Center) program, first approved in 1965 under the Office of Economic Opportunity, supported clinics for the purpose of providing health services to poor and medically underserved communities. The program was transferred in the early 1970s to HEW and was an important component in the strategy to help achieve Richmond's programmatic goals. The CHC program enjoyed Congressional support and was further validated with enactment of the Health Services and Centers Amendments of 1978 to reauthorize an array of public health services, community health and migrant health centers, and grants for primary care, preventive health services and public health programs.[2] It was Surgeon General Richmond's intent to direct health care resources to disadvantaged communities, and by 1980 the National Health Service Corps had placed over 2,000 health professionals in locales coincident with community health centers and other programs for medically underserved areas.

HHS-Related Organizational Changes

President Lyndon B. Johnson signed the Social Security Amendments on July 30, 1965, establishing both Medicare and Medicaid. The Social Security Administration was responsible for the administration of Medicare and the Social and Rehabilitation Service was responsible for administering Medicaid. In

June 1977, the Health Care Financing Administration (HCFA) was created to combine under one administration the oversight of the Medicare program, the Federal portion of the Medicaid program and related quality assurance activities under the jurisdiction of the Department of Health, Education, and Welfare. Then in October 1979, the Department of Education was created pursuant to the Department of Education Organization Act and HEW was renamed the Department of Health and Human Services (HHS) in 1980. In July 2001, HCFA was renamed the Centers for Medicare and Medicaid Services.

SMALLPOX ERADICATION

Among history's deadliest diseases, smallpox is a highly contagious and sometimes fatal infectious disease that is estimated to have caused an estimated 300 to 500 million deaths worldwide. Smallpox prevention is by vaccination and there is no specific treatment, and thus it is considered a category A pathogen that poses the highest risk to national security and public health. The global eradication of smallpox is even so considered a historic achievement in public health. Although North America and Europe were virtually free of smallpox in 1967, the disease was prevalent elsewhere in the world. In January of that year, the World Health Organization (WHO) initiated an Intensified Global Smallpox Eradication Program at a time when the disease was still endemic in 33 countries with an estimated 10 million smallpox cases and 2 million deaths. CDC played a major role in the international effort to eradicate smallpox, working in collaboration with national governments and with technical and financial support from the U.S. Agency for International Development. In 1962, CDC established a smallpox surveillance unit to monitor importation of smallpox into this nation coincident with increased air travel, and began testing a U.S. Army vaccination jet injector developed by Aaron Ismach of the Department of Defense. A foot-powered intradermal injector called the ped-o-jet was also produced to enable field use of the injector. At the request of the WHO Director-General, the Surgeon General assigned Donald Ainslie "D.A." Henderson, the chief of CDC's Surveillance Section, to lead the WHO global smallpox eradication program. The program was primarily directed to the vaccination of people in 20 Central and West African countries, and afterwards in Brazil, India and Bangladesh. Plans called for two types of CDC personnel assigned to field work: medical officer-epidemiologist advisors and nonmedical public health operations officers. Eventually, over 300 CDC staff participated in the effort. In 1966, CDC prepared a procedural document that formed the basis of the 1967 WHO field operations manual,

Donald Henderson

Handbook for Smallpox Eradication Programmes in Endemic Areas. With the recognition that smallpox vaccination alone would not eradicate the disease, an "eradication escalation" technique proposed by Dr. William H. Foege (CDC Director, 1977–1983), a former EIS officer, was introduced in 1968. The surveillance-containment strategy involved active surveillance; outbreak investigation; outbreak control by vaccination of case patients and their immediate contacts; and rapid communication of disease intelligence. Data were sent to CDC and its regional office in Lagos, Nigeria, and distributed in weekly reports. Combined with mass vaccinations, the eradication escalation strategy proved exceedingly effective. This initiative ultimately led to the last recorded case of smallpox in Merka, Somalia, in 1977. The international smallpox effort was so successful that global eradication of smallpox was certified by the World Health Assembly on May 8, 1980.[3-6]

VIETNAM WAR

In 1954, French colonial administration of Vietnam came to an end with the communism-inspired takeover of the northern part of the country. The Vietnam War began in 1955 as a conflict between Communist North Vietnam backed by China and the Soviet Union, which wanted to unify the entire country under a communist regime, and the Democratic South Vietnam backed principally by the United States. The U.S. was concerned with the spread of communism in Southeast Asia and began its military involvement in 1964 when military advisors were sent to the region. Thereafter, American presence in Vietnam vastly escalated with the deployment of Armed Forces. The lack of military progress over several years and the heavy American casualties, including nearly 47,500 combat and 10,800 noncombatant deaths, led to waning domestic support for the war. The Paris Peace Accords, signed on January 27, 1973, officially concluded direct U.S. involvement in the Vietnam War. The war finally ended in 1975 with the fall of Saigon, the capital of South Vietnam, and unification of Vietnam under Communist control.

Over 170 USPHS officers served in noncombat duty within Vietnam. Although a very small contingent, the PHS presence fulfilled important mis-

PHS medical officer Stuart Mackler, assigned to Coast Guard Cutter Yakutat, held sick calls in Vietnam coastal villages and is here examining a Vietnamese boy.
[1967, National Library of Medicine]

sions. Due to a shortage of clinical personnel in South Vietnam, a PHS Surgical Teams Program placed PHS officer and civilian physicians, nurses and technologists in Vietnamese provincial hospitals from 1962 onward. PHS CAPT Harry S. Wise, assigned to the U.S. Agency for International Development mission in Saigon, coordinated these teams. Another program, the PHS/Army Special Forces Special Epidemiologic Team (SET), operating out of CDC, was also highly active during the war on the control and prevention of oppressive diseases. SET dealt with 22 diseases and 8 vector groups, with their main focus on malaria and plague. SET produced 17 field manuals for use in the war zone. PHS CDR (later CAPT) Harold G. Scott, PhD, an expert in vector-borne diseases, served as the SET Commander.[7] Scott joined the U.S. Army and trained with the 1st Special Service Force in 1942-43. He served during WWII (battles of Leyte and Luzon) and Korea. In 1955, he joined the USPHS Commissioned Corps and was stationed at CDC in Atlanta.[8]

Harold G. Scott

Military 'Doctor Draft'

Physicians subject to the military draft were able to defer military service until after their completion of medical school and internship and/or residency training, pursuant to the Selective Service "Berry Plan" (named for Dr. Frank B. Berry, Assistant Secretary of Defense for Health and Medical Affairs), which was enacted in 1954 and ended in 1973. Physicians discharged their military obligation through service with one of the Armed Forces or by entering the USPHS Commissioned Corps. During the Vietnam War, the military's increasing need for medical personnel brought about an influx of physicians and other healthcare professionals seeking to join the PHS Commissioned Corps, which was not militarized. Those accepted into the PHS were assigned to duty throughout the nation in agency programs such as the Indian Health Service, in PHS Hospitals, and overseas. Some of the physicians applied for a highly competitive research mentorship program known as the National Institutes of Health Associate Training Program (ATP), which began in 1953 and by 1973 was at its peak with over 200 clinical associates. Notably, many of the former ATP clinical associates went on to hold leadership roles in academic medicine and research, ultimately comprising a cadre of the nation's top physician-scientists. Among those were Anthony S. Fauci (ATP clinical associate 1968-70) and three NIH Directors – Donald S. Fredrickson (1953-55), James B. Wyngaarden (1954-56), and Harold E. Varmus (1968-70).[9,10]

Nobel Prize Recipients. Some ATP associates who were PHS medical officers became Nobel Prize recipients, including Michael S. Brown (Nobel Prize, 1985), Joseph L. Goldstein (1985), J. Michael Bishop (1989), Harold E. Varmus (1989), Alfred G. Gilman (1994), Stanley B. Prusiner (1997), Ferid Murad (1998), Richard Axel (2004), Robert J. Lefkowitz (2012), and Harvey J. Alter (2020).[11]

NATIONAL INSTITUTES OF HEALTH *(See also Chapter Five.)*

In 1887, Marine Hospital Service physician Joseph J. Kinyoun set up a one-room laboratory in the Marine Hospital at Staten Island, New York, calling it a "laboratory of hygiene." In 1891, the Laboratory of Hygiene was relocated to the Butler Building in Washington, DC, and in 1904 it moved to a new building on the grounds of the Old Naval Observatory. This served as the foundation upon which arose the National Institutes of Health, the world's preeminent biomedical research enterprise. On May 26, 1930, President Herbert Hoover signed the Ransdell Act[12], renaming the Hygienic Laboratory as the National Institute of Health and directing it to ascertain "...the cause, prevention, and cure of disease." The law appropriated funds to construct and equip research facilities, and in 1938 NIH began its move from Washington, DC, to Bethesda, Maryland. By October 1940, construction of six buildings on the NIH campus was nearly complete. President Franklin D. Roosevelt stood between the columns of Building 1 and dedicated the National Institute of Health on October 31, 1940. In 1948, the National Heart Act was enacted, in which the NIH was redesignated the National Institutes *[plural]* of Health.

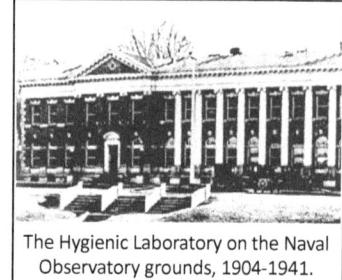

The Hygienic Laboratory on the Naval Observatory grounds, 1904-1941.
[National Library of Medicine]

NIH Building 1 with colonnade *[foreground]*, administrative center of NIH, was built in 1938 in Bethesda, Maryland, upon 70 acres of an estate known as Tree Tops that was donated by Luke and Helen Wilson.
[National Library of Medicine]

NIH Institutes

The NIH is comprised of distinct Institutes and Centers (ICs), each of which is directed to a specific disease or biomedical area. Included among those entities are the National Center for Advancing Translational Sciences, National Library of Medicine, Fogarty International Center, and the NIH Clinical Center. The National Cancer Institute (NCI) was the first research institute; established through the National Cancer Act of 1937, it was not until passage of the Public Health Service Act of 1944 that the NCI became an operating division of NIH. Passage of the National Cancer Act represented the first time that Congress provided funding to address a noncommunicable disease and foretold the categorical disease structure of NIH that has characterized the agency ever since. Between 1946 and 1949, Congress created three additional institutes for research on mental health, heart disease, and dental diseases. In 1953, a research hospital was built on the NIH campus, now called the Warren Grant Magnuson Clinical Center, opened with 540 beds. By 1970, there were fifteen NIH components, and by 1998 the NIH had 27 Institutes and Centers.

NIH Leadership

Numerous PHS officers have served at NIH. Several of those officers served in the position of an Institute Director and went on to become Surgeon General. Beginning with creation of the Hygienic Laboratory in 1887 and until 1955, seven NIH Directors were career PHS medical officers *(noted by asterisk in the following list)*. Since 1955, three NIH Directors were short-term PHS officers while serving in the NIH Associate Training Program *(two asterisks)*, and all other NIH Directors have been civilian employees or appointees.

1887–1899	*Joseph J. Kinyoun, MD	1973–1975	Robert S. Stone, MD
1899–1909	*Milton J. Rosenau, MD	1975–1981	**Donald S. Fredrickson, MD
1909–1915	*John F. Anderson, MD	1982–1989	**James B. Wyngaarden, MD
1915–1937	*George W. McCoy, MD	1991–1993	Bernadine Healy, MD
1937–1942	*Lewis R. Thompson, MD	1993–1999	**Harold E. Varmus, MD
1942–1950	*Rolla E. Dyer, MD	2002–2008	Elias A. Zerhouni, MD
1950–1955	*William H. Sebrell, Jr., MD	2009–2021	Francis S. Collins, MD, PhD
1955–1968	James A. Shannon, MD	2023–	Monica Bertagnolli, MD
1968–1973	Robert Q. Marston, MD		

PHS MEDICAL OFFICERS WHO WERE NIH DIRECTORS

Joseph J. Kinyoun Milton J. Rosenau John F. Anderson George W. McCoy Lewis R. Thompson
1887-1899 *1899-1909* *1909-1915* *1915-1937* *1937-1942*

Rolla E. Dyer William H. Sebrell Donald Fredrickson James Wyngaarden Harold E. Varmus
1942-1950 *1950-1955* *1975-1981* *1982-1989* *1993-1999*

NIH Staffing

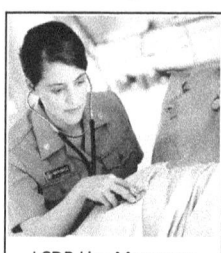
LCDR Lisa Marunycz
Senior Nurse Consultant

As of 2022, the National Institutes of Health was comprised of a staff of about 20,000 employees, of which over 200 were PHS officers. About one quarter of those officers were healthcare providers at the NIH Clinical Center Hospital, with nurse and medical officers predominating. Health services and scientist officers were also present in relatively high numbers within NIH's Office of the Director, the National Institute of Allergy and Infectious Diseases, National Cancer Institute, and the National Heart, Lung, and Blood Institute. RADM Richard G. Wyatt, who served in the Corps for 36 years beginning 1971, was a highly regarded pediatrician researcher in NIAID, later serving as Deputy Director, Office of Intramural Research in 1984. He was a participant in Surgeon General Koop's endeavor to revitalize the Commissioned Corps and served on the Surgeon General's Policy Advisory Council as NIH representative from 1987 to 2007.

Richard G. Wyatt

THREE MILE ISLAND

The Three Mile Island Nuclear Generating Station near Harrisburg, Pennsylvania, was the site of a major accident on March 28, 1979. The incident involved the loss of nuclear reactor coolant and, with the fuel core uncovered,

more than one-third of the fuel melted. The partial meltdown was followed by the release of radioactive gases. The medical response to the accident included the Surgeon General and senior HEW officials. The medical concern related to possible radiation-induced health effects, primarily cancer, in the surrounding area. Within a few days, the Nuclear Regulatory Commission advised evacuation of pregnant women and preschool age children within a 20-mile radius of the facility. HEW Secretary Califano assembled top leadership including Surgeon General Richmond, the Directors of NIH, CDC, NCI, NIOSH, EPA, and other experts, and action assignments were made. On April 2, in response to a White House request, Dr. Richmond incorporated NIH recommendations regarding the use of potassium iodide by facility workers and people living near the Three Mile Island facility. It was determined that radiation releases were minimal and well below a radiation exposure health threat. For that reason, Pennsylvania officials disputed the need for plant workers to begin taking thyroid-blocking doses of potassium iodide. Nonetheless, Congressional concerns persisted and it was Richmond who testified at a televised hearing that there was no significant danger to the population.[1,13] The accident gave rise to renewed nuclear energy safety concerns and since then, no nuclear generating plants have been built in the United States.

TOBACCO USE

Secretary of HEW Joseph Califano, himself a former smoker, was passionate about initiating a resolute campaign to reduce cigarette smoking in the nation. On January 11, 1978, in a speech before the National Interagency Council on Smoking and Health,[14] Califano called cigarette smoking "Public Health Enemy Number One" and announced a series of actions that included a major public information and education effort against smoking, proposals to ban smoking in federal buildings and on commercial airliners, and an increase of the federal excise tax on cigarettes. To provide leadership for the initiative, Califano established a new Office on Smoking and Health in HEW. His activist stance against tobacco drew the ire of the industry and its Congressional allies. In concert with Califano's campaign, Dr. Richmond released a 1979 Surgeon General's report on *Smoking and Health* concerning health hazards associated with cigarette smoking.[15] This report marked the fifteenth anniversary of the original 1964 report by Surgeon General Terry. At nearly 1,200 pages, the report detailed the overwhelming research and accumulated evidence that clearly indicted cigarette smoking as harmful to human health. And as a pediatrician, Richmond was concerned with and also included data regarding potential harm to the fetuses of pregnant women who smoke.

HEALTHY PEOPLE

As early as 1937, then Surgeon General Thomas Parran recognized that the country had accomplished what came to be known as the first public health revolution – infectious diseases had been controlled as living conditions and sanitation improved and preventive measures such as vaccines were deployed. He further noted there needed to be a shift in emphasis to chronic diseases, particularly among the underprivileged populace.[16] Julius Richmond knew that medical science and public health actions should focus on "prevention of noninfectious disease and also particularly minimizing the development of disabilities associated with illness of all kinds," a period that he called the second revolution in public health.[1] There was growing awareness about the preventability of deaths from many chronic diseases, coupled with an interest in promotion of prevention and health education as cost containment and disease management strategies. In 1979, Dr.

> There was growing awareness about preventability of chronic diseases and interest in promoting prevention and health education.

Richmond released a report that specified public health goals and quantifiable objectives for reducing disability and mortality in the United States entitled *Healthy People: The Surgeon General's Report on Health Promotion and Disease Prevention*. The report also noted that while certain factors are not entirely controllable, individual responsibility is important in making lifestyle choices that maintain personal health. There were several antecedents to the *Healthy People* initiative, especially a 1974 report issued by the Canadian Minister of Health Marc Lalonde that proposed a "health field" concept comprising four determinants of health in support of health promotion.[17] *Healthy People* was largely the work of PHS medical officer J. Michael McGinnis, founding Director of the Office of Disease Prevention and Health Promotion (ODPHP), HHS, and his staff, in conjunction with CDC Director Dr. William Foege. The Institute of Medicine provided multidiscipline background papers and a companion document on prevention and health promotion. The *Healthy People* report is updated every decade with specific 10-year objectives to address the most critical public health priorities. It has become a remarkable success and is a signature achievement of the Richmond legacy. On August 18, 2020, HHS released *Healthy People 2030*. The ODPHP leads *Healthy People* in cooperation with the National Center for Health Statistics at CDC, which oversees data in support of the initiative.[18,19] Throughout his career, Dr. McGinnis was a prodigious presence in the field of public health who served from 1977 to 1995 as Deputy Assistant Secretary for Health, HHS.

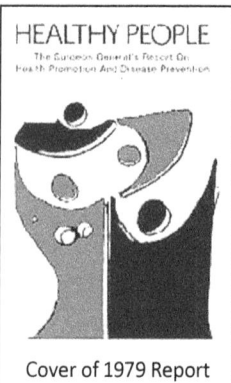
Cover of 1979 Report

J. Michael McGinnis

CHRONOLOGY • 1977–1981
SG Julius B. Richmond, July 1977–January 1981

- 1977 Julius B. Richmond is confirmed as both Surgeon General and the Assistant Secretary for Health, HEW (later HHS), the first such dual role appointment.
- 1979 Surgeon General Richmond releases report on smoking and health.
- 1979 Accident at the Three Mile Island Nuclear Generating Station.
- 1979 Release of inaugural issue of the *Healthy People* report.
- 1980 The Department of Health, Education, and Welfare is renamed the Department of Health and Human Services.
- 1980 Global eradication of smallpox certified by the World Health Assembly, WHO.

CHAPTER ELEVEN

OBRA, TOBACCO, AIDS, CORPS REVITALIZATION
1981 to 1989

THE REAGAN ADMINISTRATION assumed office on January 20, 1981, and in his inaugural address President Ronald Reagan made the declaration that "In this present crisis, government is not the solution to our problem, government *is* the problem." That statement encapsulated the administration's approach to executive management – the federal government bureaucracy would be reduced, and select programs and funding would be directed to the states in the form of block grants. Programs throughout the government were impacted, including those of the Department of Health and Human Services (HHS). The incoming HHS Secretary, U.S. Senator Richard Schweiker of Pennsylvania, was considered a moderate Republican. He resisted budget reductions for medical research and vital service programs of the Public Health Service. With regard to PHS leadership positions, Schweiker chose to re-separate the positions of Assistant Secretary for Health and the Surgeon General, and nominated Dr. Edward N. Brandt, Jr., Vice Chancellor of Health Affairs at the University of Texas, and Dr. C. Everett Koop, fellow Pennsylvanian and Surgeon in Chief at Children's Hospital of Philadelphia, respectively. Koop was seen as a staunch conservative and pro-life activist, and his nomination engendered considerable opposition among public health advocacy groups as well as members of Congress, such that his Senate confirmation did not come until November 16, 1981. Dr. Koop was officially sworn in as Surgeon General on January 21, 1982. While awaiting confirmation, Brandt served as the Acting Surgeon General and Koop served as deputy to Brandt; Koop took that opportunity to build rapport with HHS senior officials. Charles Everett Koop attended Dartmouth College for his undergraduate degree, where he acquired the nickname "Chick" (as in chicken coop), a name reserved for his friends and close associates. He received his medical degree from Cornell Medical School in 1941, followed by internship and a fellowship at the University of Pennsylvania (UPenn) School

C. Everett Koop

of Medicine, a pediatric surgery internship at Children's Hospital in Boston, and postgraduate training at the UPenn School of Medicine leading to a Doctor of Science degree in 1947. He then joined the faculty at the UPenn School of Medicine, becoming a professor of pediatric surgery. From 1948 to 1981, as Surgeon in Chief at the Children's Hospital of Philadelphia, Koop built a nationally acclaimed pediatric surgical department, and in 1956 the nation's first neonatal surgical intensive care unit.

One of Surgeon General Koop's first official acts was to appoint Faye G. Abdellah as the Deputy Surgeon General in March 1982. RADM Abdellah had served in the PHS Commissioned Corps many years at the time of her appointment. Abdellah made history – she was the first woman and first nurse to serve as Deputy Surgeon General. A graduate of the Ann May School of Nursing in 1942, she later earned an EdD from Columbia University. In 1949, Abdellah joined the Public Health Service, where she conducted pioneering research and developed some of the first patient care standards for health care facilities. Abdellah is recognized by the nursing profession as having changed the focus of nursing theory from a disease-centered to a patient-centered approach. She served as the PHS Chief Nurse Officer from 1970 to 1987. Koop declared, "She was the quintessential commissioned officer and aided the career development of every officer whose path she crossed. ...She embodied the best of service and devotion."[1]

Faye G. Abdellah

OBRA

PHS Hospital Closures

The Omnibus Budget Reconciliation Act (OBRA) of 1981,[2] signed August 13, had a very significant effect on public health programs as well as numerous other federal programs. The more noticeable change brought about by the legislation (Title IX, Subtitle J) was termination of funding and closure of the eight remaining PHS (Marine) Hospitals and 27 PHS Clinics by October 31, 1981, or transfer of the hospitals to state, local or private operation by September 30, 1982. OBRA also repealed the health care entitlement for merchant seamen, effective October 1, 1981, allowing continued hospital care for those seamen already under treatment, but only through September 30, 1982. Like prior administrations, the Reagan administration argued that the continued provision of health care to merchant seamen and other select groups was unwarranted, and that most of the facilities were underutilized. Many residents of surrounding communities also relied upon some of the hospitals, however, and fought the closures. As a result, Congress supplemented the provision for hospital transfer with sufficient funding to renovate the hospitals to conform with state building codes, thereby facilitating control of the hospitals by non-federal community entities.[3]

Block Grants

Soon after the Reagan administration took office, the Omnibus Budget Reconciliation Act was enacted. This legislation was a manifestation of the "new federalism" – taking federal authorities and budgets that had expanded over the years and returning such powers that were believed reserved to the states. As part of OBRA, 77 categorical programs were consolidated under nine block grants to the states. Consistent with Reagan's announced effort to reduce federal spending, the block grants carried about 25 percent less funding than the specific grant programs they replaced. OBRA Title IX, Health Services and Facilities, Subtitle A, amended the Public Health Service Act to add a new "Title XIX—Block Grants" to the PHS Act, which combined an array of 22 categorical health-related programs into four block grants to the states:[4,5]

- Preventive Health and Health Services – *Contained categorical programs such as fluoridation, health education, home health services, and regional emergency medical services.*
- Alcohol and Drug Abuse and Mental Health Services – *Contained programs relating to alcoholism, drug abuse, and mental health services.*
- Primary Care – *Contained programs such as community health centers.*
- Maternal and Child Health Services – *Contained programs such as maternal and child health, crippled children's services, adolescent pregnancy, hemophilia centers, lead-based paint prevention, and income for disabled children.*

The states were allowed flexibility to determine priorities in implementing the programs and determining their funding levels. The premise was that transferring programs to the states would reduce administrative costs and programmatic flexibility would result in efficiencies to offset the 25 percent decrease in federal support – that supposition would be severely challenged. In fact, adjusting for inflation and population growth, block grant funding for health, housing and social services fell markedly over time. As an example, from 1982 until 2017, funding for Maternal and Child Health Services, and Preventive Health and Health Services block grants declined by 49 and 43 percent, respectively.[6]

The impact of OBRA on the Public Health Service was very significant. The loss of its system of PHS hospitals and clinics, and consolidation of health programs into block grants to the states led to a 20 percent budget cut for the Public Health Service by 1982. There was a substantial reduction in the PHS Commissioned Corps and an overall reduction in the Public Health Service from 56,000 to 48,000 employees.[7]

TOBACCO USE

Cigarette smoking is the leading cause of preventable death and disability in the United States, and C. Everett Koop clearly understood and relentlessly communicated the devastating effects of tobacco use. He realized the issue had become something of a "raison d'être" for the Office of the Surgeon General and so became an authority on the matter. In a speech at the annual meeting of the American Lung Association in May 1984, Koop announced his ambitious goal of a Campaign for a Smoke-Free Society by the Year 2000 and carried the campaign to audiences across the country despite fierce resistance from the tobacco industry and North Carolina Senator Jesse Helms.[8,9]

Surgeon General Koop issued a *Report on Smoking and Health* nearly every year beginning in 1982, with that report stating that 30 percent of all cancer deaths were attributable to smoking. In 1986, he released the report, *The Health Consequences of Involuntary Smoking*.[10] Surgeon General Steinfeld's 1972 report, *The Health Consequences of Smoking*, concluded that smoke-filled rooms could cause discomfort and possible harm to many persons. Dr. Koop's 1986 report, which focused exclusively on secondhand smoke, concluded that involuntary smoke was a cause of disease, including lung cancer, in healthy nonsmokers; that children of parent smokers have an increased rate of respiratory problems; and that separation of smokers and nonsmokers in the same space does not eliminate the exposure to nonsmokers. Researchers studying the health effects of smoking during the 1960s and 1970s were focused on the consequences of smoking. By the late 1970s, cigarette smoking behavior was being recognized as resembling that of other drug addictions and a portion of the 1979 Surgeon General's report dealt with behavioral aspects of smoking. Scientists began researching smoking as a possible addiction and a substantial body of evidence resulted. The 1988 report issued by Surgeon General Koop, *The Health Consequences of Smoking: Nicotine Addiction*,[11] reviewed new evidence and arrived at three major conclusions:

- Cigarettes and other forms of tobacco are addicting.
- Nicotine is the drug in tobacco that causes addiction.
- The pharmacologic and behavioral processes that determine tobacco addiction are similar to those that determine addiction to drugs such as heroin and cocaine.

The report had a profound effect, changing the view from cigarette smoking was just a habit to it being addicting and as equally addictive as illegal drugs. The findings had implications for treatment as well, suggesting the possible use of nicotine replacement therapy to quit smoking. The tobacco industry continued its efforts to discredit the report long after publication, even though their own documents indicated that it had known nicotine was addicting.[12]

HIV/Acquired Immunodeficiency Syndrome

Surgeon General Koop came to prominence and elevated the stature of the Office of the Surgeon General due to his forthright stance in response to the acquired immunodeficiency syndrome (AIDS) epidemic in the United States. On June 5, 1981, the Centers for Disease Control (CDC) *Morbidity and Mortality Weekly Report* carried the article "*Pneumocystis* Pneumonia --- Los Angeles," which reported that during the period October 1980 to May 1981, five homosexual males were treated for *Pneumocystis carinii* pneumonia, all of whom eventually died. A month later, 26 cases of Kaposi's sarcoma were diagnosed in homosexual men, and by August 1981 the CDC reported 108 cases of AIDS, with 43 dead. By the fall of 1982, other persons including hemophiliac patients and drug addicts had acquired the disease. CDC, as the lead federal agency, immediately convened a task force in June 1981 and, in 1983, the Assistant Secretary for Health Edward Brandt created a Departmental Executive Task Force on AIDS to deal with the growing epidemic. However, the Surgeon General was excluded from these official groups and was directed not to involve himself in public discourse on the subject. In May 1983, Drs. Luc Montagnier of the Pasteur Institute in Paris and Robert C. Gallo of the National Institutes of Health (NIH) identified the infectious agent that caused AIDS, a virus called human immunodeficiency virus or HIV. Then in 1985, the enzyme-linked immunosorbent assay (ELISA) was licensed which could detect and measure antibodies in blood. The ELISA was the first screening test used to detect the presence of antibodies to HIV in blood, thereby making the nation's blood supply once again safe for transfusion. HIV attacks the body's immune system, specifically the CD4 T cells. Over time, opportunistic infections or cancers overcome a very weak immune system and signal that the person has AIDS, the last stage of HIV infection. By the mid-1980s, much was still unknown about AIDS, but extraordinary progress had been made. The virus and antibodies to it had been identified, the modes of transmission were known and yet the disease was fatal, it was spreading, and there was no cure. By July 1985, the CDC had reported 11,737 AIDS cases, with 5,812 deaths, and the AIDS-related death of actor Rock Hudson that summer further raised public concern. Conservative politics and personal beliefs roused antipathy toward the homosexual community and thwarted Dr. Koop's attempts to educate the public about AIDS. The situation was both frustrating and an embarrassment to Koop. In the summer of 1985, acting Assistant Secretary for Health James Mason made Dr. Koop a member of the AIDS Task Force and agreed that he should begin to publicly speak about the disease; indeed, Surgeon General Koop became the lead federal spokesperson on the public health aspects of AIDS. Koop believed that he was deliberately kept from contact with the president."[3] Finally, after remaining silent on AIDS for years, President Reagan visited HHS headquarters on February 5, 1986, and announced that AIDS should be a top priority and asked Dr. Koop to prepare a special report on the disease. Koop wrote much of the report himself. Concerned that a review of the report by Reagan's policy advisers would lead to removal of essential health information, he provided numbered copies of the final draft to the Domestic Policy Council, which he collected at the end of the meeting. The stratagem was successful – without further revision, Koop released the report at a press conference on October 22, 1986. Entitled *Surgeon General's Report on Acquired Immune Deficiency Syndrome*,[14] it was a nonjudgmental, explicit and comprehensive document that was, in certain quarters, controversial. Twenty million copies were distributed in the public domain.[14,15] There was some interest among Congress members in sending copies of the report to their constituents. Congressional hearings were held to address

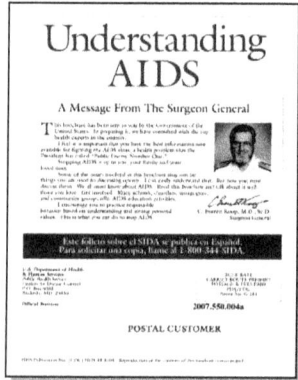
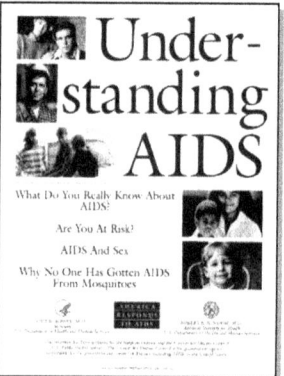

Covers of the brochure, *Understanding AIDS: A Message from the Surgeon General*, sent by PHS/CDC to 107 million households, May 1988.

the growing epidemic, which led to an appropriation of $20 million for an AIDS brochure that could be sent to all residences, with the legislators stipulating that it be cleared by health officers, not White House staffers. Based upon CDC guidelines, the brochure was largely written by Dr. Koop. The resulting eight-page mailer, *Understanding AIDS: A Message from the Surgeon General*, was sent to 107 million households in the United States in May 1988, the largest ever public health mailing. Koop's explicit language, the need for sex education, and his approach to AIDS as a public health rather than a lifestyle issue won him both admirers and detractors. He achieved his goal of educating the public with accurate and complete information about an important public health threat. The effect of Koop's forthright actions strengthened the role of Surgeon General to speak authoritatively on matters of public health and restored implicit credibility and visibility to the Office of the Surgeon General.[1,15]

> C. Everett Koop's forthright actions restored credibility and visibility to the Office of the SG.

Anthony S. Fauci

In July 1968, Dr. Anthony "Tony" S. Fauci entered the Commissioned Corps as a clinical associate in the Laboratory of Clinical Investigation, National Institute of Allergy and Infectious Diseases (NIAID), NIH. His research focused on autoimmune diseases, but he was intrigued by the 1981 reports of homosexual men presenting with *Pneumocystis carinii* pneumonia. Further reports of individuals with *Pneumocystis* pneumonia prompted Fauci to shift his focus to studying the pathogenesis of this new disease. Said Fauci, "I made the decision that we would have to switch over to research on this disease (AIDS) because, as every month went by, I became more convinced that we were dealing with something that was going to be a disaster for society."[16] In 1984, Dr. Fauci became the Director of the NIAID and he assumed the role of lead federal spokesperson on the scientific aspects of the HIV/AIDS epidemic.

Anthony S. Fauci

In Their Words
by RADM (Ret.) Anthony S. Fauci

I had assumed the role of point person for the scientific and medical aspects of HIV/AIDS when I became Director of the National Institute of Allergy and Infectious Diseases in 1984. Dr. Koop became interested in HIV/AIDS in early 1986 and he began meeting with me at night in my office to learn about the science of HIV. He then became intensely interested in HIV/AIDS and wrote the Surgeon General's Report on HIV in 1986, and from that point on we were partners and collaborators and deepened our friendship. Dr. Koop was a natural spokesperson and was a man of great courage and integrity. He became the point person on the public health components of HIV/AIDS in 1986, and I continued my role as point person on the scientific and medical components of HIV/AIDS. We were true partners in the struggle against HIV/AIDS. I am inspired to this day by Chick's legacy and the contributions of his successors.

In 1985, Dr. Fauci was promoted to Rear Admiral in the PHS and retired from the Corps in August 1996. He continued to lead NIAID and the ongoing research related to HIV/AIDS, as well as bioterrorism and emerging infectious diseases. On June 19, 2008, Anthony Fauci was recognized with the nation's highest civilian honor, the Presidential Medal of Freedom, for his extraordinary commitment to public health. Notably, Fauci went on to serve as the lead federal spokesperson for the medical/scientific community in educating the public about the novel coronavirus disease pandemic that emerged in 2019.

COMMISSIONED CORPS REVITALIZATION

In February 1982, one month after being sworn in, Surgeon General Koop received a letter from Luther Terry in which he noted that Julius Richmond, the first Surgeon General not chosen from the Commissioned Corps, had "...made a great effort to make it clear that he was a part of the team." Terry advised Koop that he "should make a concerted effort to save the PHS as a proud team. ...I hope that you can help to preserve the tradition and integrity of the Public Health Service."[17] Dr. Koop soon began wearing the uniform of the Surgeon General on a regular basis in a symbolic effort to project authority and raise the public profile of the Corps. This was important, because for some time Surgeons General preferred a business suit befitting their position as executive office physician-leaders; the Surgeon General's uniform was typically reserved for ceremonial events. Similarly, the uniform had fallen out of favor and was seldom worn by PHS officers at agencies such as CDC and NIH because, as Koop aptly noted, they "came to view themselves more as agency personnel and less as Commissioned Corps officers."[1]

The Commissioned Corps was periodically confronted by presidential administrations, members of Congress, and by the Office of Management and Budget (OMB) as being an anachronism, contending that its work could be performed by civilian employees. The fact that PHS officers often functioned alongside Civil Service employees in similar positions bolstered that assertion. Some officials were of the belief that the Corps was also languishing and not sustaining its leadership role in public health, even though PHS officers had distinguished themselves at the forefront of health care delivery, preventive services, disease surveillance, regulatory work, and research for 100 years. In 1981, the Omnibus Budget Reconciliation Act had a very significant impact on the Corps – it repealed the health care entitlement for merchant seamen and led to closure of the system of PHS Marine Hospitals and Clinics. Then in November 1982, OMB attempted to strip the Assistant Secretary for Health, Edward Brandt, of his authority over the Public Health Service and abolish the PHS Commissioned Corps.[18] The OMB effort failed, but Dr. Koop realized that he needed to do all he could to protect the Commissioned Corps, "...to save this little-known jewel in the American crown." To counter the ongoing diminution of the Corps and take action to improve Corps effectiveness and restore its prominence, Surgeon General Koop initiated a comprehensive revitalization of the Commissioned Corps in April 1987. The plan had goals formulated by working groups with four key elements:

- Reorganization and direct supervision of the Division of Commissioned Personnel, to ensure that promotion and professional development opportunities are administered in a scrupulously objective and fair way.

- Provision of career tracks for the eleven professional categories, to enhance opportunities for professional development within the PHS and thus increase retention and professional growth.
- Institution of specific programs within career tracks for career development and mobility, with periodic changes in the duty assignments and stations to permit officers to have a variety of experiences.
- Enhancement of the Corps image by wearing the PHS uniform, which embodies the concept that being a commissioned officer is a unique and proud role in the medical, public health and scientific communities.

A concerted effort was made to expand the Commissioned Officer Student Training and Extern Program (COSTEP) and improve recruitment of junior officers to strengthen the Corps. Recruitment efforts were also directed toward increasing the number of minorities and women, and a PHS ready reserve was created to allow inactive reserve officers to serve in times of need. The PHS also developed an emergency readiness capability through use of disaster mobilization teams. Dr. Koop directed that PHS officers were to wear the appropriate uniform daily, effective May 1, 1987. However, due to significant resistance, each agency was allowed to set its own uniform requirements.[19]

The credibility of the PHS Commissioned Corps and its public health mission had been recaptured, and Koop attributed the success of the revitalization initiative to the strong support and involvement of HHS Secretary Otis R. Bowen and his chief of staff Thomas Burke, Assistant Secretary for Health Robert E. Windom, and Koop's own chief of staff Edward D. Martin, described by Koop as the "quintessential commissioned officer who deserves the major credit."[1] Dr. Martin went on to serve as the Deputy Assistant Secretary of Defense, Professional Affairs and Quality Assurance, and Acting Assistant Secretary of Defense for Health Affairs; he held the rank of Rear Admiral upon retirement in April 1998. After years of challenge by OMB Surgeon General Koop and the Commissioned Corps finally garnered the support of the Office of Management and Budget.

Edward D. Martin

On December 23, 1988, President Ronald Reagan proclaimed January 4, 1989, as *National Commissioned Corps of the Public Health Service Centennial Day* (Proclamation 5926). On the occasion of the Centennial, Koop hailed the turnaround by noting OMB's congratulations on the progress made and its expression of continuing support for the revitalization initiative. The revitalization effort was a milestone event in the history of the Corps. However, it would be the first of several subsequent initiatives to revitalize the institution and activities of the PHS Commissioned Corps.[1,20,21]

> ## *In Their Words*
>
> ### by RADM (Ret.) Edward D. Martin
>
> On a regular basis, the OMB had sought major reductions in Corps strength or outright dissolution of the Commissioned Corps. Many senior officials thought the most recent OMB proposal to abolish the Corps would be successful as a result of the closure of the PHS Hospitals and Clinics and the attendant, very significant reduction in personnel. Dr. Koop and those of us in leadership positions viewed this as an existential threat that would be detrimental not only to the Corps, but to public health generally. With the support of Secretary Bowen and his Chief of Staff Tom Burke, the Commissioned Corps personnel office was moved to the Office of the Surgeon General and Dr. Koop took great personal interest in revitalizing the Commissioned Corps. As his Chief of Staff, Dr. Koop asked me to focus my attention on the revitalization initiative. We recognized that the effort needed to be assertive and comprehensive in scope, with an emphasis on (re-)instilling officership as critical to the Corps' viability. There were many differing viewpoints within the PHS and Corps regarding actions to be taken, so the effort was not easy at all. The key to its eventual success was largely the great respect that Dr. Koop had generated within the Public Health Service and the strong support of Assistant Secretary Robert Windom and most Agency heads, including Drs. Jim Mason, Frank Young and David Sundwall. Dr. Koop held town hall meetings in the agencies and elicited the active participation of Professional Advisory Committees and a large number of officers. Promotion and recruitment systems were changed significantly, and emergency response and disaster capabilities were substantially increased with hundreds of officers training in field conditions for natural disasters. Many prior criticisms of the Commissioned Corps were effectively addressed and as a result the OMB proposals were not implemented or legislated. There is little question in my mind that without Dr. Koop's efforts and the active support he elicited from PHS leadership and officers themselves that the OMB proposals would have been effected.

ASSISTANT SECRETARY FOR HEALTH, ADMIRAL RANK

Dr. James O. Mason, MD, DrPH, was sworn in as the Assistant Secretary for Health (ASH), HHS, April 21, 1989. RADM Mason had served as Director of the CDC since 1983. On July 14, 1989, he was designated the Acting Surgeon General while Dr. Koop was on terminal leave. Surgeons General hold the three-star rank of Vice Admiral. To accommodate Dr. Mason as a superior officer to the Surgeon General, a provision was included in the Vaccine and Immunization Amendments of 1990, Section 5, that the Public Health Service Act was amended to insert the following:

> During the period of appointment to the position of Assistant Secretary for Health, a commissioned officer of the Public Health Service shall have the grade corresponding to the grade of General of the Army.

That has opened the door for a *non*-PHS officer political appointee to become the ASH with the corresponding rank of PHS Admiral. That situation also presents a potential conflict with the requirement that uniformed personnel not engage in political activities. Along with appointing civilian physicians as Surgeon General, this has been a matter of general concern.[22,23]

PHS Physician Assistants

Physician assistants (PAs) are a vitally important component of the healthcare team where clinical care is rendered. PAs provide much of the direct patient care within the Bureau of Prisons (BOP), ICE Health Service Corps, Indian Health Service, U.S. Coast Guard, and elsewhere within the sphere of PHS activities. With the support of RADM Kenneth P. Moritsugu, physician assistants entered and were first commissioned in the PHS Commissioned Corps in 1989. Donald H. Gabbert, Richard C. Vause, Jr., DHSc (first Chief PA, BOP), and James Portt were the first to achieve promotions to the rank of Captain in 1998.[24] RADM Michael R. Milner, DHSc, helped advance the role of PAs in the Corps.

Michael R. Milner

A certified PA (PA-C), he transferred from the U.S. Air Force to the PHS in 1989, soon becoming Chief PA Consultant to the Director of the Indian Health Service, where he advocated for the increased use of physician assistants. From 2006 to 2010, RADM Milner served as Chief Professional Officer (CPO) of the Health Services Officer Category, which encompasses the Physician Assistant Group. Another PA, RADM Epifanio "Epi" Elizondo, PhD, served in the U.S. Navy, Army, and Air Force prior to joining the PHS. His distinguished career included serving as Chief PA in BOP, and as CPO of the Health Services Officer Category from 2010 to 2016. Milner and Elizondo both served as Regional Health Administrators for HHS Region I and Region VI, respectively.

Epifanio Elizondo

MEDEX Program. CAPT Richard A. Smith, commissioned in the PHS in 1956, became Deputy Medical Director of the Peace Corps in 1964. He is widely recognized for founding the physician assistant profession. MEDEX (MEDical EXtension) is the term for the program he developed to educate non-physician providers, to expand primary care access in medically underserved communities. Smith created the first MEDEX PA program at the University of Washington in Seattle. From 1972 to 1981, he was detailed to the University of Hawaii where the MEDEX Group produced a 7,000 page MEDEX Primary Health Care Series that was a framework for expanding medical care in low resourced countries.[25,26]

Richard A. Smith

GLOBAL ERADICATION OF POLIO

In 1988, the World Health Assembly adopted a resolution calling for the global eradication of polio by the year 2000. It marked the launch of the Global Polio Eradication Initiative, with the involvement of the World Health Organization, United Nations Children's Fund, the CDC, Rotary International, the Gates Foundation, the Global Alliance for Vaccines and Immunizations, and national governments. By 2018, wild poliovirus was eradicated worldwide, with Afghanistan and Pakistan being the only countries where the disease was still endemic. From 2011 to 2018, over 650 CDC staff supported global polio eradication efforts, of which 208 personnel including many PHS officers completed 2,120 field deployments worldwide.[27] PHS medical officer Jon K. Andrus, for example, of CDC's Epidemic Intelligence Service received the Distinguished Service Medal for his work in eradicating polio in Southeast Asia. He later served as a Deputy Director of the Pan American Health Organization.

REAPPOINTMENT AND DEPARTURE

Surgeon General Koop's actions on important health-related issues earned him the respect of many federal officials and those outside the government. Dr. Koop was reappointed to a second term by President Reagan in October 1985, and became a leading spokesperson for the Department. He aspired to become the next Secretary of HHS with the arrival of the George H.W. Bush administration in January 1989. Instead, Bush selected Louis Sullivan for HHS Secretary, and Koop completed his term of office on October 1, 1989.[8]

CHRONOLOGY • 1981–1989
SG C. Everett Koop, January 1982–October 1989

1981 *Omnibus Budget Reconciliation Act of 1981*. Closes PHS hospitals and clinics and consolidates PHS programs and budgets into block grants to the states.

1982 Surgeon General Koop issues an advisory against the use of salicylates (aspirin) for children with influenza or chickenpox. *(See Chapter Nine.)*

1983 Human immunodeficiency virus is identified as the causative agent of AIDS.

1986 Surgeon General's report, *The Health Consequences of Involuntary Smoking*, concludes that secondhand smoke is a cause of disease.

1987 Revitalization of the PHS Commissioned Corps is initiated by SG Koop to restore the Corps' prominence and leadership role in public health.

1988 Surgeon General's report, *The Health Consequences of Smoking: Nicotine Addiction*, concludes that nicotine in tobacco causes addiction.

1988 Surgeon General's brochure, *Understanding AIDS: A Message from the Surgeon General*, is sent to 107 million households in the U.S.

1988 Indian Health Service, which had been a Bureau, is elevated to Agency status within the Public Health Service. *(See Chapter Seven.)*

CHAPTER TWELVE

NEW CHALLENGES, COMMOTION & QUIESCENCE
1989 to 1998

THE GEORGE H.W. BUSH ADMINISTRATION wanted a surgeon general who was pro-life, yet lower profile than C. Everett Koop. Candidates for high level positions, including Surgeon General, were interviewed on a variety of issues to ensure consistency of their views with administration policies. Dr. Antonia C. Novello was a Public Health Service Commissioned Corps officer known to Louis W. Sullivan, Secretary of Health and Human Services. Sullivan wanted to increase diversity within the Department and it was a "driving force" in his consideration of Novello for the Surgeon General post.[1,2] On October 17, 1989, Dr. Novello was nominated for the position of U.S. Surgeon General. She would make history as the first woman and first Hispanic person to hold the office of Surgeon General, beginning her tenure on March 9, 1990. Born in Fajardo, Puerto Rico, Dr. Novello received her medical degree from the University of Puerto Rico in 1970. She completed an internship and residency in pediatrics at the University of Michigan Medical Center and held fellowships in pediatric nephrology at the University of Michigan and Georgetown University in Washington, DC. After completing two years in private practice, Novello joined the PHS Commissioned

Antonia C. Novello

Corps in 1978, her first assignment being at the National Institute of Arthritis, Metabolism and Digestive Diseases, National Institutes of Health. While at NIH, Novello earned an MPH degree from John Hopkins School of Hygiene and Public Health in 1982. She was also detailed to the Senate Committee on Labor and Human Resources where she helped draft legislation for the National Organ Transplant Act of 1984. Novello progressed through several positions at NIH, rising to Deputy Director of the National Institute of Child Health and Human Development (NICHD) in 1986. In addition, she served as the coordinator for AIDS research at the NICHD from September 1987, developing a special interest in pediatric AIDS.

From 1989 through 1997, there were few serious challenges of an administrative or public health nature that incumbent Surgeons General needed to address. Antonia Novello noted during her swearing-in ceremony that her motto as Surgeon General would be "good science and good sense." Soon after, she indicated that as Surgeon General, unlike Dr. Koop, the role of spokesperson on health issues for the administration would be a shared responsibility with physicians HHS Secretary Louis Sullivan and Assistant Secretary for Health James O. Mason. She continued that health matters, like tobacco, "will not have a person (as spokesman), it will have the triad, the three of us."[3] During her tenure she focused on an array of health issues that were also addressed in a series of articles entitled *From the Surgeon General, US Public Health Service*, published from 1991 to 1993 in the *Journal of the American Medical Association*.

TOBACCO USE

The adverse health effects of smoking cigarettes continued to be of foremost concern, causing an estimated 400,000 deaths yearly. Smoking was a main issue for Surgeon General Novello who would carry on the custom of issuing official reports on the topic, but also for the Secretary of HHS. Louis Sullivan was an ardent, anti-tobacco crusader and James Mason was outspoken on the matter. Responding to the anti-smoking coalition and to a letter sent by Sullivan, the R.J. Reynolds Tobacco Company announced in January 1990 that it was halting its planned marketing of Uptown, a new brand of menthol cigarettes targeted to Black people. Sullivan made HHS buildings smoke-free, and he tried to ban cigarettes from vending machines and stop tobacco industry sponsorship of sporting events. On November 21, 1989, a notable legislative measure was enactment of the Department of Transportation Appropriations Act of 1990 (Public Law 101-164), which included a permanent smoking ban on all domestic airline flights (except to Alaska and Hawaii).

For her part, Dr. Novello issued two Surgeon General reports on smoking and health. *The Health Benefits of Smoking Cessation: A Report of the Surgeon General, 1990*,[4] dealt with the evidence-based determination that smoking cessation had immediate and important health benefits for men and women of all ages. The subsequent report, *Smoking and Health in the Americas*,[5] prepared by the Centers for Disease Control and Prevention (CDC) in cooperation with the Pan American Health Organization, explored the epidemiologic, economic and social issues of tobacco use in the countries of Latin America and the Caribbean. It noted the high prevalence of smoking among young people, the substantial number of women that had begun smoking in recent years and the portent of an epidemic of smoking-related illness, with about 100,000 deaths annually in Latin America and the Caribbean.

Surgeon General Novello fought tobacco industry advertising aimed at children. This was particularly so with regard to the R.J. Reynolds Company advertisements for Camel cigarettes that featured the cartoon character "Old Joe Camel," first introduced in 1988. In 1991, a study showed that 91 percent of six-year olds associated Joe Camel with a picture of a cigarette.[6] On March 9, 1992, Novello joined Dr. James S. Todd, Executive Vice President of the American Medical Association (AMA), to berate the use of Joe Camel, calling on retailers to remove Joe Camel signs from their stores and urging publications to refuse to run such ads. Three months later Dr. Novello, along with AMA leaders and 200 school children, paraded through downtown Chicago to protest the use of Joe Camel in cigarette ads.  Said Novello afterwards, "We might not succeed today or in our lifetime, but there's momentum growing." Yet, R.J. Reynolds continued to market its cigarette with Joe Camel.[7,8] Despite ongoing denials by the company, internal documents released in January 1998 indicated that R.J. Reynolds' advertising strategy was meant to appeal to youth as early as 14 years of age.[9]

Following the lead of the 1986 Surgeon General Report entitled *The Health Consequences of Using Smokeless Tobacco*, Surgeon General Novello and Secretary Sullivan addressed the issue of smokeless tobacco (spit tobacco – snuff and chewing tobacco), the use of which can cause oral cancer. Sullivan delivered the keynote address at the First International Conference on Smokeless Tobacco, held April 10-13, 1991. He stated that it was "immoral" to condone the promotion of products that, when used as intended, caused disability and death, and he called upon individuals and organizations to join the effort to stop the promotion of such products.[10] In December 1992, a report requested by Surgeon General Novello was released by the HHS Office of Inspector General entitled *Spit Tobacco and Youth*,[11] which detailed the usage of spit tobacco by youth – its prevalence and patterns of use, health effects, influences on its use, product promotion and sales, regulation, and educational efforts. The report found that nearly 20 percent of male high school students in 1991 had used smokeless tobacco in the prior 30 days.

While the HHS anti-tobacco stance was appropriate for this nation, with certain limits, it did not translate into the administration's policy toward U.S. exports of cigarettes. In April 1990, in a keynote address at the World Conference on Tobacco and Health in Perth, Australia, HHS Assistant Secretary for Health Mason called it "unconscionable" for U.S. cigarette companies "to be peddling their poison abroad." Yet when summoned by U.S. Representative Henry Waxman to repeat his comments at a Congressional hearing, Mason's appearance was canceled, with HHS explaining it was inappropriate to discuss trade matters. It was evident the Bush presidency would not interfere with

U.S. cigarette companies profiting from overseas markets.[12] In September 1990, Novello made the candid remark at a press conference that "For me to talk about it would be almost disrespectful of my [political] party."[4,13] While political considerations were likely factored into some of the decisions of her predecessors, such a public statement could weaken a Surgeon General as a "truth to power" spokesperson who places science above politics on matters of public health.

INITIATIVES

Healthy Children Ready to Learn

Dr. Novello took an active interest in advocating for children's health. Her *Healthy Children Ready to Learn* initiative began with the premise that all children have a right to be healthy, which was foundational to the concept that health is essential to optimum education. The idea was to correlate activities with the National Education Goals and the related National Health Promotion and Disease Prevention Objectives in *Healthy People 2000*. The first National Education goal, "By the year 2000, all children in America will start school ready to learn," coupled with relevant National Health Promotion objectives, was the lead basis of the approach to advance progress toward school readiness, focus attention and resources on needed programs and services, and thus help achieve the goal of children arriving at school well nourished and ready to learn.[14] A successful *Surgeon General's Conference on Healthy Children Ready to Learn: The Critical Role of Parents*, was held in February 1992, providing a framework for state and local efforts in later years, to include conceptual approaches for responding to a growing childhood obesity epidemic.[15]

Hispanic-Latino Health Initiative

Hispanic-Latino Americans are among the fastest growing ethnic groups in the U.S. and Surgeon General Novello wanted to address the health-related disparities affecting this population through her National Hispanic-Latino Health Initiative. She organized the first workshop on Hispanic health, with a threefold purpose: (1) to summarize the health needs, concerns and priorities of Hispanics-Latinos; (2) to develop effective and realistic implementation strategies for meeting those needs; and (3) to provide a clear focus for coordinating HHS efforts with those of Hispanic-Latino communities nationwide. Novello convened a national conference in September 1992, a series of regional health meetings in five major cities and a culminating meeting of the executive planning committee. Key areas of concern included improved access to health care, improved data collection strategies, development of a research agenda, increased representation in the health professions and increased community-based health promotion and disease prevention activities. The conference produced a delineation of issues and strategies to respond to each issue.[16,17]

OTHER ISSUES

Underage Drinking

Novello took on the issue of underage drinking, requesting the HHS Inspector General (IG) to review the issue to better understand the range of factors that influence alcohol use among American youth. The results were published in 1991 and 1992 in a series of eight reports entitled *Youth and Alcohol*, each with a subtitle relevant to a specific topic. For two reports – *A National Survey: Drinking Habits, Access, Attitudes, and Knowledge*, and, *Do They Know What They're Drinking?* – the IG's interviews of junior and senior high school students revealed disturbing facts, such as 8 million of the nation's 20.7 million 7th to 12th graders in 1990 drank weekly. In addition to advocating for more prevention and enforcement, the Surgeon General was critical of alcohol beverage industry advertisements that appealed to youth.

Organ Donation, Immunization, Violence

Antonia Novello focused on the shortfall in the supply of donor organs and, to this end, a Surgeon General's Workshop on Increasing Organ Donation was held in July 1991 to identify strategies for boosting donations. Novello also worked with organizations to promote immunization of children. In July 1991, the Surgeon General joined with the American Academy of Pediatrics to launch a nationwide vaccination awareness campaign in response to a surge in measles cases and the fact that many children were not fully immunized. She was outspoken on the need to address issues related to an epidemic of violence in society. She called upon physicians to screen patients for domestic violence and help form community coalitions to respond to such problems.

HURRICANE ANDREW

On August 24, 1992, Hurricane Andrew made landfall in Southern Florida as a Category 5 storm. It was the most destructive hurricane to ever hit Florida in terms of structural damage. In conjunction with the HHS Office of Emergency Preparedness, a PHS Medical Support Unit was deployed prior to the storm making landfall, and multiple Disaster Medical Assistance Teams were activated after landfall. PHS officers were deployed to Florida to provide health and medical services during the recovery effort.[18,19]

HIV/ACQUIRED IMMUNODEFICIENCY SYNDROME

The HIV/AIDS pandemic is among the more significant of biomedical episodes in public health history. Dr. Novello continued the role of the Surgeon General as a principal educator about AIDS and how to protect against acquiring the disease. She had a particular interest in women and children with HIV infection, and the need for empowerment and education of women to help prevent spread of the disease to themselves and their offspring. In 1992, Dr. Novello issued a 30-page informational pamphlet entitled *Surgeon General's Report to the American Public on HIV Infection and AIDS*, which provided a comprehensive review about the disease.[20]

In 1984, Dr. Anthony S. Fauci became the Director of the National Institute of Allergy and Infectious Diseases, NIH. As a recognized national authority, he became the lead federal spokesperson on the HIV/AIDS epidemic for decades, something that could be viewed as opportune for Surgeon General Novello and her successors. While still able to draw attention to public health issues surrounding HIV/AIDS, Surgeons General were spared the unrelenting scrutiny of patients with HIV, activist groups, politicians, legislators, healthcare providers and the scientific community that Fauci endured.

On November 4, 1988, President Reagan signed the Health Omnibus Programs Extension (HOPE) Act,[21] which authorized federal funds for AIDS prevention, education, testing and research. It created the National Commission on AIDS, and the Office of AIDS Research, NIH, with Dr. Fauci becoming its first director until 1994 while also serving as NIAID Director. In 1989, Fauci endorsed the concept of a "parallel track" whereby HIV-positive persons not enrolled in clinical trials could have access to investigational drugs. RADM Frank E. Young, then FDA Commissioner, backed Fauci and implemented the policy.[22] NIAID research led to the development of effective antiretroviral drugs to treat and prevent HIV/AIDS, and it continued to pursue other therapies and a vaccine. Over the years, Dr. Fauci developed trusting relationships with Congressional leaders and presidents, including Senator Edward Kennedy, Presidents George H.W. and George W. Bush, Bill Clinton and Barack Obama. Progression of the AIDS epidemic to include the broader heterosexual population in this nation and elsewhere in the world led President George W. Bush in 2003 to create the President's Emergency Plan for AIDS Relief (PEPFAR) to control the HIV pandemic globally, of which Dr. Fauci was a principal architect. With reauthorizations in 2008, 2013 and 2018, total program funding had reached over $110 billion.[23] Since its inception, the program is credited with saving over 25 million lives and preventing millions of HIV infections in more than 50 countries.

Frank E. Young

GULF WAR

On August 2, 1990, Iraq invaded the country of Kuwait resulting in a seven-month Iraqi military occupation of that country. Iraq's refusal to withdraw from Kuwait led to a United Nations-authorized coalition of military forces from 35 nations, led by the United States, to expel Iraqi troops from Kuwait.

Known as the first Gulf War, it was comprised of Operation Desert Shield for the coalition troop buildup and Operation Desert Storm for its combat phase, culminating with the expulsion of Iraqi troops by February 28, 1991. While retreating from Kuwait, the Iraqi military set fire to about 700 Kuwaiti oil wells, the last of which was not extinguished until November 1991, causing significant regional air pollution. The U.S. Environmental Protection Agency (EPA) was given lead responsibility to address the impact of oil spills and the oil well fires in Kuwait, and it asked the PHS to prepare a plan with respect to health surveillance and risk assessment issues, and strategies and approaches to address the possible adverse health effects associated with the oil fires in Kuwait. Coordinated by RADM Frank E. Young, then Deputy Assistant Secretary for Health, Science and the Environment, an HHS/PHS *Plan of Action for Protecting Public Health* was produced by the interagency Kuwaiti Task Force on May 31, 1991. Numerous PHS officers were involved in an array of activities prior to, during and after the war, both in the U.S. and in Kuwait. The FDA made arrangement for the use of unapproved drugs and biologics needed by U.S. Forces. PHS personnel deployed to the Persian Gulf to assess hazards, plan appropriate public health measures, provide direct patient care, and assist with post-war cleanup. PHS clinicians conducted medical screening of U.S. citizens returning from Iraq, and PHS medical personnel provided staffing support at the National Naval Medical Center to cover for military staff deployed to the Middle East. The Kuwaiti mission included Agency for Toxic Substances and Disease Registry PHS medical officer CAPT John S.

CDR Seligman *(r)* at a U.S. Marine Corps camp in Saudi Arabia. He conducted field investigations within the military and among civilians on the health impact of smoke from the oil fires.

Andrews, assigned to the U.S. Army 352nd Civil Affairs Command in Saudi Arabia and Kuwait to assist in restoring Kuwaiti public health services; CDR (later RADM) Paul J. Seligman, NIOSH medical epidemiologist who was on the EPA investigative team deployed to the Gulf region to assess the health impact of the oil fires on the civilian and military populations; and CDR Ruth A. Etzel who, in collaboration with the World Health Organization, worked with the Kuwaiti government to set up a surveillance system to monitor the adverse health effects of the oil fires. All subsequently testified at Congressional hearings on the environmental impact of the Gulf War.[24,25]

> ## *In Their Words*
> ### by RADM (Ret.) Paul J. Seligman
>
> Like all Americans, I had watched intently as the events in the Middle East unfolded in late 1990 and early 1991. Before the ground invasion by coalition forces that rapidly drove Iraqi forces from Kuwait, the Office of the Surgeon General was actively engaged in a planning effort that involved multiple PHS agencies, but no one had anticipated the oil fires. The imperative was clear – to determine whether the smoke presented an immediate and potentially long-term health risk to coalition forces in Kuwait and to the civilian population. Within 72 hours after the reports of the fires, I was on a plane to Dulles airport to rendezvous with a team from the EPA, the National Weather Service and the National Institute of Environmental Health Sciences for a flight to Riyadh. Once in Saudi Arabia, we were met by U.S. Embassy staff and after a few days of preparation in Dhahran headed up the coast by road to Kuwait City in a convoy with the returning U.S. Ambassador. Imagine my delight when I arrived in Kuwait to be greeted by my CDC colleague, CAPT John Andrews. I completed interviews with medical corpsmen and civilian emergency room staff and conducted record reviews that evidenced respiratory symptoms and ocular irritation from smoke exposure, but no serious illness. In collaboration with Navy Environmental Preventive Medicine Unit 2, we conducted a rapid survey of self-reported health complaints among nearly 3,000 U.S. Marines. The air monitoring team found levels of sulfur dioxide, nitrogen dioxide and hydrogen sulfide that were well below harmful thresholds, and widely varying levels of respirable particulates against a background of sand and dust storms in the country. The increased symptoms of upper respiratory irritation we found were consistent with the environmental air sampling results. I had an opportunity to brief Senators Joseph Lieberman and John Chafee at the Kuwait airport and to testify before them in Congress two weeks later. Being able to rapidly deploy with a multidisciplinary team, with support from the military and State Department and an incredibly responsive team at the CDC, made for an extraordinarily successful, impactful mission. I returned home with great satisfaction, knowing that we had addressed an important public health question, and with heartfelt appreciation for military families and what they go through when their loved ones are deployed overseas.

NOVELLO DEPARTURE

Surgeon General Antonia Novello brought attention to a range of health issues and introduced neglected issues into public and professional discourse. However, in November 1992, president elect William J. Clinton wanted to select his own Surgeon General and so Novello's tenure came to an early end in June 1993. Nonetheless, Surgeon General Antonia Novello advanced science-based understanding about new areas of public health importance.

Limits to Independence

A NEW SURGEON GENERAL WOULD BE CHOSEN by President William J. "Bill" Clinton, reverting to the relatively recent practice of installing political appointees in the position. His choice was Dr. M. Joycelyn Elders, Director of the Arkansas Department of Health, who was appointed by then-Governor Clinton in 1987. Joycelyn Elders had a compelling record of personal accomplishment. She received a B.A. in biology in 1952, worked as a nurse's aide at the Veterans Administration Hospital in Milwaukee, and joined the Army in 1953. During her 3-year tour in the Army, she trained as a physical therapist. She then attended the University of Arkansas Medical School, receiving her MD degree in 1960. After completing an internship and pediatrics residency, Dr. Elders earned a master's degree in biochemistry in 1967. She became an Assistant Professor of Pediatrics at the University of Arkansas Medical Center, achieving full professorship in 1976 and specializing in pediatric endocrinology. During her term of office at the Arkansas Department of Health, Elders successfully lobbied for a mandated K–12 curriculum that included sex education and substance abuse prevention programs, and she pushed for school-based health clinics and making contraception available to students. By 1992, she improved childhood health screenings with a nearly doubled rate of immunizations and expanded the state's prenatal care program. She became President of the Association of State and Territorial Health Officers in 1992.[26]

M. Joycelyn Elders was sworn in as Surgeon General on September 8, 1993, becoming the first African American to hold the position. As Surgeon General, Elders worked on many of the same issues that she promoted in Arkansas. She was a strong advocate for comprehensive sex education and distribution of contraceptives in schools, getting school-based health clinics placed in underserved areas, and making family planning available to all women. She also suggested that drug legalization was an issue that should be studied, a viewpoint held by others in public health, but which the White House immediately distanced itself from. In February 1994, Dr. Elders and five former Surgeons General – Drs. Novello, Koop, Richmond, Ehrlich and Steinfeld – wrote to Senator Edward Kennedy expressing their opposition to "any proposed federal policy that would mandate written parental consent prior to counselling or providing condoms or other contraceptive aides to unemancipated minors," fearing it would reduce the hope of reaching teenagers most at risk for AIDS and unintended pregnancies.[27]

M. Joycelyn Elders

Surgeon General Elders also spoke on issues that had become associated with the Surgeon General – AIDS and the adverse health effects of tobacco use. In March 1994, the Surgeon General's Report on *Preventing Tobacco Use Among Young People* was released, marking the first time that the focus was on young people.[28] The report noted that about one-third of the nation's high school students were cigarette smokers or used smokeless tobacco, and almost all tobacco use begins by the time people graduate from high school. Nicotine addiction further ensured that adolescent smokers would regularly use tobacco as adults and lead to eventual health problems; thus, preventing tobacco use among young people was critical to end the epidemic in the U.S. Joycelyn Elders was an excellent speaker who conveyed her message with authority and passion, yet often with controversy. She was in high demand, traveling across the country to speak at conferences, colleges, schools and other forums. She had many supporters who admired her relentless public health stances, as she spoke forthrightly and publicly about abortion rights and the need for contraceptive use. There were, as well, detractors who did not agree with her outspoken positions and messaging that they deemed irresponsible. On the subject of reproductive rights, she stated that we need to "get over this love affair with the fetus and start worrying about children." Elders said that she was overbearing only to people who needed such an approach, and that "You've got to get people's attention before you can achieve change."[29] While HHS officials did not hinder Elders with respect to her speaking engagements, she was repeatedly cautioned by top officials to be more discreet in her public remarks,[30] amidst conservative politicians who increasingly called for Elders to resign. On December 1, 1994, she spoke at a United Nations-sponsored World AIDS Day conference. During a panel discussion, Elders made a controversial remark about sex education that promptly resulted in the loss of White House support, and President Clinton asked for her resignation. After only 15 months in the position of Surgeon General, her last day in office was December 31, 1994. Dr. Elders brought considerable fervor to her role as Surgeon General, but her curtailed tenure contributed to a lack of substantive programmatic achievements while in office.

Acting SG, Quiescence

PRESIDENT BILL CLINTON appointed Rear Admiral Audrey F. Manley to serve as Acting Surgeon General, a position that she held from January 1, 1995 until June 30, 1997. Dr. Manley was serving as the HHS Deputy Assistant Secretary for Health at the time of appointment. Manley received her medical degree from Meharry Medical College in 1959, with a residency at Chicago's Cook

County Children's Hospital. She held faculty appointments at the Universities of Illinois, Chicago, and California, moving to Atlanta in 1970. She was chief of medical services at Grady Memorial Hospital Family Planning Clinic until 1976, when she joined the U.S. Public Health Service. Manley studied sickle cell and other genetic diseases at the Health Resources and Services Administration and earned an MPH degree from Johns Hopkins University in 1987. In 1988, RADM Manley became Director of the National Health Service Corps, and Deputy Assistant Secretary for Health in 1989. In 1994, Manley was appointed the Deputy Surgeon General and Acting Deputy Assistant Secretary for Minority Health. It was evident that the Clinton administration wanted a Surgeon General who was an experienced HHS official and a "known quantity," who would avoid controversy. Surgeon General Manley fulfilled that expectation – she was a very capable administrator and exceptional leader who carried out the duties of the office competently and without fanfare. Two things were predominant during Manley's tenure. On July 11, 1996, *Physical Activity and Health: A Report of the Surgeon General*[31] was released at the White House, concluding that regular moderate physical activity can substantially reduce the risk of developing heart disease, hyperten-

Audrey F. Manley

Vice President Al Gore introduces the Surgeon General's Report on *Physical Activity and Health*, 1996.

[National Library of Medicine]

sion, colon cancer, and diabetes. Dr. Manley noted that the event was the major highlight that year, which included Vice President and Mrs. Al Gore, HHS Secretary Donna Shalala, Assistant Secretary for Health Dr. Philip Lee, and CDC Director Dr. David Satcher.[32] *(Note: Philip R. Lee, who previously served under President Lyndon Johnson, returned to his former position as HHS Assistant Secretary for Health under President Clinton.)*

GAO Report

On May 15, 1996, the General Accounting Office (GAO) released a report entitled *Issues on the Need for the Public Health Service's Commissioned Corps*.[33] The report questioned the need for a commissioned corps with military-like pay and benefits, and the higher cost of Corps members relative to civilian employees performing similar duties. The HHS Office of the Inspector General response to the draft report delineated the value of the Corps, while noting that, counter to GAO claims, no substantial cost savings would be realized if Corps functions were civilianized. The GAO report was widely discredited, but nevertheless was used again in 2018 as the basis for an Office of Management and Budget proposal to substantially reduce Corps strength.

SECOND ACTING SG

Dr. Manley was selected as the 8th president of Spelman College in Atlanta, Georgia, effective July 1, 1997. Upon her departure from the Public Health Service, RADM J. Jarrett Clinton was designated the Acting Surgeon General while serving as Acting Deputy Assistant Secretary for Health, HHS. He brought an extensive background in agency leadership, including serving as the Health Administrator of Region IV and Administrator of the Agency for Health Care Policy and Research. He also served as the Deputy Assistant Secretary of Defense for Professional Affairs; afterwards, from 2000 to 2001, he was the Assistant Secretary of Defense for Health Affairs. A career PHS officer, Dr. Clinton served ably until the next Surgeon General was confirmed in February 1998.[34]

J. Jarrett Clinton

CHRONOLOGY • 1989–1998

SG Antonia C. Novello, March 1990–June 1993
SG M. Joycelyn Elders, September 1993–December 1994
Acting SG Audrey F. Manley, January 1995–June 1997
Acting SG J. Jarrett Clinton, July 1997–February 1998

1991 PHS officers deploy to Kuwait and Saudi Arabia in aftermath of the Gulf War.
1991 HHS Inspector General releases a series of eight reports entitled *Youth and Alcohol*, which included a national survey of high school students.
1992 Surgeon General Novello issues a 30-page pamphlet entitled the *Surgeon General's Report to the American Public on HIV Infection and AIDS*.
1992 PHS officers deploy to Florida in response to Hurricane Andrew.
1992 HHS Office of Inspector General releases report *Spit Tobacco and Youth*, which details the status of youth use of spit tobacco.
1994 Release of first-ever Surgeon General's Report on *Preventing Tobacco Use Among Young People*.
1996 GAO releases report questioning the value of the PHS Commissioned Corps.
1998 HHS–Department of Agriculture agreement to detail PHS officers to the Food Safety and Inspection Service; number of officers were increased in 2003.
2003 Creation of the President's Emergency Plan for AIDS Relief (PEPFAR).

CHAPTER THIRTEEN

CALM & COMPETENT, 9/11
1998 to 2002

ON SEPTEMBER 12, 1997, President Clinton nominated Dr. David Satcher, the Director of the Centers for Disease Control and Prevention, to become the next Surgeon General. It was noted that there was a very intense vetting process of Satcher by the White House, "To avoid any of the controversy we've experienced in the past."[1] Dr. Satcher was sworn in on February 13, 1998, serving the statutory four year term until February 12, 2002, as the 16th U.S. Surgeon General, and he was appointed to serve concurrently as the Department of Health and Human Services (HHS) Assistant Secretary for Health until January 20, 2001, when the George W. Bush administration took office. Drs. Satcher, Julius Richmond, and Steven Galson (Acting SG) were the only Surgeons General to also serve as Assistant Secretary for Health. Satcher graduated from Morehouse College in Atlanta in 1963. He received his MD and PhD in Cell Biology from Case Western Reserve University in 1970. Dr. Satcher joined the faculty of the UCLA Schools of Medicine and Public Health, and King-Drew Medical Center in Los Angeles where he developed the Department of Family Medicine. From 1979 to 1982, he served as professor and Chair of the Department of Community Medicine at Morehouse School of Medicine, and then became President of Meharry Medical College from 1982 to 1993. In 1993, he was appointed Director of the Centers for Disease Control and Prevention (CDC), prior to becoming Surgeon General.

David Satcher

Surgeon General Satcher focused on several issues of importance to the nation's health, foremost among them being racial and ethnic health disparities. Other priority issues included tobacco use, mental health, oral health, obesity, and sexual health. These issues were addressed through a series of national conferences, Surgeon General Reports and Calls to Action. Satcher released more reports than any other Surgeon General, reflecting his motivational interest in a range of topical issues combined with his ability, as Assistant Secretary for Health, to marshal more resources within HHS than would normally be available to the Surgeon General. He also addressed many other issues such as international tobacco control, polio eradication, tuberculosis, injury prevention, children's health, mental health, global HIV/AIDS and global health disparities. Like his predecessor Surgeon General Antonia Novello, these topics were often addressed through a series of articles entitled *From the Surgeon General, US Public Health Service*, published from 1999 to 2001 in the *Journal of the American Medical Association*.

Surgeon General's Reports

Tobacco Use

In his first year as Surgeon General, Satcher released the Report, *Tobacco Use Among U.S. Racial/Ethnic Minority Groups*.[2] This was the first report to focus on tobacco use among four racial/ethnic groups: African Americans, American Indians and Alaska Natives (AI/ANs), Asian Americans and Pacific Islanders, and Hispanics. Noting that these four groups were expected to become nearly half of the U.S. population by 2050, it provided comprehensive data on each group's patterns of tobacco use, adverse health effects, societal and psychosocial factors associated with such use, and interventional effectiveness. Cigarette smoking is a major cause of disease and death in each group, with African Americans bearing the greatest health burden. Among adults, AI/ANs have the highest prevalence of use, and among adolescents cigarette smoking increased in the 1990s among African Americans and Hispanics.

In 2000, *Reducing Tobacco Use: A Report of the Surgeon General* was released, which provides a review of several effective methods to reduce and prevent tobacco use. This report reviewed five approaches to reducing tobacco use: educational, clinical, regulatory, economic, and comprehensive.

In 2002, Satcher released *Women and Smoking: A Report of the Surgeon General*, a subject first described in a 1980 *Report* released by Surgeon General Richmond when an epidemic of tobacco-related diseases among women were first being seen. By 2002, the nation was in the midst of an epidemic of lung cancer in women, accounting for 25 percent of all cancer deaths and surpassing breast cancer as the leading cause of female cancer death. The report reviewed the health effects of smoking in women, including an increased risk of cardiovascular and pulmonary disease and adverse developmental effects in pregnancy, and includes smoking cessation and prevention interventions.

Mental Health

A formal proclamation was issued by President George H.W. Bush designating the decade beginning January 1990 as the "Decade of the Brain." In June 1999, a White House Conference on Mental Health was convened, followed that December by David Satcher's release of the first-ever *Surgeon General's Report on Mental Health*.[3] The landmark report conveyed that mental health is fundamental to overall health, that mental disorders are health conditions which have a major impact on individuals and families, and that effective treatments are available which can reduce the prevalence of mental disorders. It noted that one in five Americans experiences a mental disorder in the course of a year. The report reviewed the origins of such disorders, discussed the influence of the physical and social environment on mental health, and made recommendations for prevention and mental health promotion. Two other related reports were issued by Dr. Satcher. The *Report of the Surgeon General's Conference on Children's Mental Health*, published in 2000, had recommendations for a National Action Agenda on Children's Mental Health derived from a conference conference held on September 18 and 19, 2000. And, *Mental Health: Culture, Race and Ethnicity*, released August 2001, which was a supplement to the 1999 *Report on Mental Health* that discussed disparities in access to mental health services. The 21st Century Cures Act (Public Law 114-255) enacted December 13, 2016, incorporates relevant Acts to strengthen the prevention and treatment of mental illnesses and substance abuse, and it also created the position of HHS Assistant Secretary for Mental Health and Substance Use who directs the Substance Abuse and Mental Health Services Administration established in 1992.

Oral Health

Satcher brought a new issue to the forefront with release of *Oral Health in America: A Report of the Surgeon General*.[4] While effective means to maintain oral health had benefited most Americans, Dr. Satcher wrote a "silent epidemic" of dental and oral diseases was affecting some population groups, often significantly diminishing their quality of life. Those who suffered the worst oral health were among the poor of all ages, along with members of racial and ethnic minority groups, individuals who were medically compromised or who had disabilities. Two major themes of the report were that oral health is integral to general health and oral health involves being free of all disorders of the craniofacial complex. The report, which received wide media interest, called for a National Oral Health Plan to improve quality of life and eliminate disparities.

Youth Violence

The report, *Youth Violence: A Report of the Surgeon General* reviews research into the factors that increase the likelihood that young persons will become violent, and factors that seem to protect youth from viewing violence as acceptable. The report also reviews research on the effectiveness of specific strategies and programs designed to reduce and prevent youth violence.

SURGEON GENERAL'S CALLS TO ACTION

A Call to Action is a less substantial document than a Surgeon General's Report. It briefly discusses an important public health issue, summarizes available research, and provides a framework to encourage nationwide action to address the problem. Dr. Satcher created the Call to Action as a way to more rapidly produce and disseminate information on public health issues. During his tenure, Surgeon General Satcher released three Calls to Action.

Suicide Prevention

The *Surgeon General's Call to Action to Prevent Suicide*,[5] published in July 1999, followed a National Conference on Suicide Prevention in October 1998. The Report introduces a blueprint for addressing suicide – Awareness, Intervention, and Methodology (AIM)[6] – an approach that includes 15 key recommendations and forms the basis of a national strategy for suicide prevention.

Sexual Health

In 2001, *The Surgeon General's Call to Action to Promote Sexual Health and Responsible Sexual Behavior* was released. The report noted that programs which emphasize abstinence, but also cover methods of contraception, have either no effect or a delay on initiation of sexual activity. The report's conclusion was that providing school-based sexuality education is useful to ensure that youth have a basic understanding of sexuality. The report met with conservative opposition, with the President declaring that abstinence education was the most effective approach. As noted by former Surgeon General Koop, "The President's Press Secretary, Ari Fleischer, reported the President's frustration with Satcher, but no one talked about Satcher's frustration with the President."[7]

Obesity

The prevalence of a populace with excessive weight and obesity was beginning to reach epidemic proportions. The *Surgeon General's Call to Action to Prevent and Decrease Overweight and Obesity*[8] was released in 2001, stating that 300,000 deaths yearly were associated with obesity (CDC lowered the estimate in 2005 to 112,000 deaths[9]). Satcher said that failure to reverse the situation "could wipe out the gains we have made in areas such as heart disease, diabetes, several forms of cancer, and other chronic health problems." The report identified schools as central to preventing excess weight in children and recommended that all schools provide quality daily physical exercise programs and provide healthy food and beverage options. The *Call to Action* was meant to promote recognition of overweight and obesity as a major public health problem, identify effective interventions, assist Americans in balancing healthful eating with regular physical activity, and develop public-private partnerships to help implement the vision of a healthier lifestyle.

HEALTH DISPARITY

Surgeon General Satcher brought attention to the fact that racial, ethnic and socioeconomic health disparities pervaded the spectrum of health care throughout the nation. He frequently spoke and wrote about the issue and included information about the health impact of disparities in his Surgeon General Reports and Calls to Action. Satcher believed strongly that robust public health efforts were necessary to reduce and ultimately eliminate such disparities. In addition to lack of access to quality health care, other determinants of health included biologic and genetic characteristics of these populations, personal health-related behaviors, and environmental factors. A comprehensive, science-based approach was needed that, in the context of a balanced community health system, focused on health promotion, disease prevention and early detection activities, moving towards universal access to quality health care. In 1998, President Clinton and the Surgeon General announced a national initiative to eliminate racial/ethnic disparities in health status by 2010, which was incorporated as a goal of *Healthy People 2010*. Even after leaving office, Dr. Satcher continued efforts to achieve progress on the elimination of health disparities.[10,11]

DIVISION OF PERSONNEL REALIGNMENT AND TRAINING

It was evident by spring of 2000 that the array of PHS active duty strength by rank indicated a high retention rate of mid- and late-career officers, juxtaposed with decreased recruitment and retention in the lower grades, resulting in many more senior officers than junior officers. To address this and other personnel issues, the Division of Commissioned Personnel (DCP) initiated a realignment of its office with the intent to grow and expand the Commissioned Corps. As described by RADM R. Michael Davidson, Director of DCP, the office would "shift its mission from a personnel processing center to a human resource provider. We will place heavy emphasis on the recruitment, placement, and retention of officers in positions which contribute to public health and national security." Various organizational components were consolidated into two principal branches known as the Recruitment and Assignment Branch and the Officer Support Branch, with the latter focusing on recruitment and retention through service and support. In 2001, the Commissioned Officer Training Academy initiated a pilot 5-day version of the Basic Officer Training Course (BOTC) for officers called to duty after January 1, 2001, which would replace the former 2- and 3-day BOTCs. Beginning May 13, 2007, PHS officer training began a transition to a two-week Officer Basic Course (OBC), which all "Call to Active Duty" officers are required to attend. OBC provides comprehensive training that included officership, officer competency, career development, force readiness and deployment, and other essential areas.[12-15]

In Their Words
by RADM (Ret.) Kenneth P. Moritsugu

A critical role of the Surgeon General is to provide the best possible knowledge and science to the American people to help them to be safe, healthy, and happy. To accomplish this goal, the Surgeon General has an opportunity to speak "ex cathedra" on a number of topics through Surgeon General Reports, Calls to Action, reports of deliberations, conferences and workshops, and other platforms. As Deputy Surgeon General to two prolific generators of these communiques, and as Acting Surgeon General, I had a unique opportunity to identify priority topics, organize and arrange for the preparation of relevant publications, and execute their roll out and core messaging to achieve the best possible visibility and uptake of the issues. ADM David Satcher and VADM Richard Carmona and I generated over 29 Reports of the Surgeon General, Calls to Action, and Proceedings of workshops and meetings. Given the overarching responsibility of Surgeons General, there has never been a dearth of important topics to address. There were many suggestions, and it was incumbent on us to identify priority topics on which to focus our efforts. With the stature and impact of publications of the Surgeon General, interested participants to help produce these documents were never an issue; rather, it was a challenge to cull the agencies and individuals to reasonably sized working groups comprised of the best minds (clinicians, scientists, policymakers, public health specialists, social scientists, mental health professionals) who would analyze the science, anticipate new developments, and apply this knowledge into the production of these documents. Efforts could take months or even years to generate a publication, including writing, reviewing, editing, validating the science, and ultimate sign off by the Surgeon General. Next was distilling the core message of each initiative, to be easily understandable, memorable, and consistent with the science. One example was the 2006 release of the Surgeon General's Report on secondhand smoke. Dr. Carmona crafted a simple but meaningful trope: "The debate is over; the science is clear; secondhand smoke kills!" The message was clear, easy to remember, and found its way into the mainstream media. Our target audience was not only highly educated scientists, but more importantly, the average American. For each document, we created a companion publication, a "People's Piece" written at a sixth-grade reading comprehension level to assure the broadest understanding of the message. Determining how best to issue a document created logistical challenges, such as ensuring the availability of the Surgeon General and other key personnel to maximize impact and uptake. Release on a Monday or Tuesday, rather than Friday, would allow for optimal media coverage. Subsequent to document release, we would design a continuing drumbeat of the message, so its release would not simply be a single event. Evaluation of impact, and learning and adjusting for future efforts, is essential and consistent with public health principles. For me, it was indeed a privilege and honor for me to be an integral part of this responsibility and lineage of Surgeons General of the United States.

Kosovo War

The Kosovo War was an armed conflict in the Serbian province of Kosovo that occurred from February 1998 until June 1999. Kosovo was comprised mostly of ethnic Albanians, the majority being Muslims who considered Kosovo as their country. The Republic of Yugoslavia and Serbian Armed Forces wanted to reassert control over that region and began a period of repression and ethnic cleansing that included raiding villages and forcing people from their homes. The assault led residents to flee the area, eventually displacing about one million Kosovar Albanians as refugees in neighboring countries or internally as displaced people. On March 24, 1999, the North Atlantic Treaty Organization intervened with air strikes against Serbian military targets, leading to withdrawal of Serbian forces and establishment of United Nations administration in the Kosovo province. On April 21, 1999, Vice President Al Gore announced plans to resettle up to 20,000 Kosovar refugees in the United States, as one of forty countries that were participating in the Humanitarian Evacuation Program. Designated "Operation Provide Refuge," refugees arrived primarily at Fort Dix on Joint Base McGuire in New Jersey, with the first refugees arriving on May 5. The health assessment of those persons 15 years of age and older consisted of a physical examination, laboratory work, chest x-ray, immunizations, and screening for HIV infection, syphilis and tuberculosis. Refugees also were evaluated for select chronic conditions and were provided dental and pharmacy services. Intervention and prevention services were provided as well. Where indicated, refugees were treated at a 24-hour acute care clinic and referred for specialized hospital care. HHS was the lead agency for this mission with support from the Departments of Defense and State, Immigration and Naturalization Service, American Red Cross, and New Jersey National Guard. Beginning May 3, 1999, the Office of Emergency Preparedness deployed the first team of PHS officers from the Commissioned Corps Readiness Force and PHS-1 Disaster Medical Assistance Team to staff the Fort Dix medical intake process. The team included physicians, nurses, dentists, pharmacists, laboratory technologists and medical records personnel, with CDR Kevin S. Yeskey as the medical officer-in-charge. By July 1999, the Public Health Service had medically examined over 4,000 Kosovar refugees at Fort Dix.[16,17]

Measles Eradication

HEW announced on October 4, 1978 an initiative to eliminate indigenous measles in this nation by October 1, 1982. Measles is an acute viral respiratory illness with a prodrome of fever, cough, coryza, conjunctivitis, and characteristic enanthema (Koplik spots), followed by a maculopapular rash usually appearing 14 days after exposure. Measles is a highly contagious airborne virus that can be spread to others from four days before to four days after appearance of the rash. The 1978 initiative was the second of three attempts that were made by the CDC to eliminate measles in the United States – in 1967, 1978, and 1993. The 1978 eradication strategy had three major aspects: achievement and maintenance of high immunization levels, development of strong and effective surveillance systems, and aggressive response to disease occurrence. Although the goal was not met, by 1981 reported measles cases were 80 percent less compared with the prior year. A resurgence of measles occurred during 1989 to 1991, leading to a refined elimination strategy to include administration of a second dose of measles vaccine. That led to a successful eradication campaign, and measles was declared eliminated in the U.S. in 2000.[18-20] Nonetheless, sporadic outbreaks of measles have occurred due to children not being vaccinated and travelers acquiring measles abroad. The year 2019 marked the greatest number of confirmed cases reported in the nation since 1994.

PHS Response to Terrorism Attacks

In October 2000, Congress passed the Public Health Threats and Emergencies Act (Public Law 106-505) to strengthen the public health infrastructure and improve preparedness to address the threats of antimicrobial resistance and bioterrorism. This would be an area of escalating involvement by HHS and the PHS Commissioned Corps, heightened by the September 11, 2001, attacks on the World Trade Center and the Pentagon and, soon thereafter in October, the receipt of anthrax-tainted letters principally by news media in New York City and at Congressional offices in Washington, DC.

In the immediate aftermath of the World Trade Center attacks, PHS officers were onsite in New York City. At the time, RADM Robert F. Knouss directed the Office of Emergency Preparedness which supported the medical response teams of the National Disaster Medical System (NDMS), with CAPT John Babb (RADM, 2002) directing teams of both the NDMS and Commissioned Corps Readiness Force (CCRF). A 43-person CCRF medical team was

President George W. Bush's iconic remarks amid the ruins of the World Trade Center, September 14, 2001.

deployed to the event on September 20, followed by a 44-person PHS-1 Disaster Medical Assistance Team two days later. By September 24, over two hundred Public Health Service officers had been deployed to assume roles in the incident command system and establish medical treatment stations. Teams of clinicians and behavioral health specialists operated five medical clinics close to Ground Zero, treating rescue and recovery workers for eye and respiratory problems, soft tissue injuries, and mental health issues. The NDMS deployed five Disaster Mortuary Operations and Response Teams, which CCRF supplemented with eleven forensic odontologists and data analysts to support the medical examiner's office in identifying victims. A veterinary medical assistance team was sent to care for search and rescue dogs. The CDC deployed a large contingent of Epidemic Intelligence Service officers and other personnel, including CCRF pharmacist officers to support the National Pharmaceutical Stockpile.[21-23]

In September and October 2001, another major threat was brought about by bioterrorism attacks with *Bacillus anthracis* spores sent through the mail to two U.S. Senators' offices and news media agencies, resulting in five deaths among 22 infected individuals. PHS officers were among the CDC professional and scientific staff at the forefront of the investigative response, working with other officials to determine the source of the attacks and issuing guidance on protective actions. PHS officers were also tasked with treating persons exposed to the spores and distributing antibiotics to 37,000 persons. Bioterrorism is a form of asymmetrical threat that could include contagious as well as non-contagious biological agents such as anthrax.

Commissioned Corps Readiness Force members and PHS-1 Disaster Medical Assistance Team deployed to the World Trade Center, 2001. *[Commissioned Corps Bulletin, November 2001]*

> The events of 2001 reinforced the need for all PHS officers performing response activities to be fit for duty & deployable.

By December 2001, there were over 800 deployments of PHS officers in response to the 9/11 and anthrax attacks, and ultimately over 1,000 deployments. It proved to be the broadest response, to that date, conducted by HHS. The events of September 2001 were an inflection point for the Commissioned Corps and its officers. While the Corps' response was truly laudatory, it was nonetheless transformational in prompting a conceptual return of the Corps as a deployable uniformed service – where officer readiness and deployability would once again be embraced and enforced in policy and doctrine.

Commissioned Corps Readiness Force. The Commissioned Corps Readiness Force was created by the Office of the Surgeon General (OSG) in 1994 to improve the Corps' ability to respond to public health emergencies. For several years, CCRF teams were comprised of officers who volunteered and received specialized training. In October 1997, operational management of CCRF was transferred to the Office of Emergency Preparedness. In February 2001, the definition and training requirements of a "deployable" officer serving in the CCRF were approved by Surgeon General Satcher. Following the 9/11 terrorist and anthrax attacks, however, CAPT Babb noted in January 2002 that many officers had not fulfilled the requirements for CCRF membership.[24,25] This reinforced the need to ensure that all PHS officers performing response activities were physically and emotionally fit for duty, and it set in motion a concerted, multi-year effort by OSG and HHS leadership to build up and fortify the response capabilities of the Corps and its officers. OEP was moved to the Department of Homeland Security and CCRF moved back to OSG in March 2003. In 2004, CCRF was subsumed under a new Office of Force Readiness and Deployment (OFRD). From November 1999 to October 2016, CAPT Daniel Beck was among the PHS officials that were most responsible for PHS officer deployment activities, becoming Deputy Director and Acting Director of OFRD, and later Director of the renamed Readiness and Deployment Operations Group.

Dan Beck

STRATEGIC NATIONAL STOCKPILE

The Strategic National Stockpile (SNS), originally named the National Pharmaceutical Stockpile, was created by the CDC in 1999 to ensure the nation's readiness to respond to a public health emergency such as a major natural disaster, disease outbreak, or biological or chemical threat. The Administration for Strategic Preparedness and Response (ASPR) administers the SNS, and the stockpile is maintained by the CDC Division of Strategic National Stockpile (DSNS) where PHS officers and other personnel provide oversight. The SNS is comprised of antibiotics, chemical antidotes, antitoxins, vaccines, life-support medications, medical/surgical items, and IV administration and airway maintenance supplies. SNS drugs and supplies are located in twelve strategic locations throughout the nation, with some of this inventory stored in pre-configured "Push Packages," each weighing over 50 tons, which can be transported to states and communities within 12 hours of an emergency. These packages also contain 10-day antibiotic regimens to treat over 200,000 people. A CDC team known as a Technical Advisory Response Unit deploy concurrently to advise local authorities on receiving, distributing and replenishing SNS materiel. Another SNS component is the Vendor-Managed Inventory program, with pharmaceuticals, vaccines and medical products packaged for specific types of response. An SNS User-Managed Inventory program includes CHEMPACK containers with antidotes to chemical nerve agents, and a few thousand of these are forward deployed throughout the nation, such that 90 percent of the population is within a 1-hour accessibility timeframe. The DSNS also manages and deploys Federal Medical Stations (FMS), which are caches that contain beds, supplies and medicines used to provide a temporary medical shelter within a pre-identified building during a national emergency. Each FMS offers short-term medical surge capacity for 50 to 250 inpatients with subacute health care needs.[26-29]

PHS CEREMONIAL FEATURES

RADM Kenneth P. Moritsugu, Deputy Surgeon General, took the initiative to assimilate ceremonial features into the Commissioned Corps that were consistent with military service traditions.

Honor Guard

Each major branch of the Armed Forces maintains an official Honor Guard based in Washington, DC, along with local units stationed at military bases throughout the country. Honor Guard teams consist of three distinct types: a Color Guard to present the Colors, Parade Unit, and Drill Team. Military Honor Guards are typically composed of enlisted personnel overseen by senior enlisted or officers. In January 1990, a group of Public Health Service officers equipped with a PHS sword formed an honor guard to honor Surgeons General Koop and Novello at a reception in Washington, DC. By 1993, a ceremonial Sword Honor Guard (SHG) was formally constituted and members were trained in military drill and ceremonies. Sponsorship of the SHG was assumed by the

District of Columbia Metropolitan Branch of the Commissioned Officers Association, a national advocacy group for PHS officers. Over the next few years, the SHG refined its organizational structure and processes. The SHG performed at numerous events in support of the Commissioned Corps for nearly a decade. RADM Moritsugu recognized its importance and with concurrence of the SHG, a workgroup was formed to transition the Guard into the Office of the Surgeon General. By order of Surgeon General Satcher, the SHG was formalized as the USPHS Surgeon General's Honor Cadre in October 1999. CAPT Richard C. Vause, Jr. was appointed as the first Commander of the Honor Cadre. The name was later changed to the Honor Corps, and subsequently to the USPHS Surgeon General's Honor Guard. A *Drill and Ceremonies Manual* establishes USPHS Commissioned Corps policy and the roles and responsibilities of the Surgeon General's Honor Guard. The Honor Guard is comprised of PHS officers who are expected to uphold high standards of officership. Like other uniformed services, the USPHS Honor Guard has become a prominent ceremonial component at many official HHS and non-HHS events.[30-32]

USPHS Music Ensemble

The USPHS Commissioned Corps Music Ensemble is comprised of a Ceremonial Band and a Choral Group. The Music Ensemble, like the Honor Guard, is a valued ceremonial element for the Corps. Known as the "Surgeon General's Own," it performs at about thirty events each year, including award ceremonies, promotions, retirements and special events. Notably, the Ensemble has performed at every PHS Foundation Scientific and Training Symposium *(see Chapter Eighteen)* since 2001. In 2011, the Choral Group and Ceremonial Band performed the first of several annual concerts at the National World War II Memorial on the National Mall in Washington, DC. The Ensemble performed in the presence of Vice President Joseph R. Biden during the induction of Vivek H. Murthy as Surgeon General. Ensemble members are dedicated officers who  rehearse and perform on their own time, apart from assigned duties. The idea of creating a USPHS Commissioned Corps musical group was proposed by Scientist officer CAPT (Ret.) John J. Bartko. CAPT Bartko and CAPT Derek E. Dunn, Chief Scientist Officer at the time, recognized that unlike other uniformed services, the PHS Commissioned Corps was without a musical component for ceremonial occasions. CAPTs Bartko and Dunn undertook a survey of Scientist Category officers, which revealed that a number of officers were interested in joining a musical group. CAPT Dunn proposed to the Office of the Surgeon General (OSG) and to Chief Professional Officers (CPOs) that a PHS musical group be established. The OSG and CPOs embraced the idea and surveyed active duty officers to determine Corps-wide interest. About 75 officers showed interest in forming a musical group, and respondents were invited to a meeting in July 2000, where Deputy Surgeon General RADM Kenneth P. Moritsugu welcomed the participants and planning ensued to establish a choral group, a wind group and a chamber group. The initiative was subsequently formalized within Office of the Surgeon General.

PHS March and Fanfare

The *Public Health Service March* was composed by retired Senior Chief Musician George King III, U.S. Coast Guard. In the 1970s, King was Conductor of the USCG Training Center Band in Cape May, New Jersey. When PHS dignitaries were to visit the base, he learned that the USPHS had no Service March. Other uniformed services have marches and official music, and King resolved to remedy the situation and he composed the musical score and lyrics of the *PHS March*. In 1978, Mr. King conveyed the copyright of the *PHS March* to Surgeon General Julius B. Richmond. On the occasion of the USPHS Commissioned Corps Centennial in 1989, King, upon request of the Public Health Service, also composed the *Centennial Fanfare – Anchor and Caduceus*. At the Washington, DC, gala celebrating the event in January 1989, the Coast Guard Band played and Senior Chief Musician King conducted for the premier of the *Fanfare*. Then on May 9, 2023, at the USPHS Scientific and Training Symposium, George King was the featured Guest Conductor at the evening concert of the USPHS Music Ensemble.[33,34] In 2020, the *Public Health Service March* was slightly modified, adding "air" to the lyrics.

George King III

> **Public Health Service March**
> *The mission of our Service is known the world around,*
> *In research and in treatment no equal can be found.*
> *In the silent war against disease no truce is ever seen,*
> *We serve on the land, air and sea for humanity,*
> *The Public Health Service team!*

PUBLIC HEALTH SERVICE BICENTENNIAL

The year 1998 marked the Bicentennial of the U.S. Public Health Service and several special events were held to celebrate the occasion. The first full week of April is National Public Health Week and on April 7, HHS Region I Office, along with the National Park Service and U.S. Navy, held a ceremony in the Charlestown Navy Yard National Historic Park in Boston. Charlestown was the site of the first marine hospital built with Act of 1798 funds. The event was staged in front of the *U.S.S. Constitution* (launched in 1797, it is the oldest naval warship still afloat). Senator Edward Kennedy introduced keynote speaker Dr. David Satcher, and former Assistant Secretary for Health and Surgeon General Julius Richmond also gave a presentation. A special plaque was unveiled to commemorate and mark the site of the Charlestown Marine Hospital.[35]

On July 3, 1998, a special program was also held in Independence National Historical Park in Philadelphia to mark the 200th anniversary of the PHS. Congress Hall, the building in which Congress passed the Act of 1798, along with Independence Hall, were the backdrop for an outdoor ceremony featuring Dr. Satcher who discussed the historical contributions of PHS and his principles for guiding its future. The program included a historical skit, related exhibits, and music by the Colonial Fife and Drum Company.[36]

On July 15, 1998, more than 300 PHS officers, civilians, friends and family gathered to attend a celebratory PHS Bicentennial Luncheon at the Commissioned Officers Club at the National Naval Medical Center in Bethesda, Maryland. Attendees came from several states, with ADM David Satcher delivering an inspiring presentation to the audience. All of those in attendance received a souvenir gold colored PHS Bicentennial medallion, backed in blue velvet.[37]

Satcher's Departure

Surgeon General David Satcher's last day in office was February 12, 2002. In the fall, he was appointed to a senior position at the Morehouse School of Medicine. The next day, Kenneth P. Moritsugu, Deputy Surgeon General, assumed the position of Acting Surgeon General, serving until August 4, 2002. Moritsugu received his medical degree from George Washington University and an MPH from the University of California, Berkeley. RADM Moritsugu was a consummate leader with a distinguished PHS service record, and he stayed on to serve as Deputy to the next Surgeon General.

Chronology • 1998–2002

SG David Satcher, February 1998–February 2002
Acting SG Kenneth P. Moritsugu, February 2002–August 2002

1998   Release of the first-ever Surgeon General's Report on *Tobacco Use Among U.S. Racial/Ethnic Minority Groups*.

1999   Creation of the National Pharmaceutical Stockpile, renamed Strategic National Stockpile in 2003.

1999   PHS deployed to medically screen thousands of arriving Kosovar refugees.

1999   PHS Honor Guard is established in Office of the Surgeon General.

1999   Release of the first-ever Surgeon General's Report on *Mental Health*.

2000   PHS Music Ensemble is established in Office of the Surgeon General.

2000   Release of the first-ever Surgeon General's Report on *Oral Health*.

2000   Eradication of measles in U.S. is declared.

2001   Terrorist attacks on the World Trade Center and Pentagon, and bioterrorism attack with anthrax-tainted letters; over 800 deployments of PHS officers.

CHAPTER FOURTEEN

TRANSFORMATION, EMERGENCY RESPONSE, ICE HEALTH SERVICE CORPS
2002 to 2009

PRESIDENT GEORGE W. BUSH announced the nomination of Richard H. Carmona for the position of U.S. Surgeon General on March 26, 2002. Dr. Carmona was unique to the position – a former member of the Army Special Forces and Vietnam veteran, he was a paramedic, registered nurse and physician. He received his medical degree from the University of California, San Francisco, in 1979, where he completed a surgical residency (Drs. Carmona and Koop were the only board certified surgeons as Surgeon General). He earned an MPH degree from the University of Arizona in 1998. Prior to nomination, Dr. Carmona was chairman of the state of Arizona Southern Regional Emergency Medical System with expertise in special operations and emergency preparedness. He was a Professor of Surgery, Public Health and Family and Community Medicine at the University of Arizona, surgeon and deputy sheriff at the Pima County Sheriff's Department. Through positions of progressive responsibility, he became chief executive officer of the Pima County Health Care System. Dr. Carmona was unanimously confirmed by the U.S. Senate and was sworn in as the 17th Surgeon General on August 5, 2002, serving a 4-year term. During his nomination remarks, the President stated that he wanted Dr. Carmona to address three particularly urgent issues: first, to administer the Public Health Service Commissioned Corps, preparing it to respond to any emergency and educating the public about the threat of bioterrorism; second, lead an initiative that focused on prevention and lifelong healthy living as a key component of medical care; and third, speak regularly to the nation about alcohol and drug abuse and the toll that they take on our society.[1] Carmona had the needed credentials to advance C. Everett Koop's Commissioned Corps revitalization initiative, to transition the Corps into a mobile cadre of emergency responders, and to build upon the efforts of Dr. David Satcher and other Surgeons General in advocating for health promotion and disease prevention, especially among

Richard H. Carmona

minority populations. At an October 2002 Media and Health Research forum, the new Surgeon General stated that his first priority would be disease prevention. He emphasized the preventable nature of many diseases, focusing on the morbidity and health care costs of the obesity epidemic, and pointing to the reduction of cardiovascular disease rates due to healthier lifestyles.[2,3] Other priorities were public health preparedness and eliminating health disparities.

COMMISSIONED CORPS TRANSFORMATION

Former Surgeons General Koop and Satcher had taken steps to revitalize and strengthen internal Corps operations. Now, a new effort – transformation – was being conceptualized under Surgeon General Carmona to further advance the Commissioned Corps to meet public health challenges of the 21st century. The transformation was an amalgam of elements. Initiatives were taken to increase Corps visibility and its public health capabilities, more closely align and integrate it with other uniformed services, and promote the Corps as an essential component in health emergency response activities. With the 2001 terrorist attacks in mind, the Public Health Service increasingly ramped up its readiness skills. As the only uniformed service comprised exclusively of medical, public health and biomedical science personnel, the Corps was under pressure to assert itself as the public health emergency response force for the nation.

Richard Carmona's appointment was opportune – he had the military and emergency response background that would prove vital to leading a transformation of the Corps during the period of 2002 to 2006. Dr. Kenneth P. Moritsugu, Deputy Surgeon General, had extensive and wide-ranging PHS leadership experience that helped facilitate a needed cultural change within the Corps. It was also significant that the Commissioned Officers Association had appointed CAPT Gerard (Jerry) M. Farrell (Ret.), a U.S. Naval Academy graduate and distinguished career officer, as the new Executive Director, effective November 2001. Carmona, Moritsugu, Farrell, former Army officer OSG Chief of Staff RADM Robert C. Williams, and RADM John T. Babb, Director of the Corps' Readiness Force, worked in tandem to transform and integrate the Corps into the sphere of the armed services through strategic interactions and alliances with military counterparts and the Department of Defense, with the intent to secure parity and full interoperability of the Corps with the other uniformed services. They raised awareness about the value of the Commissioned Corps among other uniformed service leaders, which led to recurring service of the Corps alongside military service members as a force multiplier and critical component of public health emergency response and international humanitarian missions.

Kenneth Moritsugu

Initiation of Transformation

Transformation of the U.S. Public Health Service Commissioned Corps was a multi-year endeavor that progressed through different administrations. The transformation process officially began on April 17, 2003, when Tommy Thompson, Secretary of the Department of Health and Human Services (HHS) sent a memorandum to HHS Operating and Staff Division Heads noting that the PHS Commissioned Corps was a "hidden treasure" that had a distinguished history of serving the nation and the world. He stated that the Corps responded admirably to events beginning with September 11, 2001, and that it was essential that the Corps be strengthened to ensure that all public health needs are met in war and peace. Several months earlier, he had directed the Surgeon General to study the Corps to identify the best organizational and management practices and "transform the Corps to meet the public health needs of the 21st century. The end product will be a visible, physically fit, highly motivated, and expert mobile uniformed service of public health professionals." Thompson requested all HHS leaders to assist the Surgeon General in accomplishing his directives for Corps transformation and building the Commissioned Corps Readiness Force (CCRF, created 1994).[4]

Secretary Thompson formally announced the vision and plan for transformation of the Commissioned Corps on July 3, 2003, at the Reserve Officers Association in Washington, DC. He stated that this would be the "biggest and most sweeping transformation" in Corps history and would bring it into parity with other uniformed services. His message encompassed the need to increase the Corps' size and scope to meet the demand for public health and primary care, particularly in areas where there were problems of access; and the need to have a Corps that had response capabilities and was 100 percent deployable to public health emergencies. Thompson also proposed improvements to the Corps' management and development structure, including a modern system of total force management. He proposed restoring warrant grades to incorporate associate degree health professionals into the Corps and to include a strong reserve component as part of the total force.[5]

On October 30, 2003, Surgeon General Carmona testified before the U.S. House Committee on Government Reform to advance the essential need for transformation to strengthen the Corps and its reserves to meet the nation's many public health challenges. His testimony also clarified certain misconceptions and described changes to the initial transformation plan, including assurance that deployments would be congruent with an officer's skills, competencies and physical capabilities. A second panel providing testimony consisted of former Surgeons General C. Everett Koop and Julius Richmond, and the Commissioned Officers Association Executive Director Jerry Farrell. Among the items discussed, they stated that the Office of Surgeon General should have complete control over all aspects of the Corps, with Dr. Richmond emphasizing the importance of involving agency heads in plan development, and CAPT Farrell recommending a mission-driven planning process and a delay in implementation until the profile of the future Corps was defined.[6,7]

Led by Surgeon General Carmona and Deputy Surgeon General Moritsugu, the transformation initiative was a complex process that involved numerous PHS officers and officials at all levels of HHS. The transformation process began by retaining the Lewin Group to evaluate force management options, and creating focus groups and a Transformation Workgroup with agency representatives and senior PHS officers to formulate policy options for recruitment and training, officer profiles and classification, position identification, allocation and billets, career development of officers, and staffing difficult-to-fill jobs. New units were established in 2003 to include:

- Office of Commissioned Corps Operations (OCCO, formerly Division of Commissioned Personnel) in the Office of the Surgeon General (OSG);
- Office of Commissioned Corps Force Management (OCCFM) within the Office of the Assistant Secretary for Health; and
- Office of Commissioned Corps Support Services (OCCSS), which reports to leadership of the Program Support Center.

In 2004, the Commissioned Corps Readiness Force was subsumed into a new Office of Force Readiness and Deployment (OFRD) in OSG.

In January 2005, Michael O. Leavitt succeeded Tommy Thompson as HHS Secretary and on January 18, 2006, he announced his vision to advance the Corps' transformation, designating it "Commissioned Corps Renewal." Deputy Secretary Alex Azar organized five interagency workgroups to formulate detailed recommendations: sizing of the Corps; recruitment, training and career development; assignments; classification and positions; and readiness and response. In June 2006, the Assistant Secretary for Health and Surgeon General announced the creation of 12 new positions in OCCFM and OCCO to lead implementation of the Secretary's decisions relative to the transformation workgroup recommendations. By December 2006, the Transformation Implementation Plan provided for the following: expand by 10 percent to a total active duty strength of 6,600; improve recruitment with an electronic Call to Active Duty system; recruit officers both to the Corps at large and to specific positions; characterize officers not only by profession, but by their clinical, public health, mental health, and research roles; upon call to active duty, require officers to attend a new 2-week Officer Basic Course (OBC, replacing a 5-day Basic Officer Training Course introduced in October 2001) and provide leadership training; identify positions of a Corps officer by a unique billet that describes professional qualifications and functional role; maintain up-to-date officer profiles to support referral of officer candidates to appropriate assignments; and institute a tiered response structure of readiness teams to tailor a response to the type and severity of event.[8] Key transformation accomplishments by December 2007 included launch of the OBC, redesign of the Corps website, production of recruitment brochures and category-specific fact sheets, completion of a recruitment plan and activation of a recruitment call center, development of incentives to officers who accept hard-to-fill assignments, completion of plans to migrate human resources activity to the Coast Guard Direct Access system, and determination of elements for category-specific billet templates.[9] Principal goals of the transformation initiative were to enhance the overall effectiveness of the USPHS Commissioned Corps; to better utilize Corps officers within HHS and non-HHS agencies; to overhaul the structure and administration of the Corps; and ensure that all officers were physically fit and deployment ready, unless granted a waiver, to meet any type of public health/medical emergency domestically and, if a threat to national security, internationally. Although considerable progress was made during Surgeon General Carmona's tenure, the transformation process would necessarily continue for several more years to achieve its objectives. Disease prevention and elimination of health disparities were central to Carmona's speaking engagements at countless venues throughout the nation, but Corps transformation and emergency preparedness were an imperative.

Mission Statement, Core Values

A new ***USPHS Mission Statement*** was released February 17, 2005:[10]

The mission of the U.S. Public Health Service Commissioned Corps is to protect, promote, and advance the health and safety of the Nation.

As America's uniformed service of public health professionals, the Commissioned Corps achieves this mission through:
- Rapid and effective response to public health needs,
- Leadership and excellence in public health practices, and
- Advancement of public health science.

New ***USPHS Commissioned Corps Core Values*** were released in 2006:[11]
- *Leadership* – Provides vision and purpose in public health through inspiration, dedication, and loyalty.
- *Service* – Demonstrates a commitment to public health through compassionate actions and stewardship of time, resources, and talents.
- *Integrity* – Exemplifies uncompromising ethical conduct and maintains the highest standards of responsibility and accountability.
- *Excellence* – Exhibits superior performance and continuous improvement in knowledge and expertise.

In Their Words

by VADM (Ret.) Richard H. Carmona

Upon becoming Surgeon General, I discovered the U.S. Public Health Service Commissioned Corps (CC) to be an extraordinary army of health warriors who were, though, fragmented and diminished in morale. These exceptional health practitioners and scientists within HHS and outside organizations were often viewed as employees who happened to wear a uniform rather than as a uniformed service member. Although a quarter of our officers had prior military service, the majority had little knowledge about uniformed service protocol. Further, other military services often did not recognize the PHS CC as a peer uniformed service. When military issues such as pay and benefits arose before Congress, the CC was often left out and had to fight for parity. Intrigued as to how this negative "branding" of the once heralded PHS CC occurred, I committed to learning the determinant factors in Corps history. Self-inflicted wounds as well as the "plague of politics" contributed to the cumulative negative perception of the Corps. Top-level factors included disempowerment of the position of Surgeon General, nomination of civilians for Surgeon General, and allowing an option to the Assistant Secretary for Health, a civilian political appointee, to become an instant 4-star Admiral. During the Vietnam War era, many physicians that joined the Corps to avoid military service rarely wore their uniform or participated in Service activities. To confront the Corps' decline, our OSG leadership team in 2002 launched a plan for effective, sustainable behavioral change to regain PHS Corps parity as a legitimate uniformed service. This mission was critical to the Corps' future and involved a multifaceted approach to create a new "brand" of health warriors much like the Army's "Be All You Can Be." Thus began a several-year journey of another transformation initiative overseen by committed OSG leaders with the support of HHS and its operating divisions. Mandatory, fortified officer basic training was instituted to teach officership and inspire each officer to, individually and collectively as a team, exceed all requirements in their assignments. We expanded CC postings throughout the federal government like the White House and various Departments including State, Defense, Agriculture, and Interior and, in time, these cabinet level Departments became powerful advocates for the Corps. As a result of remarkable improvements in professionalism, officership, physical fitness, readiness and hundreds of successful deployments to include the combat zone, Corps morale soared and the perception of a professional Corps was embedded in all who encountered us. The Corps became the "go to" uniformed service to meet unmet health-related needs of our nation and our allies. By 2005 to 2006, the Corps had self-transformed and had attained a "seat" at the table of leadership in all federal government agencies where the USPHS Commissioned Corps was needed.

Parity and Esprit de Corps
Throughout its history, the Commissioned Corps had an unparalleled record of public health achievement. However, after 1967 when line authority for PHS programs was transferred to the Assistant Secretary for Health and Scientific Affairs, the Corps began to wane and become marginalized. That situation led to C. Everett Koop's revitalization and the later transformation initiatives. Among Surgeon General Richard Carmona's achievements was to instill a renewed sense that the Corps was, indeed, a vital branch of the uniformed services and that PHS officers needed to fully embrace that view and transform themselves in a way that met officership expectations, which included the requirement to wear their uniforms when on duty. Carmona is widely recognized for leading a recovery of parity and interoperability of the PHS Corps with other uniformed services, and restoring an esprit de corps that was present during an earlier time in Corps history – these essential elements contributed to the eventual success of the transformation process. Personal esteem for Carmona endured among PHS officers due to his impact on the Corps – he was a role model and mentor for officers. Such traits are reflected by the Junior Officer Advisory Group's sponsorship of the VADM Carmona Inspiration Award.

SURGEON GENERAL'S REPORTS, CALLS TO ACTION

Dr. Carmona released three Surgeon General's Reports and two Calls to Action.

Tobacco Use
The Health Consequences of Smoking: A Report of the Surgeon General, was released in 2004. This report provides an updated, comprehensive overview of the harmful effects of smoking cigarettes. Major conclusions include the fact that smoking harms nearly every bodily organ, and the list of diseases that are caused by smoking was expanded to include abdominal aortic aneurysm, pneumonia, periodontitis, cataract, acute myeloid leukemia, renal cancer, cervical cancer, pancreatic and stomach cancer.

Exposure to Tobacco Smoke
The Health Consequences of Involuntary Exposure to Tobacco Smoke: A Report of the Surgeon General,[12] was released in 2006. It was issued twenty years after Surgeon General Koop's 1986 report, *The Health Consequences of Involuntary Smoking*, which concluded that involuntary secondhand smoke was a cause of disease. This new report updates the scientific evidence of the harmful effects of involuntary exposure to tobacco smoke, noting that secondhand smoke produces substantial and immediate effects on the cardiovascular system and that even brief exposures can pose risks to older adults. It further notes that tobacco smoke is a risk for children exposed in their homes to parental

smokers. The report concludes that any exposure to secondhand smoke is a risk to nonsmokers and the only resolution is to eliminate indoor smoking in public places. The report generated controversy with respect to the premise that secondhand smoke exposure can cause immediate cellular damage, an issue that would be addressed in a 2010 Surgeon General's Report.

Bone, Oral, Persons with Disabilities Health

Bone Health and Osteoporosis: A Report of the Surgeon General,[13] was the first-ever report to address the burden of bone disease and fractures, which is projected to increase markedly as the population ages. A foundation for the Report were the proceedings of a Surgeon General's Workshop on Osteoporosis and Bone Health held December 12-13, 2002, in Washington, DC. The report provides scientific information relative to the prevention, assessment, diagnosis and treatment of bone disease, and a framework for educating Americans and healthcare providers about the scope of the problem, and prevention and lifestyle changes to minimize the impact of bone disease.

A *National Call to Action to Promote Oral Health*, released in 2003, would build on Dr. Satcher's earlier report on *Oral Health in America*. The *Surgeon General's Call to Action to Improve the Health and Wellness of Persons with Disabilities*[14] describes the challenges to health and well-being faced by persons with disabilities. It highlights the need to promote accessible, comprehensive health care that enables persons with disabilities to have a full life in the community with integrated services. This 2005 Call to Action delineates four goals: understanding that persons with disabilities can lead productive lives; healthcare providers have the knowledge to diagnose and treat the "whole person" with dignity; persons with disabilities can promote their own good health with healthy lifestyles; and accessible health care and support services can promote independence for these persons.

OBESITY

Dr. Carmona discussed the obesity epidemic at numerous venues, noting that nearly two of every three American adults were overweight. In Congressional testimony in 2003, he declared the crisis of obesity to be "the fastest-growing cause of disease and death in America."[15] He warned in articles and speeches that "obesity is the terror within," a threat that was every bit as real as weapons of mass destruction. His prognostications drew media attention and underscored the potentially serious public health threat that obesity posed to society, particularly in children who were increasingly diagnosed with type 2 diabetes, and the economic burden estimated to be $117 billion annually in direct and indirect costs. He affirmed that increased physical activity and healthier eating habits were key factors in reducing the prevalence of obesity.[16]

Preparedness and Response Actions

Departmental initiatives and legislative measures were introduced to bolster the preparedness and response capabilities within HHS. The Office of Public Health Emergency Preparedness (OPHEP) was formed in June 2002 to coordinate efforts for responding to bioterrorism and other public health emergencies.[17] In March 2004, the National Incident Management System was created to provide a consistent incident management approach for federal, state, local and tribal governments. And in December 2004, the National Response Plan, a framework that provides for a unified national response to domestic disasters and emergencies, was released by the Department of Homeland Security. The Plan was superseded by the renamed National Response Framework in January 2008, which was updated with a third edition in June 2016 and a fourth edition released October 28, 2019.

PROJECT BIOSHIELD

Following the anthrax attack of 2001, the federal government bolstered its arsenal of pre- and postexposure medical countermeasures, to include diagnostic tests, antidotes, drugs and vaccines, to respond to chemical, biological, radiological or nuclear (CBRN) agents. Because there was little economic incentive for manufacturers to research and develop such countermeasures, the Project BioShield Act of 2004[18] was enacted to, among other purposes, fast-track research, development, and availability of effective pharmaceutical products against CBRN agents. The Act authorized $5.6 billion over 10 years to develop, procure, stockpile and distribute products, particularly vaccines (including those not tested for safety and efficacy in humans), needed to protect against bioterror weapons of mass destruction. The Pandemic and All-Hazards Preparedness Act of 2006 created the Biomedical Advanced Research and Development Authority (BARDA) to oversee the development and procurement of medical countermeasures for Project BioShield.

PAHPA

A major piece of legislation was the December 19, 2006, enactment of the Pandemic and All-Hazards Preparedness Act (PAHPA).[19] The Act amended the Public Health Service Act, incorporating OPHEP and creating within HHS a new Office of the Assistant Secretary for Preparedness and Response (ASPR). The first Assistant Secretary, RADM W. Craig Vanderwagen, served from 2007 until 2009; he was succeeded by RADM Nicole Lurie who served from 2009 to 2017. The Assistant Secretary was tasked with consolidating and improving national public health and medical preparedness and response capabilities for natural, accidental and deliberate emergency events. ASPR responsibilities are multifaceted and include advising the HHS Secretary on public health preparedness and response issues; supporting and coordinating federal, state, territorial and tribal emergency readiness capabilities; overseeing the National Disaster Medical System, the Medical Reserve Corps, and the Strategic National Stockpile; administering programs involving advanced research, development and acquisition of medical countermeasures (Project BioShield, BARDA); and developing a National Health Security Strategy (NHSS). On March 13, 2013, the Pandemic and All-Hazards Preparedness Reauthorization Act[20] was enacted and, on June 24, 2019, the Pandemic and All-Hazards Preparedness and Advancing Innovation Act[21] (PAHPAI) was enacted to reauthorize PAHPA. These legislative measures further strengthened the many provisions that support national preparedness and response for public health emergencies. As a backdrop to preparedness and response activities, the ASPR NHSS for 2019–2022 and its Implementation Plan are a comprehensive plan with a whole-of-government approach to support authorities in a public health emergency, disaster, or attack from emerging and pandemic infectious diseases or chemical, biological, radiological and nuclear (CBRN) threats. The NHSS also aligns with the National Response Framework, which builds upon the National Incident Management System. The Framework groups the capabilities of federal departments and agencies into fifteen Emergency Support Functions (ESFs). ESF #8, Public Health and Medical Services, tasks HHS with coordinating the provision of federal public health and medical assistance to states and localities for preparedness, response and recovery activities. In July 2022, ASPR was elevated to an Operating Division of HHS and renamed the Administration for Strategic Preparedness and Response.

C. Vanderwagen

Nicole Lurie

Medical Reserve Corps

The Medical Reserve Corps (MRC) is a national network of approximately 200,000 volunteer medical and public health professionals, as well as volunteers without healthcare backgrounds, organized within 1,000 community-based units. Generally, about one-third of MRC volunteers are nurses, another third are other healthcare professionals, and the remaining third are support personnel. These volunteers build community resiliency in responding to local health needs and emergency events affecting public health. The MRC, initially based in the Office of the Surgeon General, began in 2002 as

Robert J. Tosatto

a demonstration project with 42 community-based units. The Pandemic and All-Hazards Preparedness Act of 2006 codified the Medical Reserve Corps and the PAHP Reauthorization Act of 2013 reassigned the MRC to the Office of the Assistant Secretary for Preparedness and Response. CAPT Robert J. Tosatto was the first Director of the Medical Reserve Corps Program and remained in the position until his retirement in 2017. Tosatto was an exceptional leader who guided a team of committed PHS officers and dedicated civilians to advance the program to its recognized national importance.

> ## *In Their Words*
>
> ### by RADM (Ret.) W. Craig Vanderwagen
>
> The World Trade Center and anthrax attacks of 2001 and impact of Hurricanes Katrina, Rita and Wilma in 2005 led the White House and Congress to call for a variety of corrective actions at HHS to protect the health of the Nation's population. The operational shortcomings and lack of effective tools in responding to these emergency events contributed to passage of the Pandemic and All-Hazards Preparedness Act in 2006. The greatest perceived needs were to establish clear leadership, responsibility and coordination for federal public health and medical response, and to provide a risk embracing, but scientifically sound capability to speed the development of medical countermeasures to fifteen identified national threats. These expectations required significant reorganization of a variety of Departmental functions and organizational units, which was a complex and extremely challenging mission for me and my leadership team. For example, NIH processes were not intended to support research into bioterror countermeasures that would typically involve lengthy studies, nor did FDA move swiftly in evaluating and certifying the safety and efficacy of new products. Thus, BARDA was commissioned to guide and fund targeted NIH- and FDA-sponsored research in the shortest reasonable period of time. On the operational side, each of the HHS Operating Divisions (OpDivs) had up to this point responded to emergency public health events as separate entities with little coordinated strategy for deployment and use of assets. Some OpDivs were not prepared to manage operational response in an effective manner using Incident Command principles and practices, so response activities and situational awareness were chaotic. And, the National Disaster Medical Services program returned to HHS with PAHPA and needed significant re-tooling. In summary, significant change in HHS culture was envisaged (and indeed required) and many parts and pieces needed to be brought together to work as a harmonious and effective whole in support of federal, state and local responders. I assembled a uniquely mature and innovative leadership team to bring this new organization, the Office of the Assistant Secretary for Preparedness and Response, into reality and we were blessed with a Secretary and a President who were very supportive and wanted us to succeed.

Officer Deployments

Following the 9/11 and anthrax attacks in 2001, it was evident that substantial improvements were necessary to better prepare PHS officers for emergency deployment. Importantly, the transformation included an initiative to raise the standards and readiness capabilities of PHS officers to respond to public health emergencies. The Commissioned Corps Readiness Force (CCRF), created in 1994 and directed by CAPT (RADM, 2002) John T. Babb beginning July 2000, was subsumed under the new Office of Force Readiness and Deployment (OFRD) in 2004; CAPT David C. Rutstein (RADM, 2007) replaced RADM Babb as Director of OFRD in 2007. In 2013, the OFRD was renamed the Readiness and Deployment Operations Group (RedDOG) in the Division of Commissioned Corps Personnel and Readiness. In 2019, RedDOG was placed in a new Readiness and Deployment Branch (RDB) within the newly designated Commissioned Corps Headquarters.

John T. Babb

The bioterrorism events that occurred in late 2001 tested the readiness of the Corps to meet the health and medical needs of emergency responders in New York City and the preventive health needs of potentially anthrax-exposed individuals in and around Washington, DC. While the deployments in the immediate aftermath of those events was laudatory, improvements were needed in the Corps' readiness and response capabilities as still greater challenges lay ahead. Beginning in 2004, OFRD enhanced both the basic and specialty online training modules and field training. Basic readiness physical fitness standards were set, and all officers would soon be rostered into tiered, preconfigured and deployable response teams. By 2005, PHS officers had deployed to numerous disease outbreaks, natural and manmade disasters.

Major Hurricanes, 2004–2005

Hurricanes Charley, Frances, Ivan, Jeanne

The hurricane season of 2004 produced four major hurricanes in rapid succession affecting the southeast U.S. – Charley making landfall on August 13 (Category 4), Frances on September 5 (Category 2), Ivan on September 16 (Category 3), and Jeanne on September 26 (Category 3). A combined total of over 600 PHS officers deployed to Florida and Alabama in responding to the four hurricanes. Officers from every professional category were used to provide relief for victims, provide first aid and medical care to injured citizens, support local health facilities, and lead units to stabilize building structures. Nearly one-half of the deployed personnel were nurse officers. Officers represented almost every agency where PHS officers were assigned.[22]

Hurricanes Katrina, Rita, Wilma

On August 26, 2005, the states of Louisiana and Mississippi activated their emergency response plans, ordering evacuations from coastal areas in anticipation of the imminent arrival of Hurricane Katrina. An estimated over one million people evacuated the metropolitan area of New Orleans, about 100,000 remained and, of those, more than 10,000 sheltered in the Superdome. On August 29, 2005, Hurricane Katrina made landfall on the Gulf Coast at the Louisiana-Mississippi border as a Category 3 storm. The storm surge pushed water into communities, and the levees and floodwalls of New Orleans were overtopped and breached, such that about 80 percent of New Orleans was flooded. The resulting toll on human life and property was overwhelming: more than 1,800 people lost their lives, people were trapped in their houses and on rooftops, and over 800,000 housing units were damaged or destroyed in the storm leaving many people homeless. Hurricane Katrina was soon followed by Hurricane Rita when it made landfall on the Gulf Coast in southwest Louisiana as a Category 3 storm on September 24, 2005, and a large storm surge devastated coastal communities. The approaching storm prompted an evacuation of between 2 and 3 million residents of Louisiana and Texas. On October 24, 2005, another hurricane, Wilma, was a Category 3 storm when it made landfall in southwestern Florida, moving quickly across the Florida Peninsula and impacting southeast Florida, including the Florida Keys.[23-25]

Over 10,000 people sheltered in the New Orleans Superdome in the aftermath of Hurricane Katrina.

On August 31, HHS Secretary Michael Leavitt declared a Federal Public Health Emergency for the Gulf Coast region. The public health and medical needs in areas affected by Hurricanes Katrina and Rita led to the deployment of the Commissioned Corps along with a vast array of other federal health assets that included National Disaster Medical System teams and over 100 tons of pharmaceuticals and medical supplies from the Strategic National Stockpile. The Corps conducted the largest deployment in its history with 2,119 of the 6,122 officers (35 percent) on active duty deployed at least once to Hurricanes Katrina and Rita, serving a total of 2,372 missions.[26] More than 2,400 Corps officers were deployed in the combined response to Hurricanes Katrina, Rita and Wilma under the direction of the Surgeon General and RADM John Babb.

After-Action Reports

The White House report, *The Federal Response to Hurricane Katrina: Lessons Learned*,[28] issued February 2006, addressed the "significant flaws in federal, state, and local preparedness for catastrophic events and our capacity to respond to them." It included three recommendations regarding the Commissioned Corps.

> 57c. HHS should organize, train, equip and roster medical and public health professionals in preconfigured and deployable teams.
>
> 59. The Surgeon General should routinely communicate public health, as well as individual and community preparedness guidance to the general population.
>
> 60. Create and maintain a dedicated, full-time and equipped response team composed of Commissioned Corps officers of the USPHS.

Recommendation 57c led Secretary Leavitt to direct the implementation of preconfigured deployable teams. That directive evolved into three Response Tiers and a "Mission Critical" designation.

- *Tier-1 Response Teams* report to point of departure within 12 hours of notification and include five Rapid Deployment Force (RDF) Teams, ten Regional Incident Support Teams (RIST), five National Incident Support Teams (NIST), and five Capital Area Provider (CAP) Teams.
- *Tier-2 Response Teams* report to point of departure within 36 hours of notification and include five Applied Public Health Teams (APHT), five Mental Health Teams (MHT), and five Services Access Teams (SAT).
- *Tier-3 Response Teams* report to point of departure within 72 hours of notification and include all Corps officers not assigned to Tier-1 or Tier-2 Teams. Tier-3 Teams deploy to augment Tier-1 or Tier-2 teams, or provide specific technical skills and subject matter expertise.

Rapid Deployment Forces are the forward-leaning operational unit comprising 125+ PHS officers with a range of clinical and public health skill sets. Each RDF is scalable, the core mission being to set-up and provide care to patients at the emergency event in a 250-bed federal medical station(s).

HHS's Office of Inspector General subsequently reviewed the USPHS response to Hurricanes Katrina and Rita and drew the following conclusions.[27]

> State health officials credited these officers with saving many lives. Officers employed their clinical skills to provide a variety of services, including primary and emergent care, pharmacy, and veterinary medicine. Meanwhile, Corps environmental health officers and engineers helped assess and counter public health threats caused by the hurricanes and subsequent flooding. Although satisfied with the relief services the Corps provided, some needs were not met, especially in the nursing, mental health, and dental areas. Corps officers and field commanders also identified the need for more nursing and mental health professionals, the latter for both hurricane victims and response personnel.

The report found that while most deployed officers met readiness standards, "...many lacked experience, effective training, and familiarity with response plans." Among the report's recommendations was the need to institute more effective training for Corps officers; streamline deployment-related travel; stagger deployments to ensure continuity of operations; and improve ability to coordinate mission assignments and track officers in the field.

Despite the acknowledged need for improvement, the PHS response to the hurricanes of 2005 spawned a broadening recognition that the Corps was, indeed, an indispensable component of national health security. The evolving focus on officer readiness and capability to deploy to public health emergencies would serve to strengthen the vitality of, and provide further justification for the essentiality of the PHS Commissioned Corps.

AFGHANISTAN AND IRAQ WARS

The Afghanistan War (Operation Enduring Freedom) and Iraq War (Operation Iraqi Freedom) were prolonged armed conflicts that began in 2001 and 2003, respectively. The George W. Bush administration, joined by coalition allies, initiated these retaliatory operations using the predicate of the September 2001 attacks on the United States The Iraq War, also known as the Second Gulf War, began in March 2003 with the invasion of Iraq by a U.S. and British-led coalition that overthrew the government of Saddam Hussein. On May 1, 2003, President Bush declared the end of major combat operations in Iraq; however, a longer phase insurgency emerged for several years, and the U.S. did not formally complete its withdrawal until December 2011.

Many PHS officers served with U.S. military forces in Afghanistan and Iraq, deploying in various consultative roles on clinical and public health missions. Among the assignments were support and direct assistance with shoring up hospital facilities, public health services, and public works infrastructure.

CAPT Clare Helminiak *(c)* at a hospital in Charikar, Afghanistan.

DART CAPT Pete Wallis *[left]*, CAPT Joe Hughart, CDR George Havens, CAPT Brad Woodruff, CAPT Eric Noji.

The Commissioned Corps assistance was occasionally provided within the setting of active military operations, with a few PHS officers coming under enemy fire. For that reason, several officers received training in defensive driving, security, and weapons of mass destruction. Some PHS officers were detailed to the U.S. Agency for International Development (USAID) beginning in 2003. As part of USAID Disaster Assistance Response Teams (DARTs), PHS officers from various agencies deployed as a group, having diverse public health backgrounds such as health care, epidemiology, environmental health, water and sanitation. In addition to providing expertise on the public health system and public works infrastructure, officers provided direct patient care services

PHS engineering officers inspecting Al Rasheed water treatment plant located south of Baghdad, Iraq, with military protection.

and assessed local health needs, including issues related to communicable diseases, high rates of diarrhea, lack of immunizations, and poor maternal and child health care. Follow-up included collaborations with relief organizations to help the local populace obtain food, water and medicines.[29-32]

NONRENEWAL, ACTING SG, CONGRESSIONAL TESTIMONY

Surgeon General Carmona's 4-year tenure came to an unexpected end July 31, 2006, when his term of office was not renewed by the George W. Bush Administration. Many believed that political appointees instigated the nonrenewal. Once again, Kenneth Moritsugu became the Acting Surgeon General. On July 10, 2007, former Surgeons General Carmona, David Satcher and C. Everett Koop testified before the House Committee on Oversight and Government Reform that they experienced varying degrees of political interference in the administrations in which they served. Dr. Carmona stated that political appointees often applied ideological, theological, and/or political considerations and preconceived beliefs that were scientifically incorrect to public health policy discussions and public announcements. Although disputed by administration officials, the *Washington Post* newspaper stated, "Dr. Carmona joins a list of present and former Bush administration officials who assert that politics often trumped science within what had previously been nonpartisan government health and scientific agencies." The Surgeons General also noted the diminution of the Office of the Surgeon General and called for greater protection from political pressure and independence of the Office.[33-35] Political and ideological bias can undermine public health protections and until the Trump administration, the G.W. Bush administration was widely considered the most antagonistic toward science/science-based policies in recent political history.[36]

SECOND ACTING SG

RADM STEVEN K. GALSON, an officer with a distinguished PHS career, having formerly served as deputy director and then director of the Food and Drug Administration's Center for Drug Evaluation and Research, was appointed the Acting Surgeon General on October 1, 2007, upon the retirement of Kenneth Moritsugu on September 30, 2007. Galson served in the Acting SG position until October 1, 2009. Notably, he served concurrently as Acting Assistant Secretary for Health from January to June 2009. Steven Galson received his MD degree from Mount Sinai School of Medicine and an MPH from Harvard University. While Surgeon General, Galson embarked on the *Healthy Youth for a Healthy Future Initiative* in 2008, which included an outreach tour to 38 states to recognize effective childhood obesity prevention programs and to model healthy behaviors. He issued two *Surgeon General's Calls to Action: Prevent Deep Vein Thrombosis and Pulmonary Embolism;*[37] and, *Promote Healthy Homes.*

Steven K. Galson

Hurricanes Gustav and Ike. Dr. Galson's tenure covered one of the larger PHS responses to hurricanes making landfall in the U.S. In 2008, two powerful Category 2 hurricanes hit the United States: Hurricane Gustav which made landfall along the Louisiana coast on September 1, and Hurricane Ike which struck the Gulf Coast near Galveston, Texas September 13. Approximately 800 PHS officers deployed to these natural disaster emergencies, plus five Federal Medical Stations, serving alongside healthcare professionals from the Medical Reserve Corps and National Disaster Medical System to augment local and state resources.

DOD/HHS MENTAL HEALTH AGREEMENT

In April 2008, a 10-year Mental Health Memorandum of Agreement (MOA) was signed by DOD and HHS to detail credentialed behavioral health PHS officers to military treatment facility positions to treat service members who were returning from deployments with conditions such as anxiety, depression, post-traumatic stress disorder (PTSD), and flashbacks. Known as the DOD–USPHS Partnership for Psychological Health Initiative (PPHI), each position requires an initial 3-year tour with the Commissioned Corps. The MOA was renewed October 12, 2018, effective through April 30, 2025. The PHS recruits officers, especially new calls-to-active duty, to fill an array of behavioral health positions at Army, Navy, and Air Force facilities throughout the nation to provide mental health care for service members and their families.

Paul J. Andreason

PHS CAPT Paul J. Andreason, an exemplary career officer, served with the Department of Defense as the psychiatric attending physician for the combat-related PTSD day-hospital/intensive outpatient treatment program at the Washington, DC, Walter Reed Army Medical Center from 2008 to 2011 and then transferred to the new combined uniformed service Walter Reed National Military Medical Center in Bethesda, Maryland, where he continued his professional duties until 2014. Andreason noted that PHS personnel also worked in the Departments of Social Work, Psychology, Nursing, and Rehabilitation Medicine, as well as the Department of Psychiatry at Walter Reed.[38]

TOBACCO LEGISLATION

On June 22, 2009, the *Family Smoking Prevention and Tobacco Control Act* was enacted.[39] This historic legislation gave the FDA authority to regulate the manufacture, distribution and marketing of tobacco products, and created the Center for Tobacco Products in FDA to implement the Act.

ICE HEALTH SERVICE CORPS

ICE Health Service Corps' history goes back to 1980, when the "freedom flotilla" mass migration from Cuba led to the creation of the Division of Immigration Health Services (DIHS) in HHS, to which USPHS Commissioned Corps officers were detailed. The program expanded as many detention centers opened around the country. In the aftermath of the September 11, 2001, attacks on the World Trade Center, the Department of Homeland Security was created in 2002, incorporating 22 agencies, one of which was the Bureau of Immigration and Customs Enforcement, now known as the U.S. Immigration and Customs Enforcement (ICE). ICE is responsible for enforcing customs and immigration laws and is authorized to detain immigrants at processing centers and detention facilities. In October 2007, DIHS was realigned from HHS to ICE and, in 2010, DIHS was renamed the ICE Health Service Corps (IHSC). IHSC's mission is to provide the safe delivery of high quality health care to noncitizens in ICE custody. IHSC administers a detention health system that provides direct health care in ICE-owned facilities; oversees compliance with healthcare-related detention standards in contracted facilities; reimburses for off-site health care services that detainees receive; and supports special operations missions. The ICE Health Service Corps consists of a multidisciplinary staff of about 1,700 authorized positions

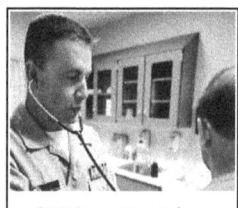

CDR Sean McMahan examining a patient.

that include federal civilians, contract personnel, and PHS officers at ICE Headquarters, field offices, and ICE-managed detention facilities. Authorized PHS positions were increased from 569 in FY 2022 to 619 in FY 2023. The IHSC workforce is multidisciplinary, comprised of physicians, nurse practitioners, physician assistants, nurses, social workers, psychiatrists, psychologists, dentists, pharmacists, and administrators. IHSC healthcare professionals provide intake screening within 12 hours of arrival and comprehensive medical screening within 14 days. They provide compassionate care that includes medical, nursing, pharmacy, dental, behavioral health, and public health services. IHSC healthcare staff are often the first to diagnose and address chronic conditions and communicable illnesses during the initial medical encounters with those who enter custody. Immigration and Customs Enforcement issued an inaugural report, *Health Service Corps, Fiscal Year 2020*, on November 5, 2020.

Aisha K. Mix

In Fiscal Year 2023, the IHSC team provided direct health care to 131,000 noncitizens housed at 19 ICE Health Service Corps-staffed facilities throughout the nation. The Field Medical Coordinator Program comprised only of PHS officers oversaw the health care for about 192,000 detainees housed in 128 non-IHSC-staffed facilities and managed more serious detainee illnesses with medical referrals. IHSC's Special Operations Unit supported ICE Air Operations and ICE Enforcement and Removal Operations, caring for 2,579 noncitizens during transport to 97 countries. And under an agreement with the U.S. Coast Guard, IHSC also provided medical services to 958 migrants rescued or interdicted at sea. IHSC expanded its telepsychiatry services to address high demand and staff shortages and, as of 2023, provided telepsychiatry services in eight ICE facilities. IHSC also implemented the Unified Patient Tracking System, a database that compiles significant event notifications, clinical updates, tracks hospitalized patients with medical and mental health concerns, and supports case management and continuity of care, for all noncitizens in ICE custody across 147 facilities.[40,41]

Diedre Presley

Notable in 2019 and 2020, the USPHS appointed two officers from IHSC – RDML Aisha K. Mix, Senior Health Policy Administrator, and CAPT Diedre Presley, Deputy Assistant Director, Administration Division – to serve as the Chief Professional Officers for the Nurse Category and the Health Services Officer Category, respectively. Further, RDML Jennifer Moon, Deputy Assistant Director, Health Care Compliance Division, IHSC, was appointed the Chief Professional Officer for the Nurse Category in 2023.

Jennifer Moon

Gene Migliaccio

Gene Migliaccio, DrPH, Professor and an Associate Dean at the Milken Institute School of Public Health, George Washington University, served 35 years in federal government. As a member of the federal Senior Executive Service, he served as Executive Director for Community Care with the Department of Veterans Affairs from 2015 to 2018, and as Director of Federal Occupational Health Services from 2007 to 2015. Prior to that, PHS officer CAPT Migliaccio was the Director of Immigration Health Services, ICE, for twelve years. A seasoned and highly regarded public health professional, Dr. Migliaccio is experienced in managing the delivery of health care services to diverse population groups, including special and underserved communities.

In Their Words

by CAPT (Ret.) Gene Migliaccio

The most professionally satisfying, challenging, and important position I held during my 35-year federal career was as Director of the Division of Immigration Health Services where I served from 1994 to 2007. PHS immigration work began in 1892 at Ellis Island – and here I was, having the honor and privilege to lead PHS commissioned officers, civil servants and contractors in our vital mission of providing health care and public health services in support of immigration law enforcement. In 1994, the organization consisted of 68 FTEs providing health care in 7 clinics and a short stay inpatient facility to about 7,000 undocumented migrants on any given day. In the mid-1990s, changes in immigration law resulted in a doubling in our population served to 14,000. We developed an integrated delivery system that included medical, dental, mental health, and environmental health services, which was quality-driven and accredited; focused on hiring and training new staff; incorporated medical claims administration; and increased our physical infrastructure. We developed new mission, vision, and value statements, and a "Spirit" statement that was our guiding light – we added dignity to the necessary process of undocumented migrant detention. Our most challenging public health threat was combating tuberculosis, especially along the Texas border, where the TB rate was five times the national rate. We went into overdrive to focus on population health, joined by CDC and State TB controllers. Our PHS officers moved from PPDs to chest x-rays via teleradiology, resulting in reductions in TB identification from 3 days to 4 hours. Our PHS leadership team was strong, creating an integrated 24/7 health care delivery system by growing the program to over 800 FTEs; establishing a leadership training program for administrative and professional staff; achieving Joint Commission accreditation for all ambulatory care clinics; opening 10 new clinics with over 200 inpatient beds; and providing exceptional care to our 28,000 daily population. We accomplished all of this due to our values of treating each person in the Division with dignity and respect, and seeking opportunities for their continued growth and advancement into positions of increased responsibility and fulfillment.

HUMAN GENOME PROJECT

Among the most noteworthy of scientific research projects is the Human Genome Project (HGP). On April 14, 2003, the International Human Genome Sequencing Consortium announced the successful completion of the Human Genome Project. Initiated in 1990, a consortium of research geneticists in the United States, China, France, Germany, Japan, and the United Kingdom successfully determined and sequenced almost all the three billion base pairs that comprise human genomic deoxyribonucleic acid (DNA). Genes are segments of DNA made up of four chemical bases: adenine (A), guanine (G), cytosine (C), and thymine (T), and over 99 percent of those bases are the same in all people. The research intent was to show each gene's functionality and, further, determine the genetic basis of diseases from which to develop new and effective approaches for disease prevention and treatment.  The HGP was initially led in the U.S. by James Watson, PhD, and later by Francis S. Collins, MD, PhD, who noted, "The availability of the highly accurate human genome sequence in free public databases enables researchers around the world to conduct even more precise studies of our genetic instruction book and how it influences health and disease." The elucidation of the human genome led to an international collaboration that developed a haplotype map, named *HapMap*, of the human genome. A haplotype is a common set of genetic variants, or polymorphisms, and the map provides a means to identify and catalog genes and genetic variations affecting health, disease, and responses to drugs and environmental factors.[42,43]

CHRONOLOGY • 2002–2009

SG Richard H. Carmona, August 2002–July 2006
Acting SG Kenneth P. Moritsugu, August 2006–September 2007
Acting SG Steven K. Galson, October 2007–October 2009

2003	Secretary Thompson announces major initiative to transform the USPHS Corps.
2003	HHS and Department of Agriculture follow-on to 1998 agreement, to detail more PHS officers to the Food Safety and Inspection Service.
2003	The International Human Genome Sequencing Consortium announces successful completion of the Human Genome Project.
2003	Iraq/Afghanistan Wars to which PHS officers deployed.
2004	Release of the first of two Surgeon General's Reports on *Health Consequences of Smoking*.
2004	Release of Surgeon General's *Report on Bone Health and Osteoporosis*.

2004	*Project Bioshield Act*. Provides authorization and funding to expedite research, development and availability of products against CBRN agents.
2005	Secretary Leavitt advances transformation with Commissioned Corps Renewal Initiative.
2005	Release of the new USPHS Mission Statement.
2005	Hurricanes Katrina, Rita and Wilma devastate the Gulf region; the USPHS responds with the largest-ever (to date) deployment of personnel.
2006	Release of the new USPHS Core Values.
2006	Transformation Implementation Plan is released.
2006	Release of the Surgeon General's Report on the *Health Consequences of Involuntary Exposure to Tobacco Smoke*.
2006	*Pandemic and All Hazards Preparedness Act of 2006*. Creates the Office of the ASPR, HHS; codifies the Medical Reserve Corps.
2007	Division of Immigration Health Services realigned from HHS to Department of Homeland Security, and renamed the ICE Health Service Corps in 2010.
2008	Hurricanes Gustav and Ike activate one of the larger USPHS responses with 800 PHS officers deployed to the region.
2008	DOD-USPHS Partnership for Psychological Health Initiative agreement; MOA is renewed in 2018.
2009	The *Family Smoking Prevention and Tobacco Control Act*. Gives FDA authority to regulate tobacco products.

CHAPTER FIFTEEN

AFFORDABLE CARE, EBOLA, CDC
2009 to 2014

PRESIDENT BARACK OBAMA'S first choice for Surgeon General was neurosurgeon and CNN medical journalist Sanjay Gupta. Obama believed that Gupta could be an effective spokesperson on health care reform while serving as Surgeon General. The Commissioned Officers Association and some Corps officials initially voiced displeasure, noting Gupta's lack of public health background. However, other public health advocates endorsed the nomination, noting that Gupta had excellent communication skills and could reinvigorate the Office of the Surgeon General. But in early March 2009, Dr. Gupta withdrew his name from consideration for personal reasons.

The President then announced his choice of Regina M. Benjamin as the 18th U.S. Surgeon General in a ceremony at the White House on July 13, 2009. In her acceptance remarks, Benjamin gave a moving account of her own family who were afflicted with preventable diseases and illness. She added, "While I cannot change my family's past, I can be a voice in the movement to improve our nation's health care and our nation's health for the future. My hope, if confirmed as Surgeon General, is to be America's doctor, America's family physician." Dr. Benjamin was confirmed by the Senate on October 29, 2009, and took office on November 3. She named RADM David C. Rutstein as Acting Deputy Surgeon General in January 2010, who served until October 1, 2010. Regina Benjamin attended the new Morehouse School of Medicine in Atlanta and because it was not yet accredited, she

Regina M. Benjamin

completed her medical education at the University of Alabama in Birmingham in 1984, taking her family practice residency at the Medical Center of Central Georgia. She also earned an MBA from Tulane University in 1991. Dr. Benjamin spent three years with the National Health Service Corps and in 1990 founded the Bayou La Batre Rural Health Clinic in Alabama, keeping the clinic in operation in spite of damage from Hurricanes Georges and Katrina and a devastating fire. She also served as Associate Dean for rural health at the College of Medicine, University of South Alabama. In 1995, she was the first African American woman to be elected to the American Medical Association Board of Trustees and was president of its Education and Research Foundation. In 2002, she became president of the Medical Association of the State of Alabama and served as the 2008-2009 chair of the Federation of State Medical Boards of the U.S. Dr. Benjamin was the recipient of several prominent recognitions, including the MacArthur Fellows Program Grant in 2008.

OBESITY EPIDEMIC

Soon after Dr. Benjamin became Surgeon General, on February 9, 2010, First Lady Michelle Obama announced the launch of an ambitious *Let's Move!* campaign with the goal to eliminate the epidemic of childhood obesity within a generation. Childhood obesity in the nation had tripled during the prior three decades and such children were at high risk of developing chronic obesity-related health problems. "The physical and emotional health of an entire generation and the economic health and security of our nation is at stake," said Mrs. Obama. Many dignitaries attended the White House ceremony including the Surgeon General, Cabinet members, members of Congress, and an array of leaders from the medical, media, sports, entertainment and business communities. The campaign included a comprehensive and multifaceted approach to combating the obesity epidemic, including improved food nutrition labels so that healthier food choices could be made; serving healthier breakfasts and lunches in school food programs; improving access to fresh fruits, vegetables and whole grains in communities where access is limited (known as food deserts); and increasing children's physical activity. An umbrella foundation, the Partnership for a Healthier America, comprised of leading children's health foundations and a new federal Task Force on Childhood Obesity comprised of key agency representatives were formed to support the campaign.[1] The Healthy, Hunger-Free Kids Act of 2010 was also enacted, which reauthorized child nutrition funding and set new nutrition standards. Work was already underway with the Food and Drug Administration (FDA) and food and beverage companies, and in June 2011 the Department of Agriculture replaced its *Food Pyramid* with *MyPlate* – a plate with four sections for fruits, vegetables, grains and protein, and a circle for dairy.

Childhood and adult obesity was a major public health issue that had been a priority of previous Surgeons General, and Dr. David Satcher underscored the problem with the 2001 release of his *Call to Action to Prevent and Decrease Overweight and Obesity*. It was evident, however, that the challenge to childhood obesity would now be led by the First Lady. While Surgeon General Benjamin appeared alongside Mrs. Obama at some events, Benjamin's overweight appearance was a topic of discussion in the media. Benjamin had critics and supporters over the matter, and to a certain extent she effectively countered with the observation that "You can be healthy and fit at different sizes."[2] Although not a direct participant in Mrs. Obama's anti-obesity campaign, Benjamin was an advocate of the initiative and aligned herself with it by incorporating the January 2010 release of *The Surgeon General's Vision for a Healthy and Fit Nation*[3] into the campaign narrative. As Benjamin declared in an article, "Both my 'Vision for a Healthy and Fit Nation' report and the First Lady's 'Let's Move!' campaign take a comprehensive approach that engages families and communities, as well as the public and private sectors."[4] The *Vision* report, like most Surgeon General reports, was largely written by subject matter experts at the Department of Health and Human Services (HHS), including the National Institutes of Health (NIH) and Centers for Disease Control and Prevention (CDC). It presented an excellent review of the problem of obesity in the nation, its causes and health consequences. The report focused on preventive measures and interventions relating to personal behaviors, and social determinants and physical environments that offer or limit opportunities for positive health outcomes.

AFFORDABLE CARE ACT

When Regina Benjamin took office as Surgeon General, one health issue was dominating the headlines – the health care reform legislation. The issue of health care reform was contentious from the beginning and would be controversial even after legislation was in place. For some time, there had been an ongoing, partisan political battle in Congress over health reform legislation. Despite Republican opposition, the Patient Protection and Affordable Care Act (Affordable Care Act, ACA)[5] narrowly passed both chambers of Congress and was signed into law by President Obama on March 23, 2010. But implementation of the law would be problematic and subject to ongoing opposition. Regina Benjamin's intent was to become a spokesperson for the administration, as indicated by her nomination remarks: "As we work toward a solution to this health care crisis, I promise to communicate directly with the American people to help guide them through whatever changes may come with health care reform." Unlike Sanjay Gupta and some of her predecessors, however, Benjamin was not generally thought of as being a commanding speaker. And, in response to a question to Dr. Benjamin about her priorities in light of past Surgeons General who had dealt with difficult and controversial public health issues, she replied: "I'm not sure if anything is going to be controversial. My priorities are wellness and prevention. Obesity is a major issue...."[6] Kathleen Sebelius, a former Insurance Commissioner and Governor of Kansas, became HHS Secretary in April 2009. It was evident from the outset that the Surgeon General, though supportive of health care reform, would not be involved in the complicated and hard-hitting battle over passage and implementation of the Affordable Care Act. Led by Sebelius, ACA messaging had to be carefully

> The extreme political partisanship about health care reform likely removed it from appropriate discourse for the Surgeon General.

crafted by experts who were conversant in the complexities of national health insurance. Benjamin was the keynote speaker at a March 2010 meeting of the American Medical Association; when asked about the policy behind health care reform, she replied: "I don't talk about legislation. That's not my role."[7] Perhaps the absence of the Surgeon General was fortuitous – the extreme partisanship and ensuing rancor over health reform had likely removed it from the bailiwick of appropriate and impartial public discourse for the Surgeon General.

Corps-Related Provisions

The Affordable Care Act effected some changes to the USPHS Commissioned Corps. It eliminated the cap of 2,800 Regular Corps officers and deemed all Reserve Corps officers serving on active duty at the time of enactment to be officers of the Regular Corps, and it replaced the Reserve Corps with a Ready Reserve Corps. However, the ACA inadvertently failed to include authority related to personnel compensation for the Ready Reserve, and so the reserve component languished until 2020 when new legislation remedied the omission *(see Chapter Seventeen).*

National Prevention Council

The Patient Protection and Affordable Care Act, Section 4001, provided for establishment of the National Prevention, Health Promotion, and Public Health Council (National Prevention Council, NPC) within HHS, composed of twelve federal department heads and any other appropriate agency, with the Surgeon General as chairperson. President Obama signed Executive Order 13544 on June 10, 2010, to authorize the Council. Its principal objectives were to coordinate prevention, wellness and health promotion practices and, with assistance of an Advisory Group, prepare a national prevention, health promotion, public health and integrative health care strategy. The *National Prevention Strategy* was published June 16, 2011. In the Introduction, Dr. Benjamin noted the *Strategy* encourages private and public partnerships to "improve America's health by helping to create healthy and safe communities, expand clinical and community-based preventive services, empower people to make healthy choices, and eliminate health disparities." In June 2012, the Council released the *National Prevention Council Action Plan* which outlined the federal commitment and actions to implement the *NPC Strategy.*[8]

PRIORITIES/INITIATIVES

The Obama administration was intently focused on getting health reform legislation passed and implemented. Benjamin was content with discussing her priorities of wellness and prevention, something everyone could agree on, weaving a narrative about how they coincided with the goals of Mrs. Obama's *Let's Move!* campaign and the Affordable Care Act. On April 1, 2013, Dr. Benjamin introduced the Surgeon General's *Every Body Walk!* initiative to promote walking and walkable communities. This outreach effort gained media attention and included appearances by Benjamin in various cities to lead a communal walk and encourage people to walk as part of a daily, enjoyable routine to gain long-term health benefits. On May 11, 2011, Dr. Benjamin along with the National Consumers League launched the *Script Your Future* public awareness campaign about the importance of medication adherence. In February 2013, Dr. Benjamin joined leaders of the federal interagency Healthy Homes Work Group to announce release of *Advancing Healthy Housing: A Strategy for Action*. This follows upon Acting Surgeon General Galson's 2009 *Call to Action to Promote Healthy Homes*. The *Strategy for Action* unifies federal efforts to assist states in remedying unsafe housing conditions and to expand the availability of affordable safe housing.

Surgeon General's Reports, Calls to Action

Dr. Benjamin released two reports updating the dangers of tobacco use. In 2010, a Report of the Surgeon General entitled *How Tobacco Smoke Causes Disease: The Biology and Behavioral Basis for Smoking-Attributable Disease*[9] provides a comprehensive, scientific discussion that substantiates evidence relating to how mainstream and secondhand smoke exposures damage human organs, and effective interventions for tobacco cessation. The other report, released in 2012, *Preventing Tobacco Use Among Youth and Young Adults: A Report of the Surgeon General*, provides updated data on the prevalence, social and other causes, and effects of tobacco use by young people. The report also identifies effective strategies that hold the potential to dramatically reduce tobacco use among youth. In 2010, HHS also released *Ending the Tobacco Epidemic: A Tobacco Control Strategic Action Plan*.

In 2011, Dr. Benjamin issued the *Surgeon General's Call to Action to Support Breastfeeding*,[10] which highlighted the benefits of breastfeeding as the best source of infant nutrition and immunologic protection. The report identifies current barriers to breastfeeding, and encourages communities, hospitals and businesses to support women who choose to breastfeed.

Surgeon General David Satcher released the first *Call to Action to Prevent Suicide* in 1999 and, on May 2, 2001, presented the *National Strategy for Suicide Prevention*. In 2012, Surgeon General Benjamin and the National Action Alliance for Suicide Prevention released an updated *National Strategy for Suicide Prevention* with four strategic directions and goals and objectives to guide suicide prevention actions for the next decade.

H1N1 INFLUENZA

In April 2009, a new novel influenza A (H1N1) virus emerged in the United States and rapidly spread worldwide. The virus was designated as influenza A (H1N1)pdm09 virus and was informally called swine flu. On June 11, 2009, the World Health Organization (WHO) declared a global H1N1 influenza pandemic, and on October 24, 2009, President Obama declared the flu a national emergency. The Centers for Disease Control and Prevention activated its Emergency Operations Center (EOC) on April 22, 2009, to coordinate a complex year-long response to this emerging public health threat. This influenza A virus was different from H1N1 viruses in general circulation at the time. While nearly one-third of those over 60 years of age had antibodies against the virus, likely from exposure to an older H1N1 virus earlier in life, few young people had any existing immunity and the 2009 flu pandemic primarily affected children and young and middle-aged adults. The prevalence of influenza waned during the summer of 2009, but a second wave that fall continued until November 2009. By May 2010, case numbers were in steep decline. The Food and Drug Administration approved four H1N1 influenza vaccines in September and a fifth vaccine in November 2009, which were initially administered to high risk persons with the launch of a national vaccination campaign in October 2009. Vaccines were not available in large quantities until

Stephen C. Redd

late November – after the second wave of illness had subsided. From April 12, 2009, when the disease was first reported until April 10, 2010, an estimated 60.8 million cases, 274,304 hospitalizations and 12,469 deaths occurred in the nation.[11,12] The U.S. public health emergency expired in June 2010, and WHO announced the end of the global pandemic on August 10, 2010. Two PHS officers, Rear Admirals Stephen C. Redd and Anne Schuchat of the CDC led the federal response to the pandemic, with Redd serving as the H1N1 incident commander overseeing the 3,000 CDC staff who participated in the response and vaccination effort, and the longest activation of the EOC at the time. Dr. Redd served as the CDC Deputy Director for Public Health Service and Implementation Science. Dr. Anne Schuchat was the Director of CDC's National Center for Immunization and Respiratory Diseases and served as chief health officer and a high-profile spokesperson for the CDC during the 2009 pandemic response. Both officers were exceptional national leaders, and each served with distinction at the Centers for Disease Control and Prevention.

Anne Schuchat

COMMISSIONED CORPS MANAGEMENT REVIEW

Assistant Secretary for Health Howard K. Koh, who was appointed in 2009, recognized the need to improve the organizational and operational structure of the Commissioned Corps. From 2009 to 2010, Dr. Koh initiated a comprehensive management review of the Corps that included senior level officials in HHS and the Commissioned Corps.[13] The review resulted in over 40 recommendations. Among key changes, a plan to create a new billeting system that went into effect in January 2010. Category specific standard billets were modified with position specific content and new personnel orders were issued. In 2012, the Division of Commissioned Corps Personnel and Readiness (DCCPR) was formed, consolidating OCCO, OCCFM, OCCSS, and OFRD (renamed Readiness and Deployment Operations Group, or RedDOG, in 2013). The U.S. Coast Guard's Direct Access system, an integrated administrative, personnel and payroll system, was acquired to support Corps operations. Another key outcome was establishing criteria for recruiting new PHS officers. The criteria limited the positions to which officers could be assigned and had the potential of reducing officer accessions, henceforth. In brief, the five "pillars" representing what all Corps assignments should encompass were as follows:

Howard K. Koh

- Service to medically underserved and vulnerable populations;
- Service in hardship locations, hazardous duty, or difficult-to-recruit positions;
- Service in positions that require rapid deployment and 24/7 availability;
- Service in positions that require regular engagement with other uniformed services; or,
- Service in key public health positions that can only be filled with a Commissioned Corps officer and address an important need.

PHS OFFICER DEPLOYMENTS

Hurricane Sandy

Hurricane Sandy (Superstorm Sandy) was the strongest hurricane of the 2012 Atlantic hurricane season. A Category 3 storm when it made landfall in Cuba, it became a Category 2 and was the largest Atlantic hurricane on record, by diameter, off the northeastern coast of the United States. On October 29, Sandy came ashore near Brigantine, New Jersey, with hurricane-force winds and moved inland. The hurricane impacted the entire Eastern Seaboard, with particularly severe flooding, structural damage and loss of utility service in communities of New Jersey and New York. In New York, streets, tunnels and subway lines were flooded, and power was shut down in and around the city.

HHS ultimately sent more than 1,000 disaster medical personnel, PHS officers and civilians, to assist with the response and recovery. PHS Rapid Deployment Force (RDF) teams, which are scalable multidisciplinary teams of up to 125 members, were among those initially deployed to New Jersey and New York. Disaster Medical Assistance Teams (DMAT) and multiple PHS response teams deployed to New Jersey – one RDF, one Mental Health Team (MHT), one Services Access Team (SAT), one Incident Response Coordination Team (IRCT); and, in New York – three RDFs, two MHTs, two IRCTs, and a National Veterinary Response Team. In all, over 400 PHS officers were deployed to New Jersey, New York and Connecticut to provide incident management, staff 250-bed federal medical stations, render clinical care within hospitals and shelters, and provide environmental health and veterinary services.[14,15]

Unaccompanied Children

In fiscal year 2014, there was an 80 percent rise from the prior year in the number of Central American children without a parent or guardian who were crossing the southern border into the U.S. The influx of nearly 70,000 unaccompanied children resulted in an urgent humanitarian situation. Unaccompanied children under the age of 18 who are apprehended by U.S. Customs and Border Protection (CBP) are placed in shelters overseen by the Administration for Children and Families (ACF). Through the HHS Office of the Assistant Secretary for Preparedness and Response, the Commissioned Corps was authorized in May 2014 to begin deploying officers for the unaccompanied children mission to assist CBP facilities and augment the ACF-contracted staff in shelters. PHS Rapid Deployment Forces were joined by other PHS teams specializing in applied public health, mental health, and social work to provide medical and public health coordination, medical screening, basic medical care, vaccinations and mental health screening for the children. Five SATs provided support for case management activities. A total of 337 PHS officers deployed for this mission.[16]

CDR Margaret Caulk counseling an unaccompanied child, Nogales, Arizona.

Accomplishments, Early Out

Regina Benjamin capably carried out her duties as Surgeon General during a challenging period for the Corps. She chaired the National Prevention Council and consistently espoused wellness and prevention. A focus on the prevalence of obesity and the need to exercise more and make good food choices was a theme that permeated her tenure. In March 2011, a gaffe occurred during the Fukushima, Japan nuclear accident when the Surgeon General responded to a television reporter that it was appropriate that Californians were stocking up on potassium iodide tablets to protect the thyroid gland as a precaution against a possible nuclear cloud drifting to the Pacific coast. State and federal authorities, however, were advising that such measures were unnecessary, and at a press conference President Barack Obama affirmed that people need not take such measures. This much publicized instance was a reminder that dependable accuracy was required in a Surgeon General's pronouncements. In June 2013, Regina Benjamin announced her intention to resign and did so on July 16, 2013, four months prior to the end of her official term of office. No reason was proffered; in an email she stated, "My goal was to create a grassroots movement, to change our health care system from one focused on sickness and disease to a system focused on wellness and prevention. With your help, that movement has begun." HHS Secretary Sebelius praised Dr. Benjamin for her service to the nation.

Acting SG, An Emerging Health Crisis

A NEW CHALLENGE WOULD EMERGE after the Deputy Surgeon General, Boris D. Lushniak, assumed the position of Acting Surgeon General on July 17, 2013, serving until December 18, 2014. Lushniak received his medical degree from Northwestern University in 1983 and an MPH from Harvard University. He began his career in 1988 with CDC's Epidemic Intelligence Service at the National Institute for Occupational Safety and Health in Cincinnati, Ohio, and served on assignments to Kosovo, Bangladesh, Russia, Ground Zero in New York, and with the anthrax team in Washington, DC. In 2004, he transferred to FDA as chief medical officer in the Office of Counterterrorism Policy and Planning and was appointed FDA Assistant Commissioner for Counterterrorism Policy in 2005. Appointed Deputy Surgeon General in November 2010, Dr. Lushniak was a personable, interactive leader and lively speaker whose leadership style was distinctly different from that of Dr. Benjamin. When he became Acting Surgeon General, he was determined not to be an interim "stand-in" and so was proactive in engaging in operational and outreach activities and releasing two Surgeon General's reports. His term as Acting Surgeon General was particularly noteworthy due to the 2014 Ebola virus disease global epidemic, including an unprecedented international health mission involving the USPHS Commissioned Corps along with multiple agencies of the U.S. Government, to include the Department of Defense, in partnership with the Liberian Government.

Boris D. Lushniak

SURGEON GENERAL REPORTS

Acting Surgeon General Lushniak released two reports, the 50th Anniversary Surgeon General's *Report on Smoking and Health*,[17] and the first-ever *Surgeon General's Call to Action to Prevent Skin Cancer*.[18] *The Health Consequences of Smoking – 50 Years of Progress: A Report of the Surgeon General* was released on January 17, 2014, at a White House briefing by Dr. Lushniak, HHS Secretary Sebelius, Assistant Secretary Koh, and CDC Director Thomas Frieden, marking the 50th anniversary of the January 11, 1964 release of Surgeon General Terry's landmark report on the health hazards of tobacco use. Although the prevalence of smoking among adults declined from 42 percent in 1965 to 18 percent in 2012, nearly one-half million premature deaths and over $290 billion in total economic costs were attributed to tobacco use yearly as of 2014. The Report is a historical review of the research, epidemiology and progress made in reducing cigarette use and preventing tobacco-related disease and death.

EBOLA – A GLOBAL THREAT

Ebola virus disease (EVD) was first identified in 1976 in the Democratic Republic of the Congo (formerly Zaire) near the Ebola River, which gave the virus its name, and also in South Sudan. Since then, sporadic outbreaks have appeared in several African countries. In March 2014, an outbreak of EVD in Guinea, West Africa, soon spread to the countries of Liberia and Sierra Leone. On August 8, 2014, the World Health Organization (WHO) declared it to be an epidemic and a "public health emergency of international concern." President Barack Obama went on September 16, 2014, to the CDC in Atlanta for a meeting with Director Thomas Frieden and other officials. While at CDC, the President announced an unprecedented U.S. response to contain the virus, which had become an out-of-control epidemic and worldwide threat. Included in his remarks was the statement that "Personnel from the U.S. Public Health Service will deploy to the new field hospitals that we're setting up in Liberia."[19] A few days prior, Dr. Lushniak had approved the plan to deploy USPHS Commissioned Corps officers to Liberia. The USPHS would be the only American entity to provide direct patient care to Ebola patients in Africa. The CDC would also send 1,900 civilian and commissioned officer personnel to Guinea, Liberia and Sierra Leone from July 2014 to March 2016, the largest response in agency history, to conduct surveillance, contact tracing, infection control training and communications.[20,21]

The mission was the largest ever U.S. Government response to an international epidemic and it required immediate action. The U.S. Agency for International Development (USAID) was the lead agency. The $700 million plan involved multiple missions, including the deployment of 3,000 military personnel to West Africa; construction of ten 50-bed medical treatment units

(Ebola treatment units, ETUs), laboratories and other medical facilities; healthcare provider training; and construction of a 25-bed hospital staffed by PHS officers to treat infected ETU healthcare workers. The 25-bed hospital was called the Monrovia Medical Unit (MMU) within PHS Camp Eason, which was named for John C. Eason, Jr., who in 1943 was the first African American commissioned in the PHS and whose assignments included work in Liberia.[22,23]

Camp Eason located in Margibi County, Liberia, about 50 miles from the capital city of Monrovia.
[FDA Voice, 2015]

Healthcare workers caring for patients with Ebola virus disease were among those who were at highest risk for contracting the disease. The White House National Security Council believed that to encourage national and international healthcare personnel to continue to volunteer in Ebola-affected

Malac (l), Sirleaf (c), Giberson (r) at MMU.

countries, it was essential to have a dedicated ETU facility – the Monrovia Medical Unit managed and staffed by PHS officers – for such workers should they become infected with the virus. Led by RADM Scott F. Giberson, Acting Deputy Surgeon General and PHS Ebola Response Commander, a small team went in October 2014 to work with the Department of Defense (DOD) and USAID to plan and build the MMU. The MMU was an Expeditionary Medical Support Unit that, with consultation from Médecins Sans Frontières, USAID and WHO, was reconfigured to function as an ETU, including adaptations for infection control. Initially, DOD provided for PHS officer billeting, food, water and other living support, security, plus medical equipment and supply chains.[24] On November 5, 2014, U.S. Ambassador to Liberia Deborah R. Malac and Liberian President Ellen Johnson Sirleaf joined RADM Giberson to mark the opening of the MMU. Supporting the Ebola mission was CAPT Dan Beck, Deputy Commander, PHS CC Ebola Response.

The first team of about 70 officers arrived in Liberia on October 27, 2014, and on November 12 the MMU accepted its first patient. Four overlapping teams of 70 PHS officers would be deployed on 60-day rotations. Team 2 transitioned with Team 1 the week of December 11-18. Teams consisted of clinical and public health specialists, including physicians, nurses, pharmacists, safety officers, laboratorians, behavioral health specialists, administration, logistics and planning staff.[23,24] From October 2014 to May 2015, over 300 officers were

Prior to deployment, PHS officers attended a CDC training course at the Federal Emergency Management Agency's Center for Domestic Preparedness in Anniston, Alabama. It was critical that healthcare providers were competent in donning and doffing personal protective equipment before being allowed to care for Ebola patients.
[Monrovia Medical Unit Walkthrough–YouTube]

deployed to the MMU, providing direct patient care for those with Ebola, malaria and other illnesses. They also assisted in research protocols and provided education to Liberian health workers.[24] The Ebola epidemic in West Africa brought about a successful collaboration of agencies in the Department of Health and Human Services, including the USPHS Commissioned Corps with the Office of the Assistant Secretary for Preparedness and Response, the Centers for Disease Control and Prevention and National Institutes of Health.

USPHS Commissioned Corps Team 3 at the Monrovia Medical Unit, March 6, 2015.[24]
Front Row: RADM Epifanio Elizondo, incoming MMU Commander (l),
MMU Commander Lushniak (c), and Officer in Charge CAPT Dean J. Coppola (r).

The USPHS and DOD overcame numerous challenges to establish quality treatment for Ebola-infected healthcare workers in the MMU. By the time the MMU was turned over to the Government of Liberia on April 30, 2015, it had treated 42 patients from 9 countries; 18 patients were diagnosed with Ebola virus disease, of which 9 died. On May 1, 2015, the USPHS flag was taken down at the MMU and on May 9 the nation of Liberia was finally declared free of Ebola. Overall, the Ebola epidemic took a devastating toll with more than 11,300 deaths in Guinea, Liberia and Sierra Leone.[24]

In Their Words

by RADM (Ret.) Boris D. Lushniak

In June of 2013, Surgeon General (SG) Regina Benjamin gathered her leadership team in her office and declared that RADM Scott Giberson, then head of the Division of Commissioned Corps Personnel and Readiness, would be the new Deputy Surgeon General (DSG). This startled me and the team as we thought that I was just unceremoniously relieved of my duties as DSG. She then declared "Boris will be the Acting Surgeon General" as she had decided to leave the SG role a few months before her term officially ended. Soon after, we lined up along the HHS driveway and saluted as the 18th Surgeon General departed by car. And thus, we entered another "Acting SG" stage. My notion was that to be "acting" meant that we as a team were "to act" – "to do" and not to be static placeholders. Although Scott and I were forewarned that our acting positions would last only a matter of months before a new SG was nominated and confirmed, we began to take action. However, days turned into weeks, weeks to months and then a year, and the challenges were many. Within the halls of HHS, we continued to fight for the existence of the Corps against formidable forces questioning the purpose of our uniformed service. In January 2014, we commemorated the 50th anniversary of SG Luther Terry's Report on Smoking and Health with a poignant ceremony at Terry's graveside with former SG Satcher, the Terry family and the public health community in attendance. A few days after, at the White House, we released the new Surgeon General's Report on the Health Consequences of Smoking—50 years of Progress. At this event I echoed the words of my hero, SG Koop, spoken by him at the 25th anniversary that "enough is enough" when it comes to tobacco use in this country. Perhaps the most difficult and dangerous challenge was leading the Corps' response to the Ebola epidemic in Western Africa. On September 16, 2014, President Obama announced that PHS Corps officers would deploy to Liberia and staff a hospital for healthcare workers who became ill. A team of officers led by RADM Giberson, CAPT Mike Schmoyer and others, working with the White House, HHS, Department of Defense, USAID and many other partners laid the groundwork to realize the Monrovia Medical Unit (MMU). DOD very ably supported this high visibility, high risk PHS mission and by November 7, 2014, the MMU was fully operational. From then until May 2015, over 300 PHS officers deployed to serve in this critical and historic mission. These officers, all volunteers, were an incredible group of compassionate and dedicated individuals who, by their service, reflected admirably upon the Corps. The Office of the Surgeon General arranged for a call from President Obama to the team in Liberia for a holiday greeting. Answering my prayers the night I committed to HHS leadership that the Corps was a "green light" for this mission – all officers returned home safely.

Presidential Unit Citation

In total, over 1,000 USPHS officers deployed in various roles to support the Ebola response mission, which included airport screenings in five major cities, reintegration missions back into the U.S., and domestic hospital preparedness actions. On September 24, 2015, President Barack Obama presented the Presidential Unit Citation (PUC) to the PHS Commissioned Corps during a White House ceremony in the Oval Office. The PUC was awarded to all Corps officers, including Ready Reserve officers on active duty between September 9, 2014 and May 1, 2015, "For extraordinary courage and the highest level of performance in action throughout the United States Government's response to the Ebola outbreak from Sept 9, 2014 to May 1, 2015."[25]

President Obama with [left to right] Calvin Edwards, Jose Belardo, Dan Beck, Vivek Murthy, Boris Lushniak, Scott Giberson, Sylvia Trent-Adams, and Dean Coppola at the White House, September 24, 2015.

CENTERS FOR DISEASE CONTROL AND PREVENTION

CDC and NIH Ebola Response

The Centers for Disease Control and Prevention was a critical partner in the campaign to end the epidemic of Ebola virus disease in West Africa. CDC's response to the epidemic was the largest ever, directed at controlling the epidemic in West Africa and strengthening preparedness for Ebola in the United States. From July 9, 2014 to March 31, 2016, approximately 4,000 CDC staff members were directly involved in the response effort and, of these, 1,897 deployed to Guinea, Liberia, Sierra Leone and other African countries affected by the epidemic. The deployed teams, comprised of Civil Service employees and PHS officers, included an array of specialists in epidemiology, infection control, laboratory analysis, medical care, emergency management, information technology, health communication, behavioral science, anthropology, logistics, planning and other disciplines.[21] CDC played a vital role in stemming the Ebola epidemic. The National Institute of Allergy and Infectious Diseases initiated a clinical research program to investigate treatment interventions for EVD. The Partnership for Research on Ebola Virus in Liberia was a research study that went through a few iterations with a focus on the efficacy of ZMapp, a biopharmaceutical drug comprising three monoclonal antibodies. The effort involved the deployment of 108 NIH staff, including 18 PHS officers. Further, a NIH/PHS research partnership led to additional commissioned officers being deployed to carry out the research protocols.[26]

Organizational Overview
The Centers for Disease Control and Prevention had its origin in 1942 as a wartime agency called the Office of Malaria Control in War Areas (MCWA), the purpose being to control malaria around military bases in the South where malaria was problematic. Its headquarters in Atlanta, Georgia, was central to endemic malaria in the nation, and it functioned within the PHS Division of State Relations headed by medical officer Joseph W. Mountin. The MCWA was renamed the Communicable Disease Center in July 1946. The National Malaria Eradication Program, a cooperative effort of CDC with state and local health agencies of Southern states, commenced on July 1, 1947 and, by 1951, malaria was considered eliminated from the U.S. Dr. Mountin envisioned a national agency to support state health departments in monitoring, investigating and controlling communicable diseases. The CDC's Epidemic Intelligence Service was established in 1951 to investigate disease outbreaks and respond to concerns about biological warfare relating to the Korean War. Much of the CDC grew programmatically by acquisition. In the early years, it acquired disease control programs including plague, venereal disease, tuberculosis, and a veterinary program. During the 1960s, CDC took on responsibility for immunization programs, foreign quarantine, smallpox eradication, and licensing of clinical laboratories. In 1970, the Communicable Disease Center was renamed the Center for Disease Control to reflect its broader mission, and it soon widened its portfolio to include nutrition, cigarette smoking, disease prevention, environmental health, occupational health and workplace safety. On October 1, 1980, the CDC was reorganized to better align its structure with the expanded mission and it was named the Centers [plural] for Disease Control, comprising several program component Centers. And in 1992, the CDC was again renamed the Centers for Disease Control and Prevention.[27,28] The CDC is an indispensable public health institution that protects the public health, safety and security domestically and globally. Its mission is to serve as "the national focus for developing and applying disease prevention and control, environmental health, and health promotion and health education activities designed to improve the health of the people of the United States." Among its many activities, CDC identifies and defines preventable health problems, maintains active

surveillance and is responsible for the control of disease outbreaks, implements environmental health programs, conducts operational research, and develops and administers occupational safety and health standards. CDC's vast portfolio pertains to infectious diseases, food borne pathogens, environmental and occupational health, injury prevention, health promotion and information, noninfectious and chronic diseases, emerging infectious diseases, and emergency preparedness. The CDC often leads emergency responses to natural and man-made threats, managed by the CDC Center for Preparedness and Response. The Emergency Operations Center (EOC) is their command center for monitoring emergency responses to major public health threats domestically and abroad. Staffed around-the-clock, the EOC supports the HHS Secretary's Operations Center. The Centers for Disease Control and Prevention is considered the gold standard for scientific rigor and integrity.

CDC Headquarters and Emergency Operations Center

In 1947, Emory University conferred 15 acres of land on Clifton Road to the CDC for a token payment of $10. The Centers for Disease Control and Prevention remains headquartered in Atlanta at 1600 Clifton Road, close to Emory University, with an affiliated Chamblee campus on Buford Highway in Atlanta. In July 1999, CDC dedicated its main campus to Edward R. Roybal, who championed the CDC while serving in the U.S. Congress. CDC also maintains several sites elsewhere in the nation for its various programs.

Until 2002, virtually all CDC Directors were PHS officers, but in recent years the position has been filled by civilian federal employees or political appointees. CAPT Louis L. Williams, Jr., was the first director of the MCWA. There have been twenty CDC Directors, thirteen of whom were USPHS Commissioned Corps officers *(noted by asterisk)*.

1942–1943	*Louis L. Williams, Jr.	1983–1989	*James O. Mason, MD, DrPH
1944–1946	*Mark D. Hollis, ScD	1990–1993	William L. Roper, MD, MPH
1947–1951	*Raymond A. Vonderlehr, MD	1993–1998	*David Satcher, MD, PhD
1952–1953	*Justin M. Andrews, ScD	1998–2002	*Jeffrey P. Koplan, MD, MPH
1953–1956	*Theodore J. Bauer, MD	2002–2009	Julie L. Gerberding, MD, MPH
1956–1960	*Robert J. Anderson, MD, MPH	2009–2017	Thomas R. Frieden, MD, MPH
1960–1962	*Clarence A. Smith, MD, MPH	2017–2018	Brenda Fitzgerald, MD
1962–1966	*James L. Goddard, MD, MPH	2018–2021	Robert R. Redfield, MD
1966–1977	*David J. Sencer, MD, MPH	2021–2023	Rochelle Walensky, MD, MPH
1977–1983	*William H. Foege, MD, MPH	2023–	Mandy K. Cohen, MD, MPH

Quite prominent was RADM Anne Schuchat, who was appointed the Principal Deputy Director of the Centers for Disease Control and Prevention in September 2015, and who retained that position following her retirement from the Commissioned Corps in 2018. Dr. Schuchat also was Acting CDC Director for short stints in 2017 and 2018. She was widely recognized as an authoritative CDC spokesperson who appeared on national broadcast media to inform the public about public health issues of national importance. Schuchat retired from federal service in 2021.

In Their Words

by RADM (Ret.) Anne Schuchat

My route to the Commissioned Corps of the U.S. Public Health Service was through the CDC's Epidemic Intelligence Service (EIS). In the fall of 1987, I flew to Atlanta for the job interviews. My last interview was with a current EIS Officer, Ned Hayes, who told me there was a stir because a new order would require CDC Corps officers to wear a uniform. For decades the EIS program has been the dominant entry point for medical officers into the Commissioned Corps. The CDC EIS Program trains physicians, veterinarians, and others with doctoral degrees in health-related fields to become disease detectives, and it has been a springboard for future leaders in the PHS. And while some of my fellow officers found their way to other HHS agencies, I spent my entire public health career in Atlanta at the Centers for Disease Control and Prevention. CDC is the largest federal agency headquartered outside Washington, DC, and now numbers over 27,000 personnel, including contractors. I began as an EIS officer assigned to Meningitis and Special Pathogens and got to work on vaccines against the same bacterial pathogens that I had seen during my medical school pediatrics rotation and internal medicine residency. From 1988 to 2005, I worked on surveillance, epidemiologic studies, outbreak investigations, and public health emergency responses such as the bioterrorist anthrax and the emergence of Severe Acute Respiratory Syndrome in 2003. I got to help make prevention of group B strep infections in newborns become a standard of care and establish a national policy to prevent foodborne listeriosis. After a focus on bacterial infectious diseases, I completed stints in a variety of leadership posts for the agency. While my uniformed service was quite different than my father's naval service in the Pacific during World War II, we shared the comradery of public service as well as amusement with the occasional pomp and circumstance. His participation in my Flag promotion ceremonies provided cherished moments for our whole family. I retired from the Corps after thirty years of service, always based at CDC headquarters in Atlanta though traveling to more than 25 countries and numerous states on official duty. Working at CDC with both Commissioned Corps and Civil Servants allowed me to see talented individuals rise to one challenge after another, placing service above self and the national and global interests ahead of career or personal advancement.

CDC Staffing

As of 2021, the Centers for Disease Control and Prevention and the Agency for Toxic Substances and Disease Registry, for which CDC performs administrative functions, were comprised of a staff of approximately 27,000 personnel, including about 12,000 full-time Civil Service employees, a similar number of contractors, and 830 USPHS commissioned officers. Programs with the largest contingent of PHS officers (approximate numbers) include the Center for Global Health (140 officers); National Center for Emerging and Zoonotic Infectious Diseases (125); Center for Surveillance, Epidemiology, and Laboratory Services (90); the National Institute for Occupational Safety and Health (80); National Center for HIV/AIDS, Viral Hepatitis, STD, and TB Prevention (70); the National Center for Immunization and Respiratory Diseases (65); the Center for Preparedness and Response (50); and, the National Center for Chronic Disease Prevention and Health Promotion (50).

CHRONOLOGY • 2009–2014

SG Regina M. Benjamin, November 2009–July 2013
Acting SG Boris D. Lushniak, July 2013–December 2014

2009	WHO declares a global H1N1 influenza pandemic.
2010	First Lady Michelle Obama launches the *Let's Move!* campaign.
2010	The *Patient Protection and Affordable Care Act*. Creates the National Prevention Council chaired by the Surgeon General.
2010	Surgeon General's Report on *How Tobacco Smoke Causes Disease: The Biology and Behavioral Basis for Smoking-Attributable Disease*.
2011	National Prevention Council releases the *National Prevention Strategy*.
2012	National Prevention Council releases the *NPC Action Plan*.
2013	The Surgeon General's *Every Body Walk!* initiative.
2014	Surgeon General's Report, *The Health Consequences of Smoking – 50 Years of Progress*, January 17.
2014	First-ever Surgeon General's *Call to Action to Prevent Skin Cancer*.
2014	Identification of Ebola virus disease in Guinea, West Africa.
2014	Monrovia Medical Unit opens November 5, staffed by 70 PHS officers.
2015	Monrovia Medical Unit closes May 1; Liberia declared Ebola-free May 9.
2015	Presidential Unit Citation is awarded to the USPHS Commissioned Corps.

CHAPTER SIXTEEN

OPIOIDS, COAST GUARD, NOAA
2014 to 2017

ANOTHER CHALLENGE WOULD EMERGE – this time, of a more political nature. After the departure of Surgeon General Benjamin in July 2013, Dr. Boris Lushniak served as Acting Surgeon General. The USPHS Commissioned Officers Association and former Surgeon General Richard Carmona made appeals for the appointment of a Surgeon General from the ranks of career officers in accordance with the law, but that went unheeded. On November 14, 2013, President Barack Obama nominated Dr. Vivek H. Murthy to serve as the next Surgeon General. Dr. Murthy was among the younger individuals and the first person of Indian heritage to hold the office of Surgeon General. Despite an impressive entrepreneurial record, he was arguably among the less experienced of Surgeon General nominees. Vivek Murthy earned his medical degree and MBA in Health Care Management from Yale University in 2003 and completed a residency in Internal Medicine at Brigham and Women's Hospital (BWH), where he became an attending physician and medical instructor. A record of accomplishment dates from 1995, when as a Harvard undergraduate he co-founded and for eight years led Visions Worldwide, an organization focused on HIV/AIDS education in India and the U.S.; and in 1997 Swasthya, a community partnership to train women in rural India to be health workers. In 2007, Dr. Murthy co-founded TrialNetworks, a cloud-based system to improve research efficiency. A co-founder of Doctors for Obama in 2008, renamed Doctors for America in 2009, it grew to 15,000 physicians and medical students to advocate for quality affordable health care and support the Affordable Care Act (ACA). In 2011, President Obama appointed Dr. Murthy to the Advisory Group on Prevention, Health Promotion, and Integrative and Public Health, which advises the National Prevention Council.

Vivek H. Murthy

PUBLIC HEALTH VS. SPECIAL INTEREST POLITICS

The nomination hearing of Vivek Murthy for the position of Surgeon General took place on February 4, 2014, before the U.S. Senate Committee on Health,

Education, Labor and Pensions (HELP). In his prepared statement Dr. Murthy espoused what had become the principal tenets of the position of Surgeon General: providing the public with the best scientific information to improve health; leading the PHS commissioned Corps; and chairing the National Prevention Council. He stated that he would focus on issues such as "obesity, diet, physical activity, and tobacco cessation."[1] Those were noncontroversial public health issues, but Murthy's affiliation with Doctors for America was a potential challenge to gaining bipartisan support. Instead, the main threat to his confirmation came from the National Rifle Association (NRA), which represented gun enthusiasts and manufacturers. The Senate HELP Committee approved Murthy's nomination and forwarded it for a vote by the full Senate, but a prior Doctors for America letter Murthy had sent to Congress members about the need for gun violence prevention measures and a 2012 tweet that guns were a public health issue were problematic for the NRA and those Senators beholden to the NRA and its opposition to any restrictive gun regulations. In spite of Murthy's Senate testimony that he did not intend to use the Surgeon General's office as a bully pulpit for gun control, the NRA sent a letter to Senate leadership suggesting "the likelihood he [Murthy] would use the office of surgeon general to further his preexisting campaign against gun ownership," thus effectively halting action on the nomination.[2]

In a May 8, 2014 editorial in the *New England Journal of Medicine*, the question was posed: "Should a special-interest organization like the NRA have veto power over the appointment of the nation's top doctor? The very idea is unacceptable."[3] The American Public Health Association and numerous professional organizations shared the view that gun violence was a major public health issue. The influence of the NRA over this nomination galvanized campaigns by health care coalitions, anti-gun violence groups and the Indian American community, prompting more than 100 national organizations to send a November 12, 2014 letter to Senate members stating that the confirmation of the Surgeon General "should be made based on protecting and improving public health, not politics," and urging confirmation of Vivek Murthy.[4] And then the Ebola outbreak in West Africa and the need for a Surgeon General moved action on the nomination. On December 15, 2014, the appointment of Murthy as Surgeon General was approved by a 51–43 Senate vote.

Surgeon General Vivek Murthy's immediate task was to assume responsibility for oversight of the PHS Commissioned Corps response to the Ebola virus disease epidemic in West Africa and attend to a measles outbreak in the U.S. The Centers for Disease Control and Prevention (CDC) and state efforts addressed the measles outbreak, and the Corps' medical mission in Liberia would soon come to completion. The most pressing issue for Murthy, instead, became the widespread opioid abuse crisis in the nation.

OPIOID CRISIS

The rapid increase in the use of prescription opioids and illegal/illicit opioids (heroin, fentanyl) in the nation gave rise to an opioid abuse epidemic. From 1999 to 2016, more than 630,000 people died from a drug overdose, and the number of such overdose deaths involving opioids was five times higher in 2016 than 1999. Of 64,000 drug overdose deaths in 2016, 42,249 were opioid-related, of which 19,413 (45.9 percent) involved synthetic opioids – primarily fentanyl. The CDC identified three distinct waves in the rise of opioid overdose deaths through the years: 1990s – rise in prescription opioid overdoses; 2010 – rise in heroin overdoses; and 2013 – rise in synthetic opioid overdoses, particularly those involving illicitly manufactured fentanyl. The startling impact of this tragedy is that drug overdoses had become the leading cause of death for people under 50 years of age.[5,6]

> The rapid increase in use of prescription opioids and illicit opioids gave rise to a persistent opioid abuse epidemic in the nation.

Legislative Measures. Two legislative measures were passed that included provisions related to the opioid crisis. The Comprehensive Addiction and Recovery Act[7] was enacted on July 22, 2016, to address the continuum of care from opioid abuse prevention to recovery support, including expanding access to addiction treatment services and overdose reversal medications. The 21st Century Cures Act[8] was enacted on December 13, 2016, designating $1 billion for state grants to implement opioid abuse prevention activities, support opioid-related training for healthcare practitioners, improve access to health care and addiction treatment programs, and to enhance state-administered prescription drug monitoring programs. The focus of the Cures Act was to support biomedical research and precision medicine at the National Institutes of Health (NIH). The NIH allocation of $4.8 billion included $1.8 billion earmarked for cancer research in the Beau Biden Cancer Moonshot initiative named to honor Vice President Joe Biden's son who died of brain cancer in 2015.

Turn the Tide Rx. On August 8, 2016, Surgeon General Murthy launched a national campaign called *Turn the Tide Rx* to educate the public and mobilize healthcare practitioners to become proactive in stemming the opioid epidemic. On August 24, Murthy took the step of mailing a letter and a pocket card with CDC opioid prescribing guidelines to 2.3 million physicians, nurses, dentists and other clinicians. The letter urged prescribers to treat pain more safely and effectively; to screen patients for opioid use disorder and, if needed, connect them with proper treatment; and to discuss and treat addiction as a chronic illness and not a personal failing. The campaign included a website with resources for clinicians. Dr. Murthy embarked on a national tour that included visits to media outlets, professional groups and treatment centers to discuss the opioid crisis and motivate the public and healthcare providers to work together to address this national public health issue. In venues around the nation, Dr. Murthy provided an authoritative and thoughtful articulation of the multifaceted nature of the issue.[9-11]

SURGEON GENERAL REPORTS

In a November 19, 2015 interview for the Washington Ideas Forum, Dr. Murthy noted that his two priorities as Surgeon General were prevention and health equity. He released two Surgeon General's Reports and a Call to Action.

E-Cigarettes

Surgeon General Murthy released the first-ever *Surgeon General's Report on E-Cigarette Use Among Youth and Young Adults*[12] in 2016. The report reviewed the scientific literature on use and effects of e-cigarettes and their marketing within the context of youth and young adults from 11 to 24 years of age. E-cigarettes include a range of devices that allow users to inhale an aerosol that typically contains nicotine, flavorings and other additives. By 2014, e-cigarettes were the most commonly used tobacco product among youth, posing a health hazard to youth, pregnant women and fetuses. On August 8, 2016, the Food and Drug Administration finalized a rule that extended its regulatory authority to include all tobacco products, including e-cigarettes. This follows upon the *Family Smoking Prevention and Tobacco Control Act of 2009*, which gave the agency authority to regulate the manufacture, distribution and marketing of tobacco products. Effective January 1, 2014, a new policy (CCI412.01, 21 June 2013), prohibited the use of tobacco products by PHS officers while in uniform, making it the first uniformed service to do so.

Alcohol and Drugs

In 2016, Surgeon General Murthy released the first-ever *Surgeon General's Report on Alcohol, Drugs, and Health*, with the lead title of *Facing Addiction in America*.[13] The report discussed substance misuse as a growing public health crisis, particularly with regard to opioids. It described the neurobiological basis for substance use addiction disorders and provided a framework for improving prevention, diagnosis, treatment of and recovery from alcohol and drug misuse. Guidance is provided on how individuals, organizations and communities can mitigate substance misuse. The report notes that a comprehensive approach is needed to address substance use problems including enhanced public education; implementation of evidence-based prevention policies and programs; improved access to treatment services; recovery support services; and policies and financing to ensure that substance misuse and use disorders services are accessible, compassionate, efficient and sustainable.

Walking

Dr. Murthy's *Step It Up! The Surgeon General's Call to Action to Promote Walking and Walkable Communities*, released in 2015, was similar to Surgeon General Benjamin's *Every Body Walk!* initiative introduced in 2013, both of which were intended to promote regular walking (and wheelchair roll) along with walkable communities to improve overall health.

VA-USPHS AGREEMENT

The Veterans Health Administration (VHA) is the largest integrated health care system in the nation, serving 9 million veterans yearly at 172 medical centers and over 1,000 outpatient sites. On January 17, 2017, the Department of Health and Human Services and VHA entered into a 5-year Memorandum of Agreement to detail PHS Commissioned Corps officers to the VHA "to promote public health in various roles, to include, but not limited to: direct patient care service delivery in rural, underserved communities." In order to gauge programmatic effectiveness, only a limited number of officers were selected initially, with preference given to new recruits.[14] *(See also Chapter Nineteen.)*

PHS DEPLOYMENTS

Throughout 2016, there were several deployments of PHS officers to urgent health-related events, a few of which were of national interest.

Water Emergency

A Flint, Michigan water crisis began in 2014 after the water source for the city's drinking water was changed to the Flint River. The failure of officials to apply corrosion inhibitors led to leaching of lead from aging pipes into the water supply, exposing over 100,000 residents to extremely high levels of lead, which is a potent neurotoxin, particularly to young children. On January 16, 2016, President Obama issued an emergency declaration. Among a wide array of federal resources were CDC personnel and 47 PHS officers deployed to support response and recovery efforts. Officers in Applied Public Health, Services Access and Mental Health Teams assisted with assessing lead exposure, health surveillance, public messaging, and behavioral health support to this widely publicized event.[15]

IHS Great Plains

The Indian Health Service in the Great Plains Area (GPA) provides health care to about 130,000 Native Americans located in Iowa, North and South Dakota, and Nebraska. In 2015 to 2016, the Centers for Medicare and Medicaid Services (CMS) cited serious deficiencies relating to the quality of patient care being provided at four of the hospitals. Beginning in early 2016, PHS officers were deployed to the Winnebago, Pine Ridge, and Rosebud Indian Hospitals to address the urgent need for healthcare staff to assist in remedying shortcomings noted by CMS. A total of about 200 officers were sent to the GPA, including medical officers, nurses, pharmacists, and experts in quality assurance.[16]

Zika Virus

In early 2015, an epidemic of Zika fever in Brazil began to spread in South and North America. The virus, carried mainly by the *Aedes aegypti* mosquito, usually causes a mild infection. In February 2016, the World Health Organization declared the outbreak a public health emergency of concern with evidence that the Zika virus could be transmitted from an infected pregnant woman to her fetus with a potential to cause microcephaly and neurological problems in the infant. Zika infections can also result in Guillain-Barré syndrome in adults. From 2015 to 2018, the CDC reported about 5,700 Zika disease cases in the U.S. and 37,000 cases in Puerto Rico, most occurring in 2016. On August 12, 2016, the Obama administration declared a public health emergency in Puerto Rico. As part of the HHS Zika response, CDC personnel completed 1,700 deployments, and 115 Commissioned Corps officers conducted surveillance, vector control and participated in health communication activities while serving in 29 states and territories and in 13 countries.[17]

Louisiana Floods

On August 11, 2016, the state of Louisiana experienced an unprecedented storm that produced catastrophic flooding. Thousands of houses and businesses were damaged, and people were displaced from homes. Louisiana's governor declared a state of emergency and the Office of the Assistant Secretary for Preparedness and Response deployed DMATs from surrounding areas. On August 14, PHS Rapid Deployment Force 3 consisting of 102 officers deployed to provide medical and behavioral health care to shelter residents, and a 250-bed Federal Medical Station was set up at Louisiana State University. In all, 200 PHS officers were deployed for this emergency to render medical and public health support and provide appropriate placements for patients.[18]

Hurricane Matthew

Hurricane Matthew was the most powerful storm of the 2016 Atlantic hurricane season and first Category 5 Atlantic hurricane since 2007. It began in the Eastern Caribbean on October 1, 2016, making landfall in Haiti, Cuba and the Bahamas. The storm then moved on October 7 along the coast of the southeastern U.S. – Florida, Georgia, South Carolina, and North Carolina – causing widespread devastation. The Office of the Assistant Secretary for Preparedness and Response sent 570 personnel to assist with medical emergency response efforts, including 146 PHS officers deployed to the region.

SG Departure

The new administration of Donald Trump took office in January 2017 and, with it, the desire to appoint a new Surgeon General. Even though the Public Health Service Act of 1944 codified the 4-year term of office for a Surgeon General, new administrations had increasingly come to consider the position as subject to political sanction. On April 21, 2017, the Trump administration asked Dr. Murthy to resign and, upon his refusal, relieved him of his duties as Surgeon General. In a Facebook post, Murthy noted that he chose not to resign because of his commitment to the Commissioned Corps, the American people, and all who worked with him to build a healthier and more compassionate America.[19]

While there was a general perception that as Surgeons General Vivek Murthy and Regina Benjamin may have interacted with PHS officers relatively infrequently, Dr. Murthy's nearly two and one-half years in office were promising in terms of what he had hoped to accomplish and he was a featured speaker at an array of events and academic forums. In early December 2020, President elect Joseph R. Biden, Jr. announced that Vivek Murthy was his choice to again serve as the Surgeon General.

Acting Surgeon General

The Deputy Surgeon General RADM Sylvia Trent-Adams, who served in that capacity from October 2015 until January 2019, was appointed Acting Surgeon General effective April 21, 2017, serving until September 5, 2017. Trent-Adams, a nurse, was the first (Acting) Surgeon General who was not a physician. She was not, however, the first nurse to serve in the SG position. Former Surgeon General Richard Carmona was a physician and a nurse. Sylvia Trent-Adams received an MS in nursing and health policy and a PhD from the University of Maryland. She served in the U.S. Army Nurse Corps for five years, joining the PHS Commissioned Corps in 1992. She held various HHS positions, including serving as Deputy Associate Administrator for the HIV/AIDS Bureau in the Health Resources and Services Administration. She also completed two internships in the U.S. Senate working on issue papers. From November 2013 to May 2016, Trent-Adams served as the Chief Nurse Officer of the USPHS. In January 2019, RADM Trent-Adams was appointed Principal Deputy Assistant Secretary for Health, and she retired on August 31, 2020. In March 2019, RADM Erica G. Schwartz, MD, JD, MPH, was selected as the new Deputy Surgeon General (DSG). Prior to becoming DSG, RADM Schwartz served four years as the Chief Medical Officer and Director of Health, Safety and Work-Life in the U.S. Coast Guard.

Sylvia Trent-Adams

Coast Guard and NOAA Health Care

COAST GUARD

The U.S. Coast Guard (CG) is one of the Armed Forces and was formed in 1915 by a merger of the Revenue Cutter Service (RCS, est. 1790) with the Life-Saving Service (est. 1848). In 1939 and 1942, respectively, the Lighthouse Service and the Bureau of Marine Inspection and Navigation were consolidated with the  Coast Guard. The principal mission of the Coast Guard includes coastal defense, maritime transportation and safety, and maritime law enforcement. The Guard has been in the Department of Homeland Security since 2003, having previously been in the Treasury Department from 1915 to 1967 and Department of Transportation from 1967 to 2003. In wartime at the direction of the President, the Coast Guard serves under the Navy Department. The 45,000 active duty members of the Coast Guard operate a multi-mission, interoperable fleet of over 240 cutters (the term used by the RCS, it now refers to Coast Guard ships 65 feet or more with permanent crews), 200 fixed and rotary-wing aircraft, and 1,650 boats (vessels under 65 feet).

Coast Guard Health Care

The U.S. Coast Guard does not maintain a medical corps. Rather, USPHS commissioned officers are assigned to the Coast Guard to provide health care and public health services. The Public Health Service Act of 1944 provided for the Surgeon General to appoint a Chief Medical Officer of the U.S. Coast Guard with the rank of Assistant Surgeon General. A PHS Corps physician fills this role as Director of Health, Safety and Work-Life (also known as Surgeon General of the Coast Guard). As of 2020, approximately 200 PHS officers render health and safety services to Coast Guard active duty and reserve personnel, whereas active duty dependents and CG retirees and their dependents often use military treatment facilities and network providers for their health care. PHS providers include physicians, dentists, pharmacists, environmental health and health services officers, and clinical and rehabilitation therapists working in a health care system of 42 clinics and 150 sick bays in coastal areas of the U.S. and Puerto Rico, and in the Coast Guard's environmental health and safety program. PHS personnel wear Coast Guard uniforms but replace CG accoutrements with the PHS insignia. In addition to PHS officers, Coast Guard enlisted personnel are trained as health services technicians who assist medical and dental officers and provide routine and emergency health care services in large Coast Guard clinics, small sick bays ashore, and aboard cutters.[20-22] The Coast Guard Academy in New London, Connecticut has a medical clinic located in Michel Hall, named for RADM Carl Michel, USPHS. Dr. Michel served as the Academy's chief medical officer and in July 1940 was appointed Chief Medical Officer of the Coast Guard, becoming the first to advance to PHS Assistant Surgeon General and Rear Admiral in November 1943.[23] PHS medical officers have served as the Coast Guard's Chief Medical Officer since 1920, earlier known as the CG medical aide, -advisor, or –chief. In 1997, RADM Joyce M. Johnson became the first woman to hold the position and first female to attain flag rank on active duty with the Coast Guard, setting a precedent for other female officers who were to become Chief Medical Officer.

PHS CHIEF MEDICAL OFFICERS OF THE COAST GUARD, 1920–2023

Henry V. Johnston, *ca. 1920-1922*	Captain Marshall C. Guthrie, *1938-1940*
James M. Gillespie, *1922-1926*	RADM Carl Michel, *1940-1946*
Surgeon Walter W. King, *1926-1932*	RADM Paul M. Stewart, *1946-1952*
Captain Allan J. McLaughlin, *1932-1936*	RADM Joseph F. van Ackeren, *1952-1957*
Captain H.McG. Robertson, *1936-1938*	RADM Richard B. Holt, *1957-1960*
	RADM Kenneth R. Nelson, *1960-1961*

RADM Carl Michel
1940-1946

Howard Fishburn
1961-1971

Robert R. Fletcher
1971-1973

William A. Cherry
1973-1977

Harry Allen
1977-1981

Leon R. Jellerson
1981-1985

Edward F. Blasser
1985-1988

Michael P. Hudgins
1989-1993

Alan M. Steinman
1993-1997

Joyce M. Johnson
1997-2004

Paul J. Higgins
2004-2007

Mark J. Tedesco
2007-2011

Maura Dollymore
2011-2015

Erica G. Schwartz
2015-2019

Dana L. Thomas
2019-2024

NOAA CORPS

The National Oceanic and Atmospheric Administration (NOAA) was formed on October 3, 1970. NOAA is a scientific agency of the Department of Commerce with the mission to understand and predict changes in climate, weather, oceans and coasts, and to conserve and manage coastal and marine ecosystems and resources. The NOAA Commissioned Officer Corps (NOAA Corps) is part of NOAA's Office of Marine and Aviation Operations. In 1807, President Thomas Jefferson created the Survey of the Coast to chart the nation's coastal  waters to ensure safe navigation. With the expansion of its responsibilities to include geodetic surveys in the nation's land mass, the Coast Survey was renamed the Coast and Geodetic Survey (C&GS) in 1878. The NOAA Corps was formed as the C&GS Corps on May 22, 1917, coincident with the United States' entry into World War I (WWI). Over half of the contingent of C&GS commissioned officers served with the Army, Navy and Marine Corps during both WWI and WWII. The Corps subsequently transitioned to the Environmental Science Services Administration Commissioned Officer Corps in 1965, and then to the NOAA Corps in 1970. The Corps was comprised of 321 officers in 2022 (authorized up to 500) who are trained in engineering, earth sciences, oceanography, meteorology, fisheries science and related disciplines. Officers operate NOAA's fleet of 15 research and survey ships and eight aircraft, manage research projects, conduct diving operations, and serve in leadership and staff positions throughout NOAA.[24]

Corps Health Care

USPHS commissioned officers are assigned to NOAA to provide medical care and occupational health services to the NOAA Corps. A PHS officer serves as Director of the Office of Health Services (OHS), which is tasked with  supporting all personnel in the Office of Marine and Aviation Operations to include NOAA officers, professional wage marine employees, aircraft operations personnel, and other personnel embarked aboard NOAA vessels and aircraft. The five medical programs – Aviation Medicine, Dive Medicine, Marine Medicine, Behavioral Health, and Medical Affairs – within the OHS render preventive, diagnostic and treatment services for medical problems encountered in high-risk operational ship and aircraft environments located in domestic and international areas of operation. OHS programs also promote mental and physical readiness, and medical staff are subject matter experts in travel medicine. PHS officers advocate for individuals in what is physically and mentally best for them in an array of operational environments.[25]

Christian Rathke

Origins of the USPHS in NOAA

RADM Christian Andreasen (NOAA Corps, Ret.)

Interviewed by CAPT Christian Rathke, USPHS [November 16, 2020]. Director, Office of Health Services and Staff Officer Support, NOAA

Background. Dr. Leonard Bachman and Dr. C. Everett Koop worked together at the Children's Hospital of Philadelphia, where Dr. Bachman served as the director of anesthesiology. The two became great friends. When Dr. Koop became Surgeon General, he brought Dr. Bachman in 1979 to head the PHS Hospitals and Clinics, until the hospitals were closed in 1981 under the Reagan administration.

1972. RADM Chris Andreasen was the Chief of Commissioned Personnel, under Admiral Nygren, and the NOAA member of the Seafarers Health Improvement Program. The intent of this initiative was to develop standards for those who came on board ships to decrease the number of individuals in ill health from sailing. Prior to this, there were no health standards for seafarers at NOAA, and it was costly to divert ships to return sick personnel to shore. The USPHS led this effort and Dr. Bachman was on the Program committee. PHS medical officers periodically augmented NOAA ships, but there were no full-time PHS officers assigned to NOAA.

1976–1978. RADM Andreasen went to sea as a Commander. He realized that the people who were promoted to Captain had budgetary experience, so he asked for his next assignment to include some budgeting aspect. He was appointed the Staff Assistant to Admiral Lippold who was head of the Office of Fleet Operations (now the Office of Marine and Aviation Operations), where he was in charge of handling negotiations for six unions, writing budgets for the fleet, preparing correspondence to the Hill and handling the health of the 600 sailing crew.

1979. RADM Andreasen informed Admiral Lippold that there were 70 people handling the engines and engineering of the fleet, but only one person overseeing the safety of 600 crew, and that individual (himself) was not qualified to work the medical policy issues. Based on previous positive work with USPHS officers, RADM Andreasen recommended creating a USPHS medical officer position. Admiral Lippold agreed and made an appointment to meet with Dr. Koop. RADM Andreasen had a USPHS Commander in mind, someone who had previously sailed with the fleet on long cruises. Dr. Koop had someone else in mind and in 1979 assigned Dr. Bachman to the NOAA Office of Fleet Operations, as the first USPHS Medical Officer. Captain Bachman* set the medical policies and worked out how to institute them across the fleet, eventually posting USPHS doctors in the NOAA Marine Centers. What began as an idea to have a USPHS officer direct and write medical policy eventually turned into an enduring collaboration of NOAA and the USPHS Commissioned Corps.

*Dr. Bachman was a Rear Admiral when he was in charge of all USPHS Hospitals; he became Captain when he came to NOAA and reverted to Rear Admiral upon rejoining SG Koop's staff.

> ## CHRONOLOGY • 2014–2017
>
> Acting SG Boris D. Lushniak, July 2013–December 2014
> SG Vivek H. Murthy, December 2014–April 2017
> Acting SG Sylvia Trent-Adams, April 2017–September 2017

2016   Launch of national *Turn the Tide Rx* campaign.

2016   *21st Century Cures Act*. Provides state grants to implement opioid abuse prevention, healthcare provider training, improved access to treatment programs, and to enhance prescription drug monitoring.

2016   Release of the Surgeon General's Report on *E-Cigarette Use Among Youth and Young Adults*.

2016   Release of the Surgeon General's Report on *Alcohol, Drugs, and Health*.

2016   Several PHS officer deployments to emergency public health-related events, including IHS Great Plains, Michigan Water Emergency, Zika Virus, and Louisiana Floods.

2017   Memorandum of Agreement to detail PHS Commissioned Corps officers to the Veterans Health Administration.

CHAPTER SEVENTEEN

OPIOIDS, MODERNIZATION, RESERVE CORPS, COVID-19 VS. POLITICS
2017 to 2021

A NEW SURGEON GENERAL would soon be named. In June 2017, President Donald J. Trump nominated Jerome M. Adams to become the 20th Surgeon General. Dr. Adams, a board certified anesthesiologist, was appointed in 2014 by former Governor (and Vice President) Mike Pence to serve as Indiana State Health Commissioner. Jerome Adams received an MPH from the University of California at Berkeley in 2000 and his medical degree from Indiana University School of Medicine in 2002. Dr. Adams served as an Associate Professor of clinical anesthesia at Indiana University School of Medicine and a staff anesthesiologist at Eskenazi Health. He served in leadership positions at several professional organizations, including the American Medical Association and in state associations. As Health Commissioner, Adams presided over Indiana's response to an unprecedented HIV outbreak and helped launch Indiana's state-based alternative to Medicaid expansion. Adams was confirmed as Surgeon General by the Senate in August and sworn into office on September 5, 2017. As stated in his acceptance speech, Dr. Adams' motto as Surgeon General was "better health through better partnerships" – maintaining strong public health relationships and forming partnerships with business and law enforcement. He also pledged to lead with science and facilitate locally led solutions to the nation's most difficult health problems.[1]

Jerome M. Adams

PRIORITIES

The Surgeon General articulated his priorities early on. His first priority was to address the opioid epidemic. Dr. Adams traveled to many communities to discuss opioid use disorder as a chronic disease that responds to medication-assisted treatment. He encouraged people to reach out "to those suffering with empathy and support." Another priority was health and the economy. He noted that living conditions had an enormous impact on overall health and wellness and that communities and businesses needed to address preventable chronic diseases and behavioral health issues to prosper. Dr. Adams' third priority targeted national security. He cited an estimate that 7 in 10 young persons aged 17 to 24 would not qualify for military service due to obesity and other health issues. Therefore, his attention focused on promoting school based physical activity which has the benefits of healthier students and greater educational achievement. Other top priorities included curbing the use of tobacco products and e-cigarettes among young adults and communicating the best available science about emerging public health threats.[2-5]

OPIOID EPIDEMIC

For the new administration, the opioid crisis came to the fore as the highest priority public health issue of the moment. On March 29, 2017, President Donald Trump signed an Executive Order to form the President's Commission on Combating Drug Addiction and the Opioid Crisis, and on October 26 he directed the Department of Health and Human Services (HHS) to declare the opioid crisis a public health emergency. The Commission's final report was issued November 1, 2017, and included 56 recommendations. The Commission called for a national multimedia campaign to fight the crisis and it urged Congress to provide federal block grant funding to the states for opioid and substance use disorder-related activities. The recommendations addressed physician and pharmacist training, prevention, treatment, overdose reversal, recovery, an expanded drug court system, and research into pain management and addiction.[6] Emanating from the report was an HHS 5-point strategy to combat the opioid crisis that included resources to support improved treatment, prevention and recovery services; improving the collection of relevant data; improving guidance on pain management; improving the availability of overdose-reversing drugs; and improving research on pain and addiction.[7]

Naloxone Advisory

Surgeon General Adams soon addressed a matter absent in the Commission report, namely, the use of naloxone, an opioid antagonist to reverse the effects of an overdose. On April 5, 2018, he released the *Surgeon General's Advisory on Naloxone and Opioid Overdose*.[8] Included in the advisory were specific directives for patients and the public, and for prescribers, treatment providers and pharmacists. The advisory was considered part of the administration's ongoing efforts to respond to the sharp increase among drug overdose deaths, with the Centers for Disease Control and Prevention (CDC) releasing new data showing a 30 percent increase in opioid overdoses from July 2016 through September 2017.[9] On March 29, 2018, HHS Secretary Alex M. Azar II announced that Assistant Secretary for Health Brett P. Giroir would coordinate HHS efforts to respond to the nation's crisis of opioid addiction and overdose.[10]

Spotlight on Opioids

In 2018, there were nearly 67,400 drug overdose deaths in the nation. Opioids were involved in about 70 percent or 47,000 of those deaths, of which synthetic opioids such as fentanyl accounted for about 67 percent.[11] A rise occurred in 2019, with a total of 70,630 drug overdose deaths; about 70 percent or 50,000 involved opioids, of which synthetic opioids accounted for 73 percent or more than 36,000 deaths.[12] In September 2018, HHS and the Office of the Surgeon General released a new report entitled *Facing Addiction in America: The Surgeon General's Spotlight on Opioids*.[13] It provides updated prevalence data on opioid misuse and guidance on the continuum of care approach for substance misuse prevention, early intervention, treatment and management of opioid use disorders, and recovery support.

E-CIGARETTE EPIDEMIC, TOBACCO, HYPERTENSION

The Surgeon General was confronted with another major challenge – the rapid growth of electronic cigarette (e-cigarette) use among youth. Federal data indicated that, among high school students, e-cigarette use had increased from 1.5 percent in 2011 to 20.8 percent in 2018; and during 2017 to 2018, usage had increased by 78 percent – from 11.7 to 20.8 percent of students. In 2019, an estimated 4.1 million high school and 1.2 million middle school students were using e-cigarettes.[14,15] In response, Dr. Adams issued a public health advisory on December 18, 2018, the *Surgeon General's Advisory on E-cigarette Use Among Youth*.[16] The advisory singled out e-cigarette company Juul Labs, which produced a cartridge containing as much nicotine as a pack of 20 regular cigarettes. The advisory proposed prevention strategies that included educational initiatives, school policy and legal restrictions. In addition to nicotine, which is highly addictive, e-cigarette aerosol can contain harmful substances. E-cigarette use, or vaping, was associated with an outbreak of lung injury that, by December 17, 2019, had resulted in over 2500 cases involving hospitalized patients.[17] On December 20, 2019, the President signed legislation to amend the Federal Food, Drug, and Cosmetic Act which raised the federal minimum age of sale of tobacco products from 18 to 21 years of age.

Tobacco Use

In January 2020, *Smoking Cessation: A Report of the Surgeon General*,[18] was released, which updates the 1990 Surgeon General's Report entitled *The Health Benefits of Smoking Cessation*. This new report summarizes more recent research, noting that smoking cessation reduces the risk of adverse health effects on reproductive health outcomes, cardiovascular diseases, chronic obstructive pulmonary disease and cancer, and can add up to a decade to life expectancy. The report provides interventions and strategies to promote smoking cessation.

Hypertension

In October 2020, the Surgeon General issued a *Call to Action to Control Hypertension*. Hypertension affects nearly 50 percent of the adult population and is a significant preventable risk factor for heart disease and stroke. Despite the prevalence of this condition, only about one quarter of those with hypertension have their blood pressure adequately controlled. The report provides strategies and interventions to address and control this chronic health condition.

HURRICANES HARVEY, IRMA, MARIA

In August and September 2017, three Category 4 to 5 (Saffir-Simpson Hurricane Wind Scale) hurricanes – Hurricanes Harvey, Irma, and Maria – caused major loss of life and property and are among the five costliest hurricanes in this nation's history.

Hurricane Harvey. Hurricane Harvey came ashore south of Houston, Texas, on August 25, 2017, as a Category 4 storm. The storm subsequently stalled over Houston, inundating the area with record rainfall, resulting in extensive regional flooding. Floodwaters damaged homes, blocked roadways, and spilled into wastewater treatment facilities and Superfund sites.

Hurricane Irma. Hurricane Irma rapidly intensified with sustained Category 5 winds and hit the U.S. Virgin Islands on September 6, 2017, causing widespread destruction. Passing north of Puerto Rico, the storm made landfall with Category 4 strength winds in the Florida Keys on September 10, causing considerable damage as it advanced across the Florida peninsula.

Hurricane Maria. Hurricane Maria continued to strengthen to a Category 5 storm in the Caribbean and on September 19, 2017, it passed over St. Croix in the U.S. Virgin Islands, destroying much of the island's buildings and power infrastructure. On September 20, Hurricane Maria made landfall in Puerto Rico, destroying one-third of all homes and the island's entire power grid.

This series of destructive storms placed an enormous strain on the response capabilities of federal agencies, particularly the Federal Emergency Management Agency, which deployed thousands of federal personnel to the affected states and territories. Surgeon General Jerome Adams visited the U.S. Virgin Islands and Puerto Rico in October 2017 and witnessed the "appalling damage to lives and property, [and] ...saw how the people of the islands were suffering."[19]

The USPHS Commissioned Corps fielded over 1,800 deployments, among the largest contingents in Corps history, to help meet the demand for emergency support in the aftermath of these three hurricanes. PHS officers cared for the medical and mental health needs of thousands of displaced persons and addressed a multitude of environmental and infrastructure disruptions arising from the devastating impact of these hurricanes. The experience of

Rapid Deployment Force-5 (RDF) is telling.[20] Seventy-eight members of RDF-5 deployed August 24, 2017, to Dallas, Texas, to await the landfall of Hurricane Harvey. Staging, checking inventories, and other preparations ensued in coordination with RDF-4 and several Disaster Medical Assistance Teams (DMATs). Augmented by PHS officers from Tier 3, the RDFs traveled to the George R. Brown Convention Center in Houston to manage a Federal Medical Station (FMS). After two weeks of response activities in Houston, most RDF-5 members were sent to Atlanta, Georgia, and to Ft. Myers, Florida, in anticipation of incoming Hurricane Irma. Part of the team took commercial flights, while others were flown by C-130 military transport *[photo]* to the Orlando, Florida airport. Upon arrival,  PHS officers were divided into four task forces, with TF3 being assigned to East Lee County High School to support special needs evacuees and their caregivers, amid the nearly 5,000 evacuees who had filled the shelter to capacity. After three weeks in the field, RDF-5 was demobilized, turning over operations to RDF's -1, -2, and -3. Within a few weeks after returning home, a combination of PHS officers from RDF-4 and RDF-5 were assigned for up to four weeks' deployment to Puerto Rico. Thirty-eight officers from RDF-5 were rostered for

PHS Engineers assess water loss from a cooling tower at Bayamon Hospital in Puerto Rico, 2017.

RDF Coqui-1 [pronounced Ko-Kee, the tiny Coqui frog unique to Puerto Rico], while other officers deployed in support of Incident Response Coordination Team (IRCT) operations in varying roles. Reports by officers indicated that they overcame many challenges including long hours, deficits in billeting, and limited or no food, water and restrooms. Nonetheless, the PHS teams recognized that citizens had lost homes and were surviving day-to-day, and so all responders "worked together in unison, with energy, love, respect, and camaraderie." Such camaraderie helped sustain responders in meeting numerous challenges. Of even greater importance, it allowed responders to focus on the important mission of placing service to others before self."[21,22]

DOD Humanitarian Medal

On November 15, 2018, more than 1,400 members of the USPHS Commissioned Corps received the Department of Defense Humanitarian Service Medal. The award recognized officers' participation in relief efforts related to Hurricanes Harvey, Irma or Maria carried out in 2017. Duties included patient care, case management for medical evacuees and help with recovery operations including rebuilding/strengthening local health care and social systems. The award for this large scale deployment was approved by the Joint Chiefs of Staff for qualified members of all branches of the uniformed services.[23]

PACE, HIV EPIDEMIC

The Prevention through Active Community Engagement (PACE) program is a chartered USPHS advisory group. PACE leverages the expertise of PHS officers to provide education about the benefits of prevention in local communities. It also provides community outreach for prevention-related initiatives of the Surgeon General and Assistant Secretary for Health (ASH). Each of the ten HHS Regional Offices has a PHS officer serving as a point of contact. ASH Brett P. Giroir announced July 8, 2019, that his office was standing up a new PACE team of highly qualified Commissioned Corps officers to support the regional "Ending the HIV Epidemic" initiatives in Atlanta, Dallas, and Los Angeles. The officers work collaboratively with HHS interagency leadership and other federal and non-federal partners to develop public health interventions specifically geared toward the communities they are trying to reach.[24]

SOUTHERN BORDER DEPLOYMENTS

Fiscal year 2019 witnessed a surge in the number of migrants apprehended between ports of entry along the nation's U.S.–Mexican border. Of the total of 851,508 individuals who were apprehended, 76,000 were unaccompanied children. HHS is responsible for providing care to unaccompanied children up to 18 years of age and PHS officers are periodically called upon to supplement the HHS mission of caring for these children. From December 30, 2018, until October 2, 2019, a reported 483 PHS officers deployed to support the Department of Homeland Security mission at the southern border. A total of nearly 7,000 deployment days were involved in this mission.[25-27]

COMMISSIONED CORPS MODERNIZATION

Conditions of Service

Consistent with recommendations of the Assistant Secretary for Health, on March 28, 2018, HHS Secretary Alex Azar issued Commissioned Corps Directive 111.03 describing new Conditions of Service, followed by Commissioned Corps Instruction 241.01 on June 22, and Personnel Operations Memorandum 821.66 on July 12, 2018, which detailed the readiness standards and duty requirements for Regular and Ready Reserve Corps officers. These requirements covered maintenance of professional competence, career progression, deployment readiness (fitness, training), clinical hours, uniforms, security suitability, and health and weight standards for retention on active duty.[28-30]

Administration OMB Plan

Despite advance written nonconcurrences from the Office of the Assistant Secretary for Health, the Office of Management and Budget (OMB) released on June 21, 2018, a reform plan for the federal government that included a proposed reduction in the PHS Commissioned Corps strength from 6,500 to 4,000 officers.[31] It postulated that "...mission assignments and functions have not evolved in step with the public health needs of the Nation," for which OMB provided no supportive data. Under the OMB plan, HHS would civilianize officers who do not provide critical public health services, require that Corps officers initially work in a hard-to-fill area and continue there or deploy to public health emergencies, and enforce standards for Corps eligibility and readiness, a stipulation already in progress by issuance of the aforementioned Corps directives. The OMB proposal was based upon the contention that PHS officers occupy positions that civilian employees could fill at lower cost, citing a 1996 General Accounting Office study that was widely considered analytically flawed. As noted in a commentary about the OMB proposal, "Civilianizing the Corps would not save money, and in fact could cost more."[32] On July 24, 2018, the Military Coalition sent a letter to Congress stating that "There are neither data nor analyses offered by OMB to justify this 2500-officer reduction."[33] And on July 25, 2018, the Congressional Research Service (CRS) noted a lack of detail and supporting evidence in the OMB plan to inform policymakers.[34]

HHS Response

With the support of Secretary Azar, Assistant Secretary Brett P. Giroir and Surgeon General Adams had been working with OMB to show the value of the Corps and were intent on maintaining control of the Corps' future within HHS. The June 21, 2018, release of the administration's reform plan led Drs. Giroir and Adams to become strong advocates for the Corps, keenly aware that the Corps, in the words of Dr. Giroir, "is absolutely vital and we need to grow."

In response to predecisional communications from OMB in February 2018 to alter and downsize the composition of the Commissioned Corps, and after extensive discussions with OMB and White House, Admiral Giroir with the support of Dr. Adams and Secretary Azar responded in March that HHS did not accept OMB's directive, but instead would engage in a data-driven, objective review and potential transformation of the Corps that would survey officers and all agency heads, account for 21st century threats for deployment, and conduct an audit of the financial implications. The need for modernization and

Vice President Mike Pence with *[left to right]* Admiral Giroir at the Podium, Surgeon General Adams, Dr. Deborah Birx and PHS officers in the White House Briefing Room on March 15, 2020; the Commissioned Corps' service during the Covid pandemic was recognized.
[C-Span]

how it needed to proceed became objectively evident in early summer 2018 and was briefed to OMB on September 20, 2018. Not up for debate, based on requirements and data, the plan was over time to replace approximately 1,100 officer billets with civilians, but also to add an additional 2,500 officer positions in critically needed roles that officers could uniquely serve. This yielded a Regular Corps of nearly 7,700 officers. In addition, a Ready Reserve of at least 1,000 officers was required, later expanded to 2,500 given the experience of the Covid pandemic. From that moment this became the official plan, with the challenge to galvanize support and make it a reality. Seizing on the opportunity presented by pandemic funding, these initiatives were ultimately funded in a bipartisan manner in 2020.[35] The Corps began modernizing its operations, to include structure, business and management practices, staffing needs, and training so as to evolve into a more responsive workforce. Giroir believed the Corps should be a highly trained, always ready, and fully deployable force to preserve public health and national security, be a fundamental instrument for nonemergent, yet critical public health needs within the nation, provide federal leadership and scientific expertise, and serve as an innovation engine for public health. Due to increased agency and deployment demand for PHS officers, an ongoing challenge was the need to meet personnel requirements, so recruitment and retention were priorities. Mission priority positions included underserved and vulnerable populations, hazardous duty or health security positions, direct patient care, difficult to recruit or retain categories, and leadership or deployment utilization positions.[25,36,37]

In Their Words

by ADM (Ret.) Brett P. Giroir

When I left DARPA in 2008, I told my family that I would only return to Washington, DC, if asked to be Surgeon General or the Assistant Secretary for Health. Although President-elect Trump's transition team initially slotted me for Defense or Intel, they understood my passion for public health and the USPHS Commissioned Corps (CC) – a service that I only knew from a distance, but had felt a calling for over two decades. During the confirmation process, when I could have no interactions with HHS, the Commissioned Officers Association made clear that our Service was under fire, mostly undeserved, but also for reasons that were accurate and justified. Indeed, on my first day in uniform, February 15, 2018, I learned that OMB wanted to dismantle the Corps entirely, or at least reduce its numbers by half within one budget cycle. And astonishingly, CCHQ was actually operationalizing a plan to implement OMB's guidance. VADM Adams and I were not going to let that happen. But it was also critical to understand, and remedy, the reasons (accurate and perceived) why our Service was on the chopping block. Thus, Modernization of the Corps was born. And the reforms proved essential, and likely lifesaving, when we took the fight to COVID-19 – from Japan to the Javitz Center, from ABC to CNN, and ultimately to multiple podium briefings at the White House. The hard fought victories of Modernization are in the history books, but the fight for the Corps' future is not over. So, I would like to leave you with three tenets that I believe are essential moving forward. First, the Corps' distributed, agency-centric organization and federated funding will continue to impede our alignment and weaken our unity. Therefore, it is vital that we view ourselves as USPHS Commissioned Corps officers first. We may work at the CDC or IHS, but foremost, we are PHS officers; everything else is secondary. Don't just wear the uniform – live the uniform. Having a service mission, motto, doctrine, and centralized strike teams will go a long way to solidify our identity, but these cannot substitute for the visceral commitment of each and every officer. Second, don't accept what is unacceptable. Insist that your leadership – SG, ASH, and Secretary – stand firm when necessary, even if it means their jobs. Be unabashedly explicit about consequences. What would have happened if there were no CC officers to implement the national Covid testing program or deploy to nursing homes, or care for the imprisoned? What would have happened on the southern border if CC officers did not extinguish outbreaks of influenza, measles, and meningitis in Customs and Border Protection? Finally, make known our Service's accomplishments – we need a public face and a Congressional presence, and strong advocates from the Armed Services. That is why we invested heavily in a modern web presence and legislative liaisons, performed numerous Congressional briefings, and nurtured new relationships with DARPA, the National Guard, the VA, and DOD leadership. The future of the Corps is bright but remains fragile. Whether you are an active duty junior officer or a retired flag, that future is our collective responsibility.

USPHS Brand Guidelines and USPHS Doctrine

In July 2020, under OASH auspices, the USPHS Commissioned Corps published *Brand Guidelines* to articulate and bring consistency to the Corps' messaging relating to its mission, principles, values, and image. The Guidelines support a very strong brand identity to increase awareness and cohesive communications about and throughout the Corps. The Guidelines further delineate the proper usage of official seals, logos and insignia, and standardize the graphic and typography elements for various types of media. It also specifies the Corp's brand messaging as the anchor for all branded content:

- As America's Health Responders, we are the first in line to defend our nation's public health against threats large and small.
- Public Health Service officers serve our nation's health every day, as well as during times of public health emergencies.
- For more than two centuries, our highly trained active duty officers have stood ready to face all challenges to protect our nation's health.
- The Commissioned Corps is for those individuals who place service over self and value leadership, integrity, adventure, and helping those in need.

The Guidelines carry the new official motto of the PHS Corps, *In Officio Salutis – In the Service of Health*. The Guidelines were updated July 2023.[38]

In January 2021, the *U.S. Public Health Service Commissioned Corps Doctrine*[39] was released. The Doctrine is a comprehensive overview of the mission, structure, values, capabilities, and traditions of the Commissioned Corps, and was catalyzed and primarily written by flag officers under the leadership of RADM Scott Giberson. In prefatory remarks, ADM Giroir notes "The Doctrine helps assure unity of perspective and purpose as well as pride among our officers, and provides a cogent narrative from which administrations, policy makers, and future leaders may develop and implement strategy."

Both the PHS *Brand Guidelines* and the *Doctrine* were much needed, coherent pronouncements about the Commissioned Corps for officials and others such as Congress members and the general public, as well as for PHS officers.

READY RESERVE CORPS

The USPHS Commissioned Corps had received periodic authorizations as it evolved to maintain a reserve component to supplant the active duty Corps. In more recent years, the Patient Protection and Affordable Care Act (ACA, Public Law 111-148) that was enacted March 23, 2010, eliminated the cap of 2,800 Regular Corps officers and deemed all Reserve Corps officers serving on extended active duty at the time of enactment to be officers of the Regular Corps. The law abolished the existing PHS Inactive Reserve Corps in which inactive reservists voluntarily activated when needed, and replaced it with a Ready Reserve Corps (RRC) whereby personnel who join the RRC are available on short notice for involuntary call to active duty to provide conventional public health services and surge capacity for emergency response missions. A drafting error in the ACA, however, failed to include statutory authority related to personnel compensation for the Ready Reserve and so the implementation of a reserve component languished for several years.

On March 27, 2020, after intense work by legislative affairs within OASH and support of multiple external organizations, especially the Commissioned Officers Association and The Military Coalition, the Coronavirus Aid, Relief, and Economic Security Act,[40] also known as the CARES Act, was enacted to provide a $2.2 trillion economic stimulus package in response to the economic downturn resulting from the COVID-19 pandemic. The legislation also incorporated many provisions derived from other bills that were pending before Congress, including the United States Public Health Service Modernization Act. Within the CARES Act is the provision (§3214) entitled *United States Public Health Service Modernization,* which provides authority to re-establish the Ready Reserve Corps. Surgeon General Adams noted that this activation of the Ready Reserve Corps "...will ensure a robust response to the public health needs of the future." The USPHS commissioned its first officers into the Ready Reserve Corps in July 2021 to fulfill the following public health roles.[41]

- Support the USPHS Commissioned Corps' capacity to respond to regional, national, and global health emergencies and improve access to health services;
- Preserve clinical care positions by maintaining a surge capacity of health professionals available for deployment without jeopardizing the service of clinicians in hard to fill roles;
- Offer an opportunity to serve for mission-driven clinical and public health professionals who cannot commit to a full-time active duty position in the USPHS Commissioned Corps; and
- Enable access to highly specialized skill sets that would be impractical in full-time active duty positions.

FRAMINGHAM HEART STUDY

The year 2023 marked the 75th anniversary of the Framingham Heart Study (FHS), considered among the most important epidemiological studies in medical history. The impetus for the study can be ascribed to the premature death from hypertensive heart disease of President Franklin Roosevelt in 1945, and a growing epidemic of cardiovascular disease as the primary cause of mortality in the 1940s. At the time, blood pressure elevations were thought to be part of the natural aging process and cardiovascular disease was poorly understood, with few therapeutic options. The National Heart Act of 1948 created the National Heart Institute (NHI, renamed National Heart, Lung, and Blood Institute [NHLBI] in 1976) and allocated $500,000 for a twenty-year heart study. The proposal for the population-based study was prepared in 1947 by PHS medical officer Gilcin F. Meadors. A suburb near Boston and Harvard University, Framingham, Massachusetts, had a stable population of 28,000 and was selected for the study site. The town's residents were receptive to the study and the original cohort of 5,209 of the town's 10,000 adults were recruited from 1948 to 1952. The U.S. Public Health Service began the longitudinal research in October 1948, but within months the National Heart Institute assumed control of the study. As of 2023, there had been four Framingham Heart Study Directors. The first three were PHS medical officers: Dr. Thomas Royle "Roy" Dawber serving from 1949 to 1966, Dr. William B. Kannel from 1966 to 1979, Dr. William P. Castelli from 1979 to 1994; and Dr. Daniel Levy appointed in 1994. The FHS Directors made prescient decisions with respect to the research study, the results of which have laid the foundation for preventive cardiology. In 1971, an agreement with Boston University provided for ongoing support through federal contract, thereby allowing the study to endure for decades. A seminal report published in 1961 introduced the term "risk factor" and established that the risk of developing coronary heart disease was related to elevated serum cholesterol levels and hypertension.[42] The Framingham Study went on to determine that there are multiple risk factors for cardiovascular disease including obesity, smoking, and lack of exercise, and atrial fibrillation predisposing to stroke. The Framingham Heart Study is iconic research that has undergone several generational iterations, including genetic correlations, producing groundbreaking findings related to determinants of cardiovascular health that continue to inform the practice of cardiology worldwide.[43-45]

Thomas R. Dawber

William B. Kannel

William P. Castelli

CORONAVIRUS DISEASE 2019 PANDEMIC

The 1918 H1N1 influenza pandemic was the most severe pandemic in modern history, causing an estimated 675,000 deaths in this country and 50 to 100 million fatalities worldwide. Since 1918, other pandemics have involved influenza A (H2N2) virus in 1957 and influenza A (H3N2) virus in 1968, with each causing roughly 100,000 deaths in the United States; and a novel influenza A (H1N1)pdm09 virus that emerged in 2009 causing 12,500 deaths in the U.S.[46] A new, highly infectious pathogen emerged in December 2019, when a cluster of pneumonia cases appeared in Wuhan, China. This outbreak would become the most serious worldwide public health crisis to occur in a century. Sequencing of respiratory samples from Chinese patients indicated that a novel coronavirus (Latin name for crown, due to crown-like surface spikes), or 2019-nCoV, was the causative agent. The World Health Organization (WHO) gave an official name to the disease – coronavirus disease 2019, abbreviated COVID-19, the causative agent being severe acute respiratory syndrome coronavirus-2, or SARS-CoV-2. 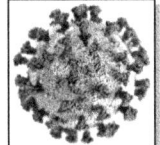 The principal mode of infection with SARS-CoV-2 is person to person, typically through exposure to respiratory droplets carrying infectious virus that is produced during exhalation, coughing or talking. Although most people with COVID-19 have mild symptoms, the disease can cause severe illness and death. Older adults and persons with underlying medical conditions such as heart or lung disease or diabetes are at increased risk of developing severe illness. Symptomatology may include fever, cough, fatigue, headache, muscle aches, diarrhea, sore throat, shortness of breath or difficulty breathing, loss of taste or smell, and persistent chest pain. Of major significance, yet unknown at the start of the pandemic, the rate of disease spread was largely driven by infected persons who were asymptomatic.

Emergency Declarations

Coronavirus cases soon began to be seen in various countries worldwide, with the U.S. confirming its first case in Washington State on January 20, 2020. WHO declared the coronavirus outbreak to be a global health emergency on January 31, 2020, and a global pandemic on March 11, 2020. HHS Secretary Azar issued a public health emergency (PHE) declaration on January 31, 2020. A PHE continues for 90 days, and the declaration was renewed several times, the last in 2022 being October 13. And on March 13, 2020, President Trump declared a national emergency, noting in an accompanying letter that 32 states had already declared a state of emergency due to the coronavirus. The letter stated, "It is the preeminent responsibility of the Federal Government to take action to stem a nationwide pandemic."[47] The national emergency declaration, continued by President Biden in 2021 and 2022, was ended April 10, 2023.

Public Health Response

New COVID-19 cases and attributable deaths continued to rise exponentially in the U.S. during 2020, and the public health response to the pandemic was challenging. Mainly at the outset, yet throughout 2020, the health care delivery system dealt with a shortage of available healthcare professionals and insufficient personal protective gear and essential equipment. The incredible efforts of healthcare providers to care for hundreds of thousands of afflicted patients around the nation was indeed heroic, with clinical personnel continually risking their own lives to save others.

> The incredible efforts of healthcare providers to care for afflicted patients were indeed heroic.

Coronavirus Task Force. A White House Coronavirus Task Force was formed on January 29, 2020. HHS Secretary Alex Azar was appointed chair, but soon Vice President Mike Pence would take charge, with Dr. Deborah L. Birx being named the White House COVID-19 Response Coordinator. Among task force members were Surgeon General Jerome Adams, Dr. Anthony Fauci (NIAID Director), Dr. Francis Collins (National Institutes of Health [NIH] Director), Dr. Stephen Hahn (Food and Drug Administration [FDA] Commissioner), and Robert Redfield (CDC Director). In March, HHS Assistant Secretary for Health Giroir became coordinator of the nation's COVID-19 diagnostic testing program, an especially difficult post complicated by a lack of testing infrastructure and test-related missteps by the CDC and FDA. The Coronavirus Task Force held regular meetings and public briefings at the White House, and it served as the authoritative face of the federal government's response to the pandemic. However, the task force was viewed with some mistrust as fewer meetings and briefings were being held toward the end of 2020, and as reports began to surface about political intrusiveness into its deliberations.

Operation Warp Speed. The federal government's announcement of Operation Warp Speed (OWS) on May 15, 2020, was a public–private partnership of historic significance to accelerate the development of COVID-19 vaccines, therapeutics, and diagnostics. Major HHS component agencies, including the CDC, FDA, NIH, the Office of the Assistant Secretary for Preparedness and Response (ASPR), and Biomedical Advanced Research and Development Authority (BARDA), worked with multiple research entities and manufacturers to facilitate the vaccine development enterprise. OWS and vaccine companies adopted several strategies to accelerate vaccine development and mitigate risk. Utilizing innovative platform technologies along with other steps such as combining clinical trial phases led to effective coronavirus vaccines made by Pfizer-BioNTech and Moderna that were given emergency use authorization by the FDA in December 2020.[48]

Public Health Agencies. The CDC utilized its expertise in disease epidemiology and surveillance, laboratory diagnostic testing, and the provision of guidance to federal and state leaders, the public, businesses and other entities to stem the disease. The FDA prioritized its activities to the development, availability and approval of testing devices, therapeutics and vaccines to combat COVID-19. These agencies were largely successful in performing these responsibilities, though both had early missteps that delayed Covid testing efforts. The CDC released a flawed diagnostic test kit, and the FDA unduly restricted the use of academic and commercial laboratory tests, though it soon reversed course.

PHS COMMISSIONED CORPS

The deployment of PHS commissioned officers in support of the response to the spread of coronavirus was without precedent in Corps history. All officers were placed on an "all hands on deck" situation, with on call alert status effective March 25, 2020. Officers would deploy without supervisory approval under the declaration of a national emergency by President Trump in March 2020 and continued by President Biden in 2021 and 2022. Over 1,800 officers were deployed during the initial four months of the pandemic and, by mid-2021, over half of all PHS officers had been deployed for the COVID-19 response mission. A total of about 4,537 officers were deployed from 2020 through 2022, with some officers serving on multiple deployments.

DEPLOYMENTS FOR THE CORONAVIRUS MISSION, 2020-2022

COVID-19 Response Time Period	Number of Officers Deployed*
January 1 through April 30, 2020	1,898
January 1 through December 31, 2020	2,981
January 1 through December 31, 2021	1,086
January 1 through December 31, 2022	470
Total, 2020-2022	4,537

*Numbers based on deployment start date and include virtual assignments. Data derived from HHS, OSG, Commissioned Corps Headquarters, in response to FOIA requests.

Deployment Roles

USPHS leadership saw the impending threat of coronavirus and began extensive training such that by the end of February 2020, the Commissioned Corps had formed ten clinical strike teams comprised of multidisciplinary healthcare and public health providers. The strike teams deployed to support the COVID-19 mission on the front lines, which encompassed a variety of settings including coronavirus testing sites, nursing homes, hospitals, airports, tribal territories and military installations. PHS officers served in vital roles, assisting civilian health care institutions in rendering clinical care to non-Covid and coronavirus-infected patients, helping set up community-based testing sites and performing nasopharyngeal swab tests, administering COVID-19 vaccinations, and providing administrative, logistical and leadership support at various venues. Between July and November 2020, strike teams composed of PHS officers and federal health personnel that included infection prevention specialists from CDC were deployed to 96 nursing homes that were facing an array of challenges to bolster facility capabilities as well as to better understand the etiology of large outbreaks and factors associated with coronavirus spread.[49-52]

Because many Commissioned Corps personnel provide direct patient care in their regular duty assignments and the newly authorized Ready Reserve Corps was in its early stages and unable to participate, a number of officers were deployed multiple times. In fact, the COVID-19 response required that PHS officers deploy more frequently and for longer periods than any prior response mission. As a consequence, the Corps' force health protection program was ramped up to deal with the increased stress placed upon officers. Introduced in 2017, the USPHS Corps Care program involves a comprehensive strategy to meet the behavioral, health, medical, and spiritual needs of all Commissioned Corps officers. The program assists officers with building and strengthening their resiliency, coordinates resources to address officer needs, and promotes wellness throughout the deployment continuum.[53]

A few widely publicized missions in early 2020 included PHS officers. On February 3, 2020, the cruise ship Diamond Princess was quarantined two weeks at the Yokohama port in Japan due to an escalating number of COVID-19 cases onboard, eventually numbering about 700 passengers and crew testing positive for coronavirus infection. Led by RADM Richard W. Childs, a 25-member PHS strike team deployed to Japan on February 15, 2020, to assist in evacuating hundreds of Americans on repatriation flights and their subsequent quarantine on U.S. military bases. The team further ensured that about 50 coronavirus-infected Americans received proper care at 25 hospitals throughout Japan, where Dr. Childs was able to secure compassionate use remdesivir for several critically ill patients, all of whom survived.[54]

Early in the pandemic, the Life Care Center nursing home in Kirkland, Washington, experienced the first significant cluster of coronavirus cases in the nation. Facility staff as well as residents were testing positive for COVID-19, with numerous deaths occurring among the residents. A strike team of 28 PHS officers, including physicians, physicians' assistants, nurses, technicians and other medical personnel, were dispatched on March 6, 2020, to supplant the overwhelmed staff and assist with controlling the outbreak in the facility.[55]

On March 26, 2020, PHS Strike Team 1 deployed to the Jacob K. Javits Convention Center in New York City, which had been transformed into a 500-bed field medical station. PHS officers served alongside military and other medical personnel to care for COVID-19 patients transferred from New York City area hospitals. The team was led by CAPT Morrisa Rice, with CAPT Renee M. Pazdan, a neurologist and former Army officer as the chief medical

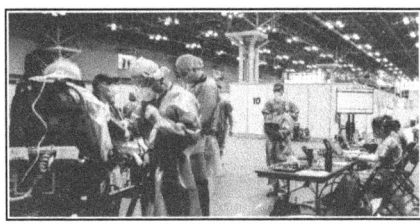

Javits Center in New York City with a scalable 250 to 2,500 bed hospital to care for COVID-19 patients.
[Comfort, Javits Center Open Care to COVID-19 Patients. Defense News, April 7, 2020.]

officer. The multidisciplinary team of 67 PHS officers included physicians, nurses, pharmacists, advanced and behavioral health providers, case managers, therapists, logisticians, and administrators. Nearly 1,100 patients were treated at the Javits NY Medical Station, with the last patient being released on May 1.[56]

The extent to which so many PHS officers, individually and within groups, were challenged to meet this crisis head-on cannot be fully known. Yet, all officers persevered and successfully accomplished the coronavirus response mission, an achievement that surely complements the history of the Corps.

ADMINISTRATION POLITICIZATION

While Operation Warp Speed was a major accomplishment of the Trump administration, the administration's response to spread of coronavirus had serious implications for the health of Americans. The United States, with only 4 percent of the world's population, accounted for about 20 percent of confirmed COVID-19 deaths in 2020, attesting to the fact that administration efforts to control the virus were markedly less effective than other developed countries. The federal government's pandemic response was broadly viewed as a striking public health failure. Given the biomedical, public health, and production capabilities of the time, the federal response was ineffectual due to an array of impactful factors, but the lack of assertive leadership predominates. Public health professionals note that there was "...a profound failure of the nation's leadership to value public health tools and expertise, even amid a historic public health crisis. The U.S. experience with COVID-19 has been a master class in the importance of leadership from the top during a crisis, demonstrated by its absence."[57] On February 7, 2020, President Donald Trump told *Washington Post* journalist Bob Woodward that the coronavirus was airborne, highly contagious and "more deadly than even your strenuous flus."[58] Nonetheless, the President proceeded to publicly minimize disease severity alleging to avoid panic, even though forthright messaging is an essential tenet during a public health crisis. Trump's focus on sustaining the nation's strong economy in an election year defied the essential need to first rein-in the virus to reopen businesses early and safely. Abetted by some elected officials and media, there was a move to reshape mitigation strategies as possible infringements on personal freedoms, while disregarding the detrimental effect such an approach might have on people's lives. This was exacerbated by the dissemination of misinformation, including intentional disinformation and conspiracy theories, by individuals and groups via social media and other communication outlets, and it was a significant factor in propagating vaccine hesitancy among a vast swath of the American populace. From a public health response standpoint, there were other factors that collectively led to suboptimal pandemic control efforts in 2020. The fact that infected, asymptomatic individuals were transmitting the virus was verified a few months after disease onset, and it resulted in shifting and possibly confusing public guidance. Periodic inconsistencies of the administration's messaging with recommendations of the CDC and public health officials may have subverted public trust and compliance with virus mitigation measures.[59,60] These multi-layered factors resulted in avoidable infection, human suffering and death. Moreover, attending healthcare providers, including PHS officers who deployed in clinical support roles for the COVID-19 mission, were placed at significantly greater personal health risk to themselves and their families due to the surge in coronavirus cases.

The *Lancet Commission on Public Policy and Health in the Trump Era* faulted the Trump administration's response to COVID-19, noting that 40 percent of Covid deaths could have been averted as compared with the other Group of Seven (G7) nations.[61] And in Congressional testimony, the former Coronavirus Response Coordinator Dr. Deborah Birx indicated that had the Trump administration promoted optimal coronavirus mitigation strategies, her belief was that there could have been 30 to 40 percent fewer deaths.[62]

The Assistant Secretary for Health and Surgeon General were national public health leaders. With the best of intentions, both as political appointees had to contend with administration talking points while trying to impart reliable evidence-based public health information. As with Dr. Anthony Fauci, this was a balancing act. Notably, Admiral Giroir appeared with some regularity in televised forums to update the public about measures being taken, including to test for, track and slow the spread of coronavirus. Although his oversight of the nation's COVID-19 testing process was fraught with ongoing technical and logistical difficulties, he did a commendable job given such a challenging mission. Dr. Adams took on a communications role consistent with his position, keeping the public apprised of recent developments with respect to mitigation guidance and status of coronavirus spread in the nation.

COMPARISON WITH THE 1918 PANDEMIC

Prior to the coronavirus pandemic, the 1918 influenza pandemic (Spanish flu; *see Chapter Four*) was the most severe pandemic in recent history, causing an estimated 675,000 deaths in the United States and at least 50 million fatalities worldwide. Historical interest in comparing the 1918 pandemic with the COVID-19 pandemic has provided a few interesting observations. At the outset of the Spanish flu pandemic, officials in some townships downplayed the severity of the disease. By late 1918, though, a highly lethal disease surge happened and its deadly impact soon became apparent. At the time, it was assumed that this was a bacterial disease; regardless, there were no influenza vaccines or antiviral drugs. Efforts to mitigate spread of the flu virus were imposed, much like those employed to stem spread of coronavirus, including wearing masks, social distancing, and limiting indoor gatherings. And similarly, localities that were proactive with mitigation measures led to slowing of the disease spread, whereas those places resistant to public health recommendations experienced considerably more persons succumbing to the disease. An important distinction in national response efforts is that, with respect to the Spanish flu, there was no leadership or guidance provided from the White House. President Woodrow Wilson, in fact, rarely if ever spoke publicly about the flu that was ravaging the country, even as some of his staff were becoming ill. Wilson was instead preoccupied with the final phases of World War I.[63] In contrast, President Trump fashioned the national coronavirus response as centered within the Executive Branch; however, the responsibility for most actionable items was consigned to the states. Out of necessity, and much like the early 1900s when the public health infrastructure was relatively absent, in 2020 medical and public health institutions had to generally fend for themselves, contending with insufficient resources of every type and the counterproductive political directives coming from some municipalities and states.

Thomas D. Tuttle

An interesting congruence was a PHS commissioned officer by the name of Thomas D. Tuttle. Tuttle resembled Dr. Anthony S. Fauci in their actions and a bit in physical appearance. As the Washington State Health Commissioner, Dr. Tuttle was lead spokesperson in the effort to minimize the impact of the influenza pandemic in that state.

Anthony S. Fauci

Like Fauci, Tuttle advised the public to make behavioral changes to limit spread of the virus, to include wearing masks, social distancing, reducing public gatherings, and quarantine. He warned of disease resurgence if restrictions were lifted early, and he raised the notion of community spread through an asymptomatic "carrier." And like with Fauci, his restrictive measures were not always well received by business and political entities.[64,65]

REFRAMING PUBLIC HEALTH

Importantly, the 1918 influenza pandemic provided the impetus to reframe the concept of disease as a societal-wide threat that acknowledges the occupational and social conditions which can give rise to illness. It brought an awareness of the importance of epidemiology as the cornerstone of public health and the collection of health data subsequently became more systematic. As a result of the experience and lessons learned from the 1918 influenza pandemic, many countries created or bolstered their health ministries and began to centralize their public health systems.[66,67]

CHRONOLOGY • 2017–2021
SG Jerome M. Adams, September 2017–January 2021

2017	Formation of Presidential Commission on the opioid crisis; HHS declares the opioid crisis to be a public health emergency.
2018	Surgeon General releases advisory on naloxone and a report entitled *Spotlight on Opioids*.
2018	Surgeon General releases advisory on e-cigarette use among youth.
2018	Release of revised Conditions of Service in the PHS Commissioned Corps.
2018	USPHS Modernization initiative proposed.
2018	Department of Defense bestows Humanitarian Service Medal to USPHS.
2018	70th anniversary of the Framingham Heart Study.
2019	Prevention through Active Community Engagement program initiated.
2019	Coronavirus disease 2019 emerges in China.
2020	Release of the Surgeon General Report on *Smoking Cessation*.
2020	Issuance of *Call to Action to Control Hypertension*.
2020	*Coronavirus Aid, Relief, and Economic Security Act (CARES Act)*. Includes authorization to re-establish the Ready Reserve Corps.
2020	Worldwide pandemic of coronavirus disease 2019 (COVID-19). The deployment of PHS commissioned officers in support of the response to coronavirus was without precedent in Corps history.

CHAPTER EIGHTEEN

COVID-19, UNACCOMPANIED CHILDREN, CLIMATE CHANGE, COA & FOUNDATION
2021 to 2023

THE NEW ADMINISTRATION of President Joseph R. Biden, Jr. assumed office on January 20, 2021, inheriting multiple challenges emanating from the prior administration, not the least of which was the essential need to rein in the COVID-19 pandemic that was ravaging the country. The promise of new, innovative vaccines to stem the spread of the disease was realized with the Food and Drug Administration's emergency use authorization in December 2020 of the Pfizer–BioNTech and Moderna mRNA vaccines, and authorization in February 2021 of the Johnson & Johnson (Janssen) viral vector vaccine.

Vivek H. Murthy

Vivek H. Murthy was a health adviser to Biden during the 2020 presidential campaign, and he would once again become Surgeon General in the new administration. Although there was some advance concern about coronavirus-related consulting to private companies by Dr. Murthy, his confirmation hearing by the Senate Health, Education, Labor and Pensions Committee was non-controversial. Murthy stated that "If confirmed as Surgeon General, my highest priority will be to help end this pandemic."[1] During testimony he noted "There are issues that have been worsened by Covid – mental health and substance use disorders – and those are my accompanying priorities as well." His nomination as the 21st U.S. Surgeon General was confirmed by the Senate on March 23, 2021.

CORONAVIRUS DISEASE 2019 PANDEMIC

The spread of coronavirus continued unabated in the country during 2021, which was largely attributed to those persons who were resistant to mitigation efforts and/or those who remained unvaccinated. The COVID-19 Delta variant had become predominant in the summer of 2021, and emergence of the highly transmissible Omicron variant overtook Delta as the dominant viral strain by late December, taking hold throughout the world. About 200 million or 60 percent of Americans were fully vaccinated in 2021, meaning that they had received the primary 2-dose series of an mRNA vaccine or a single dose of the Janssen vaccine. Centers for Disease Control and Prevention (CDC) data indicated that unvaccinated people were nine times more likely to be hospitalized and were at 14 times greater risk of dying from Covid. As a consequence, during much of 2021, more than 90 percent of all coronavirus hospitalizations and deaths comprised individuals who were among the unvaccinated within the population. By December 2021, the U.S. had reached a total of over 800,000 deaths due to coronavirus, with a reported 1.3 times the per capita deaths when compared with the European Union. This high rate of mostly preventable deaths placed a severe strain on hospital resources, healthcare professionals and the public health system.[2-4] By April 1, 2022, the more contagious Omicron subvariant, BA.2, became the dominant version of COVID-19 in the nation, accounting for over 50 percent of Covid infections. U.S. hospitalizations and deaths continued to exceed the rates seen in Western Europe due to the relatively large segment of the populace who resisted mitigation efforts, which was hindered further by some conservative governors who opposed mask mandates in their states. By mid-May 2022, the total number of Covid-related deaths in the U.S. surpassed one million persons, with most deaths occurring among the 65 years and older age group. In comparison, that number approximates an estimated total of 1.1 million military deaths in all major U.S. wars since 1775, including 500,000 deaths during the Civil War. The Omicron subvariant, BA.5, predominated in the fall of 2022 and though it spread more easily than other strains, it caused less severe illness. By January 2023, the Omicron subvariant XBB.1.5 accounted for half of Covid cases in the nation, and about 90 percent of Covid infections by April 2023.

White House Response Team
A White House COVID-19 Response Team was formed in January 2021. The Surgeon General's priority was to address the coronavirus pandemic and he was appointed to the Response Team along with Jeffrey D. Zients (COVID-19 Response Coordinator; replaced in March 2022 by Dr. Ashish Jha), and prominent public health officials including Dr. Anthony S. Fauci (Chief Medical Advisor to the President), Dr. David A. Kessler (Chief Science Officer), and Dr. Rochelle P. Walensky (CDC Director). Throughout 2021, the Response Team members held regular televised briefings regarding the spread of coronavirus, the need for vaccinations and testing, quarantine recommendations, and best mitigation strategies for the general public and for specific groups such as age-based, those with underlying medical conditions, and school bound children. In addition to the formal briefings, Dr. Fauci led pandemic-related public outreach efforts, along with Drs. Walensky and Murthy, by appearing in multiple media outlets to inform the public about coronavirus impact trends, guidances and recommendations. Dr. Fauci became the public face of the

federal response to coronavirus. An experienced infectious disease expert, he was an authoritative spokesperson about all aspects of COVID-19. He often appeared on various television outlets on the same day. However, he and other medical authorities endured attempts to discredit their recommendations in furtherance of the ongoing politicization of Covid. Dr. Walensky's public outreach included televised appearances to provide CDC's science-based analytic information. And, Dr. Murthy fulfilled the role of the nation's doctor; he was conversant on a range of public health issues and conveyed a reassuring demeanor that helped restore public recognition and importance of the Surgeon General's office.

Appearances by Drs. Fauci, Walensky and Murthy became much less frequent during 2023 due to the precipitous decline in Covid-related hospitalizations and deaths, which was in part due to rising population immunity. This was reflected in the fact that only about 60 PHS officers deployed on Covid response missions during 2023.

COVID-19 Response Plans

The Biden administration released three reports in 2021 and 2022 pertaining to its response to the coronavirus epidemic:
- *National Strategy for the COVID-19 Response and Pandemic Preparedness* [January 2021], which provided a framework and actionable plan with the goal to "guide America out of the worst public health crisis in a century"; it included steps to achieve each of seven goals, including the issuance of Executive Orders;
- *U.S. COVID-19 Global Response and Recovery Framework* [July 2021]; and
- *National COVID-19 Preparedness Plan* [March 2022], which focused on activities to deal with the coronavirus in future years.[5-7]

On April 11, 2023, the COVID-19 pandemic National Emergency declaration, first enacted during the Trump administration in 2020, was ended. The HHS COVID-19 Public Health Emergency declaration expired on May 11, 2023.

SURGEON GENERAL ADVISORIES

Health Misinformation

Online social media sites have become a purveyor of unverified content, including *mis*information and intentionally deceptive *dis*information, which is widely disseminated instantaneously. Misinformation is not limited to social media; such information is also gotten via search engines and televised media outlets. A striking escalation of health misinformation and disinformation accompanied the Covid pandemic, which hindered efforts to contain Covid and harmed the many individuals who chose not to follow mitigation measures nor be vaccinated, thereby contributing to ongoing spread of coronavirus in this country. On July 15, 2021, Vivek Murthy released *Confronting Health Misinformation: The U.S. Surgeon General's Advisory on Building a Healthy Information Environment*.[8] This Advisory was atypical by focusing on a non-medical topic. In prefatory comments, he stated: "Limiting the spread of health misinformation is a moral and civic imperative that will require a whole-of-society effort."

Youth Mental Health

During the Covid pandemic, widespread behavioral issues including anxiety and depressive symptoms were emerging and exacerbated due to restrictions on educational, workplace, and social interactions. On December 7, 2021, Dr. Murthy issued *Protecting Youth Mental Health: The U.S. Surgeon General's Advisory* to address the mental health crisis.[9] He noted in introductory remarks: "The pandemic era's unfathomable number of deaths, pervasive sense of fear, economic instability, and forced physical distancing from loved ones, friends, and communities have exacerbated the unprecedented stresses young people already faced." Recommendations are made in the report for proactive efforts to support the mental health of children, adolescents and young adults.

Health Worker Burnout; Workplace Mental Health and Well-being

In May 2022, Dr. Murthy issued a report entitled *Addressing Health Worker Burnout: The U.S. Surgeon General's Advisory on Building a Thriving Health Workforce*. And on October 20, 2022, he released *The U.S. Surgeon General's Framework for Mental Health & Well-Being in the Workplace*. These two reports address the factors that underpin burnout and the mental health issues that affect healthcare workers, and provide recommendations to promote their well-being, thereby strengthening the nation's public health infrastructure.

Social Media Use

On May 23, 2023, Dr. Murthy released a Surgeon General's Advisory entitled *Social Media and Youth Mental Health*.[10] The report states that social media may offer some benefits, yet there are indicators that such media may also be harmful to the mental health and well-being of children and adolescents. Murthy notes that the most common question he receives from parents is, "Is social media safe for my kids." The report provides recommendations that can be used to help make social media safer for young people.

Loneliness and Isolation

On May 3, 2023, Dr. Murthy released a new report entitled *Our Epidemic of Loneliness and Isolation: The U.S. Surgeon General's Advisory on the Healing Effects of Social Connection and Community*.[11] In introductory remarks, he indicates that loneliness harms both individual and societal health, and that society has an obligation "...to make the same investments in addressing social connection that we have made in addressing tobacco use, obesity, and the addiction crisis." The report states that social connection is an important determinant of health and, more broadly, of community well-being, and it provides a framework for a national strategy to advance social connection.

CNN Sanjay Gupta with SGs V. Murthy, R. Carmona, J. Elders, K. Moritsugu, R. Benjamin, J. Adams, and A. Novello meeting on the *Future of Mental Health and Wellness*, Dartmouth College, September 28, 2023.[12] *[Dartmouth College YouTube]*

LEGISLATIVE INITIATIVE

On July 27, 2023, U.S. Senators Tammy Duckworth and Ronald Wyden introduced new legislation to provide the Corps with the funding support it needs to ensure a highly trained and fully deployable national public health service. The *U.S. Public Health Service Commissioned Corps Operations and Readiness Act* would authorize dedicated annual funding to the Commissioned Corps, which is currently the only uniformed service without a budget line item for service operations and maintenance.[13]

OPIOID CRISIS

The drug overdose crisis continued to escalate in 2021 and 2022 due to the proliferation of highly potent illicit synthetic drugs. Overdose deaths reached a new record in 2022 with more than 109,000 American lives lost. Of those, about 70 percent involved synthetic opioids, in particular illicitly manufactured fentanyl and its analogues that were often added to drugs that many people used, unaware of the extreme danger. According to Dr. Rahul Gupta, Director of the White House Office of National Drug Control Policy, less than 1 out of 10 people who need addiction care receive it. On April 21, 2022, the Biden administration released the *National Drug Control Strategy*, with new initiatives to contend with the opioid crisis, including making it easier to treat patients with substance use disorders, and supporting prevention, harm reduction, and treatment initiatives. The administration, through HHS, provided over $5 billion to support substance use and overdose prevention efforts in communities. In addition, the billions of dollars that corporations paid to settle opioid-related lawsuits will be used to fund addiction treatment and health care and make it more accessible.[14-16] The CDC National Center for Injury Prevention and Control (NCIPC) is among the lead federal agencies working on the drug overdose crisis. In June 2023 Congressional testimony,[17] NCIPC Director CAPT Christopher M. Jones, PharmD, DrPH, outlined CDC's key strategies to address the crisis: using data and surveillance to monitor substance use and overdose trends; helping communities use data to drive action and implement evidence-based strategies; supporting providers, health systems, payors and employers to improve pain management practices and link people to care; partnering with public safety and community organizations to advance overdose prevention strategies; and raising public awareness through education.

Christopher Jones

In Their Words
by CAPT Christopher M. Jones

The overdose crisis is complex and it has profoundly impacted our nation over the past two decades. CDC's most recent data show that over 300 Americans are dying each day from a drug overdose and many millions more struggle with substance use and addiction. The historic increases in overdose deaths in recent years are spurred on by a rapidly changing drug market inundated with illicitly made fentanyl and other synthetic opioids, as well as a resurgence of stimulants like methamphetamine. And behind these statistics are individuals, families, and communities that have been deeply impacted. This situation continues to present emerging and novel threats to the health of our nation. At CDC, we are working urgently to save lives while also building a strong foundation of prevention to protect the next generation. CDC invests in communities across the country through a national program called Overdose Data to Action or OD2A that supports the critical work being done by health departments. This initiative is being done in concert with other federal agencies, including the Substance Abuse and Mental Health Services Administration (SAMHSA), NIH, FDA, Indian Health Service, and Health Resources and Services Administration (HRSA). USPHS Commissioned Corps officers are at the forefront of the overdose crisis, working tirelessly with communities to save lives. Across HHS, they serve on the front lines providing clinical care and services to individuals with substance use disorders and distributing naloxone and fentanyl test strips to community members. They are scientific officers and program managers of CDC, HRSA, and SAMHSA grants who work on program implementation and evaluation. CDC officers lead surveillance efforts to improve the collection, trend analysis, and dissemination of overdose data to drive public health action in communities, and they conduct innovative research to identify effective policies, programs, and practices. PHS officers also volunteer in their own communities, providing presentations on substance use and overdose prevention and participating in naloxone training programs.

DEFENSE HEALTH AGENCY, PUBLIC HEALTH

On October 31, 2022, and in compliance with the Defense Authorization Act for FY 2019, the Deputy Secretary of the Department of Defense (DOD) directed that the public health centers and public health programs within each military Service – the Army, Navy, and Air Force – be transferred to and consolidated within a new Public Health directorate in the Defense Health Agency (DHA). The purpose of the directorate is to provide a unified and coordinated approach to improve force readiness by providing force health protection to service members and their families across the DOD. Transition of the Service public health centers and programs to the directorate was ongoing into 2023 and is a challenging and complex undertaking that involves infrastructure, processes and systems, while maintaining force protection with enhanced global capabilities. To head DHA Public Health, DOD named USPHS officer Rear Admiral Brandon L. Taylor as its first Director on February 1, 2022. The fact that a PHS officer was selected for this high level position is a testament to the very exceptional abilities of RDML Taylor, a pharmacy officer, as well as recognition of the expertise that the USPHS Commissioned Corps brings in partnership with the other uniformed services.[18-20]

Brandon L. Taylor

In Their Words
by RDML Brandon L. Taylor

The public health enterprise within the Department of Defense is a passionate and often overlooked community that also includes PHS officers. While there is great anticipation among the Services for this transition to a unified command, many concerns were initially expressed regarding the convergence of Army, Navy, and Air Force public health centers into the DHA. Nonetheless, many have lauded having a USPHS Commissioned Corps officer, a neutral party, leading this effort, and it is the intent of DHA Director LTG Crosland to have a USPHS flag officer in this role moving forward. The breadth of the DHA Public Health portfolio is impressive, with an expansive array of medical services available to service members and their dependents. It is also not uncommon in the course of a day for me to meet and discuss a range of issues; for example, biosurveillance with Chem-Bio and intelligence communities, receive a classified briefing on nefarious efforts that could affect public health, discuss remedial strategy for a significant contamination event, and work on Total Force Fitness policy. Once this major transition is complete, DHA Public Health will have over 1,400 uniformed and civilian personnel and an annual operational budget of nearly $1 billion. What a joy to serve with these talented and driven public health professionals and also represent the PHS as the senior Corps officer at DHA.

Unaccompanied Children

Every year, unaccompanied children predominantly from Central American countries cross the Mexico–United States border/southern border into this nation. Unaccompanied children are under 18 years of age who have no parent or legal guardian nor lawful immigration status in the United States. When an unaccompanied child is apprehended by U.S. Customs and Border Protection authorities, the child is transferred to the care and custody of the Office of Refugee Resettlement (ORR) in the Administration for Children and Families, HHS. By law, ORR must provide food, shelter, and medical care to unaccompanied children until it is able to release them to safe settings. During most years since fiscal year 2012, the number of children encountered by the Border Patrol has been increasing, with spikes recorded in fiscal years 2014 and 2019, culminating with 145,000 children in fiscal year 2021, of which nearly 123,000 were referred to ORR. This trend continued into fiscal year 2022, with over 149,000 unaccompanied children crossing the border, of which 130,000 were referred to ORR. To ensure adequate shelter capacity, ORR activated influx care facilities and temporary emergency intake sites in 2021 to permit the prompt and safe transfer of children from DHS custody.

Unaccompanied children are provided a range of services that include health care consisting of a complete medical examination with screening for infectious diseases, appropriate immunizations, prescription medications, dental care, and mental health services. PHS officers are often called upon to support the HHS mission in providing the care for these children. In 2021, more than eight hundred PHS officers deployed to southern border states and around the nation, often on extended duration missions in support of Operation Artemis, which was the Biden administration's interagency effort led by the Federal Emergency Management Agency to facilitate the processing of unaccompanied children. Though in fewer numbers, PHS officers were also deployed in 2022 to provide health care and support services, including 91 PHS officers who went to Customs and Border Protection sites in Arizona and Texas to provide intake support. The 2021 mobilization for the Artemis operation was under the command of RADM Richard W. Childs, MD, Clinical Director of the NIH National Heart, Lung, and Blood Institute, who also led the February 2020 coronavirus mission in Japan. The complexity and scale of USPHS Operation Artemis spurred the development of a new, more effective data system to track officer deployments that would allow for dynamic reporting to the command and control team, and it was further integrated into the deployment management system at Commissioned Corps Headquarters.[21-24]

Richard W. Childs

OPERATION ALLIES WELCOME

In August 2021, amid a growing Taliban takeover of the country of Afghanistan, the United States began a withdrawal that included evacuation of embassy personnel, U.S. and certain Afghan nationals. On August 29, 2021, President Biden directed the Department of Homeland Security to lead efforts across the federal government to resettle approximately 115,000 (as of August 2023) Afghan nationals, many of whom supported the U.S. military and civilian personnel in Afghanistan, to resettle in the United States. The mission was known as Operation Allies Welcome (OAW) and involved intake processing at designated U.S. military bases. Processing included the provision of medical care services such as COVID-19 testing, health screening, performing medical examinations, administering MMR, polio, varicella, COVID-19 and other appropriate vaccinations, and case manager duties prior to being connected with nongovernmental organizations for resettlement in communities. In late July 2021, the HHS Office of Refugee Resettlement joined the whole-of-government effort. Operation Allies Welcome was ended September 30, 2022. The USPHS Commissioned Corps was a significant partner in its support of OAW, with about 550 PHS officers deployed from May 2021 to May 2022 to multiple states for the mission.[25,26]

PHS officers review medical records at Holloman Air Force Base, New Mexico, on Oct. 7, 2021. [U.S. Army Photo]

CLIMATE CHANGE

Climate change will increasingly threaten human health and create new public health challenges worldwide. The impact of climate change in this country will undoubtedly lead to greater reliance upon the response capabilities of the USPHS Commissioned Corps. In 1965, President Lyndon B. Johnson's Science Advisory Committee issued the report, *Restoring the Quality of Our Environment*, which noted that the production of carbon dioxide from fossil fuel combustion increases atmospheric carbon dioxide and "...could act, like the glass in a greenhouse, to raise the temperature of the lower air."[27] By the 1980s, evidence was mounting that human activity was having a critical impact on global warming. In June 1988, an international conference in Canada, The Changing Atmosphere: Implications for Global Security, concluded that:

> The Earth's atmosphere is being changed at an unprecedented rate by pollutants resulting from human activities, inefficient and wasteful fossil fuel use and the effects of rapid population growth in many regions. These changes represent a major threat to international security and are already having harmful consequences over many parts of the globe.[28]

Climate Change Denial

In the late 1970s and 1980s, the Exxon [Oil] Corporation provided substantial funding to conduct climate change research. This seminal research confirmed that continued high utilization of fossil fuels could have a devastating influence on global climate. However, the oil industry response, led by Exxon, was to undermine its own research findings. Exxon pursued a long-term, relentless strategy to discredit the scientific consensus by advancing climate change doubt and denial. It did this through the media, by lobbying members of Congress, and funding individuals and groups promoting climate change disinformation.[29] As of 2023, some industry companies, trade groups and Congress members continued to espouse doubt that human activity is a major contributing factor.

Impact on Health

In January 2024, the National Oceanic and Atmospheric Administration reported that global surface temperature during the year 2023 was the warmest among all years in the 1850–2023 climate record, and 2014 through 2023 were the ten warmest years since 1850.[30] The impact of continued global warming will worsen the adverse health consequences to human health, which are profound and all-encompassing. The U.S. Global Change Research Program, in its *Fourth National Climate Assessment,* noted that "Climate change affects human health by altering exposures to heat waves, floods, droughts, and other extreme events; vector-, food- and waterborne infectious diseases; changes in the quality and safety of air, [and availability of] food, and water; and stresses to mental health and well-being."[31] Health care leaders must therefore integrate climate considerations into decision-making and health policy to ensure a more resilient and equitable health care system.[32] The United Nations Intergovernmental Panel on Climate Change (IPCC), among the most authoritative bodies that assess climate change science, released its Sixth Assessment (Synthesis) Report on March 20, 2023. The Report notes that there is a rapidly closing window to secure a livable and sustainable future. Without far-reaching measures to reverse greenhouse gas emissions, the world could surpass the critical temperature threshold of 1.5°C by the early 2030s. Beyond that, escalating climate adversities will be such that people would be unable to adapt, and the Earth system would be fundamentally and irreversibly altered.[33]

U.S. Climate Initiatives

On January 27, 2021, President Biden signed Executive Order 14008, *Tackling the Climate Crisis at Home and Abroad*, a comprehensive document noting that actions must be taken "...to avoid the most catastrophic impacts of that crisis;" and that "...climate considerations shall be an essential element of United States foreign policy and national security."[34] Significantly, the Order stated the nation would rejoin the Paris Agreement (occurred February 19, 2021), the legally binding international treaty on climate change mitigation adopted by 195 countries in 2015, from which the Trump administration withdrew. Biden's Executive Order directed the implementation of a government-wide, coordinated approach to address the inherent challenges of the climate crisis. It tasked the HHS Secretary to establish an Office of Climate Change and Health Equity to address the impact of climate change on the health of Americans and establish an Interagency Working Group to decrease the risk of climate change to vulnerable persons in society. Many agencies formed climate-related programs, including the CDC which initiated a Climate and Health Program to support health agencies as they prepare for the health impacts of a changing climate.[35] In September 2021, an editorial was published simultaneously in more than 200 medical-health journals worldwide in which the authors declared that climate change is the greatest threat to global public health.[36] In May 2022, Assistant Secretary for Health Admiral Rachel L. Levine was in New York City to witness *NYC + Hospitals*, the largest municipal hospital system in the U.S., sign a pledge to reduce greenhouse gas emissions, a pledge that HHS asked the health care sector to support, because that sector accounts for 8.5 percent of the country's emissions.[37] At a conference on December 8, 2022, Dr. Levine stated that "Climate change is a massive public health risk and our office will be the center of that conversation."[38]

Climate Resilience

Agencies across the federal government have been preparing for the impact of climate change, as its effects will become increasingly evident in the U.S. and around the world. It is inevitable that with the higher temperatures, changing precipitation patterns, and more frequent and intense weather events, public health will be affected with resultant disruptions to everyday life. As a consequence, the PHS Commissioned Corps will be called upon to assist with federal responses to climate-induced public health emergencies. Climate change will disproportionately impact more vulnerable populations who are socially and economically disadvantaged. Dr. Paul Reed, Deputy Assistant Secretary for Health and Director, Office of Disease Prevention and Health Promotion, oversees disease prevention and health promotion programs, including the *Healthy People* initiative. As a physician and disaster responder, domestically and globally, RDML Reed has seen how the socioeconomic conditions of communities profoundly impact resilience and health outcomes. Resilience is the capability to prepare for and adjust to changing conditions and withstand and recover rapidly from disruptions. People must work within their communities to develop the resilience necessary to withstand the adverse health consequences and disruptions due to climate change.

Paul Reed

In Their Words

by RDML Paul Reed

The views expressed are those of the author. They do not necessarily reflect the views of the Office of the Assistant Secretary for Health or the U.S. Department of Health and Human Services.

My training as a physician and pediatrician, and my early clinical career, convinced me that being healthy – or more specifically, not being ill – was the goal I needed to seek for my patients. In fact, in the United States, we have a system of health care that is almost entirely directed in the same way – toward treating disease and injury. Our "health care" system is not principally designed to advance health and well-being. In my various public health professional roles, especially working in the humanitarian, global health, and disaster medicine spaces, I began to understand that individuals and communities are only able to improve their health and well-being through the conditions of the environments within which they live. It is this social, economic, and physical context – what the Healthy People 2030 initiative defines in the Social Determinants of Health framework – that truly determines our opportunities for healthy living and therefore better health outcomes. An even more expansive and forward-looking framework – one focused on defining the actions necessary to improve lives in terms of being healthy, well, thriving and resilient – exists in the framework of the Vital Conditions for Health and Well-Being, which identifies factors that people depend upon to reach their full potential, such as basic needs for health and security. Both frameworks offer an alternative philosophy to understanding where health and well-being are derived – one that demands a broad perspective of the daily influences on our opportunities, choices, and behaviors that may or may not be in our control. Those influencing factors vary from the conditions of people's homes and the economic realities that families face to the political decisions made at every level of government, and the profitability of fossil fuel versus alternative energy sources. The factors that determine the availability of nutritious foods, for instance, are tremendously varied and complex in their interplay. The solution to improving access and affordability of nutritious foods for all is equally daunting. One of the most profound influencers on our individual and collective lives is in the effects of climate change. Not only does climate change have obvious impact on the health and well-being of individuals and communities through large scale climactic events such as hurricanes, but climate change also has major implications on sustainable agriculture and is therefore a significant contributor to the availability of nutritious foods. Climate change also represents a determinant of health issue that is itself influenced by myriad economic, political, and cultural drivers. The climate crisis and the resilience of individuals and communities to thrive in the face of disruptions that occur with increasing frequency is to a certain extent in their control, if they are able to make informed decisions, enabled by equitable systems of governance and economy, to improve conditions such as ensuring access to suitable housing and reliable transportation.

PHS Commissioned Officers Association & Foundation

COMMISSIONED OFFICERS ASSOCIATION

The *Commissioned Officers Association of the United States Public Health Service* (COA) was established on October 16, 1951. The signatories to the Articles of Incorporation were PHS officers John M. McInerney, George F. Archambault and Thomas A. Foster. The Articles specified several purposes of the COA; among them, the principal intent was "To foster, promote and develop the interests and welfare of the USPHS and its officers...."[39] Since its inception, the COA is the only organization working exclusively  to support and advance the interests of the USPHS Commissioned Corps and its officers. It does this through representation and advocacy for the Corps, providing officers with education and training programs, and by serving as a trusted informational resource for entities such as the Office of the Surgeon General, Office of the Assistant Secretary for Health, and the U.S. Congress. A major COA priority has been to ensure that the USPHS Commissioned Corps has parity with the other uniformed services, which has largely been accomplished through effective and sustained collaborations with related organizations and The Military Coalition, a consortium of the uniformed services and veterans' groups. The Commissioned Officers Association also oversees a network of over eighty COA Local Branches throughout the nation that function at the local area level. The Local Branches work in tandem with the national organization and also independently provide their own program initiatives. Of the various categories of COA membership, active duty and retired PHS officers predominate. The COA Board of Directors administers the organization at the national level. The Board is comprised of eleven active duty officers, each representing a professional category of the Corps, plus three active duty field officers, three retired officers, and one officer from the Ready Reserve, with all serving three year terms of office.

PHS COMMISSIONED OFFICERS FOUNDATION

On February 5, 1991, USPHS officers formed the *Anchor and Caduceus Society* as an incorporated nonprofit entity in the State of Maryland. The Society's purpose was to promote activities which would enhance the heritage of the Commissioned Corps. The Society sponsored a luncheon on January 4, the anniversary date of the Corps, and on July 16, the anniversary of PHS. The highlight of the January 4 luncheon was the C. Everett Koop Honorary Lecture presented by an invited speaker of note. The *PHS Commissioned Officers*

Foundation was formed on May 3, 2000.⁴⁰ An amendment approved by the Board of Trustees and signed November 13, 2000, by Jerrold M. Michael, President, and Michael Lord, Secretary, changed the organization's name to the *PHS Commissioned Officers Foundation for the Advancement of Public Health* (COF). The Foundation is a not-for-profit charitable and educational organization to serve the needs of the Commissioned Officers Association and the broader public health community. The COF advances public health leadership through programs related to advocacy, education, research and program support, and it builds partnerships between the Commissioned Corps and the public health community. The Foundation manages a portfolio of grant and scholarship programs and, importantly, it sponsors the USPHS Scientific and Training Symposium, a responsibility that was transferred to the Foundation from the COA in 2005. The Symposium is an annual gathering of USPHS officers that includes Corps leadership for professional education and  skills training, official briefings about Commissioned Corps organizational, operational and policy issues, and to promote comradery in the Service. The Symposium's scientific program is developed by PHS officers who meet throughout the prior year. In 2005, the *Anchor and Caduceus Society* was merged with the Foundation, which carries on the tradition of sponsoring the Koop Honorary Lecture in conjunction with the annual Symposium. The Foundation Board of Trustees is comprised of fifteen members, most of whom are retired PHS officers, who serve a three year term of office. All former Surgeons General are invited to become Honorary Trustees of the Foundation.

Jerrold Michael

The founding president of COF, RADM Jerrold (Jerry) M. Michael, was highly esteemed in the Corps due to his steadfast support and mentorship of officers. Michael served as a Navy hospital corpsman in World War II. His professional career in the PHS was engineering, and keen intellect propelled him through the ranks. After retirement, Michael became Dean of the University of Hawaii School of Public Health. In 2007, the Foundation created the RADM Michael Fellowship to provide funding of university continuing education for USPHS junior officers. Over the years, the Association and Foundation have become integral to enriching the work life of PHS officers and safeguarding the viability of the Commissioned Corps in fulfilling its public health mission. COA/COF leadership, to include the USPHS Board members, have been especially proactive in advancing the status of the Corps with regard to parity and interoperability with the other uniformed services. Occasionally, COA will lobby on behalf of the Office of the Surgeon General and Assistant Secretary for Health, such as it did to obtain training funds and pass Ready Reserve

Corps legislation. Enduring relationships have been fostered with members of Congress who have provided reliable support in advocating for the Corps. Progress has also been made on numerous fronts through outreach by the COA/COF, providing authoritative comments about operational, policy and legislative matters, testifying before Congressional committees, distributing promotional materials, and collaborating with partner organizations such as the Military Officers Association of America, Association of Military Surgeons of the United States, Reserve Officers Association, and The Military Coalition.

EXECUTIVE DIRECTORS

In addition to the officers who comprise the governing Boards, the success of the Association and Foundation in sustaining the Commissioned Corps must be given to the exceptional ability of the individuals who have held executive leadership positions and staff of these organizations. The first Executive Director of COA was William J. Lucca, Jr., a graduate of Georgetown University School of Law, who served for over 30 years. As of 2022, all subsequent COA/COF Executive Directors have been retired military officers. They include Michael W. Lord, Esq., Gerard M. Farrell, James T. Currie, and Jacqueline Rychnovsky. There have been two Deputy Executive Directors, John E. McElligott and David Corrigan. Long serving staff have included Judith Rensberger, Teresa Foley, Donna Sparrow, and Erica Robinson.

EXECUTIVE DIRECTORS, COA/COF, 1962–2022

William J. Lucca	Michael W. Lord	Gerard M. Farrell	James T. Currie	Jacque Rychnovsky
1962-1995	U.S. Navy, Ret.	U.S. Navy, Ret.	U.S. Army, Ret.	U.S. Navy, Ret.
	1995-2001	2001-2014	2014-2020	2020-

DEPUTY EXECUTIVE DIRECTORS

John E. McElligott	David Corrigan
U.S. Army Reserve	U.S. Marine Corps Reserve
2012-2019	2022-2024

USPHS Corps Mascot

The USPHS Commissioned Corps welcomed its first official mascot in 2023. Commissioned with an honorary rank of Lieutenant Commander, Abigail's namesake is Abigail Adams, First Lady of the United States when the U.S. Marine Hospital Service was created in 1798.  Abigail is a Labrador Retriever that is a Warrior Canine Connection trained facility dog. Her main role involves offering therapeutic care, fostering a sense of unity, and aiding in public health communications. As a facility dog, Abigail will not only represent the USPHS at ceremonial events, but will accompany officers in their work to protect the nation's health, offering comfort and relief from stress. The USPHS Commissioned Corps mascot program was made possible by a memorandum of understanding between the USPHS Commissioned Corps and the PHS Commissioned Officers Foundation. As of 2023, Abigail resided in Maryland with her handler, LCDR Daniel R. Johnson and his family.

Chronology • 2021–2023

SG Vivek H. Murthy, March 2021–

- 2021 Formation of White House COVID-19 Response Team.
- 2021 Executive Order 14008, *Tackling the Climate Crisis at Home and Abroad*.
- 2021 Announcement of the creation of the Public Health and Emergency Response Strike Team (PHERST).
- 2021 Surgeon General releases Advisories on Health Misinformation and on Youth Mental Health.
- 2021-22 Continued deployment of PHS Commissioned Corps officers in support of the COVID-19 response.
- 2021-22 Deployment of PHS Commissioned Corps officers in response to a surge of unaccompanied children at the southern border.
- 2021-22 Deployment of PHS Commissioned Corps officers in support of Operation Allies Welcome.
- 2022 NOAA reports the nine years from 2014 through 2022 ranked among the ten warmest years on record.
- 2023 Surgeon General releases Advisory on Loneliness and Isolation.

CHAPTER NINETEEN

CCHQ, PHS DEPLOYMENTS, PHS CHALLENGES

THE U.S. PUBLIC HEALTH SERVICE COMMISSIONED CORPS is comprised of a medical, public health and science professionals organized into eleven categories corresponding with their professional/scientific education and training, to include dental, dietitian, engineer, environmental health, health services, nurse, pharmacist, physician, scientist, therapist, and veterinarian. As such, the Corps is uniquely qualified to provide comprehensive health care, public and environmental health, and science-based services throughout the nation with an array of capabilities by way of the full-time duty assignments of its officers. This network of exceptionally well trained professionals and scientists working collaboratively for the citizens of this nation is unique in the world.

PHS officers further serve as a national health security asset in responding to public health crises and emergency events such as natural disasters, disease outbreaks, or terrorist attacks, domestically and internationally. The many types of deployment missions also include, for example, providing health care for unaccompanied children who cross the southern border; providing back-up for shortages of professional staff in the military; participating in state-based missions to provide dental, vision, and medical services in underserved communities; and providing medical care and public health services on joint uniformed service humanitarian missions to other countries. Public health emergency events as declared by the President or Secretary of Health and Human Services (HHS) are part of the National Response Framework Emergency Support Function (ESF) #8 – Public Health and Medical Services. The HHS Secretary, through the Administration for Strategic Preparedness and Response (ASPR), coordinates ESF #8 preparedness, response, and recovery actions. PHS officers may deploy for such events, as well as support the urgent medical and public health needs of other federal agencies, state and local governments, and occasionally foreign governments. Officers also deploy to National Special Security Events declared by the Secretary of Homeland Security. Countless times, PHS officers have fulfilled these vital missions with personal commitment, dedication and compassion.

COMMISSIONED CORPS HEADQUARTERS

Headquarters Operations

Commissioned Corps Headquarters (CCHQ), the largest component of the Office of the Surgeon General (OSG), is responsible for command, operational and administrative activities of the Corps. It supports approximately 6,500 active duty officers through agreements with 26 different agencies in nine Departments, comprising 800 duty stations throughout the U.S. CCHQ staff perform a wide array of personnel management functions, including recruitment and retention, duty assignments, readiness compliance, deployments, career development, performance evaluations, promotions, training, policy development, awards, personnel records maintenance, and retirements. In performing its responsibilities, Headquarters solicits consultative input from the Chief Professional Officers and Agency Liaison Officers. CCHQ's multifaceted responsibility requires a dedicated staff of uniformed service and civilian personnel, led by exceptional leaders who serve in the capacity of Director.[1]

Headquarters is the nucleus of the USPHS Commissioned Corps, as its operational imperatives impact all PHS officers and the Service as a whole. CCHQ brings about a measure of unity to a system with an atypical split command structure, where officers are accountable to OSG and to the agency to which assigned. Headquarters represents the commonality of the entire Corps in its operational command structure, uniformed service precepts, and for the commitment to mission critical deployments. Those closely held activities, overseen by CCHQ, are essential to sustaining a uniformed service presence. Commissioned Corps officers are health care, public health and science professionals who serve individuals and communities throughout the nation and various areas worldwide. CCHQ is a reliable partner with those officers, providing guidance and ensuring that officers are well served and supported so that they can more optimally serve their constituents and the public. Headquarters' duty to agencies is to help ensure that PHS officers with proper skill sets are billeted to the agency to facilitate mission accomplishment.

Headquarters Directors

The Surgeon General is leader of the Commissioned Corps and serves as the nation's doctor in communicating with the public about healthy lifestyles and science-based public health guidance. The Deputy Surgeon General is tasked with working with the CCHQ Director in overseeing programmatic actions to ensure operational effectiveness in meeting policy objectives. The Headquarters Director is the senior executive officer for the Commissioned Corps and principal advisor to both the Surgeon General and Deputy Surgeon General. The Headquarters Director, in concert with OSG, works laterally and upline through the Assistant Secretary for Health to communicate resource needs, systems improvements, and operational plans that are necessary to accomplish its responsibilities and program goals. In so doing, HHS is better able to account for the Headquarters' programmatic activities and associated funding requirements, and thereby can more effectively utilize the PHS Corps.

The individuals who hold the position of CCHQ Director endure the constant burden of responsibility that comes with a uniquely demanding job. They generally have business acumen with a grasp of policies and procedures and operational efficiencies, and are capable leaders who can motivate a collegial team effort to accomplish the mission with excellence. The Director must have good interpersonal skills when communicating with officers, senior leadership and other Services, and be available to fulfill ceremonial duties. Equally important is the supportive attention and executive presence that the Director and his/her staff project to PHS officers, thereby bolstering general employment satisfaction and positive interactive relations among officers. The health and welfare of each officer is of paramount concern for the CCHQ Director, as well. With increasing officer deployments, it became apparent that the Corps needed behavioral health and well-being resources for officers. As a result, a comprehensive Corps Care program was introduced to assist officers with improving readiness and preparedness, and building resilience and healthier lives. The Corps Care program was particularly beneficial when there was an unprecedented deployment of two-thirds of the complement of PHS officers across the initial two years of COVID-19 response.

Corps Modernization

Each Director of Commissioned Corps Headquarters has had a fundamental responsibility to reimagine, transform, and modernize Corps operations and infrastructure. Strategies have included improvement of organizational structure and systems, improvement of recruitment processes, updating training, and adapting force management to improve officers' overall capabilities for public health crisis response. In 2017, the reimagine plan became the basis for a Corps Modernization effort initiated in 2018. Along with an allocation of resources to implement the plan, CCHQ improved the electronic document submission and management systems. In 2020, a framework was created within Headquarters to re-establish the Commissioned Corps Ready Reserve. A dedicated staff was formed to promulgate policies and operationalize mission requirements, including training programs, for overall management of the Reserve Corps. A substantial effort was put forth for several years to produce a USPHS Commissioned Corps *Doctrine* in order to align with other uniformed services. Published in January 2021, the *Doctrine* gives a comprehensive overview of the mission, structure, values, capabilities, and traditions of the Commissioned Corps *(see Chapter Seventeen)*.

The following USPHS officers have served in the executive position of Director, Commissioned Corps Headquarters, Office of the Surgeon General.

DIRECTORS OF COMMISSIONED CORPS HEADQUARTERS

NAME	TENURE	ORGANIZATIONAL NAME
James G. Terrell, Jr.	1947-1948	Division of Commissioned Operations
ASG Eugene A. Gillis	1948-1952	Division of Commissioned Operations
CAPT Erwin C. Dresher	1952-1954	Division of Commissioned Operations
CAPT James K. Shaeffer	1954-1955	Office of Personnel [Joint CO/CS]
CAPT Murray A. Diamond	1955-1957	Office of Personnel [Joint CO/CS]
ASG Richard C. Anderson	1958-1962	Office of Personnel [Joint CO/CS]
ASG Murray A. Diamond	1962-1966	Office of Personnel [Joint CO/CS]
CAPT Elton S. Osbourne	1961-1963	Commissioned Personnel Operations Division
Unknown	1963-1968	Commissioned Personnel Operations Division
CAPT Tamarath K. Yolles	1968-1971	Commissioned Personnel Operations Division
ASG E. Lee W. Smith	1971-1973	Commissioned Personnel Operations Division
CAPT Dale Truesdell	1973-1977	Commissioned Personnel Operations Division
CAPT Delbert A. Larson	1977-1987	Commissioned Personnel Operations Division
CAPT David W. Callagy	1987-1990	Division of Commissioned Personnel
CAPT Richard J. Bertin	1990-1992	Division of Commissioned Personnel
RADM Suzanne Dahlman	1992-1998	Division of Commissioned Personnel
RADM R. Michael Davidson	1998-2003	Division of Commissioned Personnel
RADM Denise S. Canton	2004-2006	Office of Commissioned Corps Operations
RADM Lawrence J. Furman	2006-2010	Office of Commissioned Corps Operations
RADM Scott F. Giberson	2011-2014	Division of Com. Corps Personnel and Readiness
CAPT Scott M. Helgeson (a)	2014-2016	Division of Com. Corps Personnel and Readiness
RADM Joan F. Hunter	2016-2019	Division of Com. Corps Personnel and Readiness
RADM Susan M. Orsega	2019-2021	Commissioned Corps Headquarters
RDML Richard P. Schobitz	2022-	Commissioned Corps Headquarters

Richard J. Bertin 1990-1992   Suzanne Dahlman 1992-1998   R. Michael Davidson 1998-2003   Denise S. Canton 2004-2006   Lawrence J. Furman 2006-2010

Scott F. Giberson 2011-2014   Scott M. Helgeson Actg. 2014-2016   Joan F. Hunter 2016-2019   Susan M. Orsega 2019-2021   Richard P. Schobitz 2022-

Officer Deployments

The Readiness and Deployment Branch (RDB), which manages officer deployments, resides organizationally within the Division of Strategic Deployment Operations and Readiness, Commissioned Corps Headquarters, Office of the Surgeon General. Commissioned Corps officers are deployed upon request. If the mission is an appropriate utilization of the Corps, the Surgeon General recommends and receives approval from the HHS Secretary or the Assistant Secretary for Health. Once mission requirements are determined, RDB will match requirements with the qualifications of officers on the ready roster. To prepare for emergency response roles, officers undergo didactic and field training and must be physically and mentally fit to meet readiness standards.

In the aftermath of the 2005 deployment of PHS officers to the public health emergencies resulting from Hurricanes Katrina, Rita and Wilma, HHS Secretary Michael Leavitt directed the Commissioned Corps to implement a tiered structure of preconfigured response teams *(see Chapter Fourteen)*. In 2020, the tired response framework was disbanded, ushering in a more agile, adaptable and scalable response approach. The new approach is more consistent with the concept of strike teams composed of officers with response roles that fulfill mission-specific requirements. Response assets are scalable and deployed in accordance with mission requirements. Three guidances released in 2022 updated officer readiness and deployment policies and procedures.

- Commissioned Corps Instruction 241.01, Readiness and Duty Requirements. 3 November 2022.[2]
  Establishes individual readiness (including deployment readiness) standards and duty requirements that officers must follow while on active duty in the Commissioned Corps.
- Commissioned Corps Instruction 241.02, Deployment of Public Health Service Officers. 7 November 2022.[3]
  Establishes policy and assigns responsibilities and requirements to which officers must adhere while on active duty and prescribes procedures to ensure efficient deployment of the USPHS Commissioned Corps for response activities.
- Personnel Operations Memorandum 821.76, Deployment Procedures. 7 November 2022.[4]
  Implements CCD 121.02 and CCI 241.02 and outlines the procedures for officer deployments.

Commissioned Corps Headquarters assigns all officers to a rapid deployment unit or group. CCHQ maintains a Unit Manning List (UML), a preconfigured roster of each rapid deployment unit/group, that includes deployment roles, qualifications for each role, standard operating procedures, and the unit's on call schedule. CCHQ then assigns qualified officers to a specific unit/group and, during on call months, officers must be prepared to deploy within 48 hours of receipt of deployment orders.

PHS PHERST

In April 2021, the USPHS Commissioned Corps announced a new active duty contingent known as the Public Health Emergency Response Strike Team, or PHERST, which emanated from the Corps' modernization program initiated under Assistant Secretary for Health Admiral Brett Giroir. If warranted, a Public Health Emergency Response Strike Team(s) will be "first on the ground" – the first group assigned to respond to an urgent emergency event. The PHERST is comprised of a cadre of highly skilled personnel who are trained and ready to deploy within eight to twenty-four hours to assess critical needs and provide essential clinical care in public health emergency situations such as disease outbreaks or natural disasters. The primary function of these officers is to be on standby as first responders to regional, national, and global public health emergencies. They serve as an asset for federal and non-federal systems that require surge capacity and health care sustainment during a federal public health emergency or national emergency declaration. PHERSTs are managed by Commissioned Corps Headquarters, and officers do not require agency supervisory approval to deploy. If needed, officers may deploy for extended durations to ensure continuity of care and activities, as well as leadership. When not deployed, they are assigned full time to agencies for short-term staffing needs and to remote locations or underserved communities. Beginning in 2023, PHERST officers were also assigned to military treatment facilities. Since inception, the Public Health Emergency Response Strike Teams have supported numerous federal and state collaborative operations such as repatriation, community stabilization, and population health.[5,6]

DOD MILITARY TREATMENT FACILITIES

In November 2022, the Department of Defense (DOD) completed a multiyear transition of military [medical] treatment facilities (MTFs) from the military departments – the Army, Navy, and Air Force – to the Defense Health Agency (DHA). DHA is now responsible for the management and administration of military treatment facilities worldwide, comprised of about 700 military hospitals and clinics. In October 2023, the PHERST program began a collaboration through assigning PHERST officers to full-time clinical, safety, and behavioral health provider positions at MTFs. The PHERST presence augments care for the military community by assisting MTFs with clinical staffing issues to ensure continuity of comprehensive care, while they continue to support the nation as rapidly deployable assets that are available to deploy within 24 hours of activation. The PHERST officers are on a five month on-call rotation the same as PHS Corps officers assigned to deployment teams 1 to 5. It is anticipated that this on-call schedule will limit the duration of most deployments to 30 days or less.[7]

VA HOSPITALS AND CLINICS

Billets
The Veterans Health Administration (VHA), located within the Department of Veterans Affairs, is the largest integrated health care system in the nation, providing care at 1,321 health care facilities that includes 172 medical centers, and serving 9 million enrolled veterans each year. On January 17, 2017, a Memorandum of Agreement (MOA) was approved by the USPHS Commissioned Corps with the Department of Veterans Affairs to assign PHS officers to provide direct patient care at VA hospitals and clinics. The billets were initially limited to twenty medical and nurse officers. Subsequent modifications to the MOA were made as follows: June 2018, the cap on number of PHS officers was increased to 70; in 2020, the professional categories were expanded to include nurse practitioners, physician assistants, clinical social workers, and psychologists; December 2022, the cap was increased to 250 PHS officers; and 2023, further expansion of clinical disciplines based on VA medical facility requests. As of December 2023, just over 80 PHS officers were supporting the VHA mission at 26 medical centers and 22 community-based outpatient clinics.[8,9]

Clinical Hours
On February 1, 2021, an MOA was signed between the USPHS Commissioned Corps and the Department of Veterans Affairs, VHA, to provide opportunities for licensed clinical PHS officers who are not in clinical billets to serve at VHA health care facilities to maintain their clinical skills and meet the yearly 80 hours requirement in accordance with Commissioned Corps directives. Any VHA facility is eligible to participate under the MOA, though not obligated to take part in the program.[10]

REMOTE AREA MEDICAL

Over the years, the Public Health Service Commissioned Corps has deployed on numerous Remote Area Medical (RAM) visits throughout the nation. RAM is a nonprofit organization that provides free medical, dental, and vision care to people in remote and underserved areas around the world. The organization was founded in 1985 by British philanthropist Stan Brock. RAM's first mission was in Guyana, where the volunteer healthcare professionals provided care to thousands of people over several weeks. RAM and the USPHS Commissioned Corps entered a formal partnership in 2016 to provide medical care to underserved communities in the United States. The partnership enabled PHS officers to assist in RAM setup, management and operations, and provide direct patient care at pop-up clinics across the nation. Over 100 Regular Corps, PHERST and Ready Reserve officers provided care to the community in need at the RAM held at a pop-up clinic in Tulsa, Oklahoma, preceding the 2023

USPHS Scientific and Training Symposium. The May 5 and 6, 2023 Remote Area Medical in Tulsa was a great success, with over 460 patients receiving dental, vision, and medical services. The partnership between RAM and the USPHS serves as a model for how organizations can collaborate to address the health care needs in underserved and uninsured communities.[11,12]

PHS officers at RAM event in Tulsa, OK, 2023. *[Photo Credit: Chris Cannon, RAM Media Relations]*

READY RESERVE CORPS

On March 27, 2020, enactment of the Coronavirus Aid, Relief, and Economic Security Act, also known as the CARES Act, provided authorization for the formation of a PHS Ready Reserve Corps *(see Chapter Seventeen)*. The long-sought Reserve Corps complements the Regular Corps' capacity to respond to health emergencies. It provides a surge capacity of health professionals who are available for deployment, without jeopardizing the service of essential PHS clinicians in regular duty assignments. The reserve component also provides access to individuals with specialized skill sets that might otherwise be unavailable in the Regular Corps. As of December 2023, there were 95 Ready Reserve Corps officers available for involuntary calls to active duty.

DEPLOYMENT PRECEDENCE

PHS officers are deployed as follows.
  PHERST OFFICERS — Deploy within 8-24 hours in support of urgent public health needs.
  ACTIVE DUTY REGULAR CORPS OFFICERS — Deploy within 36 hours during on-call status.
  READY RESERVE CORPS — Deploy within 5 days to augment active duty PHS officers.

EMERGENCY AND SUPPORT MISSIONS

Thousands of PHS officers have participated in deployments throughout the nation and internationally. The deployment teams might be comprised of one professional-scientific category (e.g., engineer), multidisciplinary with a range of skill sets, or specialized personnel, and certain agencies such as CDC may deploy its own Epidemic Intelligence Service officers. Notable deployments of the USPHS Commissioned Corps include the following.

USPHS COMMISSIONED CORPS
≥ 40 OFFICERS AND NOTABLE EVENT DEPLOYMENTS, 2001–2023

START DATE	EVENT	OFFICERS
2001 September	9/11 Attacks, New York City	> 1,000
2001 October	Anthrax Attacks, Washington, DC	350
2004 Aug.-Sept.	Hurricanes Charley, Frances, Ivan, Jeanne	> 600
2005 September	Hurricanes Katrina, Rita, Wilma	> 2,400
2008 January	State of the Union Address	43
2008 September	Hurricanes Gustav, Ike	800
2009 January	Presidential Inauguration	197
2010 January	State of the Union Address	25
2010 January	Haiti Earthquake, DC, Haiti	215
2010 April	Deepwater Horizon Oil Spill	168
2010 June	Operation Nexus - FTX, KY, OK, TN, TX	583
2011 January	State of the Union Address	52
2011 May	Operation Foothold - FTX, KY, SD, TX	276
2011 August	Hurricane Irene, Region 1-4	175
2011 September	Joint Sessions of Congress	40
2011 October	ACF Disaster Case Management, NY	111
2012 January	State of the Union Address	42
2012 July	Rosebud CHASM Mission, SD	70
2012 July	Operation Lone Star CHASM, TX	> 120
2012 August	Hurricane Isaac, LA	97
2012 October	Hurricane Sandy, Region 1, 2, 3	418
2013 January	Presidential Inauguration	138
2013 February	State of the Union Address	54
2013 April	Boston Marathon Bombing	19
2014 January	State of the Union Address	55
2014 May	ACF Unaccompanied Children, TX	337
2014 August	Ebola Response *(Federal: 1,191 Total)*	> 300
2015 September	Papal Mission, DC, NY, PA	97
2016 January	State of the Union Address	72
2016 January	Water Emergency Response, Flint, MI	47
2016 January	IHS Great Plains Region Support	192
2016 May	Remote Area Medical, Durant, OK	75

COMMISSIONED CORPS DEPLOYMENTS, 2001–2023 *[Continued]*

START DATE	EVENT	OFFICERS
2016 July	Republican National Conference, OH, MD	45
2016 July	Democratic National Conference, PA	44
2016-2017	Louisiana Floods, LA	200
2016 August	Zika Virus, Puerto Rico, States	115
2016 September	United Nations General Assembly	23
2016 October	Hurricane Matthew	146
2017 January	Presidential Inauguration	216
2017 June	Remote Area Medical, Chattanooga, TN	115
2017 August	Remote Area Medical, Idabel, OK	101
2017 August	Hurricanes Harvey, Irma, Maria	1,819
2017 August	United Nations General Assembly	17
2018 January	State of the Union Address	51
2018 May	Remote Area Medical, Durant, OK	125
2018 May	FEMA National Level Exercise	37
2018 September	Hurricanes Florence, Isaac, Olivia	247
2018 October	Hurricane Michael, Southeast	81
2018 Dec.-2019	ACF Unaccompanied Children, CBP Support	483
2019 May	Remote Area Medical, Minneapolis, MN	63
2019 July	Remote Area Medical, Weatherford, OK	125
2019 July	Remote Area Medical, TX, Op. Lone Star	123
2019 September	Remote Area Medical, Baltimore, MD	132
2019 December	Remote Area Medical, Camp Springs, MD	202
2020 January-Dec.	COVID-19 Response Mission	2,981
2021 January-Dec.	COVID-19 Response Mission	1,086
2021 March-Aug.	Unaccompanied Children, Southern Border	814
2021 April	Customs and Border Protection Support	94
2021 May-2022	Operation Allies Welcome	550
2022 January-Dec.	COVID-19 Response Mission	470
2023 May	Remote Area Medical, Tulsa, OK	100
2023 September	Wildfires, Maui, Hawaii	74

Data do not include National Independence Day (July 4) Celebrations, when ~50 officers deploy yearly. Data derived from HHS, OSG, Commissioned Corps Headquarters, in response to FOIA requests, and Giroir BP. The USPHS Com. Corps: America's Health Responders. AMSUS Annual Meeting, December 4, 2019.

HEALTH DIPLOMACY, HUMANITARIAN MISSIONS

The USPHS Commissioned Corps has partnered with the U.S. Navy on several multi-nationality staffed health diplomacy and humanitarian missions. The Navy's *Pacific Partnership* mission to the Indo-Asia-Pacific region began in 2006 as an annual mission to expand disaster relief capabilities and humanitarian assistance, foster enduring regional relationships, and enhance regional stability and security. The Naval hospital ship USNS Mercy is a principal platform for such missions. In March 2007, President George W. Bush declared that Navy ships would be sent on annual, four-month deployments to help Caribbean and Central/South American communities. Entitled *Continuing Promise*, the mission also helps encourage regional partnerships and enhance regional stability and security. Using medical and public health assets, the port visits provide medical, dental, optometric, surgical, environmental health, civil engineering, and veterinary services to the local populace. Navy ships used for these visits include the USNS Mercy, USNS Comfort, and USS Kearsarge. PHS Command staff normally deploy for the mission duration, often three months aboard ship, while PHS professional personnel serve one month, meeting and departing the ship at the ports of call. USPHS officers might also deploy with the U.S. Navy on international emergency missions, such as occurred in response to the Haiti earthquake in 2010. Deployments of the PHS Commissioned Corps on joint missions include the following.

DIPLOMACY/HUMANITARIAN MISSIONS, 2007–2023

START DATE	EVENT	PHS OFFICERS
2007 June	USNS Comfort, Continuing Promise	71
2008 April	USS Boxer, Humanitarian Assistance Training	34
2008 May	USNS Mercy, Pacific Partnership	46
2008 August	USS Kearsarge, Continuing Promise	38
2009 March	USNS Comfort, Continuing Promise	49
2009 June	USNS Byrd, Pacific Partnership	11
2010 May	USNS Mercy, Pacific Partnership	39
2010 July	USS Iwo Jima, Continuing Promise	29
2019 June	USNS Comfort, Enduring Promise	32

Data derived from HHS, OSG, Commissioned Corps Headquarters, in response to FOIA requests.

Commissioned Corps Challenges

REVIEW OF ONGOING CHALLENGES TO THE PHS COMMISSIONED CORPS

The USPHS Commissioned Corps mission is an essential component of public health for the nation and, like most institutions, the Corps' activities to effectuate that mission have been subject to periodic performance assessments. As with the government reform plan released June 21, 2018, by the Office of Management and Budget (OMB, formerly Bureau of the Budget), some oversight reports have contained unfavorable suppositions about the Corps, which HHS and Office of the Surgeon General leadership have viewed as threats to the Corps' preservation. Those reports have been brought by an incumbent administration, the OMB, and/or the Government Accountability Office (GAO, formerly General Accounting Office). Their assertions could be summarized as follows.

(1) The Corps was languishing as a forward-leaning public health resource by not expanding its competencies in response to new national demands.
(2) PHS Corps personnel were not maintaining officership standards, and a uniformed service framework was no longer needed.
(3) Corps officers occupied positions that could be filled by Civil Servants at substantially less cost.

Such claims have been countered by HHS in every instance. In brief *(corresponding with the enumerated items above)*.

(1) Where claims pertaining to the Corps' decline were determined to have merit, Corps/HHS leadership implemented remedial initiatives, to wit:
   • *Revitalization* (SG Koop, 1987)   • *Management Review* (ASH Koh, 2009)
   • *Transformation* (SG Carmona, 2003) • *Modernization* (ASH Giroir, 2018)
   • *Renewal* (HHS Secretary Leavitt, 2006)
(2) The necessity for a uniformed service was evident by the need for PHS officers to provide medical and public health services to special and underserved populations; the need for 24/7 personnel to be on duty and to rapidly deploy; and by the need for a network of highly trained personnel that can provide a vast array of professional and scientific services.
(3) OMB/GAO comparative analyses of PHS officers with Civil Servants were largely based upon narrowly drawn and/or dubious cost analyses that lacked incontestable validity and were generally refuted by internal HHS and third party assessments.

Contributing Factors

The basis for periodic challenges to the viability of the Commissioned Corps are to some extent the effect of ongoing institutional, structural, and funding issues, all of which have impacted the institution.

Institutional Issues

The institution of the USPHS Commissioned Corps – its role in national public health and operational impact – is generally unrecognized. PHS officers perform a wide array of vital public health functions largely unbeknownst to the general public and members of Congress. The Corps' constituents, particularly the special, underserved and vulnerable populations, are not seen as powerful advocacy groups. The periodic diminution of the Corps also makes it a reputational, "hearsay" target for oversight reviews. Thus, when administrations want to trim the national budget, susceptible programs include those that are little understood and have marginal support.

SG and ASH Appointments

Formerly, all Surgeons General were drawn from the Regular Corps as the Public Health Service Act of 1944 intended, similar to the military services. In contrast, Jesse Steinfeld served short tours of duty in the Commissioned Corps, Julius Richmond served as a civilian federal official, and C. Everett Koop never served in the federal government prior to becoming Surgeon General. Whereas the Armed Forces Surgeons General oversee the health enterprise within their respective Services, the PHS Surgeon General, while serving as commander of the PHS Corps, also personifies the "nation's doctor." A PHS career officer selected for the role of Surgeon General will have recognized leadership qualities, and considerable knowledge, experience and competence to seamlessly assume the position and advance the mission of the Commissioned Corps. Further, that person has earned the entitled rank and can comfortably interact with other uniformed service leaders. Such capability also positively impacts the parity of PHS officers with other service members.

A recurring thematic issue is that recent PHS Surgeons General are seldom drawn from among the career officer corps; rather, presidential administrations increasingly nominate civilians based on personal and political considerations. Civilian appointees to the positions of PHS Surgeon General with the rank of Vice Admiral, and occasionally Assistant Secretary for Health with the rank of Admiral, have become normalized. There are divergent viewpoints about this matter. A strong belief is that such appointments weaken the PHS Corps as a bonafide uniformed service and its parity with the other services. There is the potential conflict regarding the need for uniformed personnel to refrain from political activities. A concern is a short term civilian appointee has a protracted learning phase, and might be inclined to accede to perceived limits upon their actions and/or acquiesce to political intrusion into policy making. The contrarian view is that a political appointee serving as the senior ranking PHS officer would strive to remain independent of politics and might be strategically beneficial in advancing and protecting the Corps, noting that the Commissioned Corps has had a few excellent leaders as political appointees.

Structural Issues

Other uniformed services are organizationally structured with a unified chain of command, whereas the USPHS Commissioned Corps is encumbered by a split command structure. PHS officers are accountable for Commissioned Corps-related duties and compliance with Corps requirements to the Office of the Surgeon General (OSG), and they are accountable for their work productivity to the agency in which they are assigned. This fractured command structure is clearly disadvantageous to Corps officers who must contend with dual authorities. Because agencies disburse PHS officers' salaries, it is a proximate reason why they may view officers within their organizations principally as employees. Such a command structure also engenders sometimes contentious give and take between OSG and agencies about the priorities of the respective organizations, often as it relates to deployments, with the effect of weakening the authorities of both.

Funding Issues

The institutional and structural issues have all impacted the availability of adequate funding for the USPHS Commissioned Corps. Although fiscal years 2021 through 2023 realized an increase in funding, for several decades the Office of the Surgeon General received very limited support to conduct its operational responsibilities such that Commissioned Corps Headquarters had to occasionally call upon PHS officers to volunteer in assisting with processing administrative paperwork backlogs. Leadership and emergency response field training for PHS officers, the latter being a critical component to ensure deployment readiness, have also been notoriously underfunded for decades. These situations have been a hindrance to full implementation of the wide-ranging capabilities of the Corps.

Due to the aforementioned reasons, the USPHS Commissioned Corps has received sometimes inconsistent critiques over a period of decades. The Corps, nevertheless, has withstood the test of time and has continued to press on, advancing its expertise and capabilities to fulfill the PHS mission and proving its worth as an irreplaceable, vital component of public health and national health security.[13,14]

CHAPTER TWENTY

USPHS Professional Categories & Their Histories

The U.S. Public Health Service Commissioned Corps is comprised of officers in eleven distinct professional categories corresponding with their professional/scientific education and training: Dentist, Dietitian, Engineer, Environmental Health Officer, Health Services Officer, Nurse, Pharmacist, Physician, Scientist, Therapist, and Veterinarian. Appointment standards for each category, including qualifying academic and licensure requirements, are specified in Commissioned Corps Instruction 231.03, dated 18 April 2022.[1]

Chief Professional Officer
Each professional category is represented by a Chief Professional Officer (CPO) who serves a four year term. The CPO provides leadership, direction and coordination of their professional category, and serves as an advocate for the category in areas of interest to the Corps. The CPO is the liaison between the professional category and the Office of the Surgeon General (OSG), and he/she offers advice and guidance to the Professional Advisory Committee and Surgeon General on matters such as recruitment, retention, career development and readiness of officers within their profession. Selection of a Chief Professional Officer in the dentist, engineer, nurse, and pharmacist categories is required by statute and includes promotion to a temporary flag grade for the duration of service as a CPO, after which such officers revert to their prior highest grade if they remain on active duty. The Surgeon General customarily appoints a CPO for the other professional categories; however, there is no requirement for promotion of those individuals to a flag grade.

Professional Advisory Committee
Each of the eleven PHS Professional Categories maintains a Professional Advisory Committee (PAC). The Professional Advisory Committee provides advice on professional practice and personnel matters to its Chief Professional Officer and to the Surgeon General. The PAC also provides advisory assistance, upon request, to agencies that employ PHS personnel. PAC voting members elect a chairperson, and membership is generally representative of commissioned officers and civilian employees of the federal agencies where officers are assigned. The PAC promotes collegiality among those in its professional category/discipline and offers an opportunity to learn about and

become involved with colleagues in the issues and policies that affect their profession. Work is largely accomplished through subcommittees, so officers can become involved as a committee or working group member, which does not require formal voting membership on the PAC.

Chartered Advisory Groups

There are several OSG-chartered advisory groups that provide support, professional development and advocacy on behalf of their constituents. The two largest groups are:

- Junior Officer Advisory Group (JOAG) – members are junior officers at the rank of LCDR/O4 and below.
- Minority Officers Liaison Council (MOLC) – comprised of four Minority Advisory Groups:
  American Indian/Alaska Native Commissioned Officers Advisory Committee (AIANCOAC)
  Asian Pacific American Officers Committee (APAOC)
  Black Commissioned Officers Advisory Group (BCOAG)
  Hispanic Officers Advisory Committee (HOAC)

PROFESSIONAL CATEGORIES – COMPOSITION

- DENTIST
- DIETITIAN
- ENGINEER

Bioengineering	Civil Engineering	Material Science
Biomedical Engineering	Computer Engineering	Mechanical Engineering
Chemical Engineering	Electrical Engineering	Nuclear Engineering

- ENVIRONMENTAL HEALTH

  Environmental Health Specialist
  Industrial Hygienist
  Occupational Health and Safety Specialist

- HEALTH SERVICES

Basic and Applied Science	Health Information Tech.	Physician Assistant
Dental Hygiene	Medical Laboratory Sci.	Public Health
Healthcare Administration	Optometry	Social Work

- NURSE

  Nurse, Nurse Practitioner

- PHARMACIST
- PHYSICIAN
- SCIENTIST

  | Environmental Health | Laboratory Science | Regulatory Science |
  | Epidemiology | Psychology | Research |

- THERAPIST

  | Audiologist | Physical Therapist | Speech-Language |
  | Occupational Therapist | Respiratory Therapist | Pathology |

- VETERINARIAN

Professional Categories
Chief Professional Officers and Histories

The following section provides an overview of each PHS Professional Category, with a chronological list of chief professional officers and concise history.

Dental Category

Chief Dental Officers

RDML Michael W. Johnson	2023-2027	RADM John C. Greene	1973-1981
RADM Timothy L. Ricks	2018-2022	RADM Francis A. Arnold, Jr.	1966-1967
RADM Nicholas S. Makrides	2014-2018	RADM Ralph S. Lloyd	1962-1966
RADM William D. Bailey	2010-2014	RADM John W. Knutson	1952-1961
RADM Christopher G. Halliday	2006-2010	RADM Bruce D. Forsyth	1948-1952
RADM Dushanka V. Kleinman	2001-2006	RADM William T. Wright, Jr.	1943-1948
RADM William R. Maas	1997-2001	*DentalSurg. William T. Wright, Jr.	1941-1943
RADM Stephen B. Corbin	1995-1997	*DentalSurg. Norman V. Hooper	1938-1941
RADM Robert J. Collins, Jr.	1991-1995	*DentalSurg. Charles W. Wekenman	1936-1938
RADM Daniel F. Whiteside	1987-1991	*DentalSurg. Clinton T. Messner	1923-1936
RADM Robert E. Mecklenburg	1981-1987	*DentalSurg. Ernest E. Buell	1919-1923

*Chief of Dental Section, 1919 until 1943.

History

[Adapted from: Snyder, LP. Seventy-five Years of Dentistry in the Public Health Service and the Commissioned Corps: Public Health through Service, Research, and Prevention. PHS Dental Notes–Special Edition. Office of the PHS Historian, June 24, 1994. Chapter 4. HHS and Oral Health: Past and Present. Advancing Oral Health in America. Washington, DC: The National Academies Press, 2011. Personal histories from CPO RADM Timothy L. Ricks and other recent Dental CPOs were incorporated.]

In 1919, World War I veterans were designated as new beneficiaries for health care provided by the Public Health Service, which included dental services. Ernest E. Buell became the first commissioned dentist in the PHS Reserve and was appointed Chief of the Dental Section, Division of Marine Hospitals Relief. Dr. Buell dealt with an acute shortage of dental officers by contracting with civilian dentists. However, with the establishment of the Veterans' Bureau in 1922, most dental officers were transferred to the new agency. During the 1920s, PHS dentistry developed a career track that included postgraduate training, service, and research. Service areas expanded to include the provision of dental care for immigrants at Ellis Island, and detail of dental officers to the U.S. Coast Guard, Bureau of Prisons, and the Bureau of Indian Affairs. There were dental research opportunities in epidemiology and at the PHS Hygienic Laboratory. Dental officers also served as technical advisors to state and local health departments, and dentists became involved in public health planning. With the founding of NIH in 1930, Dental Surgeon H. Trendley Dean was assigned as head of a new Dental Section. Through ongoing collaborative research, the introduction of water fluoridation in the 1950s became a great achievement of the time. The Social Security Act of 1935 included grants to state and local health departments that included funds for new oral health programs. Surgeon General Parran established a Dental Public Health Section and assigned dentists to the PHS regional offices to support the state and local level programs. Legislation in 1943 and 1944 reorganized the PHS into four components – Office of the Surgeon General (OSG), NIH, Bureau of Medical Services, and the Bureau of State Services – and provided for a full-time chief professional officer for the Dental Category with the temporary rank of Assistant Surgeon General. A Division of Dentistry was created in OSG, and wartime experience of many young men with such poor dental health that they failed the physical examination underscored the need for more attention to dental disease. Wartime provisions to support research also resulted in formation of the National Institute of Dental Research in 1948 with Dr. Dean as its first director, who was succeeded in 1953 by Dental Director Francis A. Arnold, Jr.

The PHS assumed responsibility for the health care of American Indians and Alaska Natives in 1955, and during the first decade the number of dental providers more than tripled. Training programs for dental auxiliaries with expanded functions beyond their role in private practices were common by the early 1960s, and the IHS brought forth the ingenuity of officers to enhance dental services. A period followed that emphasized clinical research to improve patient care and planning to graduate more dentists and increase the level of productivity. There was continual growth in the dental ranks following creation of the National Health Service Corps with enactment of the Emergency Health Personnel Act of 1970, the purpose being to assign physicians and dentists in underserved areas throughout the nation. In 1973, John C. Greene was appointed Chief Dental Officer and he served as the Deputy Surgeon General from 1978 to 1981, a position in which he was able to promote public health dentistry. Dr. Greene was also known for the Greene–(Jack) Vermillion Oral Hygiene Index that was a systematic method to quantify bacterial plaque on teeth. When the closure of PHS Marine Hospitals and 27 clinics occurred in 1981, the Indian Health Service assimilated PHS dentists displaced from the closures.

In 1983, the Surgeon General formed a new Dental Professional Advisory Committee to support dental officers within the PHS. The National Institute of Dental Research intensified its research efforts, embarking on several national oral health surveys and expanding the quality and scope of its intramural program. During Surgeon General Koop's tenure, the number of PHS dental officers grew to 580 by November 1988, and dental policy was advanced through collaborations across an array of PHS programs. A Congressionally mandated *Meskin Report* led to the establishment of the Oral Health Coordinating Committee (OHCC) in 1990 to help coordinate federal activities in improving oral health. The Chief Dental Officer of the USPHS was delegated the leadership of the OHCC on behalf of the Assistant Secretary for Health. Chief Dental Officer Corbin concurrently served as OSG Chief of Staff, and also led the multi-agency response to a 1997 GAO report that concluded the Commissioned Corps was not essential to the PHS mission; the HHS response was successful in stopping any action to reduce the Corps. In 2000, *Oral Health in America: A Report of the Surgeon General* was released with a major theme being that oral health is integral to general health and, in 2003, *A National Call to Action to Promote Oral Health* was released. In April 2010, HHS Assistant Secretary for Health Howard Koh released the HHS Oral Health Initiative (OHI) to improve coordination among agency programs. CPO Chris Halliday was largely focused on HHS/DOD Health Diplomacy missions to the Caribbean, Central America and nations in the Pacific region. Subsequently, Chief Dental Officer Bailey began work on a strategic framework for the OHI. CPO Makrides presided over the revitalization effort to release the Oral Health Strategic Framework 2014–2017, which originally emanated from the OHCC.

In April 2015, the Public Health Service released its updated recommenddation that, for community water systems which add fluoride, the optimal fluoride concentration was 0.7 milligrams/liter (formerly, 0.7–1.2 mg/L). Beginning with *Healthy People 2020*, and repeated in *Healthy People 2030* released in 2021, access to oral health services was highlighted as one of the few Leading Health Indicators by the HHS Office of Disease Prevention and Health Promotion. A new report, *Oral Health in America: Advances and Challenges*, was commissioned in 2018 as the 20th anniversary follow-up to the 2000 sentinel Surgeon General's report on oral health, but due to a change in administrations and OSG leadership, it was released by the National Institute of Dental and Craniofacial Research in late 2021. In response to the COVID-19 pandemic, CPO Tim Ricks created a new national oral health coalition, the COVID 19 Public-Private Partner Dental Coordination Group in March 2020, and this group of 175 leaders from 50 dental and public health organizations, along with 12 federal agencies, met throughout 2020 and 2021 to coordinate messaging to help reopen dental practices across the country with stringent new infection control measures due to the Covid pandemic. Unfortunately, the number of PHS dental officers has continued to decrease since the early 2000s, falling from over 600 dental officers at its peak to only 160 by the end of 2021. Most of the decreases occurred due to pay parity issues and the emergence of Title 38 market pay in the federal sector for dentists, the increase in tribally managed programs in the IHS and the desire of many of those programs to hire dentists directly by the tribes. PHS dental officers have a proud heritage of exemplary service in caring for patients, innovation and professionalism throughout the federal government.

Dietitian Category

CHIEF DIETITIAN OFFICERS

CAPT Mitchel Holliday	2021–2025	CAPT Shirley A. Blakely	2000–2005
CAPT Suzan Gordon	2017–2021	CAPT Pamela Brye	1996–2000
CAPT Madeline Michael	2013–2017	CAPT Carolyn B. Przekurat	1993–1996
CAPT Edith M. Clark	2009–2013	CAPT Emma J. Luten	1989–1992
CAPT Janice Huy	2005–2009	CAPT Alberta C. Bourn	1984–1988

HISTORY

[Adapted from the USPHS Dietitian Category website.]

During the late nineteenth century, proper nourishment of hospitalized patients was under the direction of a hospital steward. By 1902, food service responsibilities were assumed by pharmacists, the only professional other than medical officers attached to hospitals, and the importance of nutrition and dietetics became recognized as a required component of hospital care. The service of dietitians and nutritionists in the Public Health Service dates to the year 1919, when the first dietetic section was organized in the PHS Division of Hospitals (DH). Hallie Corsette, the first dietitian employed by the PHS, was named Superintendent of Dietitians. Ms. Corsette planned dietary departments and recruited dietitians for PHS hospitals. By 1919, there were around 85 dietitians in the DH, which doubled over the next two years. A dietitian's duties were chiefly focused on the purchase and preparation of food. The PHS was responsible for furnishing medical and hospital care to World War I veterans and, in 1922, the Veterans' Bureau was established, transferring many PHS Hospitals to the Veterans' Bureau. Over 145 PHS dietitians were moved to Bureau facilities, and those remaining were placed under direction of the PHS Office of Nursing in the DH. Although the dietetic section was abolished due to the transfers, the dietitians continued their duties of food service administration and provision of patient nutrition education. During World War II, PHS dietitians also worked in the Civil Defense Mobilization Program, responsible for developing food-related recommendations that could be used if communities suffered bombing attacks.

In the late 1930s and early 1940s, the role of PHS dietitians expanded beyond the hospital setting as dietitians were hired by state and local health departments. In 1942, the PHS formed mobile field units to conduct nutrition appraisals in selected states. With the passage of the Public Health Service Act in 1944, the Regular Commissioned Corps was expanded to include the commissioning of dietitians and other health professionals. The Dietetic Section was reestablished in the Division of Hospitals, with Ms. Marjorie Wood being the first commissioned dietitian and first Chief Dietitian. The section was renamed the Dietetic Branch, Office of Professional Services, charged with the responsibility of developing and maintaining dietetic standards in all PHS hospitals, with a major emphasis on therapeutic nutrition and teaching programs. PHS officer Clare Baldauf developed a dietetic internship program in 1945 at the PHS Hospital in Staten Island, New York, with civil service interns accepted into the first class and subsequent classes comprised of PHS officers. The internship provided the first credentialing of PHS dietitians.

Many PHS dietitians made significant contributions in nutrition and dietetics at the National Institutes of Health. One was CAPT Edith Jones, a leader in the profession who was appointed NIH Chief Dietitian in 1952, who created the Nutrition Department for the NIH Clinical Center research hospital that opened in 1953. Other NIH dietitians of note were CAPT Jeanne Tillotson who, among other accomplishments, was nutrition expert for the Framingham Heart Study and Multiple Risk Factor Intervention Trial. CAPT Jeanne Reid was detailed to work with the U.S. space program in Houston, Texas, conducting the first studies of the effects of space on minerals. Dr. Nancy Ernst came to the NIH Clinical Center Nutrition Department in 1966 and became the primary research dietitian for the lipid service, and she served in leading roles in lipid research and helped develop diet plans for national guidances.

In 1955, responsibility for American Indian and Alaska Native (AI/AN) health care was transferred to the PHS. The following year, Dr. Bertlyn Bosley became the first Chief of Nutrition and Dietetics for the Division of Indian Health, where she was instrumental in incorporating nutrition education into the health, social and educational programs serving AI/ANs. The next IHS Nutrition Chief, Helen G. Olson, in 1969 created the IHS Foodservice and Nutrition Training Program. Other PHS dietitians have since made significant progress in advancing nutrition in AI/AN communities and IHS hospitals. In 1958, the Coast Guard Academy became the first military training facility to employ a dietitian. CAPT Jane Davidsaver was detailed to the Academy for nine years where she was involved in establishing nutritional standards and designing four new galleys. During the late 1970s, the National Health Service Corps became an important entry point for nutritionists, adding significantly to the number of PHS dietitians. And, the PHS Regional Offices have been staffed by numerous Maternal and Child Health Nutrition Consultants.

The first White House Conference on Food, Nutrition and Health was held in 1969, which established priorities for nutrition programs as an integral part of all public health programs including PHS agencies. During the early 1970s, the CDC emerged as a leader in health promotion and disease prevention, and in conducting landmark surveys of nutritional status. It provides technical assistance to state and local health departments, including guidance on nutrition and health, and its *Healthy People* publication targets proper nutrition among its health promotion initiatives. As of 2020, there were approximately 100 commissioned officers and over 400 Civil Service dietitians and nutritionists serving in HHS agencies who continue to make major contributions to the health of the nation.

Engineer Category

CHIEF ENGINEER OFFICERS

RDML Emil P. Wang	2022-2026	RADM William F. Pearson	1989-1994
RADM Edward M. Dieser	2018-2022	RADM John C. Villforth	1985-1989
RADM Randall J.F. Gardner	2013-2017	RADM Ian K. Burgess	1973-1985
RADM Sven E. Rodenbeck	2009-2013	RADM Richard S. Green	1970-1973
RADM Richard F. Barror	2005-2009	RADM Albert H. Stevenson	1966-1970
RADM Robert C. Williams	1999-2005	RADM Callis Atkins	1962-1966
RADM Thomas G. Gallegos	1995-1999	RADM Mark D. Hollis	1948-1962
		RADM John K. Hoskins	1943-1948

HISTORY

[By RADM Richard F. Barror, USPHS, Ret.]

The United States was well into industrialization and urbanization by the early 1900s, with significant adverse health consequences from the discharge of sewage and industrial waste into rivers and other sources of drinking water, and increasing air pollution from the burning of coal and trash. When the Public Health Service Act of 1912 authorized the PHS to pursue studies of sanitation, sewage and pollution, the scope of its responsibilities requiring engineering expertise was about to expand significantly. The first PHS sanitary engineer was hired in June 1913 at the Chicago Public Health Laboratory to help improve drinking water quality, resulting in the first PHS Drinking Water Standards published in 1914. Six more PHS sanitary engineers were hired in 1913 in Cincinnati to investigate river pollution and natural purification. Over the next 60 years, the PHS Cincinnati laboratory developed the fundamentals of water pollution measurements and control, including the creation of the well known Streeter-Phelps oxygen sag equation in 1925. By 1916, ten PHS sanitary engineers were investigating rural sanitation issues, coastal water pollution, sewage and industrial waste pollution, and the control of malaria. And during World War I, about 32 sanitary engineers assisted with preventing diseases and protecting the health of military encampments and nearby communities. "The nucleus of experienced sanitary engineers was to provide to a large extent the leadership and backbone for the expansion of environmental hygiene activities in the Service during the following three decades."[1] At that time, PHS engineers were in the Civil Service, not commissioned, although they did wear uniforms with insignia identifying them as engineers. During the 1920s, in addition to stream pollution studies, PHS sanitary engineers investigated and consulted on the design of ship and train sanitation systems, rural sanitation needs, sanitation systems for National Parks, mosquito control for yellow fever and malaria, and occupational health (industrial/mining dust), as well as shellfish and milk programs. In 1918, Congress authorized Reserve commissions for sanitary engineers, but no engineers saw active duty in the PHS until 1930 after passage of the Parker Act, which authorized the PHS to recruit and commission sanitary engineers in the Regular Commissioned Corps. By July 1, 1931, there were 349 active duty PHS commissioned officers, 22 of whom were sanitary engineer officers.

In the 1930s, PHS engineers expanded sanitation surveys to all federal facilities, including prisons and Indian reservations, and consulted with states on water and wastewater treatment, stream pollution and industrial hygiene. They also assisted municipalities with providing sanitation facilities in conjunction with Depression-era federal housing construction programs. And the PHS Office of Stream Sanitation in Cincinnati was instrumental in preparing the first *National Report on Water Pollution in the U.S.* issued by Congress in 1939. By July 1940, there were 37 PHS engineer officers. As part of the wartime effort, PHS engineer officers worked to ensure safe ship sanitation systems, assisted with environmental health issues affecting military bases, and investigated occupational health issues involving military arms and munitions suppliers. PHS research activities included better methods for purifying water for troops in tropical countries, and engineer officers managed malaria eradication projects in the U.S. and in tropical countries with U.S. troops. The contributions of the PHS engineer officers during World War II were recognized in 1943 with the appointment of the first PHS Chief Engineer, with the rank of Rear Admiral. During war years, the PHS doubled in size and in 1944 was reorganized. The Sanitary Engineering Division was created, which included all engineering activities except malaria control. By June 1946, there were 228 PHS engineer officers, many of whom were detailed to other federal and other agencies and overseas (e.g., United Nations, Pan American Sanitary Bureau). The wartime malaria control program developed into the Communicable Disease Center (CDC) in Atlanta, with a PHS engineer officer serving as its first director. The passage of the Water Pollution Control Act in 1948 launched the expanding national role of the PHS in establishing nationwide pollution control requirements, which culminated in the early 1970s with the passage of comprehensive Federal legislation setting and enforcing uniform national drinking water, water pollution, air quality, and occupational health standards. In the 1950s and 1960s, PHS engineers expanded their research to the adverse health effects of radioactivity from nuclear weapons testing and nuclear power plants, solid waste disposal issues, and exposures to ionizing radiation and newly invented toxic/-carcinogenic chemicals in the work and natural environments.

PHS surveys in the 1950s indicated that over 80 percent of American Indian and Alaska Native homes had no or inadequate sanitation facilities. The PHS was given responsibility for Indian health in 1955 and, in 1959, Congress passed the Indian Sanitation Facilities Construction Program, which enabled the construction of safe water, sewer and solid waste facilities; it continues to this day with most involved engineers being PHS officers. In February 1961, there were 408 active duty PHS engineers, which peaked in 1966 at about 685 engineer officers, plus an additional 115 Civil Service engineers. Most engineer officers were engaged in legacy environmental health activities, but a growing number were working on medical facility construction and biomedical engineering. The largest numbers of engineers worked in Washington, DC, the Taft Sanitary Engineering Center in Cincinnati, HEW regional offices, and in IHS area offices. From 1943 to 1970, 16 PHS engineer officers were promoted to Flag rank because of their significant leadership positions and program responsibilities. In 1970, the PHS water and air pollution, solid waste management, radiation, and drinking water programs were transferred to the newly created Environmental Protection Agency, which became the lead federal enforcement agency for the major environmental legislation that soon followed. Some 560 PHS officers, about half engineers, were detailed to the EPA to enable it to staff up quickly. PHS engineer officers headed up several EPA programs and EPA regional offices; five engineer officers were promoted to Flag rank while at the EPA. Also in 1970, NIOSH was created under CDC. Its engineer officers continued to conduct occupational health and safety research. In the 1980s and 1990s, PHS engineer officers, consistently numbering about 550, were located primarily in the IHS, FDA, CDC, NIH, and EPA. The increased number of IHS engineer officers in those decades was offset by retiring EPA engineer officers. Further, EPA was replacing PHS engineer officers with Civil Service engineers. In 1977, 203 of the 567 PHS engineer officers were in EPA, but by 2008, there were only 36 EPA engineer officers out of 400 total PHS engineer officers. Meanwhile, the number of Civil Service engineers in PHS agencies grew from 352 in 1977 to more than 700 by 2008.

Historically, PHS engineer officers have responded to emergencies and emerging health threats throughout the nation and the world. More recently, they have deployed to manmade disasters (nuclear accidents, oil spills) and natural disasters (hurricanes, tsunamis, earthquakes, floods, wildfires) to assess and reestablish damaged medical facilities and water/wastewater systems. They also deploy to humanitarian crises (refugees, Ebola) and on humanitarian missions with the Department of Defense and NGOs to support medical teams by establishing mobile medical clinics, field communications, operate medical equipment, and assess occupational and environmental hazards. "Engineering for Life," the PHS Engineer Category motto, is as relevant today as ever. The more than 1,300 engineers in HHS, including about 385 engineer officers, are vital to the missions of the various agencies in which they serve. Engineering functions have broadened significantly since 1913 to include computers, software, communications, biosecurity and bioinformatics. Yet the engineer officers located in the IHS, CDC, National Park Service and EPA continue the environmental health legacy of the first PHS sanitary engineers.

1. Williams, Ralph C. 1951. *The United States Public Health Service, 1798-1950*. Washington, DC: Commissioned Officers Association of the USPHS.

Environmental Health Officer Category

CHIEF ENVIRONMENTAL HEALTH OFFICERS

CAPT Timothy Jiggens	2021–2025	CAPT Thomas E. Crow	1998–2001
RADM Kelly M. Taylor	2017–2021	CAPT Ralph J. Touch, Jr.	1994–1998
CAPT Alan G. Parham	2013–2017	CAPT Bruce R. Chelikowsky	1989–1994
CAPT Michael M. Welch	2009–2013	CAPT Geswaldo A. Verrone	1986–1989
CAPT Craig A. Shepherd	2005–2009	CAPT/RADM John G. Todd*†	1974–1986
CAPT Randy E. Grinnell	2001–2005	CAPT Darold W. Taylor*	1963–1972

*Sanitarian Liaison Officer, †Chief Sanitarian Officer.

HISTORY

[Adapted from the USPHS Environmental Health Officer Category website.]

The Environmental Health Officer Category evolved from the Sanitarian category, which was developed in the early 1940s during the reshaping of the U.S. Public Health Service. The first sanitarians, Louis J. Ogden, Robert D. Murrill and John C. Eason Jr., were called to active duty in 1943, with assignments during and after World War II related to malaria control and environmental health services such as water purification, sewage disposal, food sanitation, and pest control. The Public Health Service Act of 1944 expanded the authority of the Commissioned Corps to include additional disciplines, and in 1948 the Sanitarian category was officially established in the Regular Corps. Initially, the category included officers who were non-sanitarians, such as individuals with backgrounds in the physical and social sciences. In 1952, non-sanitarians were removed from the category into what became the Health Services Category, and the sanitarians who remained were stationed in the Communicable Disease Center and the USPHS Division of Environmental Health (DEH). In 1963, CAPT Darold W. Taylor was appointed as the first PHS Liaison Officer for the Sanitarian category. Following a reorganization of the USPHS, the Sanitarian Career Service Board was created in 1968, subsequently becoming the Sanitarian Career Development Committee, and then the Sanitarian Professional Advisory Committee (SPAC). Name changes within the category were suggested as early as 1968 to represent a broadening of environmental health professionals. The SPAC operated until October 1, 1999, when the category name was officially changed to the Environmental Health Officer (EHO) category to better represent the growing and varied composition of the category, and the SPAC became the Environmental Health Officer Professional Advisory Committee (EHOPAC).

The passage of the Indian Sanitation Facilities Construction Act in 1959 authorized the USPHS to construct water supply and sewage and solid waste disposal facilities. It enabled the Indian Health Service to hire a large contingent of sanitarian as well as environmental engineer officers. By the 1960s, the environmental movement had increased the demand for sanitarians, and PHS Sanitarian appointment standards were changed so that a master's degree in public health was no longer required for commissioning. PHS sanitarians responsible for food safety and inspections were also moved from the DEH to the Food and Drug Administration. In 1974, RADM John G. Todd was appointed as the second Sanitarian Liaison Officer, subsequent to which his title was changed to Chief Sanitarian Officer. In the 1980s, the Sanitarian category had expanded to include professionals with expertise in industrial hygiene, occupational health, and radiation/health physics. Agency assignments likewise had grown to include CDC agencies, and CAPT Richard Driscoll became the first sanitarian accepted to the Epidemic Intelligence Service. Then in 1997, the Sanitarian category appointment standards were significantly modified to encompass four career tracks – General Environmental Health, Industrial Hygiene, Occupational Health and Safety, and Health Physics – to reflect the types of sanitarians commissioned by the PHS.

Environmental Health officers serve throughout the nation and abroad in positions vital to our nation's public health security. They are highly skilled professionals with qualifying degrees in environmental health, industrial hygiene, and occupational health and safety. Most EHOs maintain one or more professional credentials such as Registered Sanitarian or Registered Environmental Health Specialist, Certified Industrial Hygienist or Health Physicist, or Certified Safety Professional. With approximately 350 officers at any given time, EHOs carry out a wide variety of activities in diverse settings. Examples include epidemiological surveillance, disease prevention, radiological health, industrial hygiene, food safety, injury prevention, health education, ensuring adequate safe water supplies, and occupational health and safety.

With response roles that are ever evolving, EHOs respond during public health and other emergencies to protect the public from environmental threats and assist with recovery efforts. Beginning in the 2000s, EHOs were deployed with increasing frequency for federal response missions to environmental threats that result from natural and manmade disasters. When the Department of Homeland Security was created, EHOs took assignments in the new Department as well as with the new HHS Office of the Assistant Secretary for Preparedness and Response. For the COVID-19 pandemic and other deployment missions, EHOs have often served in the role of safety officers. Since inception of the category, EHOs have continually played a significant role in improving the health and quality of life in domestic and international settings, and fulfilling their commitment to protect, promote, and advance the health and safety of our nation.

Health Services Officer Category

CHIEF HEALTH SERVICES OFFICERS

CAPT Rebecca Bunnell	2024-2028	CAPT Vivian T. Chen	1999-2001
CAPT Diedre N. Presley	2020-2024	CAPT Robert G. Falter	1995-1999
CAPT Jeanean Willis Marsh	2016-2020	CAPT Evan R. Arrindell	1991-1995
RADM Epifanio Elizondo	2010-2016	CAPT Joseph Garcia, Jr.	1989-1991
RADM Michael R. Milner	2006-2010	CAPT Carl G. Leukefeld	1984-1989
CAPT Linda Morris Brown	2002-2006	RADM Karst J. Besteman	1979-1984
CAPT Nina Dozoretz (Actg)	2001-2002	CAPT Kenneth D. Howard	1978-1979

HISTORY

[Adapted from: Office of the Surgeon General. Health Services Category–"Strength Through Diversity." Commissioned Corps Bulletin. December 1999; XIII(12): 7. And, the USPHS Health Services Category website.]

In the early 1940s, health professionals were needed whose qualifications distinguished them from the principal disciplines at the time of medical and nursing officers. When the Sanitarian category (now known as the Environmental Health Officer category) was established in 1948, it initially included other commissioned officers who were commissioned as sanitarians, but who were non-sanitarians with backgrounds in the physical and social sciences. Because of the need for diverse health services specialties to carry out the mission of the Public Health Service, to include social workers, health educators, statisticians, medical record administrators and nondoctoral level scientists, the Health Services Officer (HSO) category was established in 1959 to meet the staffing requirements of a changing Public Health Service. The "health services" designation was selected by the PHS to reflect and encompass the broader functions of public health.

As the functions and responsibilities of the Public Health Service grew, the PHS required new staff with diverse training and expertise to meet the Nation's most urgent health needs. Medical record administrators gained their start in the PHS in 1947 at a time when there was concern for the medical record systems in the Marine Hospitals. By 1950, the first students were enrolled in the School for Medical Record Librarianship at the Baltimore PHS hospital, and in 1966, commissions were offered to students who went on to serve in the PHS. The first two social workers were commissioned in 1950 and they assumed key leadership positions in the NIH. These appointments established a precedent for the appointment of social workers and health services individuals representing other professional and specialty groups. The role of health educator expanded in the 1950s with the first health educator commissioned in 1953. Health education was an integral part of the Native American community health programs, which also included public health nurses and sanitary engineers. New disciplines continued to be accepted into the Health Services Category to meet changing requirements of the PHS. In 1966, the first optometrist was commissioned to serve in the Indian Health Service, and podiatry was added as a Corps specialty in 1978 with the commissioning of a National Health Service Corps podiatrist. More recent additions to the Health Services Category have included computer scientists and physician assistants in 1989, and medical technologists and dental hygienists in 1991. In 2001, the computer science discipline was expanded to include information technology curricula. Other professionals include chemists, biologists, health physicists, and environmental specialists with a background in mathematics, statistics, and epidemiology. Their importance has continued to grow tremendously as the health field expands in scope and complexity. They have served in many capacities in all agencies where the collection or evaluation of physical or environmental measurements is required, such as air quality and trend analysis performed at the Environmental Protection Agency in Research Triangle Park, North Carolina. Currently, the Food and Drug Administration employs HSOs in numerous activities, including application review, medical device testing, and food and cosmetic microbiology.

Health Services is among the largest of PHS professional categories with about 1,200 active duty officers representing 53 specific disciplines, and it is also the most diverse category in the USPHS. The professional disciplines represented within the HSO category include biological, dental hygiene, health education, information technology, medical records administration, optometry, podiatry, physical and environmental sciences, physician assistant, social work, and other public health specialties. The Health Services motto – *Multidisciplinary in Approach, Connected by Service, Advancing Public Health* – attests to the wide range of skills and expertise of this multidisciplinary team and their pride and commitment to serving in the Commissioned Corps. Within the HSO category are nine Health Services Professional Advisory Groups (PAGs) that address discipline-specific professional issues and advise the Heath Services category:

- Basic and Applied Science
- Dental Hygiene
- Healthcare Administration
- Health Information Technology
- Medical Laboratory Science
- Optometry
- Physician Assistant
- Public Health
- Social Work

Today, Health Services officers perform a wide variety of functions including direct clinical practice, program development, health planning and administration, and research. They provide these mission critical services at their duty stations, as well as on public health missions domestically and abroad.

Nurse Category

CHIEF NURSE OFFICERS

RDML Jennifer Moon	2023-2027	RADM Mary Pat Couig	2000-2005
RADM Aisha K. Mix	2019-2023	RADM Carolyn Beth Mazzella	1996-2000
RADM Susan M. Orsega	2016-2019	RADM Julia R. Plotnick	1992-1996
RADM Sylvia Trent-Adams	2013-2016	RADM O. Marie Henry	1987-1992
RADM Kerry Paige Nesseler	2009-2013	RADM Faye G. Abdellah	1970-1987
RADM Carol A. Romano	2005-2009	RADM Margaret McLaughlin	1966-1970
		RADM Lucile Petry Leone	1949-1966

HISTORY

[By RADM Mary Pat Couig, USPHS, Ret.]

With the inception of the Marine Hospital Service in 1798, nursing care was provided to the ill and disabled seamen by former seamen attendants utilizing skills they learned through practice and observation of others. A movement to open formal schools of nursing began in the 1890s, with apprenticeships as the training programs. Health inspection duties and care of immigrants were assumed by the Service with the passage of the 1891 Immigration Act, and the facility at Ellis Island occasionally hired nurses. The PHS formally employed nurses who, beginning in 1913, staffed trachoma hospitals and worked in field clinics assessing, educating and treating patients. The following year, the first nurse was assigned to participate in field studies at the Public Health Service Hospital for pellagra in South Carolina. Nurses for the U.S. Army, Navy and Public Health Service were recruited by the American Red Cross, Department of Nursing. Lucy Minnigerode, a nursing leader and American Red Cross official, was instrumental in nurse recruitment during World War I. The PHS employed more than 120 nurses for disease prevention duties in local health departments and extra-cantonment zones established around military camps and in venereal disease clinics. Ms. Minnigerode was appointed in 1919 as the first PHS Superintendent of Nurses for 23 Marine Hospitals and dispensaries. In January 1922, the PHS opened a School of Nursing located at Fort McHenry, Maryland and later that year, the PHS nursing staff expanded from 90 to 1,800 nurses working in hospitals with a bed capacity of 20,500. Additionally, in 1922 responsibility for the care of veterans was transferred from the PHS to the newly created Veterans' Bureau, and 1,400 PHS nurses were transferred to that Bureau. Toward the end of the decade, the PHS became involved with the health care of American Indian and Alaska Native people. In 1928 and over the next several decades, various PHS staff, including nurses, were assigned to provide health care to American Indian and Alaska Native people under the Bureau of Indian Affairs. In 1930, nurses became involved in correctional nursing as the PHS assumed responsibility for federal prison health care, and nurses trained in psychiatric work were assigned to two PHS narcotics hospitals from 1935 to 1938. The demands on the Service for public health nursing consultants increased greatly when the Social Security Act of 1935 assigned to the PHS the duties of assisting states and districts in establishing health organizations as well as facilitating the training of public health personnel. Pearl McIver was chief of the Division responsible for training and assigning public health nurses to health departments.

With the entrance of the United States into World War II in 1941, an already existing shortage of nurses was exacerbated. To alleviate the nursing shortage, on July 1, 1942 Congress appropriated funds for nurse education in the form of refresher classes and postgraduate courses in specialty areas. To recruit more nurses for essential civilian and military duty, Congress passed the Nurse Training Act June 15, 1943. This Act created the Cadet Nurse Corps of the Public Health Service. The PHS established the Division of Nurse Education within the Office of the Surgeon General (OSG) to administer the Cadet Nurse Corps program. Surgeon General Parran appointed Lucile Petry (later Petry Leone) as Director of the Division. She thus became the first woman to head a major PHS Division. The Corps provided scholarships and stipends to all students enrolled in accredited schools of nursing in exchange for their agreement to work for the duration of the war. These scholarships offered the opportunity of an education and career that would not otherwise have been available. More than 124,000 nurses graduated from the program before it ended in 1948. The program was developed to meet both military and civilian nursing needs. During the course of World War II, PHS nurses served at various posts to assist in the war effort. For example, PHS nurses were detailed to Service Hospitals, the military, the Office of Civilian Defense, the Coast Guard, and the United Nations Relief and Rehabilitation Administration. The Public Health Service Act of July 1, 1944 authorized the appointment of qualified nurses as commissioned officers. In July 1945, the first nurses were commissioned in the PHS, including Lucile Petry and Pearl McIver. After the war, a new Division of Nursing was located within the OSG, with Lucile Petry as the Director, which supervised all PHS nursing activities. Restructuring of the PHS in 1949 created the position of Chief Nurse Officer with the rank of Assistant Surgeon General, and Lucile Petry Leone became the first nurse and first woman to achieve flag rank in the PHS or in any of the uniformed services of the United States.

During the 1950s, opportunities for nurses within the PHS expanded as the Service acquired new responsibilities. Positions for nurses in research at the National Institutes of Health became available in 1953. In 1954, PHS Hospitals were operating specialty hospitals for tuberculosis, Hansen's disease, psychiatric disorders, and treatment of narcotic addiction where nurses were assigned. And on July 1, 1955, the PHS assumed responsibility for the health care of American Indian and Alaska Native people, establishing a Division of

Indian Health (the present-day Indian Health Service) within the PHS to administer this program including nursing services. By the end of the 1950s, research by the Division of Nursing provided a visionary direction for nursing education in promoting the nation's health, including the beginning of nurse specializations. In 1960, the Divisions of Nursing Resources and Public Health Nursing joined into a new Division of Nursing, headed by Margaret G. Arnstein. A Nurse Education and Training Branch within the Division of Nursing formed to implement the Nurse Training Act of 1964, which authorized $240 million over five years to improve nursing education and construct educational facilities. In 1970, the Division of Nursing was restructured into four primary components: Education, Manpower, Practice, and Research. The Nurse Training Acts of 1971 and 1975 provided funding to educate nurses for expanded roles. By 1980, 1.3 million nurses were practicing in the United States, with large increases of nurses with baccalaureate, graduate and doctoral degrees. Nursing research in the PHS received recognition with the creation of the National Center for Nursing Research at NIH in 1986. The Nurse Training Act of 1985 further promoted nurse role expansion with funding for nurse anesthetist and geriatric nurse practitioner programs. By 1989, 1.7 million nurses were practicing in the U.S. The Division of Nursing also promoted interdisciplinary collaboration resulting in the establishment of requirements for the roles of certified nurse midwives, nurse practitioners, and physician assistants in primary care settings. In 1993, the National Center for Nursing Research became the National Institute of Nursing Research, thus achieving equal status with the other NIH Institutes.

The PHS Nursing discipline remains committed to promoting optimum health for the disadvantaged and underserved. The Public Health Service has greatly expanded its scope of responsibilities since its inception in 1798, to include disease control, health care delivery, food and drug regulation, international health, biomedical research, disease prevention, and health promotion. Commissioned Corps nurses work in multiple agencies across the nation, with duties that include providing clinical services, developing clinical practice guidelines and evidence-based health care reports, providing education and training, performing regulatory review, and conducting research. They are also at the forefront in responding with multidisciplinary teams to public health emergencies and participating in humanitarian missions domestically and internationally. Most PHS nurses, Commissioned Corps and Civil Service, are assigned to the Indian Health Service. In the 21st century, nurses comprise the largest health professional category in the Commissioned Corps, and they contribute to the mission of the Public Health Service in a multitude of essential roles "to protect, promote, and advance the health and safety of our Nation."

Pharmacist Category

CHIEF PHARMACIST OFFICERS

RDML Kelly J. Battese	2023–2027	RADM Fred G. Paavola	1996–2000
RADM J. Tyler Bingham	2018–2022	RADM Richard J. Bertin	1992–1996
RADM Pamela M. Schweitzer	2014–2018	RADM Richard M. Church	1987–1992
RADM Scott F. Giberson	2010–2014	RADM Richard R. Ashbaugh	1981–1987
RADM Robert E. Pittman	2006–2010	RADM Allen J. Brands	1967–1981
RADM Richard S. Walling	2001–2005	CAPT George F. Archambault	1959–1967

HISTORY

[By RADM Richard J. Bertin, USPHS, Ret.]

The Marine Hospital Service, predecessor to the U.S. Public Health Service, was established in 1798 under the Department of the Treasury, with responsibility to care for sick and injured seamen in U.S. seaport locations. In 1871, pharmacist/physician John M. Woodworth was appointed lead medical officer and named the nation's first Supervising Surgeon, now known as the Surgeon General. Recognizing the importance of having professionally trained health professionals staffing the marine hospitals, Woodworth restructured the program similar to a military system. In 1889, Congress formally authorized the Commissioned Corps, but only physicians were commissioned as officers. Initially, physicians and pharmacists were the only professionally trained personnel in hospital and health care functions. In addition to serving as hospital apothecary, pharmacists served in an array of administrative and technical capacities such as hospital steward responsible for food supplies, medical purveyor, overseer of hospital operations, and as facility superintendent. It was not until 1930 that the Parker Act provided for the appointment of pharmacists in the Commissioned Corps, up to the grade corresponding to Army Captain. The first two pharmacists commissioned in the system were LT Edwin M. Holt (assigned to the Office of Indian Affairs in the Department of the Interior) and LT Edgar B. Scott. The Public Health Service Act of 1944 removed the rank limit and allowed promotion of pharmacists to the Director grade (equivalent to Army Colonel). In 1947, a pharmacy service was formed within the PHS Hospital Division with a full-time Senior Pharmacist, George F. Archambault, as its chief. Raymond D. Kinsey became the first Pharmacist Director in the Service with a temporary promotion in July 1949. Subsequently, Thomas A. Foster who was Chief of Supply and Procurement for the entire Service, and pharmacist/lawyer Archambault who was Chief of the Pharmacy Branch and served as Pharmacy Liaison for the Service in all pharmaceutical matters, were promoted to Pharmacist Director. Allen J. Brands was Chief Pharmacist for the Indian Health Service, and in 1967 he became Pharmacy Liaison Officer to the Surgeon General. In 1979, legislation authorized the rank of Assistant Surgeon General for the position of Chief Pharmacist Officer of the Public Health Service, at which time Brands accepted that role. Since then, only ten other pharmacists have held that title.

Over the long history of what is now the Public Health Service, pharmacists have played a particularly important part in a wide variety of federal health-related programs in several Departments. For many years, the majority of pharmacists served in the Bureau of Medical Services, Division of Hospitals and Clinics – successor to the Marine Hospital System. Prior to its closure in 1980, that system oversaw the operations of eight large general teaching hospitals and nearly 30 free-standing outpatient clinics, primarily in large seaport cities around the United States and on inland waterways, still caring for merchant seamen. Several of those facilities also provided care for other federal or community beneficiaries as the population of seamen and their need for federally provided care decreased. At its height, the program employed several hundred commissioned pharmacist officers in clinical practice, training, and administrative roles. All the hospitals had ASHP-accredited Pharmacy Residency programs and pioneered emerging advanced practices of the day, including bulk compounding, unit dose dispensing, and IV admixture services.

Notably, PHS pharmacist officers have been at the forefront of advanced practice innovations that were initially developed within the Indian Health Service. In 1955, responsibility for American Indian health care was transferred from the Bureau of Indian Affairs to the PHS Division of Indian Health, later named Indian Health Service (IHS). CAPT Allen J. Brands served as the IHS Chief Pharmacist until 1981. Over the ensuing years, Brands justified hiring more pharmacists to relieve physicians and nurses of pharmaceutical and administrative duties. In 1962, he introduced the practice of using patient medical records instead of prescription forms to fill medication orders. Noting that many patient visits involved minor health-related conditions, pharmacists were designated as primary care providers who delivered direct patient care for minor ailments, working under clinical protocols. This led to the use of disease management protocols under which pharmacists began to monitor and adjust medications for patients on chronic therapy. An IHS Pharmacist Practitioner Training Program was initiated, and in 1996 the pharmacist's role as primary care provider was codified in the Indian Health Service. Many of these innovative advances were adopted and are now the standards of practice within other agencies where PHS pharmacists provide professional services. Pharmacists assigned to the Indian Health Service are generally credited with developing techniques of patient counseling now used across the entire pharmacy profession. In the 1960s, they found that patients were often not following therapy as prescribed. Several Indian Health pharmacies implemented structured instructional methodologies in private areas more conducive to learning, and found marked improvement in patient outcomes.

This practice was refined and expanded throughout the Indian Health Service. Training programs were developed and shared with the larger pharmacy community. When federal legislation mandated that pharmacists offer counseling to patients under OBRA-90 in the early 1990s, the IHS model was enthusiastically adopted across the country, giving PHS pharmacy new visibility. That model was also generally adopted by colleges of pharmacy and is used by most participants in student counseling competitions today.

Currently, the Pharmacist Category is among the largest categories in the Commissioned Corps, and about 50 percent of all PHS pharmacists serve in the Indian Health Service. During recent decades, large numbers of PHS pharmacists have also served in the Food and Drug Administration, National Institutes of Health, Health Resources and Services Administration, Centers for Medicare and Medicaid Services, and Centers for Disease Control and Prevention. They have also been assigned to the Federal Bureau of Prisons, the U.S. Coast Guard, Immigration and Customs Enforcement, and to a number of Department of Defense activities, including temporarily backfilling and supplanting pharmacist positions at military installations. Pharmacists are increasingly being called upon to deploy to public health emergency events, and they have participated in national and international humanitarian missions, with their roles encompassing a broad range of clinical, administrative and technical tasks. Response to Ebola, SARS, and COVID-19 outbreaks are recent mobilization activities in which many PHS pharmacists have served.

In 2011, PHS pharmacy made another significant contribution to American pharmacy, with the issuance of the PHS Pharmacy report, *Improving Patient and Health System Outcomes through Advanced Pharmacy Practice: A Report to the U.S. Surgeon General 2011*. That document, which was written by PHS pharmacists, provides a thorough evidence-based discussion of the comprehensive patient care services that pharmacists currently provide, and it received wide recognition throughout the entire pharmacy profession. The PHS Pharmacist Category continues to stand at the forefront of national pharmacy practice, establishing models of pharmacy practice that have been adopted throughout the nation. PHS pharmacists are well educated, holding Doctor of Pharmacy degrees that provide extensive training in the clinical care of patients within all medical specialties. Many PHS pharmacists have taken advanced Pharmacy Residency training, and hold specialty board certifications and/or complementary postgraduate degrees. It is evident that PHS pharmacists will continue to make significant contributions within the Service and in the pharmacy profession more generally. PHS pharmacists will carry on that exceptional legacy of excellence in their provision of direct patient care and in their performance of other clinical and administrative services into the 21st century.

Physician Category

CHIEF MEDICAL OFFICERS

CAPT Joshua G. Schier	2021–2025	RADM David C. Rutstein	2005–2009
CAPT Brian Lewis	2017–2021	RADM W. Craig Vanderwagen	2000–2005
RADM David P. Goldman	2013–2017	RADM Joyce M. Johnson	1997–1999
RADM Clare Helminiak	2009–2013	CAPT William H.J. Haffner	1990–1996
		RADM Leonard Bachman	1986–1990

Prior to RADM Bachman, the Surgeon General served as Chief Medical Officer.

HISTORY

[Adapted from the USPHS Physician Category website.]

Physicians served for over 90 years as civilian healthcare professionals in the Marine Hospital Service (MHS) until the Commissioned Corps was authorized as a uniformed service pursuant to *An Act to Regulate Appointments in the Marine Hospital Service of the United States* on January 4th, 1889. Until 1930, physicians were the only healthcare professionals in the Regular Corps. Early in MHS history, the first physician appointed as the Supervising Surgeon (later named Surgeon General) adopted a military model for his medical staff. Physicians, now in uniform, were no longer appointed to serve in a particular facility but appointed to the general service. In this way, Dr. John Woodworth created a cadre of mobile career physicians who could be assigned and moved as needed to the various marine hospitals. From quarantine duties through passage of the National Quarantine Act of 1878 to the medical examinations of immigrants in 1891 to the expansion of the federal quarantine system in 1906, the Physician Category established a mission of fighting disease, conducting research, and caring for patients in underserved communities.

PHS physicians have led the nation's fight against infectious diseases, including establishment of the bacteriological laboratory at the Staten Island Hospital in 1887, which eventually became the National Institutes of Health (NIH), and to creation of the Office of Malaria Control in War Areas (MCWA) to control malaria around military training bases. ASG Joseph Mountin, head of the MCWA, envisioned "centers of excellence" to address the nation's public health needs for environmental issues, emerging health problems, and communicable diseases. The MCWA, renamed the Communicable Disease Center in 1946 (now Centers for Disease Control and Prevention), embraced Dr. Mountin's vision to vastly expand the scope of the CDC.

In fact, PHS physicians have played a role in the founding of the precursors for all of the U.S. Department of Health and Human Services' (HHS) 12 operating divisions and they continue to serve our nation in multiple clinical, public health, regulatory, and leadership positions within those divisions. In CDC, RADM Anne Schuchat led some of the highest profile and most consequential outbreak investigations and responses in CDC's history including serving as chief health officer during the 2009 H1N1 pandemic influenza response, CDC's incident manager for COVID-19, and support to the Washington, DC, field team during the 2001 bioterrorism response. Within the NIH, RADM Anthony Fauci served as the National Institute of Allergy and Infectious Diseases director for nearly 40 years, serving as advisor to seven Presidents, during which he oversaw research in the prevention, diagnosis, and treatments of infectious diseases, such as HIV/AIDS, respiratory infections, diarrheal diseases, tuberculosis, malaria, and emerging diseases such as Ebola, Zika, and COVID-19. ADM Rachel Levine, the 17th Assistant Secretary for Health, was instrumental in helping overcome the COVID-19 pandemic and build a stronger foundation for public health efforts.

An important aspect of the PHS physician's mission is direct clinical care of underserved populations. In 1955, the Transfer Act established the Indian Health Service (IHS) within the U.S. Public Health Service. The first IHS director was PHS physician Dr. James (Ray) Shaw. Under his leadership, the IHS began training programs for staff in cross-cultural medicine and also "taught the joint practice of public health and medical care." The Commissioned Corps continues to ensure that comprehensive, culturally acceptable personal and public health services are accessible to American Indian and Alaska Native people. PHS physicians also serve vulnerable communities and hard-to-fill positions through agencies outside of HHS, including the provision of health care to the U.S. Coast Guard personnel, Federal Bureau of Prisons (BOP) inmates, Immigration and Customs Enforcement detainees, Veterans Administration, and the Defense Health Agency. The BOP Medical Director has, until recent years, consistently been filled by a PHS officer such as RADMs Robert Brutsche, Kenneth Moritsugu, and Newton Kendig.

Throughout Corps history, PHS physicians have been ready to serve in emergent situations. They helped control the spread of major epidemic diseases such as yellow fever and bubonic plague in the 1870s, conducted investigations of human diseases including malaria and leprosy in the early 1900s, and cared for soldiers and veterans during the World Wars I and II. Physicians have been at the forefront in responding to pandemics such as Spanish Influenza, syphilis, and HIV. In modern times, PHS physicians have responded to multiple national and international emergencies, including the 9/11 attacks, and major hurricanes, Ebola outbreak in 2014 where physicians staffed the Monrovia Medical Unit, and the global COVID-19 pandemic. During the Covid pandemic, PHS physicians were among the "strike teams" that served in a variety of vital roles including caring for critically ill Americans in Japan, and providing surge capacity to support nursing homes and hospitals caring for COVID-19 patients. Leading these responses were high ranking physicians, such as ADM Brett P. Giroir and RADM Richard Childs. Today, PHS physicians continue to uphold the high standards of excellence set by their forebears with exemplary clinical and public health leadership for this nation.

Scientist Category

CHIEF SCIENTIST OFFICERS

CAPT Sukhminder K. Sandhu	2021-2025	CDR Doug A. Thoroughman	2004-2005
CAPT John Eckert	2017-2021	RADM Lireka P. Joseph	2000-2004
CAPT Martin L. Sanders	2013-2017	CAPT Derek E. Dunn	1995-2000
CAPT Sharon Williams-Fleetwood	2009-2013	CAPT Jerry M. Johnson	1991-1995
RADM Helena O. Mishoe	2005-2009	CAPT Richard P. Chiacchierini	1987-1991
CAPT Ralph O'Connor	2005-2005	CAPT James F. McTigue	1983-1987

HISTORY

[Adapted from the USPHS Scientist Category website, HHS and other public domain websites, and published documents.]

Understanding the science and dynamics of disease has been a fundamental part of the USPHS since its inception. The Public Health Service established the Hygienic Laboratory in the late 1880s, from which emanated virtually all scientific research into diseases such as cholera, yellow fever and plague. Scientist employees and consultants, as well as PHS medical officers, were involved in sentinel investigations into the etiology of an array of infectious diseases prevalent at the time. In 1902, legislation included the provision to allow the appointment of "professors" – Civil Service scientists – to head three new divisions of chemistry, pharmacology, and zoology within the Hygienic Laboratory. Passage of the Parker Act of 1930, provided for the commissioning of other professionals including scientists in the PHS Regular Corps. The law allowed for commissioning of three research scientists annually after that time. In the early 1940s, there was a PHS reorganization resulting from passage of both the Public Health Service Act of 1943 and of 1944, which among its provision expanded the eligibility of healthcare and public health professionals other than medical officers to join the Regular Corps. The Scientist Category was established in 1945 and included officers who commissioned with a doctorate level degree in a scientific or health-related specialty. In July 1946, there were eleven Scientist officers on active duty and, by January 1948, the number of Scientist officers had swelled to fifty.

In the nearly four decades that followed, PHS Scientist officers were involved in the investigation, research and scientific understanding of several key public health milestones. Drs. John Eager, Trendley Dean, and a team of scientists conducted community water fluoridation studies in Michigan during the 1940s. In 1950, Dr. James P. Leake and other public health scientists were instrumental in field investigations of poliomyelitis. In 1965, public health scientists and surgical officers were involved in efforts to control malaria and other infectious diseases in Vietnam. Scientist officers at the Lexington Hospital Addiction Research Center began mapping the brain to understand the causes of addiction. In 1969, public health scientists at the Communicable

Disease Center (later renamed Centers for Disease Control and Prevention) provided quarantine equipment and procedures for the Apollo Moon Landings. And in 1970, Scientist officers at the National Institute of Mental Health developed numerous treatment methodologies in child psychology.

While detailed to the Commissioned Corps Personnel Office and working on Surgeon General C. Everett Koop's Report on AIDS, CAPT James McTigue led efforts to further organize the Scientist Category. When the Scientist Category was chartered in 1983, CAPT McTigue was appointed the first Chief Professional Officer. The Scientist Professional Advisory Committee (SciPAC) was formed in 1984, with RADM (retired rank) Barry L. Johnson becoming the first SciPAC Chair. To celebrate the 100th anniversary of the USPHS Commissioned Corps in 1989, SciPAC organized a Centennial Science Symposium at the National Institutes of Health. During this time, Scientist officers were leaders in scientific endeavors related to widely diverse health topics, including drug and alcohol abuse, depression, AIDS, the human genome, cancer prevention, bacterial vaccines, laser technology, and biomedical research. In more recent years, Scientist officers have carried on the legacy of exceptional contributions to scientific activities across federal agencies. They are stationed throughout the nation, working with headquarters offices, field offices, state health departments and tribes, and in international assignments.

PHS Scientist officers have been at the forefront of urgent public health responses as well as advancing the science of disease prevention and health promotion. For example, they have deployed supporting surveillance and administrative activities after the September 11, 2001 terrorist attacks, contributed to a multiagency task force response to Avian Influenza in 2002, and participated in response and recovery after Hurricanes Isabel, Katrina, Sandy, Harvey, Irma, Maria, and Matthew, as well as Typhoon Yutu. Scientist officers also supported the MERS-CoV2 Response. In 2014, Scientist officers were among those providing care and epidemiologic support for the West African Ebola outbreak. And, Scientist officers mobilized to support every aspect of the COVID-19 pandemic response (2020-2023). During the ongoing COVID-19 response, officers took on numerous critical leadership roles in agency responses and nationally, led groundbreaking research on topics like transmission and treatment, and were among the first to deploy to set-up and manage medical shelters. Other deployments have involved missions related to unaccompanied children, resettlement of Afghans in the U.S., and Mpox.

The Scientist Category is comprised of officers who hold a doctoral degree and includes a wide array of specialties such as epidemiologist, laboratorian, psychologist, regulatory scientist, research scientist and others. As of 2022, there were over 400 PHS Scientist officers on active duty. The rich heritage of the Scientist Category has provided an especially strong foundation for the exceptional work carried forward into the future.

Therapist Category

CHIEF THERAPIST OFFICERS

CAPT Ronald R. West	2024-2028	CAPT Michael Huylebroeck	1994-1998
CAPT Jeffrey Richardson	2020-2024	CAPT Gene A. Diullo	1991-1993
CAPT Mercedes Benitez-McCrary	2016-2020	CAPT Robert E. Mansell	1990-1991
CAPT Scott Gaustad	2011-2016	CAPT William Fromherz	1986-1990
CAPT Karen L. Siegel	2007-2011	CAPT Alan Stone	1982-1986
CAPT Charles L. McGarvey	2003-2007	CAPT William Cox	1979-1982
CAPT Charlotte Richards	1998-2003	CAPT Dean Currier	1977-1979

HISTORY

[Adapted from the USPHS Therapist Category website, by CAPT Jeffrey Richardson and CAPT Ronald West.]

The Public Health Service Therapist Category is a multidisciplinary category comprised of healthcare providers in the professions of audiology, physical therapy, occupational therapy, respiratory therapy, and speech language pathology. The Public Health Service Act of 1944 authorized the Public Health Service to commission nurses, scientists, dietitians, physical therapists, and sanitarians. Therapist officers were called to meet the expanding rehabilitation needs of PHS. Initially, physical therapists were stationed in Marine Hospitals during the onset of the polio epidemic of the late 1940s and 1950s. Since the early 1950s, PHS therapists have played major roles in the development of the nation's medical model for the provision of health care. These therapists pioneered rehabilitation techniques, prosthetic design, and assistive devices to evaluate and treat a variety of post-war patients in a multitude of public health care settings. Many therapists' contributions have advanced their profession, setting standards of care that furthered education and research. The public health implementation of occupational therapy began at St. Elizabeth's Hospital in Washington, DC, the first federal hospital devoted to care of the mentally ill. Occupational therapists joined Saint Elizabeth's in 1931, and the first PHS commissioned occupational therapist was stationed there in the 1980s. In 1965, the Medicare and Medicaid programs were enacted, PHS headquarters directed regional therapist officers to become involved in implementing new programs. This included the establishment of standards for therapist personnel, facilities and organizational structures; provision of consultation to regional offices, local and state agencies, and service providers; and assumption of responsibility for major program components in the survey and certification processes. Through the 1960s, physical and occupational therapists at the Gillis W. Long Hansen's Disease Center in Carville, Louisiana directed efforts to the prevention and treatment of patients with deformities and wounds associated with insensitivity in their extremities. Through research, they advanced clinical solutions that are applicable for other types of clients with similar sensory conditions.

During the 1950s, the Indian Health Service utilized therapy officers to develop comprehensive plans for rehabilitation needs, which led to the design of therapy clinics and formation of IHS therapy standards of professional practice. In the late 1960s and early 1970s, physical therapist, occupational therapist, audiologist and speech pathologist officers began serving the needs of the newly built Indian Health Service hospitals and clinics. An Indian Health Service Rehabilitation Branch was formed in 1970, and by 1977 services were expanded to include home care therapy. During the 1970s, NIH occupational therapists adopted the Model of Human Occupation as the framework for clinical care and research, and PHS officers developed Physical Disabilities Evaluation and Treatment tools. Occupational and physical therapy expanded into clinical specialty practice areas in clinical care, administration, research, and education. In the 1980s, PHS therapists became principal investigators in therapy research, which broadened in the 1990s to include research resulting in the design of more than 20 clinical protocols. In 1974, the first PHS therapist joined the Bureau of Prisons, and therapy services have since expanded to other federal BOP medical centers around the country. In the 2010s these therapists developed premier services for inmate health care, wound care and telehealth that serves as a model for other services.

Since the 1990s, PHS physical therapists have been involved in creating therapy guides for U.S. Coast Guard Hospital Corpsmen, in planning physical therapy departments for USCG medical facilities, redesigning of Coast Guard officer footwear standards, and developing a new physical fitness program for rescue swimmers. Therapists continue to work on Coast Guard Training Bases to facilitate safe and efficient physical training for new personnel, and they provide rehabilitation from injury incurred during duty. PHS therapist officers have also contributed to noise and ergonomics research by the National Institute for Occupational Safety and Health. Such efforts have resulted in the issuance of standards related to prevention of noise-induced hearing loss and musculoskeletal injuries.

Therapists are also assigned to the FDA as Regulatory Review Officers to support the review of scientific, technical and clinical data in premarket applications and assess the safety and effectiveness of medical devices. After the terrorist attacks of September 11, 2001, therapists were deployed to serve in several capacities during recovery efforts. It was then that the need for respiratory therapists as a deployable asset became evident. The Therapist Category rallied and submitted the required documentation to move forward with commissioning respiratory therapists. This effort extended into 2009 when the U.S. Public Health Service became the first uniformed service to commission respiratory therapists. Since 2001, therapists of all professions have been indispensable deployable assets, serving as leaders and educators for USPHS deployment teams. In 2008, an agreement of the Department of Defense with the PHS brought therapists to staff rehabilitation centers for the treatment of brain injured service members. Specialized PT, OT and SLP therapists have advanced the treatment of concussions and led research on improving brain injury protocols. Their contributions have extended the military's ability to provide excellent care for active duty personnel and veterans who sustained brain injuries. Highly trained and skilled PHS therapists also provide teaching and mentoring in the Army physical therapy residency program. As evidenced by this brief history, the roles of Therapist Category professionals continue to expand across nearly all Department of Health and Human Services Operating Divisions. Specialization trends in all therapy fields continue to expand the roles of PHS therapists. The Therapist Category has demonstrated significant impact on the health of the American people and as a participant in response missions around the world. The foundation built by early visionary therapists has propelled the Therapist Category into becoming an invaluable, key element of the U.S. Public Health Service.

Veterinarian Category

CHIEF VETERINARY OFFICERS

RDML Kis Robertson Hale	2024–2028	CAPT Cynthia L. Pond	1998–2003
CAPT Marvin Thomas	2020–2024	RADM Michael J. Blackwell	1994–1998
CAPT John D. Gibbins	2016–2020	RADM Roscoe M. Moore, Jr.	1989–1994
CAPT/RADM Terri R. Clark	2011–2015	RADM Robert A. Whitney, Jr.	1985–1989
CAPT Hugh M. Mainzer	2007–2011	RADM Joe R. Held	1974–1984
CAPT/RADM William S. Stokes	2003–2007	RADM Ernest S. Tierkel	1971–1973
		RADM James H. Steele	1968–1971

HISTORY

[By CAPT Marvin (Tom) Thomas.]

Civilian veterinarians originally joined the U.S. Public Health Service as milk and food specialists. Beginning in 1943, veterinarians were commissioned within the Sanitarian Category, among whom was James H. Steele. Dr. Steele prepared a report entitled *Veterinary Public Health* for Assistant Surgeon General Joseph Mountin and Surgeon General Thomas Parran Jr. The report spoke to the risks posed by zoonotic diseases, which are infectious diseases transmitted from animals to humans, and also the benefits of hiring veterinarians for research and response endeavors. Resulting from that, James Steele was assigned in 1947 to the Communicable Disease Center (CDC) where he established a veterinary division. His proposal to formally establish a PHS veterinary officer category came about in the summer of 1947, when the Surgeon

General signed an amendment to the USPHS regulations, and Dr. Steele was subsequently appointed the category's first Chief Professional Officer. In 1953, Alexander Langmuir asked Dr. Steele to recruit veterinarians for CDC's Epidemic Intelligence Service (EIS) training program, thereby opening up a new sphere of scientific investigative activity for officers. The EIS veterinary officers have gone on to make substantial contributions to public health in positions with federal, state and local governments, academia, industry, and nongovernmental organizations. The history and tradition of the profession have always focused on protecting and improving both animal health and human health, and veterinary research is critical to understanding and improving human health. PHS veterinary officers have been involved with all aspects of public health and are the cornerstone to the One Health Concept, which deals with the symbiotic relationship between veterinary medicine and human medicine and the environment.

Veterinarian officers work in multiple HHS and non-HHS agencies. They provide expertise in their assignments within many disciplines, including epidemiology, biomedical research, ecosystem management, clinical response to disease outbreaks, disease prevention, preventative medicine, surgery, pathology, toxicology, regulatory affairs involving drugs and vaccines, food and water safety, and public health compliance. Veterinarians engaged in public health activities traditionally have worked in a regulatory capacity on animal health problems affecting agriculture, plant and animal health, human and animal food safety, biologic and homeland security, and wildlife and zoonotic disease prevention and control, while others have worked in applied public health roles. Veterinarians in public health careers are not limited to zoonotic pathogens, and often apply their population medicine knowledge to other roles of human disease or injury prevention and control, environmental health, and vaccine-preventable diseases. The role of the PHS veterinarian features important tasks relating to public health crisis response – before, during and after a disaster. These tasks include pre-disaster planning, disaster assessment, control of disease vectors and transmission, herd management, animal control and health care, search and rescue, maintenance of medical supplies, and information dissemination.

PHS officers are highly educated professionals with doctorate degrees (DVM/VMD), and most hold advanced degrees (MS, MPH, PhD) and are Board certified in a specialty. Veterinarians are familiar with multiple species, and their training emphasizes comparative medicine. The advanced training of PHS veterinarian officers makes them a vital response team member during deployments nationally and internationally, to include Hurricanes Katrina, Rita Ike, Gustav, Maria, Irma, and Sandy, and others such as the Ebola and Monkeypox outbreaks, COVID-19 pandemic, Unaccompanied Children missions, and the Operation Allies Welcome mission.

References

Held, Joe R., and D.J. Gregory. 1992. "Organization of Veterinary Public Health in the United States of America and Canada." *Revue Scientifique et Technique* 11, no. 1: 147-167.

Jarman, Dwayne W., Jennifer L. Liang, Richard R. Luce, et al. 2011. "Veterinary Public Health Capacity in the United States: Opportunities for Improvement." Public Health Reports 126, no. 6: 868-874.

King, Lonnie J.; Centers for Disease Control and Prevention. 2006. "Veterinary Medicine and Public Health at CDC." *MMWR Supplement* 55, no. 2: 7-9.

Moore, Roscoe M. Jr, Yvette M. Davis, Ronald G. Kaczmarek. 1992. "The Role of the Veterinarian in Hurricanes and Other Natural Disasters." *Annals of the New York Academy of Sciences* 653: 367-375.

Pappaioanou, Marguerite, Paul L. Garbe, M. Kathleen Glynn, et al. 2003. "Veterinarians and Public Health: the Epidemic Intelligence Service of the Centers for Disease Control and Prevention, 1951–2002." *Journal of Veterinary Medical Education* 30, no. 4: 383-391.

Steele, James H. "History of Veterinary Public Health in the United States of America." 1991. *Revue Scientifique et Technique* 10, no. 4: 951-983.

APPENDICES

APPENDIX A

Commissioned Officers, U.S. Public Health Service
Force Strength, Selected Years, 1900–2023

APPENDIX B

Commissioned Officers, U.S. Public Health Service
Officer Duty Stations, 2023

APPENDIX C

Surgeons General & Deputy Surgeons General
of the United States Public Health Service

About the Author

About the Contributing Editor

APPENDIX A

COMMISSIONED OFFICERS
U.S. PUBLIC HEALTH SERVICE
ACTIVE DUTY FORCE STRENGTH, SELECTED YEARS

YEAR	OFFICERS
1900	107
1910	128
1920	683
1930	289
1940	627
1945	2,342
1950	2,222
1960	3,816
1970	5,501
1975	5,510
1985	5,386
1990	6,084
1995	6,247
2000	5,704
2005	5,975
2010	6,607
2015	6,672
2017	6,509
2019	6,224
2022	5,855
2023	5,470

Source: Number of Active Duty Officers by Year. 1900–1975 Data: HHS, PHS Commissioned Corps, Report to the Senate Appropriations Committee Responding to a Request in the Committee Report on the FY1998 HAS Appropriations Bill (Washington, DC, 1998): 9. From: Hamowy, R. 2007. Government and Public Health in America. Cheltenham, UK: Edward Elgar Publishing, p. 69. 1985–2023 Data: HHS, USPHS, OSG, Commissioned Corps Headquarters.

APPENDIX B

**COMMISSIONED OFFICERS
U.S. PUBLIC HEALTH SERVICE
OFFICER DUTY STATIONS [2023]**

PRINCIPAL HHS OFFICE AND AGENCY DUTY STATIONS [OPERATING DIVISIONS]
Office of the Secretary
Office of the Assistant Secretary for Health
Office of the Assistant Secretary for Preparedness and Response
Administration for Children and Families
Agency for Healthcare Research and Quality
Agency for Toxic Substances and Disease Registry
Centers for Disease Control and Prevention
Centers for Medicare and Medicaid Services
Food and Drug Administration
Health Resources and Services Administration
Indian Health Service
National Institutes of Health
Program Support Center
Substance Abuse and Mental Health Services Administration

PRINCIPAL NON-HHS AGENCY/PROGRAM DUTY STATIONS
Department of Agriculture
Department of Defense
Department of Homeland Security (DHS)
Environmental Protection Agency
Federal Bureau of Prisons [Justice]
Immigration and Customs Enforcement, Health Service Corps [DHS]
Marshals Service [Justice]
National Oceanic and Atmospheric Administration [Commerce]
National Park Service [Interior]
U.S. Coast Guard [DHS]
Department of Veterans Affairs

APPENDIX C

SURGEONS GENERAL & DEPUTY SURGEONS GENERAL OF THE UNITED STATES PUBLIC HEALTH SERVICE*

SURGEON GENERAL *DEPUTY SURGEON GENERAL*	TERM OF OFFICE	APPOINTED BY PRESIDENT
1) John M. Woodworth	March 1871–March 1879	Ulysses S. Grant
2) John B. Hamilton	April 1879–June 1891	Rutherford B. Hayes
3) Walter Wyman	June 1891–November 1911	Benjamin Harrison
4) Rupert Blue	January 1912–March 1920	William H. Taft
5) Hugh S. Cumming	March 1920–January 1936	Woodrow Wilson
6) Thomas J. Parran, Jr. *Dep. Warren F. Draper* *Dep. James A. Crabtree*	April 1936–April 1948 July 1944–September 1946 September 1946–May 1948	Franklin D. Roosevelt
7) Leonard A. Scheele *Dep. W. Palmer Dearing*	April 1948–August 1956 May 1948–August 1957	Harry S. Truman
8) Leroy E. Burney *Dep. John D. Porterfield*	August 1956–January 1961 September 1957–June 1962	Dwight D. Eisenhower
9) Luther L. Terry *Dep. David Price*	March 1961–October 1965 July 1962–September 1965	John F. Kennedy
10) William H. Stewart *Dep. Leo J. Gehrig*	October 1965–August 1969 November 1965–April 1968	Lyndon B. Johnson
Actg. Richard A. Prindle *Dep. S. Paul Ehrlich*	August 1969–December 1969 *April 1968–December 1977*	Richard M. Nixon
11) Jesse L. Steinfeld *Dep. S. Paul Ehrlich*	December 1969–Jan. 1973 *April 1968–December 1977*	
Actg. S. Paul Ehrlich, Jr. *Dep. S. Paul Ehrlich*	January 1973–July 1977 *April 1968–December 1977*	
12) Julius B. Richmond *Dep. John C. Greene*	July 1977–January 1981 *March 1978–January 1981*	James E. Carter, Jr.
Actg. John C. Greene *Dep. John C. Greene*	January 1981–May 1981 *March 1978–January 1981*	Ronald Reagan
Actg. Edward Brandt, Jr.	May 1981–January 1982	
13) C. Everett Koop *Dep. Faye G. Abdellah*	January 1982–October 1989 *March 1982–November 1989*	
Actg. James O. Mason**	July 1989–March 1990	
14) Antonia C. Novello *Dep. O. Marie Henry* *Dep. Robert A. Whitney*	March 1990–June 1993 *March 1990–September 1992* *September 1992–January 1994*	George H. W. Bush

SURGEONS GENERAL & DEPUTY SURGEONS GENERAL OF THE UNITED STATES PUBLIC HEALTH SERVICE* [Continued]

SURGEON GENERAL *DEPUTY SURGEON GENERAL*	TERM OF OFFICE	APPOINTED BY PRESIDENT
Actg. Robert A. Whitney	July 1993–September 1993	
Dep. Robert A. Whitney	*September 1992–January 1994*	
15) M. Joycelyn Elders	September 1993–Dec. 1994	
Dep. Robert A. Whitney	*September 1992–January 1994*	
Dep. Audrey F. Manley	*January 1994–June 1997 (Actg.)*	William J. Clinton
Actg. Audrey F. Manley	January 1995–June 1997	
Dep. Audrey F. Manley	*January 1994–June 1997*	
Actg. J. Jarrett Clinton	July 1997–February 1998	
16) David Satcher	February 1998–February 2002	
Dep. Kenneth Moritsugu	*October 1998–September 2007*	
Actg. Kenneth P. Moritsugu	February 2002–August 2002	
Dep. Kenneth Moritsugu	*October 1998–September 2007*	
17) Richard H. Carmona	August 2002–July 2006	
Dep. Kenneth Moritsugu	*October 1998–September 2007*	George W. Bush
Actg. Kenneth P. Moritsugu	August 2006–September 2007	
Dep. Kenneth Moritsugu	*October 1998–September 2007*	
Actg. Steven K. Galson	October 2007–October 2009	
Dep. Robert C. Williams	*October 2007–Jan. 2010 (Actg.)*	
Actg. Donald L. Weaver	October 2009–Nov. 2009	
Dep. Robert C. Williams	*October 2007–Jan. 2010 (Actg.)*	
18) Regina M. Benjamin	November 2009–July 2013	
Dep. Robert C. Williams	*October 2007–Jan. 2010 (Actg.)*	
Dep. David C. Rutstein	*January 2010–Nov. 2010 (Actg.)*	
Dep. Boris D. Lushniak	*November 2010–Sept. 2015*	Barack H. Obama
Actg. Boris D. Lushniak	July 2013–December 2014	
Dep. Scott F. Giberson	*July 2013–Dec. 2014 (Actg.)*	
19) Vivek H. Murthy	December 2014–April 2017	
Dep. Boris D. Lushniak	*November 2010–Sept. 2015*	
Dep. Sylvia Trent-Adams	*October 2015–January 2019*	
Actg. Sylvia Trent-Adams	April 2017–September 2017	
20) Jerome M. Adams	September 2017–January 2021	Donald J. Trump
Dep. Sylvia Trent-Adams	*October 2015–January 2019*	
Dep. Erica G. Schwartz	*March 2019–January 2021*	
Actg. Susan Orsega	January 2021–March 2021	
21) Vivek H. Murthy	March 2021–	Joseph R. Biden, Jr.
Dep. Denise Hinton	*October 2021–*	

* The Public Health Service Act of 1944 included several key provisions. Section 205 provided for the Surgeon General to appoint a Regular Corps officer as Deputy Surgeon General.
** Dr. Mason was Acting SG in July due to Dr. Koop being on terminal leave July to October.

REFERENCES

[All Website URLs Accessed in 2023.]

CHAPTER ONE, Pages 5–14

1. Winslow, Charles-Edward Amory. 1923. *The evolution and significance of the modern public health campaign.* New Haven: Yale University Press.
2. Koplan, Jeffrey P., and Melissa McPheeters. 2004. "Plagues, Public Health, and Politics." *Emerging Infectious Diseases* 10, no. 11: 2039–2043.
3. The White House. 2022. "National Security Strategy, October 2022."
   https://www.whitehouse.gov/wp-content/uploads/2022/11/8-November-Combined-PDF-for-Upload.pdf

CHAPTER TWO, Pages 15–28

1. Hamilton, Alexander. 1792. "Report on Marine Hospitals, [17 April 1792]." Founders Online, National Archives.
   https://founders.archives.gov/documents/Hamilton/01-11-02-0239
2. 1 Stat. 605. 5th Congress, Session II, Ch. 77, July 16, 1798.
3. Williams, Ralph C. 1951. *The United States Public Health Service, 1798-1950.* Washington, DC: Commissioned Officers Association of the USPHS.
4. Straus, Robert. 1950. *Medical Care for Seamen. The Origin of Public Medical Service in the United States.* New Haven: Yale University Press.
5. Jensen, John. 1997. "Before the Surgeon General: Marine Hospitals in Mid-19th-Century America." *Public Health Reports* 112, no. 6: 525–527.
6. Trask, John W. 1940. *The United States Marine Hospital at the Port of Boston, 1799-1940. An Account of Its Origin and Briefly of Its History and of the Physicians Who Have Been in Charge.* Federal Security Agency, U.S. Public Health Service.
7. Woodworth, John M. 1872. *Annual Report of the Supervising Surgeon of the Marine Hospital Service of the United States for the Year 1872.* Washington: GPO.
8. 16 Stat. 169. 41st Congress, Session II, Ch. 169, June 29, 1870.
9. 23 Stat. 53. *An Act to Remove Certain Burdens on the American Merchant Marine and Encourage the American Foreign Carrying Trade and for Other Purposes.* 48th Congress, Session I, Ch. 121, June 26, 1884.
10. "The United States Public Health and Marine-Hospital Service. Part I. A Historical Sketch." 1904. *Special Articles. Journal of the American Medical Association* July 30, 1904: 326–328; August 6, 1904: 401–403.
11. Bryce, Peter H. 1918. "History of the American Public Health Association." *American Journal of Public Health* 8, no. 5: 327–335.
12. Woodworth, John M. 1876. *Annual Report of the Supervising Surgeon-General of the Marine-Hospital Service of the United States for the Fiscal Year 1875.* Washington: GPO.
13. 20 Stat. 37. *An Act to Prevent the Introduction of Contagious or Infectious Diseases into the United States.* 45th Congress, Session II, Ch. 66, April 29, 1878.
14. Shaw, Frederic E., Richard A. Goodman, and Mary Lou Lindegren, et al.; Centers for Disease Control and Prevention (CDC). 2011. "A History of MMWR." *Morbidity and Mortality Weekly Report* Suppl 60, no. 4: 7–14.
15. 20 Stat. 484. 45th Congress, Session III, Ch. 202, March 3, 1879.

16. 21 Stat. 5. *An Act to Prevent the Introduction of Contagious or Infectious Diseases into the United States*. 46th Congress, Session I, Ch. 11, June 2, 1879.
17. Furman, Bess. 1973. *A Profile of the United States Public Health Service, 1798-1948*. Washington, DC: DHEW.
18. "Obituary: Surgeon-General Woodworth." 1879. *New-York Tribune*, March 15. https://www.loc.gov/resource/sn83030214/1879-03-15/ed-1/?sp=2&st=image&r=0.33,0.296,0.493,0.277,0
19. Smillie, WG. 1943. "The National Board of Health: 1879-1883." *American Journal of Public Health and the Nation's Health* 33, no. 8: 925–930.
20. Michael, Jerrold M. 2011. "The National Board of Health: 1879-1883." *Public Health Reports* 126, no. 1: 123–129.
21. National Institutes of Health. "A Short History of the National Institutes of Health." https://history.nih.gov/display/history/A+Short+History+of+the+National+Institutes+of+Health
22. Public Law 57-236, 32 Stat. 712. *An Act to Increase the Efficiency and Change the Name of the United States Marine-Hospital Service*. 57th Congress, Session I, Ch. 1370, July 1, 1902.
23. Hamilton, John B. 1885. *Annual Report of the Supervising Surgeon-General of the Marine-Hospital Service of the United States for the Fiscal Year 1885*. Washington: GPO.
24. 25 Stat. 639. 50th Congress, Session II, Ch. 19, January 4, 1889.
25. Heiser, Victor. 1936. *An American Doctor's Odyssey: Adventures in Forty-five Countries*. New York: W.W. Norton.
26. Hamilton, John B. 1889. *Annual Report of the Supervising Surgeon-General of the Marine-Hospital Service of the United States for the Fiscal Year 1889*. Washington: GPO.
27. First Congress, Session II, Ch. 29, July 20, 1790.
28. Johnson, Joyce M., ed. 2003. *The Ship's Medicine Chest and Medical Aid at Sea*. Washington, DC: Department of Health and Human Services, PHS, OSG.

CHAPTER THREE, Pages 29–44

1. Hirschman, Charles, and Elizabeth Mogford. 2009. "Immigration and the American Industrial Revolution from 1880 to 1920." *Social Science Research* 38, no. 4: 897–920.
2. 26 Stat. 1084. 51st Congress, Session II, Ch. 551, March 3, 1891.
3. The Statue of Liberty-Ellis Island Foundation, Inc. "Overview and History. Ellis Island." https://www.statueofliberty.org/ellis-island/overview-history/
4. Bateman-House, Alison, and Amy Fairchild. 2008. "Medical Examination of Immigrants at Ellis Island." *AMA Journal of Ethics/Virtual Mentor* 10, no. 4: 235–241.
5. Treasury Department, Bureau of Public Health and Marine-Hospital Service. 1903. *Book of Instructions for the Medical Inspection of Immigrants*. Washington: GPO.
6. Fairchild, Amy L. 2003. *Science at the Borders: Immigrant Medical Inspection and the Shaping of the Modern Industrial Labor Force*. Baltimore, MD: Johns Hopkins University Press.
7. Yew, Elizabeth. 1980. "Medical Inspection of Immigrants at Ellis Island, 1891-1924." *Bulletin of the New York Academy of Medicine* 56, no. 5: 488–510.
8. Simmons, George H., ed. 1913. "Quarantine in the Maritime Cities of the United States." *Journal of the American Medical Association* 60: 194–200.
9. 27 Stat. 449. 52nd Congress, Session II, Ch. 114, February 15, 1893.
10. Wyman, Walter. 1901. *Annual Report of the Supervising Surgeon-General of the Marine-Hospital Service of the United States for the Fiscal Year 1899*. Washington: GPO.
11. Moran, Michelle T. 2007. *Colonizing Leprosy: Imperialism and the Politics of Public Health in the United States*. Chapel Hill: University of North Carolina Press.

12. Michael, Jerrold M. 1980. "The Public Health Service Leprosy Investigation Station on Molokai, Hawaii, 1909–13—an Opportunity Lost." *Public Health Reports* 95, no. 3: 203–209.
13. Public Law 64-299, 39 Stat. 872. *An Act to Provide for the Care and Treatment of Persons Afflicted with Leprosy and to Prevent the Spread of Leprosy in the United States*. 64th Congress, Session II, Ch. 26, February 3, 1917.
14. Morens, David M., Victoria A. Harden, and Joseph Kinyoun Houts, Jr., et al. 2012. *The Indispensable Forgotten Man: Joseph James Kinyoun and the Founding of the National Institutes of Health*. Bethesda: National Institutes of Health.
15. Lipson, Loren G. 1972. "Plague in San Francisco in 1900: The United States Marine Hospital Service Commission to Study the Existence of Plague in San Francisco." *Annals of Internal Medicine* 77, no. 2: 303–310.
16. Wyman, Walter. 1901. *Annual Report of the Supervising Surgeon-General of the Marine-Hospital Service of the United States for the Fiscal Year 1901*. Washington: GPO.
17. Haas, Victor H. 1959. "When Bubonic Plague Came to Chinatown." *American Journal of Tropical Medicine and Hygiene* 8, 2 Pt 1: 141–147.
18. Kellogg W.H. 1937. "The Plague Situation." *California and Western Medicine* 47, no. 1: 69–71.
19. Wyman, Walter. 1895. *Annual Report of the Supervising Surgeon-General of the Marine-Hospital Service of the United States for the Fiscal Year 1894*. Washington: GPO.
20. Cumming, Hugh S. 1903. "The San Francisco Quarantine Station." *California State Journal of Medicine* 1, no. 11: 324–9.
21. Lucaccini, Luigi F. 1996. "The Public Health Service on Angel Island." *Public Health Reports* 111, no. 1: 92–94.
22. National Park Service. 2020. "U.S. Immigration Station, Angel Island." September 6. https://www.nps.gov/places/u-s-immigration-station-angel-island.htm
23. Nauman, Russell. 2021. Operations Manager, Angel Island Immigration Station Foundation. Personal Communication, January 13.
24. Public Law 57-236, 32 Stat. 712. 57th Congress, Session I, Ch. 1370, July 1, 1902.
25. Callan, John F. 1864. *The Military Laws of the United States, Relating to the Army, Volunteers, Militia, and to Bounty Lands and Pensions, from the Foundation of the Government to 4 July, 1864*. Philadelphia: G.W. Childs, 245, 246, 285.
26. Furman, Bess. 1973. *A Profile of the United States Public Health Service, 1798-1948*. Washington, DC: DHEW.
27. Mullan, Fitzhugh. 1989. *Plagues and Politics. The Story of the United States Public Health Service*. New York: Basic Books.
28. Public Law 57-244, 32 Stat. 728. *An Act to Regulate the Sale of Viruses, Serums, Toxins, and Analogous Products in the District of Columbia; to Regulate Interstate Traffic in Said Articles, and for Other Purposes*. 57th Congress, Session I, Ch. 1378, July 1, 1902.
29. Schultz, Myron G. 2009. "Henry Rose Carter." *Emerging Infectious Diseases* 15, no. 10: 1682–1684.
30. Stern, Alexandra M. 2005. "The Public Health Service in the Panama Canal: A Forgotten Chapter of U.S. Public Health." *Public Health Reports* 120, no, 6: 675–679.
31. Frierson, J. Gordon. 2010. "The Yellow Fever Vaccine: A History." *Yale Journal of Biology and Medicine* 83, no. 2: 77–85.
32. Elman, Cheryl, Robert A. McGuire, and Barbara Wittman. 2014. "Extending Public Health: The Rockefeller Sanitary Commission and Hookworm in the American South." *American Journal of Public Health* 104, no. 1: 47–58.

33. Rockefeller Sanitary Commission for the Eradication of Hookworm Disease. 1915. *Fifth Annual Report for the Year 1914*. Washington DC: Offices of the Commission, January.
34. Fricks, L.D. 1915. "Rocky Mountain Spotted Fever: A Report of its Investigation and of Measures Undertaken for its Eradication During 1914." *Public Health Reports* 30, no. 3: 148–165.
35. Harden, Victoria A. 1985. "Rocky Mountain Spotted Fever Research and the Development of the Insect Vector Theory, 1900-1930." *Bulletin of the History of Medicine* 59, no. 4: 449–466.

CHAPTER FOUR, Pages 45–62

1. Furman, Bess. 1973. *A Profile of the United States Public Health Service, 1798-1948*. Washington, DC: DHEW.
2. Blue R. 1913. *Annual Report of the Surgeon General of the Public Health Service of the United States for the Fiscal Year 1912*. Washington: GPO.
3. Public Law 62-265, 37 Stat. 309. 62nd Congress, Session II, Ch. 288, August 14, 1912.
4. Casner, Nicholas. 2001. "'Do it Now!' Yakima, Wash, and the Campaign Against Rural Typhoid." *American Journal of Public Health* 91, no. 11: 1768–1775.
5. Woodward, Theodore E. 1992. "Epidemiologic Classics of Carter, Maxcy, Trudeau, and Smith." *Journal of Infectious Diseases* 165, no. 2: 235–244.
6. Allen, Shannen K, and Richard D. Semba. 2002. "The Trachoma 'Menace' in the United States, 1897–1960." *Survey of Ophthalmology* 47, no. 5: 500–509.
7. Bailey, Charles A. 1914. "Trachoma: A Survey of its Prevalence in the Mountain Sections of East Tennessee and Northern Georgia." *Public Health Reports* 29, no. 38: 2417–2433.
8. Siniscal, Arthur A. 1949. "Trachoma in Missouri." *Archives of Ophthalmology* 42, no. 4: 422–437.
9. Bollet, Alfred J. 1992. "Politics and Pellagra: The Epidemic of Pellagra in the U.S. in the Early Twentieth Century." *Yale Journal of Biology and Medicine* 65, no. 3: 211–221.
10. Bryan, Charles S., and Shane R. Mull. 2015. "Pellagra Pre-Goldberger: Rupert Blue, Fleming Sandwith, and the 'Vitamine Hypothesis'". *Transactions of the American Clinical and Climatological Association* 126: 20–45.
11. Kraut, Alan M. 2003. *Goldberger's War: The Life and Work of a Public Health Crusader*. New York: Hill and Wang.
12. Daniel, Thomas M. 2004. *Wade Hampton Frost, Pioneer Epidemiologist 1880–1938. Up to the Mountain*. New York: University of Rochester Press.
13. Williams, Ralph C. 1951. *The United States Public Health Service, 1798-1950*. Washington, DC: Commissioned Officers Association of the USPHS.
14. Breslin, John A. 2010. *One Hundred Years of Federal Mining Safety and Health Research*. Pittsburgh: NIOSH, CDC, Pittsburgh Research Laboratory, February.
15. Warren, B.S., and Edgar Sydenstricker. 1916. *Health Insurance: Its Relation to the Public Health*. Second Edition. Public Health Bulletin No. 76. Washington: GPO, March.
16. Wilson, Woodrow. 1917. *Executive Order 2571*. April 3.
17. Parascandola, John. 2001. "Militarization of the PHS Commissioned Corps." September. https://lhncbc.nlm.nih.gov/system/files/pub2001060.pdf
18. Public Law 65-12, 40 Stat. 76. *An Act to Authorize the President to Increase Temporarily the Military Establishment of the United States*. 65th Congress, Session I, Ch. 15, May 18, 1917.
19. Public Res. 65-45, 40 Stat. 1017. *Joint Resolution to Establish a Reserve of the Public Health Service*. 65th Congress, Session II, Ch. 196, October 27, 1918.

20. Warren, Benjamin S., and Charles F. Bolduan. 1919. "War Activities of the United States Public Health Service." *Public Health Reports* 34, no. 23, 1243-1267.
21. Blue, Rupert. 1917. *Annual Report of the Surgeon General of the Public Health Service of the United States for the Fiscal Year 1917*. Washington: GPO.
22. Blue, Rupert. 1918. *Annual Report of the Surgeon General of the Public Health Service of the United States for the Fiscal Year 1918*. Washington: GPO.
23. Public Law 65-193, 40 Stat. 845. *An Act Making Appropriations for the Support of the Army for the Fiscal Year ending June Thirtieth, Nineteen Hundred and Nineteen (Chamberlain-Kahn Act)*. 65th Congress, Session II, Ch. 143, July 9, 1918.
24. Public Law 57-244, 32 Stat. 728. *An Act to Regulate the Sale of Viruses, Serums, Toxins, and Analogous Products in the District of Columbia, to Regulate Interstate Traffic in Said Articles, and for Other Purposes*. 57th Congress, Session I, Ch. 1378, July 1, 1902.
25. Public Law 65-326, 40 Stat. 1302. *An Act to Authorize the Secretary of the Treasury to Provide Hospital and Sanatorium Facilities for Discharged Sick and Disabled Soldiers, Sailors, and Marines*. 65th Congress, Session III, Ch. 98, March 3, 1919.
26. Public Law 65-178, 40 Stat. 617. *An Act to Provide for Vocational Rehabilitation and Return to Civil Employment of Disabled Persons Discharged from the Military or Naval Forces of the United States, and for Other Purposes*. 65th Congress, Session II, Ch. 107, June 27, 1918.
27. Cumming, Hugh S. 1921. "The Work of the Public Health Service in the Care of Disabled Veterans of the World War." *Public Health Reports* 36, no, 32: 1893–1902.
28. Blue, Rupert. 1920. *Annual Report of the Surgeon General of the Public Health Service of the United States for the Fiscal Year 1920*. Washington: GPO.
29. Contagion. Historical Views of Diseases and Epidemics. Harvard Library. "Spanish Influenza in North America, 1918-1919."
https://curiosity.lib.harvard.edu/contagion/feature/spanish-influenza-in-north-america-1918-1919
30. Humphreys, Margaret. 2018. "The Influenza of 1918: Evolutionary Perspectives in a Historical Context." *Evolution, Medicine, and Public Health* 2018, no. 1: 219–229.
31. Centers for Disease Control and Prevention. 2018. "The 1918 Flu Pandemic: Why It Matters 100 Years Later." May 14. https://blogs.cdc.gov/publichealthmatters/2018/05/1918-flu/
32. Gernhart, Gary. 1999. "A Forgotten Enemy: PHS's Fight Against the 1918 Influenza Pandemic." *Public Health Reports* 114, no. 6: 559–561.
33. Blue, Rupert. 1919. *Annual Report of the Surgeon General of the Public Health Service of the United States for the Fiscal Year 1919*. Washington: GPO.
34. Snyder, Lynne Page. 1994. "Celebrating 75 Years of the Dental Corps: Origins and Early Years of Service." *Public Health Reports* 109, no. 5: 710–712.

CHAPTER FIVE, Pages 63–82

1. Lemons, J. Stanley. 1969. "The Sheppard-Towner Act: Progressivism in the 1920s." *Journal of American History* 55, no. 4: 776–786.
2. Public Law 67-97, 42 Stat. 224. *An Act for the Promotion of the Welfare and Hygiene of Maternity and Infancy, and for Other Purposes*. 67th Congress, Session I, Ch. 135, November 23, 1921.
3. Furman, Bess. 1973. *A Profile of the United States Public Health Service, 1798-1948*. Washington, DC: DHEW.
4. Public Law 67-47, 42 Stat. 147. *An Act to Establish a Veterans' Bureau and to Improve the Facilities and Service of Such Bureau, and Further to Amend and Modify the War Risk Insurance Act*. 67th Congress, Session I, Ch. 57, August 9, 1921.
5. Harding, Warren G. 1922. *Executive Order 3669*. April 29.

6. Cumming, Hugh S. 1922. *Annual Report of the Surgeon General of the Public Health Service of the United States for the Fiscal Year 1922*. Washington: GPO.
7. Public Law 100-527, 102 Stat. 2635. *An Act to Establish the Veterans' Administration as an Executive Department, and for Other Purposes*. 100th Congress, October 25, 1988.
8. Cumming, Hugh S. 1920, 1921. *Annual Report of the Surgeon General of the Public Health Service of the United States for the Fiscal Year 1920, 1921*. Washington: GPO.
9. Weisz, George. 2011. "Epidemiology and Health Care Reform. The National Health Survey of 1935-1936." *American Journal of Public Health* 101, no. 3: 438–447.
10. Williams, Ralph C. 1951. *The United States Public Health Service, 1798-1950*. Washington, DC: Commissioned Officers Association of the USPHS.
11. Public Law 71-106, 46 Stat. 150. *An Act to Provide for the Coordination of the Public-Health Activities of the Government, and for Other Purposes*. 71st Congress, Session II, Ch. 125, April 9, 1930.
12. Public Law 71-251, 46 Stat. 379. *An Act to Establish and Operate a National Institute of Health, to Create a System of Fellowships in Said Institute, and to Authorize the Government to Accept Donations for Use in Ascertaining the Cause, Prevention, and Cure of Disease Affecting Human Beings, and for Other Purposes*. 71st Congress, Session II, Ch. 320, May 26, 1930.
13. Swain, Donald C. 1962. "The Rise of a Research Empire: NIH, 1930 to 1950." *Science* 138, no. 3546: 1233–1237.
14. Public Law 64-299, 39 Stat. 872. *An Act to Provide for the Care and Treatment of Persons Afflicted with Leprosy and to Prevent the Spread of Leprosy in the United States*. 64th Congress, Session II, Ch. 26, February 3, 1917.
15. Casner, Nicholas. 2001. "'Do it Now!' Yakima, Wash, and the Campaign Against Rural Typhoid." *American Journal of Public Health* 91, no. 11: 1768–1775.
16. Cumming, Hugh S. 1930. *Annual Report of the Surgeon General of the Public Health Service of the United States for the Fiscal Year 1930*. Washington: GPO.
17. Westhoff, Dennis C. 1978. "Heating Milk for Microbial Destruction: A Historical Outline and Update." *Journal of Food Protection* 41, no. 2: 122–130.
18. Rosenau, Milton J. 1912. *The Milk Question*. Boston: Houghton Mifflin.
19. Heulings, S.M. 1925. "Commercial pasteurization, Bulletin No. 147." *American Journal of Public Health (NY)* 15, no. 8: 723–725.
20. Public Law 69-254, 44 Stat. 568. *An Act to Encourage and Regulate the Use of Aircraft in Commerce, and for Other Purposes*. 69th Congress, Session I, Ch. 344, May 20, 1926.
21. Cumming, Hugh S. 1928, 1929, 1930. *Annual Report of the Surgeon General of the Public Health Service of the United States for the Fiscal Year 1928, 1929, 1930*. Washington: GPO.
22. Allen, Diana B., and Sara B. Newman. 2021. "One Hundred Years of Health in US National Parks." *Parks Stewardship Forum* 37, 1: 95–105. Berkeley, CA: University of California Berkeley. https://escholarship.org/uc/item/8977g2b6#main
23. Public Law 70-672, 45 Stat. 1085. *An Act to Establish Two United States Narcotic Farms for the Confinement and Treatment of Persons Addicted to the Use of Habit-Forming Narcotic Drugs Who Have Been Convicted of Offenses Against the United States, and for Other Purposes*. 70th Congress, Session II, Ch. 82, January 19, 1929.
24. Public Law 71-203, 46 Stat. 273. *An Act to Authorize the Public Health Service to Provide Medical Service in the Federal Prisons*. 71st Congress, Session II, Ch. 256, May 13, 1930.
25. Public Law 71-201, 46 Stat. 270. *An Act to Establish a Hospital for Defective Delinquents*. 71st Congress, Session II, Ch. 254, May 13, 1930.

26. *Memorandum of Understanding Between the Bureau of Prisons, Department of Justice and the U.S. Public Health Service, Department of Health and Human Services*. September 30, 1991. https://www.ncr-cpl33.com/app/download/7236384628/MOU+Between+BOP++PHS.pdf
27. U.S. Department of Justice. 2016. "Review of the Federal Bureau of Prisons' Medical Staffing Challenges." 2016. Office of the Inspector General, March.
28. Bingham, J. Tyler, and Jeff J. Mallette. 2016. "Federal Bureau of Prisons Clinical Pharmacy Program Improves Patient A1C." *Journal of the American Pharmacists Association* 56, no. 2: 173–177.
29. Vause, Richard C., Art Beeler, and Mattese Miller-Blanks. 1997. "Seeking a Practice Challenge? PAs in Federal Prisons." *Journal of the Academy of Physician Assistants* 10, no. 2: 59–67 passim.
30. Brutsché, Robert L. 1989. "A Working Partnership for Health Care. The Bureau of Prisons and the Public Health Service." *Federal Prisons Journal* 1, no. 2: 32–38.
31. U.S. Department of Justice. 2008. "The Federal Bureau of Prison's Efforts to Manage Inmate Health Care." Office of the Inspector General, February.
32. Congressional Research Service. 2020. "Health Care for Federal Prisoners." *In Focus*. August 26.
33. Centers for Disease Control and Prevention. 2022. "The Syphilis Study at Tuskegee Timeline." December 5. https://www.cdc.gov/tuskegee/timeline.htm
34. Brandt, Allan M. 1978. "Racism and Research: the Case of the Tuskegee Syphilis Study." *The Hastings Center Report* 8, no. 6: 21–29.
35. Sledge, Daniel. 2017. "Linking Public Health and Individual Medicine: The Health Policy Approach of Surgeon General Thomas Parran." *American Journal of Public Health* 107, no. 4: 509–516.
36. Social Security Act of 1935. Public Law 74-271, 49 Stat. 620. 74th Congress, Session I, Ch. 531, August 14, 1935.
37. Waller, C.E. 1935. "The Social Security Act in Its Relation to Public Health." *American Journal of Public Health and the Nation's Health* 25, no. 11: 1186–1194.
38. Centers for Disease Control and Prevention. 1998. "Preventing Emerging Infectious Diseases: A Strategy for the 21st Century. Overview of the Updated CDC Plan." *Morbidity and Mortality Weekly Report* 47, no. RR-15: 1–15.
39. Centers for Disease Control and Prevention. 2023. "Core Elements of Hospital Antibiotic Stewardship Programs." September 7.
https://www.cdc.gov/antibiotic-use/core-elements/hospital.html#
40. World Health Organization. 2019. "Ten Threats to Global Health in 2019."
https://www.who.int/news-room/spotlight/ten-threats-to-global-health-in-2019

CHAPTER SIX, *Pages 83–106*

1. Social Security Act of 1935. Public Law 74-271, 49 Stat. 620. 74th Congress, Session I, Ch. 531, August 14, 1935.
2. Lyons, Michele. 2006. "70 Acres of Science: The National Institute of Health Moves to Bethesda." National Institutes of Health, Office of History.
3. Parran, Thomas. 1937. *Annual Report of the Surgeon General of the Public Health Service of the United States for the Fiscal Year 1937*. Washington: GPO.
4. Public Law 75-244, 50 Stat. 559. *An Act to Provide for, Foster, and Aid in Coordinating Research Relating to Cancer; to Establish the National Cancer Institute; and for Other Purposes*. 75th Congress, Session I, Ch. 565, August 5, 1937.

5. Furman, Bess. 1973. *A Profile of the United States Public Health Service, 1798-1948*. Washington, DC: DHEW.
6. Brandt, Allan M. 1985, 1987 (Expanded Edition). *No Magic Bullet. A Social History of Venereal Disease in the United States Since 1880*. New York: Oxford University Press.
7. Public Law 75-540, 52 Stat. 439. 75th Congress, Session III, Ch. 267, May 24, 1938.
8. Parran, Thomas. 1940, 1941. *Annual Report of the Surgeon General of the Public Health Service of the United States for the Fiscal Year 1940, 1941*. Washington: GPO.
9. Wright, John J. 1951. "Venereal Disease Control." *Journal of the American Medical Association* 147, no. 15: 1408–1411.
10. Spector-Bagdady, Kayte, and Paul A. Lombardo PA. 2019. "U.S. Public Health Service STD Experiments in Guatemala (1946-1948) and Their Aftermath." *Ethics & Human Research* 41, no. 2: 29–34.
11. Presidential Commission for the Study of Bioethical Issues. 2011. "'Ethically Impossible.' STD Research in Guatemala from 1946 to 1948." Washington, DC, September.
12. Public Law 57-244, 32 Stat. 728. *An Act to Regulate the Sale of Viruses, Serums, Toxins, and Analogous Products in the District of Columbia, to Regulate Interstate Traffic in Said Articles, and for Other Purposes*. 57th Congress, Session I, Ch. 1378, July 1, 1902.
13. Public Law 59-384, 34 Stat. 768. *An Act for Preventing the Manufacture, Sale, or Transportation of Adulterated or Misbranded or Poisonous or Deleterious Foods, Drugs, Medicines, and Liquors, and for Regulating Traffic Therein, and for Other Purposes*. 59th Congress, Session I, Ch. 3915, June 30, 1906.
14. Public Law 75-717, 52 Stat. 1040. *An Act to Prohibit the Movement in Interstate Commerce of Adulterated and Misbranded Food, Drugs, Devices, and Cosmetics, and for Other Purposes*. 75th Congress, Session III, Ch. 675, June 25, 1938.
15. Public Law 97-414, 96 Stat. 2049. *An Act to Amend the Federal Food, Drug, and Cosmetic Act to Facilitate the Development of Drugs for Rare Diseases and Conditions, and for Other Purposes*. 97th Congress, January 4, 1983.
16. Public Law 76-19, 53 Stat. 561. *An Act to Provide for Reorganizing Agencies of the Government, and for Other Purposes*. 76th Congress, Session I, Ch. 36, April 3, 1939.
17. Public Law 78-410, 58 Stat. 682. *An Act to Consolidate and Revise the Laws Relating to the Public Health Service, and for Other Purposes*. 78th Congress, Session II, Ch. 373, July 1, 1944.
18. Parran, Thomas. 1941. *Annual Report of the Surgeon General of the Public Health Service of the United States for the Fiscal Year 1941*. Washington: GPO.
19. Public Law 76-783, 54 Stat. 885. *An Act to Provide for the Common Defense by Increasing the Personnel of the Armed Forces of the United States and Providing for Its Training*. 76th Congress, Session III, Ch. 720, September 16, 1940.
20. Department of the Army. 1955. "Personal Health Measures and Immunization." *Preventive Medicine in World War II. Volume III*. Washington, DC: Office of the Surgeon General, Office of Medical History.
21. Public Law 78-74, 57 Stat. 153. *An Act to Provide for the Training of Nurses for the Armed Forces, Governmental and Civilian Hospitals, Health Agencies, and War Industries, Through Grants to Institutions Providing Such Training, and for Other Purposes*. 78th Congress, Session I, Ch. 126, June 15, 1943.
22. Parran, Thomas. 1944. *Annual Report of the United States Public Health Service for the Fiscal Year 1944*. Washington: GPO.
23. U.S. Public Health Service. 1950. *The United States Cadet Nurse Corps [1943-1948] and Other Federal Nurse Training Programs*. PHS Publication No. 38. Washington: GPO.

24. "Obituary—RADM Lucile Petry Leone, USPHS (Ret.), 1902-1999." *Commissioned Corps Bulletin* XIV, no. 2: 4.
25. Truman, Harry S. 1945. *Executive Order 9575–Declaring the Commissioned Corps of the Public Health Service to Be a Military Service and Prescribing Regulations Therefor*. June 21.
26. Parascandola, John. 2001. "Militarization of the PHS Commissioned Corps." September. https://lhncbc.nlm.nih.gov/system/files/pub2001060.pdf
27. Parran, Thomas. 1943. *Annual Report of the United States Public Health Service for the Fiscal Year 1943*. Washington: GPO.
28. Williams, Ralph C. 1951. *The United States Public Health Service, 1798-1950*. Washington, DC: Commissioned Officers Association of the USPHS.
29. Fawcett, Paul. 2016. "Coast Guard Medical in World War II." *The Cutter/Main Prop* 47: 8–10.
30. Parran, Thomas J. 1945, 1946. *Annual Report of the Federal Security Agency, Section Four, United States Public Health Service for the Fiscal Year 1945, 1946*. Washington: GPO.
31. U.S. Public Health Service. 1944. "Tuberculosis Control Division Established in Bureau of State Services, United States Public Health Service." *Public Health Reports* 59, no. 28: 917–919.
32. Fiset, Louis. 2020. "Medical Care in Camp." *Densho Encyclopedia*. October 5. https://encyclopedia.densho.org/Medical%20care%20in%20camp/
33. Public Law 79-487, 60 Stat. 421. *An Act to Amend the Public Health Service Act to Provide for Research Relating to Psychiatric Disorders and to Aid in the Development of More Effective Methods of Prevention, Diagnosis, and Treatment of Such Disorders, and for Other Purposes*. 79th Congress, Session II, Ch. 538, July 3, 1946.
34. Grob, Gerald N. 1996. "Creation of the National Institute of Mental Health." *Public Health Reports* 111, no. 4: 378–381.
35. Chung, Andrea Park, Martin Gaynor, and Seth Richards-Shubik. 2017. "Subsidies and Structure: The Lasting Impact of the Hill-Burton Program on the Hospital Industry." *Review of Economics and Statistics* 99, no. 5: 926–943.

Chapter Seven, Pages 107–126

1. National Institute of Dental and Craniofacial Research, NIH. 2018. "The Story of Fluoridation." July. https://www.nidcr.nih.gov/health-info/fluoride/the-story-of-fluoridation
2. Centers for Disease Control and Prevention. 1999. "Achievements in Public Health, 1900-1999: Fluoridation of Drinking Water to Prevent Dental Caries." *Morbidity and Mortality Weekly Report* 48, no. 41: 933–940.
3. Public Law 62-265, 37 Stat. 309. *An Act to Change the Name of the Public Health and Marine-Hospital Service to the Public Health Service, to Increase the Pay of Officers of Said Service, and for Other Purposes*. 62nd Congress, Session II, Ch. 288, August 14, 1912.
4. Public Law 80-845, 62 Stat. 1155. *An Act to Provide for Water Pollution Control Activities in the Public Health Service of the Federal Security Agency and in the Federal Works Agency, and for Other Purposes*. 80th Congress, Session II, Ch. 758, June 30, 1948.
5. Schwob, Carl E. 1953. "Federal Water Pollution Control Act: Objectives and Policies." *Journal of Industrial and Engineering Chemistry* 45, no. 12: 2648–2652.
6. Schrenk, H.H., Harry Heimann, George D. Clayton, et al. 1949. "Air Pollution in Donora, Pa. Epidemiology of the Unusual Smog Episode of October 1948. Preliminary Report." *Public Health Bulletin No. 306*. Washington, DC: Federal Security Agency, PHS.

7. Public Law 84-159, 69 Stat. 322. *An Act to Provide Research and Technical Assistance Relating to Air Pollution Control*. 84th Congress, Ch. 360, July 14, 1955.
8. US Environmental Protection Agency. 2022. "Evolution of the Clean Air Act." November 28. https://www.epa.gov/clean-air-act-overview/evolution-clean-air-act
9. Foege, William H. 1996. "Alexander D. Langmuir—His Impact on Public Health." *American Journal of Epidemiology* 144, no. 8 (Suppl): S11–S15.
10. Juskewitch, Justin E., Carmen J. Tapia, and Anthony J. Windebank AJ. 2010. "Lessons from the Salk Polio Vaccine: Methods for and Risks of Rapid Translation." *Journal of Clinical and Translational Science* 3, no. 4: 182–185.
11. Offit, Paul A. 2005. "The Cutter Incident, 50 Years Later." *New England Journal of Medicine* 352, no. 14: 1411–1412.
12. Margalit Fox. 2013. *Hilary Koprowski, Who Developed First Live-Virus Polio Vaccine, Dies at 96*. New York Times, April 20.
13. Public Law 67-85, 42 Stat. 208. *An Act Authorizing Appropriations and Expenditures for the Administration of Indian Affairs, and for Other Purposes*. 67th Congress, Session I, Ch. 115, November 2, 1921.
14. Public Law 83-568, 68 Stat. 674. *An Act to Transfer the Maintenance and Operation of Hospital and Health Facilities for Indians to the Public Health Service, and for Other Purposes*. 83rd Congress, Session II, Ch. 658, August 5, 1954.
15. Rife, James P., and Alan J. Dellapenna Jr. 2009. *Caring & Curing. A History of the Indian Health Service*. PHS Commissioned Officers Foundation for the Advancement of Public Health.
16. Public Law 94-437, 90 Stat. 1400. *An Act to Implement the Federal Responsibility for the Care and Education of the Indian People by Improving the Services and Facilities of Federal Indian Health Programs and Encouraging Maximum Participation of Indians in Such Programs, and for Other Purposes*. 94th Congress, September 30, 1976.
17. Warne, Donald, and Linda Bane Frizzell. 2014. "American Indian Health Policy: Historical Trends and Contemporary Issues." *American Journal of Public Health* 104, Suppl 3: S263–S267.
18. HHS, Indian Health Service. 2018. "Urban Indian Health Program." October. https://www.ihs.gov/newsroom/factsheets/uihp/
19. Fisher, Richard, Allen Brands, and Rick Herrier. 1995. "History of the Indian Health Service Model of Pharmacy Practice: Innovations in Pharmaceutical Care." *Pharmacy in History* 37, no. 2: 107–122.
20. Bott, Anne Marie, John Collins, Stephanie Daniels-Costa, et al.; United States Public Health Service National Clinical Pharmacy Specialist Committee. 2019. "Clinical Pharmacists Improve Patient Outcomes and Expand Access to Care." *Federal Practitioner* 36, no. 10: 471–475.
21. U.S. General Accounting Office. 1976. "Investigation of Allegations Concerning Indian Health Service." November 4. https://www.gao.gov/assets/hrd-77-3.pdf
22. Lawrence, Jane. 2000. "The Indian Health Service and the Sterilization of Native American Women." *American Indian Quarterly* 24, no. 3: 400–419.
23. Walter, George. 1989. "The Atomic Bomb, Fallout and the Public Health Service." *Commissioned Corps Bulletin* III, no. 3: 5.
24. Utah Department of Environmental Quality. 2022. "Impacts of Radiation from Aboveground Nuclear Tests on Southern Utah." January 19. https://deq.utah.gov/public-interest/impacts-of-radiation-from-aboveground-nuclear-tests-on-southern-utah

25. Environmental Protection Agency. 1987. "Off-Site Environmental Monitoring Report: Radiation Monitoring Around United States Nuclear Test Areas, Calendar Year 1986."
26. National Atomic Testing Museum. 2021. "In Memoriam: Charles F. Costa." *The Blast!* September 8.
27. Advisory Committee on Human Radiation Experiments. 1995. "Chapter 12: The Uranium Miners." Washington, DC: Department of Energy. October.
https://ehss.energy.gov/ohre/roadmap/achre/summary.html
28. Alvarez, Robert. 2013. "Uranium Mining and the U.S. Nuclear Weapons Program." Federation of American Scientists. November 14.
https://fas.org/publication/uranium-mining-u-s-nuclear-weapons-program-3/
29. Centers for Disease Control and Prevention. 2021. "Zoonotic Diseases." July 1.
https://www.cdc.gov/onehealth/basics/zoonotic-diseases.html
30. Pincock, Stephen. 2014. "James Harlan Steele." *Lancet* 383, no. 9913: 212.
31. Schultz, Myron G. 2014. "In Memoriam: James Harlan Steele (1913–2013)." *Emerging Infectious Diseases* 20, no. 3: 514–515.
32. Public Law 84-941, 70 Stat. 960. *An Act to Amend Title III of the Public Health Service Act, and for Other Purposes*. 84th Congress, August 3, 1956.
33. Henderson, D.A., Brooke Courtney, Thomas V. Inglesby, et al. 2009. "Public Health and Medical Responses to the 1957-58 Influenza Pandemic." *Biosecurity and Bioterrorism* 7, no. 3: 265–273.
34. Henderson, D.A. 2016. "The Development of Surveillance Systems." *American Journal of Epidemiology* 183, no. 5: 381–386.
35. Public Law 84-652, 70 Stat. 489. *An Act to Provide for a Continuing Survey and Special Studies of Sickness and Disability in the United States, and for Periodic Reports of the Results Thereof, and for Other Purposes*. 84th Congress. Ch. 510, July 3, 1956.
36. Division of Public Health Methods, Office of the Surgeon General, PHS. 1957. "The National Health Survey Act." *Public Health Reports* 72, no. 1: 1–4.
37. Institute of Medicine. Committee for Review and Evaluation of the Medical Use Program of the Nuclear Regulatory Commission; Gottfried, Kate-Louise D., and Gary Penn, eds. 1996. *Radiation in Medicine: A Need for Regulatory Reform*. Washington, DC: National Academies Press.
38. Wynder, Ernest L., and Evarts A. Graham. 1950. "Tobacco Smoking as a Possible Etiologic Factor in Bronchiogenic Carcinoma." *Journal of the American Medical Association* 143, no. 4: 329–336.
39. Burney, Leroy E. 1957. "Excessive Cigarette Smoking. Statement." *Public Health Reports* 72, no. 9: 786.
40. Burney, Leroy E. 1959. "Smoking and Lung Cancer. A Statement of the Public Health Service." *Journal of the American Medical Association* 171, no. 13: 1829–1837.
41. Parascandola, Mark. 2001. "Cigarettes and the US Public Health Service in the 1950s." *American Journal of Public Health* 91, no. 2: 196–205.
42. Hamowy, Ronald. 2007. *Government and Public Health in America*. Cheltenham, UK: Edward Elgar Publishing.
43. Dambach, Charles A. 1964. "A Review of the Report of the Committee on Environmental Health Problems to the Surgeon General." *Natural Resources Journal* 4, no. 2: 219–246.
44. U.S. Public Health Service. 1960. *Final Report of the Study Group on Mission and Organization of the Public Health Service*. Washington, DC: DHEW. GPO: O–553903.

CHAPTER EIGHT, Pages 127–140

1. As quoted in: Stobbe, Mike. 2014. *Surgeon General's Warning: How Politics Crippled the Nation's Doctor*. Oakland: University of California Press.
2. Mullan, Fitzhugh. 1989. *Plagues and Politics. The Story of the United States Public Health Service*. New York: Basic Books.
3. Burney, Leroy E. 1959. "Smoking and Lung Cancer. A Statement of the Public Health Service." *Journal of the American Medical Association* 171, no. 13: 1829–1837.
4. Royal College of Physicians. 1962. *Smoking and Health. Summary of a Report of The Royal College of Physicians of London on Smoking in Relation to Cancer of the Lung and Other Diseases*. London: Pitman Medical Publishing.
5. Public Health Service. 1964. *Smoking and Health. Report of the Advisory Committee to the Surgeon General of the Public Health Service*. Washington, DC: U.S. Department of Health, Education, and Welfare. PHS Publication No. 1103, GPO.
6. Centers for Disease Control and Prevention, Office on Smoking and Health. 2014. *The Health Consequences of Smoking–50 Years of Progress. A Report of the Surgeon General*. Atlanta, GA: U.S. Department of Health and Human Services, January.
7. Alberg, Anthony J., Donald R. Shopland, and K. Michael Cummings. 2014. "The 2014 Surgeon General's Report: Commemorating the 50th Anniversary of the 1964 Report of the Advisory Committee to the US Surgeon General and Updating the Evidence on the Health Consequences of Cigarette Smoking." *American Journal of Epidemiology* 179, no. 4: 403–412.
8. Dambach, Charles A. 1964. "A Review of the Report of the Committee on Environmental Health Problems to the Surgeon General." *Natural Resources Journal* 4, no. 2: 219–246.
9. "Reorganization Plan No. 2 of 1966. Water Pollution Control." Prepared by the President and Transmitted to the Congress, February 28, 1966. Effective May 10, 1966.
10. Public Law 89-97, 79 Stat. 286. *An Act to Provide a Hospital Insurance Program for the Aged Under the Social Security Act with a Supplementary Medical Benefits Program and an Expanded Program of Medical Assistance, to Increase Benefits Under the Old-Age, Survivors, and Disability Insurance System, to Improve the Federal-State Public Assistance Programs, and for Other Purposes*. 89th Congress, July 30, 1965.
11. Snoke, Albert W. 1969. "The Unsolved Problem of the Career Professional in the Establishment of National Health Policy." *American Journal of Public Health and the Nation's Health* 59, no. 9: 1575–1588.
12. National Library of Medicine. 1988. "History of Health Services Research Project. Interview with Dr. Philip Randolph Lee." Interviewer Fitzhugh Mullan. National Information Center on Health Services Research and Health Care Technology, October 5.
https://www.nlm.nih.gov/hmd/nichsr/lee.html
13. "Reorganization Plan No. 3 of 1966. Public Health Service." Prepared by the President and Transmitted to the Congress, April 25, 1966. Effective June 25, 1966.
14. Reynolds, P. Preston. 1997. "The Federal Government's Use of Title VI and Medicare to Racially Integrate Hospitals in the United States, 1963 Through 1967." *American Journal of Public Health* 87, no. 11: 1850–1858.
15. Smith, David Barton. 2015. "The 'Golden Rules' for Eliminating Disparities: Title VI, Medicare, and the Implementation of the Affordable Care Act." *Health Matrix: The Journal of Law-Medicine* 25, no, 1: 33–59.
https://scholarlycommons.law.case.edu/healthmatrix/vol25/iss1/4

16. Public Law 89-239, 79 Stat. 926. *An Act to Amend the Public Health Service Act to Assist in Combating Heart Disease, Cancer, Stroke, and Related Diseases*. 89th Congress, October 6, 1965.
17. Centers for Disease Control and Prevention. 2020. "History of Quarantine." July 20.
https://www.cdc.gov/quarantine/historyquarantine.html
18. Centers for Disease Control and Prevention. 2020. "Rubella in the U.S." December 31.
https://www.cdc.gov/rubella/about/in-the-us.html
19. National Institutes of Health. 1966. "First Effective Vaccine Against Rubella Promises Control of Infection, Defects." *NIH Record* XVIII, no. 10, May 17.
20. Jester, Barbara J., Timothy M. Uyeki, and Daniel B. Jernigan. 2020. "Fifty Years of Influenza A(H3N2) Following the Pandemic of 1968." *American Journal of Public Health* 110, no. 5: 669–676.
21. LaRocque, Regina, and Jason B. Harris. 2023. "Cholera: Clinical Features, Diagnosis, Treatment, and Prevention." *UpToDate*. Wolters Kluwer, January 29.
https://www.uptodate.com/contents/cholera-clinical-features-diagnosis-treatment-and-prevention/print
22. "Control of diarrhoeal diseases: WHO's programme takes shape." 1978. *WHO Chronicle* 32, no. 10: 369–72.
23. McPherson, Chloe. 2019. "2019: The Frog Skin That Saved 50 Million Lives." The Golden Goose Award. Awardee: David Sachar. September 10.
https://www.goldengooseaward.org/01awardees/frog-skin-cholera
24. Ruxin, Joshua Nalibow. 1994. "Magic Bullet: The History of Oral Rehydration Therapy." *Medical History* 38, no. 4: 363–97.

CHAPTER NINE, *Pages 141–152*

1. Stobbe, Mike. 2014. *Surgeon General's Warning: How Politics Crippled the Nation's Doctor*. Oakland: University of California Press.
2. Mullan, Fitzhugh. 1989. *Plagues and Politics. The Story of the United States Public Health Service*. New York: Basic Books.
3. Hamowy, Ronald. 2007. *Government and Public Health in America*. Cheltenham, UK: Edward Elgar Publishing.
4. Strosberg, Martin A. 1984. "The Commissioned Corps of the U.S. Public Health Service: A Personnel System Under Siege." *Journal of Public Health Policy* 5, no. 1: 74–82.
5. "Reorganization Plan No. 3 of 1970. Plans to establish the Environmental Protection Agency and the National Oceanic and Atmospheric Administration." July 9, 1970.
6. As quoted in: Coulston, Frederick, and Friedhelm Korte, eds. 1974. *Environmental Quality and Safety. Global Aspects of Chemistry, Toxicology and Technology as Applied to the Environment. Vol. 3*. New York: Academic Press.
7. Markowitz, Gerald, and David Rosner. 2013. *Lead Wars: The Politics of Science and the Fate of America's Children*. Berkeley, CA: University of California Press.
8. "Medical Aspects of Childhood Lead Poisoning." 1971. *HSMHA Health Reports* 86, no. 2: 140–143.
9. Rosner, David, and Gerald Markowitz. 1985. "A 'Gift of God'?: The Public Health Controversy Over Leaded Gasoline During the 1920s." *American Journal of Public* Health 75, no. 4: 344–352.
10. Nriagu, Jerome O. 1990. "The Rise and Fall of Leaded Gasoline." *Science of the Total Environment* 92, 13–28.
11. Fowler, Tristan. 2008. "A Brief History of Lead Regulation." *Science Progress*. October 21.

12. Steinfeld, Jesse L. 1971. "Remarks at the National Interagency Council on Smoking and Health Program." Washington, DC, January 11. https://www.industrydocuments.ucsf.edu/docs/#id=gykd0121
13. Steinfeld, Jesse L. 1972. *The Health Consequences of Smoking. A Report of the Surgeon General: 1972*. Washington, D.C.: U.S. Department of Health, Education, and Welfare, Public Health Service, Health Services and Mental Health Administration.
14. Public Law 91-596, 84 Stat. 1590. *An Act to Assure Safe and Healthful Working Conditions for Working Men and Women; by Authorizing Enforcement of the Standards Developed Under the Act; by Assisting and Encouraging the States in Their Efforts to Assure Safe and Healthful Working Conditions; by Providing for Research, Information, Education, and Training in the Field of Occupational Safety and Health; and for Other Purposes*, December 29, 1970.
15. Health Resources and Services Administration, HHS. 2022. *The National Health Service Corps at 50: Accomplishments, Adaptations, and Aspirations. Perspectives of the National Advisory Council on the National Health Service Corps.*
16. Public Law 91-623, 84 Stat. 1868. *An Act to Amend the Public Health Service Act to Authorize the Assignment of Commissioned Officers of the Public Health Service to Areas with Critical Medical Manpower Shortages, to Encourage Health Personnel to Practice in Areas Where Shortages of Such Personnel Exist, and for Other Purposes*, December 31, 1970.
17. Pathman, Donald E., Byron J. Crouse, Luis F. Padilla, et al. 2009. "American Recovery and Reinvestment Act and the Expansion and Streamlining of the National Health Service Corps: A Great Opportunity for Service-Minded Family Physicians." *Journal of the American Board of Family Medicine* 22, 5: 582–584.
18. As quoted in: Sullivan, Patricia. 2005. "S. Paul Ehrlich, Acting Surgeon General, Dies." *Washington Post*, January 9.
19. Public Law 93-641, 88 Stat. 2225. *An Act to Amend the Public Health Service Act to Assure the Development of a National Health Policy and of Effective State and Area Health Planning and Resources Development Programs, and for Other Purposes*, January 4, 1975.
20. Wing, Kenneth R., and Andreas G. Schneider. 1976. "National Health Planning and Resources Development Act of 1974: Implications for the Poor." Seattle University School of Law Digital Commons, 683–693. https://digitalcommons.law.seattleu.edu/faculty/372
21. Barclay, William R. 1976. "Influenza Will Not Occur in 1976 if We are Determined to Prevent It. *And*, Cooper, Theodore. 1976. "The National Influenza Immunization Program." Editorials. *Journal of the American Medical Association* 235, no. 25: 2753–2754.
22. Sencer, David J., and J. Donald Millar. 2006. "Reflections on the 1976 swine flu vaccination program." *Emerging Infectious Diseases* 12, no. 1: 29–33.
23. Honigsbaum, Mark. 2016. "Legionnaires' disease: Revisiting the Puzzle of the Century." *Lancet* 388, no. 10043: 456–7.
24. Centers for Disease Control and Prevention. 2021. "*Legionella* (Legionnaires' Disease and Pontiac Fever)." March 25. https://www.cdc.gov/legionella/fastfacts.html
25. Reye, R.D.K., Graeme Morgan, and J. Baral. 1963. "Encephalopathy and Fatty Degeneration of the Viscera. A Disease Entity in Childhood." *Lancet* 2, no. 7311: 749–752.
26. Barrett, Michael J., Eugene S. Hurwitz, Martha F. Rogers, and Lawrence B. Schonberger. 1984. "The National Reye Syndrome Surveillance System, 1983." *Morbidity and Mortality Weekly Report: Surveillance Summaries* 33, no. 3SS: 9SS–13SS.
27. "Surgeon General's Advisory on the Use of Salicylates and Reye Syndrome." 1982. *Morbidity and Mortality Weekly Report* 31, no. 22: 289–290.

CHAPTER TEN, Pages 153–162

1. National Library of Medicine. 1981. "Julius B. Richmond: An Oral History." Interviewer Peter D. Olch. History of Medicine, April 17, May 18.
   https://collections.nlm.nih.gov/catalog/nlm:nlmuid-2791102R-oh
2. Public Law 95-626, 92 Stat. 3551. *An Act to Amend the Public Health Service Act and Related Health Laws to Revise and Extend the Programs of Financial Assistance for the Delivery of Health Services, the Provision of Preventive Health Services, and for Other Purposes,* November 10, 1978.
3. World Health Organization. 1980. "The Global Eradication of Smallpox. Final Report of the Global Commission for the Certification of Smallpox Eradication, Geneva, December 1979." Geneva: World Health Organization.
4. Foege, William H., J. Donald Millar, and J. Michael Lane. 1971. "Selective Epidemiologic Control in Smallpox Eradication." *American Journal of Epidemiology* 94, no. 4: 311–315.
5. Henderson, Donald A. 2011. "The Eradication of Smallpox – An Overview of the Past, Present, and Future." *Vaccine* 29, Suppl 4: D7–D9.
6. Ogden, Horace G. 1987. "CDC and The Smallpox Crusade." Washington, DC: U.S. Department of Health and Human Services, Public Health Service, Centers for Disease Control. HHS Publication No. (CDC) 87-8400, GPO.
7. Scott, Harold G. 1995. "The United States Public Health Service in the Vietnam War." *Commissioned Corps Bulletin* IX, no. 8: 11, 12.
8. "Harold George and Bettie Scott." 2016. Leitz-Eagan Funeral Home. Metairie, LA. January 9.
   https://obits.nola.com/us/obituaries/nola/name/harold-george-bettie-scott-obituary?pid=177226147
9. Klein, Melissa K. 1998. "The Legacy of the 'Yellow Berets': The Vietnam War, the Doctor Draft, and the NIH Associate Training Program." Manuscript, 1998. Bethesda, MD: NIH History Office, National Institutes of Health.
10. Khot, Sandeep, Buhm Soon Park, and W.T. Longstreth Jr. 2011. "The Vietnam War and Medical Research: Untold Legacy of the U.S. Doctor Draft and the NIH 'Yellow Berets'". *Academic Medicine* 86, no. 4: 502–508.
11. Smith, Ethan. 2021. "Annals of NIH history: from yellow berets to Nobel Laureates." *The NIH Catalyst* 29, no. 2: 1,6,7.
12. Public Law 71-251, 46 Stat. 379. *An Act to Establish and Operate a National Institute of Health, to Create a System of Fellowships in Said Institute, and to Authorize the Government to Accept Donations for Use in Ascertaining the Cause, Prevention, and Cure of Disease Affecting Human Beings, and for Other Purposes.* 71st Congress, Session II, Ch. 320, May 26, 1930.
13. Fabrikant, Jacob I. 2010. "Decision-Making and Radiological Protection at Three Mile Island: Response of the Department of Health, Education and Welfare." Berkeley, CA: Lawrence Berkeley National Laboratory, July 29. https://escholarship.org/uc/item/90p468n9
14. Califano JA Jr. 1978. "Address by Joseph A. Califano, Jr. before the National Interagency Council on Smoking and Health." Shoreham Hotel. Washington, DC, January 11.
    https://www.industrydocuments.ucsf.edu/tobacco/docs/#id=mfnp0094
15. Richmond, Julius B. 1979. *Smoking and Health: A Report of the Surgeon General.* Washington, DC: U.S. Department of Health, Education, and Welfare, Public Health Service, Office on Smoking and Health.
16. Parran, Thomas J. 1937. *Annual Report of the Surgeon General of the Public Health Service of the United States for the Fiscal Year 1937.* Washington: GPO, 1937.

17. Lalonde, Mark. 1974. "A New Perspective on the Health of Canadians. A Working Document." Ottawa: Government of Canada, April.
https://www.phac-aspc.gc.ca/ph-sp/pdf/perspect-eng.pdf
18. Green, Lawrence W., and Jonathan Fielding. 2011. "The U.S. Healthy People Initiative: Its Genesis and Its Sustainability." *Annual Review of Public Health* 32: 451-470.
19. *Healthy People. The Surgeon General's Report on Health Promotion and Disease Prevention*. 1979. Washington, DC: U.S. Department of Health, Education, and Welfare, Public Health Service, Office of the Assistant Secretary for Health and Surgeon General, 1979. DHEW (PHS) Publication No. 79-55071.

CHAPTER ELEVEN, *Pages 163–174*

1. Koop, C. Everett. 1991. *Koop: The Memoirs of America's Family Doctor*. New York: Random House.
2. Public Law 97-35, 95 Stat. 357. *An Act to Provide for Reconciliation Pursuant to Section 301 of the First Concurrent Resolution on the Budget for the Fiscal Year 1982*, August 13, 1981.
3. "PHS Hospital Funding Ended." 1982. In CQ Almanac 1981, 37th ed., 502. Washington, DC: Congressional Quarterly.
https://library.cqpress.com/cqalmanac/document.php?id=cqal81-1173373
4. Brandt Jr, Edward N. 1981. "Block Grants and the Resurgence of Federalism." *Public Health Reports* 96, no. 6: 495–497.
5. Tomfohrde, Robert F., and Laurie A. Soman. 1984. "Local Perceptions of Federal Block Grants." *Western Journal of Medicine* 140, no. 6: 961–963.
6. Reich, David, Isaac Shapiro, Chloe Cho, and Richard Kogan R. 2017. "Block-Granting Low-Income Programs Leads to Large Funding Declines Over Time, History Shows." Center on Budget and Policy Priorities, February 22.
https://www.cbpp.org/research/federal-budget/block-granting-low-income-programs-leads-to-large-funding-declines-over-time
7. Mullan, Fitzhugh. 1989. *Plagues and Politics. The Story of the United States Public Health Service*. New York: Basic Books.
8. Stobbe, Mike. 2014. *Surgeon General's Warning: How Politics Crippled the Nation's Doctor*. Oakland: University of California Press.
9. "The C. Everett Koop Papers. Tobacco, Second-Hand Smoke, and the Campaign for a Smoke-Free America." Profiles in Science. National Library of Medicine, NIH.
https://profiles.nlm.nih.gov/spotlight/qq/feature/tobacco
10. Koop, C. Everett. 1986. *The Health Consequences of Involuntary Smoking. A Report of the Surgeon General*. Rockville, MD: U.S. Department of Health and Human Services, Public Health Service, Centers for Disease Control, Center for Health Promotion and Education, Office on Smoking and Health.
11. Koop, C. Everett. 1988. *The Health Consequences of Smoking: Nicotine Addiction. A Report of the Surgeon General*. Rockville, MD: U.S. Department of Health and Human Services, Public Health Service, Centers for Disease Control, Center for Health Promotion and Education, Office on Smoking and Health.
12. Lushniak, Boris D. 2014. "Chapter 2. Fifty Years of Change 1964–2014." In, *The Health Consequences of Smoking—50 Years of Progress. A Report of the Surgeon General*. Atlanta, GA: U.S. Department of Health and Human Services, Centers for Disease Control and Prevention, National Center for Chronic Disease Prevention and Health Promotion, Office on Smoking and Health, 2014.
13. American Academy of Pediatrics. 2006. "C. Everett Koop, MD, ScD." Interviewed by Moritz Ziegler. Pediatric History Center. Oral History Project. May 8.

REFERENCES | 355

https://downloads.aap.org/AAP/Gartner%20Pediatric%20History/Koop.pdf

14. Koop, C. Everett. 1986. *Surgeon General's Report on Acquired Immune Deficiency Syndrome*. https://profiles.nlm.nih.gov/spotlight/qq/catalog/nlm:nlmuid-101584930X1111-doc
15. The C. Everett Koop Papers. "AIDS, The Surgeon General, and the Politics of Public Health." Profiles in Science. National Library of Medicine, NIH. https://profiles.nlm.nih.gov/spotlight/qq/feature/aids
16. Office of NIH History and Stetten Museum. 1993. "Anthony S. Fauci, M.D. In Their Own Words. NIH Researchers Recall the Early Years of AIDS." Interviewers Victoria A. Harden and Dennis Rodrigues, June 29. https://history.nih.gov/display/history/Dr.+Anthony+S.+Fauci+Transcript
17. Terry, Luther L. 1982. "Letter to C. Everett Koop, February 22." National Library of Medicine. https://collections.nlm.nih.gov/catalog/nlm:nlmuid-101584930X546-doc
18. Pear, Robert. 1982. "Budget Office Urging Sharp Cuts in Scope of Public Health Service." *New York Times*, December 1.
19. Byrne, Gregory. 1987. "Koop Seeks Health Corps 'Uniformity'". *The Scientist. News*, June 1.
20. Koop, C. Everett, and Harold M. Ginzburg. 1989. "The Revitalization of the Public Health Service Commissioned Corps." *Public Health Reports* 104, no. 2: 105–110.
21. Koop, C. Everett. 1989. "Remarks Presented at the 100th Anniversary of the P.H.S. Commissioned Corps." Washington, DC, January 4. Profiles in Science. National Library of Medicine, NIH. https://profiles.nlm.nih.gov/spotlight/qq/catalog/nlm:nlmuid-101584930X134-doc
22. Public Law 101-502, 104 Stat. 1285. *An Act to Amend the Public Health Service Act to Extend Various Programs with Respect to Vaccine-Preventable Diseases*, November 3, 1990.
23. Carmona, Richard. 2017. "Instant Admirals and the Plague of Politics in the United States Public Health Service: Back to the Future." *Military Medicine* 182, no. 5: 1582–1583.
24. McKinnon, Mark F., Epifanio Elizondo, Susan M. Bonfiglio, Hunter-Buskey RN, et al. 2016. "A History of PAs in the US Public Health Service." *Journal of the American Academy of Physician Assistants* 29, no. 12: 51–56.
25. "BCOAG Presents Awards." 2000. *Commissioned Corps Bulletin* XIV, no. 3: 11.
26. University of Washington. 2017. "Richard A. Smith, MD, MPH:1932 – 2017." MEDEX Northwest, March 15. https://familymedicine.uw.edu/medex/magazine/2017/03/15/richard-a-smith-md-mph-1932-2017/
27. Centers for Disease Control and Prevention. 2023. "Global Polio Eradication." June 28. https://www.cdc.gov/polio/global-polio-eradication.html

CHAPTER TWELVE, *Pages 175–186*

1. Stobbe, Mike. 2014. *Surgeon General's Warning: How Politics Crippled the Nation's Doctor*. Oakland: University of California Press.
2. Hilts, Philip J. 1989. "President Picks Hispanic Woman to Become U.S. Surgeon General." *New York Times*, October 18.
3. Davidson, Lee. 1990. "Surgeon General is Shy But Forceful." *Deseret News,* April 15.
4. Novello, Antonia C. 1990. *The Health Benefits of Smoking Cessation: A Report of the Surgeon General*. U.S. Department of Health and Human Services, Public Health Service, Centers for Disease Control, Center for Chronic Disease Prevention and Health Promotion, Office on Smoking and Health.
5. Novello, Antonia C. 1992. *Smoking and Health in the Americas. A 1992 Report of the Surgeon General, in Collaboration With the Pan American Health Organization*. U.S. Department of Health and Human Services, Public Health Service, Centers for Disease Control, National Center for Chronic Disease Prevention and Health Promotion, Office on Smoking and Health.

6. Fischer, Paul M., Meyer P. Schwartz, John W. Richards Jr, et al. 1991. "Brand Logo Recognition by Children Aged 3 to 6 Years. Mickey Mouse and Old Joe the Camel." *Journal of the American Medical Association* 266, no. 22: 3145–3148.
7. Elliott, Stuart. 1992. "Top Health Official Demands Abolition of 'Joe Camel' Ads." *New York Times,* March 10.
8. Associated Press. 1992. "Chicago Parade Protests Smoking Cartoon Camel." *Los Angeles Times,* June 22.
9. Weinstein, Henry. 1998. "R.J. Reynolds Targeted Kids, Records Show." *Los Angeles Times,* January 15.
10. Sullivan, Louis W. 1991. "Keynote Address to the First International Conference on Smokeless Tobacco." Columbus, Ohio, April 10-13.
 https://cancercontrol.cancer.gov/brp/tcrb/monographs/2/m2_complete.pdf
11. Office of the Inspector General. 1992. "Spit Tobacco and Youth." U.S Department of Health and Human Services. OEI 06-92-00500.
12. Kluger, Richard. 1997. *Ashes to Ashes: America's Hundred-Year Cigarette War, the Public Health, and the Unabashed Triumph of Philip Morris*. New York: Alfred A. Knopf, 1996; New York: Vintage Books, 1997.
13. Hilts, Philip J. 1990. "Thailand's Cigarette Ban Upset." *New York Times,* October 4,.
14. Novello, Antonia C., Christopher Degraw, and Dushanka V. Kleinman. 1992. "Healthy Children Ready to Learn: An Essential Collaboration Between Health and Education." *Public Health* Reports 107, no. 1: 3–15.
15. Novello, Antonia C. 1992. "Parents Speak Out for America's Children. Report of the Surgeon General's Conference on Healthy Children Ready to Learn: The Critical Role of Parents." Profiles in Science. National Library of Medicine, NIH.
 https://profiles.nlm.nih.gov/spotlight/nn/catalog/nlm:nlmuid-101584932X763-doc
16. Novello, Antonia C., and Lydia E. Soto-Torres. 1993. "One Voice, One Vision—Uniting to Improve Hispanic-Latino Health." *Public Health Reports* 108, no. 5: 529–533.
17. Novello, Antonia C. 1993. "Surgeon General's National Hispanic/Latino Health Initiative. One Voice, One Vision – Recommendations to the Surgeon General to Improve Hispanic/Latino Health." Profiles in Science. National Library of Medicine, NIH, June.
 https://collections.nlm.nih.gov/catalog/nlm:nlmuid-101584932X732-doc
18. "Rapid Health Needs Assessment Following Hurricane Andrew -- Florida and Louisiana, 1992." 1992. *Morbidity and Mortality Weekly Report* 41, no. 37: 685–688.
19. Ginzburg, Harold M., Robert J. Jevec, and Thomas Reutershan. 1993. "The Public Health Service's Response to Hurricane Andrew." *Public Health Reports* 108, no. 2: 241–244.
20. Novello, Antonia C. 1992. "Surgeon General's Report to the American Public on HIV Infection and AIDS." Profiles in Science. National Library of Medicine, NIH.
 https://profiles.nlm.nih.gov/spotlight/nn/catalog/nlm:nlmuid-101584932X1-doc
21. Public Law 100-607. 102 Stat. 3048. *An Act to Amend the Public Health Service Act to Establish Certain Health Programs, to Revise and Extend Certain Health Programs, and for Other Purposes,* November 4, 1988.
22. University of Virginia. 2007. "Anthony S. Fauci Oral History, AIDS Researcher." Interviewed by Janet Heininger. Presidential Oral Histories. Miller Center, September 10.
 https://millercenter.org/the-presidency/presidential-oral-histories/anthony-s-fauci-oral-history
23. Henry J. Kaiser Family Foundation. 2023. "The U.S. President's Emergency Plan for AIDS Relief (PEPFAR)." Global Health Policy, July 26.
 https://www.kff.org/global-health-policy/fact-sheet/the-u-s-presidents-emergency-plan-for-aids-relief-pepfar/

24. Kuwait Working Party. 1991. "Plan of Action for Protecting Public Health." United States Public Health Service, Department of Health and Human Services, May 31.
25. Congressional Research Service. 1992. "The Environmental Aftermath of the Gulf War. A Report Prepared for the Committee on Environment and Public Works Gulf Pollution Task Force." Washington: GPO, March.
26. Changing the Face of Medicine. 2003. "Biography: Dr. M. Joycelyn Elders." National Library of Medicine, NIH.
https://cfmedicine.nlm.nih.gov/physicians/biography_98.html
27. "Letter From Surgeons General Letter to Edward M. Kennedy." 1994. Department of Health and Human Services, Public Health Service, Office of the Surgeon General. February 7.
https://profiles.nlm.nih.gov/spotlight/qq/catalog/nlm:nlmuid-101584930X310-doc
28. Elders, M. Joycelyn. 1994. "Preventing Tobacco Use Among Young People: A Report of the Surgeon General. Executive Summary." *Morbidity and Mortality Weekly Report* 43, no. RR-4.
29. Dreifus, Claudia. 1994. "Joycelyn Elders." *New York Times,* January 30.
30. Jehl, Douglas. 1994. "Surgeon General Forced to Resign By White House." *New York Times,* December 10.
31. Manley, Audrey F. 1996. *Physical Activity and Health. A Report of the Surgeon General.* Atlanta, GA: U.S. Department of Health and Human Services, Centers for Disease Control and Prevention, National Center for Chronic Disease Prevention and Health Promotion, President's Council on Physical Fitness and Sports.
32. Manley, Audrey F. 1996. "Surgeon General's Column." *Commissioned Corps Bulletin* X, no. 9: 1–2.
33. U.S. General Accounting Office. 1996. "Report to Congressional Requesters. Issues on the Need for the Public Health Service's Commissioned Corps." Washington, DC., May. GAO/GGD-96-55. https://www.gao.gov/assets/ggd-96-55.pdf
34. Clinton, J. Jarrett. 1997. "Surgeon General's Column. Biographical Sketch – Acting Surgeon General RADM J. Jarrett Clinton." *Commissioned Corps Bulletin* XI, no. 8: 5, 8.

CHAPTER THIRTEEN, *Pages 187–200*

1. CNN. 1997. "Clinton Names Satcher as Surgeon General. President Nominates 'True Field Commander' in Smoking War." All Politics, September 12.
2. Satcher, David. 1998. *Tobacco Use Among U.S. Racial/Ethnic Minority Groups–African Americans, American Indians and Alaska Natives, Asian Americans and Pacific Islanders, and Hispanics: A Report of the Surgeon General.* Atlanta: U.S. Department of Health and Human Services, Centers for Disease Control and Prevention, National Center for Chronic Disease Prevention and Health Promotion, Office on Smoking and Health.
3. Satcher, David. 1999. *Mental Health: A Report of the Surgeon General.* Rockville, MD: U.S. Department of Health and Human Services, Substance Abuse and Mental Health Services Administration, National Institute of Mental Health, NIH.
4. Satcher, David. 2000. *Oral Health in America: A Report of the Surgeon General.* Rockville, MD: U.S. Department of Health and Human Services, National Institute of Dental and Cranio-facial Research, NIH.
5. Satcher, David. 1999. *The Surgeon General's Call to Action to Prevent Suicide.* Washington, DC: U.S. Department of Health and Human Services, U.S. Public Health Service.
6. Satcher, David. 1999. "Public Health Service: Suicide and Public Health." *Public Health Reports* 114, no. 2: 198–199.

7. Koop, C. Everett. 2001. "The Surgeon General, the President, and the People." *COA Frontline* 38, no. 9: 5.
8. Satcher, David. 2001. *The Surgeon General's Call to Action to Prevent and Decrease Overweight and Obesity*. Rockville, MD: U.S. Department of Health and Human Services, Public Health Service, Office of the Surgeon General.
9. Flegal, Katherine M., Barry I. Graubard, David F. Williamson, and Mitchell H. Gail. 2005. "Excess Deaths Associated With Underweight, Overweight, and Obesity." *Journal of the American Medical Association* 293, no. 15: 1861–1867.
10. Satcher, David, and Eve J. Higginbotham. 2008. "The Public Health Approach to Eliminating Disparities in Health." *American Journal of Public Health* 98, no. 3: 400–403.
11. Satcher, David. 2001. "Our Commitment to Eliminate Racial and Ethnic Health Disparities." *Yale Journal of Health Policy, Law, and Ethics* 1, no. 1: Article 1, 1–14.
12. Davidson, R. Michael. 2000. "The State of the Commissioned Corps." *Commissioned Corps Bulletin* XIV, no. 5: 1–4.
13. Davidson, R. Michael. 2000. "Division of Commissioned Personnel Realignment." *Commissioned Corps Bulletin* XIV, no. 6: 3.
14. "Basic Officer Training Course—5-day Version." 2001. *Commissioned Corps Bulletin* XV, no. 8: 5.
15. "OBC 106 - A Milestone for the Commissioned Officer Training Academy." 2019. *COA Frontline* 57, no. 1: 1.
16. Chapman, Cheryl, and Carole Kuzmik. 1999. "PHS Personnel Aid Kosovar Refugees at Fort Dix." *Commissioned Corps Bulletin* XIII, no. 6: 3.
17. "Health Status of and Intervention for U.S.-Bound Kosovar Refugees – Fort Dix, New Jersey, May-July 1999." 1999. *Morbidity and Mortality Weekly Report* 48, no. 33: 729–732.
18. Sencer, David J., H. Bruce Dull, and Alexander D. Langmuir. 1967. "Epidemiologic Basis for Eradication of Measles in 1967." *Public Health Reports* 82, no. 3: 253–256.
19. "Elimination of Indigenous Measles–United States." 1982. *Morbidity and Mortality Weekly Report* 31, no. 38: 517–519.
20. Orenstein, Walter A., Mark J. Papania, and Melinda E. Wharton. 2004. "Measles Elimination in the United States." *Journal of Infectious Diseases* 189, Suppl 1: S1–S3.
21. Commissioned Corps Readiness Force. 2001. "Commissioned Officers Respond to Terrorist Attack." *Commissioned Corps Bulletin* XV, no. 10: 4.
22. Knebel, Ann R., Angela M. Martinelli, Susan Orsega, et al. 2010. "Ground Zero Recollections of US Public Health Service Nurses Deployed to New York City in September 2001." *Nursing Clinics of North America* 45, no. 2: 137–152.
23. Perritt, Kara R., and Winifred L. Boal; Helix Group Inc. 2005. "Injuries and Illnesses Treated at the World Trade Center, 14 September-20 November 2001." *Prehospital and Disaster Medicine* 20, no. 3: 177–183.
24. Satcher, David. 2001. "Surgeon General's Column." *Commissioned Corps Bulletin* XV, no. 12: 1–2.
25. Babb, John. 2002. "Changes in the CCRF Operations Plan." *Commissioned Corps Bulletin* XVI, no. 1: 5–6.
26. Centers for Disease Control and Prevention. 2014. "Receiving, Distributing, and Dispensing Strategic National Stockpile Assets: A Guide for Preparedness, Version 11." March 28. https://stacks.cdc.gov/view/cdc/77036
27. Administration for Strategic Preparedness and Response. 2023. "Strategic National Stockpile." https://aspr.hhs.gov/SNS/Pages/default.aspx

28. Board on Health Sciences Policy. 2016. *The Nation's Medical Countermeasure Stockpile: Opportunities to Improve the Efficiency, Effectiveness, and Sustainability of the CDC Strategic National Stockpile: Workshop Summary.* Washington, DC: Health and Medicine Division, National Academies Press, October 24. https://www.ncbi.nlm.nih.gov/books/NBK396382/
29. Congressional Research Service. 2023. "The Strategic National Stockpile: Overview and Issues for Congress." Updated September 26. https://crsreports.congress.gov/product/pdf/R/R47400
30. "Public Health Service Sword Honor Guard." 1998. *Commissioned Corps Bulletin* XII, no. 8: 5.
31. "PHS Honor Guard." 1999. *Commissioned Corps Bulletin* XIII, no. 8: 2.
32. "Introducing the Commander of the Surgeon General's Honor Cadre." 2000. *Commissioned Corps Bulletin* XIV, no. 1: 4.
33. "History of the Ensemble." 2020. USPHS Music Ensemble. May 28. https://dcp.psc.gov/OSG/ensemble/history.aspx#:~:text=The%20origin%20of%20the%20United,proposed%20by%20CAPT%20John%20J.
34. King, George. 2023. Personal Communication. February 4.
35. Parascandola, John. 1998. "Bicentennial Commemoration in Boston." *Commissioned Corps Bulletin* XII, no. 6: 3.
36. Parascandola, John. 1998. "PHS Celebrates Bicentennial in Philadelphia." *Commissioned Corps Bulletin* XII, no. 8: 2.
37. "Grand PHS Bicentennial Luncheon Held – ADM David Satcher, Speaker." 1998. *Commissioned Corps Bulletin* XII, no. 9: 3.

CHAPTER FOURTEEN, *Pages 201–222*

1. Bush, George W. 2002. "Remarks Announcing the Nominations of Dr. Elias Zerhouni to be Director of the National Institutes of Health and Dr. Richard Carmona to be Surgeon General." The American Presidency Project. University of California, March 26.
2. Research!America. 2002. "2002 Annual Report." Alexandria, VA.
3. "Surgeon General VADM Carmona Sets Preventions as Top Priority." 2003. *COA Frontline* 40, no. 2: 17–18.
4. Thompson, Tommy G. 2003. "Memorandum from the HHS Secretary to Agency Heads. (April 17)" *Commissioned Corps Bulletin* XVII, no. 6: 3.
5. Carmona, Richard H. 2003. "Surgeon General's Column. Remarks by Tommy G. Thompson, Secretary of Health and Human Services." *Commissioned Corps Bulletin* XVII, no. 8: 2–3.
6. Carmona, Richard H. 2003. "Meeting Our Nation's Important Public Health Challenges: Transformation of the Public Health Service Commissioned Corps." Testimony Before the Committee on Government Reform. U.S. House of Representatives. October 30.
7. "Surgeon General Carmona Announces Major Changes to Transformation." 2003. *COA Frontline* 40, no. 10: 1, 14.
8. "Transformation Update." 2006. *Commissioned Corps E-Bulletin* II, no. 15.
9. Galson, Steven K., and Sam Shekar. 2007. "Transformation Accomplishments and Future Direction – Information." Memorandum. Department of Health and Human Services, Office of the Secretary, Assistant Secretary for Health, December 6.
10. Beato, Cristina V., and Richard H. Carmona. 2005. "Mission Statement for the USPHS Commissioned Corps." Memorandum. Department of Health and Human Services, Office of the Secretary, Assistant Secretary for Health, February 17.
11. Moritsugu, Kenneth P. 2006. "The Acting Surgeon General Announces Release of Core Values of the Commissioned Corps of the U.S. Public Health Service." *Commissioned Corps E-Bulletin* II, no. 15.

12. Carmona, Richard H. 2006. *The Health Consequences of Involuntary Exposure to Tobacco Smoke: A Report of the Surgeon General*. Atlanta, GA: U.S. Department of Health and Human Services, Centers for Disease Control and Prevention, Office on Smoking and Health.
13. Carmona, Richard H. 2004. *Bone Health and Osteoporosis: A Report of the Surgeon General*. Rockville, MD: U.S. Department of Health and Human Services, Public Health Service, Office of the Surgeon General.
14. Carmona, Richard H. 2005. *The Surgeon General's Call to Action to Improve the Health and Wellness of Persons With Disabilities*. Rockville, MD: U..S Department of Health and Human Services, Public Health Service, Office of the Surgeon General.
15. Carmona, Richard H. 2003. "The Obesity Crisis in America." Testimony Before the Subcommittee on Education Reform, Committee on Education and the Workforce. U.S. House of Representatives. July 16.
16. Carmona, Richard H. 2004. "The Growing Epidemic of Childhood Obesity." Testimony Before the Subcommittee on Competition, Infrastructure, and Foreign Commerce, Committee on Commerce, Science, and Transportation. March 2.
17. Public Law 107-188, 116 Stat. 594. *An Act to Improve the Ability of the United States to Prevent, Prepare For, and Respond to Bioterrorism and Other Public Health Emergencies*. 107th Congress, June 12, 2002.
18. Public Law 108-276, 118 Stat. 835. *An Act to Amend the Public Health Service Act to Provide Protections and Countermeasures Against Chemical, Radiological, or Nuclear Agents That May be Used in a Terrorist Attack Against the United States by Giving the National Institutes of Health Contracting Flexibility, Infrastructure Improvements, and Expediting the Scientific Peer Review Process, and Streamlining the Food and Drug Administration Approval Process of Countermeasures*. 108th Congress, July 21, 2004.
19. Public Law 109-417, 120 Stat. 2831. *An Act to Amend the Public Health Service Act With Respect to Public Health Security and All-Hazards Preparedness and Response, and for Other Purposes*. 109th Congress, December 19, 2006.
20. Public Law 113-5, 127 Stat. 161. *An Act to Reauthorize Certain Programs Under the Public Health Service Act and the Federal Food, Drug, and Cosmetic Act With Respect to Public Health Security and All-Hazards Preparedness and Response, and for Other Purposes*. 113th Congress, March 13, 2013.
21. Public Law 116-22, 133 Stat. 905. *An Act to Reauthorize Certain Programs Under the Public Health Service Act and the Federal Food, Drug, and Cosmetic Act With Respect to Public Health Security and All-Hazards Preparedness and Response, and for Other Purposes*. 116th Congress, June 24, 2019.
22. "Hurricanes Charley, Frances, Ivan, and Jeanne." 2004. *Commissioned Corps Bulletin* XVIII, no. 11: 8.
23. University of Rhode Island. "Hurricanes: Science and Society. Hurricane Katrina Case Study." Graduate School of Oceanography. https://hurricanescience.org/history/studies/katrinacase/
24. University of Rhode Island. "Hurricanes: Science and Society. Hurricane Rita." Graduate School of Oceanography. https://hurricanescience.org/history/storms/2000s/rita/
25. University of Rhode Island. "Hurricanes: Science and Society. Hurricane Wilma." Graduate School of Oceanography. https://hurricanescience.org/history/storms/2000s/wilma/
26. Sumter, Jeffery L., Adrienne Goodrich-Doctor, Jill Roberts, and Thomas J. Mason. 2018. "Twenty-First Century Emergency Response Efforts of the Commissioned Corps of the US Public Health Service." *Journal of Emergency Management* 16, no. 5: 311–319.

27. Office of Inspector General. 2007. "The Commissioned Corps' Response to Hurricanes Katrina and Rita." Washington, DC: Department of Health and Human Services, February.
28. The White House. 2006. "The Federal Response to Hurricane Katrina: Lessons Learned." Washington, DC, February.
29. Carmona, Richard H. 2003. "Surgeon General's Column." *Commissioned Corps Bulletin* XVII, no. 6: 1–2.
30. PHS News. 2003. "PHS Officers Serving in Iraq." *COA Frontline* 40, no. 6: 7.
31. Helminiak, Clare. 2004. "DoD/HHS Team Site Visit to Afghanistan." *Commissioned Corps Bulletin* XVIII, no. 3: 9–12.
32. Havens, George. 2004. "Operation Iraqi Freedom: PHS Officers, Deployments, & Parity." *COA Frontline* 41, no. 3: 3–5.
33. Carmona, Richard H. 2007. "The Surgeon General's Vital Mission: Challenges for the Future." Testimony Before the Committee on Oversight and Government Reform. July 10.
34. Harris, Gardiner. 2007. "White House is Accused of Putting Politics Over Science." *New York Times,* July 10.
35. Lee, Christopher. 2007. "Ex-Surgeon General Says White House Hushed Him." *Washington Post,* July 11.
36. Berman, Emily, and Jacob Carter. 2018. "Policy Analysis: Scientific Integrity in Federal Policymaking Under Past and Present Administrations." *Journal of Science Policy & Governance* 13, no. 1.
https://www.sciencepolicyjournal.org/uploads/5/4/3/4/5434385/berman_emily__carter_jacob.pdf
37. Galson, Steven K. 2008. *The Surgeon General's Call to Action to Prevent Deep Vein Thrombosis and Pulmonary Embolism.* Rockville (MD): Office of the Surgeon General, National Heart, Lung, and Blood Institute, NIH.
38. Andreason, Paul J. 2019. Personal Communication. July 17.
39. Public Law 111-31, 123 Stat. 1776, June 22, 2009.
40. U.S. Immigration and Customs Enforcement. 2021. "ICE Health Service Corps Focused on Best Patient Outcomes." December 30. https://www.ice.gov/features/health-service-corps
41. U.S. Immigration and Customs Enforcement. 2020. "Health Service Corps, Fiscal Year 2020." November. https://www.ice.gov/doclib/ihsc/IHSCFY20AnnualReport.pdf
42. U.S. Department of Energy. 2019. "Human Genome Project Information Archive, 1990—2003." https://web.ornl.gov/sci/techresources/Human_Genome/project/index.shtml
43. U.S. Department of Energy. 2004. "International Human Genome Sequencing Consortium Describes Finished Human Genome Sequence. Researchers Trim Count of Human Genes to 20,000-25,000." October 20.
https://web.ornl.gov/sci/techresources/Human_Genome/project/pressreleases/20to25K.pdf

CHAPTER FIFTEEN, Pages 223–240

1. Obama White House Archives. 2010. "First Lady Michelle Obama Launches Let's Move: America's Move to Raise a Healthier Generation of Kids." February 9.
https://obamawhitehouse.archives.gov/the-press-office/first-lady-michelle-obama-launches-lets-move-americas-move-raise-a-healthier-genera
2. Raymond, Joan. 2010. "Top Doc: Fitness Is More Than a Dress Size." *NBC News,* February 25.
3. Benjamin, Regina M. 2010. *The Surgeon General's Vision for a Healthy and Fit Nation.* Rockville, MD: U.S. Department of Health and Human Services, Public Health Service, Office of the Surgeon General, January.
4. Benjamin, Regina M. 2010. "The Surgeon General's Vision for a Healthy and Fit Nation." *Public Health Reports* 125, no. 4: 514–515.

5. Public Law 111-148, 124 Stat. 119. *An Act Entitled the Patient Protection and Affordable Care Act*. 111th Congress, March 23, 2010.
6. Voelker, Rebecca. 2010. "Surgeon General's Prevention Priorities Dovetail With Health Care Reform Law." *Journal of the American Medical Association* 303, no. 21: 2123–2124.
7. Walker, Emily P. 2010. "HHS Secretary and Surgeon General Address AMA." *MedPage Today,* March 2.
8. National Prevention Council. 2011. "National Prevention Strategy. America's Plan for Better Health and Wellness." Washington, DC: U.S. Department of Health and Human Services, Office of the Surgeon General, June; and, National Prevention Council. 2012. "National Prevention Council Action Plan. Implementing the National Prevention Strategy." Office of the Surgeon General, June.
9. Benjamin, Regina M. 2010. *How Tobacco Smoke Causes Disease: The Biology and Behavioral Basis for Smoking-Attributable Disease. A Report of the Surgeon General*. Rockville, MD: U.S. Department of Health and Human Services, Public Health Service.
10. Benjamin, Regina M. 2011. *The Surgeon General's Call to Action to Support Breastfeeding*. Washington, DC: U.S. Department of Health and Human Services, Public Health Service, Office of the Surgeon General.
11. Centers for Disease Control and Prevention. 2010. "The 2009 H1N1 Pandemic: Summary Highlights, April 2009-April 2010." June 16. https://www.cdc.gov/h1n1flu/cdcresponse.htm
12. Shrestha, Sundar S., David L. Swerdlow, Rebekah H. Borse, et al. 2011. "Estimating the Burden of 2009 Pandemic Influenza A (H1N1) in the United States (April 2009–April 2010)." *Clinical Infectious Diseases* 52, Suppl 1: S75–S82.
13. Koh, Howard K. 2016. "Strengthening the U.S. Public Health Service Commissioned Corps: A View From the Assistant Secretary for Health." *Military Medicine* 181, no. 1: 12–15.
14. Carbone, Eric G., and Marcienne M. Wright. 2016. "Hurricane Sandy Recovery Science: A Model for Disaster Research." *Disaster Medicine and Public Health Preparedness* 10, no. 3: 304–5.
15. Iskander, John, Eva McLanahan, Jennifer D. Thomas, et al. 2018. "Public Health Emergency Response Lessons Learned by Rapid Deployment Force 3, 2006–2016." *American Journal of Public Health* 108, Suppl 3: S179–S182.
16. Burwell, Sylvia. 2014. "Statement of Sylvia Burwell, Secretary, U.S. Department of Health and Human Services, On Unaccompanied Children Before the Committee on Appropriations, United States Senate." July 10.
https://www.appropriations.senate.gov/imo/media/doc/hearings/HHS-%20Sec.%20Burwell%20Testimony-%207-9-14%20.pdf
17. Lushniak, Boris D. 2014. *The Health Consequences of Smoking—50 Years of Progress. A Report of the Surgeon General*. Atlanta, GA: U.S. Department of Health and Human Services, Centers for Disease Control and Prevention, Office on Smoking and Health.
18. Lushniak, Boris D. 2014. *The Surgeon General's Call to Action to Prevent Skin Cancer*. Washington, DC: U.S. Department of Health and Human Services, Office of the Surgeon General.
19. Obama, Barack. 2014. "Remarks by the President on the Ebola Outbreak." Obama White House Archives. September 16.
https://obamawhitehouse.archives.gov/the-press-office/2014/09/16/remarks-president-ebola-outbreak
20. Frieden, Thomas R., and Inger K. Damon. 2015. "Ebola in West Africa—CDC's Role in Epidemic Detection, Control, and Prevention." *Emerging Infectious Diseases* 21, no. 11: 1897–1905.

21. Centers for Disease Control and Prevention. 2016. "CDC's Response to the 2014-2016 Ebola Epidemic – Guinea, Liberia, and Sierra Leone." *Morbidity and Mortality Weekly Report* 65, no. 3 (Suppl): 12–20.
22. Joint and Coalition Operational Analysis. 2016. "Operation United Assistance: The DOD Response to Ebola in West Africa." Suffolk, VA: JCOA, 6 January.
23. Lushniak, Boris D. 2015. "Update on the U.S. Public Health Response to the Ebola Outbreak." *Public Health Reports* 130, no. 2: 118–120.
24. Lushniak, Boris D. 2015. "The Hope Multipliers: The U.S. Public Health Service in Monrovia." *Public Health Reports* 130, no. 6: 562–565.
25. The White House. 2015. "Presidential Unit Citation to Public Health Service Commissioned Corps." September 24.
    https://dcp.psc.gov/ccmis/PDF_docs/Presidential%20Unit%20Citation%202015.pdf
26. Pierson, Jerome F., Matthew C. Kirchoff, Susan M. Orsega, et al. 2017. "Collaboration of the NIH and PHS Commissioned Corps in the International Ebola Clinical Research Response." *Federal Practitioner* 34, no. 8: 18–25.
27. Foege, William H. 1981. "Centers for Disease Control." *Journal of Public Health Policy* 2, no. 1: 8–18.
28. Centers for Disease Control and Prevention. 1996. "Historical Perspectives History of CDC." *Morbidity and Mortality Weekly Report* 45, no. 25: 526–530.

CHAPTER SIXTEEN, *Pages 241–252*

1. Murthy, Vivek H. 2014. "Opening Statement of Vivek Hallegere Murthy, Nominee to be Surgeon General." U.S. Department of Health and Human Services. Senate Committee on Health, Education, Labor, and Pensions. February 4.
   https://www.help.senate.gov/imo/media/doc/Statement%20of%20Vivek%20Murthy.pdf
2. Mascaro, Lisa. 2014. "NRA Opposition May Sink Obama's Surgeon General Nominee." *Los Angeles Times,* March 15.
3. Curfman, Gregory D., Stephen Morrissey, Debra Malina, and Jeffrey M. Drazen. 2014. "Vivek Murthy for Surgeon General." *New England Journal of Medicine* 370, no. 19: 1843–1844. Editorial.
4. Trust for America's Health. 2014. "More Than 100 National Organizations Demonstrate Strong Support for Dr. Vivek Murthy as the Next Surgeon General." Press Release, November 12.
5. Centers for Disease Control and Prevention. 2023. "Drug Overdose." June 6.
   https://www.cdc.gov/drugoverdose/index.html
6. Jones, Christopher M., Emily B. Einstein, and Wilson M. Compton. 2018. "Changes in Synthetic Opioid Involvement in Drug Overdose Deaths in the United States, 2010-2016." *Journal of the American Medical Association* 319, no. 17: 1819–1821.
7. Public Law 114-198, 130 Stat. 695. *An Act to Authorize the Attorney General and Secretary of Health and Human Services to Award grants to Address the Prescription Opioid Abuse and Heroin Use Crisis, and for Other Purposes,* July 22, 2016.
8. Public Law 114-255, 130 Stat. 1033. *An Act to Accelerate the Discovery, Development, and Delivery of 21st Century Cures, and for Other Purposes,* December 13, 2016.
9. Murthy, Vivek H. 2016. "Opioid Epidemic: We All Have a Role in Turning the Tide." Obama White House Archives. October 5.
   https://obamawhitehouse.archives.gov/blog/2016/10/05/opioid-epidemic-we-all-have-role-turning-tide
10. Murthy, VH. 2016. "Ending the Opioid Epidemic – A Call to Action." *New England Journal of Medicine* 375, no. 25: 2413–2415.

11. News Staff. 2016. "AAFP Supports Turn the Tide Rx Campaign to End Opioid Abuse." *American Academy of Family Physicians (AAFP) News*, August 9.
12. Murthy, Vivek H. 2016. *E-Cigarette Use Among Youth and Young Adults: A Report of the Surgeon General*. Atlanta, GA: U.S. Department of Health and Human Services, Centers for Disease Control and Prevention, Office on Smoking and Health.
13. Murthy, Vivek H. 2016. *Facing Addiction in America. The Surgeon General's Report on Alcohol, Drugs, and Health*. Washington DC: U.S. Department of Health and Human Services, Substance Abuse and Mental Health Services Administration, November.
14. Commissioned Officers Association. 2017. "PHS Billets at VA." *COA USPHS News*, April 13.
15. Office of the Assistant Secretary for Preparedness and Response. 2016. "Federal Support for State and Local Response Operations. Flint, Michigan, Water Contamination Crisis." U.S. Department of Health and Human Services, February 24.
    https://www.phe.gov/emergency/events/Flint/Pages/USGresponse-24Feb16.aspx
16. Indian Health Service. 2016. "Quality and Service Improvements at the Indian health Service: Calendar Year 2016." Public Health Service, 1–15.
    https://www.ihs.gov/sites/newsroom/themes/responsive2017/display_objects/documents/2016_Letters/QualityAndServiceImprovmentsAtIHSCalendarYear2016.pdf
17. Sumter, Jeffery L., Adrienne Goodrich-Doctor, Jill Roberts, and Thomas J. Mason. 2018. "Twenty-First Century Emergency Response Efforts of the Commissioned Corps of the US Public Health Service." *Journal of Emergency Management* 16, no. 5: 311–319.
18. Iskander, John, Eva McLanahan, Jennifer D. Thomas, et al. 2018. "Public Health Emergency Response Lessons Learned by Rapid Deployment Force 3, 2006–2016." *American Journal of Public Health* 108, Suppl 3: S179–S182.
19. Sohrabji, Sunita. 2017. "'I Did Not Resign: I Would Never Abandon My Commitment', Says Former U.S. Surgeon General Vivek Murthy." *India-West News,* April 25.
20. United States Coast Guard. 2019. "Commandant Instruction 6010.5B. Administration of United States Public Health Service (USPHS) Officers Detailed to the Coast Guard." U.S. Department of Homeland Security, 05 August.
21. van Ackeren, JF. 1953. "The Medical Officer United States Coast Guard." *Military Surgeon* 112, no. 6: 414–417.
22. Marwick, Charles. 1989. "Coast Guard Turns to Public Health Service, Civilian Physicians to Meet Medical Needs." *Journal of the American Medical Association* 261, no. 19: 2784.
23. "Dr. Carl Michel, USPHS, Chief Medical Officer of U.S. Coast Guard Dies." 1946. *Coast Guard Bulletin* 3, no. 8: 165.
24. National Oceanic and Atmospheric Administration. "NOAA Corps History." Office of Marine and Aviation Operations. https://www.omao.noaa.gov/noaa-corps/noaa-corps-history
25. National Oceanic and Atmospheric Administration. "Office of Health Services." Office of Marine and Aviation Operations. https://www.omao.noaa.gov/omao/health-services

Chapter Seventeen, Pages 253–272

1. The White House. 2017. "Remarks by the Vice President and the Surgeon General at a Swearing-In Ceremony." September 5.
   https://trumpwhitehouse.archives.gov/briefings-statements/remarks-vice-president-surgeon-general-swearing-ceremony/
2. Powell, Alvin. 2018. "Opioid Epidemic Top Priority for Surgeon General." *Harvard Gazette,* January 25.
3. Mediaplanet. 2018. *"*Surgeon General Jerome Adams Outlines His Plan to Halt the Opioid Epidemic." Future of Personal Health.

4. Haskins, Julia. 2018. "Q&A With Surgeon General Jerome Adams: Gaining Better Health Through Better Partnerships: Report to Highlight Links Between US Health, Economy." *The Nation's Health* 48, no. 1: 5.
5. Adams, Jerome M. 2018. "The Value of Wellness." *Public Health Reports* 133, no. 2: 127–129.
6. Christie, Chris. 2017. "The President's Commission on Combating Drug Addiction and the Opioid Crisis: Final Report." Office of National Drug Control Policy, November 1.
https://trumpwhitehouse.archives.gov/sites/whitehouse.gov/files/images/Final_Report_Draft_11-15-2017.pdf
7. U.S. Department of Health and Human Services. 2018. "Strategy to Combat Opioid Abuse, Misuse, and Overdose. A Framework Based on the Five Point Strategy."
https://www.hhs.gov/overdose-prevention/
8. Adams, Jerome M. 2018. *Surgeon General's Advisory on Naloxone and Opioid Overdose*. U.S. Department of Health and Human Services, April 5.
https://www.hhs.gov/surgeongeneral/reports-and-publications/addiction-and-substance-misuse/advisory-on-naloxone/index.html
9. Centers for Disease Control and Prevention. 2018. "Emergency Department Data Show Rapid Increases in Opioid Overdoses." CDC Newsroom. Press Release., March 6.
https://www.cdc.gov/media/releases/2018/p0306-vs-opioids-overdoses.html
10. U.S. Department of Health and Human Services. 2018. "Secretary Azar Announces Appointments to Advance Department Priorities." HHS Press Office, March 29.
https://www.einnews.com/pr_news/439452893/secretary-azar-announces-appointments-to-advance-department-priorities
11. Wilson, Nana, Mbabazi Kariisa, Puja Seth, et al. 2020. "Drug and Opioid-Involved Overdose Deaths — United States, 2017–2018." *Morbidity and Mortality Weekly Report* 69, no. 11: 290–297.
12. Mattson, Christine L., Lauren J. Tanz, Kelly Quinn, et al. 2021. "Trends and Geographic Patterns in Drug and Synthetic Opioid Overdose Deaths — United States, 2013-2019." *Morbidity and Mortality Weekly Report* 70, no. 6: 202–207.
13. Adams, Jerome M. 2018. *Facing Addiction in America. The Surgeon General's Spotlight on Opioids.* Washington DC: U.S. Department of Health and Human Services, Office of the Surgeon General, September.
14. Cullen, Karen A., Bridget K. Ambrose, Andrea S. Gentzke, et al. 2018. Notes from the Field. Use of Electronic Cigarettes and Any Tobacco Product Among Middle and High School Students – United States, 2011-2018. *Morbidity and Mortality Weekly Report* 67, no. 45: 1276–1277.
15. Cullen, Karen A., Andrea S. Gentzke, Michael D. Sawdey, et al. 2019. "e-Cigarette Use Among Youth in the United States, 2019." *Journal of the American Medical Association* 322, no. 21: 2095–2103.
16. Adams, Jerome M. 2018. *Surgeon General's Advisory on E-Cigarette Use Among Youth.* Washington DC: U.S. Department of Health and Human Services, Office of the Surgeon General, December.
https://e-cigarettes.surgeongeneral.gov/documents/surgeon-generals-advisory-on-e-cigarette-use-among-youth-2018.pdf
17. Hartnett, Kathleen P., Aaron Kite-Powell, Megan T. Patel, et al. 2020. "Syndromic Surveillance for E-Cigarette, or Vaping, Product Use–Associated Lung Injury." *New England Journal of Medicine* 382, no. 8: 766–772.
18. Adams, Jerome M. 2020. *Smoking Cessation: A Report of the Surgeon General.* Atlanta, GA: U.S. Department of Health and Human Services, Centers for Disease Control and Prevention, Office on Smoking and Health.

19. Adams, Jerome M. 2018. "Hurricane Maria and a Generation of Resistencia." *Public Health Reports* 133, no. 3: 223–224.
20. Magill, Stephanie, and Mark Sellers. 2018. "RDF-5 Deployments for Unprecedented Atlantic Hurricane Season." *COA Frontline* 56, no. 1: 7, 18.
21. Redmon, Suzanne. 2018. "My Puerto Rico Deployment Experience." *COA Frontline* 56, no. 2: 6, 8.
22. Cole, Kristen, Candice Cottle Delisle, Chandra Jolley, and Neil Barranta. 2018. "Commissioned Corps Officers Supported Unprecedented Back-to-Back Deployments to Hurricanes Harvey, Irma, and Maria." *COA Frontline* 56, no. 2: 7, 9–11.
23. Lombardo, Tony. 2019. "In a First, Public Health Officers Receive DoD Humanitarian Medal." *MOAA News,* February 06.
24. Giroir, Brett P. 2019. "PACE Announcement – Ending the HIV Epidemic." *HIV.gov Blog*, July 08. https://www.hiv.gov/blog/pace-announcement
25. Giroir, Brett P. 2019. "The USPHS Commissioned Corps: America's Health Responders." AMSUS Annual Meeting, December 4. https://www.amsus.org/wp-content/uploads/2019/12/Giroir-Wednesday-morning-AMSUS-12-04-2019-v-FINAL-1.pdf
26. U.S. Customs and Border Protection. 2019. "CBP Southwest Border Total Apprehensions/Inadmissibles." November 14. https://www.cbp.gov/newsroom/stats/sw-border-migration/fy-2019
27. U.S. Department of Health and Human Services. 2022. "Fact Sheet. Unaccompanied Children (UC) Program." Office of Refugee Resettlement. Administration for Children and Families, December 18.
28. Azar II, Alex M. 2018. "Conditions of Service." Commissioned Corps Directive 111.03, 28 March.
29. Giroir, Brett P. 2018. "Readiness and Duty Requirements." Commissioned Corps Instruction 241.01, 22 June.
30. Adams, Jerome M. 2018. "Retention Weight Standards." Personnel Operations Memorandum 821.66, 12 July.
31. The White House. 2018. "Delivering Government Solutions in the 21st Century. Reform Plan and Reorganization Recommendations." Office of Management and Budget. https://www.whitehouse.gov/wp-content/uploads/2018/06/Government-Reform-and-Reorg-Plan.pdf
32. Bucci, Steven P. 2018. "If This Group Loses Funding, Health Emergencies Will Get a Lot Worse." The Heritage Foundation, September 4.
33. The Military Coalition. 2018. "Letter to Chairman and Ranking Member, Committee on Health, Education, Labor, and Pensions, and to Chairman and Ranking Member, Committee on Energy and Commerce, U.S. Congress." July 24. http://www.themilitarycoalition.org/uploads/4/7/6/9/47692523/tmc_ltr_cuts_to_phs__assns_.pdf
34. Congressional Research Service. 2018. "Trump Administration Reform and Reorganization Plan: Discussion of 35 'Government-Wide' Proposals." Memorandum, July 25.
35. Giroir, Brett P. 2023. Personal Communication. July 9.
36. Hobbes, Laural. 2020. "MOAA Q&A. Corps Strength. The Commissioned Corps is Growing and Ready to Hire." *Military Officer* 18, no. 1: 26–27.
37. Giroir, Brett P. 2021. "Closing Remarks From Admiral Giroir." *COA Frontline* 59, no. 1: 1, 20, 22.
38. U.S. Department of Health and Human Services. 2020. "U.S. Public Health Service Commissioned Corps Brand Guidelines." Washington DC: Office of the Surgeon General, November. https://www.usphs.gov/media/tuubjnw5/usphs-commissioned-corps-brand-guidelines.pdf

39. U.S. Department of Health and Human Services. 2021. "U.S. Public Health Service Commissioned Corps Doctrine." Washington DC: Office of the Surgeon General, January. https://dcp.psc.gov/ccmis/PDF_docs/USPHS%20Commissioned%20Corps%20Doctrine.pdf
40. Public Law 116-136, 134 Stat. 281. *An Act to Amend the Internal Revenue Code of 1986 to Repeal the Excise Tax on High Cost Employer-Sponsored Health Coverage,* March 27, 2020.
41. U.S. Department of Health and Human Services. 2020. "Trump Administration Re-Establishes Ready Reserve Corps as Part of the United States Public Health Service." HHS Press Office, June 30.
42. Kannel, William B, Thomas R. Dawber, Abraham Kagan, et al. 1961. "Factors of Risk in the Development of Coronary Heart Disease—Six-Year Follow-Up Experience. The Framingham Study." *Annals of Internal Medicine* 55, no. 1: 33–50.
43. Oppenheimer, Gerald M. 2005. "Becoming the Framingham Study 1947-1950." *American Journal of Public Health* 95, no. 4: 602–610.
44. Mahmood, Syed S., Daniel Levy, Ramachandran S. Vasan, and Thomas J. Wang. 2014. "The Framingham Heart Study and the Epidemiology of Cardiovascular Diseases: A Historical Perspective." *Lancet* 383, no. 9921: 999–1008.
45. Aronowitz, Robert A. 2011. "The Framingham Heart Study and the Emergence of the Risk Factor Approach to Coronary Heart Disease, 1947-1970." Revue d'Histoire des Sciences 64, no. 2: 263–295.
46. Centers for Disease Control and Prevention. 2018. "Past Flu Pandemics." National Center for Immunization and Respiratory Diseases, August 10. https://www.cdc.gov/flu/pandemic-resources/basics/past-pandemics.html
47. Trump, Donald J. 2020. "Letter on Emergency Determination Under the Stafford Act." The White House. March 13. https://trumpwhitehouse.archives.gov/wp-content/uploads/2020/03/LetterFromThePresident.pdf
48. U.S. Government Accountability Office. 2021. "Operation Warp Speed. Accelerated COVID-19 Vaccine Development Status and Efforts to Address Manufacturing Challenges." Report to Congressional Addressees, February. https://www.gao.gov/assets/gao-21-319.pdf
49. Bur, Jessie. 2020. "On the Front Lines of COVID Response, This Agency Makes Safety Paramount." *Federal Times,* July 17. https://www.federaltimes.com/management/2020/07/17/on-the-front-lines-of-covid-response-this-agency-makes-safety-paramount/
50. South, Todd. 2020. "From the Front Lines: USPHS Officers Were Among the First to Respond to the Coronavirus Pandemic." *Military Officer* 18, no. 6: 40–45.
51. Dolasinski, Amanda. 2021. "'Stepping Into Chaos and Doing Our Best.' USPHS Officers Tell Their Stories of the COVID-19 Fight in What Became the Service's Biggest Deployment." *Military Officer* 19, no. 6: 40–47.
52. Andersen, Lauren E., Lisa Tripp, Joseph F. Perz, et al. 2021. "Protecting Nursing Home Residents From Covid-19: Federal Strike Team Findings and Lessons Learned." *NEJM Catalyst,* June 28.
53. Myles, Ian A., Daniel R. Johnson, Hanah Pham, et al. 2021. "USPHS Corps Care: Force Health Protection for Public Health Officers During the Ebola and COVID-19 Responses." *Public Health Reports* 136, no. 2: 148–153.
54. Carter, Alexis. 2020. "NHLBI's Childs on the Front Lines of Covid-19 Health Crisis." *NIH Record* 72, no. 11: 1, 4, 5. https://nihrecord.nih.gov/sites/recordNIH/files/pdf/2020/NIH-Record-2020-05-29.pdf
55. Sternberg, Steve. 2020. "Feds Send Medical 'Strike Team' to Washington State Nursing Home Hit by Coronavirus." *U.S. News,* March 6.

56. Lopez, C. Todd. 2020. "Comfort, Javits Center Open Care to COVID-19 Patients." *DOD News,* April 7. https://www.defense.gov/News/News-Stories/Article/Article/2140535/comfort-javits-center-open-care-to-covid-19-patients/
57. Sharfstein, Joshua M., and Georges C. Benjamin. 2020. "The Exceptional American Relationship to Public Health. Why the United States Has Failed So Spectacularly to Control COVID-19." *Foreign Affairs,* August 26.
https://www.foreignaffairs.com/articles/united-states/2020-08-26/exceptional-american-relationship-public-health
58. Costa, Robert, and Philip Rucker. 2020. "Woodward Book: Trump Says He Knew Coronavirus Was 'Deadly' and Worse Than the Flu While Intentionally Misleading Americans." *Washington Post,* September 9.
59. Banco, Erin. 2021. "Emails Reveal New Details of Trump White House Interference in CDC Covid Planning." *Politico,* November 12.
https://www.politico.com/news/2021/11/12/trump-cdc-covid-521128
60. U.S. House of Representatives. 2022. "'It Was Compromised': The Trump Administration's Unprecedented Campaign to Control CDC and Politicize Public Health During the Coronavirus Crisis." Select Subcommittee on the Coronavirus Crisis. Staff Report, October.
https://coronavirus.house.gov/news/reports/new-select-subcommittee-report-details-trump-administration-s-assault-cdc-and
61. Woolhandler, Steffie, David U. Himmelstein, Sameer Ahmed, et al. 2021. "Public Policy and Health in the Trump Era." *Lancet* 397, no. 10275: 705–753.
62. U.S. House of Representatives. 2021. "Select Subcommittee Releases Initial Findings From Transcribed Interview of Dr. Deborah Birx." Select Subcommittee on the Coronavirus Crisis. *Press Release,* October 26.
https://coronavirus-democrats-oversight.house.gov/news/press-releases/select-subcommittee-releases-initial-findings-transcribed-interview-dr-deborah
63. August, Melissa. 2020. "The 1918 Flu Pandemic Killed Hundreds of Thousands of Americans. The White House Never Said a Word About It." *Time,* August 11.
https://time.com/5877129/1918-pandemic-white-house/
64. Berger, Knute. 2020. "Meet the Anthony Fauci of 1918 Washington." *Crosscut,* April 13.
https://crosscut.com/2020/04/meet-anthony-fauci-1918-washington
65. Knapp, Alex. 2020. "The Dr. Fauci of the 1918 Spanish Flu." *Forbes,* April 28.
https://www.forbes.com/sites/alexknapp/2020/04/28/the-dr-fauci-of-the-1918-spanish-flu/?sh=518a40da3547
66. Spinney, Laura. 2017. "The 1918 Flu Pandemic That Revolutionized Public Health." Arizona State University, *Zócalo Public Square,* September 26.
https://www.zocalopublicsquare.org/2017/09/26/1918-flu-pandemic-revolutionized-public-health/ideas/nexus/
67. "How the 1918 Flu Changed Public Health." 2020. Triple Innovation, March.
https://tripleinnovation.com.au/history/how-the-1918-20-spanish-flu-changed-public-health/

Chapter Eighteen, *Pages 273–288*

1. Murthy, Vivek H. 2021. "Testimony of Vivek H. Murthy, M.D. Before the U.S. Senate Committee on Health, Education, Labor and Pensions." February 25.
https://www.help.senate.gov/imo/media/doc/Murthy.pdf
2. The White House. 2021. "Press Briefing by White House COVID-19 Response Team and Public Health Officials." September 10.
https://www.whitehouse.gov/briefing-room/press-briefings/2021/09/10/press-briefing-by-white-house-covid-19-response-team-and-public-health-officials-55/
3. The White House. 2021. "Press Briefing by White House COVID-19 Response Team and Public Health Officials." November 22.

https://www.whitehouse.gov/briefing-room/press-briefings/2021/11/22/press-briefing-by-white-house-covid-19-response-team-and-public-health-officials-69/

4. Abraham, Roshan, and Aparupa Mazumder. 2021. "U.S. COVID-19 Deaths Reach 800,000 as Delta Ravaged in 2021." *Reuters*, December 12.

5. The White House. 2021. "National Strategy for the COVID-19 Response and Pandemic Preparedness." Washington, DC, January.
https://www.whitehouse.gov/wp-content/uploads/2021/01/National-Strategy-for-the-COVID-19-Response-and-Pandemic-Preparedness.pdf

6. The White House. 2021. "U.S. COVID-19 Global Response and Recovery Framework." Washington, DC, July 1. https://www.whitehouse.gov/wp-content/uploads/2021/07/U.S.-COVID-19-Global-Response-and-Recovery-Framework.pdf

7. The White House. 2022. "National COVID-19 Preparedness Plan." Washington, DC, March 1.
https://www.whitehouse.gov/wp-content/uploads/2022/03/NAT-COVID-19-PREPAREDNESS-PLAN.pdf

8. Murthy, Vivek H. 2021. *Confronting Health Misinformation. The U.S. Surgeon General's Advisory on Building a Healthy Information Environment.* Washington, DC: Office of the Surgeon General, U.S. Department of Health and Human Services, in Collaboration With the Office of Evaluation Sciences, U.S. General Services Administration, July.

9. Murthy, Vivek H. 2021. *Protecting Youth Mental Health. The U.S. Surgeon General's Advisory.* Washington, DC: Office of the Surgeon General, U.S. Department of Health and Human Services, December.

10. Murthy, Vivek H. 2023. *Social Media and Youth Mental Health. The U.S. Surgeon General's Advisory.* Washington, DC: Office of the Surgeon General, U.S. Department of Health and Human Services, May.

11. Murthy, Vivek H. 2023. *Our Epidemic of Loneliness and Isolation. The U.S. Surgeon General's Advisory on the Healing Effects of Social Connection and Community.* Washington, DC: Office of the Surgeon General, U.S. Department of Health and Human Services, May.

12. Silverstein, Hanna. 2023. "Surgeons General Connect on Mental Health at Dartmouth." Office of the President. Dartmouth College, September 28.

13. U.S. Senate. "A Bill to Amend the Public Health Service Act to Provide Additional Funding for the Commissioned Corps of the Public Health Service." 2023.
https://www.wyden.senate.gov/imo/media/doc/commissioned_corps_of_the_public_health_service_act_text.pdf

14. National Institute on Drug Abuse. 2023. *Drug Overdose Death Rates.* February 9.
https://nida.nih.gov/research-topics/trends-statistics/overdose-death-rates

15. The White House. 2022. *National Drug Control Strategy.* Office of National Drug Control Policy, April 21.
https://www.whitehouse.gov/wp-content/uploads/2022/04/National-Drug-Control-2022Strategy.pdf

16. U.S. Department of Health and Human Services. 2022. "Biden Administration Announces $1.5 Billion Funding Opportunity for State Opioid Response Grant Program." HHS Press Office, May 19.
https://www.hhs.gov/about/news/2022/05/19/biden-administration-announces-15-billion-funding-opportunity-state-opioid-response-grant-program.html

17. Jones, Christopher M. 2023. "Responding to America's Overdose Crisis: An Examination of Legislation to Build Upon the SUPPORT Act." Testimony of Christopher M. Jones, PharmD, DrPH, MPH, Before the U.S. House Committee on Energy and Commerce Subcommittee on Health. June 21.
https://d1dth6e84htgma.cloudfront.net/Christopher_Jones_Witness_Testimony_HE_Hearing_06_21_23_ee139ac33f.pdf?updated_at=2023-06-20T14:11:33.116Z

18. Hicks, Kathleen H. 2022. "Implementation of Public Health Reform of the Military Health System." Memorandum. Department of Defense, October 31.

file:///C:/Users/James%20Knoben/Downloads/Implementation%20of%20Public%20Health%20Reform%20of%20the%20Military%20Health%20System%20OSD008809-22%20RES%20Final%20(5).pdf

19. Military Health System and Defense Health Agency. "Public Health." *Health.mil*. https://health.mil/Military-Health-Topics/Health-Readiness/Public-Health

20. Aker, Janet A. 2022. *The New Public Health Director Talks About His Goals for Force Readiness.* Military Health System and Defense Health Agency. *Health.mil,* April 5. https://www.health.mil/News/Articles/2022/04/05/The-New-Public-Health-Director-Talks-about-His-Goals-for-Force-Readiness

21. U.S. Department of Homeland Security. 2021. "Homeland Security Secretary Mayorkas Directs FEMA to Support Response for Unaccompanied Children." Press Release, March 13. https://www.dhs.gov/news/2021/03/13/homeland-security-secretary-mayorkas-directs-fema-support-response-unaccompanied

22. HHS, Administration for Children and Families. 2023. "ORR Unaccompanied Children Program Policy Guide. Section 3.3. Care Provider Required Services." Office of Refugee Resettlement, June 15. https://www.acf.hhs.gov/orr/policy-guidance/unaccompanied-children-program-policy-guide-section-3#:~:text=3.3.&text=Care%20providers%20must%20provide%20educational,of%20each%20unaccompanied%20alien%20child

23. Congressional Research Service. 2021. "Unaccompanied Alien Children: An Overview." Updated September 1. https://crsreports.congress.gov/product/pdf/R/R43599

24. Deployment data derived from HHS, OSG, Commissioned Corps Headquarters, in response to FOIA requests, 2021, 2022.

25. U.S. Department of Homeland Security. 2023. "Operation Allies Welcome." Updated September 22. https://www.dhs.gov/allieswelcome

26. U.S. Department of Homeland Security. 2022. "Operation Allies Welcome Announces Departure of All Afghan Nationals From the National Conference Center Safe Haven in Leesburg, VA." September 27. https://www.dhs.gov/news/2022/09/27/operation-allies-welcome-announces-departure-all-afghan-nationals-national

27. The White House. 1965. "Restoring the Quality of Our Environment. Report of the Environmental Pollution Panel, President's Science Advisory Committee." November.

28. Canadian Meteorological and Oceanographic Society. 1988. *World Conference on the Changing Atmosphere: Implications for Global Security.* Toronto, Canada, June 27-30. https://cmosarchives.ca/History/ChangingAtmosphere1988e.pdf

29. Union of Concerned Scientists. 2007. "Smoke, Mirrors and Hot Air. How ExxonMobil Uses Big Tobacco's Tactics to Manufacture Uncertainty on Climate Science." January. https://www.ucsusa.org/sites/default/files/2019-09/exxon_report.pdf

30. National Oceanic and Atmospheric Administration. 2024. "2023 Was the World's Warmest Year on Record, by Far." *NOAA News and Features,* January 12. https://www.noaa.gov/news/2023-was-worlds-warmest-year-on-record-by-far#:~:text=Below%20are%20highlights%20from%20NOAA's%202023%20annual%20global%20climate%20report%3A&text=Earth's%20average%20land%20and%20ocean,NOAA's%201850%2D2023%20climate%20record.

31. U.S. Global Change Research Program. 2018. "Fourth National Climate Assessment. Chapter 14, Human Health." November 23. https://nca2018.globalchange.gov/chapter/14/#

32. Salas, Renee N., Tynan H. Friend, Aaron Bernstein, and Ashish K. Jha. 2020. "Adding a Climate Lens to Health Policy In the United States." *Health Affairs (Millwood)* 39, no. 12: 2063–2070.

33. United Nations Intergovernmental Panel on Climate Change. 2023. "AR6 Synthesis Report: Climate Change 2023." Geneva: IPCC, March. https://www.ipcc.ch/report/sixth-assessment-report-cycle/

34. Biden, Joseph R. 2021. "Executive Order on Tackling the Climate Crisis at Home and Abroad." The White House, January 27.
35. Centers for Disease Control and Prevention. 2022. "Climate and Health Program." National Center for Environmental Health, November 29. https://www.cdc.gov/climateandhealth/default.htm
36. Atwoli L, Baqui AH, Benfield T, Bosurgi R, et al. 2021. "Call for Emergency Action to Limit Global Temperature Increases, Restore Biodiversity, and Protect Health." *Annals of Global Health* 87, no, 1: 88, 1–5.
37. Stein, Shira. 2022. "Health Sector Gets HHS Push to Join Climate Change Fight." *Bloomberg Law News,* May 20. https://news.bloomberglaw.com/health-law-and-business/health-sector-gets-hhs-push-to-join-climate-change-fight
38. University of Arizona. 2022. "U.S. Assistant Secretary for Health Admiral Rachel Levine Introduces Online Environmental Justice Index Tool in Tucson." Udall Center for Studies in Public Policy, December 13. https://udallcenter.arizona.edu/news/admiral-rachel-levine-environmental-justice-health-equity
39. Commissioned Officers Association. 1951. "Articles of Incorporation of Commissioned Officers Association of the United States Public Health Service, Inc." October 16.
40. Commissioned Officers Association. 2000. "Articles of Incorporation of Commissioned Officers Foundation, Inc." May 3.

CHAPTER NINETEEN, Pages 289–302

1. "Department of Health and Human Services. Statement of Organization, Functions, and Delegations of Authority." 2019. *Federal Register,* 84 FR 1752, February 5. https://www.govinfo.gov/content/pkg/FR-2019-02-05/pdf/2019-00955.pdf
2. Levine, Rachel L. 2022. "Readiness and Duty Requirements." Commissioned Corps Instruction 241.01, 3 November. https://dcp.psc.gov/ccmis/ccis/documents/CCI_241.01.pdf
3. Levine, Rachel L. 2022. "Deployment of Public Health Service Officers." Commissioned Corps Instruction 241.02, 7 November. https://dcp.psc.gov/ccmis/ccis/documents/CCI_241.02.pdf
4. Murthy, Vivek H. 2022. "Deployment Procedures." Personnel Operations Memorandum 821.76. 7 November. https://dcp.psc.gov/ccmis/ccis/documents/POM_821.76.pdf
5. "Announcing PHERST." 2021. *Commissioned Corps Bulletin* 1, no. 1: 3.
6. Department of Health and Human Services. 2022. "Public Health and Social Services Emergency Fund. Justification of Estimates for Appropriations Committee. Fiscal year 2022. Public Health and Emergency Response Strike Team." pp. 196–197. https://www.hhs.gov/sites/default/files/fy-2022-phssef-cj.pdf
7. Commissioned Corps Headquarters. 2023. "Public Health Emergency Response Strike Team MTF Officer. Vacancy Announcement." https://dcp.psc.gov/ccmis/PDF_docs/PHERST%20MTF%20(Military%20Treatment%20Facility)%20Officer%20vacancy%20announcement.pdf
8. Department of Health and Human Services. 2017. "Memorandum of Agreement between the Department of Health and Human Services and the U.S. Department of Veterans Affairs – Decision." January 13. [Approved January 17, 1917.]
9. Personal Communication. 2024. Veterans Health Administration, February 9.
10. Commissioned Corps of the U.S. Public Health Service. 2021. "Veterans Health Administration (VHA) Memorandum of Understanding (MOU) for Practice Hours." April. [Updated March 11, 2023.] https://dcp.psc.gov/ccmis/VHA_MOU.aspx
11. "About RAM." 2024. Remote Area Medical. https://www.ramusa.org/
12. Stevens, Clara, and Rovigel Gelviro. 2023. "Remote Area Medical – Tulsa, 2023." *COA Frontline* 61, no. 5: 9.

13. Carmona, Richard. 2017. "Instant Admirals and the Plague of Politics in the United States Public Health Service: Back to the Future." *Military Medicine* 182, no. 5: 1582–1583.
14. Landman, Keren. 2019. "For the Uniformed Public Health Service, Existential Questions." *Undark Magazine,* June 24. https://undark.org/2019/06/24/public-health-service-commissioned-corps/

CHAPTER TWENTY, *Pages 303–331*

1. Levine, Rachel L. 2022. "Category Specific Appointment Standards." Commissioned Corps Instruction 231.03, 18 April. https://dcp.psc.gov/ccmis/ccis/documents/CCI_231.03.pdf

INDEX

A

Abdellah, Faye G., 164, 317
acquired immunodeficiency
   syndrome (AIDS), 167, 179
   PACE program, 258
   Understanding AIDS, 168
Acts of Congress, foundational
   *[1798] Act for the Relief of Sick
      and Disabled Seamen*, 16
   *[1870] Act to Reorganize the
      Marine Hospital Service*, 19
   *[1889] Act to Regulate Appointments
      in the Marine Hospital Service*, 25
   *[1902] Act to Increase the Efficiency
      and Change the Name of the US
      Marine-Hospital Service*, 38
   *[1912] Act to Change the Name of
      the PHMHS to the Public Health
      Service... Other Purposes*, 46
Adams, Jerome M., 253, 259, 260, 266
Adams, John, 16
Administration for Children and
   Families (ACF), 230, 280
Administration for Strategic Preparedness and Response (ASPR),
   196, 210, 266, 289
Advisory Committee on Immunization
   Practices (ACIP), 137
Affordable Care Act (ACA). *See* Patient
   Protection and Affordable Care Act
Afghanistan and Iraq Wars, 215
AIDS. *See* acquired immunodeficiency syndrome
Air Commerce Act, 72
air pollution control, 110
Allen, Harry, 249
Allies Welcome Operation, 281
Alter, Harvey J., 157
American Cancer Society, 107, 124
American Heart Association, 124, 128
American Indian and Alaska Native.
   See Indian Health Service
American Medical Association (AMA),
   61, 113, 177

American Public Health Association
   (APHA), 21, 128
Anchor and Caduceus Society, 285
Anderson, John F., 39, 42, 47, 159
Anderson, Richard C., 292
Anderson, Robert J., 238
Andreasen, Christian, 251
Andreason, Paul J., 218
Andrews, John S., 181
Andrews, Justin M., 238
Andrus, Jon K., 174
Angel Island Immigration and
   Quarantine Stations, 37
anthrax attack (2001), 194
antimicrobials, discovery of, 80
Archambault, George F., 320
Armed Forces Medical Library, 121
Arnold, Francis A., 305
Arrindell, Evan R., 315
Artemis Operation, 280
Ashbaugh, Richard R., 320
aspirin and Reye syndrome, 151
Assistant Secretary for Health
   (and Scientific Affairs)
   creation, 133
   political appointee, 172, 301
Assistant Secretary for Preparedness
   and Response (ASPR). *See*
   Administration for Strategic Preparedness and Response (ASPR)
Atkins, Callis, 310
Atomic Energy Commission, 119
Axel, Richard, 157
Azar II, Alex M., 204, 259, 266

B

Babb, John T., 194, 202, 212, 213
Bachman, Leonard, 251, 323
Bailey, William D., 305
Barror, Richard F., 310
Bartko, John J., 198
Battese, Kelly J., 320
Bauer, Theodore J., 238
Beck, Daniel, 196, 233, 236

Belardo, Jose, 236
Bengtson, Ida A., 48
Benitez-McCrary, Mercedes, 327
Benjamin, Regina M., 223
Berry Plan, 157
Bertin, Richard J., 292, 320
Besteman, Karst J., 315
Biden, Joseph R., 265, 273
Billings, John Shaw, 18, 21, 121
Bina, Christopher A., 74
Bingham, J. Tyler, 320
Biologics Control Act, 25, 40, 57, 88
Biomedical Advanced Research and Development Authority (BARDA), 209, 266
Birx, Deborah L., 260, 266, 270
Bishop, J. Michael, 157
Black, Fred J., 100
Black, Greene V., 108
Blackwell, Michael J., 329
Blakely, Shirley A., 308
Blasser, Edward F., 249
block grants, 165
Blue, Rupert, 36, 45
Bolton, Frances P., 97
Bourn, Alberta C., 308
Bowen, Otis R., 171
Brand Guidelines, PHS, 262
Brands, Allen J., 116, 320
Brandt, Edward N., 163
Brown, Linda Morris, 315
Brown, Michael S., 157
Brutsché, Robert L., 76
Brye, Pamela, 308
bubonic plague, 34
Buell, Ernest E., 305
Bulletin of the Public Health, 21
Bunnell, Rebecca, 315
Bureau of Indian Affairs. *See* Indian Health Service
Bureau of Mines, 53
Bureau of Prisons, 74–76
Bureau of War Risk Insurance, 58, 65
Burgess, Ian K., 310
Burney, Leroy E., 121
Bush, George H.W., 175, 188
Bush, George W., 180, 194, 201, 215
Butler, Benjamin, 24, 29, 158

C

Cadet Nurse Corps, 98
Califano, Joseph A., 153, 160
Call to Action, definition, 190
Callagy, David W., 292
Camp Eason, 233
cancer initiatives
  Beau Biden Cancer Moonshot, 243
  Richard Nixon war on cancer, 147
Canton, Denise S., 292
Carmona, Richard H., 201, 206, 216
Carroll, James, 41
Carson, Rachel, *Silent Spring*, 130
Carter, Henry R., 40
Carter, James E. (Jimmy), 153
Cash, Richard A., 139
Castelli, William P., 264
Castle Garden Landing Depot, 30
Castle Island, first marine hospital, 17
Caulk, Margaret, 230
Centennial Proclamation, 171
Centers for Disease Control and Prevention (CDC), 101, 236–240
  acquisitions, 125, 136
  Ebola mission, 232, 236
  smallpox eradication, 155
Centers for Medicare and Medicaid Services, creation, 154
21st Century Cures Act, 189, 243
Chamberlain-Khan Act, 57
Chelikowsky, Bruce R., 313
Chen, Vivian T., 315
Cherry, William A., 249
Chiacchierini, Richard P., 325
Chief Professional Officer, 303
Childs, Richard W., 268, 280
Chinese Exclusion Act, 32, 38
Cholera, 138
Church, Richard M., 320
cigarette smoking. *See* Smoking and Health
Civil Rights Act, 134
Civil War, 18
Clark, Edith M., 308
Clark, Terri R., 329
climate change, 281–284
Clinton, J. Jarrett, 186
Clinton, William J. (Bill), 183, 187

Coast Guard, 248–249
  Direct Access system, 205, 229
  World War II, 99
Cobb, Julius O., 42
Cochrane, Robert G., 69
Cohen, Mandy K. 238
Cohen, Wilbur, 132, 133
Collins, Francis S., 159, 221, 266
Collins, Robert J., 305
Commissioned Corps, USPHS
  Affordable Care Act, 225, 226
  atomic energy monitoring, 119
  Brand Guidelines, 262
  Centennial Proclamation, 171
  Ceremonial features, 197
  challenges, 124, 142,
    170, 185, 300
  Coast Guard health care, 248
  commissioning nonmedical
    categories, 67, 95
  conditions of service, 259, 293
  core values, 205
  Corps Care, 268, 291
  deployments, 293–299
  Division of Commissioned
    Personnel, 191
  Doctrine, 262, 291
  duty stations, 335
  esprit de corps, 207
  force strength, 334
  formalization of, 25
  foundations of, 15
  GAO report, 117, 185, 300
  Headquarters, 290
  Honor Guard, 197
  Humanitarian Medal, 258
  humanitarian missions, 299
  Hundley Report, 125
  inspection of immigrants, 29
  management review, 229, 300
  mascot, 288
  militarization, 54, 98
  military doctor draft, 157
  military treatment facilities, 294
  mission statement, 205
  modernization initiative,
    259, 261, 291, 300
  Music Ensemble, 198
  NOAA health care, 250
  notable events, 11
  Office of Force Readiness and De-
    ployment (OFRD), 196, 204, 212
  Officer Basic Course (OBC),
    191, 204
  OMB force reduction plan, 259
  Parker Act, 67
  Perkins Report, 142
  PHERST, 294
  PHS Bicentennial, 199
  PHS hospital closures, 164
  PHS insignia/seal, 26
  PHS March and Fanfare, 199
  PHS Professional Categories, 304
  Presidential Unit Citation, 236
  Readiness and Deployment Branch,
    212, 293
  Readiness and Deployment Opera-
    tions Group (RedDOG),
    196, 212, 229
  Readiness Force (CCRF),
    194, 196, 212
  [Ready] Reserve Corps,
    54, 61, 65, 95, 226, 263, 296
  Remote Area Medical, (RAM), 295
  renewal initiative, 204, 300
  revitalization initiative, 170, 300
  tiered response structure,
    205, 214, 293
  training, 191, 204
  transformation initiative, 203, 300
  veterans' health care,
    58, 65, 245, 295
  World Health Organization, 105
Commissioned Corps Headquarters,
  206, 284, 290
  Directors, 292
Commissioned Officers Association
  and Foundation, 285
Communicable Disease Center. *See*
  Centers for Disease Control and
  Prevention (CDC)
Community Health Centers, 131, 154
Comprehensive Addiction and
  Recovery Act, 243
Comprehensive Health Manpower
  Training Act, 147
Congressional testimony, political
  interference, 216

Continuing Promise mission, 299
Cooper, Theodore, 149
Coppola, Dean, 234, 236
Corbin, Stephen B., 305
core values, PHS, 205
Coronavirus Aid, Relief, and Economic Security (CARES) Act, 263, 296
Coronavirus disease pandemic, 265–275
 administration politicization, 269
 comparison with 1918 pandemic, 271
 emergency declarations, 265, 275
 Operation Warp Speed, 266
 Public health response, 266
 PHS officer deployments, 267
 White House Response Team, 274
 White House Task Force, 266
Corps Care, 268, 291
Corrigan, David, 287
Costa, Charles F., 119
Couig, Mary Pat, 317
Cox, Herald R., 48
Cox, William, 327
Crow, Thomas E., 313
Cumming, Hugh S., 52, 63
Currie, James T., 287
Currier, Dean, 327
Cutter incident, polio, 112
Cyclamate sweetener, 143

D

Dahlman, Suzanne, 292
Davidson, R. Michael, 191, 292
Dawber, Thomas R., 264
Dean, H. Trendley, 109
DeBakey Commission, 136
Dental Category CPO, History, 305
Department of Agriculture, Food Pyramid, MyPlate, 224
Department of Defense (DOD)
 Defense Health Agency, 279
 Ebola mission, 233
 Humanitarian Medal, 258
 military treatment facilities, 294
 PHS collaboration, 10, 202
 PHS Partnership for Psychological Health Initiative, 217
Department of Homeland Security, 218, 248, 281
Department of Interior, 73

Department of Veterans Affairs, 65, 295
deployments, PHS, 293–299
Diamond, Murray A., 292
Dieser, Edward M., 310
Dietitian Category CPO, History, 308
disinformation, 144, 270, 275, 282
Diullo, Gene A., 327
Division of Commissioned Corps Personnel and Readiness, 212, 229
Division of Strategic National Stockpile, 196
Doctrine, PHS, 262, 291
Dollymore, Maura, 249
Donora, PA, air pollution, 110
Dozoretz, Nina, 315
Draper, Warren F., 100
Dresher, Erwin C., 292
Duckworth, Tammy, 277
Dunn, Derek E., 198, 325
duty stations, 335
Dyer, Rolla E., 48, 102, 159

E

Eason, John C. (Camp Eason), 233
Ebola virus disease (EVD) epidemic, 232–237
Eckert, John, 325
Edwards, Calvin W., 236
Egeberg, Roger O., 141
Ehrlich, S. Paul, 148
Eisenhower, Dwight D., 121
Elders, M. Joycelyn, 183
Elizondo, Epifanio, 173, 234, 315
Ellis Island Immigration Station, 30
Emergency Health Personnel Act, 146
emergency preparedness, response, 209
Emergency Support Function #8, 210, 283
Enduring Promise mission, 299
Engineer Category CPO, History, 310
environmental health, 52, 120, 130
Environmental Health Category CPO, History, 313
Environmental Protection Agency (EPA), 119, 130, 142, 181
Epidemic Intelligence Service (EIS), 102, 111, 120, 237
Etzel, Ruth A., 181

F

Faget, Guy H., 69
Falter, Robert G., 315
Farrell, Gerard M., 202, 203, 287
Fauci, Anthony S., 157, 169, 180, 266, 271, 274
Federal Bureau of Prisons, 74–76
Federal Emergency Management Agency (FEMA), 234, 280
Federal Food, Drug, and Cosmetic Act, 88
federalization of quarantine, 32
Federal Medical Stations, 197
Federal Security Agency, 94, 113
Felix, Robert H., 104
Finlay, Carlos, 41
Fishburn, Howard D., 249
Fitzgerald, Brenda, 238
Fleming, Alexander, 80
Fletcher, Robert R., 249
Flexner, Abraham, 44
Flexner, Simon, 68
fluoridation of water, 108
Foard, Fred T., 114
Foege, William H., 156, 238
Foley, Teresa H., 287
Food and Drug Administration (FDA), 88–93, 113
  tobacco legislation, 218
Ford, Gerald R., 141, 149
Foreign Quarantine Service, 136
Forsyth, Bruce D., 305
Framingham Heart Study, 264
Frank, Leslie C., 71
Fredrickson, Donald S., 157, 159
Fricks, Lunsford D., 43
Frieden, Thomas R., 232, 238
Fromherz, William, 327
Frost, Wade H., 52
fuel, leaded, 144
Fuller, Justin K., 75
Furman, Lawrence J., 292

G

Gabbert, Donald H., 173
Gallegos, Thomas G., 310
Gallo, Robert C., 167
Galson, Steven K., 92, 93, 217
GAO report, 117, 185, 300

Garcia, Joseph, 315
Gardner, John W., 133
Gardner, Randall J.F., 310
Gaustad, Scott, 327
Gehrig, Leo J., 135
GenBank®, 121
Gerberding, Julie L., 238
German American relocation, 103
Gibbins, John D., 329
Giberson, Scott F., 233, 235, 236, 292, 320
Gillespie, James M., 249
Gillis, Eugene A., 292
Gilman, Alfred G., 157
Giroir, Brett P., 254, 259, 261, 266
Goddard, James L., 90, 238
Goldberger, Joseph, 48, 51
Goldman, David P., 323
Goldstein, Joseph L., 157
Gordon, Suzan, 308
Gorgas, William C., 41
Grade "A" Pasteurized Milk Ordinance, 71
great sanitary awakening, 6
Green, Richard S., 310
Greene, John C., 154, 305
Grim, Charles W., 117
Grinnell, Randy E., 313
Guatemala STD Experiment, 87
Gulf War, 180
Gupta, Rahul, 277
Gupta, Sanjay, 223
Guthrie, Marshall C., 114, 249

H

Haas, Victor H., 100
Haffner, Marlene E., 92
Haffner, William H.J., 323
Hahn, Stephen M., 90, 266
Hale, Kis Robertson, 329
Halliday, Christopher G., 305
Halperin, Jerome A., 92
Hamilton, Alexander, 16
Hamilton, John B., 22
Hansen, Gerhard-Henrik, 69
Hansen's Disease, 34, 69
Hastings, Robert C., 69
Havens, George, 215
Hawk, Floyd A., 100

Hayes, Arthur H., 90
Headquarters, PHS Corps, 290
Health and Human Services (HHS)
 Department of, creation, 154
Health Care Financing Administration
 (HCFA), creation, 154
health disparity/equity, 7, 191
Health, Education, and Welfare (HEW)
 Department of, creation, 94, 113.
 See also Health and Human Services
health insurance, 53
Health Maintenance Organizations
 (HMOs), 148
Health Services Category CPO
 History, 315
Healthy People report, 161
Healy, Bernadine, 159
Heiser, Victor G., 26
Held, Joe R., 329
Helgeson, Scott M., 292
Helminiak, Clare, 215, 323
Henderson, Donald A., 155
Henry, O. Marie, 317
Higgins, Paul J., 249
Hill, Joseph Lister, 121, 127
Hill-Burton Act, 105, 114, 136, 150
Hilleboe, Herman E., 102
Hilleman, Maurice, 138
Hirschhorn, Norbert, 139
Hispanic-Latino health, 178
Holliday, Mitchel, 308
Hollis, Mark D., 102, 238, 310
Holt, Richard B., 249
Honor Guard, 197
hookworm disease, 41
Hooper, Norman V., 305
Hoover, Herbert C., 67, 74, 124, 158
Hoskins, John K., 310
Howard, Kenneth D., 315
Hudgins, Michael P., 249
Hughart, Joseph L., 215
Human Genome Project, 221
human immunodeficiency virus
 (HIV), 167, 179
Humanitarian Medal, 258
humanitarian missions, 299
Hundley Report, 125
Hunter, Joan F., 292

Hurricanes
 Andrew, 179
 Charley, Frances, Ivan, Jeanne, 212
 Gustav, Ike, 217
 Harvey, Irma, Maria, 256
 Katrina, Rita, Wilma, 213
 Matthew, 246
 Sandy, 229
Huy, Janice, 308
Huylebroeck, Michael R., 327
Hygienic Laboratory, 23, 39, 67, 158

I

Immigration Act of 1891, 29
Immigration and Customs Enforcement
 (ICE), Health Service Corps (IHSC)
 218–220
immunization schedules, 137
Indian Health Service (IHS), 113–118
industrial health/hygiene. *See*
 occupational health/hygiene
industrial revolution, 6, 29
influenza
 Asian (H2N2), 122
 influenza A (H3N2), 138, 150
 novel A (H1N1), 228
 Spanish influenza (H1N1), 60, 271
 Surveillance Unit, 122
 Swine influenza (H1N1), 150
insulin, discovery of, 80
In Their Words
 Carmona, Richard H., 206
 Fauci, Anthony S., 169
 Galson, Steven K., 93
 Giroir, Brett P., 261
 Jones, Christopher M., 278
 Kendig, Newton E., 76
 Lushniak, Boris D., 235
 Martin, Edward D., 172
 Migliaccio, Gene, 220
 Moritsugu, Kenneth P., 192
 Reed, Paul, 284
 Schuchat, Anne, 239
 Seligman, Paul J., 182
 Taylor, Brandon L., 279
 Vanderwagen, W. Craig, 211
 Weahkee, Michael, 118
Iraq and Afghanistan Wars, 215
Italian American relocation, 103

J

Jacobson, Robert R., 69
Janney, Harold M., 75
Japanese American relocation, 103
Jarvis, Charles, 17
Jefferson, Thomas, 19, 250
Jellerson, Leon R., 249
Jenner, Edward, 28
Jha, Ashish K., 274
Jiggens, Timothy, 313
Johnson, Daniel R., 288
Johnson, Emery A., 117
Johnson, Jerry M., 325
Johnson, Joyce M., 249, 323
Johnson, Lyndon B., 131, 154, 281
Johnson, Michael W., 305
Johnston, Henry V., 249
Jones, Christopher M., 278
Joseph, Lireka P., 325

K

Kannel, William B., 264
Kelsey, Frances O., 89
Kempf, Grover, 108
Kendig, Newton E., 76
Kennedy, John F., 89, 127
Kessler, David A., 274
King III, George, 199
King, Marion R., 75
King, Walter W., 249
Kinyoun, Joseph J., 23, 35, 39, 159
Kleinman, Dushanka V., 305
Knouss, Robert F., 194
Knutson, John W., 305
Koch, Robert, 24, 28, 102
Koh, Howard K., 1, 229
Kolb, Lawrence, 73
Koop, C. Everett, 9, 163, 203, 216, 251
Koplan, Jeffrey P., 238
Koprowski, Hilary, 112
Korean War, 111
Kosovo War, 193
Krumbiegel, Stanley E., 75

L

Laboratory of Hygiene, 23, 39, 67, 158
Lalonde, Marc, 161
Langmuir, Alexander D., 102, 111
Larson, Delbert A., 292
Lasker, Albert and Mary, 107

Lavinder, Claude H., 50, 58
lead poisoning
　fuel additive, 144
　paint additive, 143
League of Nations, 64, 96
Leavitt, Michael O., 204, 213
Lee, Philip R., 133, 185
Lefkowitz, Robert J., 157
Legionnaires' Disease, 151
Leone, Lucile Petry, 97, 317
Leprosy (Hansen's Disease), 34, 69
Leukefeld, Carl G., 315
Levine, Rachel L., 283
Levy, Daniel, 264
Lewis, Brian, 91, 323
Linder, Forrest E., 123
Lin-Fu, Jane, 143
Lloyd, Ralph S., 305
Long, Gillis W., 69
Lord, Michael W., 287
Lucca, William J., 287
Lumsden, Leslie L., 70
Lurie, Nicole, 209
Lushniak, Boris D., 231, 234–236
Luten, Emma J., 308

M

Maas, William R., 305
Mackler, Stuart, 156
Mainzer, Hugh M., 329
Makrides, Nicholas S., 305
Malaria Control in War Areas, 101, 237
management review initiative, 229, 300
Manley, Audrey F., 147, 184
Mansell, Robert E., 327
March of Dimes, 112
Marine Hospital Fund, 16
Marine Hospital Service
　creation, 16
　formalization, 25
　hospital closures, 164
　insignia/seal, 26
　inspection of immigrants, 29
　Marine Hospital Fund, 16
　Marine Hospitals, 17
　Name change, 38, 46
　reform legislation, 19
　Supervising Surgeon General, 19
Marsh, Jeanean Willis, 315

Marston, Robert Q., 159
Martin, Edward D., 147, 171, 172
Marunycz, Lisa, 160
mascot, 288
Mason, James O., 172, 177, 238
maternal, child health, 64, 79, 84, 165
Maxcy, Kenneth F., 48
Mazzella, Carolyn Beth, 317
McClintic, Thomas B., 43
McCoy, George W., 47, 67, 159
McDade, Joseph, 151
McElligott, John E., 287
McGarvey, Charles L., 327
McGinnis, J. Michael, 161
McKay, Frederick S., 108
McLaughlin, Allan J., 52, 249
McLaughlin, Margaret, 317
McMahan, Sean, 218
McMullen, John, 48
McSwain, Robert G., 117
McTigue, James F., 325
Meadors, Gilcin F., 264
Measles
　eradication, 193
　vaccine, 137
Mecklenburg, Robert E., 305
MEDEX Program, 173
Medical Reserve Corps, 210
Medicare, Medicaid, 131, 134, 154
mental health/hygiene
　detail PHS officers to DOD, 217
　Surgeon General advisory, 276
　Surgeon General report, 188
Messner, Clinton T., 305
Meyer, Harry M., 91, 137
Michael, Jerrold M., 286
Michael, Madeline, 308
Michel, Carl, 248, 249
Migliaccio, Gene, 220
militarization of PHS Corps, 54, 98
military doctor draft, 157
military treatment facilities, 294
milk pasteurization, 71
Milner, Michael R., 173, 315
mine safety, 53, 119, 145
Minnigerode, Lucy, 59
Mishoe, Helena O., 325
misinformation, 270, 275
mission, PHS, 205
Mix, Aisha K., 219, 317
modernization initiative,
　259, 261, 300
Monrovia Medical Unit, 233
Montagnier, Luc, 167
Moon, Jennifer, 219, 317
Moore, Roscoe M., 329
Morbidity and Mortality Weekly Report, 125, 136
Moritsugu, Kenneth P., 76,
　147, 192, 197, 200, 202, 216
Mountin, Joseph W., 101, 111, 120, 237
Mullan, Fitzhugh, 147
Murad, Ferid, 157
Murthy, Vivek H., 236, 241, 273
Music Ensemble, 198

N

Nalin, David R., 139
naloxone advisory, 254
Narcotic Farms Act, 73
National Association of State Health Commissioners, 21
National Board of Health, 21, 23
National Cancer Act, 85, 108, 147, 158
National Center for Biomedical Communications, 121
National Center for Biotechnology Information, 121
National Center for Health Statistics, 123, 162
National Disaster Medical System (NDMS), 194, 210
National Formulary, 88
national health insurance, 53
National Health Interview Survey, 66, 123
National Health Planning Act, 136, 149
National Health Security Strategy, 210
National Health Service Corps (NHSC), 146, 154
National Heart Institute, 108, 124, 264
National Heart, Lung, and Blood Act, 148, 264
National Incident Management System, 209
National Institute for Occupational Safety and Health, 146

National Institute of Allergy and Infectious Diseases, 43, 68, 108, 169, 236
National Institute of Dental Research, 108, 109
National Institute(s) of Health (NIH), 67, 85, 105, 108, 131, 158–160, 236
National Institute of Mental Health, 104, 108
National Interagency Council on Smoking and Health, 145, 160
national leprosarium, 34, 69
National Library of Medicine, 121
National Mental Health Act, 104, 108
National Oceanic and Atmospheric Administration (NOAA), 250–251
  climate change, 282
  origins of PHS in NOAA, 251
National Park Service, 73
National Pharmaceutical Stockpile, 196
National Prevention, Health Promotion, and Public Health Council, 226
National Public Health Week, 199
National Quarantine Act
  Act of 1878, 21
  Act of 1893, 33, 72
National Research Act, 77
National Response Framework, 209, 210, 289
National Security Strategy, 10
Nelson, Kenneth R., 249
Nesseler, Kerry Paige, 317
New Deal, 78, 84
Newman, Sara B., 73
Nixon, Richard M., 141, 147, 148
Nobel Prize, PHS recipients, 157
Noji, Eric K., 215
Nomenclature of Diseases (Woodworth), 20
notable events, 11
Novello, Antonia C., 175
nuclear testing, 119
Nurse Category CPO, History, 317
Nurse Training Act, 97, 131, 147

O

Obama, Barack H., 209, 223, 225, 232, 236, 241
Obama, Michelle, 224
obesity epidemic, 190, 208, 224

O'Connor, Ralph, 325
occupational health/hygiene, 53, 97, 146, 238
Occupational Safety and Health Administration (OSHA), 146
Office for Human Research Protections, 77
Office of Civilian Defense, 103
Office of Force Readiness and Deployment (OFRD), 196, 204, 212
Office of Management and Budget (OMB), Corps challenges, 124, 170, 259, 300
Office of Public Health Emergency Preparedness, 209
Office of the Assistant Secretary for Preparedness and Response (ASPR). *See* Administration for Strategic Preparedness and Response (ASPR)
Officer Basic Course (OBC), 191, 204
Omnibus Budget Reconciliation Act (OBRA), 164
One Health concept, 120
Operation Allies Welcome, 281
Operation Artemis, 280
Operation Provide Refuge, 193
Operation Warp Speed, 266
opioid epidemic, 243, 254, 277
oral health
  Surgeon General report, 189, 208
  water fluoridation, 108
oral rehydration therapy, 138
Orphan Drug Act, 92
Orsega, Susan M., 292, 317
Osbourne, Elton S., 292
Ossenfort, William F., 73

P

Paavola, Fred G., 320
Pacific Partnership mission, 299
paint, lead-based, 143
Pandemic and All-Hazards Preparedness Act (PAHPA), 209
Parham, Alan G., 313
Parker Act, 67
Parker, Ralph R., 43
Parkman, Paul D., 91, 137
Parran, Thomas J., 68, 77, 83, 86, 105

Partnership for Psychological Health
  Initiative, 217
Pasteur, Louis, 71
pasteurization of milk, 71
Patient Protection and Affordable
  Care Act (ACA), 225
  National Prevention Council, 226
  Ready Reserve Corps, 226, 263
Patterson, Clair C., 144
Pazdan, Renee M., 269
Pearson, William F., 310
Peck, Carl C., 92
pellagra, 50
Pence, Michael R., 260, 266
penicillin, discovery of, 80
Perkins Report, 142
Petry (Leone), Lucile, 97, 317
Pharmacist Category CPO, History, 320
PHERST, 294
PHS Bicentennial, 199
PHS insignia/seal, 26
PHS March and Fanfare, 199
physician assistant, 75, 173
Physician Category CPO, History, 323
Pittman, Robert E., 320
plague, bubonic, 34
Platt, Laurence J., 146
Plotnick, Julia R., 317
Poliomyelitis, 112
  Cutter incident, 112
  eradication, 174
  Surveillance Unit, 112
  vaccine, 112
political appointee
  Assistant Secretary for Health,
    172, 301
  Surgeon General, 301
pollution control, 52, 109, 110, 130
Pond, Cynthia L., 329
Portt, James, 173
Presidential Unit Citation, 236
President's Emergency Plan for
  AIDS Relief (PEPFAR), 180
Presley, Diedre N., 219, 315
Prevention through Active Community
  Engagement (PACE), 258
Professional Advisory Committee, 303
Professional Categories, 304

Professional Category CPO and History
  Dental Category, 305
  Dietitian Category, 308
  Engineer Category, 310
  Environmental Health Category, 313
  Health Services Category, 315
  Nurse Category, 317
  Pharmacist Category, 320
  Physician Category, 323
  Scientist Category, 325
  Therapist Category, 327
  Veterinarian Category, 329
progressive era, 45
Project Bioshield Act, 209
Prusiner, Stanley B., 157
Przekurat, Carolyn B., 308
Public Health Reports, 21, 61
Public Health Service Act, 67, 94,
  98, 102, 109, 130, 172, 209, 248
Public Health Service Bicentennial, 199
Pure Food and Drugs Act, 88

Q

Quarantine
  Act of 1878, 21
  Act of 1893, 33, 72
  boarding launch, 72
  Service, CDC, 136

R

Rabeau, Erwin S., 117
radiological health, 123
Ransdell Act, 67, 158
Rathke, Christian, 250, 251
Readiness and Deployment Operations Group (RedDOG),
  196, 212, 229
[Ready] Reserve Corps,
  54, 61, 95, 226, 263, 296
Reagan, Ronald, 163, 164
Redd, Stephen C., 228
Redfield, Robert R., 238, 266
Reed, Paul, 283, 284
Reed, Walter, 40
Regional Medical Programs, 136, 150
rehydration therapy, 138
Remote Area Medical, 295
renewal initiative, 204, 300
Rensberger, Judith, 287

revitalization initiative, 170, 300
Reye syndrome, 151
Rhoades, Everett R., 117
Rice, Morrisa, 269
Richards, Charlotte, 327
Richardson, Elliot L., 142
Richardson, Jeffrey, 327
Richmond, Julius B., 153, 199, 203
Ricketts, Howard T., 42
Ricks, Timothy L., 305
Rimple, Hubert McDonald, 147
R.J. Reynolds Tobacco Company, 177
Robertson, H.McG., 249
Robinson, Erica, 287
Rockefeller Sanitary Commission, 42
Rocky Mountain Laboratory(ies), 43, 68
Rocky Mountain spotted fever, 42
Rodenbeck, Sven E., 310
Rogers, Paul, 142, 149
Romano, Carol A., 317
Roosevelt, Franklin D., 78, 84, 85, 112, 158
Roosevelt, Theodore, 38, 88
Roper, William L., 238
Rosenau, Milton J., 39, 68, 71, 159
Roubideaux, Yvette, 117
Roybal, Edward R., 238
Rubella vaccine, 137
Rucker, William C., 43
Rutstein, David C., 212, 223, 323
Rychnovsky, Jacqueline, 287

S

Sabin, Albert B., 112
Sachar, David B., 139
Saint Elizabeth's Hospital, 94, 113
Salk, Jonas E., 112
Sanders, Martin L., 325
Sandhu, Sukhminder K., 325
San Francisco plague epidemic, 34
sanitary reform, 6, 70
Satcher, David, 187, 216, 238
Scheele, Leonard A., 107
Schier, Joshua G., 323
Schmoyer, Michael, 235
Schobitz, Richard P., 292
Schuchat, Anne, 228, 239
Schwartz, Erica G., 247, 249
Schweitzer, Pamela M., 320

Scientist Category CPO, History, 325
Scott, Harold G., 157
Sebelius, Kathleen, 225
Sebrell, William H., 159
Selective Service Act of 1917, 55
Selective Training and Service Act, 96
Seligman, Paul J., 181, 182
Sencer, David J., 238
sexually transmitted disease (STD).
   See venereal disease *[outdated term]*
Shadow on the Land (Parran), 86
Shaeffer, James K., 292
Shannon, James A., 159
Shaw, James R., 114, 117
Shepherd, Craig A., 313
Sheppard-Towner Act, 64, 79, 84
Ship's Medicine Chest, 27
Siegel, Karen L., 327
Siegfried, Ernest C., 75
Silent Spring (Carson), 130
Sinclair, Upton, *The Jungle*, 88
smallpox eradication, 155
Smith, Charles E., 75
Smith, Clarence A., 238
Smith, E. Lee W., 292
Smith, Richard A., 135, 173
Smith, Richard J., 147
Smoking and Health, 124, 128
   cigarette package warning, 129
   e-cigarettes, 244, 255
   Family Smoking Prevention and
      Tobacco Control Act, 218, 244
   Office on Smoking and Health, 160
   Surgeon General reports
      SG Burney statement, 124
      SG Terry report, 128
      SG Steinfeld report, 145
      SG Richmond report, 160
      SG Koop report, 166
      SG Novello report, 176
      SG Elders report, 184
      SG Satcher report, 188
      SG Carmona report, 207
      SG Benjamin report, 227
      ASG Lushniak report, 232
      SG Murthy report, 244
      SG Adams report, 255
social media advisory, 277
Social Security Act, 78, 84

Spanish influenza, 60, 271
Sparrow, Donna, 287
Spencer, Roscoe R., 43
Steele, James H., 120, 329
Steinfeld, Jesse L., 141
Steinman, Alan M., 249
Stevenson, Albert H., 310
Stewart, Paul M., 249
Stewart, W.D., 18
Stewart, William H., 132
Stiles, Charles W., 41, 70
Stokes, William S., 329
Stone, Alan, 327
Stone, Robert S., 159
Strategic National Stockpile, 196, 210
suicide prevention, 190, 227
Sullivan, Louis W., 175–177
Surgeons General, Deputy Surgeons General 1871–2023, 336
Sydenstricker, Edgar, 51, 53, 66
Symposium, USPHS Scientific and Training, 286

T

Taft, William H., 45
Taylor, Brandon L., 279
Taylor, Darold W., 313
Taylor, Kelly M., 313
Tedesco, Mark J., 249
Terrell, James G., 292
terrorism attacks, anthrax, 194,
    World Trade Center, 194
Terry, Luther L., 127
Theiler, Max, 41
The Jungle (Sinclair), 88
The Milk Question (Rosenau), 71
Therapist Category CPO, History, 327
Thomas, Dana L., 249
Thomas, Marvin, 329
Thompson, Lewis R., 68, 99, 159
Thompson, Tommy, 203
Thoroughman, Doug A., 325
Three Mile Island incident, 160
Tierkel, Ernest S., 329
tobacco use. *See* Smoking and Health
Todd, James S., 177
Todd, James W., 100
Todd, John G., 313
Topping, Norman H., 48

Tosatto, Robert J., 210
Touch, Ralph J., 313
Townsend, James G., 114
transformation initiative, 203, 300
trachoma, 31, 48
Treadway, Walter L., 59, 73
Trent-Adams, Sylvia, 236, 247, 317
Truesdell, Dale, 292
Trujillo, Michael H., 117
Truman, Harry S., 99, 104, 107
Truman, Richard W., 70
Trump, Donald J., 247, 253, 269, 283
tuberculosis, 102, 136
tularemia, 47
Tuskegee Syphilis Study, 77
Tuttle, Thomas D., 271
typhoid fever, 52, 70
typhus fever, 47

U

unaccompanied children, 230, 258, 280
United Nations (UN), 96, 105, 282
U.S. Agency for International Development (USAID), 216, 232
U.S. Pharmacopeia (USP), 88
uranium mining, 119

V

van Ackeren, Joseph F., 249
Van Den Berg, Jessica Acosta, 116
Vanderwagen, W. Craig, 209, 211, 323
Varmus, Harold E., 157, 159
Vause, Richard C., 173, 197
venereal disease, 77, 86, 96, 136
    Chamberlain-Kahn Act, 57
    National VD Control Act, 77, 86
    Shadow on the Land, 86
Verrone, Geswaldo A., 313
Veterans Administration, 65
Veterans Affairs, 65, 295
Veterans' Bureau, 65
veterans' health care
    PHS provider of, 58, 65, 245, 295
Veterinarian Category CPO, History, 329
veterinary public health, 120
Vietnam War, 156
Villforth, John C., 91, 310
vocational education, rehabilitation, 58, 65
Vonderlehr, Raymond A., 238

W

Wagner, Carruth J., 117
Walensky, Rochelle, 238, 274
Walling, Richard S., 320
Wallis, Pete P., 215
Wang, Emil P., 310
Warren, Benjamin S., 53
War Risk Insurance Bureau, 58, 65
Wasserman, Martin P., 147
Water
  Flint, MI emergency, 245
  fluoridation, 108
  pollution control, 52, 109, 130
Waterhouse, Benjamin, 17
Watson, James, 221
Weahkee, Michael D., 117, 118
Weaver, Donald L., 147
Weekly Abstract of Sanitary Reports, 21
Wekenman, Charles W., 305
Welch, Michael M., 313
Welsh, Thomas, 17
West, Ronald R., 327
Whiteside, Daniel F., 305
Whitney, Robert A., 329
Wiley, Harvey W., 88
Williams-Fleetwood, Sharon, 325
Williams, Louis L., 101, 238
Williams, Robert C., 202, 310
Wilson, Luke and Helen, 85, 158
Wilson, Woodrow, 54, 56, 271
Windom, Robert E., 171
Winslow, Charles-Edward Amory, 6
Wise, Harry S., 157
Woodruff, Bradley A., 215
Woodworth, John M., 19, 21
World Health Assembly, 105, 156, 174
World Health Organization, 105, 155
World Trade Center attacks, 194
World War I, 53
  extra-cantonment sanitation, 56
  militarization of PHS, 54
  Selective Service Act, 55
  venereal disease control, 57
World War II, 95
  extra-cantonment sanitation, 96
  industrial hygiene, 97
  malaria control, 101
  militarization of PHS, 98
  Selective Training and Service Act, 96
Wright, William T., 305
Wyden, Ronald, 277
Wyatt, Richard G., 160
Wyman, Walter, 29, 39
Wyngaarden, James B., 157, 159

Y

Yakima County, WA, 70
yellow fever, 21, 40
Yellow Fever Commission, 40
Yersin, Alexandre, 34
Yeskey, Kevin S., 193
Yolles, Tamarath K., 292
Young, Frank E., 90, 180, 181

Z

Zerhouni, Elias A., 159
Zients, Jeffrey D., 274
Zika virus, 246
zoonotic diseases, 120

AUTHOR

JAMES E. KNOBEN holds a Doctor of Pharmacy degree from the University of California, San Francisco (UCSF) and a Master of Public Health degree from Yale University, School of Medicine. Dr. Knoben served on active duty over 33 years, retiring with the rank of Captain in the U.S. Public Health Service.

He began his PHS career in 1971 upon joining Dr. Donald C. Brodie, theoretician of the national clinical pharmacy movement at the National Center for Health Services Research. Positions held include Pharmacy Advisor, National Professional Standards Review Council; HHS Regional Pharmacy Consultant, Southwest U.S.; Director, Division of Drug Information Resources, Food and Drug Administration (12 years); and Special Assistant to Associate Director, National Library of Medicine. Dr. Knoben was the founder and co-editor with UCSF colleagues of ten editions of the *Handbook of Clinical Drug Data* – deemed a classic, the book was used worldwide in pharmacy and medical education and clinical practice.

CAPT Knoben has been actively involved in the support of USPHS officers, including the creation of three books. Along with *Pandemics, Politics, & Public Health*, he is co-author with CAPT Alice Knoben of the *PHS Officer's Guide: Leadership, Protocol & Service Standards (1st/2nd Editions)*, and co-editor with former Surgeon General Richard H. Carmona and RADM Jerrold M. Michael of *Public Health Emergency Preparedness & Response: Principles & Practice*. He also served as a PHS Commissioned Corps Liaison Officer and as co-Executive Director of the USPHS Music Ensemble. He was a member of the Board of Directors of the Commissioned Officers Association and the Board of Trustees of the PHS Commissioned Officers Foundation for the Advancement of Public Health, serving as its President from 2008 to 2010.

CAPT Knoben is the recipient of several notable awards including three U.S. Surgeon General's Exemplary Service Medals, the USPHS George F. Archambault Career Achievement Award in Pharmacy, the Washington DC Metropolitan Society of Health System Pharmacists Pharmacist of the Year Award, American Society of Hospital Pharmacists [National] Award for Achievement in Professional Practice, the UCSF 150th Anniversary Alumni Excellence Award, the UCSF Pharmacy Distinguished Alumnus of the Year Award, and he is a Fellow of the American Pharmacists Association. His service in the Commissioned Corps and work with the Association and Foundation engendered an enduring interest in the heritage of the U.S. Public Health Service.

CONTRIBUTING EDITOR

BORIS D. LUSHNIAK holds a Doctor of Medicine degree from Northwestern University and a Master of Public Health degree from Harvard University, and maintains specialty certifications in dermatology and preventive medicine. He served on active duty for 27 years, retiring with the rank of Rear Admiral, upper half, in the U.S. Public Health Service. Dr. Lushniak began his USPHS career in 1988 in the CDC Epidemic Intelligence Service and initially served with the National Institute for Occupational Safety and Health (NIOSH) in Cincinnati, Ohio. He also served on mission assignments in Bangladesh, St. Croix, Russia, and Kosovo, and was part of the CDC/-NIOSH team at Ground Zero and the CDC anthrax team in Washington, DC. In 2004, he transferred to the U.S. Food and Drug Administration and in 2005 was named FDA Assistant Commissioner for Counterterrorism Policy.

RADM Lushniak was appointed the Deputy Surgeon General in November 2010 and served in that capacity until September 2015, assisting the Surgeon General in articulating the best available scientific information to the public to improve personal health and the health of the nation. He was responsible, as well, for overseeing the operations of the U.S. Public Health Service Commissioned Corps. From July 2013 until December 2014, Dr. Lushniak served as the Acting Surgeon General, during which he released the 50th Anniversary *Surgeon General's Report on Smoking and Health* and the first ever *Surgeon General's Call to Action to Prevent Skin Cancer*. From January to March 2015, he commanded the USPHS Monrovia Medical Unit in Liberia, the only U.S. government hospital providing care to Ebola patients. RADM Lushniak is the recipient of several high level honor awards including the U.S. Surgeon General's Medallion, U.S. Surgeon General's Exemplary Service Medal, PHS Distinguished Service Medal, two PHS Outstanding Service Medals, and the American Medical Association Distinguished Service Award.

Upon retirement from the USPHS, Dr. Lushniak was appointed as Professor and Chair of the Department of Preventive Medicine and Biostatistics and Professor of Dermatology, F. Edward Hébert School of Medicine at the Uniformed Services University of the Health Sciences in Bethesda, Maryland. In 2017, he became Dean of the School of Public Health at the University of Maryland. Among other accomplishments, he developed new academic programs to meet workforce needs and launched a global health initiative. RADM Boris Lushniak's academic credentials and wide-ranging professional experiences have given him a uniquely authoritative knowledge of the public health impact of the USPHS Commissioned Corps.

www.ingramcontent.com/pod-product-compliance
Lightning Source LLC
Chambersburg PA
CBHW042030050526
44107CB00123B/1419/J